# THE LAST STAND

## -MEMORIES OF WAR-

### GARY BRIDSON-DALEY

Freedom is the sure possession of those alone who have the courage to defend it

Pericles

© Gary Bridson-Daley 2023

The right of Gary Bridson-Daley 2023 to be identified as the author of this work has been asserted in accordance with the Copyright, Design and Patents Act 1988. All rights reserved.

ISBN - 9 798394 096266

# CONTENTS

| | |
|---|---|
| Continuing Mission | 4 |
| Dedications | 5 |
| Foreword by George 'Johnny' Johnson the 'Last British Dambuster' | 7 |
| Authors Note | 8 |
| Military Veterans Stories – Beginning with HRH Queen Elizabeth II and also including Captain Sir Tom Moore | 9 |
| The Salford Lancaster – ZN-S/PB304 – A Local Story. | 244 |
| Civilian Veterans Stories – Incorporating Dame Vera Lynn | 256 |
| Mayer Hersh – A very different WW2 story from a survivor of the holocaust with related chapter, including detailed interlinked timeline | 294 |
| History on a Knife Edge in 1942 – A detailed Essay about one of the biggest 'What If's' of the Second World War | 330 |
| This is your Victory – Rousing words from Winston Churchill | 347 |
| The Journey – A Short Story from Gary Bridson-Daley | 350 |
| Interesting Observations – A Short Story from a WW2 Service Veteran | 353 |
| Tribute Poetry from World War Two Service Veterans | 356 |
| Tribute Poetry from Gary Bridson-Daley | 370 |
| Tribute Poetry from the Homeless Poet Jamie Smith | 388 |
| For the Fallen by Robert Laurence Binyon | 391 |
| Everlasting Sacrifice | 394 |
| Learning from the Lessons of the Past – Poignant words of Mahatma Gandhi | 395 |
| Looking Towards the Future – Concluding quote from Dr Martin Luther King Jr. | 396 |
| Acknowledgements | 397 |
| The Author | 399 |
| Other Works | 400 |

## **CONTINUING MISSION**

I sincerely believe it is essential to keep alive the stories of the countless sacrifices and efforts of our brave and resolute men and women from the World War Two era, and to capture and preserve these vitally important historical narratives whilst there is still time to do so, a pivotal part of our history, that of the Second World War is about to pass over the horizon of living memory, which is why I have continued the 'Debt of Gratitude Project' with this second book 'The Last Stand – Memories of War'.

Each and every veteran a hero in their own way through their very important contributions between 1939-1945, each and every one featured here making their own 'Last Stand' through giving and sharing their very unique and remarkable experiences in this book.

What's more my aims are to continue to honour all those who have ever served our country from past to present day in any and every capacity, keeping alive the vitally important message that we owe a lot to those whose service has given us the freedom that we have all been privileged to enjoy for so long now.

To all servicemen and Women

From the bottom of my heart, I thank you all for everything you have given and continue to give for your country

Gary Bridson-Daley

✳ ✳ ✳

The righteous will be remembered forever

Psalm 112:6

✳ ✳ ✳

21st April 1926 – 8th September 2022

This book is dedicated to the memory of Her Majesty Queen Elizabeth II. Former Sovereign Head of State, Head of the British Armed Forces and World War Two Veteran. We thank you for your incredible unwavering service to our country in all capacities over the decades before and during your time as our Queen.

## **FURTHER DEDICATIONS**

This book is jointly and additionally dedicated to everyone listed on this page, whether named individually or otherwise, including all those from the United Kingdom and elsewhere in the world who have ever served this country and continue to do so in the Royal and Merchant Navies, Army, Air Force, Special Forces and Intelligence Services and the many Civilian Organisations that have and continue to aid, supply and support them in all they do in defence of our country and its people.

Furthermore, to all who work in the essential lifesaving services that help us so much within our country each and every day, such as the Police, Ambulance, Fire, Mountain, Lifeboat Rescue and NHS, and to everyone who gives their time tirelessly to the numerous superb military and civilian charities in the U.K.

Each and every one play vitally important roles and do great jobs serving and helping this country in so many different capacities, your hard work is acknowledged and remembered with great appreciation for everything you continually do for us all. GBD. (Gary Bridson-Daley).

****

HRH Prince Philip Duke of Edinburgh.

The great Wartime Leader Sir Winston Churchill.

National Treasure Dame Vera Lynn.

National Treasure Captain Sir Tom Moore.

Fusilier Lee Rigby.

All those who served on the many different 'Front Lines' against the Coronavirus Pandemic.

The Men, Women and Children who were and continue to be innocent civilian casualties of war from past to present day all over the globe, all who have suffered in World Wars to more modern conflicts such as those in Iraq, Afghanistan, Syria, Ukraine and sadly any hostilities that may follow.

****

Continuously to the memory of my beautiful Mother Sylvia June Bridson; forever in my heart.

Maurice Wallman and Joanne Yates dear friends who I loved very much – R.I.P.

# FOREWORD BY GEORGE 'JOHNNY' JOHNSON MBE DFM

I consider the ongoing work of Gary Bridson-Daley to honour our service veterans in 'The Last Stand' to be a very important contribution to the conservation of this vitally important part of our nation's history.

Within this book we see the incredible results of his continuing mission to interview and preserve the precious stories of World War Two servicemen and women, those from both military and civilian backgrounds who contributed so much to the survival of our country during that conflict.

This very commendable work which is part of his 'Debt of Gratitude Project' is something I hold in very high regard indeed and I hope it achieves the great success that it rightly deserves.

*G. A. (Johnny) Johnson MBE DFM.*

### 617 Squadron 'The Dambusters'

# AUTHOR'S NOTE

All information imparted to me by veterans during the interviews and at all stages during the making of this book has been taken on trust and comes mainly from memory on their part and also from the many and varied resources provided by them. It must be remembered that each veteran has supplied personal accounts from their own experiences that are more than seventy years old and therefore should be treated, enjoyed and respected as the great factual human-interest stories that each and every one reveal themselves to be. I have, when and where possible, researched Second World War material from many additional resources in order to check, cross reference and support the accounts within this book.

The different material that was combined to compile the veterans' profiles came from the following diverse and wide-ranging sources; the stories told and information imparted to me directly both face to face and additionally in conversations over the telephone with veterans, supplementary information shared by spouses, family and friends of the veteran and material resources I was allowed to view and take notes and pictures of, such as service records, identification documents, log books, pay books and miscellaneous documents from many sources. The information also comes from the videos made during the interview process, written and audio accounts given to me, and additional notes taken during the interviews plus veterans' wartime and other photos. On the odd occasion, original quotations from the servicemen and women have been lightly edited for the sake of clarity. Further resources came from helpful veteran and military-related associations, organisations and charities, requests I made from the Ministry of Defence, online research and various other materials kindly loaned or duplicates given to me.

The content of the book is intentionally varied in order to be more engaging and interesting to the reader and comes in a few diverse forms, the core part being the veterans stories and profiles, also a chapter dedicated to the Holocaust which includes within it an interview that I conducted with a survivor of Auschwitz and eight other camps, a detailed essay called 'History on a Knife Edge in 1942', the story and unsolved mystery of 'The Salford Lancaster', two other short stories, poetry both from myself and veterans and a piece of veteran related poetry by a homeless gentleman from the streets of Manchester who also respects the sacrifices of servicemen and women.

Some of the stories I wrote from the later interviews I conducted have turned out longer, this is no negative reflection upon those that came before, just a continuing change in my writing style as time went on. An added dimension to each of these narratives is that reflected within the stories and experiences of the veterans is a little bit of my journey with them as the interviewer and creator of the Debt of Gratitude Project and additionally in the process later also as an ongoing acquaintance or friend, all of which are further important interwoven elements of the book, as it has been a big, moving, educational, incredible, and at times challenging and emotional journey.

Finally, another essential factor to mention is that everything I have written about in this or previous books is in no way a glorification or war, because as we all know war is a terrible thing, it is instead an effort to capture, preserve and share the valuable, fascinating and thought-provoking accounts of those people who by fate and circumstance were caught up in that huge part of 20th century history which has left big legacies and ramifications, yet one that still inspires and attracts a huge army of readers from all over the world right through to this very day.

# BRITISH ARMY VETERANS

# HER MAJESTY QUEEN ELIZABETH II

Served with – British Army – ATS – Auxiliary Territorial Service
Service Number – 230873
Written – 2021/2022

## Service History and Personal Stories

- Born – 21ˢᵗ April 1926, Mayfair, London, England, UK.
- Princess, later Queen Elizabeth's main World War Two experiences were as follows; Her Majesty was 13 years old when the war broke out on 3ʳᵈ September 1939, like a great many children living in London Princesses Elizabeth and Margaret were part of the mass evacuation to try and avoid the dangers of enemy bombing around the capital. They were sent to Windsor Castle which was approximately 20 miles from central London.
- Whilst there a young 14-year-old Princess Elizabeth gave her first public address from the drawing room of Windsor Castle on 13ᵗʰ October 1940 as part of BBC's Children's Hour, speaking directly to the children who had been separated from their families as a result of the evacuation scheme in order to boost their morale and show empathy for their plight.
- On the morning of her 16ᵗʰ birthday on 21ˢᵗ April 1942 Princess Elizabeth, who in order to symbolize her involvement in the war effort had been made an honorary Colonel of the Grenadier Guards undertook her first inspection of a military regiment at Windsor Castle.

- Later on in 1943 Princess Elizabeth was championing more aspects of wartime life and spirit as part of the 'Dig for Victory' campaign which strived for more self-sufficiency in food production due to shortages and rationing when she was photographed tending allotments at Windsor Castle, again to show unity with others having to do the same.
- Then after turning 18 in 1944 she insisted on joining the Auxiliary Territorial Service in order to formally be able to enlist in the women's branch of the British Army, despite initial opposition from her parents the Princess who was resolute about contributing to the war effort got her way, registering as Elizabeth Windsor. Importantly her father the wartime monarch King George VI would not show favouritism by giving any special rank to his daughter in the Army and as a result she started as a Second Subaltern (Lieutenant) and after working hard eventually became a Junior Commander (Captain).
- Her training as a Driver and Motor Mechanic began in March 1945 at No.1 Mechanical Training Centre of the ATS in Aldershot, qualifying 14th April 1945, which led to the newspapers at the time dubbing her 'Princess Auto Mechanic', and later when posted to the Mechanical Transport Training Section in Camberley, Surrey a proud King, Queen and Princess Margaret visited to see her learn about and demonstrate her engine repair skills. Princess Elizabeth was taught to drive by Maud MacLellan, commanding officer of F.A.N.Y – First Aid Nursing Yeomanry who was obliged to serve with the ATS during the war.
- On V.E Day, 8th May 1945 the end of the war in Europe was being celebrated by tens of thousands who packed the streets of London and the Royal Mall, they squeezed into every inch of space outside Buckingham Palace demanding to see the Royals who appeared on the balcony eight times throughout that day, joining them along with Winston Churchill was the young 19-year-old Princess Elizabeth in her uniform as a servicewoman of the ATS.
- At sunset with the celebrations still in full flow Princess Elizabeth along with her sister were allowed to slip into the crowds to join the huge party for a 'Night of Freedom' where they could enjoy the extremely rare delight of being a regular citizen for one night only, and partied on for a few of those historical hours, more about this later on in her story.
- Whilst in the ATS many skills were learned by a very keen Princess including how to deconstruct, rebuild and repair engines and change tires, and how to drive every kind of vehicle she worked on, including trucks, jeeps and ambulances. Her military service ended after Japan's final unconditional surrender in September 1945.
- A later 1947 article in *Collier's* magazine noted of the overalls-clad teen, "One of her major joys was to get dirt under her nails and grease stains in her hands, and display these signs of labour to her friends."
- The austerity of the Second World War continued in many ways in the lives of the nation for a number of years following that conflict, as an acknowledgement of this and in the continuing wartime spirit the then Princess Elizabeth purchased the material for her wedding dress using ration coupons ready for when she married Philip Mountbatten, Duke of Edinburgh on 20th November 1947 in Westminster Abbey.
- The legacy of her time in the ATS stayed with Her Majesty throughout her life, even into her 90's she has often been seen behind the wheel and has been known to still diagnose engine problems, a vestige of those great skills she was taught in the ATS during WW2.
- Queen Elizabeth's strong links with the armed forces continued and expanded over the decades with Her Majesty having been Colonel-in-Chief of 16 British Army Regiments and Corps, and many Commonwealth units, a time-honoured tradition which she served and maintained until her passing in September 2022.

**HM Queen Elizabeth II celebrated an incredible 70 years on the throne in 2022, her Platinum Anniversary, and as a monarch who has reigned over us for so long and been an ever-present beacon of hope throughout the many turbulent events that our country has seen during that time. I could not think of anyone who better epitomises 'True Devotion to Service' than Her Majesty, and who as a World War Two Veteran herself in the Woman's branch of the British Army called the Auxiliary Territorial Service has also truly demonstrated a real example of 'Continuity through Service'. The Queen was not only the longest reigning monarch in British history and in the world at time of writing but the only Monarch who has actively served in a branch of the Armed Forces during the Second World War. Countless volumes can quiet easily be written about the many different aspects Her Majesty's reign, her multi-faceted history being quite spectacular, but in keeping with the subject matter and emphasis of this book almost completely being on the war years I am going to focus on that aspect of her life. However, there is no doubt whatsoever that for neigh on eight decades of continuous service to her country and her people as Princess Elizabeth right through to being HM Queen Elizabeth II we truly and unequivocally owe this most magnificent lady our Late Sovereign Monarch a real 'Debt of Gratitude'.**

Princess Elizabeth's first public address, which took place on the BBC in October 1940 was made with her sister next to her in a speech aimed at fellow evacuated children of the Blitz, where in part of it she emphatically said: "Thousands of you in this country have had to leave your homes and be separated from your fathers and mothers. My sister Margaret Rose and I feel so much for you, as we know from experience what it means to be away from those you love most of all. To you living in new surroundings, we send a message of true sympathy and at the same time we would like to thank the kind people who have welcomed you to their homes in the country."

Fast forward to February 1945 and after months of debate with her parents the strong-willed yet dutiful daughter of King George VI and Queen Elizabeth (The Queen Mother) finally got her way when they relented to her numerous pleas to be allowed to do her bit for her country and join the British Armed Forces. Her parents were, as understandably all parents would be, reluctant to let their daughter join the services in a time of war especially when this young lady was the British heir to the throne, and they had also made it clear that no female member of the British Royal Family had ever joined the military! But undeterred having seen

so many around her playing their parts in so many different ways including those in the Royal Family, and seeing the general public answer their country's call and rally to the cause, with many paying the ultimate price, Princess Elizabeth felt duty bound and determined to step up, be counted and contribute as well. In the end Princess Elizabeth joined the ATS in which she served as a driver and mechanic until victory in Europe over Nazi Germany in May 1945 and victory over Imperial Japan in August 1945 had been achieved. **A lovely wartime photograph of the young Princess Elizabeth whilst in the Auxiliary Territorial Service, wearing overalls and standing in front of some of the vehicles she was training to maintain and drive, the one in the foreground showing an L-Plate and a medical lorry in the background.**

It was during that time V.E (Victory in Europe) Day took place on the 8th May 1945, and as part of that momentous day a very interesting part of Princess Elizabeth's wartime story occurred when the two Princesses went into the streets of London and joined in the huge celebrations that had erupted everywhere in the capital, something we now look at in more detail with an overview of that story and quotes both from Her Majesty and others who accompanied them that night and were also a part of that history, events that interestingly were depicted in the 2015 film 'A Royal Night Out.'

In 1985 the Queen gave a rare personal interview with the BBC in which she recalled what occurred, and later on in 2015 three other people who were part of the 16 strong party of trusted friends and security staff that accompanied the then 19 and 14 year old Princesses were also interviewed by Channel 4, they were The Hon Margaret Rhodes, Jean Woodroffe, her former lady-in-waiting and Lady Trumpington who worked at Bletchley Park and came up to London to join in the celebrations, the things some of them recounted are found within this captivating story, a small yet unique snapshot of one of the most famous days of World War Two from a very different Royal perspective:

It was the evening of 8th May 1945, and after nearly 6 long years of war the pressure valve was released and the country allowed a brief respite to celebrate the great victory over Nazism in Europe, Princess Elizabeth had already been out onto the balcony earlier with her parents King George VI, Queen Elizabeth and then again later when accompanied by Winston Churchill at 5.30pm. Around 8pm the Princesses asked if they could join the merriments that were taking place outside, after some trepidation from their parents the King and Queen, who naturally feared for their safety they were given permission to go accompanied by others from the Royal household for their protection, their parents (and everyone else for that matter) knowing full well that this would more than likely be the only time something this free and informal may be experienced by their daughters, an extremely rare break from the very formal lives they led and in future would be expected to lead in the course of their Royal lives and duties, and indeed it was to be the only time the Princess (later Queen) has ever gone incognito among her subjects! So off they went out of one of the backdoors of Buckingham Palace shortly after 10.00pm heading up the left of the Mall to join the massive party that was taking place, Margaret Rhodes, the Queen's cousin said: "We crossed the forecourt at Buckingham Palace and got to the railings and there were these masses of people. There was a general thing of, 'We want the King and Queen', which we all frantically joined in with (including the Princesses) and were amazed when, five or ten minutes later, the windows opened and they came out onto the balcony. It was a wonderful escape for the girls. I don't think they'd ever been out among millions of people. It was just freedom – to be an ordinary person."

**Pictured - V.E Day, Tuesday 8th May 1945, people celebrate on the streets of London as nearly 6 years of pent-up wartime emotions are released in one day!** In her BBC interview the Queen said: "We were terrified of being recognised, so I pulled my uniform cap down well over my eyes. A Grenadier officer among our party of about 16 people said he refused to be seen in the company of another officer improperly dressed. So I had to put my cap on normally." Lady Trumpington had caught the train from Bletchley that evening with friends to be part of the festivities, and was overjoyed at seeing the capital lit up again, saying "It had been very dim during the blackout, with only searchlights in the sky and very tiny traffic lights, and suddenly there was this sudden blaze of light. It was so exciting!' She then exclaimed: "I had a friend who was a bodyguard of the Queen, so I noticed her and Princess Margaret as they walked the streets of London. But they were people like anyone else, we didn't take any notice of them."

As the Royal Party moved on to Whitehall the Queen recalls: "Lines of unknown people linking arms and walking down Whitehall, all of us just swept along on a tide of happiness and relief. I also remember when someone exchanged hats with a Dutch sailor; the poor man coming along with us in order to get his hat back." As the night moved on so did the Royal party, and at around 11.30pm the group arrived at one of London's most famous hotels, and as Margaret Rhodes revealed: "For some reason, we decided to go in the front door of the Ritz and do the conga. The Ritz has always been so stuffy and formal, we rather electrified the stuffy individuals inside. I don't think people realised who was among the party, I think they thought it was just a group of drunk young people. I remember old ladies looking faintly shocked. As one congaed through, eyebrows were raised!"

On the way back to the palace Princesses Elizabeth and Margaret and the accompanying Royal party which also included RAF Group Captain and famed Battle of Britain pilot Peter Townsend, ended up in the Royal Parks on their way back to the palace, experiencing many things along the way, which Jean Woodroffe disclosed: "There were places like Green Park and St. James's which one would never have walked through at night in the war, and there we were. There was the usual thing of people kissing and hugging, and even making love. I was shocked by it; I hadn't experienced that sort of thing happening before in public." It was estimated that 50,000 people had gathered around the Mall by midnight, hoping to see the King and Queen one last time, the Royal party mingling amongst them, and they weren't disappointed, at approximately half past midnight their Royal Highnesses made a final surprise appearance, as the Queen told the BBC in her interview: "We were successful in seeing my parents on the balcony, having cheated slightly by sending a message into the house, to say we were waiting outside."

It is only fitting the last words regarding this very special 'Night of Freedom' should be Her Majesty's, who when reminiscing about it many years later said: "I think it was one of the most memorable nights of my life."

**Included here are further quotes from Her Majesty, which show how over the years her thoughts and feelings have been expressed regarding a deep sense of duty and other important things, which I believe truly demonstrate an unequivocal dedication to service of every kind and which are in themselves a great tribute to her:**

– "I declare before you all that my whole life, whether it be long or short, shall be devoted to your service and the service of our great imperial family to which we all belong."

– "I cannot lead you into battle. I do not give you laws or administer justice but I can do something else, I can give my heart and my devotion to these old islands and to all the peoples of our brotherhood of nations."

– "The upward course of a nation's history is due in the long run to the soundness of heart of its average men and women."

– "I have in sincerity pledged myself to your service, as so many of you are pledged to mine. Throughout my life and with all my heart I shall strive to be worthy of your trust."

– "In remembering the appalling suffering of war on both sides, we recognise how precious is the peace we have built in Europe since 1945."

**On the eve of the 70th anniversary of her accession to the throne on the 5th February 2022, (her accession being 6th February 1952), the Queen released a statement she had written that thanked the public and her family for their support over the years, again re-affirming her sense of duty to the nation, parts of which read:**

– 'As we mark this anniversary, it gives me pleasure to renew to you the pledge I gave in 1947 that my life will always be devoted to your service. This anniversary also affords me a time to reflect on the goodwill shown to me by people of all nationalities, faiths and ages in this country and around the world over these years.

I would like to express my thanks to you all for your support. I remain eternally grateful for, and humbled by, the loyalty and affection that you continue to give me.'

Your Servant

*Elizabeth R*

In the stories of Her Majesty Queen Elizabeth II, Dame Vera Lynn (with some direct feedback and exclusive content from her) and Captain Sir Tom Moore I have essentially written 'about them' as a means of honouring these revered individuals and their service to our country, very fitting and relative content indeed for this book. The narratives of all the other veterans featured within its pages have come from full interviews I conducted directly with them. The service of each and every one, known or unknown, were in their own ways hugely and equally as important during the war years, and are now here in perpetuity and for posterity as part of 'The Last Stand'.

## Additional Information and Life After Service

**Rank upon finish of service** – Junior Commander (ATS Equivalent to Captain).

**Medals and Honours** – 1939-45 War Medal, 1939-45 Defence Medal.

**Post War Years & Associations and Organisations** – As I said at the beginning I could write endlessly about the life of Her Majesty, but it is at this point at the end of her war years I finish the central focus of her story here in keeping with the majority of the stories of other World War Two veterans in this book. The main parts of her war years are covered in these accounts and the history that has occurred since is essentially known to many, from WW2 Subaltern and Junior Commander to Head of the British Armed Forces, with a legacy of incredible service in every capacity from a wonderful lady, whom a great many in this country and around the world, myself included, have and will continue to admire and respect her for greatly. Thank you Ma'am.

**Final Goodbye** – On Thursday the 8th September 2022 our Sovereign Queen passed away peacefully with her family around her in Balmoral, Aberdeenshire, Scotland at 96 years of age in the 70th year of her reign. Her loss signified, amongst many things, a huge severance with the World War Two era that my book mainly seeks to venerate. I wrote and added this final part of her story as a tribute on that very poignant day in order to honour her during that moment in history when she left us, thus ending the 2nd Elizabethan age!

**Rest In Peace**

**Women with a will to Win!** An ATS recruitment poster encapsulating the spirit of the service that Princess Elizabeth was a part of and has always exemplified, also highlighting the very important part all women from every background played and the huge contributions they all made towards the British war effort during the Second World War.

# PRIVATE MARY DOREEN CANDELIN

**Served with – Army Territorial Service, Royal Signals and Home Office**
**Service Number – 277867**
**Interviewed – Bury, Lancashire, 18th October 2018**

Important Note – Supplementary discussions took place with the veterans in this book for years after I interviewed them in order to ensure that all material within it was as correct, up to date and relevant as possible.

### Service History and Personal Stories

- Born – 3rd September 1925, Manchester, Lancashire, England, UK.
- The very unique wartime service of Mary Doreen Candelin or Doreen as she liked to be known began in April 1942, when she joined the women's branch of the British Army called the ATS - Auxiliary Territorial Service. This would lead her on a very interesting journey into the world of World War Two Intelligence gathering, where she undertook work as a high-speed Morse Code Operator.
- Her six-week basic Army training took place at High Legh in Cheshire, after further aptitude tests and also based on her having already learned basic Morse Code in the Girl Guides, Doreen was chosen to become a Specialist Morse Code Operator and sent to Douglas in the Isle of Man for this next phase of her training, run at The Hadfield Hotel.

- There she completed an intense 6-month course in Wireless Op and Morse Code Receiver training, the longest course the ATS ran, which gave her the ability to intercept and deal with up to 25 words per minute of International Morse Code; this prepared her for the secret posting for which she had already been ear-marked near Harrogate in Yorkshire.
- By early 1943 Doreen was a fully trained British Army Morse Code Receiver, with the nature of her role in communications she came under the Royal Corps of Signals and was also chosen to be part of a team of receivers with an additional affiliation to The Home Office, whom along with Bletchley Park many of her future intercepts would be shared.
- From April 1943 to May 1944 Doreen lived and was stationed at what was formally Queen Ethelburga's School, which became a requisitioned Royal Signals billet, from there teams of specially trained ATS 'Y-Operators' were taken to a secret Bletchley Park 'Y-Station' code receiving listening post and communications centre at Forest Moor, North Yorkshire.
- These teams of which Doreen was a part worked on shift patterns all round the clock at this Bletchley 'Y' or 'Outstation' intercepting German Army, SS and Gestapo transmissions on a new set radio frequency that was allocated to all of them to monitor each day.
- The messages that were captured by these ATS 'Y-Operators' and the potentially vital 'intel' that lay within them were then taken by despatch riders down to the centre of intelligence gathering at Bletchley Park AKA 'Station X', there they would be de-cyphered by their top cryptographers and any information within them that could be acted upon in any theatre of war would be passed on in order to help the allied war in many ways.
- Doreen carried out this very important work for over a year until unfortunately she became seriously ill after contracting Tuberculosis and had to be treated at York General hospital for 4 months, this led to an eventual Army Medical Discharge in September 1944.
- It wasn't until much later when being honoured by The Bletchley Park Trust and the British Government that she learned about the true extent of the intelligence network she was a part of at the Forest Moor Outstation, its connections to the vital work of Bletchley Park and as result her contribution to the overall Allied success in the Second World War.

During World War Two there was an additional and almost invisible battlefront running and being fought out alongside those of land, sea and air, that of the Intelligence War. Between 1939-1945 it had reached a whole new level of innovation and stealth by all sides engaged in the conflict, this covert war within a war extended to and affected every theatre of operations around the world during those years, the intelligence being intercepted becoming a vital part of the decision making processes and integrated into war planning at every level, which for the Allies eventually brought about the final victory over the oppressive Axis powers of Nazi Germany and Imperial Japan. In the United Kingdom Intelligence gathering was well organised and came in many forms such as a network of 'Y' or 'Outstations' that were based around Great Britain and by extension in many places around the world, they would 'eves-drop' on enemy communications by using teams of highly trained Army, Navy and Air Force personnel to try and glean whatever they could from their enemy counterpart organisations 24 hours a day! This information was in turn fed back to the Top Secret centre of operations, the GC&CS – Government Code and Cypher School at Bletchley Park in Southern England, who would as required translate and de-Cypher the intelligence and decide its level of importance, then act upon and action it accordingly in order to try and influence the outcome of any particular engagement or battle, and in the process to hopefully save as many lives as possible. Playing her crucial part in this hugely important endeavour was Doreen Candelin, who was a servicewoman in the ATS and now tells us more about her unique role as:

## **A SPECIAL MORSE CODE OPERATOR AT A BLETCHLEY PARK 'Y' STATION**

"Once I had completed my Morse training at Douglas on the Isle of Man I was able to receive and take note of up to 25 words a minute, very good for what the Army had in mind next. They posted myself and others to what I think was 'officially' called a Royal Signals Station, which was near Harrogate and used to be Queen Ethelburga's School, after we had signed the Official Secrets act and were told we could be had for treason if we spoke about anything we saw, heard or were a part of, they told us we had been chosen for work of a highly sensitive nature, which would really take place at Forest Moor out in the Yorkshire Moors, and that we would be picked up and transported by trucks each day or night and brought back after shift, we had good singsongs in the back of those trucks I can tell you, helped lift our spirits. Our work was actually at a 'Y-Station' and we were 'Y-Operators', many years later we found out it was an Outstation for Bletchley Park, a place we of course knew nothing about, we were not even aloud to tell our families what we were really doing, I told mine I was a phone Operator, the reality of course was much different! As Special Morse Code receivers, we were working around the clock in shifts that covered the whole 24-hour period because of course the war was happening every hour of the day and night, we listened into a specific radio frequency setting that you were given each day by an officer and you had to monitor and take note of whatever you managed to pick up. Almost everything was in the International Morse Code also known as the Q-Code, but even though we knew the Morse lettering being used because it was a generic international code with communications using the Latin alphabet the language we were listening to was German and we didn't understand that! But it was okay because we were there only to capture the information not de-code or translate it!

Never the less we were instructed to take down exactly what we heard as we heard it, which sometimes was in a mix of letters, numbers and I believe even coded words depending on how secret it was and the source of the message, many of us found out much later that we as British Army ATS Morse Operators had actually been set to intercept German Army, Gestapo and SS Communications! They were normally transmitted in sets of about five words per sentence with a pause, but sometimes many more, which we would have to listen to and write down very quickly, once we had filled a piece of paper we would put it in our basket and it would be whisked away and that was that as far as we were concerned! You didn't have time to think about it because on a busy night you be doing hours of that, it was mentally exhausting! Sometimes the Germans would try and jam the frequency setting that you were on, this would give loud continuous high pitch noises that you had to really concentrate on and work through to hear the message they were sending, but this also indicated it must be something useful and possibly good intelligence if they were trying to cover it up like that, so despite the ringing that you would get in your ears you would really try and catch as much of it as you could, even if you had a headache by the end of your shift! The enemy would of course try communicating any place they could, when I came to work one day I was given a frequency to tune into and eves drop on that my Commanding officer said had not been used since 1925! Those of us who were faster and keener about our work were sometimes chosen to work in the 'Special Receivers Corner', which in our big long room full of radios and code sounds coming through and essential chatter going on was at the end behind partitions for the operator to hear better, this is where as we had it explained, known frequencies of extra special importance were being homed in on, and we were ordered to pay extra attention regarding any intercepted messages. These must have contained vital intelligence because I was also given the Home Office insignia on my uniform, which I think could have only meant that part of my work and intercepts were of interest to them and that I was in some way now linked to that Government Department as well, this alongside the black and white diamond already on there to indicate that I belonged to a communications unit, i.e. the Royal Signals did make us realise that what we were doing was of some importance to the war effort even if we were not allowed for the sake of national security to see or know the bigger picture or true scale of it all! It wouldn't be until many years later that I came to fully realise that our Y Station was just one small but important piece in the jigsaw that was the huge information gathering network of Bletchley Park.

Interestingly if you did intercept a message from the beginning which we did most of the time we learned they always started off with the German words – Für meaning For, followed by station letters or numbers, then Von meaning From, that's about as much as you might understand, and at the end the letters QRZ International Morse Code for 'Closing Down Now.' After our papers were gathered together and our commanding officers looked through them I believe they went to one of our despatch riders who were always on standby 24 hours a day to take them off (to Bletchley). I was only told once about something by name that my intercepts helped directly influence in some way, and that was when a senior officer said that the Allies in Italy had achieved success at the Anzio Beach head, he obviously didn't go into more detail than that but he wanted me to know my work had helped. I felt very proud that something I'd done really had made a difference in some way."

By 1943 the ATS represented 10 per cent of the Royal Corps of Signals, having taken over the major part of the signal office and operating duties in the War Office and Home Commands, all of these which through her work Doreen was directly connected to whilst at Forest Moor. The Bletchley Park chain of intelligence gathering of which she was a part was estimated to have saved the lives of tens of thousands of people and to have shortened the war by at least two years! An intricate part of that was the 'Y' Service, a network of British signals intelligence collection sites known as the Y-Stations, the name derived from Wireless Interception (WI). The service was established during the First World War and used again during the Second World War. These Top Secret listening posts were operated by a range of agencies including the Army, Navy and RAF plus the Foreign Office, MI5 and MI6, manned by military personnel including ATS, WRNS and WAAF, they gathered their war winning information by Signit (Signals Intelligence) from Y-Stations around the United Kingdom and several British intercept sites overseas at Malta, Cairo and Sarafand in Palestine, the Japanese related intel was tracked at Abbottabad and Delhi in India, and later at Colombo in Sri Lanka and Mombasa, Kenya. There were also incept operators based on ships at sea and mobile Army incept units with British forces on the ground in theatres of war all around the world, all listening in to what the enemy radio operators were saying to each other, and their locations could be tracked down using radio direction-finding equipment; they all worked closely with their centre of Intelligence at Bletchley Park in Buckinghamshire where the vital information was eventually fed back to, deciphered and utilised accordingly.

**Doreen's contribution had certainly made a difference, which is why she was rightly honoured by The Bletchley Park Trust in 2002 with the 'Freedom of Bletchley Park' and in 2009 received the 'Bletchley Park and Outstations Commemorative Medal' from the British Government. Proving that she had performed her duties according to the motto of the Royal Corps of Signals; Certa Cito – 'Swift and Sure.' My tribute is to be able to write about this lovely lady and to have her here in my book, and by doing so to preserve her story for posterity. Doreen thank you for your valuable service to the nation.**

**The Manor house at Bletchley Park, part of the huge Top-Secret establishment that was the subject of the highly successful 2014 film 'The Imitation Game' staring Benedict Cumberbatch as the incredible breaker of the Nazi 'Enigma Code' Alan Turing, who was based there at what was also known as Station X. Doreen's valuable work and some of her intercepts ended up here and**  **contributed to the crucial 'Covert Intelligence War' that helped the Allies win the Second World War.**

## Additional Information and Life After Service

**Rank upon finish of service** – Private.

**Medals and Honours** – Bletchley Park and Outstations Commemorative Medal, Veterans Badge.

**Post War Years** – Concentrated on bringing up her family, then became a Nurse at Bury General Hospital, later qualified as a Social Worker and worked for Salford Social Services (Children's Dept.) 1963-67 and Bury Social Services 1967-1984 becoming H.O.D for Bury South Area. Retired in 1984 aged 59. Married twice, to Joseph then Eric. 3 Children, 4 Grandchildren, 9 Great Grandchildren, 1 Great-Great Grandchild.

**Associations and Organisations** – WRAC – Women's Royal Army Corps Association (which incorporates all former members of the ATS).

# STAFF SERGEANT FREDRICK DONALD HALL

Served with – 1st, 9th, 14th Survey Regiments, Royal Artillery
Service Number – 880321
Interviewed – Cannock, Staffordshire, 4th July 2016

## Service History and Personal Stories

- Born – 14th March 1920, Redhill, Surrey, England, UK.
- Don as he prefers to be called joined the Army on the 13th April 1938 at the Royal Artillery Barracks, Woolwich, London, where he undertook his basic training, following in the footsteps of his father who had been a Bombardier for over a decade and served in WW1.
- He trained as an R.A Surveyor at the Army School of Survey at Larkhill, Salisbury Plain, Wiltshire, and once this more specialised training had been completed by 1939 was assigned to the 1st Survey Regiment Royal Artillery and was now equipped with the skills for general land surveying and for military surveying for positioning of Artillery.
- On the 19th September 1939 only 16 days after the official outbreak of World War Two Don and his regiment were shipped from Avonmouth to St. Nazaire in France, then posted on the French-Belgian border as part of the BEF - British Expeditionary Force to help bolster their French and Belgian allies in Western Europe against the expected Nazi attack.
- The BEF under the command of General Lord Gort was deployed on the left flank of the French 1st Army to hold the North-Eastern front in the areas around Lille known as the Gort Line, where Don remembers being at a place called Orchies near Mouchin which was in the sector being manned by the 2nd Division of the British Expeditionary Force.

~ 22 ~

- Shortly after the German offensive in the West began on 10th May 1940 the BEF along with Don found themselves in continuous retreat and rear-guard actions all the way back to the coast where they ended up fighting for their lives on the beaches at Dunkirk, and eventually on the 27th May 1940 Don was evacuated on a Thames pleasure steamer as part of Operation Dynamo, the combined rescue effort of civilian and Royal Navy vessels.
- After returning to the U.K for the next few years Don was involved in the Coastal Defence of Great Britain, undertaking many different tasks, starting from June to December 1940 with 'Mine Securing' which was surveying and mapping coastal minefields in areas from the Humber to The Wash and Dunbar to Wick and Thurso, and also surveyed land for the RAF to build airstrips, and in March 1941 was transferred to 9th Survey Regiment, R.A.
- From 1941 until 1944 he was moved to a number of places to help install guns in regions such as Lock Tay in Scotland and Ballymena in Northern Ireland. Also to put guns around the Northern Irish coastlines and areas overlooking Southern Ireland to try and prevent German U-Boats from re-fuelling and re-supplying anywhere in the seas near those areas.
- During that time he also returned to complete further training at the Army School of Survey at Larkhill becoming a Troop Commanders Assistant, and additionally trained and was posted in 'Flash Spotting' which is the locating hostile guns by means of observing muzzle flashes. After further courses and instruction in County Durham and Yorkshire Don managed to reach the level of Advanced Surveyor and obtain the rank of Staff Sergeant.
- In early 1944 he became an Instructor at a base in Lock Tay, Scotland training troops in preparation for D-Day in many skills such as shooting, driving and surveying and also got them physically fit as he was also a Physical Training Instructor.
- On D-Day 6th June 1944 Don and the 9th Survey Regiment, R.A landed on Juno Beach as part of Operation Overlord in the joint British-Canadian sector, under the command of the British 2nd Army as part of the delayed 2nd wave Anglo-Canadian landing force around 4pm.
- Whilst on patrol on a road heading towards Caen the jeep in which he and his driver were travelling was ambushed by the Germans, they came under machine gun fire and a grenade was thrown in the back and exploded causing Don 15 shrapnel wounds on the right side of his body Inc. leg, arms and eye, then evacuated to the U.K on 10th June 1944.
- Recovered in hospital at Leatherhead near Guildford and at the Queen Elizabeth Hospital, Birmingham followed by convalescence until September 1944. After which he was posted to the R.A main depot at Woolwich, then Don transferred to the 14th Survey Regiment near Canterbury and returned to being an instructor for R.A Surveying and as a P.T.I there and other places between 1945-46 such as Oswestry, Shropshire and Sennybridge, Wales.
- De-mobbed on 13th March 1946, then put on 'Section B' Regular Army reserve from 28th May 1946 until 12th April 1950, when he received a Class 'A' Release, bringing to an end 8 years of active service, 4 years on reserve, 12 years in total given to his country. Fast-forward another 70 years and on the 14th March 2020 Don reached yet another great milestone and achievement when he celebrated his 100th Birthday at the Black Swan Residential Home in King's Lynn, Norfolk, East Anglia.

I began writing about Royal Artillery veteran Don Hall on 4th June 2020 which was the last day of the 80th Anniversary of the evacuation of Dunkirk, and Don's connection to that event is a direct one, because he was one of those who as part of the British Expeditionary Force was rescued from that beach on 27th May 1940. Don's service is very unique because at time of writing not only was he one of the few Dunkirk veterans left, but four years later he returned to France under very different circumstances as part of the invading D-Day force landing at Juno Beach on 6th June 1944, making him a very rare veteran of both these huge World War Two events. When I met Don at Juno Beach in Normandy during the 72nd D-Day Remembrance Service in 2016 and found out about his exceptional service I immediately asked if I could interview him once we had returned to the United Kingdom. What an amazing contribution to any book I put him in I thought, and as I found out on the day of the interview Don's incredible story is one of him also carrying on a family tradition with a number of parallels, because his father James Thomas Hall was a Bombardier in the Queen's Royal Regiment before, during and after WW1, and who like Don was injured in Battle. As this book is to honour all who have ever served in our armed forces both these connected family stories will be featured here, starting with Don Hall who now tells us about his:

### EXPERIENCES OF SURVIVING BOTH DUNKIRK AND D-DAY

"My job in the Royal Artillery was as a Surveyor, whether in support of a Troop which was 6 Guns or a Battery which was 18 Guns and their crews using 25 Pounders or 4.5 Inch Howitzers, we would help find the best position for our Artillery pieces either in a defensive or offensive role depending on the situation, the terrain we faced and the positioning of the enemy which we had to locate, we worked on grid systems for things and our input and feedback would help determine how and where we would engage the enemy in operations and how we would work in support of other units and formations." I took this rare opportunity to ask Don about his various memories regarding going one way out of France at Dunkirk in 1940 and coming back the other way on D-Day in 1944, he recalled; "In 1940 we were fighting a constant defensive battle against a very strong and well organised enemy and were getting a taste of Blitzkrieg first hand and the results for us and the poor refugees who were also caught up in it and mown down were devastating! I remember we were in a place called Orchies near Lille in France and we were driven back via Amiens to Dunkirk, fighting to survive and fighting for our lives all the way until eventually I was saved when I boarded what I think was a Thames Pleasure Steamer. Those civilian boatmen were very brave coming back again and again to save us whilst under constant attack from the German Dive Bombers. Later in 1944 it was still very difficult but at least we were on the attack, I landed on D-Day at Juno beach with the Canadians, a lot of devastation around, and after a few days I was seriously injured when we were ambushed by some Germans, I returned fire with my Sten Gun but as we were making our escape they threw a grenade into our jeep which exploded and injured me with shrapnel wounds in 15 places! That was my war in Normandy over by about the fifth day, I was eventually evacuated on an amphibious Duck to an LCI makeshift hospital ship and returned home to the U.K for full medical treatment and recovery. Very regrettable on both occasions was the loss of life and seeing a lot of death around you, these were hard but unfortunately commonplace things, yet still very sad, even when I recall them to this very day, I saw things you would never want to see, then, again or anytime in your life!"

**Above; Left - Escaping annihilation in Dunkirk 1940, Right - Returning for liberation on D-Day 1944, Don Hall experienced and survived both!**

## HRH KING GEORGE VI

Four years ago, our Nation and Empire stood alone against an overwhelming enemy, with our backs to the wall. Tested as never before in our history, in God's providence we survived that test; the spirit of the people, resolute, dedicated, burned like a bright flame, lit surely from those unseen fires which nothing can quench. Now once more a supreme test has to be faced. This time, the challenge is not to fight to survive but to fight to win the final victory for the good cause.

Part of King George VI D-Day statement that reflects within it both the time when Great Britain stood alone and was on the defensive, through to the time when she had many allies with her and took the fight to the enemy on the offensive, both of which are particularly and directly relevant to Don who vividly experienced each of these periods first-hand through his service at Dunkirk and D-Day.

### James Thomas Hall – Bombardier - Queen's Royal Regiment (West Surrey)

Service Number: 1005930. Born: 14.02.1892. Joined Army: July 1910 in Guildford, Surrey at eighteen and the half years of age. James came from the very hard working but sedate life of being a Farm Labourer in Lewis, Sussex in the parish of Plumpton, to a very different life in the military that would take him all over the world, but seeing that world mainly through bloody battles. He would serve bravely in many military campaigns as his extraordinary service record attests, namely;

South Africa 1911-12, India 1912-14, France 1914-16, Salonica 1916-17, Egypt 1917-19. James was awarded the 1914-15 Star, British War Medal and British Victory Medal (WW1). He was injured during trench warfare on the Western Front in the First World War where he survived many battles including the Somme and was later engaged on the Macedonian or Salonika Front in the Balkans. James continued in the Army until February 1921 when he finished his 10.5 years of service at the Royal Artillery Barracks, Woolwich where his 'Rank and character on Discharge' were described as – Bombardier, Very Good. It would be in the very same place 17 years later that his son Fredrick Donald Hall would start his career as a Gunner/Surveyor in the R.A and continuing in his father's footsteps would serve in the Second World War of the Twentieth Century.

Thank you both for courageously undertaking your duties in the cause of freedom and serving according to the Royal Artillery Motto 'Ubique' – 'Everywhere'.

### Additional Information and Life After Service

**Rank upon finish of service** – Staff Sergeant. (Acting RSM at Oswestry).

**Medals and Honours** – 1939-45 Defence Medal, 1939-45 War Medal, 1939-45 Star, France-Germany Star, Legion D' Honneur, Defence of Dunkirk Medal (French) and Albert Medal (Belgium).

**Post War Years** – Don worked at British Industrial Sands in Nutfield near Redhill, Surrey for 36 years becoming Commercial Manager, retired aged 63 in 1983, was married to Gladys 4 years, Mair 34 years and Joan 35 years, they have 3 Sons, 7 Grandchildren, 12 Great-Grandchildren.

**Associations and Organisations** – Dunkirk Veterans Association in Stafford, RBL in Nutfield serving 6 years as Chairman, Served on Nutfield Parish Council and became its Chairman in 1973-74.

# LANCE BOMBARDIER NEVILLE FOOTE

Served with – 79th (The Scottish Horse) Medium Regiment,
51st Highland Division, Royal Artillery
Service Number – 987674
Interviewed – Bury, Lancashire – 9th March 2019

## Service History and Personal Stories

- Born – 29th February 1920, Elton, Bury, Lancashire, England, UK.
- Neville or Nev as he was affectionately known was called up 20th June 1940, and was sent to do his basic training which included square bashing and small arms, he then chose to go into the Royal Artillery and trained to be a Signaller and Bombardier, along with motor transport all were undertaken over six months at Redford Barracks in Edinburgh, Scotland.
- After successfully completing every aspect of his training he joined the 79th (The Scottish Horse) Medium Regiment, which was a Regiment of the Royal Artillery whose roots can be traced back to the Original Scottish Horse Regiment raised by the 7th Duke of Atholl in 1900 to participate in the Boar War, his family at Blair in Scotland are still the only nobility in the country who have an official private military formation/army to this very day.
- From 1941 until 1944 Nev was posted with the 79th on Coastal defences and training at many locations throughout the United Kingdom as part of 'The Defence of Britain' such as Humberside, Yorkshire, Norfolk, Kent & Aldershot. He also trained to become a Motorbike Dispatch Rider and

took messages to and from Regional and Divisional Commands in the U.K, this additional role was also needed in case of radio communication failure in battle.

- During this time on the 19th August 1942 Neville was attached to part of the forces involved in Operation Jubilee, the seaborne attack on Dieppe, France. The 79th Regiment being of Scottish heritage was chosen to be involved alongside mainly Canadian Regiments also of Scottish Heritage such as The Queen's Own Cameron Highlanders of Canada, the Essex Scottish Regiment and the Royal Hamilton Light Infantry, sadly the operation was a failure with huge loss of life, Nev wasn't disembarked but witnessed the massacre unfold.
- Nearly two years later on D-Day 6th June 1944 Neville Foote and elements of the 79th Regiment landed on Juno Beach, once again with the Canadians, this time from the North Nova Scotia Highlanders of the Canadian 3rd Army, where they came under heavy artillery fire as they were in the second wave to hit the beach and the Germans had some time to re-group. Their first job as an advanced party of Signallers was to find, set up, and if required under attack help hold positions for his units artillery to link up with upon arrival.
- After this once the Normandy beaches and bridgeheads were established he was involved in many battles with the 79th Regiment which now operated as part of the 51st Highland Division as it moved outwards across France and gave artillery support to various units as ordered, and was involved in tough actions at Caen, Falaise Gap where they decimated 3 German Armies, Lisieux, Le Havre, St. Valery, onto Belgium to liberate Brussels & Antwerp.
- In September 1944 as part of another secondment, this time with the Guards Armoured Division in XXX Corps, 2nd British Army, they were involved with their 5.5-inch Howitzers in the land (Garden) part of Montgomery's ill-fated Operation Market Garden around Arnhem in Holland, where they managed to reach and take their objective of the bridge at Nijmegen but regrettably for 1st Airborne Division at Arnhem theirs was 'A Bridge Too Far'.
- The next big battle that Nev was involved in and gave artillery support for was the Battle of the Bulge in the Ardennes area of Belgium when the Germans launched a massive surprise counter-attack in December 1944. His unit was at Waterloo sight of the famous battle in 1815 when they were rushed to Dinant to help reinforce the line in that area. After this once the Germans were being pushed back in January 1945 he was engaged at a place called Rochefort as part of what was known as The Battle of Bure cleaning up the Bulge with the XXX Corps and aided by the 6th Airborne Division, also rushed in to help.
- By February 1945 Nev was with formations of the 2nd Army/XXX Corps that had experienced breaking through the very heavily fortified Siegfried Line, and battles in the Reichswald Forest region, and on the 23rd of March 1945 he was involved in the Rhine Crossing in Operation Plunder supported by the airborne landings of Operation Varsity.
- The atrocities that they faced on the 15th April 1945 when they were with some of the first units to be involved in the liberation of Bergen-Belsen Concentration Camp in Lower Saxony, Northern Germany they could never have anticipated, the scenes of mass murder that awaited them would give Neville nightmares and flashbacks for the rest of his life.
- The following month on V.E Day 8th May 1945 the war finished for Nev in Bremerhaven in Northern Germany. After this whilst still part of the 2nd Army he spent the next 8 months in Oldenburg in Lower Saxony as part of the forces of occupation known as BAOR – British Army of the Rhine. Whilst there he carried out many duties created by the aftermath of war such as the disarming of German troops, dealing with German prisoners of war, and helping displaced civilians and refugees. He was demobbed in Oldenburg on 15th February 1946, ending an incredible journey of nearly 6 years from Dieppe to D-Day to De-mob. Amongst his well-deserved honours came the French Legion D' Honneur in 2015 which reflected the amazing service and sacrifice that Neville had given.

**There are many extraordinary stories from veterans of the Second World War that come from well-known battles and places which have become almost hallowed ground and are now part of military folklore. Sometimes we might hear of veterans who were at one or two of these famous actions, and if we are very lucky as with a number of those whose stories are in this book we have some who were present at and survived many renowned campaigns and engagements. Yet at times I am still astounded when I hear what some people were involved in, went through and survived all rolled into the experiences of one individual, and Neville Foote is one such example. A serviceman who by fate and circumstance was at Dieppe, D-Day, Caen, Falaise Gap, Arnhem, The Battle of the Bulge, Siegfried Line, Rhine Crossing and was with one of the first units to be present at the liberation of Belsen Concentration Camp, finishing at Bremerhaven on the North-Baltic Sea coast and later was part of the British Army of Occupation after the war, which from an historical perspective is simply quite astounding. It is with these things in mind that we now hear from Neville as he recalls:**

### EXPERIENCING EMINENT WARTIME EVENTS IN THE LINE OF DUTY

"Well I think we need to start with Dieppe in 1942, where I was already in B Troop, P Battery of the 79th The Scottish Horse, Medium Regiment, Royal Artillery. During that raid we were in our landing craft ready to go in but did not have to disembark at the beaches as planned as the operation had been under way for some time by then. It was lucky for us that we didn't have to be landed as the whole thing turned out to be disastrous, but not lucky for the poor souls on the beaches where a complete massacre had taken place, clearly evident from the view we had, glad I wasn't sent fully into that hellish situation, but other difficult experiences awaited me in the years to come because as an artillery regiment we would be seconded to many other formations as, when and where needed as situations, offensives and emergencies unfolded, this would lead us into many more battles throughout Western Europe! From the moment we returned to France on D-Day 6th June 1944 until the end of hostilities on the 8th May 1945 we spent much of the time in the thick of the action, like it or not. As soon as we hit Juno Beach with the Canadians in Normandy right through to Bremerhaven in Germany we were almost continually in action after action, battle after battle, having to press forward and try to keep moving against a very well trained, disciplined enemy that fought with very stubborn and fierce defensive tactics when we were engaged in combat against them. On example was the problem with snipers, I remember once in Normandy we had to call in flame thrower tanks to eliminate those hidden in houses, their screams were horrifying, but it was them or us and they had already killed many good men in our ranks! I was injured a couple of times, once when a Bren Carrier I was in hit a mine, it killed my good friend Kenny Muir who was driving. Our artillery was continually pounding them and giving offensive cover but also we were subject on many occasions to a lot of incoming fire from weapons like their deadly 88mm guns, and despite our huge and in many cases rapid advances and victories we didn't have it all our own way for sure, at Caen it took a lot longer than expected to take the objective because of fierce resistance, at Arnhem we got beaten and held, and just when we thought the Germans were pretty much a spent force they attacked in a massive offensive that no one saw coming that ripped through the Ardennes in Belgium, we were involved in all those battles and I can tell you they were hard fought against the enemy and the elements! Like many others I felt fortunate to have survived everything, when I look back especially at the many now famous battles that I was a part of in Western Europe in the closing year of the war, I give thanks that I was lucky enough get through, and all these years later to be able to recall with clarity most things and to pass them on and relay them to people like yourself who are genuinely interested to hear and record them for posterity."

These kind sentiments led me to think that it is a truly remarkable and beautiful thing some of the wonderful people we are fortunate and privileged to meet on life's journey. We met as members of The Borough of Bury Veterans Association in Greater Manchester, Neville was in his 99th year and I was 50, approximately half his age, and I felt so happy to get to know such an incredible World War Two Veteran who had seen and done so much and was willing to share so many of his precious life experiences with me, and when I interviewed him at his home in Tottington, Bury on a lovely Saturday afternoon in March 2019 it was time very well spent indeed. Nev went on to divulge more as I asked him about his role in the R.A and further experiences: "I was a Signaller so I would relay vital information back and forth such as orders from HQ and officers, coordinates and updates on enemy movements and so on, in the early days this was still done by Morse code, later it was by radio contact and as a back-up in an emergency if all else failed or communications broke down in battle by motorbike if required, all of which we were trained to do. As I was also a trained Bombardier I could if and when required load or fire an artillery piece, we used 6" Howitzers in the early years for general artillery bombardment and later we had a 5.5" version which could be rotated to use as a general artillery piece or as an anti-tank weapon. Talking of weapons soon after we got into Normandy I found that my Sten Gun was not very reliable as it kept jamming, not what you want when caught up in close quarter situations with the enemy, so I disposed of it! I found a German Schmeisser so I kept that and had it with me all the way through to the end of the war, getting ammunition was no problem as retreating Germans often left spare clips at the roadside or in fields. Using an enemy weapon against the enemy, funny, but it was really reliable. When I was demobbed I was charged 17/6 pence by the Army for the Sten Gun I had 'Lost'." **The 5.5-Inch Howitzer in action, the same artillery piece as used by Neville and his battery in the 79th (The Scottish Horse) Medium Regiment in Europe.**

Next came the part of the interview I knew would be the hardest for Nev, when I asked him to recollect his experiences of being amongst some of the first Allied troops to enter Bergen-Belsen Concentration Camp, this would be the first WW2 veteran I had spoken to that had encountered the holocaust from the perspective of a liberator, I braced myself for what he would say next regarding:

### THE LIBERATION OF BERGEN-BELSEN CONCENTRATION CAMP

"It is still extremely difficult to talk about even after nearly eight decades, the absolute horrors we witnessed there are almost beyond words, nothing could have prepared us for what we were about to experience on the 15th April 1945. During that first day of 'Liberation' we were with various units which were part of the 2nd Army sent in to help and try and do what we could. It was overwhelming, thousands of dead and walking dead in the open and in huts, the living were lying and dying amongst the corpses of those who had been there for some time, their decaying bodies many heaped up into huge stacks others just littering the ground everywhere you looked, all giving off the most sickening and overwhelming smell. It was a horrendous attack of the senses in every way, physically and mentally traumatising to see what men and women of the SS and others who helped them could do to other human beings! Later figures that I have since read say there were over 60,000 emancipated and barely living that were in need of sustenance and medical treatment, and 13,000 others lay dead around the camp when it was found. It was of course a hotbed of disease and Typhus was declared as present. Shortly after mass graves had to be dug and bodies disposed of as soon as possible to try and limit the further spread of disease, former SS men and women and Hungarian guards were made to put the bodies into the huge pits, others were pushed in by allied servicemen with big bulldozers it was a living hell unfolding before the very eyes of all who witnessed it! When solid food was given with good intention by some British troops it later caused serious problems and even death for many eating it because their bodies could no longer digest or handle such things properly, terrible! I believe the Royal Army Medical Corps had to start with liquid supplements first along with de-lousing for the infestation that was present on everybody!

As prisoners were being processed former SS would try and hide amongst them to attempt an escape, they were pointed out by prisoners, I understand that later some were killed in revenge for the hell they had inflicted upon the inmates! One thing is for sure, myself and all others who witnessed the horrors of Bergen-Belsen and those who had liberated camps elsewhere, if they had been uncertain before about the war they had been fighting were left in no doubt whatsoever then that the evil Nazi regime and the ideology we were up against had to be utterly defeated, and the war we were engaged in was completely justifiable! Eisenhower said to get pictures and film of the camps for those who might deny it happened in the future, but I can tell you it happened, I was there, heard it, smelt it, saw it, will never forget it! I observed a lot of death and destruction during the war in many battles and places, but it is what I experienced at Belsen that has haunted me the most, given me countless sleepless nights, and the flashbacks are still regular, even at 99 years of age, some things it seems never leave you!"

**Prisoners at Bergen-Belsen after liberation in April 1945, amongst the tens of thousands of victims who died there was Anne Frank, pictured, who would later posthumously become famous because of her diaries, in which incredibly, regardless of all the terrible things that were increasingly happening to her, she wrote; "It's really a wonder that I haven't dropped all my ideals, because they seem so absurd and impossible to carry out. Yet I keep them, because in spite of everything, I still believe that people are really good at heart." (The Diary of a Young Girl).**

On a lighter note as we came to the end of his story, I asked Nev did he ever see any well-known people during his war years, he told me: "Yes, a few. Montgomery in Normandy, Eisenhower in Brussels after the Battle of the Bulge, Churchill when he visited Horrocks, Monty and Tedder near the Siegfried Line, also German Admirals Doenitz and Raeder near Bremerhaven on their way to the truce near the end of hostilities."

**I wish to finish by honouring Neville Foote, who sadly is no longer with us but was a true 'Gentle Man' in every sense, with some of the words from his Citation when awarded the Legion D'Honneur, which read; 'We must never forget the heroes like you who came from Britain and the Commonwealth to begin the liberation of Europe by liberating France. We owe our freedom and security to your dedication, because you were ready to risk your life.' A fitting tribute. R.I.P Nev.**

## Additional Information and Life After Service

**Rank upon finish of service** – Lance Bombardier.

**Medals and Honours** – 1939-45 Defence Medal, 1939-45 War Medal, 1939-45 Star, France-Germany Star, Legion D' Honneur.

**Post War Years** – After De-mob in February 1946 Neville returned to work in the family painting and decorating business called Sam Foote Ltd, which at that time was still being run by his father Sam. Later he took over the business and ran it until his retirement aged 64 in 1984. He married Elizabeth AKA Lena in 1946. They have 1 Son, 2 Grandchildren and 1 Great-Grandchild. Both devout Christians who have been parishioners of St. Anne's Church in Tottington, Bury for many years.

**Associations and Organisations** – Freemasons Grand Lodge of East Lancashire, Bury Lodge of Relief No.42, Member for 50 years, Scottish Horse R.A Association, Normandy Veterans Association, Market-Garden Association, Member and former President of Royal British Legion Bury Branch, B.O.B.V.A - Borough of Bury Veterans Association.

# SERGEANT LAURIE BURN

Served with – 13th/18th Royal Hussars (Queen Mary's Own),
Royal Armoured Corps
Service Number – 14402732
Interviewed – Harrogate, Yorkshire, 10th July 2021

### Service History and Personal Stories

- ❖ Born – 4st May 1924, Bradford, Yorkshire, England, UK.
- ❖ World War Two started for Lawrence Andrew Burn AKA Laurie as it did for many who later became servicemen, on the Home Front in the U.K, in his case at the small village of Killinghall, North Yorkshire from where amongst other things he witnessed the only bombs to land on nearby Harrogate in September 1940 where incidentally he worked at Montague Burton, a Tailors shop where he was a Shop Assistant and Fire Watcher.
- ❖ Later when he was part of the Killinghall Home Guard, which he had joined in January 1942 he also witnessed the bigger more destructive bombing of the beautiful city of York in April 1942, and remembers the flashes and glows that lit up the night sky during what were known as the 'Baedeker Raids' taking place on cathedral cities around that time, named as such because as the story goes Hitler enraged by the bombing of the historical cities of Rostock and Lubeck by the RAF picked up a Baedeker guidebook and ordered that every historical city marked with 3 stars in England be bombed in retaliation! *The cities of Exeter, Bath, Canterbury, Norwich and York were heavily hit.
- ❖ On 20th August 1942 Laurie volunteered for the army at the recruitment office on Victoria Avenue in

Harrogate, some of his previous training with various weapons whilst in the Home Guard which ironically included anti-tank weapons, stood him in good stead for the full Army training he undertook when he was sent off to Bovington Camp in Dorset having joined a tank regiment, the 13/18 Royal Hussars (Queen Mary's Own) based at Skipton.

- Laurie undertook 3 months of intense and varied training with the 58th Training Regiment RAC from October 1942 until January 1943, doing square bashing and basic soldiering skills such as hand-to-hand combat and use of firearms and as Bovington was and still is home of the British RAC - Royal Armoured Corps they were also trained to be proficient in many aspects of and positions in a tank included being a Driver, Radio Operator and Gunner.
- After being evaluated by their instructors the new recruits were allocated what would become their ongoing position within the tank and tank crew. Laurie was selected to become a Tank Gunner and as part of the 13/18 Hussars QMO continued with a lot more ongoing and specialist training as his regiment was one those earmarked to use new Amphibious tanks that were being developed in preparation for the invasion of Europe.
- These special tanks known as 'Hobart's Funnies' were developed along with other curious and ingenious tanks and armoured vehicles to overcome different kinds of natural challenges that the terrain at sea and on land would pose for the allied invasion force.
- Laurie and the 13/18 had ongoing training from Jan 1943 until shortly before D-Day in June 1944 in many places on different land and amphibious sea exercises, they first trained on land with Valentine tanks near Wickham Market in Suffolk and in the water with them at Fritton Lake in Norfolk. Later when moving onto live-firing exercises in Wales and the Lulworth Ranges in Dorset the tank crews had moved on to using what would become their main weapon of war, the more modern American Sherman M4 Tank fitted with a deadly 75mm main gun and two 0.3 Browning machine guns.
- Next as the training was ramped up they moved to Tain in the Highlands of Scotland where they were based at Fort George and practiced with the amphibious version of the Sherman Tank called the DD – Duplex Drive, given that name because of its ability to switch between the use of tracks on land, propellers and other equipment in the water, more about this later. Here they were being prepared for the rougher and more realistic conditions of the sea that they expected to face during any anticipated sea-based invasion.
- Finally after this and other 'Specialist Training' that Laurie talks about afterwards in this story they were ready for the main event itself, Operation Overlord, the Allied invasion of Western Europe on the 6th June 1944 known to most as D-Day, which began for Laurie and the other Amphibious tank crews of the 13/18 Hussars in their DD's when they landed at the Queen White sector of Sword Beach at around 7.25 am on that historical day.
- From that point on an 11-month battle lay ahead from Deliverance Day taking them across France, Belgium, Holland with many hard-fought battles along the way whilst attached to a lot of different formations such as the 27th and the 8th Armoured Brigades and XXX Corps, until Laurie and some of the Hussars finished their path of liberation in Bremen, Germany.
- Along the way they and their Sherman's would be involved in some legendary engagements including those at Caen, Falaise, Brussels, Antwerp, Arnhem, Ardennes, the Rhine crossing and many more, serving all the way throughout with his brother Peter as part of his crew, a very rare thing indeed, by the war's end they had got through 4 tanks!
- Then from 1945 to 1947 Laurie swapped tanks for armoured cars when he became part BAOR – British Army of the Rhine forces of occupation in what was now a divided post-war Germany, serving in Hannover and the Hertz Mountain areas as part of the 5th Infantry Division. After 4 years, 5 months Army service Laurie was demobbed in Hull 22nd April 1947.

The wartime service of this born and bred Yorkshireman would take him far from home and into the dangerous territory of Nazi occupied Europe. In fact on D-Day it is well documented that the Amphibious tanks of the 13/18 Hussars of which Laurie Burn was a part were the very first mechanised units in that 1st attacking wave to reach Sword beach in what was known as Operation Neptune, the initial amphibious part of the much bigger Operation Overlord, and as a result when they hit Normandy that morning they spearheaded the Allied invasion of Europe from that sector using a new secret weapon the Sherman DD – Duplex Drive tank, which after being launched from an LCT – Landing Craft Tank Ship used its very ingenious special duel mechanism to work by propellers in the water in a sea-going role and then convert to the use of tracks on land where it went straight into combat as a normal tank, which they did from D-Day on the 6th June 1944 until the end of war in Europe on the 8th May 1945 engaging in many tough battles along the way. Gunner Laurie Burn and all the crews in the different regiments using these DD's were very few in number even on that morning in June 1944 when they came out of the water and appeared on the 5 landing beaches at Normandy during the D-Day invasion, so to find with the kind help of the Bovington Tank Museum and interview one of these 'very few' remaining kinds of unique veterans 77 years later is something truly remarkable! When I did I couldn't believe how good, concise and clear Laurie's memory was as he told his very interesting and action-packed story, also his ability to deliver the information full of facts, figures, names and places, again reminding me of how fortunate I was as the interviewer to meet such amazing people and capture such precious and important history for my Debt of Gratitude project, this was reinforced as he told me about:

## BEING A GUNNER IN A SHERMAN DD TANK FROM D-DAY TO V.E DAY

"We were in the 13th/18th Royal Hussars Queen Mary's Own, it was originally a cavalry regiment with a proud history and some of the old traditions were still there such as all crews when in training, being inspected or forming up standing by their tanks and then being told by a Commanding Officer to 'Mount Up', then we would jump into our positions inside and on we would go, it was a little respectful nod to our origins, from when the Hussars were on horseback! Times had of course moved on and as a mechanised regiment in World War Two we were now part of the RAC – Royal Armoured Corps, not Royal Automobile Club, which by then had various kinds of tanks that we trained on and eventually went into battle with, the training is a good place to start especially as later we had been chosen to be one of the few regiments that would be using tanks both in special ambitious and traditional land-based roles that required different kinds of training. I volunteered for the Army with my older brother Peter and we chose to join the 13/18 which was based at Skipton in North Yorkshire, we were sent to Bovington Camp and ranges in Dorset 1st October 1942 where we completed our 12 week basic training during which time we were taught the skills required for almost every position in the tank as a Driver, Gunner, Wireless Operator and Loader, Assistant Driver and Bow Gunner whilst being assessed by our instructors, the 5th position was that of the Commander. It also meant if needs be that any of us could multi-task and take up the position of a fellow crewman if he was injured or killed in battle, the kind of thing that might save your life one day! Similar I believe to what some aircrewmen also did to a certain extent in Bomber Command.

Anyway by early 1943 with basic passed I was chosen to be a Tank Gunner, our early training was on Valentine tanks, this continued when we went on to Wickham Market in Suffolk and when we went to do early amphibious exercises with them in the water at Fritton Lake inland from Great Yarmouth in Norfolk, later that year when we moved on to other places in Wales and at Lulworth Cove back in Dorset we had been given a new kind of tank to practice our firing on, the American Sherman with its big 75mm gun, that could pack a punch. It was these M4's that would remain our battle tanks from there on and would eventually take us all the way through Western Europe, but before any of that we had to work on the amphibious elements of our specialist training with them, something we were in full flow with by early 1944 when we were sent down to a

Naval Submarine station in Gosport, near Portsmouth in Hampshire. It was there were we practiced for weeks with submarine escape equipment so that we were prepared for the worst-case scenario of being trapped in our tank if it went down in the water, where you could lose your life in the same nightmarish way many submarine crews met their fates, that's why we were repeatedly drilled there amongst other things in a huge water tank, when it was empty we had to climb down a 20-foot ladder and into a Sherman tank at the bottom. Once inside we had to sit in our positions and then the water was released into it, thousands of gallons, we had to wait until the water was up to our chins then put on a nose clip and switch on the oxygen from our packs called ATEA – Amphibious Tank Escape Apparatus, at some point the submariners dived down in their scuba gear and tapped us on the shoulder, that was our que to get out of the confined space of our Sherman and make our way to the surface, it was essential training but a bit of a strain on the nervous system to say the least! We progressed from there to amphibious exercises in open water conditions up in Tain, Scotland where we practised in the Moray Firth from our base at Fort George in Spring 1944 with some bad weather conditions, but it certainly gave us a more of a feel for what we could realistically expect in the English Channel later on and pretty much what we got on the day of the invasion when it came."

When it did come the D-Day assault began at each of the five Allied landing beaches with a massive aerial and naval bombardment of German coastal defences and artillery positions. The plan was that this would be followed by the Amphibious Squadrons landing with Sherman DD Tanks whose initial task was to neutralise the beach defences, followed by the arrival of the Assault Engineers in their AVRE's – Armoured or Assault Vehicle Royal Engineers which consisted of various odd-looking specialized vehicles such as flail and demolition tanks that were also known as 'Hobart's Funnies' who were to create tracks through the minefields for the safe movement of vehicles from the beach, this was to also assisted the infantry and other vehicles that were landed soon after. Once the initial enemy fire had been suppressed as best possible and the exits opened the job of the DD tanks, which now with their protective water screens down had become regular tanks, was to move off the beach to support the infantry in capturing their inland objectives. **A very good example of Sherman DD Tanks of the 13/18 Royal Hussars in action, here just off Sword beach at Riva Bella near Ouistreham where they are providing fire support and cover for the men of No. 4 Commando in fierce house-to-house fighting, note the folded flotation 'skirts' and twin propellers clearly visible on the closest tank. After subduing some quite stubborn enemy opposition, No. 4 Commando had moved inland and by 1pm had linked up with elements of the 6th Airborne Division who were holding the vital bridges over the River Orne.**

For the assault on Normandy 10 tank battalions were distributed among British, Canadian and American Forces. On Sword and Utah Beaches the majority of the DD tanks successfully swam ashore, on Gold Beach the tanks were brought directly to the shore by landing craft because of high seas. On Juno only some of the tanks were launched due to high seas, but on Omaha Beach, 27 of the 29 tanks sank at sea in six-foot waves after being launched three miles from the beach, the lack of tank cover available at Omaha leading directly to the initial very high losses of U.S infantry landed there! Numbers vary slightly from different sources, but during the entire D-Day operation approximately 290 DD – Duplex Drive tanks were used, of which around 45 sank or foundered in rough seas whilst trying to swim in. There were 4 Tank 'Squadrons' in the 13/18 Royal Hussars QMO at Sword Beach they were A,B,C,HQ, each consisting of 10 Tanks per Squadron, the first to go in were A & B Squadrons with 4 columns of 5 tanks, 1 tank failed immediately upon launch and 3 were lost on the way in, leaving 16 to 'Touch Down' on the beach, one of these being Laurie and his brother Peter's. The 13/18 landing at Sword beach was concentrated on Queen Red and Queen White areas in front of the coastal village of Hermanville-sur-Mer, where by 07:25 Laurie Burn and others in their Sherman DD's were the very first to make landfall in that sector on D-Day in support of the 8$^{th}$ Infantry Brigade and were immediately engaging the enemy. The Regiment was one of the three Armoured Regiments of the 27th Armoured Brigade, commanded by Brigadier Erroll Prior-Palmer who were a vital key element of Operation Neptune the Amphibious part of the bigger Operation Overlord. We now re-join Laurie as he shares his experiences from the extremely unique perspective of being one of the very few remaining amphibious 1$^{st}$ Wave to hit the beach veterans of D-Day;

"My brother Pete and I were part of the same Sherman tank crew in 'A Squadron', Pete was the co-driver and I was the Gunner. The Sherman was one of the 'Swimming Tanks' known as DD's because they were Duplex Drive vehicles, AKA Donald Ducks. They floated by means of a collapsible canvas screen fitted to the hull of this 32-tonne tank and raised or lowered by means of compressed air in bottles that inflated tubing that lifted the floatation screen, once it was raised the tank was driven by two propellors from the main engine and steered by a rudder and a very long tiller, actually they were very seaworthy, and survived in all but the highest seas! In case of emergency we also had our personal escape breathing apparatus and inflatable rafts. We'd departed from the Solent near Portsmouth, as we travelled across the channel there began the most terrific bombardment off the French coast, standing on our tank cupola we could see a vast armada of ships; battleships blazing off their big guns, rocket projectile ships launching hundreds of rockets; and the RAF bombing the landing area. We had all seen photos of the area at Ouistreham, where we were to land, and about 5000 yards from the beach we heard the order 'Floater' – we knew we were off! The landing craft stopped, and we moved down the ramp and floated into the sea, and the officer steered us to shore. We were all so low in the sea we looked like rowing boats, but that was part of the surprise plan.

When we came ashore that morning the 13/18 Hussars were the first on Sword Beach, there was nothing and no one in front of us, except the Germans, who from their defensive positions soon let all hell lose upon us and the other units coming in close behind us, as soon as we dropped the floater screen we were 'swamped' by the incoming high tide, which flooded the engine compartment, but what must have been real dismay to the enemy when that canvas dropped was they were staring into the barrel of a 75mm gun, one that still worked and which along with the other tanks returned fire trying to take out as many positions as we could see enemy action coming from, but we had become a sitting duck in our swamped tank and with incoming mortar and Artillery fire reigning down on us and the beach getting quickly filled with many men, vehicles and casualties there was nothing left to do but evacuate - that was our baptism of fire, that was when, like it or not, boys very quickly became men, me amongst them! It was then that our troop sergeant, who had safely landed his tank, reversed to us and took us on board, and then, amid all the shooting and mayhem, calmly dropped us off by the sea wall. I believe eventually about 33 out of our 40 tanks launched made it onto the beach but some were swamped like us, but we were enough to make a real contribution to the battle that day! That evening after receiving a new tank from the reserves we brought over with us we were camped up in an orchard in Hermanville when we were duly 'Stonked' – that is, we came under mortar attack. We had dug trenches under our tanks so we felt quite safe, but from that day on we always slept in our tanks! Our first day of war was over, a day which we had trained as a crew for two years, and we were ably led. It never crossed my mind that we could lose the war; we were too young to think otherwise. I was only just 20 years old on D-Day but many more tough engagements lay ahead across Europe before we eventually did win that war, and through the efforts and endeavours of each and everyone who was a part of all the allied forces we did exactly that!"

**The Sherman DD – Duel Duplex Tank, similar to the one in which Laurie was a Gunner, shown here with the canvas floatation screen in both positions. It was able if and when required to fire its main gun whilst approaching the shore. A marvel of design which was deemed necessary to help aid and greatly increase the chance of any amphibious led invasion of Western Europe being successful, after costly lessons learned from the disasterious Operation Jubilee at Dieppe on the 19th August 1942, which led to this and other ingenious tank-based designs being developed to cope with all beach terrains by Major-General Sir Percy Hobart, hence the nickname of 'Hobarts Funnies' which were used in many Allied offensives.**

The order of battle for the 13th/18th Hussars QMO and main places they fought in Western Europe 1944-45 began at D-Day where they were part of and came under the British 2nd Army, British 1 Corps, 3rd British Infantry Division, as part of the 27th Armoured Brigade (Amphibious). They remained part of the latter until the end of July 1944 having now moved inland engaging in support of various other units in the Normandy campaign at Caen and Caumont (near Villers-Bocage where Waffen SS 'Panzer Ace' Michael Wittmann and Heavy SS Panzer Battalion 101 had over a month earlier ambushed and were estimated to have destroyed approximately 14 tanks, 2 anti-tank guns and 13 to 15 transport vehicles in less than 15 minutes mainly with the heavily armoured Tiger 1 tanks, highlighting the real dangers that Allied tank crews like Laurie's faced). After Caumont the 13/18 were assigned to and came under the 8th Armoured Brigade, who they remained with until the wars end. We now pick up Laurie's story again from this point where as part of the 8th A.B he tells us about his and the 13th/18th's advance across Europe beginning with the dreaded Tiger Tank:

"As we continued to fight the Germans who were a very tough adversary, we went through Normandy at Mont Pincon, Falaise to the Seine, then on to Belgium with more fierce engagements, Brussels, Antwerp, the Albert and Escaut Canals. We sometimes encountered the feared Tiger tanks who we saw destroy a lot of our tanks and kill many of our lads, so if we spotted them in the distance we would call in Tactical Air Support to help destroy them, when our aircraft were close we would fire shells near the Tigers that released red smoke to mark where the enemy was so that our boys could take them out! Along the way we all witnessed a lot of suffering and casualties, British, American, Canadian, German and the poor civilians who got caught up in the line of fire, very sad.

Tank like artillery units were seconded and became ad-hoc parts of other formations along the way as, when and where needed by the army at any given time. For example in Holland during Operation Market-Garden in September 1944 where we were part of 30 Corps failed attempt to reach the 1st Airborne Division trapped at Arnhem, (the 13/18 got as far as Elst a town between Arnhem and Nijmegen), and later when the Germans broke through during the Battle of the Bulge in December 1944 we were sent as reinforcements operating from the Roer to Ardennes to help units if needed which included the 6th Airborne Division. We even had some memorable visits and situation briefings from Field Marshal Montgomery himself. In January 1945 as we advanced we were involved in engagements in Germany at Sittard in the Roer Triangle alongside the famous

7th Armoured Division (Desert Rats), in February 1945 we had hard battles at Cleve and Goch and went on to be part of Operation Plunder, the Crossing of the Rhine at Rees in March 1945, then continuing to fight on in the direction of Bremen, crossing the River Weser, by late April Bremen had been reached, and this is where we were when the Germans surrendered and we celebrated V.E Day on 8th May 1945. Can't forget it because we had just captured one of those lethal German 88mm Guns and there were long columns of German POW's marching everywhere and one of our officers told us at last the war in Europe was over, seemed unreal after nearly a year of almost continuous hard fighting! From late May I was based in Hannover and afterwards also the Hertz Mountain areas in the British Army of the Rhine from 1945-1947 as part of the 5th Infantry Division."

**Left – The Seahorse Logo of the 27th Armoured Brigade showing that the few who wore it were also in an amphibious unit including those who, as in Laurie's case were part of the D-Day landings. Right – The logo of the 8th Armoured Brigade who the 13/18 Hussars QMO fought directly under for most their campaigns in Western Europe whilst working alongside and being seconded to other various fighting units along the way.**

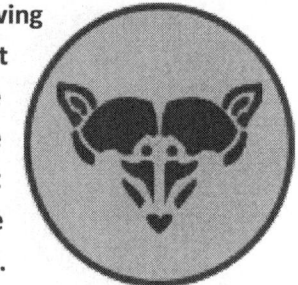

"I nicknamed our first tank Icanhopit 1, and it really was a case of 'I-Can-Hop-It' because by the time we finished our war in Germany nearly a year later we'd hopped onto Icanhopit 4, the fate of the other 3 being; one as mentioned before 'Swamped' on D-Day, one blown up when we hit a mine, one destroyed by enemy action with an anti-tank weapon whilst I was on leave which killed the Commander, the last one eventually having to be swapped for an armoured car when we became part of BAOR after the war. Very different and quite strange to experience most of our war from inside a tank and in my case through a periscope! I think to have me and Peter as two brothers in the same crew survive all that was incredibly lucky, that was why they didn't normally allow family members to serve directly together, in case they all copped for it together, would have been too much for any family to bare! As a result of those experiences and many others in battles along the way Peter had what we called shell shock, now PTSD, and wasn't too good afterwards, I Didn't talk about the war for over 50 years and since 1944 until now (2021) have only been back to Normandy once in 2002. But as I've got older and the years have passed I feel that it is important to share with those who are interested to know, like yourself Gary, what we now see as very important historical events, if we don't how else will people know what happened and what we as young lads all went through for our country and the others we helped liberate back then." 
**Laurie with his last Sherman Tank - 'Icanhopit 4' in May 1945 outside Bremerhaven in Germany with the Union Jack proudly flying high on top of the turret.**

**The 13th/18th Royal Hussars QMO is one of the very few regiments in the British Army which has 2 official mottos, both I think can be viewed as a tribute to Laurie Burn and all those who served in World War Two; they are; Viret in Aeternum – May Their Name Flourish Forever. And; Pro Rege Pro Lege Pro Patria Conamur - For King, For Justice, For Country we Fight.**

~ 38 ~

# Additional Information and Life After Service

**Rank upon finish of service** – Sergeant.

**Medals and Honours** – 1939-45 War Medal, 1939-45 Defence Medal, France-Germany Star, Legion D'Honneur (2016).

**Post War Years** – After leaving the Army in 1947 Laurie worked for the Cooperative Insurance Society for 42 years as an Insurance Salesman, from 1947 until 1989 when he retired. Married Dorothy at Bar Methodist Church, Harrogate in August 1952. Together 59 years until her passing in December 2011. They have 3 daughters, 6 Grandchildren, 3 Great-Grandchild.

**Associations and Organisations** – USDAW – The Union of Shop, Distributive and Allied Workers, as a Group Secretary, Yorkshire Area Secretary and Member of the National Committee. 13/18 Royal Hussars Association now Yorkshire Hussars Association, Life-long member of the Methodist Church.

# SAPPER FRANK MOUGUÉ

Served with – 263 Field Company & No.10 Bomb Disposal Squadron, Royal Engineers

Service Number – 14416828

Interviewed – Royal Hospital Chelsea, London, 19th February 2016

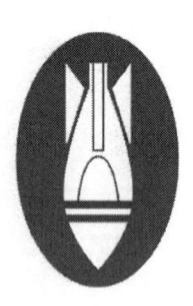

## Service History and Personal Stories

- Born – 4th February 1925, Putney, London, England, UK.
- When war broke out in 1939 Frank Mouqué became a child evacuee and was sent from Putney in Southwest London down to the seaside resort town of Bognor Regis in West Sussex. He was there from age 14-16 then in 1941 returned to his family back in the capital and worked as an Usher at the Regal Cinema in Putney.
- In January 1943 on the run up to his 18th birthday Frank volunteered for the Army, and once 18 in February 1943 he had been officially enlisted and had begun 6 weeks basic training at No.1 Primary Training Centre at Saighton Camp, Chester, after which he transferred to the Royal Engineers and was posted to the Royal Engineers Depot at Chatham, Kent, where as part of B Company, No.1 Training Battalion he undertook 6 months intensive training in every aspect of Military Engineering until October 1943.
- Eventually he would join what became his main wartime unit the 263 Field Company, it was with them that Frank would undergo a lot of training in the months running up to D-Day in preparation

~ 40 ~

- for the invasion of Western Europe. This included 2 weeks of beach landing training on various amphibious craft at a coastal area called 'The Witterings' in West Sussex, coincidently close to where he was evacuated as a child a few years earlier.
- D-Day, 6th June 1944 truly began for Frank when he landed as part of the British 3rd Infantry Division under the XII CTRE – 12th Corps Troops Royal Engineers, 5th Assault Regiment RE, 263 (Sussex) Field Company on Sword Beach at approximately 8.30am in the 'Roger/Green Sector'. The various RE Field Companies were 'loaned' to the assaulting divisions as obstacle clearance parties on the British Gold (280 Fd Coy) & Sword (263 Fd Coy) and British/Canadian Juno beach (262 Fd Coy) areas of the invasion force.
- After getting across the beach under heavy fire his first of many dangerous tasks was mine clearance, making a safe pathway from the beach to the nearest road to help incoming troops and vehicles get off the beach and inland as soon as possible.
- This was just the beginning for Frank, those of 263 and all other R.E Field Company's under XII CTRE as they moved Westward from the sands of Normandy across Europe until they finished the war in Germany nearly a year later. Along the way under fire from land and air they would complete many tasks as they were seconded and posted to many areas, assisting different units of the British Army during their hard fought and costly advance.
- This led to him being involved in many well-known parts of that campaign such as reaching the famous Pegasus Bridge on 7th June, a day after it had been liberated in the first action of Operation Overlord, then helping build the first two bridges of the allied advance that moved across the River Orne and Caen Canal, and later being involved in the evacuation of the remnants of the beleaguered 1st Airborne Division out of Arnhem in assault boats across the Lower Rhine as part of Operation Berlin in September 1944.
- Frank also took part in the bridge building required on the bigger Rhine Crossings in the full-scale assault into Germany in March 1945 as part of Operation Plunder, once across moving onto the Northern Rhine-Ruhr area via Herne, following parts of the XII Corps final advances into Germany which led to more bridges being built by XII CTRE of which 263 Coy (Company) was a part, this included bridging the Rivers Aa and Weser.
- They were also tasked with repairing roads and other infrastructure required by both the armed forces and civilian populations in the areas and countries they passed through, and whilst moving through Lower Saxony Frank recalls having to help repair and temporarily restore the water supply at the horrendous Belsen Concentration Camp. Later when the Germans Surrendered in May 1945 Frank finished his war in Hamelin, Lower Saxony.
- After this they were involved in the restoration of Hamburg Docks and later the Sappers of XII CTRE assisted other units in erecting and dismantling Bailey bridges and were involved in other civil engineering works in rebuilding the Occupied Zone of West Germany. The XII CTRE and its companies were disbanded by March 1946.
- Frank went on to serve as part of BAOR – British Army of the Rhine until 1948, and that same year returned to the U.K where he completed specialist training in Bomb Disposal, dealing with UX – Unexploded devices found around the South of England until December 1949. His final posting was to the 31 Assault Park Squadron where he remained until April 1952 when he received a Medical & Honourable Discharge, bringing to an end a very respectable 9 years and 3 months of service as a Royal Engineer in the British Army.
- During that time he had seen a lot of action, risked his life on many occasions and served his country well, so it was very fitting for Frank to end up as one of the famous Chelsea Pensioners at the Royal Hospital Chelsea in London.

'Soldiers, Sailors, and Airmen of the Allied Expeditionary Force; You are about to embark upon the Great Crusade, toward which we have striven these many months. The eyes of the world are upon you. The hopes and prayers of liberty-loving people everywhere march with you. In company with our brave allies and brothers-in-arms on other fronts you will bring about the destruction of the German war machine, the elimination of Nazi tyranny over oppressed peoples of Europe, and security for ourselves in a free world. Your task will not be an easy one. Your enemy is well trained, well equipped, and battle-hardened. He will fight savagely. But this is the year 1944. Much has happened since the Nazi triumphs of 1940-41. The United Nations have inflicted upon the Germans great defeats, in open battle, man-to-man. Our air offensive has seriously reduced their strength in the air and their capacity to wage war on the ground. Our Home Fronts have given us an overwhelming superiority in weapons and munitions of war, and placed at our disposal great reserves of trained fighting men. The tide has turned. The free men of the world are marching together to victory. I have full confidence in your courage, devotion to duty, and skill in battle. We will accept nothing less than full victory. Good Luck! And let us all beseech the blessing of Almighty God upon this great and noble undertaking.' Dwight D. Eisenhower.

This 'Order of the Day' written by 'Ike' 5 Star General and Supreme Commander of the Allied Expeditionary Force in Europe (pictured here on the front of LIFE Magazine soon after D-Day on 19th June 1944) was distributed by leaflet to this 175,000-member force on the eve of the invasion to personally encourage those taking part in D-Day, of whom Frank Mougué was one! Because he like all the others was involved in the biggest amphibious landings ever attempted, a truly historical moment in history that would bring about the liberation of millions of people under Nazi Occupation in Western Europe. It would lead to all those who were involved having to contribute in their different ways as they advanced through France, Belgium, Holland and finally into Nazi Germany itself. Frank and others of the Royal Engineers played a very important part in that, clearing mines for the safe passage of allied armies, building vital bridges for them to overcome natural obstacles, rebuilding damaged roads and many other types of essential facilities. All these things helped bring about an Allied victory over the evil of Nazism in Europe and bring about the demise of Adolf Hitler's Third Reich. Frank now tells us more about the part he played in this as:

### A SAPPER IN THE ROYAL ENGINEERS HELPING LIBERATE WESTERN EUROPE

"If anything needed building up, blowing up, clearing or fixing the Royal Engineers were the men for the job! We were trained to do all that and much more, and for me and the other lads from 263 Company or Coy as we called it this truly began at 8.30am on the 6th June 1944 when came off down the ladders of our LST – Landing Ship Tank as they were called and waded forward through choppy waters with full kit which included a 30lb pack of plastic explosives ready primed with detonators, these were meant for the sea defences like the 'Rommel's Gates' which had Teller Anti-Tank mines attached to them, but we were delayed by one hour and the tide was too high for us to deal with them! So on we went under fire mainly from incoming mortar and artillery from behind the beach, like tens of thousands of other troops making their way on to the beaches in the allied landing zones all the way down the coast of Normandy at that exact moment, we had to just keep going because this was D-Day and we were here to try and liberate 'Fortress Europe' in what was known as Operation Overlord! The amphibious part of that plan that we were involved in at that time was called Operation Neptune, this was where we had to successfully land on and take the beach areas, expand outwards from there to create bridgeheads inland, support incoming airborne reinforcements and then the initial bigger plan was to attempt link-ups with those who had already landed by air at Pegasus Bridge and with the troops coming in by sea at the next allied landing beach to us called Juno. As we were approaching by sea and whilst in the water we could see huge amounts of men and material including armour had built up on the beach and that there had been a lot of casualties, it looked chaotic so forging inland was essential to meet the goals I just mentioned, that is where we came in because as soon as we got across our part of the beach called the Roger-Green sector near Ouistrehem we were immediately instructed to get to work on clearing the way forward of mines from the beach to connecting roads behind so we could get the troops off there and as far inland as possible ASAP, otherwise it would just continue to be a killing zone that would intensify if the Germans were able to bring up reinforcements including more of the deadly 88mm anti-tank artillery pieces. We were able to meet these initial goals and at the same time supress Nazi sniper fire, later on we were ordered by our section Sergeant to move on to Colleville-sur-Orne where we had to clear a landing area for another wave of incoming gliders by using our explosives to bring down 'Rommel's Hedgehogs', these were telegraph poles erected as anti-glider weapons that would seriously damage or destroy any glider that landed on them, deadly, we started to blow down the poles but after about 15 minutes we were ordered off as the gliders were arriving, and too early for some they earned the title 'Flying Coffins', not a nice thing to see when they're your own boys! Later we dug in for the night and prepared for any possible German Counter-attack, next morning at dawn we set off to join and bolster the forces that had relieved the 6th Airborne at 'Pegasus' canal Bridge in Bénouville, where our first task was to remove the German explosive charges and fit our own, then we built a 224ft Bailey Pontoon Class 40 Bridge nearby over the Caen Canal, we called it 'London Bridge', and a second one a 286ft Bailey Pontoon Class 40 Bridge over the River Orne at Ranville, they were completed in around 3 days, and for the next two weeks we were constantly repairing the two bridges as they were damaged by shell fire! We built the first Bailey Bridge in France, over that canal and it was our OC's proud boast 'this Coy will bridge every river and canal to Berlin', in the end I think we weren't far off achieving that!" **A military transport crossing the Orne bridgehead in a picture taken by Sergeant Laing of No.5 Army Film & Photographic Unit with the tongue in cheek 'London Bridge' sign clearly showing. This was one of the two bridges Frank helped build in the early stages of the Normandy Campaign which he mentioned to me by name during the interview. 263 Field Company assisted 71 Field Company R.E in building these two Class 40 Bailey Pontoon Bridges known as London I & II to duplicate the Pegasus and Ranville Bridges across the River Orne and Caen Canal. *The Baileys were extensively used portable, prefabricated bridges.**

I went on to ask Frank about other well-known operations he participated in, the next one he described was of special interest to me because I had previously interviewed veterans who were involved in various aspects of it, but this was from a very different part and angle indeed, this was Arnhem: "What we experienced in Normandy was just the beginning, as the months rolled on we were involved in many other situations during our active service as we continued pushing through the countries of Western Europe, and I found myself in the heart of all sorts such as Operation Berlin in Holland where we evacuated the battered remnants of the 1ST Airborne Division from Arnhem back across the Neder Rhine or Lower Rhine to the safety of Allied lines on the evenings of 25-26th September 1944, this was the last part of the unintentional outcome of Montgomery's Operation Market-Garden, if it had of worked there was a possibility of reaching Berlin by Christmas '44, not meant to be! Anyhow we were bringing them back with the help of the Dorset Regiment and Royal Canadian Engineers before they were totally encircled, using 'Storm Boats' which were light flat-bottomed canvas plywood boats with a 40 horse power engine and once again found ourselves in the thick of it under heavy

German machine gun and mortar fire, we also had to contend with strong currents and fast moving water and we had to persuade the troops to leave their packs, guns and ammo behind because it was too much excess weight on a light boat, they threw most of the gear in the drink! I believe that in the end we all rescued over 2000 men, many of them were thanking us as they got off safely on the other side near Driel I think it was, but we didn't have much time for chit-chat we had to get back across and try and save as many of the remaining men as we could! During our advance through Europe we built many Pontoon bridges over many rivers like the Seine in France, the Halsche and Dommel rivers in Belgium and Holland, along the way working alongside many other well-known formations such as the 7th Armoured Division (Desert Rats) and the 51st Highland Division (of which Neville Foote was a part). In February and March 1945 we received special training in rafting and Folding Boat Equipment (FBE) bridging in preparation for Operation Plunder, the big allied crossing of the Rhine into Nazi Germany, and we eventually assisted in making a big 1093-foot Bailey Pontoon Class 40 Bridge at one of those crossing points in a place called Xanten, we finished it in around 2-3 days, some going, especially when again we sometimes found ourselves under fire from the Germans and taking casualties! As part of 12 (XII) CTRE we followed the advance of 12 (XII) Corps when they worked closely with 30 (XXX) Corps to get across the Rhine, which was really symbolic as we were now in Germany proper, on their soil and in their homeland, very significant! We later continued with 12 Corps as they advanced deeper into Germany which meant that further bridging took place over the Rivers Aa and Weser.

Our next job took us up into Lower Saxony to a place called Bergen near Celle, and nothing could prepare us for what we would witness and experience there when we were sent to help repair the water supply at Belsen Concentration Camp, most people have seen the film footage of those horrible things but to see and smell that for real, that wasn't war that was something else, too hard to explain, horrible things even for hardened soldiers to take, those who saw it will never forget it, don't wish to talk much more about that! Afterwards we were down in Hamelin when the war in Europe finished on the 8th May 1945, and like many others in many countries we seriously celebrated V.E Day in good company or 'good Coy' as we say in the R.E's, after all we had helped bring about that victory, and I think the next morning the world woke up with the biggest hangover ever! During different operations and depending on the task given we would sometimes be in forward front line situations carrying out duties like mine clearance by prodding methods and sometimes the use of mine detectors, and as mentioned before bridging rivers and other times if behind the lines doing road re-building which we did using pebble, wood and tough corduroy, bomb crater filling, removal of heavy concrete road obstructions, operating bulldozers, and sometimes using AVRE - Assault Vehicle Royal Engineers which were armoured military engineering vehicles, also doing the repair of many facilities including docks, aerodromes and runways, despite being seconded here, there and everywhere we still remained under the umbrella command of 12 Corps Troops Royal Engineers, all these different kinds of tasks led to the R.E's unofficial motto - 'First In-Last Out', how true that was!"

After completing repairs at Hamburg Docks and at other places in the allied sectors of what was now a divided Germany Frank went onto to become part of the forces of occupation in what was known as BAOR – British Army of the Rhine, spending time in the Hertz mountains, but mainly based in Hamelin, where amongst other things after completing an Army correspondence German language course with the added opportunity to practice it each and every working day Frank soon became fluent. This led to him becoming the Clerk and Interpreter between his Commanding Officer and local German staff and also dealing with German POW's, this position led to him receiving the unsubstantiated rank of Corporal until his return home in 1948. From late 1948 to early 1949 Frank trained in Unexploded Bomb Disposal and in 1949 served for 8 months in No.10 Bomb Disposal Squadron, based at Broadridge Heath BD HQ near Horsham in West Sussex, and whilst there amongst other dangerous UXB's they dealt with up and down the South coast Frank and pals were called out to take care of a big device that had been found on Brighton Beach. Frank's last posting from December 1949 to April 1952 was to the 31 Assault Park Squadron, whilst with them he spent a lot of that time at Swinton

Barracks in Perham Down, Wiltshire near Salisbury Plain, undertaking the repair and maintenance of tanks, motorbikes and all manner of military vehicles, and finished his time as a Sapper in the British Army on 1st April 1952 after being medically discharged. In retirement Frank very aptly went on to become a resident of the Royal Hospital Chelsea in London. I asked him what's it like to be one of the famous Chelsea Pensioners, instantly recognisable by their scarlet coats and tricorne hats, and was told: "Well the first thing is this is the finest care home in the country, without a doubt, and for those who reside here it is an honour to be part of such a great place with such an amazing history with all its traditions, everything one wants here your given the opportunity of it, delivered with care, servility, consideration and respect, I'm very happy here, this is Rolls-Royce, absolute, everything you can conceivably think of is catered for, after 400 years of practice they're very good at it now!"

**Royal Hospital Chelsea, the oldest purpose-built military veterans care home in the United Kingdom, founded by King Charles II and opened in 1692. Located on Royal Hospital Road in Chelsea this 66-acre site sits on one side by the banks of the River Thames. It is a Grade 1 listed heritage site designed by Sir Christopher Wren as a military Alms-house which in the ancient sense of the word is where 'Hospital' is derived from, a place of care and 'hospitality', something it has done for generations of veterans in recognition of their loyal service to the nation. Home to the world-famous Chelsea Pensioners it is an independent charity and as such relies partly upon donations to cover day-to-day running costs to provide care and accommodation for veterans of the British Army. It is also the resting place of Margaret and Dennis Thatcher who were big supporters and donors of the establishment. I am very happy to have interviewed resident veterans at this great place for my books and to have a good ongoing connection with them and by extension to this incredible and historical abode. This view of the South Front is where the words of their founding principles are etched, which state; FOR THE SUCCOUR AND RELEIF OF VETERANS BROKEN BY AGE AND WAR.**

**The motto of the Royal Engineers is; Ubique Quo Fas et Gloria Ducunt - 'Everywhere and Where Right and Glory Lead'. Which seems very fitting when describing Frank's service years. The Ubique part being a shared motto with the Royal Artillery.**

After our interview back in 2016 he signed a keepsake for me and with his well-known witty humour added regarding his story; 'Make a good job or Else!' Well Frank I hope you like the job I have done and that it makes you smile. It is a tribute written about a great guy and great veteran.

## Additional Information and Life After Service

**Rank upon finish of service** – Sapper.

**Medals and Honours** – Legion D' Honneur (2018), 1939-45 Defence Medal, 1939-45 War Medal, 1939-45 Star, France-Germany Star.

**Post War Years** – Frank returned to Mann Crossman & Paulin Brewery from 1953 to 1983 first at their bottling plant in Putney then at their Albion Brewery in Whitechapel, finishing as a Senior Supervisor of Production. After this he worked as a Teaching Assistant at Linden Lodge School for Blind Children in Wimbledon 1983-1986, and from 1986 was a Maintenance Man at Rivermead Apartments in Fulham until his Retirement in 1990. Later he Volunteered at St. Georges Hospital Audiology Department repairing hearing equipment for 12 years from 1999-2011, he was a great help as almost deaf himself mainly from Army service and knowing the equipment. Married Margery 1949 in Putney, together until 2004. Has 1 Son, 1 daughter, 2 Grandchildren, 5 Great-Grandchild.

**Associations and Organisations** – Member of the Institute of Supervisory Management, Royal British Legion - Putney Branch, Former Normandy Veterans Association - Kent.

# SERGEANT FRANK ASHLEIGH

Served with – 'A' Squadron, Glider Pilot Regiment, Army Air Corps
Service Number – 14417002
Interviewed – Wembley, London, 2nd August 2017

## Service History and Personal Stories

- Born – 23rd December 1924, Bethnal Green, London, England, UK.
- Frank Ashleigh, a true Cockney from East London, started his very diverse military career in late 1938 after leaving school aged 14! The clouds of war were already gathering and he joined the 1st Cadet Battalion, Royal Fusiliers, City of London Regiment, where he got a taste for military life and rose to the rank of Corporal, remaining a part of the Regiment until he was 17 years old in December 1941.
- By this time he was working and learning a trade as a Welder, first with T.C Jones as part of the George Cohen 600 group of engineers and then on to Strachans Limited, a firm of coachbuilders in Park Royal. They were impressed with his welding skills, and through them he became an A.I.D. (Aircraft Inspection Department) approved welder.
- During that period he had left the Cadet Force and moved on to the Home Guard which he did in addition to his full-time welding job, and spent a lot of time posted around the Childs Hill area near Golders Green. Then the same as many young lads at the time Frank wanted more adventure and to do his bit by serving directly in the Armed Forces, so on his 18th Birthday on 23rd December 1942 he joined the Army. Release to the Army was opposed by Strachans as he was in a 'Reserved Occupation' and this big engineering company was engaged in the building of military vehicles and they felt that Frank's skills were needed on the factory floor on the Home Front, but eventually they

- did release him and the following February in 1943 he received his calling-up papers and reported to Arnold camp, Nottingham where he undertook his Army Infantry training.
- After this he was posted to R.E.M.E – Royal Electrical and Mechanical Engineers due to his working background and sent to Woolwich Arsenal to await his next posting. Then he was bizarrely sent to Letchworth Garden City to learn arc welding, then to the British Oxygen Company in Cricklewood to learn gas welding, skills in which he was already proficient! His next posting was to the big Odeon Garage at Southend-on-Sea, where despite being a Craftsman with welding skills he was made a Regimental Policemen, with duties of logging the comings and goings of a fleet of Dodge built Army transport and supply lorries.
- All of this took place throughout 1943 and into 1944, and whilst at Southend Frank who by this point was yearning for change and to see some 'Real Action' saw that applications were open for those wishing to join the GPR – Glider Pilot Regiment and duly stepped forward and volunteered for this special branch of Army service in February 1944.
- A rigorous selection process followed, first through the RAF at St. Johns Wood, London for 'Flying Aptitude Assessment', after successfully passing this selection process the real training began when Frank was sent to the GPR Regimental Depot at Fargo Camp, Salisbury Plain near Larkhill, Wiltshire.
- It was there a 6 week 'Weeding Out' process including heavy PTI was carried out, at the end those still remaining in April 1944 were promoted to Corporal and went on to start their flight training, Frank was one of them. This training took place in three phases in three places between April to July 1944, beginning with learning in the aircraft almost all flying recruits started in, the Tiger Moth. Training with an instructor and finally Solo took place at RAF Denham near Gerrards Cross in Buckinghamshire, once students completed this Glider Pilot instruction would begin.
- It was at RAF Stoke Orchard near Cheltenham in Gloucestershire, home of No.3 Glider Training School RAF (3 GTS) where he and other hopefuls were introduced to the Hotspur glider and Miles Master tugs, and as Frank explained 'where the trainees had learned what you could do, or could not do in a plane without an engine!'
- Once he successfully passed this phase of his training next was the move onto the bigger Horsa glider and the Whitley twin-engine tug used to tow it. This took place at RAF North Luffenham, Rutland, East Midlands, (then Leicestershire) home of the HGCV – Heavy Glider Conversion Unit, it was here that Frank became a qualified Glider Pilot and was awarded the special Glider Pilot Regiment wings AKA The Army Flying Badge.
- He was now posted to an Operational Squadron at RAF Harwell near Harwell, Oxfordshire in July 1944, here Frank became part of No.2 Flight, A Squadron, and paired up with 'Lofty' Cummings, and after many operations being cancelled over the weeks that followed in the middle of September 1944 they finally got the 'Green Light' to go into battle.
- This was something they had waited a long time for but as fate would have it this would be Operation Market-Garden and their target was to capture a key bridge at Arnhem in Holland which turned out disastrous for them and most of the 1st Airborne Division involved there. Frank was part of the 2nd wave on 18th September; four days later he'd been captured and ended up as a POW at Stalag Luft VII at Bankau, Germany, now Poland.
- Later in January 1945 as the Russians advanced they were forced to become part of the 'Long March' from Bankau to Goldberg over 80 miles in minus 15-30 degrees, then put onto trains and taken to Luckenwalde to Stalag IIIA, 32 miles South of Berlin. They were liberated by the Red Army on the 22nd April 1945, bringing to an end a hellish ordeal. Frank was repatriated to the U.K soon after and sent to Sandhurst where he was 'killing time', then posted to run an Army Hostel in Camberley, London, later de-mobbed in May 1946 at Woking Army Depot, bringing to an end a roller-coaster 3.5 years of military service.

Frank Ashleigh was what was known as 'A Total Soldier' having been trained to be a Glider Pilot in the air and an Infantryman on the ground. When he did finally go into battle both of these skills would be needed one directly after the other, such was the unique role of those soldiers within the Glider Pilot Regiment of the British Army. After intense training his one and only mission would see him engaged in the hastily put together and fateful Operation Market-Garden in September 1944 at the zone allotted to the British 1st Airborne Division that would later become synonymous with the operation, that of Arnhem. When Frank landed he wasn't to know that his troubles had only just begun, and 4 days later he would be a prisoner of War, captured by SS troops, sent to a Nazi POW Camp and kept in grim conditions until early 1945 when he would then be put with many others on a forced march over great distances from what is modern day Poland into Germany in sub-zero temperatures, where he would eventually end up near the heart of the Third Reich outside of Berlin, only to be liberated by the advancing Russian Army. This is an incredible story of tenacity and survival from someone who after living through these extremely difficult experiences was only 20 years of age! It is also a unique one from the perspective of a rare kind of World War Two veteran, that of a Glider Pilot, so here is Frank to share with us his:

### WARTIME EXPERIENCES AS A SERGEANT IN THE GLIDER PILOT REGIMENT

"Well it seems the best place to begin is with the training because being a Glider Pilot was something quite different, I wanted more action and excitement and that's what I got right from the very beginning once I was in the GPR! Although later it was neither of those, due to circumstances it became more of a fight for survival! Anyway, training to fly gliders, a great responsibility to learn and do it well because when it came down to it going into battle the Pilots were of course not only responsible for their own lives but for those of the men they were flying into combat, and getting these men and their material safely to where they were needed was vital, so you had to do your utmost to get it right. Once we had got to RAF North Luffenham we were training on and were getting used to Horsa Gliders and the Whitley twin-engine bomber tug that was towing it at that time, in real airborne invasions all manner of aircraft were used to pull Gliders from two engine Dakotas to four engine Sterling and Halifax and even Lancaster bombers. The pilots would be recruited from the Army but would be trained by the RAF. All tuition was first in high tow, above the tug's slipstream and then once reasonably competent in the more comfortable low tow, always remembering to return to high tow before pulling off, the Horsa was a wonderful aircraft, it would not go into a spin, it simply did a stall turn, it was very light on controls and with flaps like barn doors it was very responsive. You had to become skilled in keeping your glider as steady as possible in all sorts of cross winds and turbulence so as to stay attached and not have the worst-case scenario of casting adrift or having to be released early by your towing aircraft if a dangerous situation was arising, these were just some of the things you had to learn to deal with and that is before you had the later adage in active service of potentially encountering hostile enemy action from the ground or in the air! Different kinds of skills have to be honed when flying an aircraft that has no engines, you really do have to be a very instinctive flyer because you are of course gliding and working with the natural elements more, you don't have any engine power to call upon to assist you if needs be once you've cast off, I think strong nerves, good training and confidence in your own ability were the main things that were required to succeed as a Glider Pilot! Once training was over and we were in active service we became what was known as 'Corps Troops' which meant you could be allocated anywhere, to the 1st or 6th Airborne Divisions, this also meant along with having attained our 'Wings' an automatic promotion to Sergeant would follow for all GRP Pilots, in fact it was because of this that we were known as 'The Regiment of Sergeants'. All the attributes mentioned earlier along with a bit of good luck were certainly needed for what was coming up next because for us it was time for the real thing, and as history testifies for many it didn't come much harder than Arnhem!" Fascinated by hearing these unique insights from one our last WW2 Glider Pilots and knowing much more lay ahead in the active service part of his story, I asked Frank to continue and listened eagerly as he went on to tell me;

"On Monday 18th September 1944 me and Lofty, who interestingly had transferred from the Fleet Air Arm, flew in on the second wave or lift as we called it on day two of Montgomery's Operation Market Garden, touching down behind enemy lines luckily without any opposition at LZ X – Landing Zone X-Ray near a place called Wolfheze, and unloaded our precious cargo consisting of a jeep with two trailers which were carrying a radar set and its four-man crew from the Royal Corps of Signals. Once the tail was taken off the glider and the ramps put in place, the men along with their jeeps and trailers sped off and we never saw them again. In the GPR we were part of the Army Air Corps and so as the name suggests we flew and fought, that was the incredible thing about this unique and as some have described it elite Regiment, as soon as you had flown your glider in and landed it then you ceased to be a Pilot and immediately took up the next role of being an infantryman and doing whatever was required of you in that job, real duality, if you didn't have both sets of training and skills you would have been little or no use to anyone once you had touched down! **A Horsa Glider being unloaded, whilst another flies overhead, depending on the type of equipment being carried they could be unloaded from the side or the back. The GPR was officially formed in 1942, their Commander was Lieutenant-General Frederick Browning, before Arnhem its pilots were made up of volunteers only from within the Army. After Arnhem their losses were so great that RAF crews were seconded to the regiment, next time out these mixed crews flew together in the largest single airborne lift and final operation of the Glider Pilot Regiment in World War Two over the Rhine into Germany in March 1945, Operation Varsity.**

We spent the first night in Wolfheze, the next morning at dawn we went off to Oosterbeek, about three and the half miles away, (intriguingly areas where Wilf Oldham, also in this book was located around that time). Once there being part of HQ Company we made our way to the Hartenstein Hotel, formally the H.Q of the German General Model, which had become the H.Q of the British Airborne Division, where we dug in and awaited orders. After a couple of hours a Captain O'Malley from I think the South Staffordshires along with another two glider pilots and myself volunteered to go out on patrol, we only got about a quarter of a mile before realising we were totally surrounded by Germans, they were coming from everywhere! We dived into St Bernulphus RC Church and climbed a winding staircase right up into the organ loft, realising the enemy didn't know where we were and being almost out of ammunition from earlier exchanges of fire, we continued to lay low for four days in total, by which time a German had come up and seeing the Captain first had shot him in the stomach with his Luger! Needing immediate medical attention he rightly gave himself up, and I think out of pure shock told the German that there were three more British higher up in the roof, so that was it for us, after an ultimatum we disabled our weapons then me, 'Wag' Watson and Ray Osbourne came down and from that moment onwards on Friday 22nd September 1944 we 3 glider pilots were Prisoners of War, captured by the dreaded SS who I must say treated us very fairly, myself included despite my dog tags indicating my Jewish faith! The Geneva Convention thank goodness was adhered to, I read much later that this was due in most part because the elite SS units battling against us at Arnhem despite being the victors there respected us for the fight we put up and for the tenacious resistance of the British Airborne troops!

We were then taken over the river to an interrogation centre in Oberusal where we were held for a few days, all they got out of us was our 'Name Rank and Number' and shortly after we were on our way to a POW Camp called Stalag Luft 7 at Bankau in Germany, where if I recall correctly I became prisoner number 902. We were in that camp until January 1945 then we were put on what became known as the 'Long March' this was the infamous forced movement of POW's, in our case around 1500 men who were made to walk over 80 miles in temperatures well below zero, with the threat that for every man who could not go on five more would be shot, conditions were appalling, people died along the way and we slept in cow sheds when we were lucky, we soon learnt that cows give off heat, horses don't! I found out much later we were one of a number of forced marches from POW and Concentration Camps that were going on around that time. Eventually after crossing the River Oder we reached a place called Goldberg in early February where we were put on trains to an enormous camp, this was Stalag IIIA just south of Berlin at a place called Luckenwalde, the total journey taking around 20 days. In that camp along with the different nationalities we brought were prisoners from Great Britain, Ireland, America, Canada, Australia, New Zealand, South Africa, Holland, Belgium, France, Yugoslavia, Czechoslovakia, Malta, Poland and in the worse condition were the Russian POW's who were really like skeletons, some had been there for years. The advancing Red Army finally arrived and liberated us on the 22nd of April 1945 and some of the former German captors who were handed over to Russians and other POWs didn't last long, the following day I was flown home followed by 6 weeks leave with double civilian rations, I had been through a lot for a young lad who had not yet reached his 21st birthday! There were times when I was scared but you just soldiered on and did your best regardless of what was thrown at you. After recovery time was over I returned to service but I think they didn't know what to do with me, so for my final interesting posting I was sent to form the London District Leave Hostel Unit, for troops on leave, this consisted of 3 converted houses in Victoria, where I had a staff of 4 Sappers, 30 ATS Girls and 300 beds, another terrifying experience! After this I was demobbed at Woking in May 1946. I found out later that my good pal and co-pilot 'Lofty' had been killed in Arnhem, every year when I go back there for the anniversary I go and pay him a visit, and for as long as I am capable I will continue to do so, he was my friend, never to be forgotten! Regarding Arnhem; I know this is a well-used adage but for the many who died like my mate Lofty Cummings and many who were captured like me it truly was *A Bridge too Far!*" **Pictured – An example of the stark and sad reality of war which Frank spoke about, here a Grave in Arnhem marked in German 'Unknown British Soldier' clearly showing multiple bullet holes in the paratroopers helmet!**

As a closing dedication to Frank I feel that this quote written during the operation is very fitting: "If in the years to come any man says to you 'I fought at Arnhem', take off your hat to him and buy him a drink' for this is the stuff of which England's greatness is made."

War Correspondent Alan Wood in the Daily Express, 24th September 1944

**We take off our hats and raise a glass to you Frank and all the other veterans of Arnhem, and to all your brothers-in-arms who didn't survive Operation Market Garden.**

## Additional Information and Life After Service

**Rank upon finish of service** – Sergeant.

**Medals and Honours** – 1939-45 Star, France-Germany Star, 1939-45 Defence Medal, 1939-45 War Medal, Dutch Liberation Medal.

**Post War Years** – Spent all his working life in the Toy industry rising from trainee to Sales Director for many companies such as Bell Toys & Games, Timpo and Childs Play International. Retired aged 73 in 1997. Married Mavis in 1951, together 67 years. Has 2 Sons, 3 Grandchildren, 2 Great-Grandchildren.

**Associations and Organisations** – Glider Pilot Regimental Association, Glider Pilot Regiment Society, AJEX – Association of Jewish Ex-Servicemen and Women.

# PRIVATE-MEDIC DAVID WHITEMAN

Served with – 125th Field Ambulance RAMC, British Expeditionary Force &
181st Air Landing Field Ambulance RAMC, British 1st Airborne Division
Service Number – 7363389
Interviewed – Basildon, Essex, 3rd August 2017

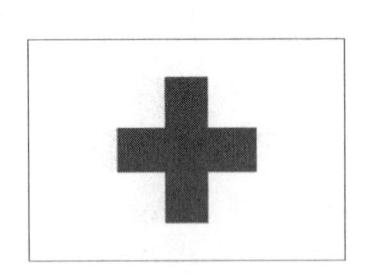

### Service History and Personal Stories

- Born – 7th August 1919, Barrow-in-Furness, Cumbria, England, UK.
- David was called up in October 1939 and went into the British Army, he had already been a practising first-aider for a few years and as such was happy to be assigned to the Royal Army Medical Corps, then sent up to Scotland soon after to train at the Dalkeith Army Medical Facility in Dundee.
- By 1940 David was a fully trained Army Medic and was part of a Medical unit called the 125th Field Ambulance RAMC. They were later based at Barracks in Newbury, Berkshire from where they proceeded to join the BEF ready to go into Europe against the Nazis.
- Soon after David was sent to France as part of the 42nd (East Lancashire) Infantry Division which was one of 5 Territorial Infantry Divisions deployed to reinforce the BEF - British Expeditionary Force, arriving on the 12th April 1940. By May the division was eventually moved into the front line on the River Escaut which flows between Northern France and Western Belgium, but within a few weeks they were in a headlong retreat to the coast.

- Amongst all the chaos and confusion David ended up on the beaches at Dunkirk tending to a continuous stream of wounded with very limited medical supplies, he ended up at the Mole or Pier (vividly depicted in the 2017 Dunkirk film by Christopher Nolan) where with injured soldiers he was evacuated by Royal Navy Destroyer HMS Malcolm in early June.
- After Dunkirk David was posted back to Newbury and whilst completing refresher courses, continued as a Medic and also put on regular Army tasks such as guard duties until 1942, he then volunteered for Airborne Forces and undertook Parachute training at RAF Ringway in Manchester and Glider training at Boston, Lincolnshire leading to new postings abroad.
- By 1943 with combined Airborne and Army Medic training David was now part of the 181st Air Landing Field Ambulance RAMC, 1st British Airborne Division, and was posted to Tunisia, North Africa doing further training in camps near Oran and Sousse to prepare for Operation Husky the Allied invasion of Sicily.
- On the evening of the 9/10 July 1943 the Airborne part of the invasion force flew in to secure its objectives, and due to stormy weather and devastating fire from the enemy and 'friendly fire' from the allied navies the fly-in became dispersed and 78 gliders ended up in the sea, David's being one of them! Very luckily they were saved by an allied ship that was heading back from the invasion to Africa which returned them safely.
- The next invasion which was on mainland Italy with the 1st A.B Div was more successful for him when they went ashore at Taranto during Operation Slapstick on September 9th 1943, this time in Landing Craft and by the end of September they had advanced 125 miles (201 km) to Foggia before being withdrawn in preparation for the Allied invasion of France.
- But it wasn't until a year later after more U.K postings and training that David would find himself in the thick of it once again, this time arriving in a Horsa Glider near Oosterbeek in Holland on the 17th September 1944, once more as part of the 181st and with the 1st Airborne Division in what would become the ill-fated Operation Market Garden.
- As this Operation started to fall apart and the Airborne forces began to get decimated Army Medic David along with his unit asked the owner of the Old Vicarage in Oosterbeek, a lady called Kate Ter Horst if they could use her home as a first-aid post.
- She agreed and as the battle raged on over the following days she became known as 'The Angel of Arnhem' for her kindness and hard work helping the RAMC tend to the injured and dying soldiers as her home was getting destroyed around her due to enemy action.
- Eventually the remaining soldiers of the 181st RAMC escaped across the Rhine to Nijmegen. A true bond between Kate, her family and the surviving soldiers was formed that lasted for decades after and continued with David all his life and on subsequent visits to Arnhem. After surviving so much action in the field David finished his Army days in quieter surroundings at the Aldershot Garrison where he was de-mobbed in 1946.

I was searching for a long time for a World War Two veteran who could represent the Medical services in my book as I felt compelled to write about this branch of the armed services because of the vitally important life-saving role they played during that conflict, and in one form or another in every battle in our military history. Wherever armies have campaigned and fought there have been those with them who have dealt with the aftermath of fighting in many ways to relieve pain and to try and preserve life. During the Second World War this already highly organised branch of the British Army was known as the RAMC- Royal Army Medical Corps and consisted of people who served in many roles such as Doctors, Surgeons, Medics, Dentists, Nurses, Medical Orderlies, Ambulance Drivers to name but a few. They undertook their duties both at the front and behind the lines and amongst them was Army Medic David Whiteman who was in the thick of the action numerous times from Dunkirk to Arnhem and under very dangerous battle conditions had to treat the most horrendous injuries of servicemen, some of whom he personally knew and served with and for many he would be the last face they would see! When I was given the opportunity to interview David through the kind help of Dick Goodwin from the Taxi Charity for Military Veterans I wasted no time in going down to London where in a fascinating interview David told me about:

### BEING AN RAMC MEDIC IN THE HEAT OF BATTLE DURING WORLD WAR TWO

"So much happened in so many places I think it is best I give you accounts of the most historically well-known parts of my service starting with Dunkirk where I was a Medic with the 125th Field Ambulance. Just to clarify a Field Ambulance or FA was the name used by the British and most other Commonwealth armies during World War Two to describe a mobile medical unit that treated wounded soldiers very close to or in the examples I will give you directly in the combat zones. Being in the RAMC meant playing a very different role, not one of engaging in direct combat and expecting to take life but quite the opposite, engaging in order to save life! This was our calling, our choice and our remit! At Dunkirk in 1940 we really did have our backs up against the wall, or in this case to the sea, pretty much the same because we were encircled and until you could escape you had nowhere to go and we were being bombed and shelled night and day by the Germans, terrible! For most that would mean only looking after himself when avoiding incoming fire and air attacks, but for us as medics we had the added dimension of duty of care so we were tending to the injured and dying regardless of whatever else was going on around us, same in every battle we were a part of during the war no matter where we were, which as you can imagine brings with it many added dangers such as becoming casualties ourselves, as many in the RAMC did! On the beaches it was pure hell, virtually no cover at all and I was treating soldiers with all kinds of injuries from shrapnel to bullet wounds, we tried to get the boys off onto the small boats about 50 at a time but that wasn't working, especially when consistently under attack, so sadly we realised that the seriously wounded would have to be left behind on the beaches! We helped who ever we could carry but by this time the dressings and essential materials were running out, near the end as the situation became much worse it was almost every man for himself! We stayed to help as many as we could for as long as we could, and in the last days of the evacuation in early June we were saved ourselves, picked up from a concrete pier called the Mole by a Royal Navy ship called HMS Malcolm, leaving behind us a scene of total carnage, not the last time I would find myself in a situation like that!"

David was right, it wouldn't be the last time he'd be a part of and experience such frightful and difficult things, four years later he would be involved in another historical military engagement around Arnhem in Holland, where as a Medic he would again have to evacuate under fire! David who was one of those 'Dwindling Band of Warriors' from that Airborne Brotherhood now tells us about:

### OPERATION MARKET GARDEN AND THE ANGEL OF ARNHEM

"As soon as we landed in our Horsa Gliders at Oosterbeek near Arnhem things started to go wrong, I was already having to tend to casualties with broken legs and other injuries from bad glider landings. I was now an Army Medic in the 181st Air Landing Field Ambulance attached to Light Artillery units, of the 1st Airborne Division, and I would once again need every bit of my experience and training during Market Garden. Enemy opposition increased day by day as did the wounded that came as a result of intensifying actions and our situation just got worse in every way. By then we had already set up a first aid post at the house of a Dutch family headed by Kate Ter Horst who had five children there with her! Over an eight-day period more than 250 wounded paras were treated there in the Old Vicarage and 57 men buried in her garden, whilst her own family were hiding bravely in the cellar, all very traumatising for those young children. Kate found water to share with everyone at great risk to herself from German snipers, she remained undaunted and read the bible to the wounded paras as bullets whirred through her house and comforted them as they were operated on without painkillers. When you see soldiers with their guts hanging out, and men screaming with arms and legs blown off, others with visible shrapnel wounds and some with no visible wounds, yet dead or dying, then you realise or in my case are reminded what war is all about. Finally when we could do no more and were in danger of being captured ourselves we had to make the very hard decision to try and escape in the heat of battle, which we managed to do across the Rhine to Nijmegen, I couldn't believe I was having to do the same thing again years later when the allies had almost seemingly won the war in Europe!

A remarkable picture of a British Army Medic, armband visible, tending a wounded soldier next to a knocked out German Panzer which is still on fire, indicating that they are still in a very active combat zone, this being similar to many situations that David found himself in during the course of his duties, some of which he has described here in his story.

Kate rightly became known as 'The Angel of Arnhem' to the soldiers and in the film 'A Bridge Too Far' was depicted by Liv Ullman, later she was awarded the MBE in recognition of her selfless actions. I am so proud to have met her and talked to her in that house as the battle raged around us and all those years later to have contact with her family, a very, very special connection to have and a lovely silver lining to what is otherwise a story about an operation with many dark clouds!" **Left; Kate Ter Horst - 'Angel of Arnhem', and Right; Medical Orderlies, a Nurse, a Surgeon and a Medic escort an injured soldier at a Field Ambulance station.**

**From Florence Nightingale in the Crimean War, to the RAMC in WW1, WW2 through to Afghanistan and other conflicts of the modern day, they all including David certainly performed their duties according to the motto of the corps; In Arduis Fidelis – 'Faithful in Adversity', and as I shook his hand at the end and thanked him for everything, from his past service to the lovely interview that day, I wondered how many lives those very same hands of his had saved during the distinguished service he had undertaken as a Medic in World War Two? A couple of months later in November 2017 David passed and so I felt very lucky to have been able to interview him when I did and to now be able to honour his memory in perpetuity with his inclusion in my book.**

# Additional Information and Life After Service

**Rank upon finish of service** – Private-Medic.

**Medals and Honours** – 1939-45 Defence Medal, 1939-45 War Medal, 1939-45 Star, Africa Star, Italy Star, France-Germany Star.

**Post War Years** – After his demob in 1946 David worked for Vickers-Armstrong ship building company back at his hometown of Barrow-in-Furness for 6 years as a Store and Maintenance man. After it was a big move to Salisbury now Harari in Rhodesia, where he worked as a Foreman of a painting and decorating firm for Standard Bank until his return to the U.K in 1976 with his family. He then worked as spray painter in Laindon, Essex and retired in 1994 aged 75! David married Eileen in 1942, they were together 69 years until her passing in 2011. They have 1 daughter, 4 Grandchildren.

**Associations and Organisations** – RBL Laindon Branch, Southend Normandy Veterans Association, Taxi Charity for Military Veterans, Rhodesian Freemasons.

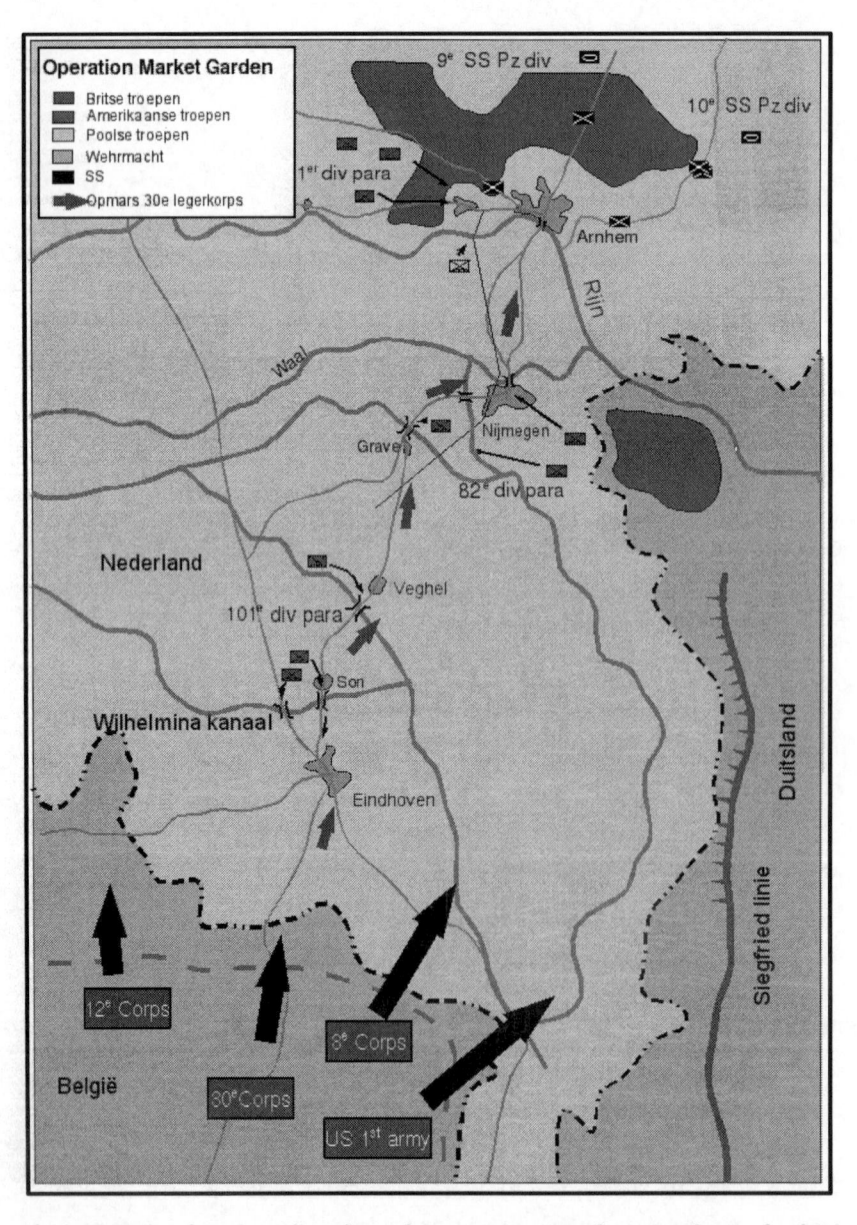

**A map, quite fittingly in Dutch, showing the plan of Operation Market-Garden, of which David was a part, and the disposition of Allied Airborne & Ground formations and also those of the opposing Axis forces.**

# SERGEANT WILFRED EDWARDS OLDHAM MBE

Served with – 1st Battalion The Border Regiment, 1st Airborne Division
Service Number – 3391058
Interviewed – Radcliffe, Greater Manchester, 6th August 2018

## Service History and Personal Stories

- Born – 28th August 1920, Salford, Lancashire, England, UK.
- Wilf as he is known to many volunteered for service at the armed forces recruitment office in Greymoor Street, Bolton in June 1940 aged only 19, and became part of The East Lancashire Regiment. Little was he to know then of the huge experiences that lay ahead in the years to come and the many places life in the Army would take him during WW2.
- This started with his basic training at Squires Gate in Blackpool from September 1940-January 1941, followed by a driving course at Salisbury Plain in Wiltshire and Wool in Dorset after which he was sent to a 'Holding Battalion' on the Isle of Anglesey from February-August 1941, then onto Harrington Barracks between Crosby and Formby where he re-joined the East Lancashire Regiment from August 1941-February 1942.
- He was then posted to a Battalion of the Kings Liverpool Regiment which was a Home Defence Unit, and was sent from February 1942-February 1943 to guard airfields near Newbury in Berkshire and later to Swanage in Dorset where he was helping protect special radar equipment near the coast.

- Whilst at the latter Wilf volunteered for Airborne Forces at Dorchester in February 1943 and had the choice to become part of either the Glider Bourne or Parachute Troops.
- ❖ He chose gliders and as a result was transferred to the 1st Battalion of the Border Regiment which was part of the 1st Air Landing Brigade, then sent for training to the Glider Regiment as part of T (Training) Company on Hotspur Gliders at Barton Stacey, Hampshire, after which they continued their instruction on bigger Horsa Gliders before leaving the UK.
- ❖ Once all the UK based training was finished in May 1943 they were then sent as part of a convoy from Liverpool to Scotland and onto Oran in Algeria, where in various camps in Algeria and Tunisia May-July they undertook drills, acclimatization exercises and further Glider training on the American WAKO Gliders, this was all completed by early July 1943.
- ❖ Wilf was now a fully trained Airborne Infantryman, and as a Bren Gunner in 12 Platoon, B Company, 1ST Battalion The Border Regiment, 1st Air Landing Brigade, 1st Airborne Division took part in his first active combat mission, Operation Husky the allied invasion of Sicily, unfortunately whilst on the way in on the airborne part called Operation Ladbroke his Waco Glider ditched into the sea with loss of life and only after 8 hours were they rescued.
- ❖ Next came the invasion of Italy at Taranto on 9th September 1943 in Operation Slapstick, this seaborne landing put the 1st Airborne Division at this vitally strategic port from where they advanced up the peninsula 125 miles/201km to Foggia before they were withdrawn.
- ❖ After return to the U.K it would be almost another year until they were in combat again, this time it would be as part of the hard fought but disastrous Operation Market Garden in Arnhem, Holland where unfortunately the 1st Airborne Division was all but decimated. Wilf landed in a Horsa Glider near Oosterbeek on 17th September 1944, by 25th September after heavy fighting he and other remnants of units retreated over the Rhine to Nijmegen.
- ❖ When Wilf along with others of the 1st A.B. Div returned to the U.K they were rested, re-fitted and brought back up to strength, during that time the war in Europe had finished, V.E Day had come and gone but the 1st A.B.Div was on the way to Norway to oversee the disarming of the remaining large German forces of occupation that were still there.
- ❖ Once this was successfully completed he returned to the U.K in August 1945, and after training new recruits at Perham Down Army Camp near Salisbury Plain, Wiltshire had to exchange his Red Beret for a Khaki Beret in October 1945 as his airborne days were over.
- ❖ Finally he was sent with the Border Regiment to Brunswick, Germany to be part of the allied forces of occupation in BAOR – British Army of the Rhine where he undertook guarding duties and small arms training and became a Sergeant. Wilf was demobbed there in May 1946, bringing to an end a very action-packed 6 years in the British Army.

"I want to say before we start, in many ways this is the end of the story, not the beginning! I would like to say this to everybody, I would like the whole world to know this, for one nation to inflict war on another nation is the most dreadful thing that can ever happen between nations, because all it brings is death and the destruction of almost everything, and in a war when it does come to an end, there is no victory, nobody has really won the war, one side is supposedly victorious but both sides have lost most things if not everything! Also this word 'Hero' is banded about a lot and is used far too easy, to me any battle throughout the history of the world what's been fought, the real heroes of any battle, any country, any part of the world, and people may say different, but to me are ones that lie buried in that soil, they've lost their lives, they only have one and they've lost it, men as young as 17, 18, 19 with all their life in front of them! So to me the 'Real Heroes' are the dead ones!"

These were the opening words of World War Two Airborne Veteran Wilf Oldham who felt moved to begin his interview with this very poignant message especially to future generations, which comes from someone with a century of life experience to draw upon, and who as the reader can already see from main bullet points of his story has had within that time a lot of first-hand experience of the hard, vicious and destructive nature of war. I first met Wilf at the Imperial War Museum North at Salford Quays in Greater Manchester and was enthralled with his account of what he did during the war years, and touched by the calm temperament and kind nature of this very humble and wise old warrior, I knew I had to interview him so I could share his remarkable story with you, so here it is from the man himself who tells us about:

## SERVING IN THE AIRBORNE FORCES DURING THE SECOND WORLD WAR

"It is almost unbelievable the things you see and experience in wartime, whether you're in battle situations or not. Once we were at a training exercise on a makeshift airfield near the Kairouan-Sousse area in Tunisia where we were based when we were preparing for the invasion of Sicily, I was already on the ground and looking up at the other gliders as they were making their way down and suddenly the tail end of one of them just fell off and the men inside were thrown out, they looked like parachutists but they had no parachutes, they just tumbled out the back of their glider falling to their death! Poor guys didn't stand a chance, I didn't look as they hit the ground, even though it was in the distance a bit I didn't want to see men meeting their ends like that, especially knowing they were some of our boys! The glider which looked like a Waco went into an uncontrollable spin with more parts falling off it and crashed, and I thought that could easily have been us if we had been put in that particular one which was only a few minutes behind us, 'there but for the grace of God go I', it certainly wouldn't be the last time I thought that! **During preparation for the invasion of Sicily a jeep is loaded onto an American WACO CG-4A Glider, these would be flown by members of the GPR – Glider Pilot Regiment.** Soon after that incident and with battalion, brigade and divisional exercises completed we were involved in the real invasion of Sicily on the 9th-10th July 1943 during the airborne part of Operation Husky called Operation Ladbroke, our Waco Glider like many others crashed into the sea and it was us that nearly copped for it this time! *(During the same operation this was also the experience of David Whiteman from the RAMC who also features in this book). On the way into our drop zone whilst still out over the sea the weather changed for the worst, that along with pretty heavy AK-AK fire meant we were cast off too early by the pilots of the towing Dakota, soon after we were told to prepare for a crash landing, within seconds of going into the sea around 10pm, which I believe was in the Maddalena Peninsula south of Syracuse, our damaged glider was filling up with water, terrifying! I tried to open the door but the water pressure meant I couldn't do it, we were trapped! Private Hurley took his rifle and smashed a hole in the canvas so that we could escape, once we were out into open sea we scrambled to hold onto the floating wings, there was no sign of Hurley again, his quick thinking had help save us but sadly it seems he was washed away and drowned, we had also lost our head glider pilot. We were in the water, in the dark with a heavy swell until we were rescued 7-8 hours later around 5.30-6.00am by a ship of the invasion force, by which time we had lost half a dozen men and without seeing any of the main action I had nearly died as well! The losses for the 1st Air Landing Brigade were heavy with many gliders in the sea and many men drowning before even reaching targets, I believe the war office were on the verge of disbanding glider battalions after Operation Ladbroke, thankfully they didn't or what was at that time the biggest action by glider borne troops could have been their last action of that war!"

It certainly wasn't the last action for Wilf and the men of the 1st Battalion, Border Regiment, as part of the British 1st Airborne Division. I listened attentively as more of Wilf's story unfolded regarding:

## SEABORNE AND AIRBORNE OPERATIONS IN EUROPE AND SCANDINAVIA

"When we took part in the invasion of mainland Italy on the 9th September 1943 which I now know was called Operation Slapstick, we went in on ships of the Royal Navy, leaving from Bizerte in Tunisia and put ashore in Taranto at the bottom of Italy. On the journey over we saw the Italian Battleship Fleet under Royal Navy escort steaming off to Malta and into captivity, quite a sight. Once we were in Italy we advanced throughout September up from Taranto over a hundred miles to a city called Foggia on the East coast, and on the way only had skirmishes with the Germans who had not yet made a stand as they were retreating to more fixed positions in mountains that could be better defended, before this happened we had been withdrawn from the line and were on the way back down to Taranto again and by November 1943 had left Italy for the U.K in preparation for D-Day, which for us didn't happen, in the end they used the 6th Airborne Division for that, instead it would be September 1944, nearly a year later before we saw real action again, this time at Arnhem in Holland as part of Operation Market Garden. **Field Marshal Montgomery, who formulated the daring two-pronged plan for Market-Garden, here pointing out strategic moves to King George VI in his Mobile H.Q in Holland.**

To summarize, because much has already been said about the glorious failure of this epic battle, 1/Borders flew from RAF Broadwell in Oxfordshire, we arrived safely in our Horsa Gliders on the first day of the operation on 17th September 1944 at Landing Zone 'S' at Wolfhenze near Oosterbeek, our objectives were to move on to Renkum and capture the ferry area and protect against any enemy troop movements towards the Landing Zones and Drop Zones, this we did, temporarily. The German Artillery, Mortar and Machine Gun attacks became much stronger and more constant, eventually to save us being surrounded we were ordered to withdraw to Divisional HQ at Oosterbeek, by which time we had lost half of 12 Platoon, B Company and as each day passed things became much more desperate in every way, we were obviously losing the battle! At one point me and a pal were in a slit trench and as shells rained down he asked if we could say the Lord's prayer out loud together, which we did, because we both believed we might not make it out alive! A realistic thought because all around us death had become an everyday part of our life! As fate would have it eventually we did get out by escaping over the Neder-Rhine to Nijmegen in a rowing boat on 25th September, with Arnhem not taken and the 1st Airborne seriously mauled they were a badly wounded Division and what was left of it returned home to the U.K to lick its wounds and re-group, me with them! **A Bren Gunner poised for action, this was Wilf's main role in battle, to provide attacking and defending fire with his Bren LMG - Light Machine Gun.** From our original B Company of 120 men only 23 made it back! In May 1945 having recovered our 1st Airborne Division was sent to Norway as part of Operation Doomsday to help with the disarming and dismantling of the German Forces there, we thought they might give us a bit of trouble, but in the end they were no bother, they knew the game was up! I was flown over with other troops in a Lancaster Bomber to Oslo and was involved in liberating POW Camps and other duties, to end with a happy memory I was also part of the Guard of Honour on the streets of Oslo when King Haakon and the Norwegian Royal Family returned from years of exile in London on 7th June 1945."

## LIEUTENANT-GENERAL FREDRICK ARTHUR MONTAGUE 'BOY' BROWNING

General Fredrick Browning GCVO, KBE, CB, DSO has been called the 'Father of the British Airborne Forces'. He was the commander of 1st Airborne Corps and deputy commander of the 1st Allied Airborne Army, a part of this was the 1st Airborne Division, which during Operation Market-Garden he personally led, and despite being such a high-ranking officer he landed with his Tactical Headquarters near Nijmegen to directly command his troops. During the planning of the operation he had his doubts about it and was the officer who memorably and prophetically said; "I think we might be going a bridge too far." Browning had been the first GOC – General Officer Commanding the 1st Airborne Division since its inception in November 1941 and the man chosen by Winston Churchill to establish, organise and lead Britain's newly founded Airborne Forces in World War Two. He was also responsible for other small but important touches that defined and gave the British Airborne Forces their identity, and still do, such as choosing the distinct maroon colour of their beret and standardising it for all soldiers in that branch of service, and he assigned the artist Major Edward Seago to design the Parachute Regiment's now famous emblem from Greek mythology of the warrior Bellerophon riding the winged horse Pegasus who was aptly 'the greatest hero and slayer of monsters.' This insignia, shown at the start of Wilf's profile became the shoulder flash of the British 1st and 6th Airborne Divisions.

Browning had also been awarded the DSO for valour in WW1 at the Battle of Cambrai in November 1917, he was part of the British Olympic Bobsleigh team at the 1928 Winter Olympics in St. Moritz, Switzerland and in July 1932 married the famous author and playwright Daphne du Maurier. After Arnhem his next appointment in December 1944 was as Chief of Staff to Admiral Lord Louis Mountbatten at SEAC Headquarters in Kandy, Ceylon until July 1946. The final part of his military service from September 1946 to January 1948 was as Military Secretary of the War Office. **King George VI (Left) with then Major-General Browning (right) on 21st May 1942 at Airborne Forces Southern Command inspecting a modified jeep fitted with a Vickers machine gun, also note the Airborne insignia, described above, mounted as a plaque on the front bumper.**

In later conversations with Wilf in July 2020 whilst enquiring more about his service years I asked him about his thoughts regarding another huge and important piece of history that he was living through, the Coronavirus Pandemic, his view was such a moving one I felt I had to add it to his story: "During the war we knew who our enemy was we could see them, this enemy is invisible and doesn't discriminate with its victims and takes them regardless of race, colour, creed, religion or age. As the world is coming together to try and defeat the Coronavirus, this is probably wishful thinking, but once we do that wouldn't it be great if the nations of the world thought that this proves well if we unite and work together we can do anything, achieve anything, can stop anything if we really want to, so why don't we stop fighting and stop all wars and conflicts, then there would be much less suffering and the world would be a much better place for everyone to live in!"

His story and World War Two legacy continued when he was recognised in the 2020 New Year Honours List and made an MBE for 'Services to Commemorations and UK/Dutch relations in the Diplomatic Service and Overseas List.' The achievements don't stop there, because on the 28th August 2020 Wilf Oldham reached another milestone, his 100th Birthday and became a Centenarian.

As the motto of his first regiment, The East Lancashire says; Spectamur Agendo – 'Judge us by our Deeds', as this story and his MBE show history is judging him in the very good and positive way that this great veteran truly deserves. Wilf it is an honour to have you in my book my friend.

## Additional Information and Life After Service

**Rank upon finish of service** – Sergeant.

**Medals and Honours** – 1939-45 Defence Medal, 1939-45 War Medal, 1939-45 Star, Italy Star, France-Germany Star, Commemorative Dutch and Norwegian Liberation Medals, MBE (2020).

**Post War Years** – After leaving the Army in 1946 Wilf worked at Robert Fletcher and Sons Paper Mill in Kersley, Lancashire as a Loadings Mixer in the Preparations Dept. until his retirement in 1981 aged 61. Married Jessie in Bury in 21st Jan 1943, they have; 2 Daughters, 2 Grandchildren, 1 Great-Grandchild.

**Associations and Organisations** – Arnhem 1944 Veterans Club, Border Regiment Association, Parachute Regiment Association – Bolton Branch.

**Wilf Oldham's portrait looking towards the 'John Frost Bridge' at Arnhem. Seen here in 2023. A very nice tribute to a great man. The Dutch remembering and honouring 'The Heroes of Arnhem' to this very day.**

# PRIVATE ARNOLD HUTCHINSON MBE

Served with – 7th (L.I) Parachute Battalion, 5th Brigade, 6th Airborne Division
Service Number – 14701259
Interviewed – Stafford, Staffordshire, 28th November 2017

## Service History and Personal Stories

- Born – 17th September 1924, Bradford, Yorkshire, England, UK.
- Arnold Hutchinson or 'Arnie' as the likes to be known was in the early part of the war a child refugee like others in this book. He stayed with 3 families in Yorkshire between September 1939 to September 1940, then like them he went on to do great service in the Armed Forces. He would be part of some very well-known engagements during the latter end of that conflict and after, in his case as part of the famous Airborne Infantry, as a Para.
- Arnie began his service aged 19 when he undertook his basic training at Brancepeth in County Durham with the Durham Light Infantry in January 1944, he was then transferred to the KSLI – King's Shropshire Light infantry where he completed 13 weeks of more intense Corps training in Shrewsbury, Shropshire after which he volunteered for the Paras.
- After this decision the Airborne part of his training naturally followed and in July-August 1944 he was sent to RAF Ringway, now Manchester airport, home of No.1 PTS - Parachute Training School, learning the Para fundamentals, and did his jumps over Tatton Park, Cheshire. With wings earned

~ 63 ~

- Arnie and the KSLI finished with field manoeuvres at Totley, Sheffield, South Yorkshire, now fully trained they were ready to be allocated a Para unit.
- Arnie officially joined the 7th (Light Infantry) Parachute Battalion on the 31st August 1944 at Bulford in Wiltshire, and whilst based at this huge camp witnessed big formations of aircraft and gliders forming up overhead as part of Operation Market-Garden on the 17th September 1944, his 20th Birthday. Luckily he was not part of that disastrous undertaking but in December 1944 he was dispatched with 7 Para into Battle in Europe.
- On the 16th December 1944 the Germans smashed through the Ardennes area of Belgium in a major surprise counter-offensive which would become known as the Battle of the Bulge, the 6th Airborne Division, Arnie amongst them were on their way to help stem this tide, on Christmas Day they left Southampton and went via Calais overland to allied lines in the area of Namur and Dinant in Belgium, eventually ending up in Eprave on January 10th 1945.
- The danger of the Bulge now over and the offensive now beaten back 7 Para and Arnie advanced up into Holland where they finished near Venlo before being withdrawn at the end of February 1945, then returned to Bulford and prepared for their next big operation.
- This was to be Operation Varsity, the airborne drops over the Rhine into Germany on the 24th March 1945 in support of the ground and amphibious parts of Operation Plunder. The 6th Airborne Division was charged with capturing areas around Hamminkeln and Wesel, it was here that Arnie made his 11th and final Parachute Jump.
- After this successful undertaking the battalion had supported offensive actions all the way up to Wismar on Germany's Baltic Coast, it was there that elements of them including Arnie had one of the famous link ups with the Russians on the 7th & 8th May 1945, V.E. Day. Soon after that 7 Para was moved with the 5th Parachute Brigade to a very different theatre of war out in South-East Asia preparing for the intended invasion of Japan.
- Jungle training and acclimatization followed but after the Atomic bombs were dropped and Japan surrendered in August 1945 they were switched to other duties, and between September 1945 to August 1946 Arnie and 7 Para were involved as forces of occupation and containment in India, Malaya, Singapore, Siam (Thailand), Java (where he met his future wife Sienie), Sri Lanka, all under the control of SEAC - South East Asia Command.
- The next posting was again under very different conditions, this time in the Middle East in what was then British Mandate Palestine, where the 7th Battalion was returned to the 6th Airborne Division on what they called 'Policing Duties', Arnie was based at Tulkarm Army Camp near Netanya as part of the HQ Company Administration Staff from August 1946 until July 1947. Whilst there he had varied experiences such as peaceful visits to Bethlehem, Nazareth and Jerusalem to coming under attack by insurgents at Tulkarm!
- Once those duties were finished Arnie returned to the United Kingdom that same month, was demobbed in York on 27th August 1947, and after everything was only 22 years old.

'O God, The creator of all who has promised that those who trust in thee will rise on wings like eagles and, finding their strength renewed, will run and not get weary; will walk and not grow weak.. Grant that we of the Parachute Regiment may, in trusting in thee, find ourselves truly ready for anything in furtherance of thy kingdom and in the service of our king/queen and country.. Through him, who in thy service was strong until death, Jesus Christ our Lord. Amen.'

These opening words are 'The Prayer of the Parachute Regiment' that seems a very apt way to continue the story of a young man who served in what is a very well-respected part of our armed forces. I have been very fortunate over the years to interview a lot of WW2 Airborne Veterans from different regiments of the British Army, but Arnold 'Arnie' Hutchinson was the first I had interviewed who was in one of the direct standing Battalions of the Parachute Regiment.  As part of the 7th Parachute Regiment during the Second World War he saw service in places as diverse as the battlefields of Europe, to the Jungles of South-East Asia to desert terrain of the Middle East.  He like all others in the Airborne Forces was a volunteer who put himself forward, come what may, into the unknown dangers that lay ahead of him.  He fulfilled his duty and was lucky enough to survive all that he encountered and as a result be able to share his story with us about:

## BEING AN AIRBORNE INFANTRYMAN IN THE PARACHUTE REGIMENT

"I am very proud to say that I earned my Red Beret and was in 7 Para, or to give my unit its full title the 7th Light Infantry Parachute Battalion which along with the 12th and 13th Battalions and their company HQ's made up the 5th Parachute Brigade of the 6th Airborne Division.  We served under an excellent Commanding Officer called Lieutenant Colonel Pine-Coffin a brave leader and holder of both the Distinguished Service Order and Military Cross, and I mean this jokingly but respectfully an ironic surname for someone leading us into battle! **British Paras kitting up with a Douglas C47 'Dakota' behind, the 'Sky Train' that would drop them into war zones.** Anyway there were 4 companies, HQ, A, B and C within each Battalion, I was part of HQ company in 7 Para but of course was still a fully trained Airborne Infantryman, this meant that although my main duties were HQ related including communications between us and other company HQ's, we still served in and near the thick of it all and were shipped in, moved overland or parachuted into war zones.  Like everyone else we came under fire, as the Germans didn't give us any special treatment just because we were HQ, if anything it could lead to you being in more danger sometimes because the enemy knew if they could take out a HQ they'd reduce the capability of an opposing force to operate well and also cause confusion in its ranks!  As we were all fully armed, me with a Sten Gun, there were times like during The Battle of the Bulge and when we dropped into Germany where you might end up engaged with the enemy and have to return fire!  When the Battle of the Bulge started we were rushed to Belgium and were at a village called Wavreille, on the defensive line around Dinant and Namur, the latter we saw being bombed in an air raid, and eventually we ended up around Rochford and Eprave, during those battles I think the bitter cold was claiming as many casualties as the enemy, very hard going, at a village called Bure the Germans concentrated an attack on another of our Battalions killing 91 of our people and elsewhere we came under sniper fire! During operations as things unfolded we found ourselves in all sorts of situations, and once after we had jumped in during Operation Varsity one of our guys called Jordan was injured and lying in an open field, we were under very heavy fire from stubborn German defenders and I thought if he stays there he is going to die, somehow I summed up the courage to run out into the field with my other Para mates laying down covering fire to get him and bring him back, bullets were whizzing by and churning up the ground all around us, how we weren't hit I'll never know!  Sometime later at another fierce engagement at the Neustadt Bridge in April 1945 my other friend Tommy was not so lucky he was killed in battle there and was only 19 years old, had his whole life ahead of him!  That could have been any of us at any time!  Death was never far away and we saw it in one form or another as we went along, both amongst our lads and the enemy.  Even as we went in during Varsity the sky was a mass of aircraft towing gliders, and as far as the eye could see thousands of Paratroopers streaming out of their Dakotas like us, and heavy anti-aircraft fire was bringing down aircraft which you could see plummeting to the ground, they had become casualties before they could even engage the enemy!

Later on in some places we encountered very badly injured German soldiers and some would look at you and you could see it in their eyes, they just wanted you to finish them off, I could never bring myself to do that, to kill unarmed troops who were close to death, not very heroic, others might, not me, I wouldn't be able to live with that, it was one thing maybe having to shoot the enemy in battle, but not this way! When my war was finished I came out with a clear conscience, having served well.

A mass drop of Allied parachutists by Dakotas, and Horsa Gliders already on the ground, similar to what Arnie witnessed and was himself a part of during Operation Varsity, which was the largest airborne operation in history to be conducted on a single day and in one location, dropping approximately 17,000 British and American troops over the Rhine into Germany on the 24th March 1945.

On the morning of our Airborne drops over the Rhine in Operation Varsity I composed a short piece of poetry, it was called 'Eve of Battle' which I think was written as a young man expressing his inner thoughts and fears of jumping into the unknown, and if fate was to dictate that I didn't make it out alive someone might have found that on me and been inspired by it, luckily that didn't happen so it is me that has shared it with you and others, many years later I also wrote other pieces called 'Young Friend Tommy' about his very untimely loss, and 'The Seventh in S.E.A.C' about our very different duties out in South-East Asia (all pieces included in the poetry section of this book), although some would now regard it as just history I believe it should be remembered any way possible, poetry is one of those poignant and good ways which you can do that!" This was something I could totally relate to and agree with as a writer of conflict and remembrance poetry myself, and in tribute to all the brave men of the Parachute Regiment who went into battle like Arnie Hutchinson, and others such as Tommy Cairns who paid the ultimate price, I include this fitting tribute to reflect upon, known as:

## THE PARACHUTE REGIMENT CHARTER

"What manner of men are these who wear the maroon red beret? They are firstly all volunteers, and are then toughened by hard physical training. As a result they have that infectious optimism and that offensive eagerness which comes from physical well-being. They have jumped from the air and by doing so have conquered fear. Their duty lies in the van of battle: they are proud of this honour and have never failed in any task. They have the highest standard in all things, whether it be skill in battle or smartness in the execution of all peace time duties. They have shown themselves to be as tenacious and determined in defence as they are courageous in attack. They are, in fact, men apart - every man an Emperor."

**Dedication by Field Marshal The Viscount Montgomery of Alamein.**

The precious testimonies of Arnie and every other veteran in this book truly are 'Memories of War' and I thought it was very important that those words are part of the title of this book. In fact it was the name for a book that I had in my mind and was originally inspired to write from my teenage years when I was a pupil at Moston Brook High School in the early 1980's! The seed was planted then after first becoming interested in the history of the Second World War. All these years later I am very happy that it has become the major 'Debt of Gratitude Project' which I have been undertaking for some time now, and has really evolved more than ever into a passion to honour our WW2 veterans from all the services and backgrounds such as Arnie, who have been in the words of Parachute Regiment motto: Utrinque Paratus 'Ready for Anything'.

Thank you Arnie, Thank you All.

## Additional Information and Life After Service

**Rank upon finish of service** – Private.

**Medals and Honours** – 1939-45 War Medal, General Service Medal with South-East Asia Bar and Palestine Bar, 1939-45 Star, France-Germany Star, MBE (in 1976). PRA Membership Medal.

**Post War Years** – After leaving the Paras in 1947 Arnie studied and became a Chartered Accountant, from 1952-1976 he worked for Price Waterhouse in The Hague, Holland and in Copenhagen, Denmark. After this from 1976-1989 he was Chief Accountant for WCE – Wasey Campbell Eweld Advertising Agency in the U.K. Arnie retired December 1989 aged 65. He married Sienie in Bradford on 19th November 1947, and were together until her passing in 2008, they have 4 Children, 4 Grand-Children.

**Associations and Organisations** – PRA - Parachute Regimental Association Wolverhampton & Stafford Branches, FCA – Fellow of Chartered Accountants.

# CAPTAIN SIR TOM MOORE

Served with – 9th Battalion Duke of Wellington's Regiment & 146th Regiment, Royal Armoured Corps

Service Number – 193763

Permission given for Inclusion in this Book – October 2020

Final Revisions – 2023

### Service History and Personal Stories

- Born – 30th April 1920, Keighley, West Riding of Yorkshire, England, UK.
- Thomas Moore, a born and bred Yorkshireman attended Keighley Grammar School and later completed an apprenticeship as a Civil Engineer before being conscripted into the British Army in May 1940, where he became part of an infantry unit, the 8th Battalion, Duke of Wellington's Regiment (8 DWR) at Otley in West Yorkshire, he was then sent to be trained at Wadebridge, Cornwall and with other new recruits was involved in coastal defence for the predicted German invasion of the U.K.
- He was soon promoted to Corporal and later that year was selected for officer training and sent to an Officer Cadet Training Unit at Droitwich Spa in Worcestershire and became a Second-Lieutenant on 28th June 1941. Whilst with 8 DWR he became a member of the 145th Regiment Royal Armoured Corps on 22nd October 1941 when it was re-designated to become an armoured unit which operated Churchill Tanks. Later that year he was posted to India and whilst there had been transferred to the 9th Battalion (9 DWR) which had also been re-designated as 146th Regiment Royal Armoured Corps.

~ 68 ~

- ❖ They were based in Bombay (now Mumbai) and then Calcutta (now Kolkata) and whilst in India he was tasked with setting up and running a training programme for Army motorcyclists due to his expertise in the sport. In October 1942 he was promoted to War- Substantive Lieutenant and on 11th October 1944 he became a temporary Captain.
- ❖ His regiment, now in Burma, were equipped with M3 Lee tanks, and from 1944 until 1945 Tom and the 146th were involved in the hard-fought Battles for the Arakan coastal region and Ramree Island (Operation Matador) on the Southern Front in the Burma campaign as part of the Fourteenth 'Forgotten' Army.' Whilst there as a Tank Commander he survived vicious Japanese attacks and the dreaded Dengue Fever.
- ❖ In late 1945 Tom went on to be part of the allied occupational forces in Sumatra after the Japanese surrender by which time he had risen to the rank of Captain. On his return to Britain he served as an instructor at the Armoured Fighting Vehicle School in Bovington, Dorset until he was demobbed in spring 1946.
- ❖ Tom Moore's military and other accolades did not stop when his military service stopped, as most of the United Kingdom and indeed the World now knows, and much later in life his extraordinary fundraising efforts in 2020 for the 'NHS Charities Together' fund led amongst other things to him becoming an Honorary Colonel and after 800,000 people had signed a petition calling for Tom to be knighted the Queen doing so that same year.

Captain Sir Tom Moore is another great example of that incredible wartime 'Greatest Generation' standing up and coming forward as they did 75 years earlier to once again help their country in a time of national crisis, then it was World War Two this time the Coronavirus Pandemic. Since early 2020 we have seen very well-known veterans of World War Two such as Dame Vera Lynn and Her Majesty the Queen offer words of kindness and support to the nation during an increasingly difficult time, and a once lesser-known gentleman also began with what was a charity fundraising idea branded as 'Tom's 100th Birthday Walk for the NHS' to try and raise £1000 to help the NHS by walking 100 laps of his garden by his 100th birthday on the 30th April 2020. This he did, starting on the 6th April and finishing 16th April 2020, and on that day watched at a safe distance by a guard of honour from the 1st Battalion of the Yorkshire Regiment, the regiment into which the Duke of Wellington's Regiment were merged in 2006. He then stated that he would keep on going to raise as much money as possible by his birthday, which was also the final day his 'Just Giving' page would run, by that time he had absolutely smashed that original target by raising a staggering 39 million pounds with the final gift aid tax rebates included, that had come in from what were now worldwide donations! William the Duke of Cambridge praised him as a 'One-man fundraising machine', and he has justly been applauded by the likes of Sir Mo Farah, Sir Lewis Hamilton, Gary Lineker, David Williams and many others. He has influenced and inspired a huge amount of people of all ages and backgrounds to undertake fundraising for the NHS and other great causes and charities in the United Kingdom that needed more help than ever during the Covid 19 crisis, and was described very aptly by then Prime Minister Boris Johnson as; 'A true National Treasure who has provided us all with a beacon of light through the fog of Coronavirus.'

Alas I had not met Captain Tom or interviewed him like I normally do with the other veterans I write about, despite trying this was not possible, understandably due to how incredibly popular he had become in such a short time meaning so many other people wanted to interview him and do things with him and were trying to get a piece of his very precious time. When I got in touch with Carver PR the Company that in conjunction with his family deals with his publicity and told them about my Debt of Gratitude Project to honour veterans, I was very kindly granted permission to write about him for inclusion in my book. So with all these things in mind and in place the next part of his story is a collection of quotes from this very inspiring veteran regarding many aspects of his life from wartime recollections to his charity work, accolades, thoughts and opinions, through to some of the things that have happened since he became famous, so here are:

# THE INSPIRATIONAL WORDS OF CAPTAIN SIR TOM MOORE

**Starting with his World War Two service as a commissioned officer serving in Burma, he said:**

"Being conscripted didn't do me any harm at all. The reason for conscription was that the country had become desperately short of soldiers. It was an entirely different world to anything I'd been in before but we survived. I was at the front along with the Indian Army, we all battled together, we were under fire constantly, there was an element of discomfort shall we say, I was only 21 or 22, you don't get very frightened at 22! Part of the adventure of life, and if I was capable, I'd do the same thing all over again." **A British Crew in action on an American M3 Lee Medium tank, seen here as it crosses a river north of Imphal to meet the Japanese advance in Burma, 1944, the same kind of tank Captain Tom manned during the Burma Campaign in WW2.**

**Whilst out there he also saw and heard a certain well-known performer called Vera Lynn and was lucky enough along with many others to meet her, as he now recalls:**

"One day this charming young lady appeared who turned out to be Vera Lynn, and was produced amongst men who had not seen girls for a long time, it was quite something, she did a little song for us so it really boosted morale of everybody, she was great. **Tom went on to say with a smile on his face;** "All I know is that she appeared amongst us with Lord Mountbatten, I thought at the time the top people get all the best jobs!"

**At the outset of his special NHS charity fundraising walk the target as mentioned before was £1000, as things spiraled and he reached the £5,000 000-mark Tom explained more about his motivation:**

"I am absolutely thrilled, they have done incredible things for me and my family, and I am glad that I have been able to give something back to them, especially at this deeply challenging time."

"When we started off with this exercise, we didn't anticipate we'd get anything near that sort of money. It's really amazing. All of them, from top to bottom, in the National Health Service, they deserve everything that we can possibly put in their place. They're all so brave. Because every morning or every night they're putting themselves into harm's way, and I think you've got to give them full marks for that effort. We're a little bit like having a war at the moment. But the doctors and the nurses, they're all on the front line, and all of us behind, we've got to supply them and keep them going with everything that they need, so that they can do their jobs even better than they're doing now."

**When Tom was chosen as the guest of honour to open the new Nightingale hospital in his native Yorkshire on 21st April 2020, done via video link, the World War Two veteran had this to say:**

"I'm honoured to be opening the NHS Nightingale Yorkshire and Humber and to get to thank many of the NHS workers directly. I know that having extra beds available for the sick, if needed will be reassuring to those workers, as it would have been to me when I was on the front line."

On the 17th July 2020 he became Sir Tom when Queen Elizabeth knighted him in the grounds of Windsor Castle with the ceremonial sword that belonged to her father King George VI who led his nation through World War Two, and presented him with the insignia of Knight Bachelor in a special and personal investiture, of which he said: "It was an absolutely outstanding day, you could never believe at 100 I would get such an honour that I have today. Never have I been so privileged as to be so close to the Queen and to speak to her, that really was outstanding."

**The Queen personally praised Captain Sir Tom telling him:** "Thank you so much, an amazing amount of money you raised."

On the 10th September 2020 Captain Sir Tom visited the Army Foundation College at Harrogate, Yorkshire in his capacity of Honorary Colonel, awarded by them on his birthday, which he described as "truly a great honour", and where addressed as 'Colonel Tom' was invited that day to be Chief Inspecting Officer at their annual graduation parade, and gave these very positive words:

"To go up the ranks so quickly, I'm really delighted, I know it's only an honorary one but really I'm absolutely thrilled with the fact the honour has been placed on me." His advice for junior soldiers was "To try to be the best." He continued "When I was conscripted, I looked round to see all the other people and thought I'm going to the best, without climbing over anyone's shoulders, just quietly get on and do your best and be your best."

Continuing his great work after the success of the Just Giving campaign Sir Tom and family launched 'The Captain Tom Foundation' on 17th September 2020 to carry on raising funds for a number of charities close to their hearts on what he views as 'The next part of his journey.' Another key aim of the foundation is to inspire a new generation of 'Captain Toms' and he elaborated more on this:

"I never dreamt that this could happen, the overwhelming generosity of people, during a period of darkness, has shown the resilience and caring people are capable of during a time when there was anguish and instability. After all we have achieved over the last few months, and with the world still in recovery, it made sense to us to create a legacy. To raise money and push towards our vision of a more hopeful world. So, together with my family, we have created The Captain Tom Foundation."

**In relation to this he also Tweeted:** "I'm so proud of all we have achieved but we're not done yet!"

Prior to the release of his autobiography in September 2020, amidst the Coronavirus Pandemic he had these rousing and motivating words, some of which became the title of his book, when he said: "My message to the nation right now is, 'tomorrow will be a good day.' We will get through this and come out of it stronger, more united and ready to face any challenge together."

And to finish, this small yet lovely and hopeful message and parting gift from a veteran of the wartime generation to those of all generations:

"For all those finding it difficult: the sun will shine on you again and the clouds will go away."

'Virtutis Fortuna Comes' meaning 'Fortune Favours the Brave' this is the motto of the Duke of Wellington's Regiment of which Tom was a part, and those words are very apt when describing the efforts and achievements of Captain (Honorary Colonel) Sir Tom Moore. A man who became a household name and whom the nation took to their hearts, and a very fitting veteran to have as part of my book, so on behalf of myself and countless others I say a huge thank you for all you have done and all you have represented during difficult times, your words are and will forever be a source of great inspiration and one of your many great legacies. Thank you Sir.

# Additional Information and Life After Service

**Rank upon finish of service** – Captain – Later Honorary Colonel (2020).

**Medals and Honours** – 1939-45 Defence Medal, 1939-45 War Medal, 1939-45 Star, Burma Star, Yorkshire Regimental Medal (2020), Knight Bachelor (2020).

**Additional Accolades & Achievements** – So many have been bestowed and so much attained since his extremely successful 'Just Giving' campaign in 2020 that only a few are listed here: On 23 April 2020 Tom was given a Pride of Britain award in recognition of his efforts. He featured in a cover version of the song 'You'll Never Walk Alone' sung by Michael Ball, the single topped the UK music charts with all proceeds going to the NHS Charities Together and did so on time for his 100th Birthday on 30th April, where amongst other things he received 150,000 cards including a personalised birthday card from Queen Elizabeth II, presented in person by the Lord Lieutenant of Bedfordshire, Helen Nellis. Also Birthday congratulations were made by Prince Charles and he took a video call from the Secretary-General of the United Nations, António Guterres and had fly-overs from a RAF Battle of Britain Memorial Flight Spitfire and Hurricane, later followed by Wildcat and Apache helicopters of the Army Air Corps and that same day named a 'Point of Light' by the Prime Minister. On the 12th May, he was granted the Freedom of the City of London. In July Tom Moore became the first member and captain of the Football Association and England National Football Team's Lionhearts squad. This honour was presented by former England captain David Beckham, and Cranfield University near his home in Bedfordshire, awarded him an Honorary Doctorate of Science. A number of artists have painted portraits of 'Captain Tom' and on 14th August an official portrait painted by Alexander Chamberlin was unveiled. It is in the collection of the National Army Museum. The fame does not stop there, he has given over 150 media interviews, and on the 6th May BBC One even changed its advertised schedule to screen a 30-minute BBC News Special, *Captain Tom: We Salute You*, and ITV, screened a 30-minute documentary, *Captain Tom's War*, on the 8th May, in which Captain Tom reminisced about his military career, followed by the hour-long *The Life & Times of Captain Sir Tom* on 13th August and he was also the special guest on an episode of Piers Morgan's Life Stories on 13th September. On 17th September his autobiography 'Tomorrow will be a good Day' was released as part of a £1.5 million book deal and soon after made it onto The Times No.1 Bestsellers Booklist. Great Western Railway named a Class 800 train, 800 025, *Captain Tom Moore*, in October 2020 he was presented with the first ever 'Military Veterans Railcard' by Transport Secretary Grant Shapps, and at time of writing Captain Tom Moore holds two *Guinness World Records*: as the fundraiser raising the greatest amount of money in an individual charity walk, and as the oldest person to have a number-one single on the UK charts. December 2020 at Sports Personality of the Year Dame Jessica Ennis-Hill presented him with The Helen Rollason Award which recognises outstanding achievement in the face of adversity, a great end to 2020, and to start 2021 he appears on the cover of GQ Magazine as their oldest cover star and named 'Inspiration of the Year'. Sadly, on 2nd February 2021 Captain Tom passed away, taken by that terrible great leveler - Coronavirus, another National Treasure gone. Rest in Peace. GBD.

**Post War Years** – After leaving the army, he worked as a sales manager for a roofing materials company in Yorkshire, and later as managing director of a Fens-based company in Norfolk manufacturing concrete called Cawood Concrete Products Ltd, which was renamed March Concrete Products Ltd. after he led a management buyout in 1983, the company was sold to ARC in 1987. Married Pamela in January 1968, who passed in 2006. Has 2 Daughters, 4 Grandchildren.

**Associations and Organisations** – Army Foundation College, Harrogate, Duke of Wellington's Regiment Association, for 64 years he organised the DWR's annual reunion.

# GUNNER JOHN BOOTH

Served with – 5th Searchlight & 137th Field Artillery Regiments, Royal Artillery
Service Number – 1628864
Interviewed – BLESMA Care Home, Blackpool, 22nd August 2014

### Service History and Personal Stories

- Born – 14th March 1918, Chadderton, Manchester, England, UK.
- Called up in 1940 at 22 years of age, completed basic training at Kinmel Park Army Camp near Abergele in North Wales. As part of the 5th Searchlight Regiment and later the 137th Field Artillery Regiment John learned to use various calibres of Anti-Aircraft and Artillery weapons as well as searchlights used against enemy aircraft for night time combat.
- John married Irene Bell on the 22nd February 1941, picture above, a few months later he was posted with the 137th R.A Regiment to Singapore, the Regiment was captured when Singapore fell to the Japanese on the 15th February 1942 during the biggest defeat the British Army suffered in its entire history, John became one of 80,000 prisoners that day!
- He was a Prisoner Of War for three and the half years from February 1942 to September 1945, held under dreadful conditions and treated horrifically, sent as a POW to Saigon in Vietnam from March 1942 until moved by rail in cattle trucks via Phnom Penh in Cambodia to Non Pladuk in Thailand in June 1943 to begin work on what history would call the 'Death Railway.'
- It was there that John would be a slave labourer at various points and dreaded internment camps on the River Kwai such as Kinsaiyok from June until October 1943, then relocated to Chungkai

~ 73 ~

- where just as work on the railway was completed he lost both legs after sepsis led to them having to be amputated without anaesthetic!
- John remained in Chungkai until it was closed in June 1945, the final part of his ordeal in captivity was in a camp near Bangkok called Nakhon Pathom until his liberation on the 2nd September 1945. Then he returned on a long journey via India, Egypt and the Suez Canal arriving in Southampton November 1945 to be re-united with his wife and loved ones.
- After a few weeks in hospital in Birmingham John was home for Christmas 1945, and in 1946 he was fitted with new prosthetic legs at Chapel Allerton Hospital in Leeds and was then ready and equipped to bravely begin his new life as a civilian once again.

As you read through the pages of this book you will find the stories of numerous extraordinary and diverse World War Two veterans, those who were in the Royal Navy, Royal Air Force, the Army, Intelligence and Home Front capacities, men and women from the U.K, from the Caribbean and India/Pakistan and elsewhere, those who came through the conflict unscathed, at least physically, some who were injured, and others who suffered sight and hearing impediments either as a direct result of action or naturally through age and the passing of time. The variety represented here gives a very rich tapestry of personal histories and poignant narratives that deliver stimulating and thought-provoking reading. A very good example of this is the story of our next veteran, who when he joined the Army could never have imagined the horrors and personal ordeals that lay ahead when he went as part of His Majesty's armed forces to serve King and Country in South-East Asia, leaving home as an able-bodied young serviceman and returning as a limbless veteran, this is the poignant story of Royal Artillery Gunner John Booth who now takes us in quite sobering detail through some of his difficult personal journey, telling us how it was:

### SURVIVING THE HARDSHIPS AND HORRORS OF THE FAR EAST AND THE DEATH RAILWAY

"When we were beaten by the Japanese in Singapore it came as an utter shock and was a huge and humiliating defeat. We were reduced almost overnight from being proud fighting soldiers of the British Army to a disposable Slave Labour Army at hands of our merciless captors! In Spring 1942 I was first sent for 14 months with around 700 men to work on the docks in Saigon, Vietnam, now known as Ho Chi Minh City, and held in the Saigon Prison Camp, after this in mid-1943 we were transferred somewhere even worse to the jungles of Thailand to a prison camp called Kinsaiyok to work on the infamous River Kwai. Once the Japanese had decided to build a railway line and its connecting bridges from Thailand up into Burma to support and supply their military ambitions up there we immediately became expendable. It was irrelevant to them how many lives it cost to build it as long as it was completed for the Empire and the Emperor, as a result allied POW's started to forge out of the unforgiving landscape what became known as the 'Death Railway' and it lived up to its name, every sleeper representing a life or more of our poor boys who were forced to build it under appalling conditions and utter brutality. The cruelty and ruthlessness were continuous both in the camps and on the railway and bridge construction, once strong men that were in their prime had become walking skeletons, now suffering from malnutrition and racked with illnesses such as malaria, beriberi, cholera, dysentery, barely able to stand as they became more and more incapable, all were senselessly battered with clubs and bamboo sticks, all these things happened to me and everyone I knew and we witnessed many beaten to death for not being able to work, or for the slightest indiscretion or just because the sadistic Japanese and Korean guards felt like it in their random daily outbursts of vicious spontaneous violence. Bodies of the victims were thrown into mostly unmarked shallow graves in makeshift cemeteries that followed the railway mile after mile! Add to that the intolerable heat, draining humidity, rats, endless flies, mosquitoes and other parasites, the months of relentless torrential downpours of monsoon rains, the merciless terrain we had to smash through whether solid stone or the deep jungle with razor sharp thorns that could rip a man's skin open in an instant, which was my undoing later on, the gruelling work of having to carry heavy logs, railway sleepers and all other materials by men with little and sometimes nothing on their feet, and you have the cocktail of unrelenting misery and unceasing torment, one which when I look back I really still cannot understand how I survived and how 12,000 other broken souls didn't!"

**A sketch by Leo Rawlings in 1943, himself a POW on the 'Death Railway.' Here depicting four POW slave-labourers carrying a large log, waist deep in the water of that river. Similar to the hardships and experiences detailed by John Booth in his accounts of that time, where he worked on both railway lines and bridges whilst in captivity. One of John's camps Chungkai was located near a stretch of river called 'Mae Klong' where Bridge 277 the original so called 'Bridge Over the River Kwai' was located, later made famous in the 1957 film of the same name directed by David Lean.**

I listened, most of the time in utter silence, stunned almost in disbelief at what I was hearing and shocked at how inhumane people, in this case their guards could be, as John continued to tell me: "I was involved in the last few months of construction on the Death Railway and by October 1943 was in a camp called Chungkai. They were all horrific places if I was asked to compare them I could only answer how do you compare hell with hell…? Yet the worse part of my personal hell was to come, when my skin on one leg was ripped open by a bamboo thorn in the jungle and the other had a nasty insect bite, both happened in Kinsaiyok by the time we had reached Chungkai which had big makeshift hospital facilities, I had sepsis which if not treated quickly was a sure death sentence! So it was both legs off with a chance I might live, otherwise die there as another statistic of the Death Railway! I chose amputation which was carried out with no anaesthetic whatsoever with 4 men holding me down and something in my mouth so they couldn't hear my screams whilst I had one leg after another sawn off! Pain and trauma beyond description! The Japanese rarely supplied medicines and were even known to withhold them even if not used! Passing out was my only temporary escape. Some of the inner strength I summoned up to get through that stayed with me for the rest of my days and was translated into determination which helped me get through all the obstacles and difficulties that life threw at me later. But believe me if you survive having your legs taken off without pain relief then most other things in life don't seem too hard after that, in fact it became quite the opposite, I valued life even more having been given this second chance to do so, and wanted to live it to the fullest and do the very best I could, from the small day to day issues through to the bigger life achievements! Later I went back to work, raised a family with the help of a wonderful wife Irene, making sure that despite disability I was the best father to my children and best grandpa to my Grandchildren I could possibly be, it was very hard and took much adjusting for her too, I drove cars, went on holidays and had hobbies all this even with prosthetic legs! So I think to a large degree I succeeded in most things."

# THE DEATH RAILWAY – A SHORT OVERVIEW

In order to give John's story more historical context I have included some brief background information regarding what is known as the Thai-Burma Railway, Siam-Burma Railway or ultimately the 'Death Railway' along with this map showing its layout indicating important places en-route.

The Japanese began their wartime construction of the railway in October 1942, using Prisoners of War captured from when Singapore fell in February of that year. It was built in order to provide logistical support to planned attacks of the Burma campaign and also against the British in the Indian sub-continent.

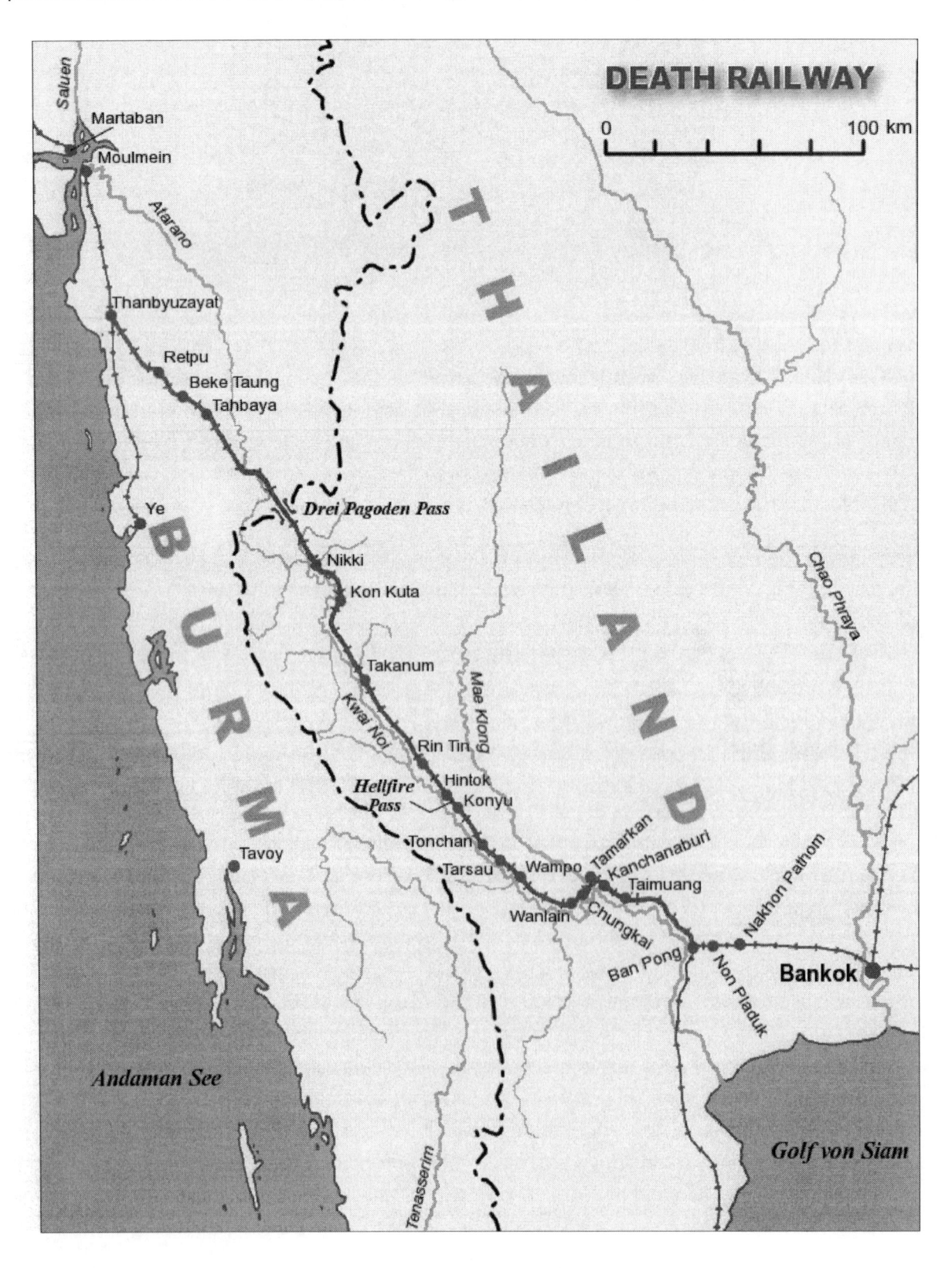

When completed a year later in October 1943 the railway spanned a 415 Kilometre/258-mile link from its starting point at Ban Pong in Thailand, where it connected to a main line running to the Capital Bangkok, all the way up through harsh unforgiving terrain to Thanbyuzayat in Burma where it linked up with the line running up the Capital Rangoon, it consisted of 688 bridges and over 60 stations. This maps out the geography of pure suffering that was achieved at the expense of many!

In fact the Japanese would use the forced labour of approximately 60,000 Allied POWs of mixed nationalities and 200,000 South-East Asian civilians known as Romusha, Japanese for 'Labourer.' Of these around 12,000 allied troops and 90,000 civilian labourers died or were killed during its construction! The death rate of Western POWs in Japanese camps was an incredible 27.1%, seven times higher than that of servicemen held by German and Italian forces. When completed despite allied bombings the line continued in use until the war in the Far East ended in September 1945.

**I felt honoured to have spent time with this incredible man who really had been to 'hell and back', privileged to have captured his very moving story and humbled by what I had heard and learnt from being with this most inspiring veteran. Thank you John, your suffering was not in vain, and your story and personal sacrifices will be remembered here in permanence now you are a part of The Last Stand – Memories of War.**

## Additional Information and Life After Service

**Rank upon finish of service** – Gunner.

**Medals and Honours** – 1939-45 Defence Medal, 1939-45 War Medal, 1939-45 Star, Pacific Star.

**Post War Years** – 1946-1976 Worked 30 years at CWS (COOP) Main Factory in Middleton, Manchester as a Store Keeper. Retired in 1976 and went to live in Blackpool. Married Irene Bell at St. Gabriel's Church, Middleton Junction, Manchester in 1941, Irene passed 1998. Children, they have 2 Sons, 4 Grandchildren, 4 Great-Grandchildren (at time of interview). He came to BLESMA at South Shore, Blackpool in January 2013.

**Associations and Organisations** – BLESMA – British Limbless Ex-Servicemen's Association. FEPOW – Far East Prisoner of War Association.

# COLOUR SERGEANT IAN NIVEN MBE

Served with – 1st Battalion, Lancashire Fusiliers & Chindit Special Jungle Force
Service Number – 14408980
Interviewed – Sale, Cheshire, 1st October 2014

## Service History and Personal Stories

- Born – 23rd January 1924, Manchester, Lancashire, England, UK.
- Ian Volunteered for the Army on 20th October 1942 at Oxford Road Army Recruitment Office, Manchester aged 18, he was already in the Home Guard as a Fire Watcher at Manchester Royal Infirmary and had done some basic shooting and drilling which stood him in good stead for the real thing when he was finally sent for in late December 1942.
- He had initially chosen the Royal Scots, following in the military footsteps of his father John Carmichael Niven who as a Scotsman served in The Royal Scots (The Royal Regiment) in the last year of the First World War and had re-joined the same regiment again in World War Two, but first Ian had to complete intensive infantry training with the Scottish Lowland (Holding) Regiment at the Cameron Barracks in Inverness, Scotland.
- Whilst there he undertook further training to become a Signaller which included learning Morse Code, Radio Transmission and Maintenance, Flag Communication (Semaphore), drilling and military exercises as an Infantryman and Signaller with and without a full radio pack on his back to prepare him for this dual job that he would carry out later in combat.
- After successful completion of this training Ian was then transferred to his father's Regiment the Royal Scots in May 1943 based at Hunstanton in Norfolk and was with them until August 1943.

Next he was shipped out from Liverpool to India on the SS Empire Pride to begin active service overseas. During that journey he was seconded to the K.O.S.B - Kings Own Scottish Borders Regiment whilst working for their officers on board.

- ❖ His potential had already been spotted and Ian was selected to become part of a very special Jungle fighting force that had been created by Orde Wingate to try and help stop the Japanese advance in Burma, with the use of Guerrilla tactics and attacks in that terrain to take the fight directly to the enemy and disrupt their ability to wage war effectively by hitting them hard behind their own lines of advance. This effective force was in time to become legendry, and was known as the Chindits.
- ❖ In order to teach the soldiers this kind of warfare, Ian and others who became part of this 'Special Jungle Force' were taught unique warfare and survival skills in similar terrain in Silchar, India, on the India-Burma border from October 1943 until February 1944. Whilst there Ian was transferred to the 1st Battalion Lancashire Fusiliers where he would meet and train with fellow 'Mancunion' Tommy Hopper who he would next see 70 years later!
- ❖ All of this training was leading up to the huge Airborne offensive that took place on 5th March 1944 which was called Operation Thursday where a staggering 10,000 troops, 1000 mules and supplies were eventually dropped into dense jungle clearings in the heart of enemy territory in Burma, using C47 Dakotas and Waco CG-4A Gliders. This type of operation had never been attempted before in such terrain and was the largest Allied airborne operation ever conducted until forces under General Eisenhower landed in France as part of Operation Overlord three months later in June 1944.
- ❖ Ian went in as part of the 77th Brigade in the 2nd wave of glider landings that first night under the Command of Brigadier Michael Calvert at an area codenamed 'Broadway', after this from March until July 1944 Ian and fellow Chindits were engaged in fierce battles in many areas in the Sagaing Region Northwest of Burma, and also defending points such as 'White City' where they had established a rail and road block at Mawlu, north of Indaw.
- ❖ The 77th Brigade fought on until finally capturing the 'Pin Hmi Bridge' and after a 20-day siege of Mogaung captured the town on the 27th June 1944, but at the cost of 50 percent casualties! It was the first place in Burma to be liberated from the Japanese, and also marked the last major Chindit campaign of the war.
- ❖ By July it was clear the Chindit Force was exhausted, it was withdrawn from Operations in Burma, and the British 36th Division was transferred from Arakan to replace them. At the end of this their second campaign in Burma they had lost 1,396 killed and 2,434 wounded, additionally over half the remainder, like Ian Niven had to be hospitalised for treatment of various diseases and for special diets to re-build their strength and health again.
- ❖ After lengthy hospital treatment and recuperation in India and with the war now over Ian was transferred for further duties at the British Army Headquarters in Lucknow, Uttar Pradesh, he had now been promoted to Colour Sergeant and served in more peaceful surroundings as an Orderly Room Sergeant for the 1st Battalion Lancashire Fusiliers until the end of July 1946, after which he travelled home on the Cunard ship MV Britannic from Bombay to Liverpool.
- ❖ Upon his return to the U.K Ian still had ongoing and re-occurring health problems from his time in the Jungle such as bouts of Malaria and Amoebic Dysentery, injury to his left knee, and spent time in hospital in Chester, after which he was demobbed on 14th August 1947.

Ian Niven was at time of writing one of the very few remaining World War Two Special Jungle Force 'Chindits' left in the U.K, and his story here in The Last Stand is a direct connection to the story of Tommy Hopper from my first book, as they are both linked through their service together in India and Burma as Lancashire Fusiliers and as Chindits. I first saw them featured together in a Manchester Evening News article in 2013 saying '70 years on, War heroes reunited' and with them being within Greater Manchester, having some shared military history and very reachable in the early days of my veterans interviewing,

I thought it would be great to interview them both which I did individually in 2014 with the idea of spreading them out over two books so I have a Chindit in each. Years later that is exactly what is happening. Ian's story starts in Manchester where he joined the Army in 1942, after extensive training in 1943 he was sent out that same year to India and then Burma where he had been selected to become one of Major-General Orde Wingate's elite jungle fighting force which was charged with taking on the Japanese in deep jungle terrain using the same kind of Guerrilla tactics that the enemy had employed against the allies up until that point with great success. This led to Ian and the other Chindits being involved in fierce close quarters combat from when they were dropped into the battle zone in Gliders as part of Operation Thursday in March 1944 and continued on in active combat until July 1944 after which they were taken out of 'The Line' in August when suffering from severe fatigue and many with diseases, Ian being one of those seriously ill with amongst other things Malaria and Dysentery picked up from long exposure to the harsh environment which was their battleground over those hard months. Now sharing his memories of these and many other things is Ian Niven who recalls:

## BEING ONE OF WINGATE'S SPECIAL FORCE CHINDITS

"I am very proud to say I am a Chindit, because once a Chindit always a Chindit! We earned that lifelong title through blood, sweat and tears in the jungles of Burma where we fought a tough, vicious and determined enemy who knew the lay of the land well and who were already masters of jungle warfare! What our training taught us was to beat them at their own game using similar tactics plus the element of surprise that came from Operation Thursday, a huge force being dropped in by gliders and supply aircraft of the United States Air Forces 1st Air Commando Group **(Emblem shown)** right into the heart of their territory, something they never expected, and taking them on from behind their lines using additional guerrilla hit and run tactics that left them in tatters, we were essentially a big 'Long-Range Penetration Force' hitting them hard and hurting them hard as they had done to others, now it was their turn! These attacks helped de-stabilise a well-established enemy force and along with the other allied forces they were fighting in the country as they tried to move up into British ruled India, we would eventually help prevent them from achieving this very dangerous goal in the region. If they had have got into India and got hold of the vast resources there the war could have lasted a lot longer with far more devastating consequences, realising this is why General Wingate had the full backing of Churchill and the Americans to try and stop this big threat and to hopefully try and speed up and bring about the defeat of the Japs in the Far East. My little part in all this, well by the time Operation Thursday happened I was a Lancashire Fusilier, an infantry soldier in the Special Chindit Force which was part of the 77th Brigade, under the 14th 'Forgotten' Army, which was a componant of SEAC – South East Asia Command, headed by Louis Mountbatten. Just before we were to go into battle we were making final preparations at a place called Lalaghat in Assam, India, a big camp and airfield with Gliders, towing aircraft and servicemen everywhere, you could tell it was a huge and very important operation, so much so that our C/O was told to find the youngest and the oldest soldier who would be going in and to have them ready for inspection and to be prepared to meet some very important people. This happened two days in a row, and lo and behold on the 4th March we met Major-General Orde Wingate, mastermind of everything going on around us and the next day, the day of our departure and start of Operation Thursday, on the 5th March 1944 we met the overall Commander of SEAC Lord Louis Mountbatten himself, very special experiences and some of the fonder memories of that campaign, but much harder was to follow!

**The Glider, a key component in any Chindit Operation, vital for delivering the troops into harsh battle zones.**

**The flag of SEAC with the emblem of the 'Pheonix rising from the Flames' in this case from the earlier defeats in that theatre of war such as the devastating fall of Singapore in February 1942.**

This started with our glider-borne descents into specific landing zones in the jungle at night guided only by some torches on the ground! When you see war footage of glider landings in open fields in the day these seem hard enough, can you imagine coming down in narrow cleared out areas in the jungle with virtually no light! We, the Lancashire Fusiliers were in the second wave. There were of course casualties I saw gliders and the bodies of our comrades in the tree tops, they were from the 1st King's Liverpool Regiment in the first wave, one of the many not so nice memories of war. Once down each battalion normally consisting of around 1000 men was split into 2 columns, A and B, each having a HQ Company, which as a signaller I was attached to, and of course the other essential component for this extreme terrain with its stifling humidity, our loyal companion the Mule, **(Pictured here as part of a Chindit column)** my radio set was carried by a mule most of the time, they had to be flown in as well. I don't know what was harder, fighting the elements or the enemy, also I was an infantryman and signaller so I had to do both jobs, we spent a lot of the time with our senses naturally heightened through adrenaline and being in the dangerous jungle environment, sometimes apprehensive, sometimes fearful of not knowing what was literally around the next corner. In a heartbeat you could go from only seeing and hearing the sights and sounds of nature to those of the terror of pitched battle, gunfire, explosions, men screaming and all hell let loose! That applied if you were being ambushed or doing the ambushing! If you didn't get shot, your nerves certainly would be after prolonged exposure to those very harsh conditions! **Major-General Wingate, in the centre, and senior officers, including Brigadier Calvert, 3rd from the left, waiting for a night time supply drop at their make-shift landing zone and airfield called 'Broadway'. Both Chindit incursions into Burma, Operation Longcloth in 1943 and Operation Thursday in 1944 were Wingate's brainchild, sadly shortly after this picture was taken he was killed in a plane crash on 24th March 1944 in Manipur, Northeast India. Wingate was an exponent of unconventional military thinking and the value of surprise tactics which worked increasingly well against the Japanese in the jungle warfare that took place in Burma.** We saw a lot of vicious fighting under our commanding officer Brigadier 'Mad' Mike Calvert who earned that name for his continuous bravery and ferocity in hand-to-hand fighting, and for leading by example when taking his men into battle with himself at the front, no wonder he won a DSO and bar whilst commanding the 77th Brigade with the Chindits, and no surprise he later led an SAS unit in Europe near the end of the war. Many years later he paid me a surprise visit at the pub I was running called the Fletchers Arms in Denton, Manchester, it was great to reminisce about our Chindit days in Burma, despite all the ups and downs of everything we went through out there the one thing that anyone who has served together will tell you, especially if you have been in the heat of battle together, are that the bonds of comradeship never disappear regardless of how many years come to pass." This feeling was certainly apparent when Ian saw Brigadier Calvert again, and he wrote a special message to him in a book about the Chindits called 'To be A Chindit' which read;

**To Ian Niven C/Sgt.   29 July '72.**

**Who had the misfortune to serve under my command in Burma and is therefore lucky to be alive!  He took part in the glider landing, defence of White City, operations outside White City, advance to Mogaung, attack on Pin Hmi Bridge and final capture of Mogaung.  He suffered all the tropical diseases.  I am glad to see you so fit now.  My best wishes   Yours Sincerely   Michael Calvert.**

"Whether we were on the defensive like at White City, called that because of all the white parachutes stuck in the trees with our supplies on them from air drops, containing essential ammunition to fight with and desperately needed food, whilst we were going hungry beneath them, and which us and the enemy couldn't and didn't dare to try and reach for the fear of being shot by snipers from either side, or if on a gruelling and costly offensive like at Mogaung, and additionally in heavy monsoons, and heat that regularly reached over 100 degrees fahrenheit or being effected by one or more of the many diseases you could catch out there, it was hard for all concerned and many, me included, became very fatigued and very ill indeed.  I remember after more than four months of active service in Burma when I was being flown out of there in a Dakota on the way to hospital in India, thinking 'if we die then hell won't be as bad as what we have been through and experienced.'  I was suffering from Bacillary Dysentery and at one point was close to death, they had to put me in a bath of ice water to cool me down, when I regained consciousness I remember looking round and seeing many sick people and many bodies with blankets over them and being told 'Your lucky mate, you could easily have been one of them!'  A lot to go through for myself and other young lads like me who were bearly 21 years old, all of that as part of an army and a theatre of war which sadly to a large extent was 'forgotten!'  War when even seemingly essential in order to beat an evil enemy is still a crazy state of affairs, yet one I am pleased to say despite all difficulties we helped the allies win."

## THE IMPORTANT CONTRIBUTIONS OF OVERSEAS PERSONNEL IN WW2

Many came from all over the world from countries that were then part of the British Empire, Commonwealth and elsewhere, different colours and creeds to help Great Britain and her ally the United States win the war in Burma, it is very important to remember the contributions of people who helped us there and in all other theatres of that war between 1939-1945, and those who paid the ultimate sacrifice whilst doing so!  The war in Burma was undoubtedly one of the greatest examples of this diversity in action with servicemen and women coming to join us from many places and backgrounds such as Hindus, Sikhs, Muslims and Christians from all over the Indian Contenent, this included the already famous and fearsome Gurkhas from Nepal, those from the African Continent such as Nigerians, Ugandans, Kenyans, Belgian Congolese and Rhodesians both black and white.  In addition to this was the invaluable help of the local native tribesmen the Kachin and Karin, who knew their land inside out and as a result were able to work closely with us against the Japanese who had been brutal occupiers.  Also our other valuable allies in that theatre of war were the Chinese.  Each and everyone of these brave peoples should rightly be honoured and remembered alongside our own, they were all heroic individuals who chose to stand up and be counted and fight against oppressive regimes like Imperial Japan, they were with us when it mattered.  Deep gratitude to you all.  **Above - A great example of that diversity from the campaign in Burma.  Gurkha Bhanbhagta Gurung VC, a soldier of the 3rd Battalion, 2nd Gurkha Rifles, he won the highest military honour for gallantry possible, the Victoria Cross, for his actions on 5th March 1945 at Snowdon-East, near Tamandu, where he took out a Japanese sniper and 5 enemy positions single-handedly.  The VC was awarded personally to Gurung by King George VI at Buckingham Palace on the 16th October 1945.**

The Lancashire Fusilier's motto is; Omnia Audax 'Daring in all Things', words that I think and his story truly testifies sums up Ian's service and a life well lived by this truly inspirational veteran.

## Additional Information and Life After Service

**Rank upon finish of service** – Colour Sergeant.

**Medals and Honours** – Burma Star, 1939-45 Star, 1939-45 Defence Medal, 1939-45 War Medal, M.B.E – Awarded 12th June 1999 for services to Manchester City Football Club and the community.

**Post War Years** – After finishing the Army in 1947 for the next two years Ian had a number of diverse part-time jobs that he ran simultaneously, these included Credit Collector, Market Trader and Progress Clerk, Ian already had experience as a Clerk from when he worked on the L.M.S Railway for 2 years before joining the Army and mastered as a Clerk whilst in it in 1946. In 1949 ever eager to try new things he began working for Richard Johnson and Nephew who were a firm of ironmasters and wire drawers, and interestingly during WW2 were the suppliers of the galvanised wire used for the Pluto fuel pipeline, then worked for them as a Junior Buyer and later moved up to become an Engineering Buyer, this lasted well into the 1960's by which time he had studied for and got his Licence Trade Diploma and also began working in the pub trade part-time. By the 1970's Ian had moved into this line of work full-time and managed his own pubs such as The Fletchers Arms in Denton, were there is still to this very day 'The Niven Room' named after him, and The Royal Scott at Marple Bridge near Stockport, both in Greater Manchester. In 2015 I organised another re-union for ex-Chindit buddies Ian Niven and Tommy Hopper and along with some family members we all went very fittingly to The Fletchers Arms. He retired from the pub game in 1999. His other great life-long passion has always been Manchester City Football Club, where he has been involved directly in one capacity or another since 1947 and still was at time of writing in 2021. He was a part of the original Supporters Club from 1949, also did a lot of work with the Junior Blues and grass roots football from its early days and later became a Senior Director on the Man City board of Directors which he was a part of for 25 years from 1971-1996. Since then in recognition for his service to the club he has been made a life-long Honorary Vice-President, which amongst other things means he always gets to see his favourite club at home or away matches gratis from the Directors Box with his close friend Mike Summerbee, himself an ex Man City player who also starred in the 1981 WW2 cult film 'Escape to Victory' with Sylvester Stallone, Michael Caine, Bobby Moore, Osvaldo Ardiles and Pele', and in recent years Mike has become the Club Ambassador. Ian enjoys keeping this continuous tradition of attendance, something very close to his heart and that he very rarely misses. On Sunday 10th November 2019 after being a special guest of Boris Johnson at 10 Downing Street for breakfast, Ian and a few of the remaining Chindits were part of the Remembrance Parade at the Cenotaph in London, this was followed by his swift departure in a car laid on by Mike Summerbee that drove him quickly up the country to Anfield Football Stadium to join the Directors so he wouldn't miss the important match between Man City and Liverpool, he arrived complete with medals and wearing his traditional Chindit hat in time for the 4.30pm kick off, what a legend! Later remarking: 'What a great treble that day was!' In honour of the Chindits the British Army created the new 77th Brigade in January 2015 using its old formation badge, and Prince, later King Charles III is its Patron, through this association Ian has met him a number of times. Ian Married three times, first to Olive (whilst on leave Oct 1945), later Dorothy, finally Marjorie. He has 1 Son, 1 Daughter, 4 Grandchildren, 6 Great-Grandchildren.

**Associations and Organisations** – The Chindits Old Comrades' Association, The Chindit Society, The Burma Star Association, British Institute of Inn Keepers.

# LANCE CORPORAL ALEC BORRIE

Served with – Gordon Highlanders, Highland Light Infantry,
1st SAS - Special Air Service Regiment
Service Number – 14002888
Interviewed – Kent, Greater London, 4th February 2022

## Service History and Personal Stories

- ❖ Born – 17th September 1924, Soho, London, England, UK.
- ❖ Alec came from a Military family background, his father William Arthur Borrie served in the Queen Victoria's (Rifle) Regiment for 4 years on the Western Front from 1914 to 1918 in France and Belgium and fought in many historical battles including at the Somme, he went on to win the Military Medal for his courage in combat and was injured and returned to the U.K right near the end of the conflict. His Uncle Alexander Borrie was part of The Machine Gun Corps and was killed whilst fighting against the Turks in Palestine in 1917.
- ❖ So it was no surprise that once the Second World War had broken out that a young Alec (named after his brave Uncle) and being quite liberal about his age, followed in their footsteps and started to play his part as soon as he could, and from 1940 until 1942 was in the Barnhurst Home Guard in Kent, where during the London Blitz of 1940 and 1941 he was helping guard the big Vickers

munitions factory at Crayford and from a distance witnessed the devastation of the German bombing on the docks at Tilbury.

- Whilst in the Home Guard Alec was undertaking an apprenticeship in carpentry and in one of his last jobs worked at Vickers Dartford woodwork shop, further helping the war effort on the Home Front by making bomb boxes. Having grown tired of this by early 1942 Alec volunteered for the Army at the recruiting office in Bexleyheath, Kent with the help of his dad who stated that he was over 18! Having Scottish family roots he volunteered for the Gordon Highlanders and in February 1942 was sent up to the Bridge of Don barracks in Aberdeen, Scotland for basic training lasting 12 weeks.

- After returning from later leave with his family down in London Alec was transferred to a new regiment in November 1942, the H.L.I – Highland Light Infantry based at Wick near John o' Groats not far from the most Northerly part of mainland Scotland. The H.L.I's were later given a 6-month posting at Stromness in the Orkney Islands to help guard the British Royal Navy Home Fleet based at Scapa Flow. In January 1944 when Alec's battalion of the H.L.I's was disbanded he chose to join the SAS and so another big adventure began.

- In February 1944 intense training began, and with the new regiment that Alec had volunteered for being an airborne Special Forces unit the first part of his training was held at RAF Ringway in Manchester, where after successfully completing 8 parachute jumps he was awarded the S.A.S wings. After this Alec and the other successful intake went onto the next phase of their training up in Darvel, Ayrshire, Scotland learning to use all sorts of weapons and vehicles and become proficient in different types of covert warfare tactics.

- By the end of July 1944 with all training completed and with their Commanding Officer Paddy Mayne feeling his men were fully proficient, capable and ready for battle the real tests were about to begin, and in August 1944 with the Allied invasion of Western Europe already well established the remainder of the 1st SAS Regiment were deployed to France.

- Between August 1944 to April 1945 Alec Borrie and the other men of C Squadron, 1st S.A.S were engaged in operations that took them through France, Belgium, Holland and eventually into Nazi Germany itself. During that time they undertook dangerous covert actions against the enemy behind their lines which included ambushing German troop convoys, training and working closely with Resistance fighters to hit other targets of importance that involved acts of sabotage on German supply and infrastructure.

- Amongst his other wartime experiences whilst in Antwerp, Belgium Alec and others witnessed a V1 Flying Bomb shoot over their heads on its final decent and explode into a housing block near them, and in Holland they were sent over the border into Germany to search for wanted war criminals.

- Later in April 1945 near the end of the war in Europe whilst on operational duty behind the lines in Germany his jeep struck a mine that caused Alec injuries to his mouth, head and right leg and a return to the U.K for medical treatment, after recovery he re-joined his unit at Chelmsford, then sent out for the latter end of the German surrender in Norway (Operation Doomsday), next he took part in training and preparations to go to the Far East and fight the Japanese, which after the dropping of the Atomic Bombs was not needed.

- In October 1945 the SAS Regiment was disbanded and Alec was given the choice of joining other regiments and went back to the Highland Light Infantry, after qualifying to be an Instructor he taught weapons training to new recruits at the Bridge of Don Barracks, Aberdeen where it all began for him 3 years earlier with the Gordon Highlanders, later he served 6 months at Maryhill Barracks in Glasgow, home of the H.L.I's.

- Alec was demobbed at York on the 14th February 1947 and left the Army with 56 days paid release that expired on the 11th April 1947 bringing to an end an extraordinary and diverse period of service in both the regular Army and 1st Regiment of the Special Air Service.

When I was privileged to spend time with Alexander Campbell Borrie AKA 'Alec' for my first veteran interview of 2022 I knew I was gaining an insight into someone very special due to the nature of his World War Two activities in the 1st Special Air Service Regiment, known to most as the SAS. Not only was he part of this hand-picked formation, initially the very first of its kind and the absolute foundation of its modern-day famous successor, but as I was informed on the day by Alec according to the SAS Association as far as they know he is incredibly (at time of interviewing) one of only two of the original remaining Second World War veterans from the 1st SAS Regiment in the United Kingdom! His combat missions in Western Europe from shortly after D-Day in 1944 until just before V.E Day in 1945 led to him operating in France, Belgium, Holland and Germany. During that time he served directly under the revered leadership of Lieutenant Colonel Robert Blair 'Paddy' Mayne, who led Alec and the other men in many covert actions behind enemy lines directly engaging the enemy, especially in France and Germany. These and many other facts make this story, one of the longest in my book, even more amazing, a very rare part of military history that I have been able to capture in the nick of time, and using the first-hand resources gleaned from our interview and some quotes with Alec's permission from his self-published autobiography it has become a wonderful and unique addition to my Debt of Gratitude Project. So here now to give us his very Special Air Service story is Alec Borrie who tells us much more about how it was:

## TO BE A TROOPER IN THE ELITE 1ST REGIMENT OF THE SAS DURING WORLD WAR TWO

"When I first joined the Army I had served with both the Gordon Highlanders and the Highland Light Infantry both touching on our family's Scottish heritage, something I was not allowed to forget with a middle name like Campbell. Anyway when it was decided that our Battalion of the H.L.I's was to be disbanded in early 1944 we had the choice of joining the Commandos, the Paratroopers or the SAS, I didn't fancy the first two and wanting to be away from the Orkney Islands I applied for the S.A.S, not really knowing what they did! After being interviewed by their Commanding Officer Paddy Mayne, who liked to select and hand pick his own troops, I was accepted and I reported to Darvel near Kilmarnock in Ayrshire, Scotland. I found out that from the 300 men interviewed in that intake only 30 were considered suitable, just 10 per cent of us were chosen for what was, as we soon found out, a tough unit, and it had to be because a lot of the things we would be expected to do in operations were not going to be those that a regular Army unit would undertake. The nature of the Regiment we had volunteered for started to become more apparent when we began training, then we started to get a very good idea of the kind of behind the lines, covert type operations we may well be expected to carry out, just by the sheer diversity of what they were teaching us to do and things we were learning to operate!" I was really intrigued to know more about how the early wartime SAS was trained, and listened intently as Alec went into further detail: "All the new men were placed in different sections; I was placed in C.Squadron, B.Troop, which comprised of several groups of six men, there was as you would expect for any 'Special Unit' a lot of hard physical training that took place and these were done by the groups mainly on their own so that they could operate as small units and be able to last independently for fairly long periods behind the enemy lines, key to what we would be doing later of course. We undertook demanding survival training which involved slogging with very heavy packs on our backs over long distances and being dropped off in isolated and difficult terrain out in the Scottish Moorland and having to get back to base, sometimes as a group and sometimes in pairs, within a given time which was never long enough! You were taught all sorts, to be hardy and live on whatever natural resources you could get hold of, navigation and compass training where we had to find our way to places more than 40 miles away, hand-to-hand combat, the use of knives and almost every conceivable weapon available to you from hand guns, machine guns and mortars to 25 Pounder Field guns, and to become proficient with munitions for sabotage, know various ambush tactics, right through to learning to drive the special jeeps that were designed for the SAS with their 5 mounted machine guns on them, we even got basic training on how to pilot a plane on a given compass bearing and do the same with the huge Horsa Gliders and even how to operate a steam locomotive, which could be used for many destructive purposes in the right hands! This fully-comprehensive all-round training having for the most part been developed by our very capable and battle-hardened C/O Paddy Mayne, who from his and the extensive combat experience of others who served with him in North Africa, Sicily and Italy had been designed to give us as many skills as possible to do the job that this Regiment was created for! It was now becoming clear that the invasion of Europe by the allied forces was going to take place quite soon as the squadron was joined by French S.A.S to act as interpreters who would be helping us in operations and also to liaise with the French Resistance (The Maquis) if needs be who we would working with and training later on. Eventually the Squadron had been moved to RAF Fairford in Gloucestershire where we were camped in a field beside the Airdrome, more firearms training took place and our jeeps were sent away for further protective modifications. A few days before the invasion of Europe the SAS had dropped a section well into France, initially A and B Squadrons did June and July, when it was the turn of C and D squadrons to be deployed the beachhead at Normandy had already been well-established. In early August we were flown over with our jeeps in Dakota transport aircraft then drove through German lines to Auxerre in central France and made a camp in a nearby wood called The Floret de Merry Vaux. This and other bases were used over the next few months right up till the end of hostilities in the country. Supplies of food, petrol and ammunition dropped by Parachute were stored there and used by any section in the area to hide, rest or restock whenever they needed to."

**A specially adapted SAS jeep the same as that driven by Alec Borrie during operations in Western Europe with C Squadron of the 1st Regiment Special Air Service, equipped with bulletproof front windows and armed with 5 Vickers K. model machine guns, 1 that was mounted on the driver's side, 2 with armoured plating on the passenger side and 2 mounted at the rear with no protective shielding (in this picture covered). The fuel capacity was also increased in this modified jeep with three 12-gallon petrol tanks fitted, two self-sealing ones behind the driver and passenger seats, and one under the** passenger seat, making a total of 48 gallons of fuel which enabled the troops to travel over extended distances which was a great advantage when travelling to and operating in combat and being able to escape further distances after in order to evade capture by the enemy! Alec mentioned an additional skill the driver was taught was to be able to use the machine gun on his side whilst driving to give additional blasts of covering fire if needed when the passenger was reloading his twin Vickers, sometimes very useful in battle. These jeeps were used by both the British 1st and 2nd SAS Regiments that were operating in Western Europe at that time (1944-45), who were joined in supportive operations by the Free French 3rd & 4th SAS and the Belgian 5th SAS, the latter three having been formed by the renaming of parachute units.

"Now we were truly behind enemy lines it was time to get on with the job we came to do, which was to harass the Germans as much as possible, and in our first operation we ambushed a convoy of lorries carrying troops by waiting for our chosen target at a main road that had a long U-shaped bend, we waited for them to appear round the other side of the bend and opened fire with our forward facing guns, that is a lot of fire power brought to bare from a few jeeps with twin Vickers all blazing at the same time! We later found out that we had wiped out about 60 of the enemy, for the loss of 1 jeep and a soldier injured! As you can imagine in the months that followed as we advanced and made our way through France, Belgium, Holland and Germany many more varied experiences, both good and bad, in and out of combat happened! As we gradually made our way southwards through France we met up with groups of resistance fighters that we sometimes helped out with weapons and a bit of additional know-how and acts of sabotage such as railway lines and logistical targets, one such group we met near Autun after having a supply drop by air and shooting up some more targets was interestingly led by an RAF Pilot who had himself been shot down nearby. We worked closely with the resistance a number of times in France as they were also the people with good local knowledge that helped us find a lot of decent targets to hit such as a house that we shot up which we were told contained Gestapo officers. It was shortly after this that one of the lighter moments happened, also good to share as it wasn't all continuous battling and hard stuff, stress relieving things occurred as well which were of course good for us, anyhow back to the story, after taking out the Gestapo target we were motoring along a narrow lane when one of the leading jeeps knocked over a goose. A couple of our pals, Woody and Smudger Smith stopped and picked it up to have for dinner later. A few miles on and we heard a lot of shouting as the goose came to and had both of them out of the jeep and the rest of us laughing our heads off. With five machine guns and two pistols between them these Special Forces guys were being chased by an irate bird! Talking of which once we took charge of a special delivery that was parachuted in at night, a female agent of the SOE - Special Operations Executive, a spy, who was told by one of our lads to get a f***ing move on, something she didn't take kindly to, and the next day we put her on a train to Paris so she could go and do her bit behind enemy lines as well, brave woman. We later moved on to Dijon and Lyon, but by October we were in Belgium where it was our turn to be rested up, so for us that meant 6 weeks of R&R (rest and relaxation) in Brussels during which time we also serviced the jeeps and weapons, obtained food and fuel and restocked ammunition for all our guns, in the case of the machine guns this meant emptying the 100 round drum magazines, cleaning, oiling and then refilling them with a mixture of bullets; 1 ordinary, 1 tracer, 1 armour piercing, 1 explosive in this order all the way through, a lethal combination, then rewind the springs to the correct tension."

**Left; SAS Pals from the Troop on leave in Brussels 1944, L to R, Joe Craig, Arthur Middleton and Alec Borrie, wearing the Red SAS Beret issued for those engaged in operations in Europe, (the Beige Beret is still also officially worn by veterans).**

**Right; Another interesting picture of Alec in Brussels during that same leave period, which he remembers because they had taken the twin guns off their jeeps to be serviced as explained earlier, also note the SAS insignia on front of the jeep. As Alec told me; "There were 4 Squadrons in the 1st SAS Regiment: A,B,C,D. 2 Troops in a squadron, A & B. Normally each troop had 4 jeeps, 2 men to a jeep, sometimes more jeeps if we had interpreters or extra men with us. Each troop had a Troop Commander, mine was Derek Harrison."**

"After Brussels it was time to move on, get back into active engagements again and were ordered to proceed on into Holland where we made our way to a town called Velno near the German border on the Dutch side of the River Maas, where our section was attached to the Headquarters of the Field Security Police based by the river, our remit was to cross over into Germany to capture and bring back wanted War criminals for interrogation, our tasks certainly were varied! By Christmas of 1944 we had moved on to Eindhoven and joined up with the rest of C Squadron in one of the areas that a few months earlier was part of the failed Operation Market Garden. After spending Christmas there and undertaking patrols by late January 1945 we were told to make our way one troop at a time to Antwerp in Belgium, which unfortunately for us roughly coincided with the Germans deciding to try and wipe out the docks there, through which most the Allies supplies were being landed, and they tried to do this using their new frightening long-range V1 Flying Bombs and V2 Rockets, most of which fell not on the docks but in and around the city and led to a very near miss for us on one occasion!" I was intrigued to hear more about this and what Alec told me next was the closest and nearest encounter with a V1 that I had heard from a veteran in any of my interviews, truly astounding: "These missiles caused so much devastation wherever they landed, which is why we were billeted singly in houses all over the outskirts of the town because a lot of these 'Vengeance Weapons' were blowing up all over the place, so much so that it became known as the 'City of Sudden Death'! Our section stayed in a place called Berchem and met up at a central point every day, the idea being to potentially minimise casualties by spreading us out, during that time myself and a pal were walking into Antwerp down a long wide street in a residential area and suddenly we heard a loud strange humming noise, we looked up and around only to find to our horror that it was coming from a V1 Flying Bomb which came in right over our heads, literally at roof top level, we dived flat onto the pavement as it went straight down the end of the long street in front of us and smashed into a tower block, exploded and left the block standing with a big hole right through it! Not the usual final decent of a V1 that you see on newsreel footage where it cuts out and drops down, don't know why? In that encounter with a flying bomb we were very lucky that day! These attacks went on for all the 4-5 weeks we spent there, we in the SAS didn't have any casualties but we did spend quite a lot of time helping the local Civil Defence in any way we could to recover injured people from the wrecked buildings, in a strange way it was like having the Blitz all over again! During our stay in the city we were shown where the Gestapo tortured and shot anyone suspected of anti-German activities, it had been left untouched, the 2 posts the victims were tied to and the rough pine coffins stacked against the walls, chilling, these people had suffered terribly at the hands of these sadists as many had in all the lands the Germans had occupied and terrorised, so we didn't feel bad about dispensing a bit of justice when we came across them! By March 1945 we had returned home to the U.K, from Antwerp to Tilbury and before being given 28 days leave we spent some time at the new Headquarters of the 1st SAS at Chelmsford where we found out about a whole Troop from B Squadron who had landed in France by Parachute and been captured after being betrayed by someone in the French Resistance, then taken into a wood and shot by German SS, it brought home once again the real danger of what we were doing. Just when I was really enjoying being back home after so long and thinking maybe I'd get lucky and might not be needed with it being so evidently near the end of the war in Europe, we got recalled to Barracks, effective immediately, just after the Allies had crossed the Rhine into Germany at the start of their Spring offensive in late March 1945, I was soon to find out I would again be in the thick of it!

A few days later having checked the jeeps and guns we were on our way, I had a new partner this time Sergeant Alexander (Sandy) Davidson from Aberdeen who had been in the SAS from its early days in the North African desert, one of the 'Real Originals' of the Regiment. We drove to Tilbury and went from there in a tank landing craft to Amsterdam, Holland then proceeded as a Squadron towards Germany. After crossing the Rhine by a temporary pontoon bridge near Nijmegen, it soon became obvious that it would be a different type of war, Germany was now fighting for its very life on its own soil and everybody was the enemy. It wasn't long before this became all too apparent when we lost our Intelligence Officer Major Bond, this led to our C/O Lt. Colonel Paddy Mayne personally taking out the roadside pill box and its German inhabitants that had caused this which led to him winning his 2nd bar to his DSO medal for bravery. We were now on forward reconnaissance, up to 30 miles ahead of the advancing Canadians who were making for Wilhelmshaven, and keeping them informed of where the heavy concentrations of German tanks, guns and men were, and in one village reported clear 2 hours earlier we came under very heavy mortar fire and lost all four of our jeeps and with minor injuries managed to escape along a ditch to safety. Our later replacement jeeps had heavier guns put on them, the .50 calibre M2 Browning Heavy machine gun mounted on the front instead of the twin Vickers, an absolute brute of a weapon that could penetrate brick walls and kill anyone inside houses when loaded with our usual cocktail of bullets (described earlier). Not long after this we came unstuck again, when the whole Squadron led by Paddy Mayne got trapped in a wood right in the centre of the Herman Göring Panzer Division with its heavy armour and tanks, over the following days whilst many of them were surrendering to us we had to keep moving as the remaining ones who did want to fight kept shelling the positions we were moving out of, eventually there were more prisoners than us, and interestingly we even got some of them to drive vehicles as we made our way back to Canadian lines, where we eventually handed them over to become official POW's. By this point in the war there were only 2 types of German soldiers, the die-hard fanatics who kept on fighting to protect their 'Fatherland' or those who had simply had enough and just wanted to give up in order to live! As we kept on in our recon role, moving towards Oldenburg, we were losing more men and jeeps more often than we did in France, Belgium and Holland, but it was also becoming more obvious that the Germans were well and truly beaten and their army preferred when possible to give up to the Allied Forces rather than the advancing Russians."

**Right; Under heavy fire in German woods as described by Alec, this extremely rare and interesting picture was taken by Alec with a camera that he explained with a grin; 'was acquired from a German who no longer needed it'. In this photo you can clearly see the newer Browning Heavy machine guns now mounted on their SAS jeeps, and men of C Squadron taking cover as they were being attacked, with as Alec pointed out their C/O Paddy Mayne in the bottom right-hand corner** sitting up and surveying the situation. It was quite exceptional for someone in any of the Special Forces to have and use a camera during wartime and capture action like this as it was happening! Alec still described his wartime Commanding Officer Paddy Mayne (pictured) all these years later very respectfully as; "A great leader of men, calm under fire, brave, always addressed us by our first name, asked us to do things in a courteous manner, only in the heat of battle as you would expect having to sometimes shout orders, and not the man I have heard some public speakers who didn't even meet or know him describe him as, I served under his command and was led by him for over 12 months and if it wasn't for the many great skills and qualities he possessed there is a pretty good chance I wouldn't be here today to tell you these things in person!"

"By now it was late April 1945 and little did I know that my time in active combat with the SAS would be coming to an end sooner than I expected, as it would for my jeep partner Sandy, but for him in a different way. This all came about when we were following a set of tyre tracks on a gravel road leading up to a farmhouse and we struck a mine. There was a mighty flash and the jeep rose in the air, the next thing I knew I was sitting in the field at the side of the road, temporarily deafened and with leg and facial injuries. Later after being taken to a casualty clearing station they took Sandy to one side and covered him with a blanket and told us he had died most probably from shock. I couldn't believe it, he had fought with the regiment from the beginning all the way from the deserts of North Africa right through Europe, only to die now in the heartland of his enemy, right near the end of the war, tragic! In 2007 I went on an SAS Association trip to Belgium, Holland and Germany during which I visited the Grave of Sandy Davidson, paid my respects and laid a cross. Getting back to the story, I was transferred to a nearby hospital that was only captured the day before and had my bottom lip stitched back in place by a German surgeon, curiously the ward I was on had a mix of German, Canadian and British casualties in beds next to each other, needs must I guess. After a few days I was flown in a converted Dakota (DC3) Air Ambulance to Blackbushe Airdrome (RAF Blackbushe) in Hampshire, followed by a long train journey up to Manchester where I was admitted to Crumpsall Hospital, and as I was getting better

I could go into Manchester dressed in wounded soldiers uniform of bright blue jacket and trousers, white shirt and red tie which allowed me to take advantage of free bus travel, tea and cakes in some big department stores and cinema visits, very nice. After treatment at other rehabilitation centres near Dartford and at Richmond Park I was on an RTU – Return To Unit with 1st SAS at Chelmsford by the summer of 1945, and was then sent to join my Squadron now out in Norway helping with the German Surrender and disarmament, however by the time I got out there they were beginning to get packed ready to come home! So after returning preparations and training then began for deployment to the Far East for the final stages of the war out there, but before that happened the A-Bomb drops on Hiroshima and Nagasaki took place and that was that, the Japanese had surrendered and the Second World War was over by September 1945. By November 1945 the powers that be had decided that there was no longer any need for a unit such as ours and had disbanded the SAS, only to later realise that was not a good decision and reformed 'The Regiment' in 1947 and we have been involved in pretty much every conflict since then! Back to 1945, were all given the choice to join the Parachute Regiment, as we were an 'Air Service' or returning to your own regiment, I chose the latter, re-joining the H.L.I's where I later qualified and became a fire arms and drill instructor, and promoted to the lofty rank of Lance-Corporal and mainly spent my time training new recruits until April 1947 when I was finally demobbed in York and became a free man once again, ending 5 years of the most exciting and worst times of my life, but it was never dull, and the friends I made in the SAS and after at reunions since are true friends and are for life, and all who served in the war, those who didn't survive and those who did, I think each man did his best according to our motto: *Who Dares Wins*."

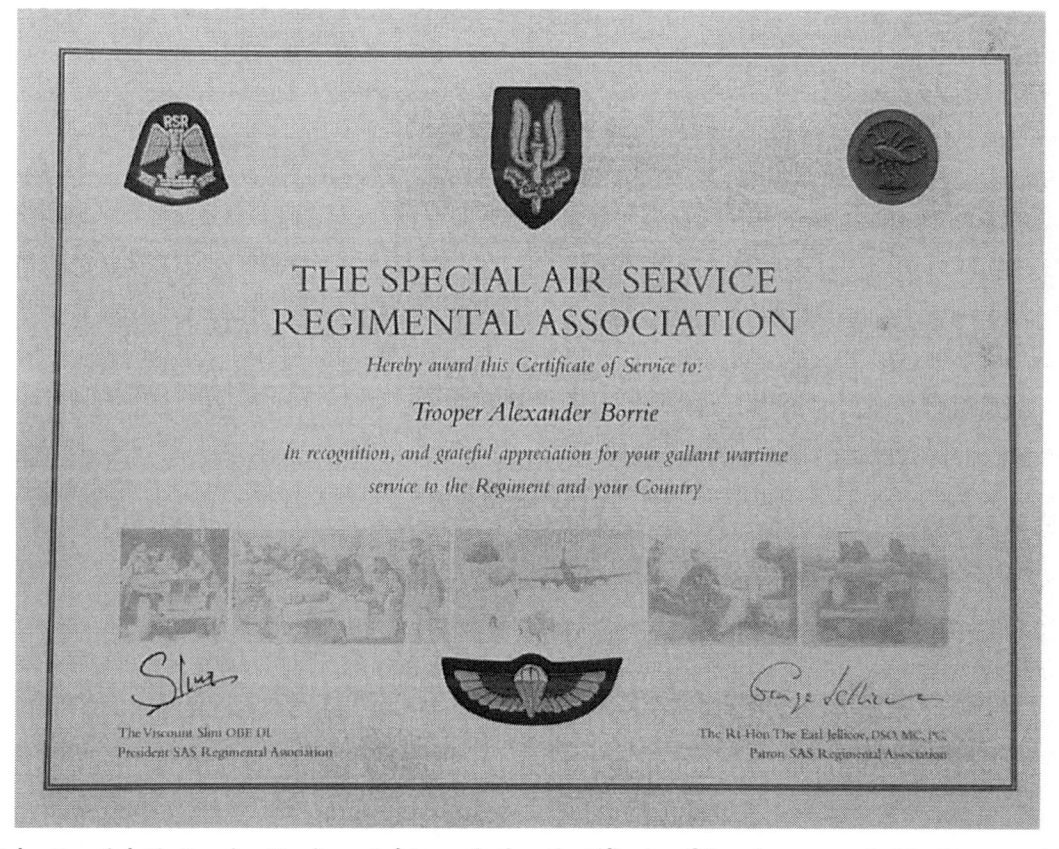

**Above – The Special Air Service Regimental Association Certificate of Service, awarded to Trooper Alexander Borrie (in recognition of his wartime service in the 1st SAS Regiment). Alec joined the SAS Regimental Association in November 1945 which was formed as he explained "to help any member in need for the rest of their life" and he has attended annual reunions ever since.**

**When I went to interview Alec I ended up spending most the day with him, we talked on and off camera about his exploits, shared a few laughs, had lunch, did more interviewing, I was cherishing every moment, I thanked him for his service, and was so grateful that I was allowed to have this precious time with one of**

the last World War Two veterans from 1st SAS, but like all good things we had to finish at some point. So I asked him a couple of questions to conclude:

**Out of interest, did you meet any well-known World War Two Leaders, Politicians or Royalty?** "Monty came to visit us before D-Day up in Darvel, Scotland for a bit of moral boosting, during which he said; 'If you do your job properly most of you won't be coming back!' Bloody great I thought, not exactly encouraging words! On another occasion I met Princess, later Queen Elizabeth, after my recovery from the mine incident in 1945, I think on an inspection with others at the Aberdeen Barracks, anyway she was still wearing her ATS uniform so I guess she was still in the Army."

**Do you find there is a lot of interest in your WW2 SAS service now?** "Yes, but there wasn't for a great many years because people hardly knew anything about us and what we did, and we didn't talk about it publicly, only a little at SAS reunions! It was only when the Iranian Embassy SAS action took place in 1980 that things started to change because of it being televised around the world live. Then people knew a bit about the SAS and their interest increased as a result of it, not sure if that is good or bad, but people these days also know a lot more about the SAS because of ex-members of the Regiment writing about it (e.g. Andy McNab and Chris Ryan) and everything they read on the internet and see in documentaries, but of course right through to now the day to day operations taking place is still closely guarded and restricted information, as it should be to protect those involved, but yes people do seem to be more interested about my service and others of the SAS, but in the end we are pretty much ordinary men who've just had to do a few out of the ordinary things!"

**From its inception by David Sterling in July 1941 during the desert Campaign in North Africa, and after his capture in January 1943 with its continued leadership by Paddy Mayne until the end of World War Two, through to the modern day where 'The Regiment' is part of UKSF – United Kingdom Special Forces, the Special Air Service has served with distinction in hotspots and areas of ongoing conflict around the globe. It is true to say of all those who have served from past to present day in the SAS including the remarkable Alec Borrie whose story is written here to honour him, that in the true 'Espirit de Corps' this commemorates all those; "Who Dared All, To Win All"**

## Additional Information and Life After Service

**Rank upon finish of service** – Lance Corporal.

**Medals and Honours** – Legion D'Honneur, 1939-45 War Medal, 1939-45 Defence Medal, 1939-45 Star, France-Germany Star, Netherlands Commemorative Medal.

**Post War Years** – In 1946 Alec went back to the job he had started before the war as an apprentice Carpenter, working long hours on jobs such as the Festival of Britain until completing his City & Guilds finals in Carpentry and Joinery at Woolwich Polytechnic in 1951. After that he worked for a few companies on many jobs that required his skills as a now qualified Carpenter, eventually employed by RALCO – Roof and Lining Construction Company, who Alec stayed with for 27 years working both locally and around the country and was with them until his retirement in 1989 aged 65. On 18th May 2019 Alec flew in Spitfire MJ627 from Biggin Hill, Kent and as 2nd pilot took control for 20 minutes. Alec married Jean Sturgeon on the 7th June 1952 at Christ Church, Bexleyheath, Kent and they were together until Jean's passing on 29th January 2000. During World War Two Jean was a Nurse in the WRENS specialising in burns care for badly injured servicemen, based at Great Yarmouth and Portsmouth eventually becoming a Lieutenant. Children; 1 Son. 2 Grandchildren.

**Associations and Organisations** – The Special Air Service Regimental Association (Member No.1000) and the Bexleyheath & District Sea Angling Society.

# DEMS GUNNER KENNETH ASHWORTH

Served with – Royal Artillery – DEMS – Defensively Equipped Merchant Ships
Service Number – 14220977
Interviewed – Prestwich, Manchester, 14th July 2014 &
Broughton House for Ex-servicemen and Women, Salford, 2019

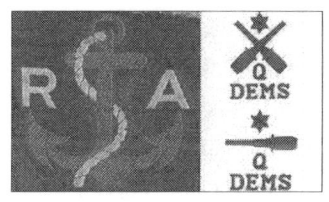

## Service History and Personal Stories

- Born – 7th September 1923, High Town, Manchester, England, UK.
- It all started for Ken Ashworth when he served in the Home Guard in Manchester between 1939-1942, where he and others from his unit which was part of the Manchester Regiment were tasked with guarding and patrolling shops and businesses on Anti-looting duties after air raids to try and stop theft which was quite common place during the war.
- Ken joined the Army aged 18 on 2nd July 1942 at Queens Road, Manchester choosing the Royal Artillery, he went on to do R.A training at Salisbury Plain, Wiltshire and after successful completion of that became a Gunner and was transferred to the Royal Artillery Maritime Regiment by the Autumn of 1942 then found himself in active service soon after, starting with No. 4 Maritime AA Battery and serving in many others throughout the war.
- During the next three years Ken saw a lot of action when he served on 4 ships and remarkably was involved amongst other things in 4 major amphibious based invasions, these were Operation Torch in Algeria in November 1942, Operation Husky in Sicily in July 1943, Operation Avalanche in Italy in September 1943 and Operation Overlord in France in June 1944.

- The ships that Ken served on were the Fort Bourbon a 7000-ton Cargo Ship, MV Devonshire a 12,000-ton purpose-built troop ship which was later converted to an LSI – Landing Ship Infantry (Large), SS Empire Foam a 7000-ton CAM – Catapult Aircraft Merchantman Ship (for launching a fighter aircraft), RMS Andes a 27,000-ton Fast Ocean-Going Passenger Liner that was requisitioned and used as a troop ship during hostilities.
- On D-Day 6th June 1944 Ken was on board MV Devonshire which sailed from Tilbury Docks, London to the British-Canadian landing beach called Juno in Normandy, France, and for some months after did re-supply journeys between the U.K from docks such as the Solent, Seine Bay and Southend taking men and supplies to various landing beaches in Normandy.
- After this Ken went on to serve in the Mediterranean once again, later by mid-1945 with the war in Europe over he had been transferred from the Maritime Artillery back to the regular Royal Artillery where he served in various training establishments in Greece and Great Britain undertaking different duties including driving and maintaining of vehicles in the motor transport section, his last posting being with the 30th Field Regiment, R.A, after which he was de-mobbed May 1947 in London.

Kenneth Ashworth's story is a special one because he was the 1st World War Two veteran I found when I began my 'Debt of Gratitude Project' back in 2014, he was the 2nd ever veteran I officially interviewed, and has now ended up here years later in 'The Last Stand – Memories of War'. Funny how things have played out due to me intentionally spreading the stories of veterans who were in the same branch of service over the books I have written, and Ken really was the connection that began it all. His is a great narrative because it's one that is quite unique and is about cooperation and a cross-over between two completely different services. Ken joined the Army and trained as a gunner in the Royal Artillery and after this was transferred to the Maritime Artillery on the DEMS – Defensively Equipped Merchant Ships in order to help provide protection on various Merchant Navy shipping that ranged from a Converted Cruise Liner which became a Troop Ship to carry thousands of American and Canadian servicemen from New York, U.S.A and Halifax, Canada to Liverpool, U.K for D-Day, to actually being involved in seaborne invasions on other big vessels such as an LSI(L) – Landing Ship Infantry (Large) and was part of amphibious assault landing forces in North Africa, Sicily, Italy and France, each in the capacity of what was essentially a soldier at sea. After giving so much Ken very fittingly ended up at Broughton House care home for ex-Servicemen and Women in Salford, Greater Manchester, maintaining along with others in this book the continuity of having a veteran from there in each of my books so far. He now shares with us in his own words his great story of how it was:

### TO BE AN ARMY ARTILLERYMAN ON MERCHANT NAVY SHIPS

"When I joined the Army I had no idea I would end up at sea, that wasn't quite the plan, but it turned out to be something very interesting because I ended up serving in two services during the war which is something especially as I have got older and there are far fewer of us around meant is quite rare, an unusual kind of veteran, I guess. It meant doing our training on land then using what we learnt and taking it to sea, which was harder to apply when you're sometimes pitching, rolling and moving about, more skills to learn and keep practicing. We had to know all sorts of weapons from the regular artillery pieces that were around in the Army at that time, some of which were put on ships, through to doing extra courses as we went along to learn various Anti-Aircraft guns so we could man and use most things as and when needed, the kinds of ships we were on varied a lot and so did the array of weapons on board them, so as you'd expect they wanted crew that were trained as best possible to be able to defend their ship as best possible! I learned to use low-angle guns which could be used against surfaced submarines, enemy ships and land defenses these were anything between 3–6-inch (75-150mm), and high-angle AA Guns such as the Oerlikon 20mm cannon and also 12 pounders and Bofors (40mm) guns. Although I was at sea I didn't end up taking on any kind of Naval rank,

I was a Maritime Gunner but still part of the Royal Artillery, a DEMS Gunner, and when on board any ship we came under the command of the Master of the vessel as a soldier on loan if you like!

**A BL 4-inch Mk VII Low-Angle gun, one of the many weapons used by Ken during the war, shown here on the stern-aft deck of a Defensively Equipped Merchant Ship in 1943.** It was a very dangerous job because we had to contend with the real threats from below of U-Boat attacks that were constant and sinking huge amounts of Merchant shipping during the war, as most people know the Merchant Navy suffered some of the highest losses of any of the services in the World War Two! Also the threats came from above with attacks from German and Italian air forces which is why we were there as Gunners on the DEMS, these were the realities for me and the others who had to fight off enemy attacks numerous times on the different ships which we served on. We had certain types of guns we were allocated to once on board but you never knew what you might be called on to do or man if things happened, that was the thinking, and it proved right, in the heat of battle if men got injured or killed which certainly was not unusual others could and would jump in and take over if needs be! The Royal Artillery motto is 'Ubique' which means 'Everywhere' and with our combination of Army and Navy service we were exactly that, we certainly got around, saw a lot of action in a lot of places such as North Africa, Sicily, Italy and France, and had some close scrapes and right old ding-dongs, sometimes you were ready for the enemy so your adrenaline was already going, you were pumped up and you dealt with the attacks as scary as they were and got on with trying to stop them but other times they took you by surprise and that was even scarier because frightening things just happened! I remember one particular time like that when we were at Algiers during the time of Operation Torch near the end of 1942, I think on the Fort Bourbon supply ship, my memory is getting a little hazy these days, anyway we were attacked by two German aircraft that came down on us very quickly, looked like JU 88's, they machine gunned and try to bomb our ship, we were all really terrified, it was so close I thought I was going to die, bullets ricocheting everywhere and luckily the bombs missed, only just! Once they were gone I had a feeling of absolute peace like never before, I am not a religious man but I felt like God had put his hands around me and was protecting me and comforting me, it's the only way I can describe it! Serving on board and alongside men of the Merchant Navy was also very different because they were civilian seamen in a civilian service and we were military, but after working alongside them I have a lot of respect for what they did doing their best to keep the war effort, our country, our armies and invasion fleets supplied, without them we could not have won that war, they went through the same dangers as regular servicemen and I believe that the moment they were sunk for the many who were that unlucky, all money that was for or would have gone to their family immediately stopped, after all they went through, unbelievable!"

I went on to ask him more about his time in the DEMS and particularly what he remembered about D-Day and was told: "We were on a big Landing Ship Infantry, also known as an LSI, which is a ship that carries men and equipment and smaller beach vessels for shore landings, ours was called the Devonshire and we were in Operation Neptune, the first amphibious part of the bigger Operation Overlord on that historical day! I was manning my gun as usual, we didn't have any bother from above or much incoming fire from shore out where we were as our bombers and battleships had given them a real pounding, quite a sight, but once the British and Canadians had set off in their smaller LCI (Landing Craft Infantry) vessels and hit the beaches it looked like they were taking quite a few casualties in both men and material! It took them quite a while to overcome the beach obstacles, and there were a number of bodies around the place and things burning. Luckily after some fierce fighting and reinforcements they got the upper-hand and later pushed on inland, and after D-Day we concentrated on supply and re-supply going backwards and forwards between England and different landing zones along the Normandy coast in France, but I couldn't help thinking what if we had been Army soldiers like we were trained to be and ended up on one of those beaches instead of becoming Marine Artillery, then that could easily been me or my pals lying dead on one of those beaches like the other poor boys we saw that day!"

**Above – RMS (Royal Mail Ship) Andes – Flagship of the Royal Mail Lines fleet and the biggest of the vessels Ken served on whilst seconded from the Royal Artillery to the Maritime Artillery for active war duties as a DEMS Gunner.**

### DEMS – DEFENSIVELY EQUIPPED MERCHANT SHIPS

The type of merchant ships Ken served on were such an interesting category of vessels that I have included here some relevant overview information about them that connects directly to his story. DEMS was an Admiralty Trade Division programme established in June 1939 with the aim of arming 5,500 Merchant Ships to help protect and give them adequate defence against enemy aircraft and submarines whilst undertaking vital convoy duties on oceans around the world during the conflict. By the end of 1940 some 3,400 ships had been armed and all ships had been armed by 1943. The acronym DEMS was used to describe the ships carrying the guns, the guns aboard the ships, the military personnel manning the guns, and the additionally the shore establishments supporting the system. DEMS guns were manned by an interesting assortment of servicemen, they consisted of 24,000 Royal Navy personnel, 14,000 men of the Royal Artillery Maritime Regiment and 150,000 Merchant Sailors who were trained in support roles by passing ammunition, loading and replacing casualties, and on troopships transporting RAF personnel, troops from the RAF Regiment crewed the guns. The six maritime regiments of the Royal Artillery remained active until the end of the war in 1945, examples being; 1st Battery 1st Maritime Regiment RA, 6th Battery 3rd Maritime Regiment RA. DEMS Gunners were commanded by a Petty Officer or a Royal Marine Sergeant, sometimes on larger ships they embarked a Junior Naval Officer to oversee these crew, all members of the armed forces that served on board a DEMS ship were required to sign on as members of the crew, i.e. as Merchant Seamen, and were as a result under the authority of and answerable to the Commander of the Vessel. This very interesting military-civilian cooperation meant that as Merchant seaman on board these specially fitted vessels, military personnel could visit neutral countries without being interned, consequently DEMS Gunners are listed on crew lists, very useful for historical reference. In 1943 WRENS (Women's Royal Naval Service) personnel were appointed as Boarding Officers, to help inspect merchant ships when in harbour. They were tasked with various duties such as delivering sailing orders, explaining route alterations, mustering confidential books, and also checking guns, ammunition and armaments stores and 'keeping an eye on the gunners' and checking their welfare.

To help summarise Ken's 4 years and 8 months of service on land and at sea as part of the Royal Artillery which was classed as 'Exemplary', I include this reference from his 'Notification Pending Release' document written by one of his Commanding officers, which described Ken as:

**A quiet and conscientious soldier. He has a very fair knowledge of wireless and telegraphy. He has recently been employed as a driver, and has proved very competent on vehicles up to 5-tons; he has, in addition, a fair knowledge of MT maintenance and repair. A hard working and reliable man.**

Major H.G Battes, Commanding Officer, 117th Field Battery, R.A.  16 Feb 1947.  Greece.

Additionally I think when describing Ken, who I have known since 2014, his character and the continuous bravery he showed during his service can be fittingly summarised in the Motto of the Maritime Artillery – 'Fearless over the Oceans of the World'.

## Additional Information and Life After Service

<u>Rank upon finish of service</u> – Gunner.

<u>Medals and Honours</u> – 1939-45 War Medal, 1939-45 Defence Medal, 1939-45 Star, Africa Star, Italy Star, Atlantic Star with France-Germany Clasp.

<u>Post War Years</u> – From 1947-48 Ken worked on Manchester trams, after this from 1948 until his retirement aged 60 in 1984 he worked on British Railways as a Junction Controller finishing his time at the big Crewe junction. Married Catherine Nee Durkin in Southport on the 28th August 1948. Children; 2 Daughters, 3 Grandchildren, 2 Great-Grandchildren.

<u>Associations and Organisations</u> – RBL Cheetham Branch - Waterloo Road.

Where it all began, back in July 2014, pictured here shaking hands with Ken the first World War Two veteran I had found at the very start of my 'Debt of Gratitude Project' over a few drinks at Sinclairs Oyster Bar, Manchester, after attending the monthly 'Turning of the Leaves' ceremony on the book of Remembrance at Manchester Cathedral with him and other Armed Forces Veterans.

Respectfully, despite the Royal Navy being the 'Senior Service', with the book being jointly dedicated to HRH Queen Elizabeth as well as others, it was Her Majesty's Army story which started the book and therefore meant that the order of it became Army and next Navy. It is with this in mind that the story of Ken Ashworth, who essentially due to the rare nature of what he did with both Army and Merchant Navy during his service, acts a very good bridge between the two and very good continuity between the land and sea services featured in 'The Last Stand'.

~ 97 ~

# ROYAL & MERCHANT NAVY VETERANS

# LEADING SEAMAN ALFRED LONSDALE

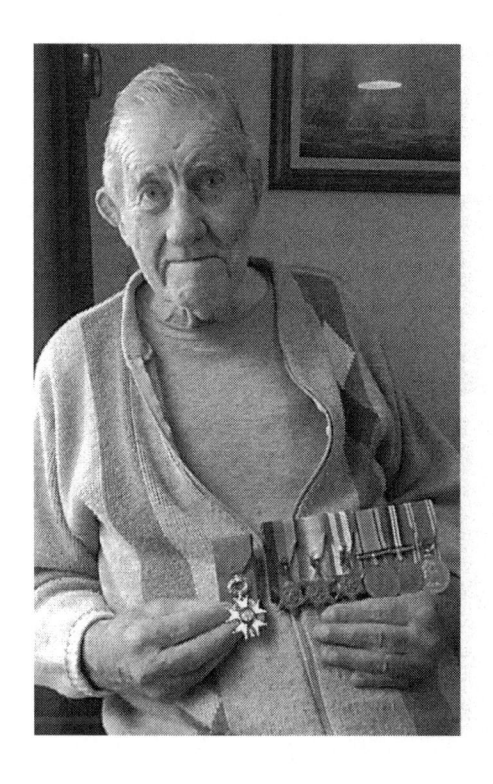

Served with – Royal Navy, HMS Glengyle, HMS Valiant, HMS Malaya, HMS Excellent, MOD Tug TID 116.
Service Number – PJX315589
Interviewed – Horley, Surrey, 18th September 2017
Further Telephone Interview – April 2021

## Service History and Personal Stories

- Born – 12th May 1925, Outwood Surrey, England, UK.
- Seeking adventure Alf joined the Royal Navy at HMS Collingwood in Fareham in Hampshire aged 16 in May 1942 and completed his basic training at HMS Victory a Royal Navy depot and training establishment in Portsmouth, where he finished in June 1942.
- In July 1942 Alf joined his first ship HMS Glengyle (4.196), a cargo ship that was converted into an LSI - Landing Ship, Infantry (Large) for amphibious operations, where he saw his first action aged 17 on the 19th August 1942 when he was involved in the ill-fated Operation Jubilee at Dieppe, France

where as a Q.R 2 – (Quarters Rating Two) Anti-Aircraft Gunner manning 4 Inch Guns he witnessed the disastrous attack and its slaughter unfold, a tough baptism of fire!

- Later from January to December 1943 he was seconded to and served on one land base, known in the Navy as a 'Stone Frigate' which was called HMS Hannibal at Algiers in Algeria and 2 ships in the Eastern and Central Mediterranean as part of the Mediterranean Fleet, HMS Valiant (twice) and HMS Malaya and became an AB/S – Able-Seaman.
- The 2 Royal Navy Queen Elizabeth Class Battleships HMS Malaya (01) and HMS Valaint (02) had been in the British Grand Fleet and taken part in the famous Naval Battle of Jutland in World War One, and now Alf was part of their on-going prestigious history.
- Whilst on HMS Valiant Alf also took part in Operation Avalanche on 9th September 1943, which was the Allied invasion of Italy at Salerno, during which he witnessed HMS Warspite get hit with a new revolutionary type of German air launched radio guided missile.
- 1944 was also a big year for Alf AKA 'Lonsy', in February at HMS Excellent training facility on Whale Island near Portsmouth, Hampshire he passed the higher course for Anti-Aircraft Gunner and got the rating of AA/3 on various guns, including the 4.5", and with D-Day fast approaching the next posting was to be a very interesting and different one indeed.
- Alf was transferred to a Ministry of War Transport Tug called TID 116 to be the Royal Navy serviceman on board this civilian vessel, although put on board in a R.N communicator, liaison and AA Gunner role (on twin Lewis guns), being the kind of all-round seaman he was Alf ended up doing all sorts of additional hands-on work that was required for the special operations to take over alongside other tugs the artificial harbours called Mulberry for the allies to Normandy, France.
- The tug and its crew made half a dozen trips in support of the D-Day landings to set up this vital sea to land supply route just off Gold Beach at Arromanches. Taking one and sometimes two sections at a time, they also helped the Army assemble this marvel of engineering as well, on return they towed landing craft of injured troops back to the U.K.
- After finishing his Mulberry work Alf was promoted to Leading Seaman and his very interesting and varied service continued when he was drafted to be part of the Commodore's Home Fleet Destroyers Staff on HMS Vindictive at Scapa Flow, whereas replacement and reserve crew they were always on standby to be put on short-term secondments to various Destroyers as, when and where needed for different kinds of operations, which he did from July to December 1944.
- This led to him serving on HMS Greenwich (F10), HMS Orwell (G98) and HMS Onslo (G17) in patrols and anti-U-Boat operations in the North Sea and Western Approaches, also part of Royal Navy Escorts on in-coming and out-going Atlantic Convoys at various U.K ports.
- The action didn't stop there, after this Alf was sent out to Australia on HMS Berwick and after arrival at Sydney in spring 1945 he and others were sent by steam train to Brisbane where everything came full circle, when as a Leading Seaman and Gunner he re-joined his first ship HMS Glengyle where he first began his sea-going days as a Boy Sailor in 1942.
- For the next few months the Glengyle which had been transferred to the Australian Naval Board transported Australian troops from Queensland to various islands in the Pacific such as New Guinea, Solomon Islands and repatriating other units back, these operations continued after the A-Bomb drops on Hiroshima on 6th August 1945, Nagasaki on the 9th August and final Japanese surrender on 2nd September 1945, later in February 1946 they came to the Japanese harbour of Kuri where another unique experience would follow.
- Whilst berthed there Alf and others were detailed to a big working party and sent into Hiroshima to help clear roads to try and restore a bit of infrastructure from amongst the utter devastation that was once a city, where they saw first-hand the A-Bomb destruction.

- ❖ After this it was the count down to the return home and after picking up hundreds of British POW's and wounded Soldiers from Subic Bay in the Philippines for repatriation to Great Britain, by June 1946 HMS Glengyle had dropped off her troops and was on the River Clyde, and by October 1946 she had been released to her owners The Glen Line, ending her service as part of the Royal Navy/Royal Fleet Auxiliary and was undergoing work by Vickers-Armstrong at Newcastle on Tyne to reconvert her for commercial service.
- ❖ It was then also Alf's time to finish after his incredible service of 4.5 years, and after saying goodbye to his ship for the last time he was demobbed on the 26th October 1946.

Over the years as I have travelled around the country being fortunate to interview many World War Two veterans, and I've seen that they have very rightly received various medals and awards for their bravery and service from different countries. One of those awards was the French Legion D' Honneur which I have seen bestowed upon those who fought in France jointly at Dunkirk in 1940 and at D-Day in 1944. Not until I met Alf Lonsdale had I come across a WW2 Veteran who was awarded one for his roles at Dieppe in 1942 and for the part he later played at Normandy in 1944. It is very rare indeed to find a veteran that was involved in Operation Jubilee, but in Alf's case this is only the start and a part of an action-packed remarkable career where he served in and experienced many varied Naval operations all over the world, and did so on many types of sea-going craft such as legendry World War One Battleships, a converted Landing Ship Infantry vessel, Ministry of War Transport Deep Sea Tug and Destroyers of the Home Fleet. Each one of those has a special story and part of Second World War Royal Navy history attached to it, we are now going to hear in Alf's own words a number of those very important recollections, starting with his:

### VERY FIRST ACTIVE SERVICE ON THE DISASTEROUS OPERATION AT DIEPPE

"The Glengyle was part of Operation Jubilee, the Dieppe raid. Along with other LSI's – Landing Ship Infantry, Princess Beatrice was one, we embarked about 500 Canadian Essex Scottish Infantry and six tanks, possibly Churchill's, of the Calgary Tank Regiment, and with minesweepers leading headed Eastward up Channel. As we passed other harbours more craft joined up, I believe the total passed 60. Having levelled with Dieppe it was 'Line abreast', and straight on to the five landing beaches selected. It was here that things stated to go wrong. The units on our Eastern flank ran into a Westbound German coastal convoy and all surprise was lost. We landed our full contingent on Red Beach the right side of the harbour entrance, opposition was stiff and the tanks never got off the beach. Talk had it that some pre-arranged timber ramps had never arrived. Glen laid off about 1000 yards employing 4" covering fire, not exactly easy due to the close proximity of the opposing forces. The situation was fully under review and after about 5 hours around 1100 hours, evacuation was broadcast and by 1200 about 1000 men from all units had been recovered from the shore. We the Glengyle recovered about 400, mainly wounded, and were about the last to leave. It had become very tricky, several landing craft were lost as was destroyer HMS Berkley, bombed, and HMS Calpe, HQ Ship, was also hit. I can't swear to the following figures but I believe from later research 6000 troops, mainly Canadian, went ashore, 73% of the force were killed, wounded or taken prisoner. All equipment landed was lost. The RN lost 34 ships and 550 men, the RAF flew 2617 sorties, losing 106 planes in the largest single day air battle of the war. What is true. It was the Allies blackest day since September '39! This was a lot for a 17-year-old teenager to take in on his first engagement on active service, on our LSI we came under attack from enemy aircraft strafing and I returned fire and we were all in the thick of it. Judging by what was going on around us that day, I think we were lucky to get away with our ship and our lives! When I returned to Dieppe for the 75th Anniversary in August 2017 it was very emotional, there were very few of us left who could make it, and when I saw the widows crying that really hit me, still so much pain all those years later! Every battle leaves its mark and its scars of every kind, for those directly involved in it and those such as the families who also indirectly suffer as a consequence of it, I am sure it has been that way since time immortal and probably always will be!"

**Left - Part of the aftermath of the disastrous Operation at Dieppe, burning landing craft, destroyed Churchill tank and Canadian casualties, similar to what Alf had witnessed from a distance high up on his AA position overlooking Red Beach. Right - HMS Glengyle the LSI where Alf started and finished his career at sea, he served on her in many significant places from Dieppe to Hiroshima!**

It was truly incredible to hear my first personal and in this case very detailed account of the Dieppe from a very rare veteran of that ill-fated engagement, a part of World War Two history I had been trying to find and record for such a long time. Then followed other great stories which were a nice mix of Alf's experiences: "During my years in the Navy I visited Malta many times as it operated as one of the three main Naval bases in the Mediterranean, the other two being Alexandria and Gibraltar, anyway on one occasion whilst manning a tender as Coxswain I was given the task of taking a ships' Captain and a certain Junior officer who happened to be Prince Philip for a run ashore into the Grand Harbour in Valetta, Malta. After showing him the new steering gear which was a bit tricky I handed over to Philip, and whilst on the helm, and quite easily done, I've done it myself, he turned the wheel the wrong way, but instead of going astern we went full ahead up a set of steps, and the Captain goes flat on his back in the back, legs in the air and very unhappy, I thought I would lose a stripe for that but I got away with it! From what I heard and saw Prince Philip seemed to be a very liked officer, no doubt about that, and many years later during one of his official visits, this one was at the Maritime Club in Birmingham, whilst we were at the bar I mentioned to him the steps at Grand Harbour, Salima steps I think they were called, he remembered quite well and we had a good laugh about that. **HRH Prince Philip, served with distinction at both the Battle of Matapan near Crete in March 1941 and at the invasion of Sicily in July 1943, he was also present on HMS Whelp at the Japanese surrender in Tokyo Bay on 2nd September 1945. Here in Royal Navy Uniform with HRH Queen Elizabeth II who as outlined at length earlier in her opening story also served during the Second World War in the ATS – Auxiliary Territorial Service, as a mechanic and military truck Driver. The Queen is the only female member of the Royal family to have entered the armed forces and at time of writing the only living head of state that has served in World War Two, both of them are fine examples of the contributions of Great Britain's 'Greatest Generation.'**

On a more serious note later on in 1944 I was transferred to be part of a crew on the tug *TID 116 in preparation for D-Day, and we were totally engaged in positioning barges, LCA's, LCT's, caissons, and tracks for Mulberry 2 around the South and South-West Coasts, some came down from Scotland and how Jerry never spotted it all beats me. From D-day we were almost entirely involved in Mulberry in one way or another for quite a while, bringing parts of it over to Normandy, also helping position those huge pieces and put them together, and taking injured troops and other materials back as instructed. We got our orders secretly from 'Proserpine' (HMS Proserpine) a Royal Navy H.Q and Communication Centre up in the Orkneys. **\*TID – A Ministry of War Transport classification meaning – Tug, Inshore and Dock. 182 of these tugs were built and they numbered TID-1 to TID-12 and TID-14 to TID 183. Number 13 not being included due to sea-going superstition! Pictured – A good example of a Wartime Tug, similar to the one Alf served on along the Normandy coastline, France.**

Another memorable experience was when I was back on my first ship HMS Glengyle for the last time and we were in the Pacific and around Asia in 1945-46, after Japan had surrendered and shortly before we were due to come home we came into the Japanese port of Kuri, whilst berthed there I was detailed as part of a working party for Hiroshima, not at all nice! Really didn't want to be there. Luckily I've not had any long-term effects! About 12 of us chosen from our ship, put in a truck and sent off into the city where we joined about 100 others and were put to work. We were sent to help clear roads and help repair any infrastructure in any way we could, but the place was just mile after mile of complete devastation, it was an apocalyptic landscape, as far as the eye could see the city had been utterly destroyed, unbelievable, very hard to describe! It was evident in a very short time that there was little we could do in the midst of such absolute desolation, bridges on their side, everything flattened and burned, whole areas gone! Where could we even start? The few people we came across were trying to survive and there was even an active black-market that the Japs already had in operation. I'll never forget that amongst all that we even saw shadows in the shapes of human beings in some places where they had obviously been totally vaporised by the A-Bomb blast, incinerated, we found out later tens of thousands of lives were wiped out in seconds! Hard to comprehend as we stood there in the midst of it all, still is even looking back over seven decades later. In the end all part of the many things that occurred during my eventful years in the Navy!"

**Hiroshima after the A-Bomb dropped by Enola Gay on 6th August 1945.** This was the 'Apocalyptic Landscape' that Alf described and actually walked through. When I interviewed him there was little doubt that I was talking to one of the last people alive who had seen and experienced the aftermath of Hiroshima first-hand. Adding this to the interview that I did with Royal Navy POW Geoff Stott in my first book who was near to and witnessed the second deadly A-Bomb dropped on Nagasaki three days later on the 9th August 1945, means I have now met and captured the stories of two veterans who have direct links with both A-Bomb drops of the Second World War, quite incredible, again truly 'Connecting with History.'

After sitting with Alf Lonsdale a veteran who experienced and came through Dieppe, Salerno, Atlantic Convoys, D-Day, The Pacific, Hiroshima and much more, when it comes to describing him and his combined Navy and Fire service of 32.5 years I can only echo and quote the Motto of one of his ships, HMS Valiant, to say thank you 'Lonsy' for being both - 'Valiant and Vigilant'.

## Additional Information and Life After Service

**Rank upon finish of service** – Leading Seaman Gunner.

**Medals and Honours** - 1939-45 Defence Medal, 1939-45 War Medal, 1939-45 Star, Atlantic Star, Italy Star, France-Germany Star, Legion D'Honneur, Fire Brigade Service Medal for Exemplary service.

**Post War Years** – After demob from 1946-48 Alf was a truck driver for L. Young & Son in Horley, but was still very motivated to continue helping others and so went on to serve an incredible 28 years in the Fire Service around Surrey 1948-1976, then worked from 1976-1988 as Operations Supervisor for Tradewinds Airline Cargo Company until he retired in 1988. Alf never married or had children.

**Associations and Organisations** – RBL Horley Branch and President of Horley Royal Navy Association.

# EFFICIENT DECKHAND DERRICK CORFIELD

Served with – Merchant Navy, RMS Orion
Service Number – R 301772
Interviewed – Salford, Greater Manchester, 3rd September 2019

## Service History and Personal Stories

- Born – 31st March 1927, Irlams o'th' Height, Salford, Lancashire, England, UK.
- During the Second World War Derrick Corfield had a full range of wartime experiences, starting at aged 12 in 1939 when he was sent to Lancaster as a Child Evacuee, he returned a year later to Salford after which the Manchester-Salford Blitz began in December 1940.
- Derrick left school aged 14 and later on between 1943-1944 was working in factories as part of the civilian war effort for Freedlands Furniture in Trafford Park as a Driller, where he made Lancaster Bomber door hinges and during that time joined the Home Guard and was attached to the Manchester Regiment on guard duties around Trafford industrial area.
- He went on to work at Cunliffe Engineers in Pendleton, Salford as a Copper Roller and at that point had transferred over to a Home Guard unit that was part of the Lancashire Fusiliers doing fire arms and combat training, in between all these things he was able to pursue the love he already had for being on the water by also being part of the Sea Scouts.

- Wanting to do more and be fully involved in the war effort but knowing he was too young to directly go into the regular armed forces Derrick joined the Merchant Navy aged 16 in December 1943, he left his job at Cunliffes' to begin basic Mariners training in January 1944 at Wallasey Sea Training School in Liverpool and finished as a Cadet Petty Officer.
- On the 26th February 1944 Derrick embarked on the Ocean-going passenger liner RMS – Royal Mail Ship Orion, a ship of the 'Orient Steam Navigation Company' (flag with crown shown on his intro page), now converted into a troop ship, he served on her until the 24th October 1945.
- RMS Orion was re-fitted to carry 7000 troops which she did when they ferried American and Canadian servicemen on the 'Atlantic Run' from America to Britain to take part in D-Day as part of a convoy system where they had to travel far slower than they wanted.
- In April-May 1944 whilst his ship was undergoing maintenance at Clydeside, Scotland Derrick was sent on a 'Crash' Gunnery course at a Royal Navy Gunnery School in Greenock where he received Anti-Aircraft weapons training, after this if ever the ship was at 'Action Stations' he had to man one of the Oerlikon 20mm Cannons, not bad for a teenager of 17!
- After D-Day in June 1944 Derrick would experience many kinds of sailings all over the world, which included picking up Yugoslavian Guerrilla Fighters in Port Said in Egypt and taking them to Naples, Italy in the Autumn of 1944, they would then go on to fight the Germans in Partisan operations to help free their country from the Nazi occupiers.
- Once the war was finished Derrick and the Orion were involved in transporting and returning Allied servicemen of all nationalities back home to places such as North America, New Zealand and Australia. They also travelled to Bombay and Calcutta in India to collect returning Special Forces Chindits and also collected British 'Death Railway' POW's who barely survived the horrific Japanese camps and as Derrick recalled 'Were like Skeletons!'
- Later after disembarking from RMS Orion Derrick served on SS Cara, SS Fort Reliance, SS Manchester City and MV Moorby which was his last ship, he finished his time on her and 'Came Ashore' on 22nd August 1948. His official cessation of Merchant Navy service was on 1st December 1948 by which time he had been to war, travelled most the world, worked his way up from Deck Boy to become an E.D.H - Efficient Deck Hand, a rank that was equivalent to an A.B - Able-Bodied Seaman in the Royal Navy, all by 21 years of age.
- Derrick's love for the sea remained as did his will to help and serve others and he would go on to combine these two things in civilian life, when many years later he passed and got his Yacht Masters Certificate and gave his time freely to work with the 'Ocean Yacht Club Charity' taking young people on sailing and Tall Ship Experiences between 1979-1986.
- A 1ST Time interview for Derrick and the first time I have interviewed a crew member of a World War Two Troop Carrying Liner. Another very different aspect of WW2 service captured for posterity from a Merchant sea-going sailor and serviceman's perspective.

The story of Derrick Corfield is one of lifelong service to others, proven beyond any doubt by 4 years in the Merchant Navy during and after the Second World War, followed by 25 years in the Fire Brigade and continuous Voluntary work over the years. The Merchant Navy of which he was a part was a vitally important service and as the Commercial Navy it was the absolute supply lifeline that kept Great Britain from starving and kept her equipped with almost everything needed to maintain the war effort during the Second World War. Additionally the movement of troops and supplies to conduct operations all over the world in all theatres of war depended on the valiant efforts of the Merchant Navy who it must not be forgotten alongside Bomber Command suffered the highest losses of personnel during that conflict! Despite these things and all the dangers that went along with being in any of the services during wartime Derrick was determined to get involved and serve before the war ended and as a result due to being too young to join any of the main armed services he cleverly found a way to be directly in the action by volunteering for the Merchant Navy where he could go to sea as a Deck Boy and still be able to play his part, such was the determination of this brave young man who was only 16 years old when he went to serve his Country on board HMS Orion. Additionally and astoundingly by the age of 17 he had been trained to man and use Anti-Aircraft Guns to help defend his ship against any possible air attack. Proving that where there truly is a will there is a way! An admirable example to us all. I met Derrick at Salford Veterans Breakfast Club as I did Robert Hayfield, both friends and both shared that same sense of duty and need to continue remembrance in many forms, Derrick was still at time of writing active in the organising of veterans remembrance events around Salford and we have done a few together. The interview I conducted with Derrick was the very first he had given, as I have touched on before when as an author and in essence an historian who is the first to capture and have wartime events relayed to you this brings something extra to the experience making it even more special. At 92 Derrick was the youngest World War Two service veteran that I can recall interviewing in recent years and his interview was undertaken symbolically on the 80th anniversary of Britain declaring war on Germany in 1939. So here is another incredible story from another incredible World War Two veteran who now very kindly opens up to tell us about:

### EXPERIENCES ON THE HOMEFRONT AND IN THE MERCHANT NAVY DURING WW2

"My war had already begun in earnest a few years before I joined up when I had been a child evacuee and had found myself shipped off for my own safety out of the high risk target cities of Manchester and adjacent Salford up to a more rural area near Lancaster in 1939, and like so many other children at that time found myself in new and unfamiliar surroundings where I was kindly looked after and adopted by a nurse, but I was only 12 years old, and it was hard to be away from your family, your home and everything that was familiar to you and at that age all you had ever really known, and sometimes I was quite lonely. So twelve months later in 1940 after the 'Phoney War' and after the RAF had beaten back the German Air Force in the Battle of Britain it was deemed safe enough for me to return home, which I did late on that year, ironically just in time for the Manchester Blitz! That arrived around Christmas time with all the dangers and experiences that came with it when the city was heavily bombed and I remember the air raid sirens sounding, the search lights going up in the night sky, the thunder of the Anti-Aircraft Artillery as there was a battery not that far from us, blasts high up above, sometimes the sounds of bombs dropping and their explosions as they landed on the poor people below and the glow of fires in the distance with the centre of Manchester burning, and elsewhere which in a lot cases would have been the homes and work places of local inhabitants! A strange thing I also recall hearing during a raid was what sounded like bits of metal hitting the ground in the road right near us, I'm pretty sure it was shrapnel or similar that was falling from the skies, and once even saw a parachute mine coming down, hard to believe what we all went through back then when you see normal life today in those same places! Later after I had left school and was at work, in one job I was making hinges for the doors on Lancaster Bombers as part of a factory work force contributing to the war effort in that way at that time, I had also volunteered to be part of the Home Guard and was in two Home Guard Battalions over 1943 and into the start of 1944, the Manchester Regiment and the Lancashire Fusiliers doing guard and fire duties in important places. But I really wanted to get more directly involved and although mum didn't like it, and who could blame her I was only 16 years old, she reluctantly let me volunteer for the Merchant Navy and once I got in I had to leave my job and the Home Guard when I went for my basic training at a Merchant Navy Maritime School in Wallasey in Merseyside, my next stop which would be my main ship was the converted Cruise Liner now troop ship RMS Orion, which as you can imagine even though we were at war opened up the world to me."

I listened intently to the next part about his time on board the troop ship and ex-liner Orion with great interest as I had worked on cruise liners and been at sea all over the world myself, albeit in peace time yet on similar Merchant vessels as Derrick, including on the famous Queen Elizabeth 2 for the entire World Cruise, this for me gave an additional dimension as I could relate in some way to the stories that he went on to tell me:

"When we came over from New York via Newfoundland, where we picked up our convoy and on to Liverpool we had over 7000 souls on board who would make up part of the forces for D-Day, and it was very worrying for us to be on a ship that was capable of over 20 knots speed but ordered to do 9 knots in order to be part of a convoy! We were easily able to outrun any potential U-Boats but instead at that lower speed we really were a sitting duck if we had got unlucky. The threats were still very real in the war at that time, U-Boats were still operating, mine fields were around and new ones being sown and there was also the danger closer to land that you might run into German E-Boats, these fast motor torpedo boats were known for their destructive 'Hit and Run' attacks that had claimed many lives already. These things combined meant that despite better Royal Navy and Coastal Command convoy protection the threats were still out there and still tangible to any slow moving vessels like ours! Another time like that was when we were adrift in the Indian Ocean for 48 hours whilst one of the ship's pistons was being fixed on the open deck, we would have been a very easy target for the Japanese this time, but we didn't just sit around doing nothing, instead we made the most of it, fished and caught sharks and enjoyed grilled shark steaks! We were aware that Merchant Navy losses were high, but of course you didn't get figures in the war, that would have been very bad for morale, we just got on with the job at hand whether it was delivering servicemen or partisans to their destinations during the conflict or returning troops and POW's after it was finished, we did all that, and luckily in the end we came through unscathed, too many others were not as lucky as us and didn't make it back, don't forget them, we must not, ever!"

**RMS Orion, in peacetime a luxury Cruise Liner, during wartime converted to a Troop ship that could carry up to 7000 troops. It was on this Merchant Vessel that Derrick was a crew member throughout all his wartime service. Orion a 23,371 ton ship was built by Vickers Armstrong at their yard in Barrow-in-Furness, Lancashire, and was in service from 1935 until 1963. From 1940-1946 she carried over 175,000 personnel and had steamed over 380,000 miles/610,000 Kilometres.**

During the Second World War, German U-boats sank nearly 14.7 million tons of Allied Merchant shipping, which amounted to 2,828 ships (around two-thirds of the total allied tonnage lost). The United Kingdom alone suffered the loss of 11.7 million tons, which was 54% of the total Merchant Navy fleet at the outbreak of the Second World War. Over 30,000 Merchant Navy seafarers were killed aboard convoy vessels in the war, but along with the Royal Navy, the convoys successfully imported enough supplies to keep the United Kingdom 'Afloat' sustained and functional as a country and as a result eventually contributed greatly to an Allied victory.

**THE RISKS THEY RUN FOR YOU**
BOMB
SHELL
TORPEDO
MINE

# Under the 'RED DUSTER'
## they sustain our Island Fortress

*Nearly one third of the world's Merchant Ships fly the RED ENSIGN*

The 'Red Duster' nickname for the red Merchant Navy flag, shown here in this British Wartime poster which was aimed at making the general public aware of the dangers that those who crewed these merchant vessels faced in order to keep Great Britain sustained and able to continue in the war. Despite huge losses in every part of the world where they operated during 6 years of war, and even when facing the dangers of enemy bombs, shells, torpedoes and mines as depicted here, they were steadfast throughout and succeeded in doing an incredible job. Derrick was one of those who contributed to this brave hard-earned success that should be evoked when possible. These are the thoughts and sentiments of many and as a result of this in honour of those lost, representatives of the Merchant Navy lay wreaths in reverence alongside the armed forces in the annual Remembrance Day service on the 11th November each year, and following many years of lobbying to bring about official recognition of the sacrifices made by merchant seafarers in the two world wars and since, Merchant Navy Day became an official 'Day of Remembrance' on the 3rd September 2000, which coincidently was the day I interviewed Derrick in 2019.

Such was the importance of the Merchant Navy, something already proven in the First World War, that when the United Kingdom and the British Empire entered the Second World War in September 1939, King George VI issued this message:

*'In these anxious days I would like to express to all Officers and Men and in the British Merchant Navy and the British Fishing Fleets my confidence in their unfailing determination to play their vital part in defence. To each one I would say: Yours is a task no less essential to my people's experience than that allotted to the Navy, Army and Air Force. Upon you the Nation depends for much of its foodstuffs and raw materials and for the transport of its troops overseas. You have a long and glorious history, and I am proud to bear the title "Master of the Merchant Navy and Fishing Fleets". I know that you will carry out your duties with resolution and with fortitude, and that high chivalrous traditions of your calling are safe in your hands. God keep you and prosper you in your great task.'*

Between 1939 to 1945 up to a third of ocean-going vessels in British Merchant service were owned by other countries, many ships and seafarers from countries that had been invaded and occupied by Nazi Germany including Poland, Denmark, Norway, Belgium, Holland, France, Greece, Yugoslavia and to a large degree Russia had placed themselves under British control and protection. Interestingly the British government also regularly hired ships and crews from neutral countries such as Sweden to help with the war effort. This along with other factors such as Great Britain having a big Merchant Fleet, and at the outbreak of war the biggest and strongest Navy in the world to help protect it, along with the shipping of her Commonwealth and Empire territories and substantial American Aid, would all be desperately needed in the war years that lay ahead as considerable casualties and a huge attrition rate (some figures outlined earlier), mainly attributed to the German U-Boats, took its toll on men, material and ships on active service throughout the seas of the world.

The biggest and arguably most important trade route was the North Atlantic, and 'The Battle of the Atlantic' was the longest running battle of World War Two, from the first to the last day of the conflict! In order to coordinate a defence for this huge vital artery and supply line a big bomb and gas proof bunker/underground headquarters was set up in a labyrinth below Derby House, Liverpool called 'Western Approaches Command'. This nerve centre had the combined branches of the Royal Navy and Royal Air Force (15 Group, RAF Coastal Command) and the intelligence input from Bletchley Park working together with the Merchant Navy to provide the best convoy protection system possible for their ships, and later to take the fight to the enemy with much improved and advanced Anti-U-Boat fighting tactics which were mainly devised at the HQ by WATU – Western Approaches Tactical Unit. The C-in-C's of this around the clock HQ were Admiral Sir Martin Dunbar-Nasmith VC (1939-41), Admiral Sir Percy Noble (1941-42), Admiral Sir Max Horton (1942-45). After the war this facility was mothballed and sealed up for nearly 50 years until this Gem was 're-discovered', it reopened as the 'Western Approaches Museum' in 1993 and is a place I can recommend for a visit to all interested in WW2 and history.

As a further tribute to Derrick and all those who served in the Merchant Navy in the War Years, and as a nice way to pull together and finish this Merchant Navy related story, I have included part of an apt quote to honour the sailors of these Commercial vessels and their vitally important work:

**"He wears no gold braid or gold buttons, neither does he jump to the salute briskly. Nobody goes out of his way to call him a 'hero', or pin medals on his breast.**

**No – he is just a seaman of the British Merchant Service. Yet he serves in our Front Line today."**

**Montague Smith, The Daily Mail, November 1939.**

## Additional Information and Life After Service

**Rank upon finish of service** – E.D.H – Efficient Deck Hand.

**Medals and Honours** – 1939-45 War Medal, 1939-45 Star, Atlantic Star, Pacific Star, Fire Brigade Long Service and Good Conduct Medal.

**Post War Years** – After the Navy Derrick was 25 years in the Fire Service at The Crescent Fire Station, Salford until 1973, later he was a Project Team Manager in the Probation Service, Salford, retired in 1986. Married to Marjorie 1951-2017. Children; 1 Son, 1 Daughter, 3 Grandchildren, 1 Great-Grandchild.

**Associations and Organisations** – Merchant Navy Association, Royal Navy Association, Ocean Yacht Club Charity, Royal British Legion Pendleton Branch, Salford Veterans Breakfast Club.

# PETTY OFFICER & LEADING COOK ROBERT HAYFIELD

Served with – RNPS – Royal Navy Patrol Service
Service Number – MX85148
Interviewed – Salford, Greater Manchester, 18th August 2019

## Service History and Personal Stories

- Born – 11th November 1921, Pendleton, Salford, Lancashire, England, UK.
- World War Two and the experience of war was already very real for Robert Hayfield before he joined the Armed Forces, because he had lived through and seen the damage inflicted all around him by the ongoing heavy bombing attacks of the Luftwaffe during the terrible Manchester Christmas Blitz of 1940 and on the Trafford-Salford Docks in 1940-41.
- Robert went on to serve in a very interesting but little-known part of the Royal Navy called the RNPS – Royal Navy Patrol Service on fishing trawlers that were converted into Minesweepers and sent on operations around the Coastline of Britain, out to Africa and elsewhere, where they would undertake many interesting and different duties.
- He was already an experienced Baker before joining the Navy at age 19 in August 1941, so choosing to be a Cook was a natural way for him to go. After 6 weeks basic Naval training in Skegness he went on to general Chef/Navy Cook training at the RN Cookery School at HMS Europa in Lowestoft in Suffolk, where he finished in November 1941.

~ 111 ~

- Robert sailed from Greenock, Scotland in December 1941 as part of a 30-ship convoy to Freetown in Sierra Leone and soon after he joined converted trawler Scud VI which would be the first of four vessels he would serve on during the war, he was on her from January 1942 until February 1943 on mine-sweeping duties along the West African Coast from Sierra Leone to Ghana.
- During that time alongside his regular duties in the galley Robert was given a short course in the use of AA Guns whilst on board, and when at 'Action Stations' helped man the ships' magazine below to supply ammunition to the guns above to help keep them equipped.
- After this he had a couple of months posted to the 'Edinburgh Castle' Accommodation Ship at the Lagos Port complex, Apapa, Nigeria, then to the U.K for a very interesting but short Top-Secret assignment from May to June 1943 out from Portsmouth on the Solent.
- Robert was a crew member on what was Admiralty Hopper Barge No.24, converted to carry a huge drum with 3" Diameter Hamel pipes and renamed HMS Persephone, which was carrying out initial trials on what was to become the Pluto pipeline that would run under the Channel to France and fuel the proposed allied invasion of Western Europe after D-Day. On board during these exercises were representatives from all the 'Combined Services' there to view this equipment which was being trialled by Army Royal Engineers.
- Next was HMS Blackthorn which Robert served on from July 1943 until September 1944 and he was now promoted to 'Leading Cook'. This vessel undertook a convoy support role and operated in home waters clearing the way for shipping convoys moving up and down the coast from Portsmouth to the Thames Estuary and also to nearby Chatham Docks, during that time they sometimes came under fire from long range land based German Artillery in France and even an E-Boat attack on one of the convoys they were escorting.
- Whilst his trawler was docked in Portsmouth in January 1944 as part of protection for a Royal Navy Cruiser, Robert saved a fellow crewman who had fallen into the water and could not swim well at all, without hesitation he jumped into the freezing water and saved the drowning man's life. For this he was mentioned in despatches and commended for his bravery with the Oak Leaf clasp which he later wore on his 1939-45 War Medal.
- Robert and the crew of HMS Blackthorn were also part of very important and dangerous night time operations minesweeping covertly under the cover of darkness in the week running up to D-Day to clear safe sea lanes for the invasion fleet and putting down Dan Markers to guide them nearer the time. Amazingly they weren't spotted by the Germans, in some cases they were only a mile from the occupied French coast. For his involvement in these brave actions Robert later received the French Legion D' Honneur in July 2016.
- His last assignment on HMS Blackthorn (T 100) whilst based at Portland Naval Base was Weymouth Bay mine clearance on the Dorset coast. This was followed by his posting to what would be his final converted trawler HMS Kuvera, he would serve on her from October to December 1944. During that time he would sail out of South Shields and West Hartlepool escorting convoys on the way to Lerwick, Scotland and up to the Faroe Islands, a very rough ride in Winter in the freezing and unforgiving North and Norwegian Seas.
- Robert's remaining service would all be on Terra Firma, after spending time at HMS Colombo in Plymouth, a Naval 'Holding Base' for sailors awaiting further postings, he was then sent back to where he began 4 years earlier at the RN Cookery School at HMS Europa in Lowestoft, Suffolk, now training others as a Leading Cook and Baker, and also at a hotel run by the Royal Navy in Lowestoft teaching the same to prepare and give skills to those returning to 'Civvy Street'. All of this from January 1945 until his demob in March 1946 and along the way in 1945 he had again been promoted, this time to Petty Officer, helping to conclude what had been a very good and diverse 4.7 years of service to his country.

**Robert Hayfield is a great example of a veteran that served in a rare and lesser known branch of one the Armed Forces during the Second World War called the Royal Navy Patrol Service, who on converted civilian fishing trawlers and purpose built Royal Navy trawlers modelled on the design of their civilian counterpart, some with the prefix HMS – His Majesty's Ship others with HMT - His Majesty's Trawler and with a mixture of civilian and Royal Navy crews, took to the seas around the United Kingdom and other parts of the world wherever they were posted in order to undertake vital Mine-Sweeping and Anti-Submarine duties to patrol and protect coastal areas, hence the M/S and A/S on their insignia. They also escorted and helped keep coastal convoys safe by minesweeping lanes ahead and around them, undertaking anti-submarine detection and counter measures and in those functions also served as another layer of defence for convoys when working alongside regular Royal Navy escort ships. A Minesweeper could be created by replacing the trawl with a mine sweep. Alternatively adding depth charge racks on the deck, ASDIC Sonar equipment below, and a 3-inch (76mm) or 4-inch (102mm) gun on the bow equipped the trawler for anti-submarine duties. These robust vessels with their hardy mixed crews consisting of ex-fishermen who knew those vessels and seas well served alongside Royal Navy Gunners, Communications Officers and other sea-going personnel. RNPS trawlers were involved in some fascinating undertakings in both well-known and secret operations, and due to the nature of their work essentially became a Navy within a Navy. They were unfairly known by some as 'Harry Tate's Navy' after the comedian Harry Tate who during his shows had things falling apart around him, but as the war went on and the work of the RNPS and their crews became known that same nickname came to represent something quite different, a worthy password for courage! In any conflict all military personnel from the Navy, Army and Air Force march on their stomachs, and without the vitally important rarely acknowledged Cooks who work hard night and day behind the scenes to feed them they wouldn't get very far or be able to carry out their duties. Robert was one of those servicemen preforming a role I haven't featured in my books until now but one that really deserves to be here, now in his own words are some of his own unique experiences:**

<u>**BEING A CHEF ON THE HIGH SEAS IN THE ROYAL NAVY PATROL SERVICE**</u>

"Whether you're a Cook in Military of Civilian life one things for sure, as long as you can and want to work you'll always have a job because people always need feeding! So when it was time to do my bit during the war with already being a Baker it seemed like very good way to go to train as a Cook. **Class 128 during basic Naval training in Skegness, Lincolnshire, August 1941. Robert, 2<sup>nd</sup> Row, 4<sup>th</sup> on the right.** Ending up in the RNPS led to a lot of wide-ranging experiences and as you would expect some tough times and some good times. I spent a total of 15 months posted down in West Africa over 1942-43, mostly on the Scud VI where we carried out minesweeping duties whilst I got to grips with cooking at sea and working on what was sometimes a pitching and rolling Galley doing my best to produce meals that would keep the crew happy, whilst on her I also got some training on AA Guns but I was better at cooking, although when we saw some action I did help with getting the ammo up to the guns. Scud VI was also used as a 'Coffin Ship' which meant she sometimes had to pick up bodies of Merchant Seamen that had been killed in action and carry them on to the next assigned port for burial, we felt a bit uneasy when we had that kind of cargo! I got up on deck quite a lot for many different reasons, and that meant I witnessed some very interesting things over the years, and being on these kinds of requisitioned and Converted Fishing Trawlers with mixed civilian and Navy crews was very different, something that didn't exist elsewhere in the Navy apart from maybe on the Tugs a little bit, close cooperation was needed and that led to good comradeship and some great friendships being forged.

**A converted trawler very similar to Scud VI that Robert served on.** My next vessel in May-June 1943 was HB24 AKA HMS Persephone where we were doing the secret trial runs for what would later become Operation Pluto *(Pipeline Under the Ocean or Pipeline Underwater Transportation of Oil. This was a joint operation between the British Armed Forces, British Engineers and Oil Companies in support of Operation Overlord, which supplied the fuel by 2 big underwater pipelines from the U.K to France to the invasion forces after D-Day), I saw piping being coiled out from a huge drum on the deck as they laid it on the sea bottom, on board were all sorts of military personnel and officers, obviously it was a very important project, I didn't know until many years later how important it was and what I was in a very small outside way a part of, interesting.  When I was serving on my next trawler HMS Blackthorn from July 1943 till September 1944 loads happened on there and by then I was also a 'Leading Cook', whilst moored at Portsmouth in January 1944, we had a 'Man Overboard', he was in real trouble so I jumped in the icy water and saved him and got a commendation for bravery, and the story made it in to my local paper back home, the Salford City Reporter on the 21st January 1944, my family were very proud.  Soon after that on the way from Chatham Docks to Portsmouth in what was known as 'E-Boat Ally' the convoy we were escorting was hit by a devastating attack off the Sussex coast near Bognor Regis by German E-Boats that sunk 3 cargo ships and HMS Pine another of our trawlers.  Other times there was random shelling from the big German coastal guns in France that landed near us, unbelievable.  When D-Day was looming there was a huge amount of activity all around Portsmouth, Southampton and the Solent area, we saw sections of the Mulberry Harbour under construction in 'Dry Dock', there were one-man submarines, ships and craft of every kind everywhere, even the Royal Yacht was around.  We were transferred to a new anchorage at Bembridge, Isle of White where we undertook minesweeping covertly at night to clear lanes for the invasion force, it was dangerous, especially when we got close to the coast of France, if the Germans saw us they could have despatched their deadly E-Boats and I might not have lived to tell my tale! On the 5th-6th June we were able to watch the huge D-Day Armada of ships and many aircraft towing gliders, all heading for France, an incredible and historic sight, by the end of the day ships were returning bringing prisoners back.  Many, many other things happened, enough to fill a book, in the end I came full circle and finished as a Petty Officer and Leading Cook back where I was trained at HMS Europa at Lowestoft in Suffolk, except this time I was doing the teaching. I want to end with this, something very important to me, please remember all those who didn't come back, those who paid the highest price and made the biggest sacrifice, they can't tell their story like I am doing, so it's up to us to keep their stories alive and honour the fallen, remembrance is so, so important!" Robert was himself born on Remembrance Day 11th November 1921 and 'Crossed the Bar' on 13th July 2020.

**These words from a very good friend of mine Glenise Jones of the Royal Naval Association, Manchester are a poignant tribute to him and a fitting end to his sea-going story;  Home is the Sailor, home from the Sea.  RIP Sir, thank you for your service.  Calm seas and a fair wind.**

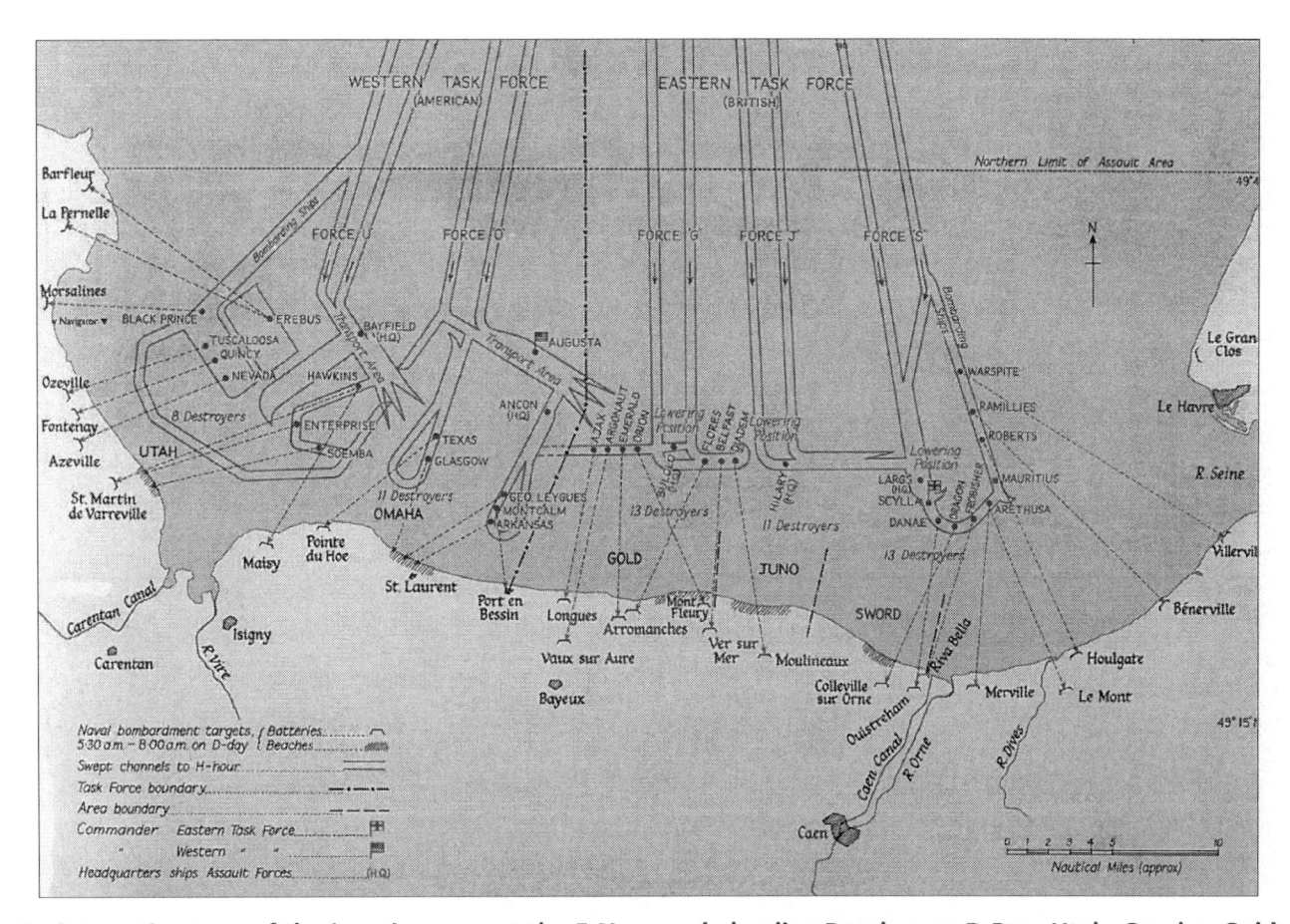

An interesting map of the invasion area at the 5 Normandy landing Beaches on D-Day; Utah, Omaha, Gold, Juno and Sword, showing the sea channels cleared of mines to create safe passage for the maritime invasion force. Very dangerous pre-invasion work which the vessel Robert served on was a part of, and also indicating the location of Allied Naval vessels engaged in bombardment in the Operation Neptune element of Operation Overlord, and their targets on shore.

Winston Churchill knew the importance of the Royal Navy Patrol Service when he wrote a message of thanks to them at the end of the war, which said amongst other things; No work has been more vital than yours, no work has been better done. The Ports were kept open and Britain breathed. The Nation is once again proud of you! A fitting accolade to all who served in the RNPS including Robert who we remember here through this impressive story.

## Additional Information and Life After Service

**Rank upon finish of service** – Petty Officer and Leading Cook.

**Medals and Honours** – 1939-45 Defence Medal, 1939-45 War Medal with Oak Leaf Clasp, 1939-45 Star, Atlantic Star, Royal Navy Patrol Service Silver Badge (awarded 13/11/1943), Legion D' Honneur.

**Post War Years** – After the Navy Robert worked in, managed and owned Bakeries in Manchester up until the 1970's. Then worked as Health and Safety Officer at Hotpoint in Colwyn Bay, retired age 65 in 1986 and returned to Salford. Married Irene in July 1943 at St. Paul's Church Pendleton, Salford. Children; 1 Son, 3 Daughters, 6 Grandchildren, 7 Great- Grandchildren.

**Associations and Organisations** – RBL Pendleton, RBL Colwyn Bay, Salford Veterans Breakfast Club.

# ABLE SEAMAN GUNNER VICTOR BURGESS

Served with – Royal Navy, HMS Queen Elizabeth, HMS Devonshire,
HMS Foxhound, HMS Cumberland
Service Number – CJX140851
Interviewed – Bolton, Greater Manchester, 30th April 2019

## Service History and Personal Stories

- Born – 9th August 1918, Isle of Sheppey Kent, England, UK.
- Victor knew from very early on that he wanted a life and career at sea and this began when he undertook Naval training at Greenwich Royal Hospital School and Naval College in 1930 at only 12 years of age! He completed 3 years there and then went on to finish his final year at Holbrook Royal Hospital School in Ipswich, Suffolk which is owned by the Crown Naval Charity, Greenwich Hospital where he graduated in 1934 aged 16.
- After this the natural progression for Victor was to formally join the Royal Navy which he did in 1934 where he underwent rigorous training at the RNTE – Royal Naval Training Establishment for 'Boy Sailors' called HMS Ganges in Shortly near Ipswich, Suffolk.
- Once he had successfully passed the initial R.N training in seamanship at this Royal Navy 'Stone Frigate' by November 1934 he was posted to his first ship the mighty Dreadnought HMS Queen Elizabeth (00), she was the flag ship of the fleet whilst in the Mediterranean, quite a first assignment for 16-year-old Victor who was on her until September 1935.

- After this he was posted to HMS Devonshire (39), a County-class Heavy Cruiser from October 1935 until November 1936, which was assigned to the Mediterranean Fleet and whilst on her at 18 years of age he became an O/S - Ordinary Seaman.
- This was followed by his next posting between February 1937 until November 1937 on the F-Class Destroyer HMS Foxhound (H69), she was involved in enforcing the Non-Intervention Agreement during the Spanish Civil War of 1936-39, imposed by Great Britain and France on both sides during that conflict.
- He then had time away from sea-based duties, when in 1938-39 he was based at HMS Pembroke, the R.N Barracks at Chatham Dockyard in Kent, and also undertook a Seaman Gunner training course during that period to get that rating, and additionally was a Bosun.
- Then came Victor's biggest and main deployment of his Naval career on the County-class Heavy Cruiser HMS Cumberland (57), from March 1939 until November 1945, this encompassed all his extensive WW2 sea-going action, during that time when aged 21 he became an AB/S - Able-Bodied Seaman (Gunner), this would lead to many experiences.
- Some of these were as follows, Victor was involved in the first major sea battle of World War Two, The Battle of the River Plate at Montevideo, Uruguay, where HMS Cumberland arrived to give support to HMS Exeter, Ajax and Achilles, then on the 17th December 1939 witnessed the Germans scuttle their own vessel the Pocket Battleship the Graf Spee.
- In June-July 1940 his ship escorted the first of the WS 'Winston Special' Convoys, when WS1 went from Liverpool to Ceylon, this very special convoy contained the three troop carrying Super Liners, the MS Aquitania, MS Mauritania and the MS Queen Mary.
- During September 1940 the ship was deployed along with the Aircraft Carrier Ark Royal and other Royal Navy Battleships to help as part of Operation Menace, the Free French landing in Dakar, Senegal. During that operation the Cumberland took a direct hit from a shore battery and sustained damage and casualties.
- Whilst back in the U.K under a later refit in dry dock at HM Dockyard Chatham between July to September 1941, the ship got caught up in a German night air raid, where Victor and others were involved in returning fierce anti-aircraft fire from the ship's 4" Guns.
- Joined the 18th Cruiser Squadron in the Home Fleet at Scapa Flow and between January 1942 to March 1943 HMS Cumberland escorted 4 outward and 4 return journeys on the hazardous Russian convoys to and from the U.K and from bases in Iceland to Murmansk, Russia. During some convoys worked with HMS Belfast, now moored in London. On one of those journeys they had the Government Foreign Secretary Sir Stafford Cripps on board.
- It was whilst undertaking these duties that Victor and HMS Cumberland were part of the Home Fleet cover for what was to become the ill-fated passage of Arctic Convoy PQ17. As part of their outer-perimeter protection force they received the order along with other Royal Navy vessels 'The Convoy is to scatter' which led to its decimation by the Germans.
- Supported the Operation Torch landings in North Africa in November 1942 with a screen of 5 destroyers that helped cover the US landings on the Atlantic coast, and also acted as part of a perimeter guarding force laying off shore to shield against possible enemy attacks.
- In September 1942 HMS Cumberland took part in Operation Gearbox 1 and in May-June 1943 Operation Gearbox 2 on the Arctic Island of Spitzbergen North of Norway. Then from March 1944 until September 1945 was assigned to the Far East where she served in various Cruiser Squadrons and task forces as part of the Eastern Fleet and supported many operations in places such as the Indian Ocean, Sumatra at Sigli, Trincomalee, Malaya, Burma and the bombardments of Sabang, Nicobar Islands and Port Blair amongst others.

- ❖ Victor took part in the big victory parade in Rangoon, Burma in June 1945 with the salute taken by Lord Louis Mountbatten. In September 1945 Victor witnessed the Japanese surrender of Java on board HMS Cumberland and took part in the Allied Victory parade in Singapore and by November 1945 was home in the U.K and his sea-going days were over.
- ❖ The rest of his Navy days were spent between HMS Pembroke and HMS Ganges as a 'Messman' in the Petty Officers Mess until he received his Class A release on 17th Oct 1948.

The life and service of Victor Burgess and the history he has been a part of and witnessed, detailed above, is nothing short of extraordinary. Born during World War One he served before, all the way through and after World War Two, defending his country for a very impressive 15 years in the Royal Navy. When I was the first person to ever interview him in April 2019 he was 100 years old and as sharp as a button, with a memory that could recall the finest details of dates, times, places and experiences which as a result brought his recollections and narratives starkly and very interestingly to life, they contained and spanned many important parts of Royal Navy history that took place during various conflicts. He was part of so many important maritime engagements and deployments around the world in U.K Home Waters, Mediterranean, Atlantic, Arctic and Pacific Oceans, in the Spanish Civil War, Russian Convoys including PQ17 and part of Naval actions against both our German and Japanese adversaries in WW2, and continued to serve on into Cold War period. When interviewed in December 2019 for an ITV Grenada Reports feature about the 80th Anniversary of the Battle of the River Plate, he was one of the last known veterans alive in the United Kingdom who took part in that first momentous Naval engagement of the Second World War. Victor now touches on some of these historic events as he tells us about:

## 15 ACTION PACKED YEARS IN THE ROYAL NAVY

"I think the inspiration to go to sea was always there, my father Robert John Burgess was a Royal Marine during WW1 and I had brothers that were serving in both the Royal and Merchant Navies over many years, it was in the blood so to speak. Even before going to sea I can recall memorable things such as when I was a boy at the Royal Hospital-Naval School at Greenwich and we all came out to witness the British Airship R101 going over in October 1930, a magnificent thing for us young boys to see but the next day we heard that sadly it had crashed in France! I also got to see close up some of the Royals, in 1933-34 whilst I was completing the final part of my schooling at Holbrook near Ipswich I saw The Prince of Wales arrive, he later became King Edward VIII who abdicated to marry Wallis Simpson in 1936. When I was a Boy Sailor on my first ship HMS Queen Elizabeth we were present at Spithead, Portsmouth as part of the Royal Review to mark the Silver Jubilee of King George V who inspected us on July 16th 1935, and later whilst on my main ship HMS Cumberland we were inspected by the wartime monarch King George VI at the Home Fleet base of Scapa Flow on March 19th 1943, we had to keep eyes forward whilst he passed but still all exciting moments along the way." Victor then went on to tell me about his involvement in both the Spanish Civil War and key Naval events of World War Two and I listened intently to some WW2 Naval History I had never heard before in a veteran interview such as the River Plate and PQ17 accounts, as he said: "Then of course there were far more serious moments, when I was on HMS Foxhound we were helping enforce the Naval Blockade against the Spanish Nationalist and Republican sides during that Civil War and saw action when fired upon by the Spanish cruiser Almirante Cervera which mistook us for an enemy ship until we signalled that we were British! Trying to police a Civil War, a very tricky, delicate and dangerous thing to do, but in some ways with being on a real war footing and actually seeing some action it was a warm up and useful preparation for what would follow with 6 years of a World War! I served on one ship throughout the Second World War in many theatres of that conflict, the County Class Heavy Cruiser HMS Cumberland on her I was involved in the first British-German sea battle of the conflict and after we had raced down to support other Royal Navy ships at the Port of Montevideo in Uruguay, we were at action stations ready for what we thought would be a full blazing battle, instead when she started to move out from port on December 17th 1939 we were very surprised when she began to explode as the Germans began to scuttle their own ship! We later came very close by her and our commanding Officer Captain Fallowfield ordered most the crew up on top and to give three victory cheers as we went passed her smouldering wreckage, quite a sight to behold!"

**A dramatic picture of the Graff Spee taken from HMS Cumberland where Victor got a very good view with being on the Upper Deck 4" Guns on Midships. Shortly after the scuttling of this Deutschland Class Cruiser her Commanding Officer Captain Langsdorff went on to commit suicide by shooting himself whilst lying on the ships battle ensign in the Naval Hotel in Buenos Aires, Argentina. This photo and the one of the Cumberland in the Arctic were taken by the ships' official photographer and copies of them became part of Victor's own personal collection.** "We saw service all over the globe between 1939-45, from the South Atlantic to the icy conditions of the Arctic Convoys to the heat of the tropics. During that time we did escort cover on PQ17 and I thought it was very strange that we were told to leave that convoy as we were supposed to be there to help protect her, and as we found out later those Merchant ships and their poor sailors paid a very heavy price for that confusion and for our withdrawal orders having been issued! During the sub-zero conditions we encountered on the Russian convoys myself and others manning guns got the worst of it because we were outside totally exposed to the elements for hours at a time, it was hellish, and when we got into Murmansk there were constant air raids by the Germans and we always had to be at action stations. **Right - HMS Cumberland in December 1942, with a picture that totally encapsulates conditions on a freezing Arctic Convoy, a harsh reality for Victor and his crewmates.**

As you would expect along the way as we moved around the world because we were involved in and saw a lot of action, the possibility of injury or death was never too far away, as it always was for most on active service in war zones. A good example of that was when we supported the Free French landings in Dakar and took a direct hit from heavy shore defences that sadly maimed and killed a few of our fellow shipmates on the Cumberland, **(Pictured)**, bad things for us all to witness and experience. We were also involved in giving Naval protection to the American landings in North Africa during Operation Torch, at that time this along with Rommel's defeat at El-Alamein seemed to signify that the Axis forces in the desert were on the run and didn't have long left in that theatre of war! Later on the other side of the world when we were defeating our other wartime enemies the Japanese, the threat of the suicidal Kamikazes was never far away, and amongst other things we were there when the Japanese top brass arrived to negotiate the surrender of Java which took place on board our ship, and so much more. We saw a lot and survived a lot! They were years that tested you to your limits mentally, physically and emotionally but the bonds between those who served remain there to this very day, I am still in touch with ten families of those I served with, I write and receive letters to and from Australia, Scotland, Portsmouth and Bournemouth etc, and it reminds me of 15 years of my life very proudly spent in service to my country." **That he did and with great courage survived it all, as the motto of one of his former ships' HMS Devonshire states – Auxilio Divino: 'By the help of God.'**

After the main surrender of Imperial Japan on 2nd September 1945 a high-ranking Japanese delegation came on board HMS Cumberland on the 15th September to negotiate the terms by which the Allied forces would take control of Java, Dutch East Indies, now Indonesia. One of the many World War Two events that Victor Burgess was a part of, witnessed or was around during his 6 years on the ship. He had seen all these officers arrive for this historical meeting, amongst them, pictured here under the ship's pennant and with the Union Jack victoriously mounted behind is Major General Yamamato (Front row third from the Left) and Rear Admiral Meada (Next to him at the end).

## Additional Information and Life After Service

**Rank upon finish of service** – Able-Bodied Seaman Gunner.

**Medals and Honours** – 1939-45 Defence Medal, 1939-45 War Medal, 1939-45 Star, Arctic Star & Clasp, Atlantic Star, African Star, Burma Star, Russian Government Arctic Convoy Medals.

**Post War Years** – Worked at Warburtons Bakery, Bolton for 35 years, retired as a Foreman in 1983, married to Jean from 1947 until 2017, they have 2 Sons, 4 Grand-Children, 6 Great-Grandchildren.

**Associations and Organisations** – HMS Cumberland Association, Greenwich & Holbrook Old Boys Association.

# LEADING STOKER HARRY SHARPLES

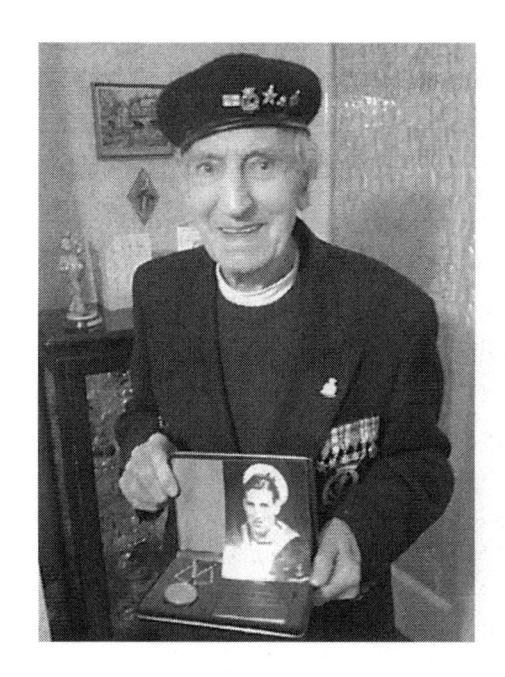

Served with – Royal Navy, Aircraft Carrier HMS Unicorn
Service Number – DKX 159329
Interviewed – Swinton, Greater Manchester, 17th November 2014

## Service History and Personal Stories

- Born – 29th July 1923, Swinton, Salford, England, UK.
- Harry's War began on the Home Front where he was part of the Civil Defence from 1940-1942 in the Home Guard around Walkden and Swinton in Salford, during his patrols he help keep safe important areas and facilities such as key railway junctions and tunnels and Chlorine Gas storage facilities.
- Next came service in the Armed Forces when he volunteered for the Navy in September 1942 at Dover Street in Manchester, he then undertook Naval training to be a Seaman and Stoker at HMS Duke in Great Malvern, Worcester from October-December 1942, and HMS Drake aka HMNB Davenport, in Plymouth, Devon from December 1942-January 1943. Harry also completed further training as an Electrical Welder something he was already doing with engineering firms in Civvy Street before joining up.
- Interestingly during that training period he worked with other seamen in November 1942 on a refit and to convert a British RN Submarine called HMSM – His Majesty's Submarine Thunderbolt to carry two 'Chariots', a type of manned torpedo. Originally named HMSM Thetis (N25), she was in an earlier tragic accident in June 1939, re-commissioned and re-named in 1940 only to be lost again with all hands in March 1943 in the Mediterranean.

- Upon successful completion of his training he was posted to the new aircraft carrier HMS Unicorn in Jan 1943 and was there for her sea trials which took place in the Atlantic between Northern Ireland and Scotland and later in the Clyde area up until May 1943 after which she joined the Home Fleet based at Scapa Flow in the Orkney Islands in Scotland.
- A huge array of experiences awaited Harry during his sea-going days on board HMS Unicorn where he undertook Active-Duty postings all around the world to a number of theatres of war such as The Atlantic, Scandinavia, Arctic, Mediterranean and the Pacific.
- He assumed many responsibilities aboard HMS Unicorn as a Stoker specialising in engine room duties and as a General and Electrical Welder repairing the vessel as required, whether it be from regular wear and tear, accidents or after enemy attacks! Harry was also a Fire Fighter as Part of the Damage Control Team that was often at 'action stations'.
- The aircraft carrier Harry served on provided air support for convoys and was also part of invasions and other strategic tasks such as Operation Governor, an offensive Home Fleet sweep off Norway, a big diversionary manoeuvre during the real Allied attack on Sicily in July 1943.
- Operation Avalanche, the Allied invasion on the coast at Salerno, Italy in September 1943 as part of Force V. Whilst there Harry was part of a joint U.S-British Fire Damage team that tried to help HMHS – His Majesty's Hospital Ship Newfoundland that had been attacked by the Luftwaffe on the 12th & 13th September with 21 killed including 12 British Medical Staff.
- Later that year Harry also completed a Russian Convoy as part of a Distant Cover Force out of Scapa Flow for Convoy JW54A from Lock Ewe to Murmansk in November 1943.
- HMS Unicorn was nominated by the Royal Navy at the end of 1943 to become part of the Eastern Fleet and transferred to the Pacific, during 1944-45 the ship and its crew were deployed in a few roles such as Fleet Aircraft Carrier, aircraft transportation, and utilised for mobile aircraft repairs due to her special on-board maintenance facilities, and did so in many places including Sumatra, Cochin, Trincomalee, Bombay, Durban, Philippines, Leyte.
- In 1945 the Aircraft carrier with a nearly 1000-man crew along with Stoker Harry Sharples was transferred to the new BPF - British Pacific fleet, which when it later came under U.S command became Task Force 57 and was involved in the amphibious invasion of the Japanese island of Okinawa in Operation Iceberg I in April and Operation Iceberg II in May.
- After this HMS Unicorn went to Sydney, Australia and then onto Brisbane where she was in dry dock when the Japanese surrendered on August 15th by which time Harry had become a Leading Stoker. Shortly after the ship began to ferry aircraft, equipment and men including released Allied POW's back to Australia, in December 1945 she departed for home arriving at Plymouth in January 1946, she was decommissioned, placed in reserve and later re-activated to serve in the Korean War 1950-1953 and scrapped in 1959-1960.
- Once his carrier was mothballed at the end of its World War Two service Harry was stationed at RN bases HMS Drake & HMS Drake IV, finishing in the Navy November 1946.

When I met Harry Sharples at Manchester Town Hall back in 2014 at a special event hosted by the Russian Government to honour Arctic Convoy Veterans and found out that he was a Leading Stoker and Electrical Welder on the Aircraft Carrier HMS Unicorn, I was presented with a great opportunity to interview an ex-serviceman who could give a very different kind of story from the unique perspective of being on this type of vessel. Harry was the first mariner I had met who had completed all his Second World War and later sea-going service on an aircraft carrier, and did so from 1943 until 1946 involved in many theatres of war all over the globe, where HMS Unicorn along with various squadrons of the Royal Navy Fleet Air Arm risked their lives to provide valuable air and anti-submarine cover during all these extremely dangerous tours of duty. We now hear this unique perspective from the man himself, Leading Stoker Harry Sharples who enthusiastically divulged:

## HOW IT WAS TO SERVE ON AN AIRCRAFT CARRIER DURING WORLD WAR TWO

"I had so many experiences whilst I was on board the Unicorn during the war, almost too many to tell you, we were all over the world and involved in so much, but here are a few that I remember that stick out. Before I even got to sea proper we were sent to work on a submarine called the Thunderbolt, before that she was the Thetis which had been in a bad accident back in 1939, the Navy were using her again and as I was already a Welder I ended up being sent to work on her. Many seamen had died on board that sub and mariners are by nature a superstitious lot so this was seen as really bad luck, which proved to be right as I believe she was tragically lost at sea again later with all hands! **HMSM Thunderbolt (N25), previously HMSM Thetis, seen here stationary in harbour, it was this submarine that Harry did refitting work on in late 1942, as Thetis she had been lost once on the 1st June 1939 in Liverpool Bay during sea trials, then salvaged, repaired and recommissioned as Thunderbolt in 1940, before finally being lost in action off Sicily on the 14th March 1943.** Once I got to my one and only vessel the aircraft carrier HMS Unicorn where I served from 1943 to 1946 above and below decks as a Stoker and Welder, then the real action began! Quite a few Aircraft carriers were lost before we were out in battle zones ourselves, you eventually heard about them, very sobering as we were a big target for anyone who wanted to try and sink us, as the enemy did with HMS Ark Royal, HMS Hermes, HMS Eagle and others, they had a good go at us too, a number of times. We got dive bombed by the enemy when we were around the Bay of Biscay and Gibraltar area during one of our operations in the Mediterranean and I had to do some makeshift welding work on the Unicorn to help repair the damage. But we were lucky compared to the poor hospital ship that got hit by the Germans at Salerno, that I now know was the Newfoundland, I was involved in trying to put her out, she was ablaze for a couple of days and we were sent to help the Americans as part of Damage Control, as trained ships' firemen we worked all through the night on a floating fire tender hosing her down but she was really burning fiercely, I believe nurses and doctors died on her, bombing a big and clearly marked hospital ship, that for sure is a war crime!" **The vessel Harry spoke about, HMHS - His Majesty's Hospital Ship Newfoundland here in Spring 1943 leaving port in Algiers, the picture shows her distinctly identifiable as a Hospital Ship, painted white and bearing standard Red Cross markings to indicate her function and as such was given due protection under the Geneva Convention, or so those who manned her thought!**

**Her fate** - Assigned as a hospital ship to the Eighth Army, of North Africa fame, for the Allied invasion of Italy, and whilst at Salerno on the 12th September 1943 along with two other hospital ships she was attacked twice by enemy dive bombers, and on the 13th September when moored out at sea was hit by a German Henschel HS 293 air-launched 'Glide Bomb' that had been unleashed from a Dornier Do 217 Bomber. This revolutionary new radio-guided flying bomb was essentially the first ever type of Cruise Missile! 6 British Medical Officers and 6 nurses were killed and the ship eventually had to be scuttled!

I remember sitting and listening intently as one amazing sea-going story after another was recounted to me by Harry who had so much Naval history to share, it reminded me of why I loved interviewing veterans so much and I was all ears as he continued to tell me more carrier based stories: "When we were up on the flight deck there were a whole bunch of added dangers with people and equipment moving all over the place and aircraft taking off and landing, you had to pay extra attention to what you were doing on top of trying to do your job. Once when we were working on aircraft crash barriers a Squadron of Seafires were taking off, and the last one to go had an accident and flipped over on top of us, luckily we were in what was like a bunker, we weren't hurt but there was wreckage around and we were trapped underneath the plane. The Seafire was starting to burn and could explode any second because it had full fuel tanks as it was just starting out on its mission, which meant we could easily be burnt alive, so the Skipper who saw this from the tower had to think and take action real quick. As most of the plane was hanging over the side of the carrier he ordered an immediate 'Turn hard to Port' and as the ship dipped down and round to the left it created enough angle for the plane, with the aid of some crew pushing, to slide off the flight deck into the water, the plane was gone but he had saved our lives! Lots of crazy close scrapes and difficult things like that happened, all you could do was brush down, be grateful you were alive and carry on!"

**The Supermarine Seafire was the conversion of the illustrious and much-loved land-based version of the Spitfire to its versatile sea-going variant essentially becoming 'The Spitfire at Sea'. This sister adaptation was used with great efficiency by the pilots of the Royal Navy Fleet Air Arm who also had to learn vital additional skills of how to manage perilous landings on the moving runways that were the aircraft carriers. It was a Seafire like the one pictured here that nearly killed Harry during the accident in his story.** "We went through all sorts, from full scale invasions in Europe and the Pacific, to convoy escorts in the Mediterranean, Atlantic, North Sea and in the freezing Arctic where we were always up against German U-Boats, to the heat of the Far East with those Japanese Kamikazes buzzing around and launching ferocious suicidal attacks, whilst serving on the Unicorn I lost my best mate Leading Stoker Brombill who got a burial at sea with full military honours, he was only 21, a life lost so young! During our many operations whilst working below decks on action stations and when enemy attacks were taking place we also heard what were essentially the demise of ships, the eerie sounds of their munitions exploding as they were sinking and the heavy thuds of trapped air escaping from inside doomed vessels tearing them apart, all these noises magnified by the water and sometimes the force of what was happening making our ship shudder, but we also shuddered in a different way inside ourselves because we knew that at the exact moment we were hearing these death knells that fellow Merchant and Royal Navy seamen were also losing their lives! Moments like that were very sobering! That's when you knew you were at war. We all had some tough and dangerous times but I can say hand on heart that we all did our duty and to the best of our ability, something I can look back on with a certain amount of pride." **Above - A rare picture showing five fleet aircraft carriers of the British Pacific Fleet together at anchor c. 1945, the 3rd being Harry's ship HMS Unicorn (172).**

A closer look at HMS Unicorn (172), she was Classed as an Aircraft Repair Ship and Light Aircraft Carrier, and this is where Harry Sharples served from 14th January 1943 until 6th July 1946, for 3.5 years this was his home, as it was for many others. During her service in WW2 alongside her regular crew HMS Unicorn hosted a number of Fleet Air Arm Squadrons and their varied aircraft that included: 818 Squadron with Fairy Swordfish Torpedo Bombers, Squadrons 809, 824, 887, 897 with Supermarine Seafire Fighters and 817 Squadron with Fairy Barracuda anti-submarine aircraft.

After speaking to Harry again in 2020 I thought to myself, HMS Unicorn, all the other ships, aircraft and submarines that are in his story are all gone now, and here is Harry who managed to outlive them all, and here am I lucky enough to capture the important history of this great man and all he was a part of and survived, which as his story testifies he successfully did in the true spirit of his ships' motto 'Vox non Incerta' - 'Against All Odds'.

## Additional Information and Life After Service

**Rank upon finish of service** – Leading Stoker.

**Medals and Honours** – 1939-45 War Medal, 1939-45 Star, Africa Star, Italy Star, Burma Star with Pacific Bar, Atlantic Star with France-Germany Bar, Arctic Star, Russian Ushakov Medal, Russian 75 years Commemorative Victory Medal (2020).

**Post War Years** – After his demob from the Navy Harry went back to his pre-war work as a Boiler Maker and Welder and worked for various big companies from 1947 onwards such as Metropolitan-Vickers, Wimpy, Humphrey & Glasgow, Stone & Webster, Mathews & Yates until his retirement aged 65 in 1989. He married Lilian Bateman in May 1947 at Eccles Registry Office, Salford. They were together 63 years until Lilian's passing in October 2010. They have 1 Son, 1 Daughter, 1 Grandson.

**Associations and Organisations** – Life member of the Royal British Legion, The Burma Star Association and the Boiler Makers Union.

# FLIGHT LIEUTENANT KEITH QUILTER DSC

Served with – Royal Navy Fleet Air Arm & Royal Naval Volunteer Reserve
Service Number – FX91692
Interviewed – Wittersham, Kent, 31st May 2018

## Service History and Personal Stories

- Born – 6th March 1922, Leyton, Greater London, England, UK.
- In September 1939 at the start of World War Two Keith began a 4-year Aircraft Engineering course with the De Havilland Aircraft Company and was based at their Hatfield factory and Aerodrome in Hertfordshire which was a major development and production facility.
- During his time there on the 3rd October 1940 they were attacked by a German Junkers JU88 and Keith narrowly escaped with his life, others were not so lucky as four bombs hit the '94 Shop' building, killing 77, injuring 25 and disrupting work on the famous Mosquito.
- Being a man of action from the very beginning Keith also contributed in other ways to the war effort whilst at De Havilland by being part of the Home Guard as a Despatch Rider in the evenings at Hatfield, and at the weekends he volunteered to be part of the 'Upper Thames Patrol' at Maidenhead on C6 Motorboats, all undertaken from 1939-1942.
- At the age of 20 Keith applied for the Royal Navy in early 1942 to pursue his dream of becoming a Naval Aviator, he was accepted and finally went in November 1942 and was allowed to leave his job at De Havilland which was a 'Reserved Occupation.'

- Keith was sent to HMS Daedalus, RNAS – Royal Naval Air Station at Lee on Solent, near Portsmouth in Hampshire for basic Naval Training, then onto HMS St. Vincent at Forton Barracks in Gosport, Hampshire for 7 weeks of classroom instruction and further training as an officer cadet and had successfully completed these basic stages by February 1943.
- Over a year of flight training programmes followed in the United States of America at various locations such as U.S.N.A.S – United States Naval Air Station Pensacola in Florida where Keith successfully completed his EFT – Elementary Flight Training and received his wings in November 1943, the same month received his commission as Second-Lieutenant.
- This was followed by operational training at U.S.N.A.S Miami in Florida where he trained on the North American Aviation Harvard aircraft and U.S.A.A.F – United States Army Air Force base at Lewiston, Maine with No. 738 Squadron to complete conversion training on Grumman F4F Wildcat and Vought F4U Corsair carrier-based aircraft.
- The last parts of his intensive overseas training between March 1943-June 1944 were completed at U.S.N.A.S Brunswick in Maine where the new No. 1842 Squadron was officially formed on 1st April 1944 as a single seat fighter squadron, they finished by flying down to Norfolk, Virginia to complete with the challenging aircraft carrier landing training.
- Active service for Keith with 1842 Squadron began in Aug 1944 as part of the 2nd Carrier Air Group when he was involved in three attacks as part of Operation Goodwood against the German Battleship Tirpitz in Kaafjord in Norway. After this he saw extensive action in the Pacific as part of the BPF – British Pacific Fleet AKA Task Force 37 of the U.S 3rd Fleet, between February to September 1945 during which time he was involved in Operation Iceberg, the invasion of Okinawa and in total flew over 30 combat missions.
- In July 1945 whilst on a low-level strafing and bombing mission on a Japanese destroyer in a harbour at Owase, mainland Japan he was shot down and had to ditch in the water, incredibly he was rescued by the U.S search and recovery submarine USS Scabbardfish, he spent 3 weeks on her during which time war with Japan had come to an end. Keith was awarded a DSC – Distinguished Service Cross for his actions between July-August 1945.
- Whilst with the FAA – Fleet Air Arm 1842 Squadron he flew from HMS Formidable (67) and also HMS Victorious (R38) aircraft carriers on the Vought F4U Corsair as a Flight Leader during the war, and after the war continued as a commissioned officer flying the Supermarine Seafire whilst part of 1832 Squadron on the aircraft carriers HMS Implacable (R86) in 1949 and HMS Theseus (R64) in 1950 during the early part of the 'Cold War' era.
- In between and after the post-war carrier-based assignments Keith was also on land based Royal Navy Air Stations such as R.N.A.S Anthorn/HMS Nuthatch near Carlisle, Cumbria January to March 1946, after which he was demobbed but remained on reserve, then returned to active service based at R.N.A.S Culham/HMS Hornbill in Culham, Oxfordshire November 1947 to January 1952 with the interim carrier-based periods shown above. These Naval Air stations served as ARDU's – Aircraft Receipt and Dispatch Units that accepted aircraft from their manufacturers and tested/prepared them for operational use.
- Once his military service was over Keith returned to work with the De Havilland Aircraft company and later at the Aviation Division of Smiths Industries until his retirement, dedicating his whole working life to aviation and the defence of his country before, during and after the war in both civilian and military capacities spanning 48 years from 1939 until 1987, truly amazing service that really deserves to be acknowledged and commended.

Thursday 31st May 2018 was quite simply an incredible day, as I was fortunate to spend it with two outstanding veterans. That afternoon I was with Keith Quilter at his home in Wittersham near Tenterden, Kent, the very first Fleet Air Arm Royal Navy pilot that I had interviewed and who had a remarkable service history full of amazing stories and achievements. This followed on from having been with Dame Vera Lynn that morning at her home in Ditchling, East Sussex near Brighton. Keith's unique career as a Naval Aviator and Commissioned Officer of the RNVR – Royal Naval Volunteer Reserve spanned from 1942 until 1952. During World War Two he was carrier based and flew Vought Corsair F4U fighter-bombers as part of FAA – Fleet Air Arm 1842 Squadron from the pitching and rolling decks of HMS Formidable (67) and HMS Victorious (R38) and soon proved himself in action. His bravery and leadership led to him being entrusted to take his men into battle as a Flight Leader during which time he served mainly on the Formidable as part of the Home Fleet, Mediterranean Fleet, Eastern Fleet and BPF – British Pacific Fleet and whilst on active duty in these theatres of war was involved in extensive fighting in all these areas as one of the young pilots who truly were the 'Top Guns' of their time. Keith now tells us how it was to be:

## A NAVAL AVIATOR SEEING COMBAT AGAINST THE GERMANS AND THE JAPANESE

"Pilots of the Fleet Air Arm were known by many as 'Flying Sailors' and our bases were on aircraft carriers of the Royal Navy, and as a result our landing strips were mobile and went wherever the action was to be found or a mission was to be carried out! My first combat missions were three attacks against the feared German Battleship the Tirpitz up in Norway as part of the naval Operation Goodwood in August 1944 with 1842 Squadron where we gave 'Top Cover' to Fairy Barracuda Torpedo Bombers, did low-level strafing of Flak positions in the Kaa and Alton Fjords and on the 24th August I was also one of those who carried out a direct dive-bombing attack on the heavily defended Tirpitz itself at her anchorage in Kaafjord, where I dropped a 1000 pound device that just missed her, real baptisms of fire for a young 22 year old! At that time our attacks were the latest of a number of attempts to try and seriously damage or sink this real threat to allied shipping, unfortunately we were not successful but in November 1944 the Tirpitz was finally sunk by Lancaster Bombers using the enormous 12,000 pound 'Tallboy' earthquake bombs developed by Barnes Wallace of Dam Busters fame. The Tirpitz was the sister ship of the Bismarck and both shared the same eventual fates of being destroyed by the allies."

A 1942 sketch drawing by U.S Naval Intelligence of the dreaded Tirpitz showing her deadly eight 15" guns, a real danger to any ships it might engage. This powerful battleship in military terms was known as a 'Fleet in Being' which means it was a naval force that extended a controlling influence without having to leave port, (Just as the German battleships of World War One did), but were the 'fleet' to leave the port and face the enemy, it might lose in battle and no longer influence the enemy's actions, however whilst it remains safely in port, the enemy is forced to continually deploy forces to guard against it. Therefore as a strategic weapon a 'Fleet in Being' can be part of a sea denial doctrine, but not one of sea control.

| | |
|---|---|
| SOLO | BOMBED TIRPITZ (NEAR MISS) AND STRAFFED FLACK POSITIONS IN KAA AND ALTON FIORDS. LANDED ON INDEFATIGABLE |
| SOLO | INDEFATIGABLE TO FORMIDABLE |
| SOLO | STRAFFED FLACK POSITIONS IN KAA AND ALTEN FIORDS |

**Written History, the entry in Keith's flight logbook showing his attack on one of the most famous battleships in World War Two, the mighty Tirpitz!**

As the interview progressed Keith went on to talk about his service on the other side of the world: "The greater part of the action I saw in the war took place in the Far East-Pacific region between February to September 1945 in operations against the Japanese which took place as we moved closer to mainland Japan, whilst doing this their opposition got stiffer and eventually due to their mind set and 'Bushido' warrior code became suicidal in the form of Kamikaze attacks. I was part of the BPF – British Pacific Fleet or 'Forgotten Fleet' as it became known, which was a huge fleet that included 6 aircraft carriers and many other ships and despite its valuable contribution was seen as being in a 'Support Role' next to the much bigger Fleets deployed by our American allies, most people don't even know that the Royal Navy and Fleet Air Arm served in the Pacific campaign in the Second World War, and after we became only a footnote in the World War Two history books! Out there we were tasked with attacking Japanese aerodromes in islands between Okinawa and Taiwan to try and prevent or limit Kamikaze suicide missions against Allied ships and to prepare for a possible ground invasion of the Japanese mainland, and along the way were involved in Operation Iceberg in April 1945 to help support the landings on the vitally strategic island of Okinawa, twice our aircraft carrier HMS Formidable received direct hits from Japanese Kamikazes and I narrowly escaped with my life! We served alongside our U.S Allies out there, stood shoulder to shoulder with them as they had done with us elsewhere and took a lot of losses on board ships of the BPF during air attacks, one of those was a very personal loss to me, my cabin mate and very close friend Walter Stradwick, who died during an attack on an aerodrome 18th July 1945, we were going in at around 50 feet to destroy Japanese aircraft on the ground and suddenly Walter's Corsair which was close alongside me plunged into the ground and exploded into a huge ball of flames and he was gone in a second, it really profoundly hit me when I returned to the ship and walked back into an empty cabin to complete silence knowing he was gone! **Above - Friends and Flying Brothers. A group picture of 1842 Squadron FAA Pilots with one of their Vought F4U Corsair Fighter-Bombers. Keith Quilter (fifth right) and best friend Walter Stradwick (fifth left, in the middle, buttons showing), lost in battle.** Less than a week after Walter died I was shot down during the run in to another low-level dive bombing attack, this time on a Japanese Destroyer in the Harbour at Owase as were now hitting targets on mainland Japan, somewhere the FAA saw action and the RAF did not as far as I am aware, anyway I was downed by Anti-Aircraft fire but remarkably saved by a U.S Submarine called USS Scabbardfish undertaking what was called 'Lifeguard Duty', incredible, they came right into the harbour under fire and saved me! During my three weeks on board her the Americans had dropped A-Bombs on Hiroshima and Nagasaki and the Japanese had surrendered by mid-August finally bringing hostilities to an end in that momentous war in which I played a part!"

I feel a very appropriate and different kind of dedication to conclude Keith's story and honour his remarkable service, which also highlights his skill and bravery as a Naval Aviator are these words from the Commander of HMS Formidable Captain Phillip Ruck-Keene RN who wrote Keith's reference on September 17th 1945, and stated:  To my entire satisfaction.  A first-class flight leader and squadron officer who showed excellent offensive spirit in operations.

## Additional Information and Life After Service

**Rank upon finish of service** – Flight Lieutenant.

**Medals and Honours** – 1939-45 Defence Medal, 1939-45 War Medal, 1939-45 Star, Atlantic Star, Arctic Star, Pacific Star, Distinguished Service Cross.

**Post War Years** – After leaving the FAA Keith returned to De Havilland Aircraft Company at Hatfield until 1962 where he was Deputy Contract Manager.  After this he worked for Smiths Industries in Cheltenham as a Programme Manager in their Aviation Division from 1962 until his retirement in 1987.  Married twice, 35 years to Ilene, 20 years to Julia.  2 Step-Daughters, 1 Step-Son.

**Associations and Organisations** – Member of the Isle of Oxney R.B.L, Fleet Air Arm Officers Association, Kent Air Arm Association, former HMS Formidable Association.

# MARINE GEORGE SIMMS

Served with – Royal Marines, 41 Commando, 4th Special Service Brigade

Service Number – PL/X106639

Interviewed – Broughton House for Ex-servicemen and Women, Salford, Greater Manchester, 14th February 2018

## Service History and Personal Stories

- Born – 24th December 1923, Withington, Manchester, England, UK.
- George Simms spent a life in service to others, beginning as a volunteer for The Salvation Army between the age of 16-17 in 1939-1940, where he helped Armed forces personnel and Veterans in their welfare services, in December 1940 just after his 17th birthday he volunteered for the Royal Navy at Dover Street Recruitment Centre in Manchester where he was interviewed and accepted for the Royal Marines, and from 1941-Mid 1943 found himself posted around the U.K learning many aspects of special Commando warfare.
- This started with three months of very tough basic training at The Commando Training Centre at Lympstone, Devon and after passing there George went on to do specific Endurance and Mountain Training in various places around the South of England, and then onto the Isle of White to do Amphibious training on different types of Landing Craft.
- After this he was sent up to the Commando Training Centre in Achnacarry in the West Highlands of Scotland known as 'Commando Country' doing live ammunition training with Bren Guns, Grenades and other explosives. As their first active combat mission drew closer George and the Marines of 41 Commando took part in 'Combined Forces' exercises around and on Scottish islands such as Skye

in preparation for a big operation in the Mediterranean that as mid 1943 approached would soon be revealed to them.

- Instructions in these diverse forms of combat were designed to create hardened all-round amphibious infantry assault troops that could and would be deployed on a wide range of operations. For George this would mean being involved in hard fought engagements undertaking 'Hit and Run' commando raids during the first Allied large-scale assault on German occupied Europe, this was the invasion of Sicily known as Operation Husky.

- As part of Husky George was with 41 R.M.C, D Company, 8th Battalion, and was active on day and night raids to take out German Coastal strongholds in the British invasion sector on the South East of the island. This he did from the beginning of the invasion on 10th July 1943 until being seriously injured on 17th July, when the Assault ship he was on called 'Queen Emma' was attacked at night by the Luftwaffe whilst in Augusta Harbour waiting to sail for an Op North of Catania, causing 18 dead and 70 injured, of which he was one.

- After treatment in North Africa and later at a hospital in Inverness, Scotland, he became part of 'Y' Troop 41 R.M.C. When his next big challenge came nearly a year later George was fully recovered and once again ready to go into action, this time as part of the biggest invasion force in history when the Allies began Operation Overlord, the liberation of Western Europe at Normandy, France on what would become known as D-Day.

- On the 6th June 1944 at 8.45am the 5 LCI(S) containing 41 Commando, which was part of the 4th Special Service Brigade, along with Marine George Simms hit Sword Beach near Lion-Sur-Mer. These were involved in the first amphibious part of Overlord called Operation Neptune. George was now part of '41' Advance HQ for 'Y' Troop as an MOA – Marine Officers Attendant to his direct Commanding Officer a certain Major Taplin.

- Then on D-Day+1 history repeated itself for George when an air attack by Heinkel Bombers with Spitfire's on their tails and in hot pursuit dropped 3 sticks of anti-personnel bombs, one of which straddled the 41 Commando HQ killing three and injuring several others badly, including George, who was medevacked back to England for treatment in Hereford.

- Some months later after convalescence in Wrexham and having recovered from his second lot of shrapnel wounds he received an R.T.U - Return To Unit, was made acting Lance Corporal and posted to a Royal Marine Training School in Deal, Kent where he was the Marine Officers Attendant in charge of the Officers Mess. George remained there until the end of his military service and was finally demobbed in Plymouth, July 1945.

The prestigious 'Green Beret' of the Royal Marines is a symbol of pride and is in itself a hard-earned accolade worn by those tough enough to make it through the rigorous training and on into battle, of which George Simms was one. Their origins can be traced back to 1664 and they have been involved in almost every war since that time, in fact their battle honours are so numerous that on the official Royal Marines insignia they only show one, that of Gibraltar. Early in World War Two Winston Churchill ordered the formation of Commando units, these began in June 1940, at first they were all drawn from the British Army, eventually they came from all branches of the British Armed forces and also included volunteers from France, Belgium, Netherlands, Greece, Norway, Poland and elsewhere. By February 1942 the Royal Marines were asked to organise Commando units of their own, a total of nine RM Commandos (Battalions) were raised during the war, numbered from 40 to 48. Various Commandos saw action in many places from North Africa, Europe and Scandinavia through to Malaya, Singapore and Burma in South-East Asia. To this day they are the U.K's Commando force and the Royal Navy's own amphibious troops and through the centuries there are countless examples of those who have served with distinction within its ranks. We now concentrate on the story of one of them, a serviceman who saw action during World War Two first in July 1943 as part of a special Commando force hitting coastal targets during the invasion of Sicily, where at 19 years of age during that campaign he was seriously injured when his landing ship was badly damaged as a result of enemy action, and a year later in June 1944 after having recovered he was back in the thick of the action once more aged only 20, this time in France at Sword Beach on D-Day. George's luck ran out on 7th June 1944 when he was again seriously wounded after his position was hit by a German air attack! Not only that but later on in Civilian life when he had become, like other veterans in this book, a long serving Fireman, he was injured again this time in Greater Manchester. His continuous desire to serve led to him being hurt on those three occasions whilst risking his life in the line of duty numerous times! For these things he was rightly awarded the Legion D' Honneur by the French Government and an award for valour from the Fire Service. So here is the story of a very brave man, the story of Royal Marine Commando George Simms who now tells us in his own words about being:

### PROUD TO SERVE AS A ROYAL MARINE COMMANDO

"My first taste of combat came in Sicily when we attacked well defended German and Italian positions and although we had been toughened up and trained continuously it was not easy, frightening in fact, but somehow you had to find the courage to overcome that, which to a large extent I did, after all I was only 19, but that in some ways helped because at that age you'll have a go at anything and also think you are indestructible! I soon found out the last part wasn't true when I ended up peppered with shrapnel after the Queen Emma was bombed, leaving many casualties, me being one, needing months of medical treatment to have as much of it as possible removed, first in a hospital in North Africa, after when I was transferred to a more specialised hospital in Scotland to have the bigger pieces taken out, which were probably parts of that ship they were that big!"

Now we jump forward a year to the 6th June 1944 to D-Day, and in between George telling us of his experiences in his own words I have inserted something a bit different at this point which vividly sets the scene and describes what was unfolding before their eyes as they approached the British Landings on Sword Beach. These quotes are from the 41 Commando Official War Diary written by their Commanding Officer Lt. Col. E.C.E Palmer, R.M. He stated:

08.25 – Coastline now perfectly visible and Troop Commanders were able to identify their beach from previous study of low obliques during the briefing. The beach appeared a bit of a shambles. It was littered with dead and wounded and burnt-out tanks and with Flails flailing through wire and mines, Bulldozers clearing gaps etc. The beach was quite obviously still under fire as mortar bombs and shells were crashing down fairly plentifully. It appeared however that Red Beach was getting a better share of this than White.

08.30 – Shells started falling around the craft and several near hits were reaching the ships damaging ramps etc. on some craft but caused no casualties to personnel.

08.40 – Due to land.

08.45 – At this point we now return to George to pick up the story and get his personal account from when he landed, which was 300 yards down the from their intended target of the area codenamed White Beach in what was actually the Red Beach sector, (detailed above as receiving more incoming fire). The horror of what they experienced is further described by him with these words and difficult memories about what this 20-year-old young man saw that day:

"When we went in I was so surprised that no hard helmets had been issued, just our Green Berets were being worn, this might have been a matter of pride on the part of the senior officers or whoever made that decision, I don't know, but this was catastrophic for many of the boys in the first wave that had gone before us, as the

Germans seeing this set their machine guns at head level and as the poor boys came storming out of their landing craft many were shot in the head and killed or had serious head injuries, it was horrific to see that, I will never forget it, having to run past the dead and dying, fellow marines, whilst being told to keep moving, and the ground being ripped up with explosions all around us, you knew it could easily be you who could get it next, so if we wanted to live we could see we had to get off the beach as quickly as possible! I was the Marine Officers Attendant to Major Taplin my direct Commanding Officer and was attached to the H.Q part of 'Y' Troop due to my serious injuries from the year before I was given that role, but when required I was still an active fighting Royal Marine, especially on D-Day, I arrived on Sword Beach that morning fully armed and like everyone else had to return fire and engage the enemy during that time! I felt so lucky to get off the beach safely that day, but within 24 hours that had all changed, because the next day on the 7th June whilst we were at a forward 41 Commando HQ we were attacked by Heinkel Bombers and just like the year before I got hit and seriously injured, the next thing I knew I was waking up on an LCT – (Landing Craft Tank) troop ship, and realising I was still alive and had survived, that was the best moment of all the things that happened at Normandy, the rest was hell!"

Despite everything that had happened to him I was very touched by how amazingly positive this incredibly brave man was and how his thoughts were still with those who didn't make it back, when he exclaimed: "Two invasions, two lots of serious injuries in two consecutive years and all by the age of 20! Two lots of very bad luck some might say, but I say Two lots of very good luck because I was fortunate enough to get through both and live on to a ripe old age, many others in those campaigns, my friends and some of our Commanding Officers never survived to have all the lovely things I was blessed with, such as a family that you can love and watch grow up, and other special things that I have experienced such as another 70 or more Christmas' and birthdays, they didn't get anything, instead they lie in the ground, many in the soil of a foreign country that they helped liberate, far from their loved ones! They were the boys who 'Said goodbye to it All.' God rest their souls."

**Royal Marine Commandos – Past to present Day. Past – Commandos of the 1st Special Service Brigade led by Brigadier Lord Lovat DSO MC (in the water to the right of the column of his men) arriving on the 'Queen Red' sector of Sword beach on D-Day 6th June 1944. The figure nearest to the camera is the Brigade's celebrated bagpiper (pipes just showing near his head), Bill Millin. Interestingly this picture was taken at approximately 08.40 in another part of 'Red Beach' in the Queen Sector where George Simms and 41 R.M.C landed as part of the 4th Special Service Brigade. Present – R.M.C's on a 'Green Ops' exercise around Woodbury Common and Tregantle Ranges in Devon. These pictures along with those of WW1 veterans in this book depicting and bringing it in line with the overall dedication to all those across time who have ever served our country.**

**As I sat there hearing over seven decades later what he had been through I was very grateful that George was one of those who made it back, and felt that it was me who was blessed this time by being able to spend precious time with him, to sit and capture his priceless memories in a home full of stories, and whilst doing so to hear how in the true spirit of the Royal Marines motto he undoubtedly lived and served his country 'Per Mare Per Terram – 'By Sea, By Land.'**

# BROUGHTON HOUSE VETERAN CARE VILLAGE

During the writing of 'The Last Stand' George Simms, Derrick Corfield, Kenneth Ashworth and Joan Jones (all in this book) and many other veterans from all other services and backgrounds were residing at Broughton House for Ex-Servicemen and Women in Salford, Lancashire, which outside of the Royal Chelsea Hospital in London has been, starting with its original building, one of the oldest purpose made care homes for veterans in the country. Opening at the height of World War One in 1916 it has, rightly, a proud history of high-quality care from that time until this day, provided by very hard working and compassionate staff. The new 'Veterans Care Village' (pictured above in the original architect's drawing, and below the finished reality as it is today), revealing the biggest change and expansion that Broughton House has undergone since it was founded in 1916. As George once said; 'I've spent nearly all my working life in one uniform or another', now after a life serving others he's been very well looked after in a very fitting place for any veteran to have as his or her home, and what they do superbly there is encapsulated in their motto which is part of the official logo - 'We care for those who served Us.' In order to maintain all this fantastic work and over a century of tradition this charity needs all the help it can possibly get from kind people who care about the welfare of our veterans, those who served in their past and gave so much to ensure that we have a better present to live in now. It is with these things in mind that I hope you will help support this great charity with whom I have been associated for some years now, this can be done through the online link below:

## www.justgiving.com/broughtonhousehome

## Additional Information and Life After Service

**Rank upon finish of service** – Marine (Private).

**Medals and Honours** – 1939-45 Defence Medal, 1939-45 War Medal, 1939-45 Star, Italy Star, France-Germany Star, Legion D' Honneur, Fire Brigade Long Service Medal.

**Post War Years** – After leaving the Royal Marines in 1945 George continued to serve, this time in a Civilian Capacity, when he went into Greater Manchester Fire Service, where he trained at Ardwick Fire Station then dutifully served at Macclesfield, Stockport and Reddish Fire Stations for a combined 25 years until 1972. During that time he was involved in some important events such as when the 'Big Freeze' came in 1947 and brought one of the coldest Winters in British history, George and other fire crews were sent to break the ice on reservoirs to help keep the water supply running into Greater Manchester, and in 1949 they helped fight a huge fire at Liverpool's Gladstone Dock when they were called in all the way from Manchester to help bring the inferno under control. Also during his service he was injured whilst fighting a fire at a night club in Reddish, when a big pane of glass came down on his hand in the middle of the blaze, and at another incident he attended George saved the life of a woman in a house fire at Bredbury, Cheshire, for which he received a Fire Service Bravery Award. After finishing at the Fire Brigade in 1972 he worked for 17 years as Head of Security at the Department of Health and Social Security in Longsight, Manchester and retired in 1989. He married Connie on 19th May 1945 just after the war in Europe finished. They have 3 Sons, 9 Grandchildren, 8 Great-Grandchildren.

**Associations and Organisations** – Royal Marines Association, Royal British Legion – Stockport.

# STOKER GEORGE WOODWARD

Served with – Royal Navy Submarine Service
Service Number – DKX164677
Interviewed – Stoke-on-Trent, Staffordshire, 13th January 2015

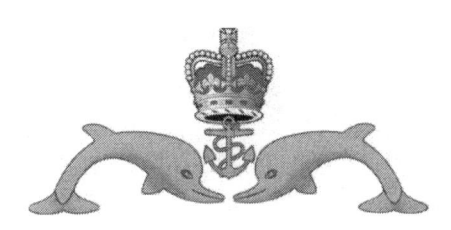

## Service History and Personal Stories

- Born – 8th July 1924, Stoke-on-Trent, Staffordshire, England, UK.
- Before World War Two began George Woodward like almost everyone else had a very different and much more peaceful life. He was working for the Coop which he had done since leaving school aged 14 in 1938, and was now part of their horse drawn bread and milk deliveries with drays around Stoke-on-Trent. A legacy of an almost bygone era.
- He continued in this work once war arrived in 1939 and also did the additional job of being a Firewatcher as part of the Civil Defence at the main Co-op Dairy in Stoke, he volunteered for the Royal Navy aged 18 on 10th November 1942, as his official record states; 'until the end of the period of the present emergency', i.e. for as long as World War 2 continued, leaving the old local life behind for the much bigger and wider world in the Navy.
- George had chosen the branch of the navy he wanted to go into, the Submarine Service, and in 1943 trained to become a Seaman and Stoker at a number of Royal Navy establishments including HMS Duke in Worcestershire, HMS Pembroke in Kent, HMS Drake in Devon, HMS Dolphin in Hampshire and Submarine Depot Ship HMS Cyclops (F31).

- During his time in the Royal Navy George served on 3 Submarines beginning with HMSM – His Majesty's Submarine H33, he joined this H-Class Submarine as part of his training in home waters and the North Sea around Northern Scotland and Northern Ireland in 1943.
- His next submarine, on which he spent most of his service, over two years from January 1944 until April 1946 was HMSM Thule (P325), this new state of the art T Class sub was equipped with LORAN - (Long Range Navigation), which was a radio navigation system and also had radar decoy balloons. Once they had tested this equipment by August 1944 they were posted to the Far East-Pacific area.
- Whilst in transit they travelled via the Mediterranean and North Africa where in certain places dangerous elements of the German Navy and Air Force still operated. Once they reached the Far East in October 1944 the Thule undertook 7 'War Patrols', this active service saw them engaged with the enemy many times up until the end of July 1945.
- During that time the Thule sank a number of Japanese vessels, in one 12-day period in particular between 17$^{th}$ to 29$^{th}$ December 1944 her actions were quite prolific, hunting down and sinking 13 Junks, 2 Lighters and 5 Sampans by various means in the Malacca Straits. Later she attacked a Japanese Submarine believed to be Ro-113 and went on to sink 5 other sailing vessels and 3 Coasters as well as laying a number of mines.
- Her Captain Lieutenant-Commander A.C.G Mars DSO, DSC and Bar, RN went on to write a very interesting book in 1956 detailing the exploits of this submarine called H.M.S Thule Intercepts in which George's name appears in the crew list. After VJ Day the Thule visited some Australian ports then Hong Kong, early November she departed for the U.K arriving back in December 1945 after which she had a refit, George had left her by April 1946.
- His last posting was HMSM Tabard (P342), this was another T Class Submarine and George served on her from April to September 1946 in Home Waters, she was part of the third group of the T Class that was selected along with a number of other boats from her class to try out new streamlining techniques based on advanced German Type XXIII submarine, which incredibly also continued to influence designs of future post-war subs elsewhere as well such as the Type 206 that were in service with the German Navy up until 2011.
- George returned to HMS Dolphin from September to December 1946 where he was finally demobbed ending a remarkable 4 years of active service that took him into many theatres of war worldwide. His love for the submarine service continued on in civilian life and he stayed affiliated to it by joining the Submariners Association as member number 4168.
- His passion about keeping alive the important contributions of the Submarine Service led George to be a founding member of the North Staffordshire branch of the Submariners Association in 1975, as part of that George proudly has a submarines blazer badge sporting the words very relevant to his branch of the Royal Navy - 'We Come Unseen.'

When we think of submarines in World War Two we tend to immediately think about U-Boats of the German Kriegsmarine or Navy, as their fleet especially as the war progressed was by far the biggest and their activities far better known and more documented, but the British Navy also had its submarine service, a lesser known branch of its mighty surface fleet which at the outbreak of war in September 1939 was still the largest in the world, and included 60 submarines, mainly modern with nine being built. The kind of stealth underwater warfare they undertook gave it the nickname of the 'The Silent Service' because by its very nature it was virtually always unseen and unheard until it struck the enemy or by chance was encountered by it. Either way the subs soon slipped away and disappeared after the engagements they were involved in and as a result their actions were less acknowledged, recounted or lauded either by the Royal Navy or the general public in the Great Britain as opposed to Nazi Germany who had a totally different approach and for good propaganda made successful submariners national heroes. Also the fact that this part of the Royal Navy was so small means there were far less crew who served in those kinds of vessels over seven decades ago, which of course means far fewer of these rare kind of WW2 veterans to potentially interview all these years later, and of those still alive from that branch of service to find one who served and survived being on not just 1 but 3 Royal Navy Submarines in many theatres of war is incredible. This person is George Woodward who went from the relatively sedate existence of delivering bread and milk for the Coop by horse and cart in his 'Home Town' of Stoke to seeing active service later on in one of the Royal Navy's most technologically advanced and newest submarines HMSM Thule, and was involved in the conflict that was the Second World War in places all over the world such as the North Sea, Mediterranean, North Africa and Far East going up against the might of Nazi Germany and Imperial Japan. So in 2015 when I was fortunate get the opportunity to interview him through the Submariners Association I made sure I took it, this led to a lovely interview with a lovely veteran, who had this to say about:

### FIGHTING A WAR FROM UNDER THE SEA AS A SUBMARINER

"They call the people from Stoke 'Stokies' so you could say I was a Stokie that became a Stoker! Anyway, being in submarines was of course a totally different kind of warfare than anything else in the Royal Navy simply by the nature of it being conducted from under the water, most the time. The tactics used to stay as unseen as long as possible before striking to try and keep the element of surprise and if needs be to get away from the enemy were very important, and sometimes tracking a ship if it was employing the zig-zagging technique using a well worked out torpedo launch that had the best chance of successfully striking its target, not an easy one for any Captain, Skipper or Commander as we used to them to do effectively, during this or any kind of engagement we would be getting our orders passed down below via our Engineer Officer, who on the Thule was a very good one called Lieutenant Bedale, he was awarded a DSC – Distinguished Service Cross for his actions on submarine patrols. *(In the Navy a DSC is; 'awarded in recognition of an act or acts of exemplary gallantry during active operations against the enemy at sea'). Life on board a submarine was not easy, very sparse conditions, living and working in very close proximity to each other in very cramped spaces for long periods of time, and not seeing natural sunlight for days sometimes weeks, subs had to come up mostly at night for maintenance and to get fresh air into the sub and for ourselves to get some too, it had to be mainly at night during operations, weather permitting, to avoid possibly being spotted by the enemy. Also as a Stoker working in the intense heat of the engine rooms added to these difficulties, and something always in the back of the head but very rarely mentioned, what if we were hit and sunk, a submariners death is a bad one, the fact you could possibly end up on the 'Eternal Patrol' at any time was a very real one that you felt when the submarine went into action against the enemy, excitement, uncertainty and occasionally a bit of fear all in the mix and adding to what could sometimes be a bit of pressure cooker feeling, but these conditions led to a lot of comradery with our pals, we were a close lot, we had to be to get through everything as best possible, as you can imagine like all sailors we made the most of shore leave as and when we got it. A lot of the time as Stokers we were as you would expect below decks when a lot of things were happening, especially when we were at action stations, but there were a couple of occasions when the submarine surfaced to finish off lighter vessels with its mounted deck guns outside and some of us were allowed to witness it, quite something to see the action as it unfolded rather than just hear it from below, then it really came home to you what you were a part of! As Stokers we operated all sorts of machinery, the subs engines, ballast and vents for when the sub dived and descended down into the deep and for when she ascended back up again, made sure equipment didn't overheat, repair all things mechanical as and when needed, kept an eye on fuel, oil, power and pressure gauges and all sorts of other devices, there was a lot to know because there was a lot of machinery needed to make such complex bit of kit like a submarine kept working." **Below decks in a WW2 British Submarine, a world with which George was very familiar.**

**HMSM Thule, seen here in Greenock, Scotland June 1944 during her 'Working Up' period, this was George's main wartime submarine, he served on her for over two years and it was where he saw the most action whilst in the Far East on board this T-Class sub, very similar to HMSM Tabard.**

Whilst on the Thule George served under a Skipper who was very well-known within the Royal Navy and who was one of their best, I asked George to tell me what he thought of him: "Alastair Mars was a very good and very well-respected Commanding officer, always looking to find and engage the enemy and destroy as many Japanese vessels as possible, that's why we sunk a lot of ships whilst out in the Far East. He used to lecture us quite a lot and give us speeches, great for moral and so we knew more about where we were, what we were doing and what was expected of us as different tactics were used to get the enemy ships, from using torpedoes if under the water to using our guns up on the top and even ramming them, we did it all, because by that time in the war the Japanese were using a lot of smaller vessels to move supplies around and so that they could hug the coastline for their own protection, that didn't stop us though because many of the places we went looking and would know to find those smaller boats like sampans and trade wind ships were in locations just like that, a lot of the action happened in the Malacca Straits around Malaysia, Indonesia and Sumatra, but of course if you were going in for an attack in areas closer to shore you had to be extra careful to make sure you weren't spotted by other possible enemy forces land, sea or air that could be in those areas, you didn't want to go from being the hunter to the hunted!

Whilst we were in the Far East we also did other types of interesting Covert or 'Unseen Missions' such as delivering secret service agents and commandos ashore onto enemy shorelines and picking them up again, and also retrieved downed airmen with the help local resistance fighters. I had other experiences whilst I was a submariner during that conflict, some good, some not so, as you would expect when in active service during a World War, once we brought a very badly injured Japanese POW on board who we had rescued from an action we had just fought where we sunk his vessel, he had one leg missing, his other leg in a mess, he also had bad chest wounds and as they brought him on board and I looked at him he still managed a smile, I will never forget that, I think he might have been on morphine, don't know, but I do remember feeling sorry for him because in the end he was only human after all, and a mariner, later on the Coxswain had to saw his other leg off, that understandably proved to be too much for him and he died.

Another time we took a few Japanese prisoners on board, again from a ship we had sunk, who were none too happy about having their ship blown up from under them and later tried a mutiny on-board, if that rebellion had succeeded it might of meant we us losing our submarine, but after it was quashed and they'd had a good hiding we had to take it in turns to be part of a 24 hour armed guard to make sure nothing like it happened again until we could get them off the Thule and hand them over as POW's, as if we didn't already have enough to do! A lot to take in for us young lads, but sadly that was the nature of war. We did have some good times of course, one nice memory was whilst we were in Ceylon, now Sri Lanka a female singer came on-board called Cherry Lind, she stood on the conning tower steps and sung *One Fine Day* from the opera *Madam Butterfly* and there we were a big group of sailors all stood round her, looking up entranced, whenever I have heard that song since it has always taken me back to that lovely moment.

**The crew of the Thule up on deck as George recalls for 'a photograph and a laugh' with their homemade 'Jolly Roger' the traditional symbol of the pirates or hunters of the high seas, and as this story testifies successful hunters they were! He pointed out to me that in this picture he is bottom row, 7th from the left! Very well done for knowing and also remembering that George.**

The years I spent in the Royal Navy were very interesting and for a young lad who had spent all his life just around Stoke-on-Trent before being a submariner it was also pretty thrilling, all those different countries we experienced and kinds of people we met and the action we were involved in, like for many young people who went in the forces then it was in many ways probably one of the most exciting parts of our lives. Those very significant years have always remained with me and after the war I made sure I kept a link to the Royal Navy and the Submarine service by being a member of the Submariners Association and co-founder of the North Staffs branch of it, after all we were part of something very special that needs to be remembered." **Pictured - The Submariners Association logo.**

**A quote George told me he heard whilst on submarines, liked a lot and which always stuck with him was; 'Whilst We Breath, We Hope', that hope which got him through some trying and difficult times still shone through when I interviewed him. George you're truly a credit to your service.**

## Additional Information and Life After Service

**Rank upon finish of service** – Stoker.

**Medals and Honours** – 1939-45 Defence Medal, 1939-45 Star, Atlantic Star, Africa Star, Italy Star, Burma Star.

**Post War Years** – Soon after leaving the Navy George returned to work for the Co-op in 1947 and delivered milk in the Cheadle Area for many years, except this time round things were mechanised and he had a van to help him do his job instead of the hand cart and horse and cart of pre-war years. He later went on to become a Round Supervisor for the Co-op Dairy back in Stoke-on-Trent and in total completed a staggering 40 years working for them by the time he retired in May 1986 aged 61. He married Hilda on the 17th August 1946 at St. Paul's Church, Burslem, Stoke and they were together for 54 years until her passing in 2000. They have 1 Son, 1 Daughter, 4 Grandchildren, 6 Great-Grandchildren.

**Associations and Organisations** – North Staffordshire Submariners Association – Co-founder and Honouree Life Member, Submariners Association.

# WREN JUNE FLETCHER

Served with – WRNS – Women's Royal Naval Service – Fleet Air Arm
Service Number – WRNS78948
Interviewed – Salford, Lancashire, 15th January 2015 & 11th January 2016

## Service History and Personal Stories

- Born – 30th June 1925, Higher Broughton, Salford, Lancashire, England, UK.
- After finishing Liverpool Physical Training College in Mid 1944 June Phyllis Cassel, later Fletcher Volunteered for the Royal Navy and by August of that year had begun selection which took her to a place called Tullichewan near Balloch in Dunbartonshire, Scotland.
- This was undertaken at HMS Spartiate, after passing selection and rigorous basic training June was chosen for something quite exciting, a job where she had to learn to fly some Navy Fleet Air Arm aircraft, then use and combine that experience to help her teach Royal Air Force and Royal Navy pilots how to land at night with the guidance of Morse Code.
- For these things June was posted to RNAS – Royal Naval Air Station – Eglinton, (AKA HMS Gannet), County Londonderry, Northern Ireland, home of 1847 Naval Air Squadron, where she would teach these skills in a Link Flight Simulator, (AKA Link Trainer) it was there pilots would sit inside and 'fly'

in low light with instrumentation lit and conditions similar to night flying in a regular aircraft with June guiding, monitoring and assessing their progress as a 'Link Trainer' during their course.

- ❖ The term 'Link Trainer' referred to both the person doing the training and the special piece of equipment used to train pilots, this flight simulator was also known as the 'Blue Box' due to early models being painted blue and 'Pilot Trainer', they were produced between the early 1930's to the early 1950's by Link Aviation Devices, founded and headed by Ed Link from New York. During the Second World War they were used as a key pilot training aid by almost every combatant nation as many Link Trainers were bought by both sides pre-war, it is estimated that more than 500,000 pilots were trained on Link Simulators.
- ❖ Many of the pilots who June taught these skills to in that part of their overall and ongoing training would find these things invaluable when put into real-life use, whether in Bomber Command on return from Bombing missions over enemy occupied Europe or Coastal Command and FAA Anti U-Boat patrols and convoy escorts over the Atlantic or elsewhere.
- ❖ During her time in service June was delighted to meet King George VI when he made an official visit to Northern Ireland in July 1945 where she briefly described her job and its use of Morse Code and recalls the King saying that he had learnt Morse Code as a Boy Scout.
- ❖ June's complete service as a WREN ran from 23rd August 1944 to 26th August 1946, after which she was 'Released to Shore' (de-mobbed) in Class A at HMS Gannet in Northern Ireland, having successfully trained scores of pilots in her specialism of landing an aircraft at night. Her love for teaching continued for the rest of her life, something she perused in civilian life for another 70 years until and long after her 'Official Retirement'.

The Women's Royal Naval Service – WRNS; popularly and officially known as the Wrens, was the women's branch of the United Kingdom's Royal Navy. This part of the service was first formed during the latter end of the First World War in 1917, and was disbanded in 1919, it was then revived at the start of the Second World War in 1939, remaining active until integrated into the mainstream Royal Navy in 1993. During these conflicts WRNS undertook many important jobs which helped free up men for more of the front-line positions in the Navy. The numerous roles they successfully carried out included being Radar Plotters, Wireless Telegraphists, Ordinance WRENS, Air Mechanics, Drivers, Cooks, Clerks and among other duties were prominent as support staff at the Government Code and Cypher School at Bletchley Park where they assumed many tasks including the operating of Alan Turing's huge De-Cyphering machines called Bombe's. At its peak in 1944 the WRNS had 75,000 active servicewomen, one of whom was June Fletcher, nee Cassel who had a very interesting and different kind of job as a Link Trainer. This involved her first undergoing some pilot training aged 19 with the Fleet Air Arm in order to be able to perform her role more efficiently so she could help train and better equip other already qualified pilots for their real situations with the vital added skills of night time landings, which once attained by the use of the Link Trainer Flight Simulator, additionally guided by voice and Morse Code would help them navigate more safely and effectively in the darkness or if bad weather conditions arose that seriously affected visibility for aircraft and crews on active duty missions, which already contained many other kinds of dangers with which they had to contend.

Fast Forward 70 years and I was very fortunate to be introduced to this incredible, gentle, intelligent and kind-hearted lady, then aged 89, with her characteristic big positive smiles who I interviewed twice and visited at her home on other occasions and really enjoyed spending time with every time I called. I was fascinated to hear and record her service and life story, during which I thought how rare it was to speak to a World War Two servicewoman with flying training, the only other one I have interviewed being Joy Lofthouse from the ATA. What I also was reminded of was how much this wartime generation seemed to achieve in their lives both during and after service which certainly was the case with June Fletcher who is now going to tell us more about how it was to be:

## A WREN PILOTING AIRCRAFT AND GIVING LINK TRAINING IN THE FLEET AIR ARM

"I thought I would join the Navy because I liked the uniform, I wasn't to know when I first joined what I would end up doing, which was very interesting indeed. After rigorous selection and basic training at Balloch in Scotland I asked them what am I going to do now, they said you're going to fly a plane! So I looked at them in amazement and said I can't even drive a car properly, let alone fly a plane, you'll learn I was told and I had those words said to me the whole of the time that I was in the Navy, you'll learn, and I did! Starting with the Fairy Barracuda aircraft and later moving onto a two-engine plane as well, I think it was an AVRO Anson, I flew a lot under instruction, taking off, landing, many different manoeuvres and scenarios, gaining many flying skills, it was very challenging and exhilarating, and yes I'm very happy to say I did learn how to fly! This in turn gave the first-hand knowledge of a pilot's job which really helped me prepare for what I would do next as a Link Trainer, the idea being that to teach a job related to flying you had to first understand flying, and of course they were right! **Pictured Below; Left – June, smiling and in full flying kit with parachute ready to go. Right – A Fleet Air Arm Fairy Barracuda the same aircraft June flew as part of her flight training.** I had been posted to my main base The Royal Naval Air Station Eglinton, which was also known as HMS Gannet, in County Londonderry, Northern Ireland where I spent my two years of active service whilst I was in the Navy and where I undertook everything." I went on to ask June to describe more about what that job entailed and she told me: "As a Link Trainer I was based in what was essentially a hanger with my own specially designed desk, which had flight instruments on a separate part at the front and on top at the side, some the same as those the pilot would have inside his simulator for me to guide and observe everything and the main desk had a glass top with maps you could put under it. This was all connected to a mock single-engine plane that was on a concertina, and we went up and down and right and left we could go anywhere in this plane, turn around do whatever we wanted. I'd lead and have to tell the pilot what to do and be a bit like an air traffic controller, I would make up for example we are going so many miles this way at that height and turning in this or that direction, some of the time when needed I spoke to the pilot through a microphone which was part of a radio set, and I would also give some of the important signals in Morse Code such as when guiding them to different airfields, each one had its own specific identifying code within that message, this was so the pilot got used to working with both methods which he would need and would be relayed to him during missions which included the secretive airfield codes. The course I set would be monitored by an electronic device called 'The Crab' it was a motorised claw that marked out everything from his 'Flight' in red removable ink on the glass topped map on the surface of my desk, from this we could evaluate how well each pilot had followed the course I had set them, it clearly plotted out the pilot's actions, path of the plane and how accurate his night landing turned out, and if required what we needed to work on until the landings were a perfect as possible, vitally important to prepare them for the real thing! Also if we changed the course or airfield it would aid in and record that amended landing too. Essentially it meant I had to merge the three skills I had learned, Flying, Morse Code and link training to simultaneously to be able to deliver this training.

**June seen here at her desk on busy her microphone communicating with a pilot in the Link Trainer, the back wing of which can be seen in the picture, also note 'The Crab' on the pole in front of her fed and powered by the connecting wire.** Interestingly I had all the numbered codes for all the different RAF and Navy Stations around the U.K which was why I think I was the only one doing that job at that station because those codes were very secretive information, and I imagine the thinking was the less people doing the job and in possession of that information the better, it was made clear to me and all others, whatever their jobs that we could not discuss our work, unless given permission or it would lead to instant dismissal and possibly much worse! This additional Link training that I and everyone else who did the same job was giving to pilots on bases all over the country and elsewhere taught some very important additional skills to help airmen get back from their missions safely, as the British bombers did almost all their operations at night, also very useful if they had to be guided in using this method because of having to switch to other airfields they didn't know in the dark or possibly due to other added factors such as bad weather or damage to their aircraft, this system could for many be the different between getting back safely or not, the difference between life or death! I was happy to be doing a job deemed important during my time as a WREN in the Navy, and one as mentioned before that really could make a difference and save lives by the skills taught and training given. It is said join the Navy and see the world, I joined the Navy, I didn't see the world but I saw life, a life one couldn't possibly experience except in the company of hundreds of friends whom you have to learn to live with in peace and harmony, it's not easy but it can be done, it takes tact, diplomacy and a sense of humour, and whilst on that journey some great friendships were forged and great memories attained, at weekends we would go many places such as Moville, Greencastle and Dublin just over the border in neutral Southern Ireland and in Northern Ireland to Belfast, and at the end of the war whilst at Lisahally in Lough Foyle near Londonderry we saw lots of German U-Boats in the Harbour, the matter was obviously secret because when we asked about them we were told, 'You didn't see anything!' *(These surrendered U-Boats were later scuttled as part of Operation Deadlight). On Friday nights we were able to keep the faith as all Jewish Wrens were invited by the distinguished and hospitable Spain family for Shabbos meal. During the war I met people of all faiths who served in our forces, it was good to see that and very important to mention and remember all those valuable contributions. Those couple of years have always remained very special to me, and additionally I was proud to have come forward and played my part at a time during the war when the nation really needed it!" **Pictured - A Wrens WW2 recruitment poster.**

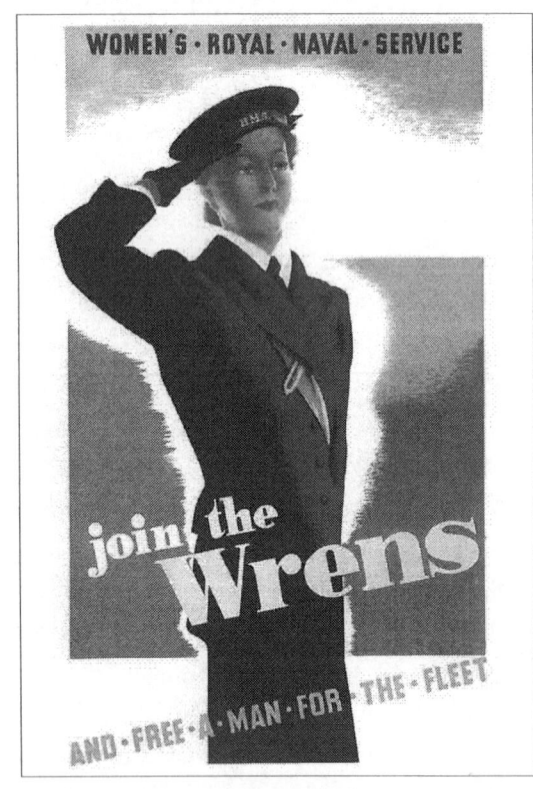

**June really was 'A WREN that Flew'...... when piloting aircraft in the Navy and as a teacher in class who flew into the hearts and minds of many who she taught in her incredible 70-year career, and many more who have been lucky and blessed to meet this wonderful lady, myself included.**

# Additional Information and Life After Service

**Rank upon finish of service** – WREN (Equivalent to Able Seaman).

**Medals and Honours** – 1939-45 War Medal, HM Armed Forces Veteran's Badge.

**Post War Years** – After leaving the Navy June went onto teach Physical Education and coach Tennis in Schools such as the Jewish High School for Girls in Higher Broughton, Salford, something she was well-equipped to do having trained to teach those things before the war in Liverpool. Unlike others when they reached retirement age June just kept on going part-time in education never really retiring both as a student and a teacher. This incredibly inspirational lady wrote 2 books, Tally's Suitcase (1993) and Tally's Children (2003), then went on to study for a Bachelor of Arts degree in English Literature and Creative Writing between 2004-2007 and on 26th June 2007 Graduated with a BA (Hons) as the oldest ever successful student of Salford University aged 83! (Picture enclosed). June's absolute love for children led her to continue as a Classroom Assistant teaching phonics, reading and elementary maths to young children at the Yesoiday HaTora Jewish Day School in Manchester until she finally retired in 2015 aged 90! She has been greatly missed by the teachers she helped and the many classes of children whose fondest memories of 'Grandma Fletcher' were when they would gather round her for story reading, something she loved doing and something they loved as well. June Married Ellis Fletcher, a Solicitor, in Manchester in 1947, he passed in 2010, they have 1 Son, 1 Daughter, 4 Grandchildren and 'Many Great-Grandchildren' as June said.

**Associations and Organisations** – Association of WRENS.

# LEADING HAND DONALD HITCHCOCK

Served with – Royal Navy, HMS Narborough
Service Number – P/JX 619231
Interviewed – Berkswell, West Midlands, 20th July 2019

## Service History and Personal Stories

- Born – 15th November 1924, Colne, Lancashire, England, UK.
- Don's involvement in the Second World War began when he was part of the Civil Defence (flag above left) between 1940-1942 as a Fire Watcher in his home town of Colne in Lancashire, which he joined aged 16. It was from that small town up there in the Pennine Hills that he witnessed the glow of Manchester burning as it was ruthlessly bombed by the German Air Force during the Christmas Blitz of 1940.
- In December 1942 Don was called up and joined the Royal Navy in Preston, but was granted a special dispensation to finish his studies in order to secure a scholarship at Cambridge University, something he managed to do and after service would return to undertake successfully. In October 1943 he completed basic training at HMS Royal Arthur Shore Station in Skegness which was a Butlins Holiday Camp requisitioned for military use.
- His academic strengths were soon spotted and as a result he was given the opportunity to become a 'Code and Cypher Operator' and was sent to train at the Royal Navy Signal School and Shore Station HMS Cabbala at Lowton St. Marys near Leigh in Lancashire from October until December 1943. Whilst there he undertook various special communications training including Morse Code and the Naval number and letter-based codes called Playfair, these would help prepare Don for his tasks once in active service on board a ship.
- This was followed by a short time at HMS Victory Barracks, Portsmouth and HMS Mercury II Shore Station, Petersfield, Hampshire before joining HMS Narborough (K578) in January 1944 at Lisahally, County Londonderry, Northern Ireland, the ship he would serve on for the rest of the war.

After working up exercises at Tobermarry, Isle of Mull Don and his new ship undertook Coastal and Atlantic Convoy escort duties up until mid-April 1944.

- In late April 1944 HMS Narborough escorted in company with HMS Bulldog (H91) some of the LST - Landing Ship Tank craft involved in the large week-long US led D-Day rehearsal exercises at Slapton Sands on the Devonshire Coast, called Exercise Tiger. But these big amphibious military manoeuvres ended in disaster when they were intercepted by German E-Boats from Cherbourg that wreaked havoc causing the deaths of over 700 American servicemen, it was covered up so as not to effect morale and to give away as little as possible regarding D-Day preparations.

- Throughout May 1944 on the run up to D-Day HMS Narborough was given a very special assignment and became one of the floating weather stations in the Atlantic, mapping and gathering vitally important Meteorological data for the up-and-coming invasion of Western Europe. This was relayed by Don back to the Admiralty in London and was fed into the allied planning to help predict the best time to launch Operation Overlord.

- On D-Day 6$^{th}$ June 1944 HMS Narborough sailed from Milford Haven, Wales and joined Support Group B where she escorted 4 troop ships, and as they moved down the Normandy coast that day they witnessed the invasion unfolding on Sword, Juno and Gold Beaches as they made their way towards Omaha Beach.

- During those escort duties on the following day, D-Day+1 they were involved in a rescue mission that saved 2689 U.S servicemen and ships' crew including one General Williams from converted cruise liner come troop ship USS Susan B. Anthony (AP-72) that struck a sea mine on the way to Omaha Beach. The quick and skilful evacuation meant that all on board were saved, which the Guinness Book of World Records lists as the largest rescue of people without loss of life (at sea during wartime).

- In addition to this between June to September 1944 Don and his ship completed 34 very interesting escort missions that they were assigned to such as protecting vessels to and from various D-Day beaches, escorting interned vessels from Bilbao, Spain and undertaking escort duties with Free French ships to Bordeaux.

- Also within that period on 15$^{th}$ August 1944 HMS Narborough working closely with HMS Ramillies (07) was part of the seaborne force involved in the 2$^{nd}$ invasion on the French mainland in Operation Dragoon at Provence in the South of France. Then throughout October and November 1944 came escort duties in a very different theatre of war on the dreaded Arctic convoys to Russia as part of the 15$^{th}$ Escort Group, taking out Convoy JW61 to the Kola Inlet and escorting convoy RA61 back to the United Kingdom, during that time they clashed with Nazi U-Boats on the approach to Murmansk.

- Upon return to the U.K Don and the Narborough were moved to the Royal Navy base at Davenport in December 1944 and took part in other very interesting duties such as coastal convoy protection, and being part of the liberation of the German occupied Channel Islands when supporting forces at the surrender of Guernsey in May 1945, through to his final big job on Operation Cabal when his ship towed German U-Boat U3041 all the way from Northern Ireland through to the Baltic and Latvia finishing there in December 1945.

- HMS Narborough made its final trip back to Portsmouth in December 1945 where Don disembarked, and the ship was paid off ending his sea-going days. After this he continued his work as a 'Code and Cypher Operator' when in January 1946 he was posted with Naval Party 1734 to Naval Shore bases in what was now Post-War Allied occupied Germany at HMS Royal Alfred, HQ of the Flag Officer (subsequently Senior Naval Officer) at Plön and later postings in Hamburg and Kiel, where he again worked on the 'Type X' De-coding machine which was based on the German Enigma design. Don returned to the U.K and was de-mobbed in Portsmouth in August 1946, ending a fascinating 3 years of service.

As a Code and Cypher Operator on board the Captain Class Frigate HMS Narborough (K578) Don Hitchcock had a very important job dealing with highly sensitive information of every kind, some of which was used to help plot the positions of friendly and enemy vessels during 'Action Stations' which could influence the outcomes of encounters with opposing forces, and other information concerning things of great worth such as up and coming weather fronts that would influence military planning for the allied invasion of Europe that we all know as D-Day. Don and his ship were also involved in that invasion of Northern France as part of Operation Overlord on 6th June 1944 and the later invasion of Southern France as part of Operation Dragoon on 15th August 1944, the first Royal Navy veteran I have interviewed to have taken part in both, for which he later was awarded the French Legion D' Honneur in December 2015. In addition to this he served on board the Narborough when she also took part in Atlantic and Arctic Convoy escort duties, the latter affording him the well-earned right to also wear the White Beret of an Arctic Convoy veteran. I was very fortunate to meet Don at the 75th Anniversary of D-Day when we were both at the Remembrance Ceremony at Bayeux Cemetery in Normandy with Prince Charles and the Duchess of Cornwall and the then Prime Minister Teresa May and heads of all other political parties also in attendance, all of whom we met. As soon as we got talking I could see from his 1939-45, Atlantic and Arctic Stars plus Legion D' Honneur and White Arctic Convoys Beret that this would be a veteran with some very interesting stories indeed, and I wasn't wrong. That along with the great added bonus of him being a writer of World War Two poetry which he recited very eloquently on the day meant that as a WW2 writer and poet myself I totally appreciated what I heard and I knew this was a veteran I just had to interview, and was very glad I did, Don now tells us how it was:

## TO BE A CODE AND CYPHER OPERATOR ON HMS NARBOROUGH

"My job on board HMS Narborough as a Code and Cypher Operator or 'Coder' as we were known entailed a number of things, mainly these, I would work in the Communications Office on board ship where we would receive incoming coded messages from our surface or underwater vessels, I would de-cypher them and send them to the bridge where the officers would decide how to action them and based on the content would prioritise the information they had, if for example they were incoming orders from a higher source within the chain of command or intelligence from vessels that were conversing about immediate action that might be required within our sphere of influence where a battle was imminent or taking place, or maybe an important manoeuvre that was required, then I would be ordered to send out replies in code to the vessels that sent them and possibly on to other ships as well, and in some cases depending on the nature of it even back to Admiralty HQ in London. On those occasions when we were at 'Action Stations' I would also if needed be working alongside crew at the plotting table, this was what was called being 'On the Plot', very important as that would be our guide to what was going on with both enemy and our own vessels above and below water to the best of our knowledge and also assist us as a battle plan which in coordination with the officers, bridge and other departments would help dictate our actions. We were involved in all sorts of things that were an important part of World War Two, some that were obvious and we realised there and then like D-Day of course, and others we didn't such as Slapton Sands, and when we were in the Atlantic on the weeks running up to D-Day where we were being used along with other ships to gather weather data to feed back to the Admiralty, I didn't really know or realise at the time the importance and gravity of the weather information I was sending back to the U.K, how it was being used and its potential bearing on the huge history changing events that would follow, namely D-Day! I would receive and send messages via Morse Code and Type X Cipher and reply using those means as ordered. On D-Day itself as we progressed southwards down the coast escorting four U.S vessels we witnessed it all unfolding before our very eyes, we had a panoramic view of the big battleships firing as they pounded German defences, amphibious craft going into battle, thousands of ships everywhere, aircraft going over, incredible sights that if you hadn't witnessed you would find hard to believe and we were a part of that momentous day, a very small but like all the rest in that enormous undertaking important part! The following day near Omaha Beach we found ourselves helping to save thousands of troops of the stricken 8000-tonne troop ship USS Susan B. Anthony, our C/O Lieutenant Commander Wilfred Muttram did not hesitate to assist and for that he later received the U.S Navy Bronze Star.

**The ship from which Don and the crew of the Narborough helped save so many, the Susan B. Anthony.**

Looking back now I was fortunate to be a part of and safely come through so many other things as well, such as the Arctic Convoys in 1944 where we were engaged by U-Boats and the ferocious winter conditions, and in 1945 being at St. Peter Port, Guernsey for the surrender of the Island and escorting 8 German ships from the Channel Islands to Cawsand Bay, Plymouth where they formally surrendered, attending Naval week in Cardiff, going to Wilhelmshaven, Germany to escort 4 modern type IX U-Boats back to Lock Ryan in Scotland, and finally towing U3041 on a month long arduous journey all the way from Lough Foyle in Northern Ireland through the almost frozen Baltic Sea to Liepaja in Latvia where we delivered what became known as 'Uncle Joe's Souvenir', a lot of special experiences packed into 3 years of service, and no regrets!"

**Right – The Captain-Class Frigate HMS Narborough, originally U.S Navy Buckley-Class Destroyer Escort DE-569, pictured here in Latvia in December 1945 after delivering U3041 to the Russians. This would be** her last assignment; she was returned to the U.S in February 1946 and scrapped December 1946.

As his story shows Don Hitchcock has seen, done and achieved a lot whilst in the Royal Navy, and when we finished what was a delightful interview we enjoyed a tot of vintage Navy rum together that he kept for special occasions, a perfect Maritime ending. It is with that little memory in mind I would like to say; Cheers Don, thank you for your kind hospitality and your inspiring Royal Navy service.

**The Association which Don was very proudly a member of for many years.**

## Additional Information and Life After Service

**Rank upon finish of service** – Leading Hand.

**Medals and Honours** – 1939-45 War Medal, 1939-45 Star, Atlantic Star with France-Germany Bar, Arctic Star, Legion D' Honneur, Russian Order of Ushacov Medal & 75 Years of Victory Jubilee Medal.

**Post War Years** – After the Navy Don attained a Degree in Geography from Cambridge University through his scholarship and perused a career in teaching, this included working for the War Office as part of the British Family Education Service on Army, Navy and Air Force bases in Cologne, Munster and Hamburg in Germany, and later at King Edward VI High School, Stafford and Queen's University, Belfast. He married Mary on 20th December 1953 in Nelson, Lancashire, they have 4 Children, 4 Grand-Children. He retired aged 65 in 1991. Don 'Crossed the Bar' 13th March 2020. Rest In Peace.

**Associations and Organisations** – Royal British Legion (West Midlands Branch), Royal Naval Association, Captain Class Frigate Association, Arctic Convoy Club (Midlands), Destroyer Escorts Sailors Association (U.S).

**ARMS FOR RUSSIA** ... A great convoy of British ships escorted by Soviet fighter planes sails into Murmansk harbour with vital supplies for the Red Army.

**A very interesting British wartime poster which is honouring those who like Don and other veterans in this book risked their lives in the treacherous Arctic Convoys to deliver 'Arms For Russia', depicting the British and Soviet forces, then allies, working together against their common German enemy to deliver vital supplies for the Russian war effort.**

# ABLE-BODIED SEAMAN NAWAB DIN

Served with – British Royal Navy/Royal Indian Navy & Royal Pakistan Navy
Service Number – 26883
Interviewed – Radcliffe, Manchester, 22nd March 2016

## Service History and Personal Stories

- Born – 30th July 1923, Ghansia, Gujrat, Pakistan.
- Nawab Din came from the humble background of a rural farming community in Ghansia, in the Gujrat area of what is now Pakistan, but with the Second World War raging, effecting and reaching every part of the globe including what was then British Colonial India he decided at the age of 20 to join up and play his part for the Allied cause.
- This led to him initially becoming part of The Royal Indian Navy, which operated as the Navy of that country, but until later partition of that continent in August 1947 was under British Royal Navy Command with its vessels carrying the prefix of HMIS – 'His Majesty's Indian Ship' in the same way that the British vessels carried the prefix HMS – 'His Majesty's Ship' (both acknowledging the wartime monarch King George VI).
- Basic Naval training began for Nawab on the 20th March 1944 at HMS Akbar that was a direct entry Training Establishment in Bombay, India (a Royal Indian Navy Facility AKA 'Stone Frigate' that operated until 1946), where he completed 3 months rigorous instruction until 16th June 1944, giving him the basic sea-going skills required to become an O/S – Ordinary Seaman on board whichever ships he would be posted to during his active wartime service.

- Nawab's wartime vessel was HMIS Cornwallis (U09), which was a 'Specialised Convoy Defence Vessel' AKA a 'Sloop' or 'Sloop-of-War' that served as part of the Eastern Fleet on convoy escort duties in the Indian Ocean, and like the Black Swan Class ships he later served on was well-equipped with good anti-aircraft and anti-submarine capabilities which amongst other things meant they could and did undertake extensive minesweeping and AA Defence roles.
- In between his postings to different ships Nawab like many sailors spent various periods of time at or assigned to land based Navy establishments either for training or other Naval duties, subsequent training at these 'Stone Frigates' led to him achieving the higher rating of AB/S – Able-Bodied Seaman AKA Able Seaman, he also received some instruction in Anti-Aircraft Gunnery.
- In September 1945 once the war against Japan in Asia and the Pacific was over and the Second World War was finished and between the partition of India in August 1947, Nawab served on 3 ships, the Minesweeping Sloop HMIS Khyber (J190) for 16 months, the Escort Sloop HMIS Kistna (U46) for 3 months and the very next day after finishing there was then assigned on the 16th July 1947 to the Black Swan Class-Sloop HMIS Godavari (U52).
- HMIS Kistna and HMIS Godarvari were named in Naval documents as vessels which, quote; 'Have been placed at the disposal of the Admiralty by the government of India. Operational control C in C Eastern Fleet and designated part of the 12th Frigate Flotilla...' Showing the close cooperation between the Navies of what was essentially a British Colonial possession up until the partition and part of the Commonwealth thereafter.
- Very interestingly as his Navy record shows the dates Nawab served on the Godavari, July-November 1947, ran through the period when the official Partition of the Indian continent took place and sharing of its Navy between the new Independent Countries of India and Pakistan.
- Whilst serving on this very special vessel that had been transferred from the Royal Indian Navy to the newly formed RPN - Royal Pakistan Navy called HMPS – His Majesty's Pakistani Ship Godavari later re-named PNS – Pakistan Navy Ship Sind she was given the honour of being the first ever Flagship (Admiral's Command Ship) of the new Navy of Pakistan and Nawab was one members of the first crew on this very important vessel, as a result he was at the epi-centre of his country's new naval history as it was happening!
- Now performing his duties in the Pakistani Navy having chosen this new country in keeping with his Muslim faith, upbringing and background he remained as a sailor during the troubled period of transition in that continent and served on another 2 ships the Black Swan Class sloop HMPS Narbada (U40) and Escort Sloop HMPS Hindustan (U80) for 12 months, finishing on the latter his final Navy vessel on 25th July 1949. After being shore based in Karachi, Pakistan awaiting his release he was Demobbed there, or as it officially states on his record 'Discharged from service as Engaged' on the 10th August 1949.
- During his 5 years, 4 months of loyal Naval service Nawab Din saw a lot of changes both historically in the continent from which he originated and in the branch of the Armed Forces he served, it was this combination that interestingly led to him being part of, under the command of and affiliated to 3 Navies, namely those of Great Britain, India and Pakistan, (their flags shown at the beginning of his profile), something special and quite different indeed, making him a rare kind of veteran and one that should and has rightly been acknowledged here with his amazing story in my book.

During World War Two over 2.5 million men from the Indian continent volunteered and served as part of the British Armed Forces, they came from all backgrounds, Sikh, Hindu and Muslim and represented a huge proportion of the very important contribution made by Commonwealth troops in that conflict and the largest all-volunteer force in history! Over 70 years later I was privileged to meet and interview Nawab Din, one of the very last of that generation of volunteers left from those brave people who at great risk to themselves came forward from a continent thousands of miles away from Great Britain to help her and the other Allies in their fight against the Axis powers. But Nawab's story does not finish there, because he served from the end of the Second World War through the period of great turmoil and transition in what was the partition of the Indian continent over which time he was a part of three Navies, the Royal Indian Navy, working closely with and as a part of the bigger British Royal Navy and the Royal Pakistan Navy. On the historic day of the 14th August 1947 which signified both the creation of Pakistan and the birth of the Royal Pakistan Navy, Nawab was at the centre of both these important events when the ship he was serving on, which the day before was part of the Royal Indian Navy was now in this new country the Admiral's flagship. That event which Nawab witnessed, was a part of and heard has been officially described in the following way; 'At 0800 on 14 August 1947, the flag of Rear Admiral J W Jefford, Flag Officer Commanding Royal Pakistan Navy was hosted on his flagship HMPS Godavari. The Admiral's first signal addressed to the officers and men of the RPN was flashed to all ships and shore establishments.' Incredible to think that even back then nearly 8 decades ago there were only a couple of hundred men present at this historical event on board that vessel (ship's compliment 180-192 men), so to find and speak to one here in my home city of Manchester is quite amazing, here are some of the things Nawab had to say about his Navy service, taken from notes I wrote down, translation help in parts from his daughter Abida, and some video footage taken on the day of his interview regarding:

## SERVING AS A SAILOR IN 3 NAVIES DURING AND AFTER WORLD WAR TWO

"My training for the Navy began in Bombay, at a place called HMS Akbar, and I remember we lived in a place called the Castle Barracks learning how be sailors, that was when the war was still going on and we had volunteered to go and help our country and the British because they were still fighting in that part of the world mainly against the Japanese. Later when we went to sea I was in many places on the ships I served in the different navies, and because of that over the years we were on all the seas around India and later Pakistan, in the Arabian Sea, Indian Ocean and the Bay of Bengal, in Bombay, Karachi, Sri Lanka and many other ports in those areas that I can't even remember the names of right now all these years later. The ships I worked on did many different things, some worked on minesweeping, others protected ships that were bringing supplies in and out of India to many places, to protect them we had big guns on the ships to help against any planes or other ships that might try to attack us and on others mines against submarines and ships as well. I was a sailor doing many different duties around a ship, helping to keep things clean, working and maintained, the ropes when we came to and left ports, also as a lookout for danger and I knew how to use some of the ships guns against planes if I was ordered to do that, and later when I had much more experience we would sometimes be ordered to help steer the ship on a course they gave us, (the job of Helmsman as it was known was sometimes given to Able Seamen, where they would steer a steady course as directed by the mate or officer on the bridge, relying on visual references, compasses and rudder angle indicator, all of which they were trained to do having already reached that rank and acquired a lot of sea-going proficiency and know-how in the Deck Department). During my time in the navy I saw a couple of ships sunk and we had been fired at from a distance and fired back but luckily we were not hit."

The times during which Nawab served as a sailor were turbulent, from World War Two through to the partition of India, as a result of this he as mentioned before ended up being a part of and under the command of three different navies during the period he was at sea from 1944 until 1949. Importantly I have included an overview of what was happening around that time to give a backdrop to the bigger historical events that occurred mainly during his service and also a few related key dates thereafter. Something I found additionally interesting to gain various perspectives was having interviewed two Second World War veterans, both who served as a part of the British Armed Forces but later lived on different sides of the partition, in this book and in the Navy, Nawab Din from a Muslim background who chose to live in Pakistan and in my first book Sucha Singh Grewal from a Sikh background who was in the Army and chose to live in India. Overview as follows:

The 'Partition of India' in 1947 divided British India into two self-governing independent Dominions, those of India and Pakistan, as announced by Lord Mountbatten at a press conference on the 3rd June 1947 that outlined this division and its date of Independence in what became known as the 'Mountbatten Plan' or the '3 June Plan', and on the 18th July 1947 the British Parliament passed the 'Indian Independence Act' that finalised the arrangements for partition and essentially resulted in the dissolution of the British Raj, i.e. Crown rule of the Indian Subcontinent which in the end existed from 1858 until 1947. *Raj a Hindi word meaning State, Realm, Kingdom or Empire. On the 14th August 1947, the new Dominion of Pakistan came into being, with Muhammad Ali Jinnah sworn in as its first Governor-General in Karachi. The following day on the 15th August 1947, India, now Dominion of India, became an independent country, with official ceremonies taking place in New Delhi with the office of Prime Minister being assumed by Jawaharlal Nehru, and with Viceroy Mountbatten staying on as the country's first Governor General. Another key figure Mahatma Gandhi remained in Bengal to work with new refugees there from the partitioned subcontinent. This partition mainly involved the division of two provinces, Bengal and Punjab, based on district-wide non-Muslim or Muslim majorities. The partition also saw the division of the British Indian Army, the Royal Indian Navy (of which Nawab Din was a part), the Royal Indian Air Force, the Indian Civil Service, the Railways and the Central Treasury, immense undertakings.

The partition displaced between 10-20 million people along religious lines and created overwhelming calamity in the newly constituted dominions, as a result it has often been described as one of the largest refugee crises in history. There was large-scale violence accompanying the partition with varying estimates on the loss of life disputed between several hundred thousand and two million. The violent nature of the creation of these two new nation states produced an atmosphere of hostility and suspicion between India and Pakistan that sadly still affects their relationship to this day. Following its creation as a new country in August 1947, Pakistan applied for membership of the United Nations and was accepted by the U.N General Assembly on the 30th September 1947, India continued to have an existing seat as it had been a founding member of the United Nations since its inception on the 24th October 1945. On 26th January 1950 India became the Republic of India, and on 23rd March 1956 Pakistan became the Islamic Republic of Pakistan and still was at time of writing in 2022 along with the People's Republic of Bangladesh, originally East Pakistan.

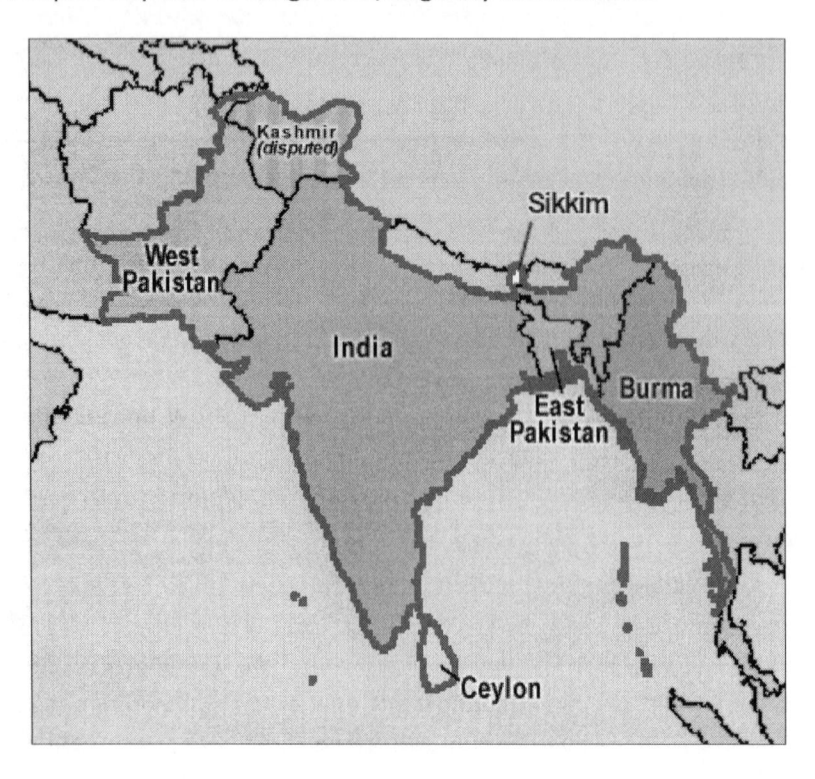

**Above – A map showing the Partition of that vast country/continent.**

Regarding the specific division of the Royal Indian Navy following India's independence, which is additionally mentioned here as another overview because of and in relation to Nawab Din's service within it, went as follows. The Armed Forces Reconstitution Committee divided the ships on the basis of two-thirds of the fleet to India and one third to Pakistan, based mainly on the size of their countries. The committee allocated to the RPN – Royal Pakistan Navy 3 of the 7 active sloops, HMIS Godavari, HMIS Hindustan, HMIS Narbada (all of which Nawab eventually served on), 4 out of 10 serviceable Minesweepers, 2 Frigates, 2 Naval Trawlers, 4 Harbour Launches and a number of Harbour Defence Motor Launches, 358 personnel and 180 officers, most of whom were Muslims or Europeans, volunteered to transfer to the RPN (including Nawab). India retained the remainder of the RIN's assets and personnel, and many British officers opted to continue serving in the RIN.

**Above left, the crest of the Indian Navy. Above Right, the crest of the Pakistan Navy, both of which Nawab served in. Above centre a picture from one of his ships, HMIS Narbada (U40), later HMPS Jhelum, showing the mixed Indian and British crew and in the background its blistered guns after extensive use in battle.**

Due to the transition of power and the dividing of the armed forces on the Indian continent during partition, as described above, Nawab was effectively one day a part of the British Royal Navy/Royal Indian Navy and the next day part of the Royal Pakistan Navy, which interestingly led to him as touched on before being part of the historical event that took place on the Admiral's Flagship where he was serving at the time, and as his daughter Abida found out later was also during that period where her father briefly met and shook the hand of the first Governor-General of Pakistan Muhammad Ali Jinnah **(Pictured)** also revered and known as Quaid Azam (Great Leader) and Baba Qaum (Father of the Nation), but other events also unfolded in the confusion of that tumultuous period and led to different experiences which Nawab mentioned during the interview when he said: "During the time they split up India and made Pakistan in 1947 it was a very big thing that was hard for many and changed the lives of millions of people who had to leave their old homes and make a new one with their families in other parts of the country, there were many refugees and in a lot of places violent things happening and people being killed, it changed the lives of people for good and bad but had an effect in one way or another on everyone living everywhere in India at that time. Even where we were in the Navy, and I think it was the same for all the different forces that were split between India and Pakistan, in our case we were in the Navy of one country before the partition and then in the Navy of another directly after! Not something many people in the military experience, we kept the same uniforms with the only difference being that we had a 'P' on the hat for Pakistan Navy and the ships flew some different flags, but even then in those early days things happened because people were nervous and there was much tension around and new borders and many problems.

~ 157 ~

Once we were fired on quite heavily with big guns by Pakistan forces that for some reason thought we were an Indian ship, many of us jumped overboard, even the ship's cat, in the end we were on shore for three days before we could re-join our ship and be on our way again, these kinds of confusions happened during the partition! I had many good years, friends and memory's and saw a lot of places thanks to the Navy, but in the end it was time for me to make the new life and think about my family and our future in our new country and so after more than five years in service I got permission to leave and the next part of my life began, but I was very happy that I volunteered and played my parts in those Navy's, I still laugh and smile when I think of those years." **Nawab served on all three of the sloops that were transferred to the Royal Pakistan Navy after the partition, the one shown here was his last, HMPS Hindustan later renamed HMPS/PNS Karsaz, she stayed in service with the aft retitled PN – Pakistan Navy until 1960.**

In his service record Nawab Din was described by a Commanding Officer-Captain as having a 'Very Good Character', something I certainly found to be true when I met him, with good humour he told the stories he could remember from his Navy days that still made him light up when he was sharing them. A great man who saw a lot, lived a lot and gave a lot, to the countries he served, to the family he loved and those who he met, which I am happy to say included me when I came to interview him, it was a pleasure to meet you Nawab, thank you for your service Sir. R.I.P. Gary.

## Additional Information and Life After Service

**Rank upon finish of service** – AB/S – Able-Bodied Seaman.

**Medals and Honours** – British 1939-45 War Medal, Pakistan Service Medal, Good Conduct Badge 1st Class (Awarded by the RPN in 1948 after service on the Admiral's Flagship 'Godavari').

**Post War Years** – After leaving the Navy in Karachi in 1949 Nawab had a very interesting and varied work history, he was in the Police Force 4 years and for a time was sent to help guard a prison in the city of Sahiwal (formerly known as Montgomery), later he changed his job and worked for many years in clothing and fabrics and had a shop in Lahore until 1962, both those cities in the Pakistani province of Punjab. In 1962 he changed his life completely by relocating to the United Kingdom and at first was living in Glasgow, Scotland where he was a Postman. By 1965 he and his family had moved to Rawtenstall in Lancashire where he became a bus driver around the Borough of Rossendale for 14 years until 1979, from then until retirement in 1988 aged 65 he regularly paid working visits to his home country of Pakistan where he was in charge of overseeing the building of commercial property around Ghansia in the Gujrat area of Pakistan where he originated from, later in 2008 he moved to Accrington in Lancashire, then by 2014 had moved to Radcliffe in Manchester where he remained close to his family until his passing on the 26th August 2019 aged 96. Nawab was married twice, first to Khurshid Begum (Din) from 1950 until her passing in 1987, and after this to Ismat (Din) from 1990 onwards. One of his greatest legacies was his huge family, having an incredible 5 Children, 1 Son & 4 Daughters, 19 Grandchildren and 23 Great-Grandchildren, all stemming from his first marriage.

**Associations and Organisations** – None.

# ROYAL AIR FORCE VETERANS

R.A.F. day raiders over Berlin's official quarter.

**INTO ACTION**

# LEADING AIRCRAFTMAN NEIL FLANIGAN MBE

Served with – Royal Air Force, Bomber Command, Ground Crew
Service Number – 713039
Interviewed – WASP HQ, London, 24th January 2015

## Service History and Personal Stories

- Born – Kingston, Jamaica, Date Not Disclosed.
- Neil joined the RAF in Kingston, Jamaica in Dec 1943 in response to a Recruitment drive being advertised in the Jamaican Gleaner where he signed up to be part of the British Commonwealth Forces, after coming to the United Kingdom in 1944 he completed basic training at RAF Cardington in Bedfordshire.
- He then went on to the No.12 School of Technical Training at RAF Melksham in Wiltshire which specialised in training Ground Crew and Technicians, the two main trade schools, Instrument and Electrical formed the main purpose of the station. Incredibly at its Zenith this major RAF Training Station housed over ten thousand personnel.
- After specialising in Instrument repair Neil was posted to a number of RAF Stations throughout his career which spanned from 1944 until 1948, mainly with No.4 Group 299 Squadron these included RAF Shepherds Grove in Suffolk, RAF Bramcote in Warwickshire.
- Whilst serving at RAF Keevil in Wiltshire he helped maintain and repair Sterling Bombers and Horsa Gliders for Field Marshal Montgomery's Operation Market Garden in Holland, mainly undertaken by the British 1st Airborne Division from 17th-25th September 1944.

- During his time in the RAF through completing specialist trade training as an Instrument Mechanic and attaining the practical experience gained through his hard work on many types of Aircraft such as the Lancaster, Oxford, Anson, DC 3 and those mentioned above, Neil managed to become an LAC – Leading Aircraftman.
- His service continued until after the war when Neil was finally demobbed at an RAF Clearing Station in Preston, Lancashire in 1948, he then went on to put the many skills he learnt in the Royal Air Force to very good use by continuing a career in the Civilian Aviation industry throughout the Caribbean and in the United Kingdom for another 35 years from 1948 until 1983, after this contributing greatly to his adopted country in many ways which led to a very well-deserved MBE – Most Excellent Order of the British Empire.

This book is full of incredible people from many parts of the United Kingdom who served our country during the Second World War and in Neil's case one who came from other side of the world from the safety of Jamaica in the West Indies. Neil and many other brave men and women like him made up a significant force of around 16,000 in total who came forward from the Caribbean Islands to serve the allied cause and who answered the county's call to arms during World War Two and were represented in all branches of our Armed forces, where like Neil they served with distinction. They did not have to come thousands of miles to help us when our country was genuinely in a great time of need, but still despite the very real danger to themselves they volunteered to do so regardless. Each contributing in their own special way through the determination they brought and the skills they learnt truly helped Great Britain and her Commonwealth forces defeat Nazism. Neil is another fine example of this, as a young man who had to leave his family to come to a strange unknown place far away affectionately known the 'Mother Country', where he learned a new trade in order to play his part in our war effort. From his hometown of Kingston to his service in RAF Bomber Command at Keevil, Neil arrived, did his bit and succeeded in many ways. Not quite sure what to expect before coming to England to serve in the RAF he now reflects and shares various thoughts from those early days, starting with being:

## THE 39th MAN TO VOLUNTEER FROM JAMAICA

"When I joined the Royal Air Force in Jamaica in Dec 1943 I did not think I would be in England, I did not know what war was all about, the tragedies, the traumas, the difficulties, and the other side of war, the death and the destruction. However, I was the 39th man to volunteer from Jamaica, and I was one of a batch of about 20 men from Jamaica coming over at that time on a long convoy across the Atlantic to Southampton, once in the UK we started our basic training at RAF Cardington in Bedfordshire, this we all did along with other Englishmen who were conscripted, because as you probably know Jamaicans were not conscripted, they were volunteers. Once we were reasonably trained after eight weeks we were marched out at a parade and then we were despatched to training camps to learn a skill or to join a squadron of the Royal Air Force. I was shipped off to learn how to repair instruments on the bombers and on the transport aircraft at RAF Melksham in Wilshire at the No.12 School of Technical Training. Naturally like with all new skills you have to spend many weeks in training and pass the exams and have the confidence to do the job on your own even at an early stage because manpower was short and the job difficult and you just had to get on with it, then after that you were sent to an operational base. You didn't realise the gravity of your responsibility at first but you soon learnt it, you had to get aircraft flying, you had to get them serviced, you had to keep them going, whether it be snowing or raining or it be sunshine, you were trained to take responsibility and do your job efficiently, we had to keep them flying, because if they weren't in the air then we could not help win the war! Your confidence grew as you grew older and to this end I suppose I survived well and became accustomed to it all. We all worked very hard but were treated equally and fairly in the Royal Air Force, as long as you pulled your weight and did what was expected of you and more when needed then you gained respect and were dealt with justly".

A wartime poster with a personal message from King George VI thanking all who came forward from the Commonwealth/British Empire to serve the United Kingdom during her darkest hours, of which Neil was one. Volunteers came forth from all corners of the earth to help when called, from as far away as Australia, New Zealand, Canada, Africa, Nepal, India, The Caribbean, and countries throughout Asia and the Middle-East. There was a huge ongoing recruitment drive in many countries to try and enlist as much manpower as possible and employ as many resources as possible to fight against the Axis powers in all theatres of war around the world. When the United Kingdom went to war in 1939 she effectively took with it her British Empire and was a major global power, with direct or de facto political and economic control of 25% of the world's population, and 30% of its land mass and the assets that lay within. But mobilizing and utilising these to fight their enemies would prove to be a massive worldwide logistical challenge, one which ran continuously throughout the war years.

"Throughout this bitter and terrible conflict, I have never doubted that the response of my colonial peoples to all calls made upon them would be swift, wholehearted, and complete. It is a wonderful thing for me to reflect that the promises of loyalty and support which so many of you sent to me in the darkest days of our history have been redeemed many times over." GEORGE R.I.

I have interviewed a number of veterans involved in Operation Market Garden from different perspectives, servicemen who were dropped as Airborne troops directly into the Arnhem battle zone and fought there, Glider Pilots who brought them in and Bomber Pilots who towed them, through to others who were with the XXX Corps trying to reach them on the ground and also involved in the final evacuation of the remaining troops across the Rhine in Operation Berlin. This interesting contribution from another unique viewpoint of Ground Crew is described here as Neil tells us about:

### OPERATION MARKET GARDEN AS SEEN BY THE GROUND CREW

"I was rather fortunate I went to work on many camps and went to work on one that had Sterling bombers, which was an aircraft that bombed the Germans but also had the capacity to pull gliders across. That was RAF Keevil near Trowbridge in Wiltshire as part of the 299 Squadron. We worked on Sterling Bombers and Horsa Gliders and helped prepare them for a very special airborne mission about to happen in Holland. I can recall the day the operation began, it was the 17th September 1944 and the sky was full of our planes and the gliders that were taking off loaded with men strapped with guns, bombs, and shipped off to the battle of Arnhem which unfortunately was not a success at that time, and after some of our planes did not come back. The casualties were high, the weather awful and the Germans especially later knew the British were coming, so it was a massacre, a terrible thing indeed, and I was there when we were seeing them off on that fateful day, us as ground crew watching all those young men going off to battle, so many of whom would not return, such a shame all those smiling soldiers not knowing what awaited them as they went on a mission which we later found out was meant to help bring the war to an end much sooner had it succeeded!"

The main purpose of 299 Squadron was to work with the airborne forces, both towing gliders and carrying paratroopers which they did on Operation Overlord on D-Day, Operation Market Garden at Arnhem, Operation Varsity into Germany. During Market Garden between 17th-23rd September 1944 the Squadron flew 54 glider towing sorties and 72 supply dropping missions, losing 5 aircraft.

The Short Stirling Bomber towing off an Airspeed Horsa Glider, this is what Neil would have seen on that September morning in 1944 at RAF Keevil as they embarked to join the great air armada flying to Holland for Operation Market Garden. In March 1944 RAF No.196 and 299 Squadrons along with Short Stirling glider tugs of No.38 Group RAF arrived at Keevil, later followed by large numbers of Horsa Gliders, crewed by Army pilots of the Glider Pilot Regiment. All those who were involved knew a big operation was afoot.

The motto of 299 Squadron which Neil worked closely with was; Par Nobile Fratrum – 'A Noble Pair of Brothers', symbolising their close association with the Army Airborne Forces, and is also I think a fitting motto to remember those people like Neil Flanigan who came thousands of miles to stand by and serve with us, those who through their personal sacrifices became our brothers. Thank you Neil for standing up, coming forward and being one of those who helped when it really mattered.

## Additional Information and Life After Service

**Rank upon finish of service** – LAC – Leading Aircraftman.

**Medals and Honours** – 1939-45 Defence Medal, 1939-45 War Medal, MBE.

**Post War Years** – 1948-1955 Returned to Jamaica and worked for Public and Private aircraft companies such as British Overseas Airways, British Caribbean Airways, British West Indian Airways, as a Senior Instrument Mechanic and Aircraft Engineer servicing planes in a number of locations in the Caribbean including Jamaica, Bahamas, Trinidad. In 1955 Neil came back to England and worked for Private and Public Airlines such as Airworks, Silvercity, Dan Air, British European Airways and British Airways as an Aircraft Engineer until he retired from the Aviation Industry in 1983. From 1983-2002 Neil became a Freelance Financial Consultant and being semi-retired put the rest of his time into a lot of community related work in and around Lambeth, London, listed below. In 2002 Neil was honoured with an MBE for his very commendable work on various committees and associations and on community and veteran related projects in the London borough of Lambeth. He married Mavis in 1951 and they were together for 59 years, and has 2 Sons, 2 Daughters and 4 Grandchildren, and as Neil said "A Great Many Great-Grandchildren, about 15 I think!"

**Associations and Organisations** – President of WASP - West Indian Association of Service Personnel and various other positions within the organisation over the years such as Chairman, Vice-Chairman, Secretary, Director/Coordinator and Trustee over a 17-year period. Also Vice-Chairman for Victim Support in Lambeth, Vice-Chairman of Community Police Consultative Group for Lambeth, Independent Adjudicator for Hampshire under the Children's Act.

# FLIGHT SERGEANT WALTER BENTLEY

Served with – Royal Air Force, Bomber Command, 570 & 196 Squadrons
Service Number – 1549633
Interviewed – Salford, Greater Manchester, 19th April 2018

## Service History and Personal Stories

- Born – 5th September 1921, Lower Broughton, Salford, Lancashire, England, UK.
- Walter volunteered for the RAF in April 1942 in Manchester, after this he was sent down to London to an ACRC – Air Crew Recruitment Centre for selection and aptitude tests to ascertain if he was capable of becoming a Pilot, after which a very long process of ongoing training and assessment took place that would last 2.4 years from May 1942-September 1944.
- This consisted of the following; In 1942; ACDW – Air Crew Drill Wing, Brighton, Sussex. No.3 ITW – Initial Training Wing, Torquay, Devon. Followed by No.28 EFTS – Elementary Flight Training School, Wolverhampton, West Midlands (flying Tiger Moths). ACDC – Air Crew Dispersal Centre, Heaton Park, Manchester. RMS Andes; Gourock, Scotland to Nova Scotia, Canada.
- In 1943; No.5 BFTS – Basic Flying Training School, Clewiston, Florida, U.S.A for 8 months intense training (flying Boeing Stearman and North American Harvards). RMS Queen Elizabeth return crossing from Nova Scotia, Canada to Gourock, Scotland. No.18 AFU – Advanced Flying Unit, RAF Snitterfield, Warwickshire, (flying Airspeed Oxfords).

~ 164 ~

- In 1944; No.1514 BAT – Beam Approach Training Flight, RAF Fiskerton, Lincolnshire. No.42 OTU – Operational Training Unit, RAF Ashbourne, Derbyshire (flew Whitworth Whitley Bombers/Trainers). No.1665 HCU – Heavy Conversion Unit, RAF Tilstock, Shropshire (flew Short Stirling four-engine Bombers, his operational aircraft during active service).
- On 21st August 1944 Walter qualified as a First Pilot, 1 month after this he was on his first active service posting at RAF Harwell in Berkshire with 570 Squadron 'A-Flight' (serving there from 23.09.44 until 06.01.46), on 23rd September 1944 every bit of previous training would count when he was sent to Arnhem as part of Operation Market Garden on his 1st flight and was shot down in Stirling LK 191, safely crash landing near Nijmegen, saving the lives of his crew, 7 days later on the 30th September he was 'back in the saddle' and flying once again! 570 Squadron was relocated to RAF Rivenhall in Essex on 7th October 1944.
- Walter's very busy Flight Log Book also revealed that during 'Active Duty Flying' he and his crew completed over 30 missions of many different kinds during the war in Europe, these included bombing Operations in support of advancing ground troops in key strategical locations such as Xanten, Germany as part of Operation Veritable in February 1945, towing a glider into battle as part of Operation Varsity on 24th March 1945 for the Rhine crossings, dropping SOE Agents into Holland, Denmark and Norway and doing other resupply drops.
- Dozens more missions followed after the war in Europe finished for things such as flying in Airborne troops of the 1st A.B Division to Norway for surrender of German forces during Operation Doomsday in May 1945, repatriation of Allied serviceman and Women of every description including bringing back A.T.S Nurses and returning Allied POW's from Belgium, Germany, Czechoslovakia and Cairo, Egypt, plus internal troop and supply flights between many bases in Europe and Allied glider retrievals and tows plus much more.
- The post-war operations which Walter piloted on took place between May 1945 to March 1946, during that time he was posted to his 2nd Squadron still flying the Short Stirling Bomber, this was 196 Squadron 'B Flight' at RAF Shepherds Grove in Suffolk (serving there from 08.01.46 until 21.03.46). After this Walter was sent to an ACHU – Air Crew Holding Unit at RAF Pocklington in the East Riding of Yorkshire, and finally on the 9th July 1946 he was demobbed at SHQ – Station Head Quarters at RAF Ossington in Nottinghamshire.

Walter Bentley, a very unassuming gentleman, a Bespoke Cabinet maker and lover of model trains who if you passed him in the street or saw him in a pub you'd never imagine or have any indication of what he did in World War Two in what he called his 'previous life.' What this local Salford lad actually did at age 20 was volunteer for the Royal Air Force, putting away his tools switching off his machines and leaving his very safe, settled and steady life at the CWS Furniture Factory in Radcliffe, Greater Manchester to learn how to fly huge 4 engine Heavy Bombers in the U.S.A and around the U.K and then go headlong into battle undertaking very dangerous missions over Nazi Occupied Europe and Scandinavia, which along the way led to remarkable events such as being shot down at Arnhem on his very first operation where under enemy fire he showed amazing skill for such an inexperienced pilot when he safely crash landed his burning Stirling bomber managing to save himself and all the crew on-board, and within a week was again behind the controls of a new aircraft! Then during the next 1 year and 10 months of active flying duty he was involved in everything from Bombing missions to dropping SOE Agents on special 'Covert Opps' against the Nazis, and later towing gliders as part of a massive allied invasion force over the Rhine into Germany to doing eventual repatriation flights for servicemen returning from war zones throughout Europe and North Africa! Then after demob in September 1946 came back home to Salford, took out his tools again and returned to his old steady job as a skilled Cabinet Maker at the CWS where he stayed for the next four decades diligently chipping, sanding and machining away with his daily tea and biscuits on the go and never getting behind the controls of an aircraft ever again! A brave man who came forward when his country needed him, did his duty and when his service was over simply went home again and with no fuss got on with his life! Over seven decades later I was very fortunate to meet him and secure this first official interview to capture his incredible story. So here is First Pilot Walter Bentley sharing with us what it was like:

**FLYING IN THE RAF AND BEING SHOT DOWN AT ARNHEM ON HIS VERY FIRST MISSION**

"It all started in the spring of 1942 when I went to a recruitment office in City Centre Manchester that I think was near the Cathedral, I only popped in to make enquiries and eventually ended up being a pilot! Silly boy what was I thinking? Well actually the main reason I went to see the RAF was that I didn't want to go in the Army because I always remember as a young lad growing up, I'd had a few conversations with men who'd been in the First World War, there were still a lot of them around in those days, and what they described about the trenches and the things they'd been through and witnessed sounded horrific, I remember it really shocked me and always stuck with me! I thought to myself I don't want anything like that to happen to me, and also from what we could gather the Navy were having a really rough time of it with the U-boats and I didn't fancy going to sea anyway, but flying sounded good and might be safer, how wrong I turned out to be! During the recruitment process I was told by an officer that my maths might not be good enough to pass as a Pilot, to which I replied 'I thought I was going to have to fight the Germans, not educate them!' Anyway two years later after finishing training in America and Britain I had got my wings and was the First Pilot of a four-engine Stirling Bomber in 570 Squadron, and on the 23rd September 1944 was on the way to a place called Arnhem on the 'Market' part of the huge Operation Market-Garden. A very memorable day alright, we were doing supply drops to the men of the 1st Airborne Division who by all accounts were in a fair bit of trouble on the ground, the Nazis were really giving them a serious mauling, but as we soon found out a lot of aircraft that were going in to try and help were also getting same treatment and becoming casualties as well, and we soon joined them after getting shot down by heavy German Anti-Aircraft fire. I had to do my best to land a bomber that had two engines and a wing on fire and hopefully save my crew. It was a real struggle but I managed to crash land it, wheels up in a farmer's field, and we were all able, thank God, to scramble out of the wreckage unscathed and walk away, not only that but we were also lucky enough to have landed behind our lines so we were picked up by our own troops, which led to us being back in England with me behind the controls of a new Stirling Bomber within a week!"

I asked Water to tell us more about his wartime flying and he explained: "We were sent on many different kinds of operations, daytime and nighttime missions, a big one in the day was Operation Varsity which was a 'Mass Lift' as they called it where many of us towed a glider, a Horsa I think, again under heavy AA fire to drop troops over the River Rhine into Germany as part of the big allied push going on there in March 1945, when we were in the air I remember saying to myself I wish this bloody bugger behind would fly straight, not be all over the sky, he jerked down and up you know, dangerous because if they shot up or down too quickly they could take you with them! At the end of the war in Europe we also flew men and supplies into Gardermoen near Oslo in Norway on the ominously named Operation Doomsday as part of the German surrender there, that involved helping the 1st Airborne Division again who I don't think had done anything since what happened to them at Arnhem! In between those things we flew a lot of missions at night as well such as some bombing raids to soften up targets and support ground forces ahead of their advances in Germany, and very interestingly dropped SOE (Special Operations Executive) agents into Holland, Denmark and Norway along with their supplies, and other times we just flew in much needed equipment on resupply drops to them at locations on certain coordinates of the map in parts of occupied Europe. We also did troop repatriations after the war collecting our forces from Europe, Scandinavia and North Africa. Interesting times!" **Above - The Badge of Royal Air Force No.196 Squadron.**

A nice photo as it shows First Pilot Walter (top left) pictured with his crew (top row) and also ground crew (bottom row) with their Short Stirling bomber behind them as part of 570 Squadron at RAF Harwell in Berkshire. During his time as a pilot Walter flew the Mark III, IV and V Stirling's.

As his Flight Log book indicates he undertook many Operations and accumulated an impressive total flying time of 1023 hrs 30 mins a lot of which was on active service under intense battle conditions completing a full tour and more, and I asked him did he ever do any more flying as a pilot after the war? He replied in his very relaxed and modest manner; "No I didn't, I decided once was enough, you know that was good enough for me, I didn't want any more after everything we'd been through! I was happy to just return home and go back to cabinet making, a lot more peaceful, no one shooting at me there! He added; I was proud to achieve what I did in becoming a pilot, but I was just an ordinary bloke doing my bit, that was all!" My reply; 'An ordinary bloke who did extraordinary bits!'

Some of those 'Extraordinary Bits' from Walter's Flight Log Book, which makes for particularly interesting reading, relating to the story he told us earlier, showing an entry in red ink for his very first active-duty mission on September 23rd 1944 as - Ops 'Market' Resupply, shot down Arnhem. Followed a week later by his next flight on the 30th which simply states – Air Test.

~ 167 ~

Walter was an unassuming yet matter of fact 96-year-old veteran when I interviewed him in 2018 and one of the very few WW2 Stirling Bomber Pilots left in the country. He still had a cheeky smile and a twinkle in his eye which led me to believe that he lived his life and served his country in line with one of his RAF Squadrons mottos, shown on its badge within the pages of his story, that of 196, which says; Sic Fidem Servamus – 'Thus We Keep Faith'. It's a privilege to have met you Sir.

## Additional Information and Life After Service

**Rank upon finish of service** – Flight Sergeant.

**Medals and Honours** – 1939-45 War Medal, 1939-45 Star with Bomber Command Clasp, France-Germany Star.

**Post War Years** – From 1946 until his retirement aged 65 in 1986 Walter returned to the place where he did his apprenticeship before the war at the CWS Furniture factory at Dumers Lane Radcliffe, there he went back to his old job as a Cabinet Maker and used to cycle to work and back, 5 miles each way every day in all weathers for 40 years! He married Gladys in 1951 in Salford. No Children.

**Associations and Organisations** – The Manchester Model Railway Society, Macclesfield Model Railway Group, Salford Veterans Breakfast Club.

# FIRST PILOT JIM GARDENER DFC

Served with – Royal Air Force, Bomber Command, 51 Squadron
Service Number – 187435
Interviewed – Whitefield, Manchester, 22nd July 2015

### Service History and Personal Stories

- Born – 25th August 1921, Heaton Park, Manchester, England, UK.
- Jim began his wartime service on the Home Front with a spell in the Home Guard between 1940 to 1941, and was posted to help guard Heaton Park Reservoir in North Manchester. Quickly realising the army was not for him he volunteered for the RAF at Dover Street Recruitment Centre, Manchester in June 1941, and soon after was sent to RAF Padgate in Warrington where he passed selection for aircrew.
- Then on to an ACRC – Air Crew Receiving Centre at St. John's Wood London for Pilot aptitude tests, once these were successfully completed Jim began training to be a pilot in earnest, starting with basic drilling at an ITW – Initial Training Wing at Thorney Island near Chichester, West Sussex, then back up to his home area at Heaton Park, Manchester, Lancashire which was being used as a huge ACDC – Air Crew Dispersal Centre where Jim awaited his next big move which would be overseas.

- This would see him sent to Canada for most of 1942 as part of a massive joint military aircrew training program known as the BCATP – British Commonwealth Air Training Plan AKA EATS – Empire Air Training Scheme often simply referred to as 'The Plan'.
- 1942 like the war years that followed would be an action packed time for Jim, as he trained at the No.33 EFTS – Elementary Flying Training School at Caron in the province of Saskatchewan completing 50 hours on De Havilland Tiger Moths, then onto No.35 SFTS – Service Flying Training School at North Battleford, Saskatchewan flying 150 hours on Airspeed Oxfords after which he received his wings there in August 1942 followed that same month by him celebrating his 21st Birthday in New York whilst on leave. Eventually in November that year Jim returned back to the U.K on the famous Liner Queen Elizabeth.
- As he was originally earmarked for Coastal Command the next part of his training continued with them in 1943 at various RAF Coastal Stations around the U.K with No.5 OTU – (Coastal) Operational Training Unit at RAF Turnberry, Scotland, at RAF Long Kesh, Northern Ireland where he flew Bristol Beauforts, then returning to RAF Turnberry where he completed torpedo training on the Clyde, and he also gained more flying experience on the Beaufort with No.306 Ferry Training Unit at RAF Templeton, South Wales.
- Now being proficient with flying that aircraft Jim was chosen to pilot one of 15 new Bristol Beaufort twin-engine torpedo bombers on a mammoth 39.5-hour ADF – Aircraft Delivery Flight from RAF Portreath, a Coastal Command Station in Cornwall, destined for Ceylon (Sri Lanka). They flew via Gibraltar, Morocco, Libya, Egypt, Palestine, Iraq, Bahrain, Karachi, after a change of plan ending up at Jodhpur, India, then spending time in Poona. Returning to the U.K via the Suez Canal on the troopship RMS Strathmore arriving early 1944.
- Once back Jim's destiny would change as he was re-designated to continue flight training this time with Bomber Command and was sent to RAF Watchfield BAS - Beam Approach School in Swindon, Wiltshire. Next moving onto heavier bomber aircraft at No.10 OTU - Operational Training Unit at RAF Abingdon and RAF Stanton Harcourt, Oxfordshire on the Armstrong Whitworth Whitley then finally progressing to RAF Marston Moor at Tockwith, North Yorkshire, home to No.1652 HCU – Heavy Conversion Unit flying Handley Page Halifax MK II Heavy Bombers, preparing them for their jump to an active-duty squadron.
- Their instructor Reg Levy had previously completed a full tour with No.51 Squadron at RAF Snaith near Goole in Yorkshire and suggested Jim and his crew apply to go there, they were accepted and between September 1944 to April 1945 undertook 37 Active-duty Operations with 51 Squadron as part of 4 Group, Bomber Command on the Halifax MK III Heavy Bomber over the perilous skies of enemy occupied Europe.
- More variation followed once Jim had finished his 'Tour' and in the following 12 months he went on to train as an Instructor at RAF Montrose in Scotland and with No.7 Flying Instructors School at RAF Upavon in Wiltshire, was Commissioned and became a Flying-Pilot Officer and received the DFC – Distinguished Flying Cross.
- As a qualified Instructor Jim taught on Airspeed Oxfords at RAF Charmy Down in Somerset and after VJ Day had been posted to RAF Croughton in Northamptonshire teaching Army personnel on General Aircraft Hotspur Gliders and the Miles Master aircraft that towed them. He demobbed in late May 1946 at RAF Uxbridge, Middlesex after 5 years of service.
- In a later achievement Jim was one of the key people behind the RAF Aircrew Memorial plaque that is located on Heaton Hall Orangery at Heaton Park, Manchester, close to where he lived most his life and where he was one of the 133,516 RAF personnel to pass through this big training and ACDC – Air Crew Despatch Centre during World War Two.

Back in the summer of 2015 Jim Gardener was the first bomber pilot and the first DFC – Distinguished Flying Cross holder I was fortunate enough to interview. I found this veteran of 37 very dangerous Operations quite by chance when told of him by an acquaintance who said he lived opposite a World War Two bomber pilot, at first to be honest I was not completely convinced because that was a claim I had heard before on a number of occasions from people and the individuals involved were respectfully part of a bomber crew but not a pilot. In this particular instance it proved to be absolutely true and showed that every lead is worth following, thank you for that Samir. As a result of this I was delighted to get a great interview with this very interesting Royal Air Force veteran who despite being in the thick of the action completed, survived and brought his crew through more than the 30 'Ops' that were required for one full tour of duty, something not many crews achieved with the terribly high attrition rate of Bomber Command. During his diverse time in the RAF Jim flew and delivered a Bristol Beaufort from the UK all the way to Jodhpur in India in a flight that took just under 40 hours, piloted a Handley Page Halifax hitting many different targets during the air war over heavily defended enemy countries in Europe and near the end of his service became an instructor on General Aircraft Hotspur Gliders. Jim now shares with us some of his thoughts, feelings and experiences and tells us how it was:

### COMPLETING 37 OPERATIONS OVER NAZI OCCUPIED EUROPE

"As you can imagine all sorts of things occurred during raids, for example there were cases of bombers opening their bomb doors and unintentionally dropping devices on friendly aircraft below them, not something you hear a great deal about generally but it did occasionally happen when you had hundreds of bombers flying on the same headings towards a target and other factors that could sometimes come into play that could add to difficulties, such as being caught up temporarily in a slipstream of another bomber and having your vision impeded and turbulence created that could lead to you inadvertently straying under the path of other aircraft, once my mid-upper gunner told me to move quickly and do a corkscrew manoeuvre because he could see what he thought was that same scenario unfolding on an aircraft above us during an op, I managed to take us out of harm's way that time and avoid what I guess they call 'Friendly Fire!' More common dangers that every Bomber Crew faced were things like Anti-Aircraft fire, very heavy flak coming up with tracers lighting up the sky at night or countless puffs of smoke with accompanying explosions all around you if it was day, we had to continue working through it when hitting heavily defended targets such as Cologne, Hamburg, Essen and others, and it could be a bit unsettling to see aircraft getting hit and going down in flames, sometimes later on you'd find out that they were your mates from the squadron and on a few occasions when back at the station we saw the WAAF girls tearful as they did their job and cleared out the lockers of the friends they had lost! But on the whole compared to many others our crew was very lucky, we had a few scrapes and close calls such as one shell exploding near us and shrapnel coming through our windscreen, which made it a bit cold on the way home and encountering a couple of night fighters on missions but with evasive actions we got through and managed to survive 37 operations with no crew member losing their life that's the most important thing!" I went on to ask Jim about one operation in particular that I wanted to elaborate on because of its (somewhat controversial) historical significance and that was Dresden, having previously interviewed a veteran that we both knew who was directly involved in that operation I was interested in the part Jim had to play in it on the 13th February 1945 which was a little different, as he was in the diversionary force not the main attack on the city itself, and I was told: "On the way in we headed the main force who were well behind us, the idea being to try and divert some of the defences off the main force, initially we moved towards Dresden then we sheared off to create the impression the force was going to head that way, eventually we bombed a port area called Bohlen which was near Leipzig and hit what I think was a chemical factory, but we of course saw the raids on the city developing, they were that prolific you could see the fires of Dresden long after, even as we approached the Dutch coast! There was a glow in the sky from the firestorms, we knew what the hell it was and we also read all about it the next day. During our 'Tour' we conducted raids over Holland, France, Germany, the heavily defended Krupps Works at Essen in the Ruhr, I.G Farben Chemical Works at Mannheim and areas around the Rhine, also at Chemnitz (where there was also Sachsenburg Concentration Camp). We hit cities, docks and marshalling yards, fuel storage depots, synthetic oil plants, did area bombing, Army support and part of the diversionary forces on raids at Lubeck and as mentioned here at Dresden. It was heavy bombing but remember places over here had similar experiences during our Blitz, Manchester, Coventry, London and many others with thousands of our people killed in a war we didn't start and didn't want! As Churchill said 'they will reap the whirlwind' and they did, big paybacks maybe but as they say all is fair in love and war!" **A Handley Page Halifax like Jim's shown here along with the positions of the 7-man crew in this interesting wartime RAF 'Join An Air Crew' recruitment poster.**

The most famous and well-known bomber of the Second World War for most people is the AVRO Lancaster, but of course there were other very effective Bombers that the RAF had at its disposal and in its arsenal, and for this reason I have included some additional information regarding the aircraft in which Jim undertook his 37 missions with No.51 Squadron. The Handley Page 4-Engine Heavy Bomber has an impressive service record, the first beginning with the Royal Air Force in 1940 and the last finishing with the Pakistani Air Force where they were retired in 1961. During their service with RAF Bomber Command in World War Two Halifaxes flew 82,773 operations, dropped 224,207 tons of bombs! The Halifax was additionally flown in large numbers by other Commonwealth and Allied nations, such as the RAAF - Royal Australian Air Force and the RCAF – Royal Canadian Air Force and also by the Free French Air Force and Polish Forces. 6176 were built, sadly of these 1833 aircraft were lost. They were also used in HCU's – Heavy Conversion Units as part of pilot training. Various improved versions of the Halifax were introduced with further upgraded features such as more powerful engines, an increased payload and a revised defensive turret, it remained in service with Bomber Command not only in bombing roles, but specialised versions of it were also developed and used for Paradrop and Troop Transport operations, but following the end of World War Two the RAF quickly phased out and retired the aircraft, after the type was succeeded as a strategic bomber by the Avro Lincoln, the advanced derivative of the Lancaster.

**Above - A Handley Page Halifax MK.1 with Ground Crew doing vital maintenance work.**

Halifax Bomber series production, began at Handley Page's factory at Cricklewood in London, (shown here in the picture), and at English Electric's site at Samlesbury, Lancashire. The 'Halifax Group' was established to oversee a massive manufacturing programme, and at its height during the war years consisted throughout the U.K of a staggering 41 separate factories and dispersed units, along with 600 subcontractors and 51,000 employees! Within that umbrella group were some big companies such as London Aircraft Production Group, Fairy Aviation and the Rootes Group, the latter through its 'Rootes Securities' arm of the business managing a big 'Shadow Factory' on behalf of the Air Ministry at what became RAF Speke in Liverpool, where they built an impressive 1070 Halifaxes, one-sixth of all those produced during the Second World War! This bit is being expanded upon because of a direct and proud personal connection I have to this part of the story, with my Grandad George Weir Bridson (Pictured) having worked there during the war years as an Aircraft Engineer involved in the Halifax Heavy Bomber project, and later he was chosen to be a 'Liaison Officer' for Rootes Securities, partly responsible for, amongst other things, public relations/contracting and procurement.

Crew picture with Jim in the centre under MH 'V' for Victor their Halifax MK III, taken on 8th April 1945 after the 37th and final mission on 51 Squadron flying from RAF Snaith in North Yorkshire, Jim fondly stated about his RAF days: "I have got to say I really enjoyed and embraced my time serving in the RAF, on the Squadron we flew hard and we played hard!" Jim's RAF achievements can be very appropriately summed up in the 2 mottos most directly connected to his branch of service, that of Bomber Command (Strike Hard Strike Sure) and of 51 Squadron (Swift & Sure), they are a great tribute to both him and all the brave men of Bomber Command who went out on dangerous 'Ops' day and night, many of whom never returned!

## Additional Information and Life After Service

**Rank upon finish of service** – Flying Officer.

**Medals and Honours** – 1939-45 War Medal, 1939-45 Defence Medal, 1939-45 Star with Bomber Command Clasp, France-Germany Star and DFC – Distinguished Flying Cross.

**Post War Years** – From 1946 until his retirement aged 60 in 1981 Jim worked as a Salesman for some big insurance companies such as Guardian Assurance and Marine Insurance, and for the latter he ended up as an Insurance Inspector. Married Grace in 1948, they were together for 50 years until her passing in 1998. Children; 1 Daughter, 1 Grandchild, 1 Great-Grandchild.

**Associations and Organisations** – Aircrew Association (Manchester Branch), Old Waconians' Association (Cheadle Hulme School Alumni), ACII – Association of Chartered Insurers Institute.

# OPERATIONAL TOUR
## FLYING OFFICER J.C. (JIM) GARDNER D.F.C.
### 51 SQUADRON RAF, SNAITH, 4 GROUP BOMBER COMMAND
### HANDLEY PAGE HALIFAX III

| OP | DATE | TARGET | DAY | NIGHT | NOTES |
|---|---|---|---|---|---|
| 1 | 3rd Sept. 1944 | Venlo | 3.45 | | 675 a/c, raids on 6 airfields in Holland |
| 2 | 23rd Sept. 1944 | Neuss (Ruhr) | | 4.55 | 549 a/c, docks & factories |
| 3 | 25th Sept. 1944 | Calais | 3.15 | | 872 a/c, defensive positions |
| 4 | 26th Sept. 1944 | Cap Gris Nez | 3.05 | | 531 a/c, defensive positions |
| 5 | 27th Sept. 1944 | Calais | 3.30 | | 341 a/c, defensive positions |
| 6 | 6th Oct. 1944 | Sterkrade | 4.20 | | 320 a/c, synthetic oil plant |
| 7 | 7th Oct. 1944 | Cleve | 4.45 | | 351 a/c, Army support target |
| 8 | 9th Oct. 1944 | Bochum | | 5.35 | 415 a/c, factories |
| 9 | 14th Oct. 1944 | Duisberg | | 5.10 | 1013 a/c, docks etc. |
| 10 | 15th Oct. 1944 | Wilhelmshaven | 1.15 | 3.40 | (Part in daylight) 506 a/c, business & residential areas |
| 11 | 23rd Oct. 1944 | Essen | | 5.35 | 1055 a/c, Krupps |
| 12 | 16th Nov. 1944 | Julich | 5.05 | | 1188 a/c, Army support |
| 13 | 18th Nov. 1944 | Munster | 5.00 | | 479 a/c, area bombing |
| 14 | 29th Nov. 1944 | Essen | | 5.05 | 316 a/c, Krupps |
| 15 | 30th Nov. 1944 | Duisberg | | 6.10 | 576 a/c, area bombing |
| 16 | 2nd Dec. 1944 | Hagen | | 6.15 | 504 a/c, industrial area |
| 17 | 5th Dec. 1944 | Soest | | 6.00 | 497 a/c, railway installations |
| 18 | 6th Dec. 1944 | Osnabruck | | 5.15 | 453 a/c, railway yards, factories |
| 19 | 28th Dec. 1944 | Opladen | | 5.30 | 328 a/c, marshalling yards |
| 20 | 2nd Jan. 1945 | Mannheim / Ludwigshafen | | 6.50 | 389 a/c, I.G. Farben chemicals |
| 21 | 5th Jan. 1945 | Hannover | | 5.25 | 664 a/c, city area |
| 22 | 13th Jan. 1945 | Saarbrucken | | 6.35 | 274 a/c, railway yards |
| 23 | 14th Jan. 1945 | Dulmen | | 6.20 | 115 a/c, fuel storage depot |
| 24 | 28th Jan. 1945 | Stuttgart | | 6.30 | 602 a/c, railway yards |
| 25 | 13th Feb. 1945 | Bohlen (Leipzig) | | 8.15 | Diversion for Dresden main force. 368 a/c, synthetic oil plant |
| 26 | 18th Feb. 1945 | Wesel | 4.50 | | 298 a/c, Army support |
| 27 | 21st Feb. 1945 | Worms | | 6.45 | 349 a/c, area attack |
| 28 | 24th Feb. 1945 | Kamen | 5.45 | | 340 a/c, synthetic oil plant |
| 29 | 2nd Mar. 1945 | Cologne | 5.30 | | 858 a/c, area bombing |
| 30 | 3rd Mar. 1945 | Kamen | | 6.30 | 234 a/c, synthetic oil plant |
| 31 | 5th Mar. 1945 | Chemnitz | | 8.35 | 760 a/c, city area damaged & Siegmar factory |
| 32 | 8th Mar. 1945 | Hamburg | | 6.00 | 312 a/c, shipyards |
| 33 | 11th Mar. 1945 | Essen | 5.35 | | 1079 a/c, area bombing |
| 34 | 13th Mar. 1945 | Barmen | 6.05 | | 358 a/c, area bombing |
| 35 | 15 Mar. 1945 | Hagen | | 5.55 | 267 a/c, area bombing |
| 36 | 4th April 1945 | Hamburg | | 5.50 | 327 a/c, Rhenania oil plant |
| 37 | 8th April 1945 | Travemunde | | 5.35 | Diversion for main force on Lubeck. 22 Halifaxes of 4 Group, including 51 Squadron |

Totals- Day/Night    61.45    144.15
Grand Total            216.00

Information about the overall operations of Bomber Command on the dates in question are printed in blue.

Above – A printed sheet put together by Jim detailing his 37 Operations between 3rd September 1944 to 8th April 1945, showing a real variation of targets during day time and night time missions.

# FLIGHT LIEUTENANT RUSSELL WAUGHMAN DFC AFC

Served with – Royal Air Force, Bomber Command, 101 Special Duty Squadron
plus RAF Training Command & RAF Transport Command
Service Number – 171904
Interviewed – Kenilworth, Warwickshire, 10th July 2018

## Service History and Personal Stories

- Born – 19th January 1923, Shotley Bridge, County Durham, England, UK.
- Russell Ray Waughman AKA Rusty, the nickname he prefers, began his extremely interesting service at the age of 16 when he joined the LDV – Local Defence Volunteers, which later became the Home Guard and from 1939-1940 guarded a number of key places of importance in the North-East such as the Tyne Bridge in Newcastle-upon-Tyne.
- In order to pursue his dream of becoming a pilot Rusty volunteered for the Royal Air Force in April 1940 aged 17, whilst waiting for formal acceptance at the required age of 18 he joined the ATC – Air Training Corps (King George VI was their Air-Commodore-in-Chief) still in its infancy, where he undertook drills and lectures ready for the RAF from 1940-1941.
- Then in April 1941 went for his medical at RAF Padgate in Warrington and in May 1941 was sworn in at RAF Heaton Park in Manchester. Later in August 1941 he was sent to an ACRC – Air Crew Reception Centre based at London Zoo in Regents Park and another at Lords Cricket Ground where further aptitude tests were undertaken.

- After passing all these entry tests Rusty's journey with the RAF was now really getting underway, in September 1941 he went to ITW – Initial Training Wing, Newquay to do the PNB – Pilot/Navigator/Bomber ground training which due to circumstances he completed at Stratford-upon-Avon, with the practical flying part taking place at No.28 EFTS – Elementary Flying Training School, Wolverhampton on Tiger Moths until 10 hours solo was completed.
- Once all this basic training was successfully undertaken by May 1942 Rusty was back at RAF Heaton Park ACDC – Air Crew Distribution Centre in Manchester from where he was sent to Liverpool to board the converted Polish Cruise Liner SS Batory. This was to take him and many others over to Canada to be part of the ETS – Empire Training Scheme.
- After arrival in Canada Rusty was sent to No.31 EFTS – Elementary Flight Training School at RAF Station De Winton in the province of Alberta, training on single-engine Tiger Moth and Stearman aircraft from June to August 1942. Then came the next step which was the conversion to twin-engine Oxford aircraft during training at No.34 SFTS – Service Flying Training School at Medicine Hat, Alberta and No. 32 SFTS at Moose Jaw, Saskatchewan.
- It was whilst at No.32 SFTS on the 5th December 1942 that Rusty qualified as a pilot and received his wings at only 19 years of age, a huge achievement. But there was still a lot of training ahead. He returned to the U.K on the famous cruise liner RMS Queen Elizabeth in January 1943 with thousands of other allied troops from New York to Greenock, Scotland.
- Then throughout 1943 it was on to the next stages of pilot training at other units such as No.28 OTU – Operational Training Unit at RAF Castle Donnington, now East Midlands Airport, where he flew the two-engine Vickers Wellington Bomber with 5 crew who would stay with him the rest of the war, and onto No.1662 HCU – Heavy Conversion Unit at RAF Blyton in Lincolnshire where he moved up to flying the four-engine Hanley Page Halifax.
- Then by November 1943 he had completed the last phase of his Pilot training at the LFS – Lancaster Finishing School which was also based at RAF Blyton, after conversion onto what would become his main wartime aircraft the AVRO Lancaster.
- 2 years of Pilot training were now complete and active service on an Operational Squadron commenced for Rusty in November 1943 and would last until June 1944, during which time he flew and unlike many other pilots survived 30 Operations or 'Full Tour' with the No.101 SDS – Special Duty Squadron flying over Germany, France and Belgium.
- He flew specially converted 8-man Lancaster bombers with secret radio jamming equipment called Cigar to help stop interception by the German Luftwaffe, more about this later when described by Rusty, and they completed many missions including Berlin, which he did on 5 occasions and dreaded by aircrew because of very high casualty rates.
- During his time with No.101 Squadron at RAF Ludford Magna in Lincolnshire Rusty became a Commissioned Officer on 6th February 1944, and was awarded a Green Endorsement for exemplary flying when returning his Lancaster to base after a mid-air collision during an operation on marshalling yards at Hasselt on the Belgium-German border, 11th May 1944.
- On the run up to D-Day Rusty also flew in a number of operations including diversionary bombing at Sangatte near Calais on 4/5th June 1944 which helped the Operation Overlord landings on the 6th June 1944, for which he was later awarded the French Legion D' Honneur by the French Government in 2016.
- After this full tour of duty he was transferred off the squadron to No.82 OTU at RAF Ossington in Nottinghamshire to take up his new role of instructing pilots on aircraft conversions, then later at various RAF Operational Training Units around the country such as No. 00 OTU, No.30 OTU and No.105 OTU from June 1944 until September 1945.

- By September 1945 Rusty had also become a qualified RAF Instructor/Examiner and had been transferred to RAF Transport Command at No.1381 TCU – Transport Conversion Unit based at RAF Nuneaton and with them later to RAF Desborough, teaching pilots how to fly the Douglas C47 Skytrain (Dakota) transport and supply aircraft. After this he was the Training Officer for No.238 Squadron at RAF Abingdon, Oxfordshire until November 1947.
- His next posting and promotion saw him move to RAF Oakington in Cambridgeshire where he became the Flying Wing Training Officer between November 1947 and October 1949 and was responsible for training within 4 RAF Squadrons based there, Nos.10, 27, 30 & 46, during that time he volunteered and flew 27 Sorties in the Berlin Airlift in September 1948.
- Later he remained with No.30 Squadron Training & Examining until November 1950, then when the Squadron moved to RAF Abingdon he went with them in that same capacity, interestingly at that base during that posting there was also a VIP Flying Unit which he trained crew for and also became a part of, Rusty flew VIP flights from the U.K for Ambassadors, Government Cabinet Staff, and Royal Messengers travelling to Europe, Malta and Africa.
- His extremely varied service continued when he was also involved in both towing gliders and dropping paratroopers in military exercises in the U.K for British soldiers who were part of the NATO forces during what had become the 'Cold War'.
- In April 1952, after 11 years of service Rusty resigned his commission but remained part of the Reserve of Officers until May 1960, bringing to an end a very action-packed, varied and interesting RAF career during which time he was awarded the DFC – Distinguished Flying Cross in July 1944 and the AFC – Air Force Cross in November 1951.

When I went to Kenilworth near Coventry on the 10th July 2018 to interview Flight Lieutenant Rusty Waughman DFC, AFC, Legion D' Honneur, I was very privileged to have found and spent time with my first World War Two Lancaster Bomber Pilot. That day very fittingly also happened to be the 100th day of special events to mark of the official 100th Anniversary of the creation of the Royal Air Force, and we started the day by sitting together and watching the RAF flyover at Buckingham Palace held to mark that historical occasion, and I thought what a great way to begin what I believed would be a very special interview, with a veteran who had such intrinsic links to the RAF. I was certainly not disappointed knowing he had such a great story to tell as a Pilot of one of the most legendry British Bomber aircraft that has ever flown, a man who had completed and survived a full tour of duty, 30 operations in Bomber Command over Europe by the time he was 21, a feat few managed amongst their horrendous attrition rates. Rusty's diverse career also led him to fly as an instructor on a number of squadrons and units in RAF Training Command and RAF Transport Command, and whilst with the latter was involved in another famous part of aviation history in 1948 when he flew 27 sorties back to Berlin under very different circumstances, this time in an American Dakota in the post-war Berlin Airlift. It is quite rare to find a pilot who served in three different RAF Commands, this he did and much more during his 11-year career in the Royal Air Force from April 1941 to April 1952, Rusty now gives us a fascinating insight as tells us how it was:

<u>SERVING IN THREE DIFFERENT ROYAL AIR FORCE COMMANDS DURING AND AFTER THE WAR</u>

"Well service for me began before I was in the RAF when as teenager I volunteered to be part of what was the forerunner to the Home Guard, the L.D.V or Local Defence Volunteers, our tongue in cheek abbreviation for it was 'Look, Duck, Vanish' as it really was a 'Dad's Army' in every sense. But for me service to our country was something that ran strongly in our family because in the First World War my father was in the Royal Navy and my mother a Nurse so it was natural to volunteer when the Second World War and second great test of our nation came along! I was fortunate to be able to realise my dream of becoming a Pilot and at such a young age, 19 when I got my wings, then to survive all the operations that sadly many others didn't and of course the very harsh reality and experiences that war brings with it! Once on active duty I was part of the 101 SDS – Special Duty Squadron, where we had specially fitted jamming equipment called A.B.C – Airborne Cigar, which worked to intercept and block transmissions between German ground tracking stations and the night fighter squadrons that the Luftwaffe would send up to try and cause us maximum casualties. This additional equipment meant that an extra crew member was required on board to operate it who was German speaking in order to translate the intercepts, he was called a Special Duty Operator, our Lancasters were all fitted with 3 huge and powerful transmitters that covered up to a 50-mile advanced radius, these slightly different looking Lancs were spaced throughout the Bomber streams at 90 second intervals to try and help safeguard as many aircraft as possible during an operation. In addition to undertaking that function during a raid we also continued in the role as a regular bomber with full bomb loads that we used to deliver, as we still contributed to and were a part of the squadrons sent on any given mission any night and fulfilled those duties as well."

**A picture from Rusty Waughmans' personal collection, showing one of the ABC adapted Lancaster Bombers, note the two transmitter aerials on top of the fuselage, the third was located under the starboard side of the nose. This Lancaster, flown by Rusty is showing the squadron and aircraft identifying lettering SR-W or 'OOR WULLIE' as the crew named her, from No.101 Special Duty Squadron at RAF Ludford Magna, shown here whilst being prepared by ground crew for an Operation in May 1944.**

I asked Rusty to tell me about some of the difficult operations and incidents that occurred during his full tour of duty on the Special Duty Squadron and sat transfixed as he told me how a young man between 20-21 years of age survived so much during his 30 missions over Nazi occupied Europe: "I first began flying on this operational squadron during what was known as the air 'Battle of Berlin' in November 1943 which was a real baptism of fire and one in which we suffered many casualties. The hardest parts, well in a few words 'All of it', simply getting there and back and surviving everything, from the very heavy anti-aircraft defences such as AK-AK and the night fighter attacks that came at us, these things combined led to the demise of many aircraft and aircrew and to see burning aircraft going down was not easy, as there could and sometimes would be your friends in them! We all had a lot of close shaves as well, once a piece of shrapnel came up through our aircraft just missed my head, bounced around and landed on the floor, I later picked it up and still have it as a curious keepsake. We were all scared, how could you not be, but we kept our fears under control as we had a job to do and focused on that as best possible, and as pilots who were leading their crews into very dangerous operations we were drilled, trained and constantly told not to show trepidation or any negative emotions whatsoever, we had to keep up morale and do our best to get our crew safely there and back. On many operations we went through such difficult and stressful things that you simply didn't expect to make it out alive or return at all, and no matter what traumatising events were unfolding around you we had to maintain radio silence between all aircraft involved in a raid, as this might help give away your position and important information or potentially cause panic within the squadrons if they heard men fearful or screaming in blazing aircraft as they went down, this silence of course helped you to focus on the job at hand and the welfare of your own crew but also added to the psychological pressure of it all. **Pictured - The official badge of 101 Special Duty Squadron RAF of which Rusty was a part.** I remember when we were on a raid and hitting the Krupps armament factories at Essen in the Ruhr Valley area of Germany in April 1944, the flack was so thick you could walk on it, the only time I was totally terrified, and for a few seconds inwardly felt panic, but I managed to remain outwardly composed and for the first time ever during operations I said a prayer, after which a feeling of calm came over me! I adjusted my seat a little lower so as not to see much outside and flew on instruments only for a short time, I felt the power of prayer had worked and had steadied me, after which I re-adjusted my seat and continued as normal, I guess it is easy to forget when looking back and describing these things that after all I was only 21 years old!"

Rusty continued to describe in more detail one of the many operations where significant things occurred where his skills as a pilot were seriously put to the test: "On the weeks running up to D-Day many operations were undertaken to hit a lot of vital German infrastructure in many places and on the 3rd/4th May 1944 we were involved in an operation to destroy a large German tank and lorry depot and Panzer training centre at Mailly-le-Camp, East of Paris, France. It was undertaken by 346 Avro Lancasters and 16 De Havilland Mosquitoes from RAF Bomber Command's Nos 1 & 5 Groups, with Pathfinders led by the famous Wing Commander Leonard Cheshire. It was thought to be a lightly defended target but when we had confusion in the mission plan and things were not being communicated well it began to get messy and unravel a fair bit, especially when we were held up at a mid-air assembly point where we were told to circle and await further orders, not good as we became sitting ducks and it gave German night fighters time to slip in amongst the bombers with devastating results, claiming many victims, if we just kept moving and jamming their communications as much as possible as we normally did things would have been quite different! The target was eventually reached and successfully bombed but on the way back the Anti-aircraft fire was heavy and the Lancaster directly below us received a direct hit and blew up, the explosion completely flipped us and turned our aircraft upside down and the only way I could retrieve it was do a full 360-degree barrel roll using only instruments to guide us as it was a night raid. A very difficult and hair-raising manoeuvre to try and pull off at the best of times in a four-engine Bomber, which with no bombs and only half fuel still weighted around 40,000 pounds or 18 tons and rapidly plunging 10,000 to 1000 feet in an inverted role under combat conditions with AK-AK fire everywhere, just to give a mental picture of the unfolding events, but thankfully I managed to pull her round just in time taking back full control of the aircraft and keeping us all alive to fly another day! Many others on that raid were not so lucky, from the 364 aircraft involved we lost 42 of them, over 11 per cent, 258 young aircrew in one night, tragic!"

We then went on to cover a little more about Rusty's fascinating service in the RAF after completing his full tour on an operational Squadron: "After finishing Ops at 101 SDS a new direction and opportunities open up for me within the RAF to be an instructor which I went on to do both in RAF Training and Transport Commands which I really embraced, during that time I became an Instructor and Examiner for a whole Wing comprising of Four Squadrons and whilst with No.30 Squadron took part in the Berlin Airlift. **Left - Whilst an instructor with T-Squadron, based at RAF Oakington, Rusty here with fellow instructors and a Dakota aircraft, bottom row 5th from right, was seconded to Fassberg and Lubeck from 1st-14th September 1948 to take part in Operation Vittles.**

Interesting returning to Berlin later in a very different capacity all together, in 1943/44 we flew over delivered our bombs and didn't stop in order to defeat Germany, in 1948 we went back and landed to deliver food to help save Germany, funny how it can all change in such a short period depending on the politics of the time!" When I spoke to Rusty on the 18th June 2020 the day Dame Vera Lynn passed away, I told him the sad news and asked him of his thoughts regarding her and he said: "I saw her sing live once in Egypt and she was a wonderful performer, and came over as very natural, like the girl next door with a voice that made you feel very relaxed, and when you listened to her she made you forget about the war for a while and represented the comfort of home. Every now and then we used to think of her on the way back from raids over Europe as we occasionally came back in over the White Cliffs of Dover and mentioned or sang a couple of lines from that famous song of hers for fun and relief as we saw the familiar sight of home shores. I am happy she was honoured in many ways she truly deserved it; she really was the 'Forces Sweetheart' and I was fortunate to have experienced that during the war." Kind words from a true gentleman.

**Rusty later went on to do a test flight in the British Meteor MK VII Jet fighter at RAF Ablingdon in 1952 taking his flying experience through from the propeller to the jet age and bringing to an end a career of remarkable achievements in the RAF, proving anything is possible when applying the motto of his former No. 101 Squadron: Mens Agitat Molem 'Mind Over Matter'.**

## JAMES SAMUEL WAUGHMAN DSM & LAVINIA MARY WAUGHMAN R.R.C

Leading Seaman J.S Waughman 235200 undertook many roles during WW1 including being a gunner on the secret Navy Q Ships, he was also a Royal Navy Diver and served on the warship HMS Agamemnon and the Ice-Breaker HMS Alexander, whilst on a trip to Russia incredibly he witnessed the start of the Revolution in 1917, James was awarded the Distinguished Service Medal for bravery. L.M Waughman, Nee Green 251928 worked at Union Infirmary in Darlington which became a Military Hospital during WW1, whilst there Lavinia eventually became an Assistant Matron and was awarded the Royal Red Cross for her outstanding work. Both Rusty's parents are great examples of those who truly served our country and in whose footsteps he followed, and are counted amongst those men and women to whom my books are dedicated. All the service histories and stories recounted here are a bridge from past to present day that give a wonderful continuity in my work to honour veterans and help carry it on to whatever comes next.

## Additional Information and Life After Service

**Rank upon finish of service** – Flight Lieutenant.

**Medals and Honours** – 1939-45 Defence Medal, 1939-45 War Medal, 1939-45 Star with Bomber Command Clasp, Aircrew Europe Star, Distinguished Flying Cross, Air Force Cross, Legion D' Honneur.

**Post War Years** – After leaving the RAF in 1952 until his retirement in 1979 Rusty worked for Ridged Containers Ltd at Desborough near Kettering where he became Manager of their Midlands factory. He married his first wife in Patricia in 1948 who sadly passed away in 1951, and married Diane in 1952, they were together until her passing in 2007. They have 2 Sons, 2 Daughters, 10 Grandchildren and 7 Great-Grandchildren. During a 1977 reunion Rusty went up in a Lancaster at RAF Waddington.

**Associations and Organisations** – RAF Association 310 Branch (Leamington Spa-Warwick), Lincolnshire Bomber Command Centre, Lincolnshire's Lancaster Association.

# FLIGHT SERGEANT HARRY LEDGER

Served with – Royal Air Force 155 Squadron Fighter Command & 76 Squadron Transport Command

Service Number – 1523562

Interviewed – Shaw, Lancashire, 15th May 2018

## Service History and Personal Stories

- Born – 12th September 1921, Rochdale, Lancashire, England, UK.
- After being called up in February 1943 Harry went to RAF Padgate in Warrington for his medical, then after passing this was sent to an ACRC – Air Crew Receiving Centre in London near Regents Park for 6 weeks basic training from February to mid-March during which time he was billeted at nearby Viceroy Court.
- Next was 3.5 months training at an ITW – Initial Training Wing based at Downing College in Cambridge from mid-March to July 1943, followed by a month at RAF Desford in Leicestershire home of No.7 EFTS – Elementary Flying Training School where flying instruction took place on their de Havilland Tiger Moths from early July to early August.
- Once this aptitude, selection and basic flight training was completed, Harry and other pilots who had passed to go onto the next level of flight training were billeted at the large ACDC – Air Crew Dispersal Centre at RAF Heaton Park in Manchester, it was there they found out where their overseas training would take place and a long journey lay ahead.

- They finally arrived in Rhodesia, Southern Africa and began the next phases of their fighter pilot training as part of the RATG – Rhodesian Air Training Group from November 1943 until October 1944, beginning at an ITW - Initial Training Wing at Bulawayo Ground Station, followed by No.25 EFTS – Elementary Flying Training School at Belvedere Airfield, and No.20 SFTS - Senior Flying Training School at Cranborne Airfield, both near the Rhodesian Capital Salisbury, flying on Tiger Moth, Cornell and Harvard aircraft.
- Whilst in Rhodesia Harry received his flying wings in September 1944, and upon completion of those three courses was then transferred with other successful pilots up to Egypt for the final part of their intense training.
- Once they had passed through No.5 ARC – Airforce Receiving Centre near Port Said they joined No.73 OTU – Operational Training Unit flying out of RAF Fayid near Ismailia, continuing on Harvard's then finally being switched up to their goal of flying the Spitfire.
- This training included Aerial Combat skills, Air to Ground and Air to Air firing drills and much more on this faster fighter aircraft! Harry was then sent to No.22 PTC – Personnel Transit Centre in Almaza, Egypt awaiting transfer out on 'Active Service' to wherever needed in any allocated theatre of war. All of this taking place between October 1944 and finally finishing as a fully trained fighter pilot in February 1945.
- Harry didn't have to wait long to find out that he was going to be involved in the Far East, and he was soon flown out that same month in an AVRO York, the modified version of the AVRO Lancaster converted to carry troops, to No.9 Transit Camp at RAF Mauripur near Karachi, India, today Pakistan.
- Followed by a transfer down to RAF Poona ARC – Airforce Receiving Centre near Bombay, then to an area south of there called Mahabaleshwar, a hill station in India's forested Western Ghats Range where all the new pilots had to undertake a very special kind of survival or JSPT course at the RAF School for Jungle Self Preservation Training.
- This equipped these young aviators with many very useful skills to help survive the harsh natural elements of the jungle if they were shot down over enemy territory and to also evade capture by the Japanese. Then a return to RAF Poona this time to be put on an RFU – Refresher Flying Unit where they were also trained in dive bombing with Spitfires. All completed between late February to late May 1945, to prepare them for active duty.
- Next came that front line combat they had trained so long and so hard to undertake when Harry and the other new pilots were sent by train from Poona to Calcutta, then flown to Rangoon and driven up to RAF Toungoo near Mandalay to join No.155 Squadron to be a part of the war in Burma. From here they undertook a number of air support and fighter-bomber missions over the Burmese Jungles from June until the Japanese surrender in mid-August 1945. Harry continued to be officially attached to 155 until October 1945.
- During that time he was in transit September-October 1945, first on a troop ship from Rangoon to Singapore. Whilst in Singapore for a few weeks he was billeted at RAF Tengah, and was asked to go and test fly a Spitfire at RAF Seletar that had engine trouble, this would be last Spitfire Harry would fly. After this he was flown from Seletar in a Sutherland Flying Boat to Colombo in Ceylon, today Sri Lanka, and then later in another aircraft onto Bangalore and RAF Yelahanka, spending a few days there before his onward journey.
- Then a long passage by train up to 229 Group in Delhi, and when his next posting and further orders came through Harry found out he was to fly another very different and renowned aircraft the Douglas C47 'Dakota' AKA 'Skytrain.' After some quick familiarisation he became a 2$^{nd}$ Pilot and part of No.76 Squadron and with RAF Transport Command flew round trips returning Army personnel from Madras to Poona and up to Karachi for their onward journey of repatriation back to the U.K. This took place from November 1945 until June 1946, many flying hours being gained in the process.

- Then in late June 1946 Harry was transferred to No.77 Squadron in Karachi at RAF Mauripur and whilst awaiting his next orders was told he was to be de-mobbed. For this he was sent in July 1946 all the way down to RAF No.3 REC – Release Embarkation Centre in Worli, South Bombay, today Mumbai, where his departure was processed by the RAF.
- It was from that big port city in India that Harry would make the return journey to Liverpool on the cruise liner the MV Britannic, and after returning home would finally be released from service altogether at RAF Kirkham near Blackpool in August 1946, bringing to an end Flight Sergeant Harry Ledger's days as a Spitfire and Dakota Pilot.

The Spitfire is an historic and exemplary aircraft, without doubt one of the most well-known of all fighting machines and symbols of World War Two and indeed of all aircraft that has ever graced the skies. Normally we tend to associate it mainly with The Battle of Britain in 1940, but this incredible fighter aircraft had many variants from Mark I to Mark 24 which spanned the entire six-year conflict from 1939-1945 when over 20,000 were made, as a result they were present and saw action in all theatres of war over that period. As with all RAF aircraft from Fighter to Bomber, Coastal, Training and Transport Commands it was manned by very brave crew, young men who put their lives on the line wherever and in whatever capacity they were sent to serve. Harry Ledger is another fine example of one of those 'Magnificent men in their flying machines' who did exactly that! He did a lot of his training under RATG – Rhodesian Air Training Group at RAF Stations in what was then Rhodesia, now Zimbabwe in Southern Africa, at that time a self-governing British Colony. I have interviewed RAF crew who were trained in many places before such as Canada, America, the Middle-East and of course in the U.K, but this is the first time I had interviewed a Spitfire pilot who was trained in Africa. What also makes Harry's story very interesting and different is that after qualifying as a pilot he wasn't sent to join a squadron providing air cover over Europe but instead was sent out to the Far-East and saw combat whilst serving under and as part of SEAC - South East Asia Command, where he flew close support and fighter air cover attack missions with 155 Squadron from a base in Burma, operating against the Japanese in mainly Jungle terrain, again a theatre of war that most people don't associate the Spitfire with much, but as with everywhere the Spitfire squadrons were sent they played a vitally important strategic role, and both these extremely adaptable aircraft and their crews acquitted themselves very well in battle. After the war finished whilst still with the RAF Harry flew a very different but again well-known kind of aircraft, the Dakota, and as a 2nd Pilot in 76 squadron he was involved in repatriating allied troops who were returning home after long years of fighting in the Jungles of South-East Asia. These are some of Harry's unique experiences given during the interview and in the many other conversations we had that followed, regarding:

<u>**TRAINING AS A SPITFIRE PILOT IN RHODESIA AND EGYPT THEN SERVING IN THE FAR EAST**</u>

"When we were sent to Rhodesia to be trained it was of course very different than anywhere else I had been, the people, the country, the culture, the weather, how could it not be it was Africa, and not many people travelled to places like that in those days! But like everything and everywhere else you go in life you kind of get used to it after a while, the main thing was that we were there to train as fighter pilots and had a lot of skills and knowledge to learn and a lot of things we were getting tested on before we could move up to the next level of training, that is where most of our energies and concentration went because your career and life depended upon it! I was at different RAF Stations whilst in Rhodesia from November 1943 until October 1944 at Bulawayo, then Belvedere and Cranborne near the capital Salisbury which is now Harare, on those bases we got trained on the Tiger Moth, Cornell and Harvard aircraft learning all sorts of aerobatics, it was very pleasant and I think because of where we were in the world it really didn't seem like there was a war going on at all, it's there that I passed all my basic training and got my wings on the of 15th September 1944."

# The RATG – Rhodesian Air Training Group

This part of Harry's pilot training reflects the global nature of World War Two, it is for this reason I have added some information about the RATG which is another fascinating part of his story.

The Rhodesian Air Training Group - RATG was part of the bigger global British Commonwealth Air Training Plan - BCATP or Empire Air Training Scheme - EATS. This was a huge joint aircrew training program created and run-in close cooperation by the United Kingdom, Australia, New Zealand and Canada and simply referred to as 'The Plan'. From May 1940 until March 1954 the Royal Air Force was present in Rhodesia in the form of the RATG, which trained 8235 Allied Pilots, Gunners, Navigators, Radio Operators, Ground Crew and others for all of the RAF Commands, in total around 5% of the overall Empire Air Training Scheme output, of which Harry was one! They trained aircrew from Great Britain, Canada, South Africa, USA, New Zealand, Australia, Greece, France, Poland, Yugoslavia, Czechoslovakia, Kenya, Tanzania, Uganda, Fiji and Malta. This incredible scheme was quoted as: 'Undoubtedly Southern Rhodesia's greatest single contribution to the Allied victory.'

As Harry's account continued to unfold he went on to tell me about how his training progressed when he went up to North Africa: "Things would change of course as myself and other pals moved onto other places and things went up a level or two and intensified both with our training and where we would go geographically, this was the case with our next location which was Northern Egypt from October 1944 till February 1945 based at RAF Fayid close to Ismailia and near the Suez Canal where I trained more on the Harvards and where I began flying on my first Spitfires, Mark V's, now we were starting to feel like real fighter pilots, how could you not when you're behind the controls of that legendary fighter aircraft!" **The unmistakable sight of Spitfires in formation, those shown here are Mark XII's from No 41 Squadron, with camouflage markings used in the 'Far East'.**

Whilst in Egypt Harry was awarded a prestigious 'Green Endorsement' which is both an award and acknowledgement by the RAF for aircrew who display 'Exceptional flying skill or judgement in handling an aircraft.' This citation, traditionally written in green ink within a pilot's flight logbook, was awarded by Harry's direct Commanding Officer who outlines his brave actions and wrote:

**Commendatory Endorsement**

On the authority of the Air Officer commanding No.203 Group. This pilot is commended for his display of airmanship at RAF Station Fayid, on the 11th Dec 1944, when he made a forced landing successfully in Spitfire B.S.134 under difficult circumstances. He showed admirable presence of mind and saved the aircraft, when, after experiencing very rough running of the engine followed by loss of power, he executed a down-wind landing on the runway, at the same time giving a clear running commentary of his movements over the c/t thereby considerably assisting the flying control in clearing the aerodrome for the emergency landing. Subsequent examination of the engine revealed the collapse of the flame-traps and a part of the induction manifold blown away by backfire.

**O.R Cain R.A.F Station, Fayid. 23/12/44.**

Now returning to Harry who after finishing his Spitfire training with No.73 O.T.U was next sent out to RAF Poona in India, 100 miles East of Bombay and then after spending some time there eventually onto Toungoo Airfield in Burma, approximately 150 miles North of the then capital of Rangoon as a fighter pilot in the Burma Campaign. It was from there that he flew with 155 Squadron, and served with them on active operational duties from June until mid-August 1945 on a number of missions which he now tells us about: "When I was out in Burma I was flying on the Spitfire Mark 8 on ground attack missions hitting the retreating Japanese as hard as possible in support of our forces on the ground, essentially the 14th Army, who had been engaged in fierce fighting with the brutal Japs for years. Our planes carried 500-pound bombs, that along with strafing could really do some damage, I remember at least half a dozen missions like that over dense Rainforest, where a lot of the time the enemy was well hidden in the Vegetation and our attacks were guided by a lot of 'on the ground intelligence.' If the Squadron was lucky enough to catch them out in the open that was different, fair game! Then they would get shot up! Other times 155 would be used as escorts on transport aircraft missions, I arrived in the closing phases of the war in Burma, the last few months up until Japanese surrender, still a hard-fought campaign though against man and the natural elements which included stifling heat and monsoons in what as I am sure you've heard became known by many since as 'The Forgotten War'."

Part of that war and the valued contribution of RAF 155 Squadron and its pilots was later detailed by their Commanding Officer Squadron Leader Gordon Conway DFC, who amongst other things stated:

'The Battle of the Sittang River Bend was a deciding factor in the closing stages of the epic Burma Campaign. RAF Spitfires which supported the Army in this battle played an important part in the successful action, and were responsible for thousands of Japanese troop casualties. One Squadron in particular, No.155 Spitfire Fighter Squadron, earned the heartfelt thanks of the Army and guerrilla parties for the magnificent support given by the pilots during the battle.'

### RAF Public Relations, Cathay Buildings, Singapore. 06/10/45.

"By September 1945 with the war in the Far East over and World War Two at an end my duties would change and so would the planes I had to fly, and from November 1945 until July 1946 I became 2nd Pilot on twin engine Douglas Dakota Mark 4 transport aircraft with No. 76 Squadron, transporting our troops on part of their long journey home, we took them from Madras to Poona in India and onto Karachi in what is now Pakistan. I had to learn to fly a new type of aircraft, that was interesting, and I had gone from being a fighter Pilot in Fighter Command to a Transport Pilot in Transport Command, but either way I enjoyed the challenge and adventure of my service years and am proud to have been a part of the Royal Air Force!"

Harry was 99 years of age when I wrote this profile in 2020 and one of 'the few' Spitfire pilots left in Great Britain, and of course it would be impossible to interview him without asking about what he thought of that famous aircraft that he once flew, which led to these very thought-provoking words:

"Yes the Spitfire was an iconic aircraft and during the war it was involved in almost every front and most battles from the skies over England, to those of North Africa, Middle-East and Europe including the invasions of Sicily, Italy and at D-Day in France, and was also involved where I served in South-East Asia in very different yet equally as demanding environments over areas of dense jungle. It undertook many diverse types of operations such as escorting bombers, working in ground attack and even dive bombing roles in support of our ground forces, giving air cover to shipping and invasion fleets everywhere, it had a variation that worked in a vital reconnaissance and intelligence gathering role photographing enemy positions right through to the Seafire version based on aircraft carriers that went all over the world giving vital assistance wherever required with the Fleet Air Arm. Everywhere and in every way it was engaged it did well and there wasn't much it didn't do with its many squadrons of brave pilots who came from all over the United Kingdom, the Commonwealth and Occupied countries to fly against our enemies, who it must be remembered were also very determined, brave and well-equipped. The Spitfire was a dream to fly, after getting used to its very responsive controls you seemed to mould into it, a good description would be that you became a part of it, it became a part of you, the noise and resonance given off by that Merlin engine was unique as you pushed it to the edge of its limits and capabilities, in all an aircraft with a superb design that is almost instantly recognisable both by sight and sound, by pilot and admirer alike!"

Harry taking a photo opportunity with a Spitfire Mark IX of No.152 Squadron (Identity letters UM), whilst at RAF Tengah in Singapore, it was here that he would fly that legendary aircraft for the last time. *No.155 Squadron (Identity letters were MP).

The service and dedication to duty Harry showed and gave during the Second World War are summed up in the mottos of the two squadrons of which he was a part, 'Eternal Vigilance' (155 Squadron) and 'Resolute' (76 Squadron), for these things Harry you are highly revered.

## Additional Information and Life After Service

**Rank upon finish of service** – Flight Sergeant.

**Medals and Honours** – Burma Star, 1939-45 Star, 1939-45 Defence Medal, 1939-45 War Medal.

**Post War Years** – In 1941 before being called up for the RAF Harry obtained a law degree at Manchester University. After finishing his RAF Service Harry was employed by Guildford-Gibson & Weldon Solicitors whilst finishing his final Law examination, which he successfully completed in November 1947 with honours. His brother Brian who served in the British Army during World War Two also passed his final law examination in 1949 with honours. As fully qualified Solicitors Harry and Brian were now part of their father's business which in 1950 became Alfred Ledger & Sons. Harry and Brian stayed there the rest of their working lives, eventually becoming Senior Partners in the family business specialising in property law until their retirement in 2004, by which time Harry was aged 82. The family business still continues to run successfully from their Rochdale office with the tradition being continued by Harry's daughter Nancy who now runs the firm. Harry Married Jean in August 1957 in Rochdale, they have 1 Son, 2 Daughters and 2 Grandchildren.

**Associations and Organisations** – The RAF Association, The Law Society.

# CORPORAL HARRY GARSTANG

Served with – Royal Air Force & RAF Regiment Ground Crew
Service Number – 1354227
Interviewed – Radcliffe, Manchester, 30th & 31st July 2018

### Service History and Personal Stories

- Born – 15th September 1920, Leigh, Lancashire, England, UK.
- Harry joined the RAF aged 18 in June 1939 at Wigan Recruiting office with the intention of becoming a Navigator on Lancaster Bombers, however as fate would have it he didn't pass the exam, something which would set him on an entirely different course altogether when he took one of the alternatives offered him and opted to become an Aircraft Armourer.
- This also probably helped his chances of survival as well due to the very high losses incurred by Bomber Command, and it would in time lead to a lot of wartime experiences of many kinds both in the U.K and overseas. These formally began with basic training at RAF Blackpool followed by a Gun Armourers Course at RAF Jerby in the Isle of Man.
- Once this training was completed by late 1939 Harry then 19 was sent to RAF Duxford in Cambridgeshire and later to her satellite Aerodrome RAF Fowlmere in Hertfordshire, he served on both those RAF Stations over a pivotal time in Royal Air Force and British history during The Battle of Britain, where he helped keep the Supermarine Spitfires of No. 19 Squadron which was part of

- No.12 Group RAF Fighter Command armed with the ammunition needed to keep flying and fighting against the German Luftwaffe.
- ❖ Despite being vastly outnumbered during the Battle of Britain, the RAF as history recalls fought very bravely to win that battle in the summer and autumn of 1940, and No.19 Squadron which was the very first RAF squadron to receive what would become the legendry Spitfire was at the forefront of things and as a result also came under direct attack at Fowlmere on 31 August 1940, something Harry saw and experienced first-hand.
- ❖ Harry finished at RAF Folwmere in late 1940 after which a very different posting in a very diverse setting awaited him when he was sent to join the Desert Campaign in North Africa where he served from 1940 until 1943, during that time he worked with the DAF – Desert Air Force where he was seconded to both British and Australian Squadrons working with ground crews in their very important roles arming both fighters and bombers at established, hastily adapted and captured airfields throughout Egypt, Libya and Tunisia.
- ❖ This led to him seeing action close to the front lines in support of Montgomery's 8th Army in many places and well-known battles such as Benghazi, the siege and relief of Tobruk 1941 & 1942, and the long-awaited Allied victory at El Alamein in November 1942 right through to the eventual surrender of Rommel's Afrika Korps at Cape Bonn, Tunisia in May 1943. During that time they had to also contend with extreme and adverse weather conditions of an unforgiving desert terrain and sporadic attacks from enemy aircraft.
- ❖ The diverse postings and experiences continued from the end of the campaign in Africa until the end of 1944, during which time Harry was again seconded, this time to the RAF Regiment on postings in the Middle East that took him to Palestine, Trans-Jordan, Lebanon and whilst there he was sent on one occasion to accompany a special convoy on a secret operation to deliver military supplies to 'neutral' Turkey to be handed over to the Turks on the Syrian-Turkish border, he believes as a means of 'persuading' them to remain neutral.
- ❖ Also whilst based in British Mandate Palestine he and others from the RAF were sent for a while over to the Greek Islands to bolster Allied presence there during the period of the main Nazi withdrawals from mainland Greece and some of the islands, as a result Harry remembers being on Samos around the time of its liberation-surrender in October 1944.
- ❖ After returning to the U.K and having much deserved leave by early 1945 Harry was back at RAF Fowlmere for a few months before being selected to go to Trondheim, Norway as part of the forces of liberation in what was known as Operation Doomsday, helping with the transition of power from the Nazi occupiers to the Allied forces led by the 1st Airborne Division where he worked in 'Civilian Affairs' as a Liaison Officer, from May-October 1945.
- ❖ His final return to the U.K during his service led to another very different posting at an RAF depot in Salford, Lancashire, dealing with servicemen being demobbed as many were at that time. Then to finish Harry was sent to RAF Cardington, Bedfordshire for a few weeks on equipment maintenance before being demobbed there in December 1945, bringing to an end 6.5 years of diverse and loyal service to the RAF and his country.

79 years after getting his first active duty posting in the Royal Air Force aged 19 in 1939 Harry Garstang shared his incredible story for the first time and I was privileged to be the one he told it to and who has captured it for posterity! A story from a very different perspective, that of a vitally important and sometimes overlooked part of the RAF, the Ground Crew. Without the Ground Crews the pilots of every aircraft they serviced and supplied could not have stayed operational and been able to engage in or have won any battle, offensive or operation they were a part of anywhere in the world during the Second World War, something cited and mentioned by many pilots and aircrew in numerous interviews I have conducted.

As a result Harry and many others like him who did numerous different and vital aircraft maintenance jobs were very much near or in the thick of the action in their support roles. In Harry's case as an Aircraft Armourer he found himself in very close proximity to enemy attacks and operations whilst on RAF bases in the U.K during The Battle of Britain and throughout the entirety of the campaign in the Western Desert as it ebbed and flowed up and down countries on the North African coast. But his service was far from over after that as he was posted and worked throughout the Middle East all the way up to Turkey, and then as the war came into its latter stages Harry was involved with support units such as the RAF Regiment to oversee the surrender of German Forces in the Greek Islands and at the end of the war in Europe was sent onto Norway which still had a very sizable Axis presence of over 350,000 troops to help as a Liaison Officer with the allied forces involved in the peaceful transition of power and 'Policing Duties' that followed. Harry had served throughout the whole duration of the Second World War and I felt extremely lucky when I interviewed him in 2018 to be able to hear and obtain these memories from one of the last and rare living links to the Battle of Britain, El Alamein and many more incredible parts of that conflict, which led to Harry explaining:

## HOW IT WAS SERVING IN THE RAF AS GROUND CREW FROM 1939 TO 1945

"There's so much for me to tell you, I will try and remember as much as I can, at least the more interesting parts and of course some facts and figures as well, as I know you are very keen to hear and get as much as you can Gary. Let's start with the Battle of Britain you've heard about the brave pilots of Fighter Command, they were famously known as 'The Few', well I think we were less famously 'The Many', because there were a lot more of us on the ground taking care of every aspect of every fighter before they went into battle and after they returned from battle, the Ground Crew took care of everything from mechanical problems to fuelling, repairing any structural damage, to the arming an aircraft, the latter being my trade and speciality. Along with the pilots the ground crew made up the 'complete team', we worked closely together and it was our responsibility to make sure we sent both the pilots and their planes into combat in the best condition possible because we really did care about them both and wanted to see them return. During the Battle of Britain in that long summer of 1940, the fate of the nation and direction of the war was hanging in the balance, and on 19 Squadron like all others in Fighter Command ground crews lost pilots and aircraft that we had all grown attached to, and when they died, especially being so young as they nearly all were, a part of you felt like it died too, only one slightly positive thing that may have helped with this was that so much was happening and we had such a short turnaround time with everything you couldn't dwell on these losses for too long, good job really! Even on the RAF Stations we were posted to the war was sometimes brought home to us in many stark ways, for example, I remember I think it was at RAF Duxford a Spitfire coming in that was in trouble, it had been shot up quite badly and the pilot had managed to crash land but it exploded and the pilot was trapped inside and the fire teams couldn't get him out in time as it was a real inferno and he burned to death, horrible! On another occasion at RAF Fowlmere the base came under direct attack from German aircraft, Dorniers, they dropped a few bombs, people ran for cover, explosions around, AA battery's returning fire, they managed to shoot one down, very chaotic, those were the kind of things that reminded us we really were at war and that whoever you were wherever you were, no one was ever truly safe in wartime, you could easily be here one minute, gone the next! For me personally those kind of 'Reminders' would re-occur many times in the years to come in the different places I served." **Left – A Dornier DO17 twin-engine Light Bomber like the one described by Harry, here being engaged by a Supermarine Spitfire, in an interesting 1940 photo from German archives.**

**BATTLE OF BRITAIN ARMOURERS WORKING AT NO.19 SQUADRON RAF FOWLMERE**

Ground Crew Aircraft Armourers at work between sorties rearming a Supermarine Spitfire MK 1 of No.19 Squadron at RAF Fowlmere during The Battle of Britain. This picture was taken in September 1940 at the time Harry was posted to that RAF Station, and interestingly shows the reloading of machine gun bullets into the wing of the fighter whilst a petrol bowser waits to refuel so that the pilot and aircraft could go back into action soon after, quick turn-arounds being an absolute necessity in order to aid victory in that crucial air battle for our country's very survival.

'Without the Ground Crews we couldn't have done Anything', something I have heard many times when I have been interviewing Air Crew from Fighter, Bomber and Coastal Commands. This was of course very true because without this 'Other Half of the Team' taking care of the many essential jobs on the ground such as fuelling, arming, mechanical and other maintenance all Royal Air Force aircraft simply wouldn't have continued running and been able to take part in operations, from The Battle of Britain to the Western Desert and Beyond! Above – Fred Roberts a colleague of Harry's re-arms a Supermarine Spitfire Mk 1A at RAF Fowlmere in Cambridgeshire.

~ 190 ~

It was at this point that we moved on to his experiences in a very different terrain, that of the Western Desert, an extremely diverse theatre of war that brought with it many new challenges, incidents and events, various aspects of which Harry touched on: "In late 1940 I was sent along with many others on a troop ship from the U.K around the Cape of Good Hope, South Africa, up the Suez Canal to Alexandria, Egypt, once we got there a new adventure started, one that would last the next three years and see a number of us in RAF Ground Units seconded to different Squadrons, air arms and air fields throughout Egypt, Libya and Tunisia as part of the Desert Air Force whilst the war in North Africa raged over hundreds of miles up and down those parts of the Mediterranean coastline. During that time both our allied forces and the axis forces were either moving forward on the offensive or backwards on the defensive, and between 1940 to 1943 I saw the fortunes of war change for all concerned many times. We were close to many front line battles as we were on different kinds of airfields that mostly weren't far from the action as the front lines moved around, this meant we were in places such as RAF Fayid with No.462 Squadron of the RAAF – Royal Australian Air Force, I believe the only one to be equipped with the Handley Page Halifax Heavy Bombers for quite some time in the Desert Campaign, we also worked on makeshift desert airstrips as battles raged at Tobruk, Benghazi and many other places, I think if I recall correctly one of the RAF squadrons we worked with was No.227, there were so many we dealt with it's hard to remember them all, at the famous battle of El Alamein in October to November 1942 I was first based at an airfield near Borg El Arab then as the 8th Army advanced we would move up with rear units being posted to various RAF squadrons on forward airfields. Later on I was awarded the 'Alamein Rosette' to be pinned on my Africa Star for being a part of that battle all the way through, proud of that! Along the way I also saw Winston Churchill during his visit to the troops in August 1942 waiving and giving the 'V for Victory' salute from the back of his car, and another time we were inspected by General Montgomery.

Many things happened along the way of course, when we moved in columns over the long desert roads being quite vulnerable there were occasions we came under air attack from the Luftwaffe and were strafed by ME 109's and 110'S and dive bombed by Stukas with their screaming sirens, frightening, people were injured and some killed and vehicles destroyed! Once when we were moving through some mountainous terrain a Messerschmitt 109 was chased and shot up by a Spitfire and then with smoke trailing behind it slammed into a hill near us and exploded, quite a thing to witness! Being up against the elements was as big a struggle as the enemy most the time, desert conditions that were raging hot in the day and freezing cold at night, plagued by flies and sometimes mosquitos, the need to have constant supplies of fresh water, living on rations that a lot of the time consisted of 'Bully Beef' and biscuits, men obviously got sick. Eventually when Monty and Rommel had slugged it out all the way down the coast I was there to witness the massive surrender of the German forces at Cape Bonn in Tunisia in May 1943, the Africa Corps was beaten at last and after all those years it was finally over, at least in that part of the world. It wasn't all war and no play, we had enjoyable pass times as well, I had a camera with me and when possible took quite a few interesting pictures during my time in the desert, capturing certain things we came across (some shown exclusively later), and we'd celebrate big victories with drinks and lively get togethers and sing our songs to keep morale up, such as the famous wartime desert song borrowed from the Germans called 'Lilly Marlene', but with lyrics changed here or there to make the RAF version, sang with the same melody but with new lines like 'we've been to bomb Benghazi, we've been to bomb B.G'….. About our jobs, well we had been trained to do a wide variety of armoury related tasks for fighters and bombers such as bomb priming, bomb loading, bullet re-arming in all calibres of guns such as 303, 0.5 and 20mm, we also did Machinery Maintenance on gun turrets and bomb racks, stripping and servicing of all manner of guns on a wide range of aircraft on the various squadrons we were loaned to out there, as a result we worked on Spitfires, Hurricanes, Marauders, Blenheims, Beaufighters, and as mentioned before Halifaxes. As Armourers we'd also been trained in the use and maintenance of many kinds of small arms from hand guns and rifles to light and heavy machine guns and at some bases we had to run firearms courses for everyone from cooks to drivers as Montgomery wanted every man trained as a standard thing regardless of their jobs, just in case stuff occurred like their positions being overrun by the enemy which happened a few times over the years!

Much more followed but I'll try my best to summarise it or we'll be here all day! After Africa I was posted to many places in the Middle East through 1943 to late 1944 such as bases near Jerusalem and Hadera in Palestine, Amman in Jordan, and also spent time in Aleppo, Syria and Beirut, Lebanon and even ended up being part of what seemed like an 'Unofficial' convoy delivery of military hardware to the supposedly 'Neutral' Turkey to help keep them that way, I guess they didn't want a repeat of World War One with them becoming allies of Germany again! In the Middle East we ended up seconded to the RAF Regiment and in October 1944 as part of I think 2020 squadron we were sent over to Samos in the Greek Islands in a support role during the surrender of a number of those Islands, the following year from May until October 1945 I was sent to Trondheim in Norway this time with 'T' Flight 101 Embarkation Unit RAF working as a Liaison Officer in Civilian Affairs dealing with released allied POW's, new German POW's now the tables had turned, repatriations, and helping Norwegian civilians with problems and much more, very interesting, and as we were serving under the umbrella forces of occupation headed by the 1st Airborne Division I was lucky enough to meet their commander Major-General Urquhart, another one of the top-brass who had popped in to pay us a visit along the way. After returning home my postings were far less exciting, as I was sent to work in a demob centre in Salford, then servicing equipment at RAF Cardington until my demob there in December 1945, bringing to an end my many adventures in the Royal Air Force. Wow now I am telling my story in full for the first time I am realising actually we did go through, see and do a lot during those war years, many things that I haven't thought about for decades, it feels good to recall those distant memories from six years of service."

**Very fittingly Harry's can-do attitude and many achievements during the war years, can be summed up by the motto of No.19 Squadron who he served with during The Battle of Britain; Possunt quia posse videntur – 'They can because they think they can'. Thank you Harry for a very funny, revealing, insightful and special interview which is another great and very important contribution to this book and the preservation of World War Two stories as a whole.**

## Additional Information and Life After Service

**Rank upon finish of service** – Corporal.

**Medals and Honours** – 1939-45 War Medal, 1939-45 Defence Medal, 1939-45 Star, Africa Star with Rosette for El-Alamein.

**Post War Years** – From 1945 until 1985 Harry worked for Lancashire United Transport as a Bus Driver in the Leigh, Warrington and Bolton areas of Lancashire and then for British Gas as a Stores Supervisor in Loughton near Warrington, retiring in 1985 aged 65. Married Emma at Loughton St. Mary's Church in Leigh, on the 18th March 1940 whilst on leave. Children; 2 Daughters, 1 Son, 3 Grandchildren, 5 Great-Grandchildren.

**Associations and Organisations** – RAF Association (Leigh Branch), Chairman of the Royal Naval Association in Atherton.

## HARRY GARSTANG'S EXCLUSIVE WARTIME PHOTOS

The photographs you see above were Harry Garstang's taken during his time in the Western Desert during the African Campaign and are from his personal collection. It is because of this that I have dedicated a special page to them, a layout I have not done previously in my books. They were taken in 1942 and 1943 showing an Axis army in retreat and defeat. Encapsulated in these 6 pictures are images depicting the shattered remnants of Rommel's once mighty Afrika Korps. From top to bottom and left to right we have the following; Messerschmitt BF 109, Junkers JU87 'Stuka', Heinkel HE 111, Junkers JU 52, Panzer MK III, and German Prisoners of War. As Harry was in the Royal Air Force seeing downed, wrecked and abandoned enemy aircraft was of particular interest to him hence there being more of those shown here, a fascinating window into World War Two through this captured history.

# LEADING AIRCRAFTMAN CHARLES HANSON

Served with – Royal Air Force, Mobile Air Crash Recovery Team
Service Number – 1010877
Interviewed – Swinton, Salford, Greater Manchester, 25th April 2018

## Service History and Personal Stories

- Born – 13th February 1914, Winton, Salford, England, UK.
- Charlie joined the RAF at their recruiting station at Padgate, Warrington in 1940 aged 26 and after basic training at RAF Station West Kirby in Merseyside he was posted to RAF Watnall in Nottinghamshire, this was the operational headquarters for No.12 Group RAF Fighter Command. Whilst there in 1940-1941 he was an Orderly at their underground Filter/Plotting Room.
- By 1942 Charlie had volunteered for and become a driver with the RAF Motor Transport Section and had become part of an Air Crash Recovery Team, being sent out to recover as much wreckage as possible from hills and rural areas of North Wales where aircraft had come down, the team were directed to known crash sites or had to try and locate lost aircraft in the last known areas and coordinates they were flying over before contact was lost.

- After this in spring 1942 he was posted out to North Africa to join those engaged in the Desert war against Rommel and the Afrika Korps, involved with the MTS undertaking many different kinds of transport related duties which again included being part of an Air Crash Recovery Team and came under attack many times as they followed the ebb and flow of the war in the desert as it moved across Egypt, Libya and Tunisia and during that long period of service was never granted any leave for 3 whole years!
- During those years Charlie had ongoing training and learned to drive every conceivable type of vehicle and operate every kind of machinery that was required for the many elements of his job that he had to undertake, which included amongst many things delivering spare aircraft parts and at crash sites salvaging usable parts, he also had to learn the maintenance of these as well and as a result became an LAC – Leading Aircraftman.
- Charlie his crew and supporting units of the Mobile Air Crash Recovery Team were attached to Montgomery's 8th Army and was with them at the famous battle of El-Alamein in Egypt in November 1942 right through to the German surrender in Tunisia in May 1943.
- After the Allies had won the campaign in North Africa Charlie stayed on as an Officers Driver with the Motor Transport Section from May 1943 to April 1945, during which time he drove officers all the way from Tunis in Tunisia to Cairo in Egypt and was then based around Cairo and Northern Egypt where he would also have additional duties of driving people and delivering goods and supplies to many RAF bases and stations as instructed.
- Charlie was back in the U.K by V.E Day in May 1945 and after continued his job as a driver with the MTS where he had to go to U.S bases around the country to collect aircraft parts and deliver them to the Liverpool Docks. This he did through to the following year until his demob at RAF Squires Gate also known as RAF Blackpool on the 10th January 1946.

When I interviewed Charles Hanson in 2018 this incredible 104-year-old RAF veteran was one of the oldest ex-servicemen in Greater Manchester and the oldest veteran I have spoken to for inclusion in this book, and despite the loss of eyesight this inspirational man was in amazing condition and had all his faculties about him. To get an idea of the times he had lived through and experienced we must look at his life and longevity in a historical context, Charlie as he was known was born before World War One even began and only two years after Titanic had sunk! He lived through the great depression of the 1920's and went on to serve our country in World War Two meaning of course he lived through both World Wars of the 20th Century! In 2018 the centenary year of the Royal Air Force he was actually older than the force in which he had served! This is the wonder of history, this tangible sense of reaching out to touch the past which is experienced when you are face to face with veterans such as Charlie and hearing their stories first-hand and being very moved by words that capture important moments in time. So here is Charlie Hanson, an incredible centenarian who did a rare and interesting job in the RAF and now shares with us:

<u>**WHAT IT WAS LIKE TO BE PART OF AN AIRCRASH RECOVERY TEAM IN WW2**</u>

"I joined the RAF in 1940 and ended up in the Motor Transport Section, transporting everything and everyone to everywhere, part of that included a very different and interesting job in an Air Crash Recovery Team which was a bit of a specialist unit in the MTS, I did that over here in Great Britain and abroad in North Africa, and in all the places we served we saw a lot of interesting but sometimes gruesome things, I tried to forget, get them out of my head, didn't want to think too much about that, or I wouldn't sleep at night, but it was also a big adventure in some ways after all I had only been in Salford before that because in those days only rich people or those in the services got to travel and see the world not regular folk or window cleaners like me. But when there is a war anything can happen and it did, even before we went abroad while we were at home things occurred even on your bases and airfields, we were at one once I can't remember the name of it but a young

Canadian Spitfire pilot had a pretty bad and unexpected ending, he was flying around after an engine refit and was doing a little salute with his plane, dipping the wings slightly like they did and he clipped the chimney of the officers mess and crashed into some woods nearby, when we arrived on the scene there were parts of the plane and him all over the trees, very sad only a young lad. It was tough to see but that's what happened in a job like ours, you were there to clear up after air crashes so I guess it's to be expected, we did exactly what it said on the tin, air crash recovery, and all that came with it, but there weren't always bodies at the crash sites though, sometimes we were there later to just salvage what was re-usable or take all the wreckage away whenever possible."

I asked Charlie to tell me more about the different jobs he had to undertake in the Motor Transport Section and about his time in a theatre of war overseas and as I listened intently he told me about:

**WAR IN THE WESTERN DESERT AND THE VARIED TASKS IN THE MTS**

"When we were in North Africa and working in and around various battlefields, we had so many different tasks that had to be done as part our support roles, everyone was trained to use whatever was needed to do the job and we were attached to many different units as the desert war progressed. During my time in the Motor Transport Section I transported all sorts of supplies and people and drove all sorts of vehicles such as HGV's, Flat Bed Lorries, Tractors, Jeeps, Diggers and Petrol Tankers through to Military Motor Bikes and Officers Staff cars, if it had wheels or tracks we drove it, if it was mechanical we worked with it! **Left – A chaotic scene similar to many Charlie saw and had to deal with whilst serving as part of the Aircrash Recovery Team.** We worked at and delivered parts to many RAF Stations, make shift airbases and forward positions of the Desert Air Force and sometimes to other units if ordered, right through to being totally mobile and out there in the desert with other supporting elements of the RAF Aircraft Recovery Team locating aircraft that had been shot down or gone down for whatever reason. The main thing was to recover important equipment like the weapons and munitions, radio sets, code books to make sure they didn't fall into enemy hands and to take whatever else we could salvage that could be re-used, and if we had time and weren't in too much danger and had all the equipment we needed such as a mobile crane and flat-bed truck then we'd try and take the lot. Remember though we were at war so we could run into danger at any time such as mines and our convoy coming under attacks from German and Italian aircraft that just fell out of the skies, we had all those things happen, from Stuka Dive bombers **(like those pictured)** screaming down and trying to blow us up to fighters like the Messerschmitt shooting us up, strafing I think it is called? Very dangerous when you've got petrol tankers with you for long trips, you had to run off into the desert away from the attack or jump into a ditch if you could find one because if an oil tanker went up then a lot more people could get it! We saw a few of our lads get finished off in those kinds of attacks and lost a fair bit of equipment as well, and during the Battle of El-Alamein I was delivering lorry loads of ammunition to the front to help keep Monty's 8th Army and his Desert Rats supplied, another dangerous one if you came under enemy attack by land or air.

**Charlie, 3rd Left, in the middle, and the rest of the crew sat on a high-octane fuel tanker as described in his story.** Sometimes we were the first to arrive at a crash site and if you were it meant you could be greeted by anything, during one recovery we arrived to find a Czech pilot that had been ejected through the front of the aircraft, there he was lying dead and splayed over the engine in the burning wreckage. We removed the body and when we were transporting him back to base the clothes for some reason re-ignited and began to burn again and we had to stop and put them out in the back of the lorry then carry on back to base. As if the recovery of the deceased pilot wasn't bad enough in the first place, we had to endure a lot of difficult things like that, sights you don't want to see, but so did the Army lads, there was so much happening all the time, you couldn't grasp it, but we persevered, all the way from Alamein to Tunis and in the end we won the desert war and we began to see what Churchill called: The beginning of the End!"

After the war and all he had experienced and the many hard and sometimes shocking things he had seen, Charlie returned to a completely different reality and very sedate existence, (just like Walter Bentley also in this book), when he went back to the job he started in 1927 as a window cleaner, this he did until he retired aged 65 in 1979 and when asked about his longevity he attributed it to his work when he said: "Being 104 doesn't worry me, I am still here. I have always worked outside and the fresh air and keeping active has helped me reach a ripe old age" and jokingly added "You could live as long as me if you clean some windows!"

When I interviewed him he still looked back with a certain fondness and with great clarity at those WW2 events from so long ago, knowing that when his country called he put down the tools of one trade, his ladder and bucket of soapy water, picked up and learned to work with the tools of another, the heavy machinery of the Air Crash Recovery Team, put himself in the line of fire, and was proud to have served when needed and to have done his duty, for this selflessness Charlie you deserve to be honoured and remembered.

## Additional Information and Life After Service

<u>Rank upon finish of service</u> – LAC – Leading Aircraftman.

<u>Medals and Honours</u> – 1939-45 Defence Medal, 1939-45 War Medal, 1939-45 Star, Africa Star. Although entitled to these medals he did not collect or apply for them.

<u>Post War Years</u> – 1946-1979 returned to his pre-war work as a window cleaner and had rounds in Winton and Worsley. Married Connie in 1935 at St. Mark's Church, Worsley, they were together 63 years until her passing in 1998. Children, 1 Son, 3 Grandchildren, 5 Great-Grandchildren.

<u>Associations and Organisations</u> – RAF Comforts Committee – Volunteer Worker.

# LEADING AIRCRAFTMAN DON HOLLIS

Served with – Royal Air Force, Ground Personnel, Radar Operator

Service Number – 1866526

Interviewed – Bletchley Park, Buckinghamshire, 1st July 2015

## Service History and Personal Stories

- Born – 21st November 1924, Wembley, London, England, UK.
- After leaving school aged 14 in 1938 Don worked for 3 years as a Booking Clerk for the London, Midland and Scottish Railway covering the Euston to Watford Suburban areas. As the clouds of war gathered Don already knew he wanted to play his part and which service he wanted to join, as a result he also spent over 3 years from 1938 to 1942 in the Air Cadets until he formally began service in the Royal Air Force on 27 January 1942 aged 17.
- After basic training at RAF Blackpool Don was sent for specialist training in his chosen area of RADAR – Radio Detection and Ranging, he would learn his new skills in this developing technology at the No.9 Radio School at RAF Yatesbury in Wiltshire which came under RAF Technical Training Command and part of No.60 Group RAF that controlled the electronic Air Defence Radar network across Britain and was responsible for the civilian and service personnel who operated, maintained and calibrated all 'Chain Home' Radar Stations.
- Having finished RADAR training by late spring 1942 Don was posted to RAF Swingate near Dover where for a year he served as a RADAR Operator at this important CH – Chain Home station in Kent, which formed part of the Air Defence network in the south-east of England. This was based on successive zonal layers centred on the capital London, which provided an early warning system against incoming enemy aircraft by use of giant detection masks that identified any potential

danger, in addition to these were the eyes and ears on the ground who were the 'Spotters' of the Observer Corps, and protected by anti-aircraft gun batteries both within the complex and at the Langdon Battery nearby.

❖ By the middle of 1943 Don was on the other side of the world in a posting that had taken him all the way out to India where he was part of No.225 Group RAF and had been specially trained and assigned to an RAF Mobile Radar Unit, along with other Radar units they were seconded out and operated in many places along the India-Burma border regions and around the Bay of Bengal, where they used their long-range equipment to mainly monitor Japanese aircraft movements over the skies of Burma.

❖ These would be reported to designated RAF HQ Stations who then sent out messages to RAF Squadrons in Burma for them to intercept the enemy in the skies over the battle zones of jungle, mountain and other terrains to help positively influence the outcome of operations for the allies engaged in combat in those areas. During that time as Don was an LAC – Leading Aircraftman he undertook a number of duties as part of the team which included the driving of the units HGV vehicles, Radar Operation and maintenance.

❖ By mid-1945 Don was down in Bangalore, India spending most his time at RAF Adgodi which was part of the No.2 Indian Group RAF, where he was involved in all sorts from the upkeep of Radar, vehicles and other equipment especially after the end of hostilities in Asia, to driving Dodge lorries for supply deliveries, through to being the chauffeur driving the car of F.F Waring the A.O.C – Air Officer Commanding of No. 225 Group RAF.

❖ After approximately 3.5 years in India Don was sent home to the shock of an English winter near the end of 1946 where he was demobbed at No.101 PDC – Personnel Dispatch Centre in Kirkham near Preston, Lancashire on New Year's Eve, 31st December 1946. He then returned to civilian life and remained on a short reserve until his final release on 22nd March 1947, bringing to an end 5 years and 2 months of service in the Royal Air Force.

Over the years I have been fortunate to interview a huge array of incredible World War Two veterans around most of the country in some very interesting places from care homes to their homes, at servicemen's clubs, libraries, museums and art galleries to name but a few. On the 1st July 2015 when I interviewed World War Two RAF veteran Don Hollis I was very fortunate indeed to have been granted permission to do so in a very special place directly related to and in many ways at the heart of that conflict when I captured his wartime time memories at the centre of codebreaking at the now famous Bletchley Park in Berkshire. It was possible to do so because Don has a number of ties with the place, it is somewhere close to where he lives and where he visits most days and has done so for many years, spending his time greeting people with a big smile and striking up friendly conversations with the visitors, which is how I met him during one of my visits there. In fact he has spent so many of his days there that the staff affectionately calls him 'one of their veterans' and after the war whilst working on the railways he also spent 15 years as a signalman at the Bletchley Station Power Signal Box across the road from B.P. During his war years he served in the RAF doing the important job of a RADAR Operator in the U.K which was an intricate part of what was known as the 'Chain Home' system of Radar stations that stretched around and gave coverage over Great Britain as an early warning system to detect enemy bomber formations on their way to try and devastate our country, the ever evolving and at that time relatively new Radar technology was a crucial part of the 'Dowding System', Britain's very sophisticated and highly effective air defence network. Later on in his service he was posted to a mobile version of the bigger static stations he first trained and served on when he was sent to India to help track enemy aircraft in and around Burma, which then meant he had undertaken Radar Opps against both our wartime enemies the Germans and the Japanese and contributed in both the European and Far East theatres of war, something he now reveals to us in interesting insights and perspectives about:

## AN RAF RADAR OPERATORS JOB AND HOW THEY FITTED INTO THE BIGGER PICTURE

"Everyone's war was different depending on which service they were in, where they were posted, the things they saw and experienced and mine was no exception, because whilst doing the main part of the job as a RADAR Operator it meant a lot of the 'war action' that me and others doing that same job saw was what we were tracking on a screen, which in some ways was like an early form of video game except it was deadly serious as the dots on the screen were real aircraft and real people and it was real people's lives we were working to protect in the important job we did, and that is no game! The equipment we manned and were trained to use allowed us to calculate a number of things about the incoming raids such as the range (distance), strength, height and bearing (direction) of the approaching enemy aircraft, which is a lot of information and it worked by sending out radio waves which would bounce off solid objects at a distance and enable us to estimate the four things I listed; hence the system and the apparatus being called RADAR - Radio Detection and Ranging. To the best of my knowledge this fitted into the bigger picture in the following way, the tracking was done from RADAR Stations including ours at RAF Swingate and the information passed on to the big plotting stations like RAF Stanmore, where they would have a huge table with the WAAF plotters at work collating all the incoming information about German aircraft formations, and from there they would ring it out to the squadrons nearest to enemy who would then scramble Spitfires and Hurricanes to intercept and attack the bombers, and depending on the size of the attacking force the RAF would decide how many squadrons to send up against them! But our Chain Home network of Radars that were dotted around the coastlines of the United Kingdom and covered the approaching airspace of our country were largely undetected by the Germans who were for the greater part totally unaware of how established and advanced this network of detection posts was and how they fed into the integrated system of air defence I have just mentioned, it was for these reasons that we were sworn to secrecy about the job we did at Radar stations and had to sign important paperwork to that effect.

In fact it was on the whole such a well-kept secret that even people in the local areas around them didn't know what the big RADAR towers were for and could only guess, as they were huge imposing structures and not really possible to hide, usually a set of four big ones and four smaller ones, as a result you heard from different sources that some though they might be something like death ray technology and crazy things such as that. I remember hearing an interview with a German airman many years after World War Two and he said that they weren't aware we had such an advanced system in place and even when on bombing raids passing over them they were hardly ever targeted because they were thought of as transmitting towers for the BBC or similar, maybe for the use of propaganda and as such were not viewed as a priority target. Good job really because if they had of become a valued target the Luftwaffe may have hit them harder like they did our RAF airfields during the Battle of Britain and I might not be sat here to share these things with you! In that interview he also said that the German aircrews and when fed back those higher up were always surprised that the RAF used to just pounce on them and seemed to be ready for them and know where they were and the direction they were heading, it was only after the war he learned about the extensive network that was in place and shocked how well-organised it was, more so than their own, no wonder he said the German air force had so many casualties over British skies at the hands of RAF Fighter Command! Sometimes if needs be we also got special transmissions from our planes called IFF – Identification, Friend or Foe to help us identify our own, and we would of course when needed help our aircrew and aircraft without hesitation when for example planes in distress transmitted another special and wider signal called 'Broad IFF' or SOS if they were damaged in any encounter with the enemy, or if they were making their way back to base after bombing raids where they might be flying low and limping in slowly, we gave extra special attention to these tracks and were sometimes requested by Stanmore to concentrate on certain ones so that if they ended up in the water the accuracy of our last plot would be essential to help air sea rescue have the best possible chance of finding and saving the lives of the downed crew, another different and very good function and use of Radar, I have wondered how many of those crews ever knew of our behind the scenes help in our inter-linked system? Overall though I am happy to say that I contributed in some small way to that air defence system being an ongoing success during the war years and did my bit to help try and keep our nation as safe and well defended as it could be under the circumstances."

**Above – The 'Chain Home' RADAR system inside and out, showing on the left a photo Don took of his colleague working in the same role as a Radar Operator on their control panel at RAF Swingate near Dover, the main Radar screen can be seen on the right-hand side of the picture, and another Radar Operator can be seen in the background helping calibrate or set the transmission frequency. On the right is a picture showing a good example of the masts of a Radar installation, this one at RAF Poling in Sussex where you can see three of the original four bigger 360 feet transmitter towers (left) and four 240 feet receiver towers (right) and the receiver building in the middle. The British 'Chain Home' system was quite an achievement and move forward in defence technology as it was the first early warning Radar network in the world, and the first military Radar system to reach operational status, its contribution was pivotal in winning the Battle of Britain and the ongoing defence of our nation throughout the entire war, tracking every kind of incoming threat from enemy aircraft to V1 and V2 rockets, and it continued in use well into the Cold War.**

It wasn't only here that Don would serve and apply his RAF trade as a RADAR Operator and Leading Aircraftman, he would end up in Asia tracking the air force of our other wartime enemy the Japanese whilst on a Mobile RADAR Station moving in many areas between India and Burma, tracking enemy aircraft movements something he now tells us more about: "When I was sent out to India in 1943 we were there to observe and report on the activities of the Japanese this time, a different part of the world and theatre of operations altogether. This time we were on self-contained RAF Mobile Radar Stations that were sent to many different areas along the India-Burma border regions and up and down coastlines in the Bay of Bengal undertaking long range Radar surveillance and tracking of enemy aircraft over the battle zones in and around Burma. Our units moved from area to allocated area in big specially adapted HGV's that had full fold out erectable Radar equipment along with support vehicles with power generators and all other manner of spare parts and supplies needed to keep us going. As an LAC – Leading Aircraftman and R.O –Radar Operator I was trained for a number of things including being a 'Motor Transport Driver' on all manner of vehicles from staff cars to trucks and HGV's, all of which I drove a lot, especially our heavy Radar Units because as a team we shared the driving in addition to our other main jobs, and who said men can't multi-task! Once in situ with equipment set up all good and useful real-time signals were tracked and as in the U.K relayed back to main HQ Plotting Stations that then got in touch with front-line fighter squadrons that would intercept the incoming enemy to hopefully bring them down before they could support operations or actions that were going on anywhere. So we were aware that we could well be contributing to the eventual outcome of some of the battles that were raging over in Burma during those periods, it felt like we were doing something useful, I later got the Burma Star for my work out there during that campaign, a nice acknowledgement for us who were really contributing behind the scenes on Terra Firma to what was happening up in the air."

Those last words lead nicely into this final summary and tribute to Don's contribution during the Second World War, which comes in the form of the motto of RAF Technical Training Command under which he trained as a RADAR Operator, that is: Labore Terrestri Caelestis Victoria – 'Victory in the air by dint of work on the Ground'. Very fitting. Thank you for everything Don.

Left – Don leaning against the cab of his 5-ton Mobile Radar Station in India, where he served from mid-1943 until the end of 1946.

Right - The Author together with WW2 Radar Operator Don Hollis on the day of the interview 1st July 2015 at Bletchley Park, Buckinghamshire, home of the top secret Second World War GC&CS – Government Code and Cypher School which post-war became acknowledged and famous for its code breaking. The Radar chain in which Don worked and served was a key component in our network of wartime defences around Great Britain and was also quite secretive work, some enemy transmissions that were intercepted at B.P which were of use to the RAF were passed onto them and acted upon to help alert this and other parts of the air defence system when required, as the encryption work undertaken there affected and was fed into all the armed forces at different levels depending upon the relevance and importance of the intel that was intercepted, which in turn as we now know helped shape and change the direction and shorten the longevity of the conflict over all, saving countless lives in the process and helping immensely to bring about an Allied victory in World War Two.

## Additional Information and Life After Service

**Rank upon finish of service** – LAC – Leading Aircraftman.

**Medals and Honours** – 1939-45 War Medal, 1939-45 Defence Medal, 1939-45 Star, Burma Star.

**Post War Years** – After demob Don returned in 1947 to his pre-war job on the railways where he worked for the next 42 years, during which time he was a Signalman at a number of places including Bletchley Station and later became an Inspector at London Euston Station and retired in 1989. In his spare time he also spent 50 years singing wartime songs in retirement homes. Don married Enid in 1952, his childhood friend, later sweetheart, who he met at 12 years of age in 1936. They were together until her passing in 2009. Children; 2 Daughters, 3 Grandchildren, 3 Great-Grandchildren.

**Associations and Organisations** – Lifelong member of the Royal Air Force Association.

# CHAIN HOME RADAR COVERAGE AROUND THE UNITED KINGDOM

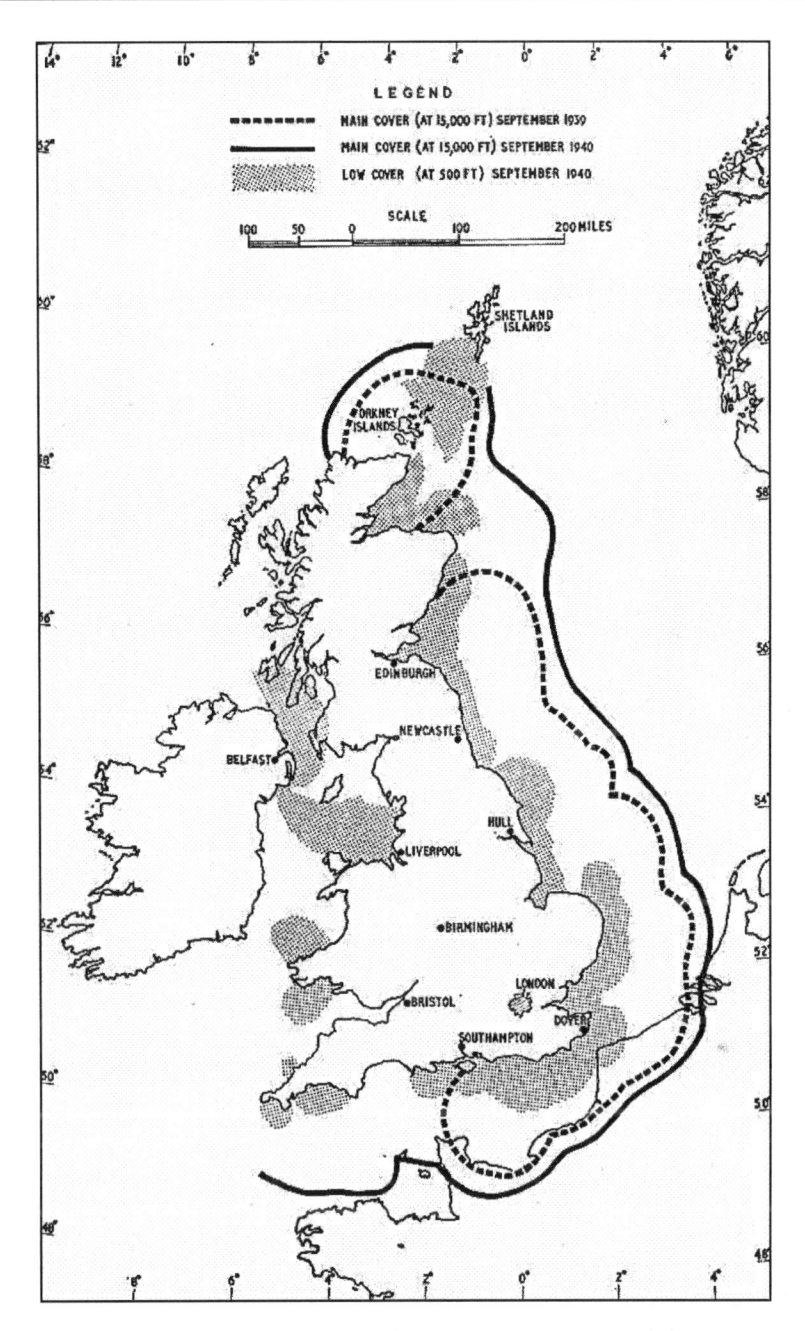

**Chain Home** – The early warning RADAR apparatus that was a very powerful weapon in the Royal Air Force defence system which surrounded most of the United Kingdom during World War Two. Shown here in this map with the dotted lines when war broke out in September 1939 is the extent of what was already a well-established defensive 'Chain' covering our 'Home' air space up to 15,000 feet and out across the English Channel to the French coast. One year later at the height of The Battle of Britain in September 1940 the solid line shows the increase in main cover expanding further into the continent, and with the Fall of France in June 1940 giving the Germans new bases much closer to the United Kingdom to launch aircraft from the Chain Home cover was expanded and extended further round the South West coast, this also helped give early warning regarding incoming Luftwaffe bomber formations that were heading for key Royal Navy port installation targets such as Plymouth, Portsmouth, Southampton and targets that were part of the 'Baedeker Raids' on towns and cities of cultural and historical significance in 1942 at a time when Don was serving at RAF Swingate. The C.H system continued to help protect Great Britain from subsequent Luftwaffe air raids until the end of the war, and also as new threats emerged in the post-war era.

# AIRCRAFTWOMAN JOAN JONES

Served with – WAAF – Women's Auxiliary Air Force – RAF

Service Number – 2127964

Interviewed – Broughton House for Ex-Servicemen & Women,
Higher Broughton, Greater Manchester, 16th September 2018

### Service History and Personal Stories

- Born – 6th June 1925, Penzance, Cornwall, England, UK.
- World War Two happened in two distinct phases for Joan Jones as it did for most men and women who served in many capacities during the years of that conflict. First as a civilian and second in the armed forces, and the very interesting experiences that occurred in their lives on the Home Front and in the military make for some interesting reading.
- The war became very real for Joan as a 15-year-old teenager in 1941 when during the Plymouth Blitz her street took a direct hit and many houses including hers were badly damaged. Then from 1942-1944 from the age of 16 to 18 Joan was part of the Civil Defence as a Fire Watcher around Plymouth, shortly after this she became directly involved in a different way when she joined the Royal Air Force as a WAAF.
- During her time in the WAAF from the summer of 1944 until the spring of 1946 Joan was trained at RAF Wilmslow in Cheshire and RAF Cranwell in Lincolnshire, and after her training had finished in

the Summer of 1944 went on to 'Active Service' at RAF Portreath in Cornwall which took her through to the early spring of 1945, then onto RAF Harrowbeer in Devon until Spring 1946 where she worked at both bases as a Teleprinter Operator.

- ❖ Joan's important job included receiving, sorting, typing up and sending on valuable messages from RAF Stations around the United Kingdom and forward airfields and bases out in the theatre of operations as the allies pushed westwards across Europe after D-Day, working on versions of what was at the time quite a modern piece of communication equipment, helping keep the vital flow of information going for it to be acted upon.
- ❖ Some of these messages were of a very secret nature and were received by Joan only in code which she immediately passed onto to her Commanding Officer, who would make sure they were relayed to the correct High Command and Intelligence branches elsewhere.
- ❖ Her contribution and that of all the WAAF's doing the same job at other RAF Stations that had these Teleprinters and indeed those in other branches of the armed forces elsewhere, helped provided essential parts of a military communications network that helped the allies win the Second World War. Joan was de-mobbed Spring 1946 in Exeter, Devon.
- ❖ In February 1945 Joan had married her sweetheart Albert who was a Royal Marine Master Tailor at the RM Barracks at Durnford Street, Plymouth, an extended part of HMNB – His Majesty's Naval Base Davenport, after they were both de-mobbed in 1946 they came to live in Manchester where Albert originated from and where his family had a Tailoring business and made a new life for themselves in post-war Britain.
- ❖ The dates of service within her story are based on information given from Joan's very good memory, and as with the story of Robert Walsh in the absence of service records.

When I recorded the memories of World War Two Women's Auxiliary Air Force veteran Joan Jones in September 2018 it was coincidently the centenary year of the Royal Air Force of which she was a part, it was also the first time I had interviewed a WAAF and the first time I had interviewed a female resident at Broughton House for Ex Servicemen and Women, so these and other things such as the role Joan played and her wartime experiences made it all very interesting indeed. Even before joining for the RAF in 1944 aged 18 Joan had already got a first-Hand taste of war whilst on the Home Front in Plymouth when experiencing air raids from the German Luftwaffe that damaged her house and on another occasion a near miss that nearly got Joan and her mother! Once she became a WAAF as with all those who joined the different services a new and interesting life awaited, in her case this would lead to postings at various RAF Stations in the U.K where she would be working as a Teleprinter Operator receiving important incoming messages from various RAF Stations including those forward H.Q's near front lines of battle zones, these would be sorted into order of importance and given to certain commanding officers when required, others would be typed up by Joan and sent onto the correct bases and people as directed on the messages, and interestingly some would arrive in code, these would be the most secret of those received. This interview with Joan now insures that within the book alongside stories of our servicemen there are stories of servicewomen from the main branches of the forces and other organisations that include ENSA, FANY/SOE, ATS/Home Office, WRNS and now WAAF, part of this varied and interesting cross-section again being captured and reflected here in Joan's engaging story as a servicewoman in World War Two, where she tells us about her:

<u>**WARTIME EXPERIENCES AND BEING IN THE WOMEN'S AUXILIARY AIR FORCE**</u>

"My wartime experiences and memories started as they did for many as a civilian on the Home Front as they called it. The Royal Navy had very big establishments, ports and presence around the city of Plymouth, that made it an important and big target for the Nazis, as a result both military and civilian targets were bombed as we found out on a number of occasions. We had some serious air raids in 1941, that is when the war really came home to us personally and to many other innocent people in the city, we lived on Union Street and during an air raid a neighbour's house two doors down got a direct hit, many houses around including ours were badly damaged and we all had to move out of our homes for a while until repairs made it possible for us to return. On another occasion when the air raid sirens sounded, people were running for their lives to shelters as bombs began to drop and as we were going into a public shelter a bomb landed nearby and the force of the explosion blew my mother on top of me, a very close and terrifying experience, we got inside safely, I think others were not so lucky!" The morale of the nation was sorely tested during the Blitz, and it is estimated that about 40,000 civilians were killed, 46,000 injured, and more than one million homes destroyed and damaged in Britain, staggering numbers. Many cities such as Manchester, Liverpool, Birmingham, Coventry, Hull, Edinburgh, Glasgow, Cardiff, Belfast, London, Portsmouth and Plymouth suffered serious damage, with this in mind I asked Joan about how she thought from her experience this effected the civilian population, and was told by her in a soft Cornish accent; "Hitler was trying to bomb the life and soul out of our great country but he failed because we as a nation mentally and physically were too strong to be beaten in that way! In fact on the whole I think it had the opposite effect and strengthened people's resolve to resist and made most people want to join the forces to fight more against him and all he stood for! Also we had a great wartime leader in Winston Churchill, who toured these war-torn cities as did the Royal Family, to show support for the people, sympathise with them to try and maintain morale. Churchill especially with his great and rousing wartime speeches and the posters we used to see around, all these helped the people a lot, I remember one which was good for Civilians and Military alike, it had a quote from him that said; "Let us go forward Together", very inspiring! **The famous wartime poster quoting Churchill, a good example of British morale boosting during the war years, something that Joan and many of that generation remember well.** I had to join something because I was soon to be 18, and at that age you either volunteered and could choose where to go or you were called up and they would then assign you anywhere doing anything, that you might not necessarily like! I could have ended up in the cook house or something like that, I wasn't going to wait to find out, my father wanted me to join the Navy and go into the WRNS because he had previously served in both the Merchant and Royal Navies, had served in World War One and later had become a Tug boat Captain in Plymouth, but I didn't fancy the Navy, at the time I was working in a hairdressers in Plymouth and went with a good friend of mine Marjorie first to the Army recruitment office to see about the ATS, and was told 'We are Full', how strange I thought, they then advised us to go up the road to the RAF recruitment office which we did and that is where we signed up for the WAAF. Surprisingly Marjorie and I ended up being posted to all our RAF Stations together and served all our time right through from start to finish experiencing many good times, very rare for this to happen for friends in any branch of the Armed Forces. We started in June 1944 by being sent for basic training at RAF Wilmslow in Wilmslow, Cheshire, where drill and discipline were the order of the day, after a few weeks of that we were

ready to be moved on to where we would get the specific training that we required for the option we had chosen which was to be a Teleprinter Operator. For this we went to very big training facility at RAF Cranwell near Sleaford in Lincolnshire (home and H.Q to No.22 Training Group in Technical Training Command, responsible for all training in 'Ground Trades' from electronics to cooking) this is where we received instruction in every aspect of the use of a Teleprinter. Luckily before the war I had already taken a secretarial course and could type well, that was an advantage both in the training and the job.

**Pictured: 'Serve in the WAAF' Recruitment poster, like those of other services reaching out to women, encouraging them to play their wartime part, which of course a great many did, and with distinction.** Once we had completed and passed our course we then put into action the things we'd learned when we were posted to RAF Portreath at Redruth in the country of my birth, Cornwall. Now on active duty our job was to operate these Teleprinters which were big noisy machines that were a cross between a typewriter and early kind of computer used to receive and send messages. They came out from the machine in front of us on printed sheets of paper, we would read them, most came through in plain English others in mixed letter and number codes, then we would decide what went where depending on its content and who and where it was meant for which in most cases was detailed as part of the message, in the case of the coded things they would be passed directly onto commanding officers who I believe would deal with that higher level of intelligence or sometimes tell us where to send it. Some of the messages were duplicates of those sent to multiple locations which included ours, others directly to us as we were one of the communications hubs for incoming RAF information. We would then type up and send on messages as directed using specific identifying codes for the onward recipients of this point-to-point contact. As we were dealing with information coming in from many places both in the U.K and elsewhere such as Europe we knew in the case of the coded messages that we were dealing with some very important information that had to be processed and passed on as quickly as possible, people's lives might depend on it. This work continued at my next and longest posting at RAF Harrowbeer which was an RAF Station at Yelverton close to my adopted home city of Plymouth. I was there when V.E Day came and we were allowed to go and join in the celebrations in town, happy people laughing, drinking and dancing everywhere, throughout the day into the night, even up on Plymouth Hoe which was the big open park in the south of the city where lots of people danced on the grass to music by the sea, near a lighthouse, can you imagine, lovely. By the Spring of 1946 I was demobbed and as I was now married to Albert a new life awaited us both. The war was over and had been won, the Germans and the Japanese had been defeated, thank goodness, and through our work we both felt we had been part of something important, and that we had contributed in our own way with the things we had done, and luckily we'd come through safely. I only had one slight 'injury' of sorts which I think has come from working in rooms that had many Teleprinters where the noise was thunderous, and after prolonged exposure to this noise I had developed very bad hearing in my left ear which later went completely, I am sure it was from my work in the WAAF, anyhow, no regrets!"

The Teleprinter that Joan worked on was also known as the teletypewriter, teletype or TTY, an electromechanical device that can be used to send and receive its important messages through various communication channels, in both point-to-point or point-to multipoint configurations. Some models could be used to create punched tape for data storage, either from typed input or from data received from a remote source, and to read back such a tape for local printing if required or onward transmission. A good example of both these options in use is in this picture from World War Two showing servicewomen busy at work on Teleprinters. These machines could work on a variety of different communication media such as dedicated non-switched telephone circuits (leased private lines) and switched networks that operated similarly to public telephone networks (telex) and later radio and microwave links (telex-on-radio, or TOR).

Women's Auxiliary Air Force as with all other female branches of the armed services contributed a lot during World War Two. It was mobilised in June 1939 and by July 1943 a peak strength of 182,000 had been reached, the women of the WAAF undertook a huge variation of jobs such as nurses, clerks, kitchen staff, telephony, telegraphy, the interception of codes and ciphers including those at Bletchley Park, aerial photographic intelligence interpreters (RAF Medmenham), mechanics, engineers, electricians, aircraft fitters, drivers, barrage balloon operators, radar control system reporters and plotters, some such as Noor Inayat Khan (who features in more detail later in the story of Jean Argles) became radio operators for the SOE in occupied Europe. Women joined the WAAF both from the U.K and many from overseas, with local recruitment taking place in the Caribbean, the Middle East and elsewhere with volunteers coming forward from the Egyptian, Palestinian, Jewish, Polish, Greek & Cypriot communities. Australia, New Zealand, South Africa and Canada all had WAAF sections in their air forces, 48 nationalities were represented within the force! In 1949 they became the WRAF - Women's Royal Air Force. All these hard working and bold women again reflecting the range of people from all backgrounds, cultures, religions and sexes that served within the British Armed Forces during the Second World War.

To finish as a tribute to one of the great women involved, Joan Jones, are these words that I feel reflect her personality, demeanour and values, a poem from her school days that Joan kindly shared with me during one of my visits, taught by her Headmistress Miss Austin;

"Whatever you are, be that. Whatever you say, be true. Straightforwardly act, be honest. In fact, be nobody else but you. Give every answer pat. Your character true unfurl. And when it is ripe. You'll then be the type. Of a capital English girl."

# Additional Information and Life After Service

**Rank upon finish of service** – ACW – Aircraftwoman.

**Medals and Honours** – HM Armed Forces Veterans Badge. No medals claimed.

**Post War Years** – After leaving the RAF in 1946 Joan settled in Greater Manchester, and for a number of years was a housewife and mother to their 2 children whilst her Husband Henry Albert Jones ran the family business as a Bespoke Tailor which was H. Jones Tailors in Market Street, Manchester. Joan subsequently returned to work pursuing a career in fashion, something she had started before the war. She worked for Richard Shops and Grafton House Store in Altrincham, Cheshire as a Fashion Clothing Sales Assistant. Later Joan utilised her secretarial skills once again and became a Personal Assistant to the Manager of GMTC Tools and Equipment in Timperley, Cheshire and retired aged 60 in 1985. Joan Married Albert on 1st February 1945 in Plymouth and were together until he passed in March 1996. They have 2 daughters, 4 Grandchildren, 7 Great-Grandchild.

**Associations and Organisations** – None.

**The contributions of women like Joan in all branches of the British and Commonwealth Forces and Civilian Occupations during World War Two, as highlighted throughout this book cannot and should not be underestimated nor forgotten. Various recruitment posters were created throughout Great Britain and her other Commonwealth countries and Dominions to help entice women into the many much needed and essential jobs that had to be filled, most of which then released men for front line service. This Australian poster 'Join Us in a Victory Job' is a great example of the varied roles women played during WW2, these roles being mirrored throughout many Allied countries involved in the conflict.**

# WARRANT OFFICER ROWLAND HILL

**Served with – Royal Air Force, SEAC – South East Asia Command**
**Service Number – 1234168**
**Interviewed – Urmston, Manchester, 16th March 2017**

## Service History and Personal Stories

- Born – 31st October 1921, Moss Side, Manchester, England, UK.
- Rowland volunteered for service in March 1941 at the Armed Forces Recruitment Centre in Dover Street, Manchester, where he chose to go into the Royal Air Force but wasn't called up to begin training until September 1941, after which he was sent to RAF Blackpool.
- Whilst there he also had to learn Morse Code as he had chosen to become a Wireless Operator, this instruction took place at the requisitioned Tram Sheds near the Manchester Hotel on the Blackpool Seafront, after which in 1942 he was sent for further advanced Morse and Wireless Training to the No.4 School of Signals at RAF Madley in Shropshire.
- This was followed by Gunnery training at RAF Evanton in Ross and Cromarty, Scotland, after passing as a Wireless Operator-Air Gunner he gained 3 strips and became a Sergeant.

- Then he was posted to RAF Ringway which is now Manchester Airport, where he was sent up with aircrews in Whitley Bombers as an Observer on the parachute training jumps being undertaken by new Paratrooper recruits over Tatton Park, Cheshire.
- Rowland was a trained pianist and before the war played in a dance band called The Meridians whose regular spot was in the Rainbow Dance Hall in Openshaw. During his time at RAF Ringway he was also part of the RAF Band which entertained the troops there.
- By 1943 his active service had taken him out to the Far East where he served with the RAF in SEAC - South East Asia Command, (Phoenix rising insignia on the first page), and as a Wireless Operator in the crew of a Consolidated B24 Liberator was part of 159 Squadron and undertook 32 bombing operations between December 1943 and November 1944.
- During that period Rowland flew on one of the longest missions of World War Two when on the night of 27th-28th October 1944 he was involved in a secret operation that took him on a 3000 mile round trip in a specially adapted B24 from Kalagphur in India to Panang near Kuala Lumpur in Malaya, where they dropped sea mines to blockade the Japanese held port and restrict enemy movement against the American Forces under Admiral Nimitz that were conducting operations on Japanese held islands in the Pacific.
- Interestingly soon after this Rowland flew as part of the crew in a test flight of a B24 Liberator to check its equipment which was flown by Group Captain Leonard Cheshire VC, who had come out as an observer for the special long-distance mission previously detailed.
- His next posting from November 1944 until June 1945 was with a very special yet lesser-known RAF Squadron called the BBC - Bengal and Burma Communications Squadron which was part of Transport Command where he undertook a further 33 operations in DC3's and various other aircraft.
- This also included some dangerous missions such as dropping essential supplies far behind enemy lines deep into the jungles of Burma to Special Operations units known as the Chindits, who were conducting close combat attacks on the Japanese.
- At that time he was involved in other intriguing operations such as flying planes full of South-East Asian POW's, some of whom were suspected of collaboration with the enemy from Burma for interrogation by the British in India, using a Vickers-Armstrong Warwick that had been converted for passenger carrying use in mainly second line roles.
- During these active-duty postings with 159 and BBC squadrons Rowland completed an incredible 65 operations, more than 2 full operational tours over the hostile enemy territory of Burma, French Indochina (modern day Vietnam, Laos and Cambodia), Malaya and India.
- Then to finish his flying days, but not active service, Rowland and the crew of his Douglas DC3 were chosen for another very different task when they flew the well-known entertainer George Formby and his wife Beryl around Burma for a week in March 1945, taking them to entertain the troops with ENSA, where he saw all the shows George performed, another interesting part of a very diverse career in His Majesty's Royal Air Force.
- Rowland then finished on the BBC Squadron and was sent to be one of the Instructors at RAF ASTR Signals School in Calcutta, India were his skills and huge amount of experience were required to train aircrews who were being sent over from Bomber Command in Europe, where they had been on Halifax and Lancaster Bombers with the R1155 and T1154 U.K radio equipment and needed to learn the different RCA U.S radio equipment that they were converting onto for operations in SEAC, he finished instructing there in late 1945.
- He was then sent to his final posting at a parachute school in Rawalpindi, India, now Pakistan, where he said 'I was playing sports and passing time until the end of service'.
- After returning home a few months later Rowland, now a Warrant Officer, was finally demobbed at RAF Kirkham in Lancashire, ending a very eventful time in the service of his country.

During his active service in World War Two Rowland Hill completed a staggering 65 operations as part of SEAC in South-East Asia. If you find an RAF veteran who completed and survived even half that number in any of the various Royal Air Force commands during that conflict you would be quite lucky. For me to find someone who had achieved that was in itself something to be very happy about, but when I found out that I had the great added privilege of being the first person to ever interview Rowland about his Second World War service I was both surprised and elated. There is always something extra special about being the first person to ever officially talk to and record for posterity the experiences and service history of a veteran, and I am so glad I did because Rowland has such a great story to share with us all. As a Wireless Operator on bombing and minelaying missions through to supply and transport missions carried out on a number of different aircraft throughout South-East Asia and flying as part of aircrew to many areas in what was then British ruled India, and finishing with him and his crew being selected to fly a well-known entertainer of the day George Formby and his wife Beryl to ENSA shows that were held very close to the frontlines in Battle zones around Burma, Roland now divulges to us what it was like to be:

## SERVING AS AIRCREW IN SOUTH-EAST ASIA COMMAND

"I was very fortunate to have had a very interesting time and quite varied service in the RAF, starting even from the time of recruitment, when I was going through my selection process they thought I would be best suited for the role of Wireless Operator because I was already a pianist and believed I would have finely tuned hearing for things like Morse Code and radio communications, and so the adventures began. Once I had passed training for W.O and Gunnery we sailed from Scotland to Egypt on the famous Queen Mary Cruise Liner which carried myself and around 8000 others to North Africa, from there we flew a Bristol Blenheim Bomber **(like the one pictured here on the left)** through to Iraq then down the Persian Gulf and delivered it all the way to India, quite a journey, after which we got posted out to 159 Squadron as part of SEAC and ended up doing 32 bombing missions on American Liberators from airfields such as Salboni, Digri and Dhubalia in West Bengal, India, flying over enemy territory all around South-East Asia attacking all legitimate targets of value such as Japanese airfields, railway stations and lines, ammunition dumps, communication facilities and ports. We also did an extremely long 18-hour mission which was 1500 miles each way from India to Malaya, 15 B24's each with four 1000-pound acoustic mines that we laid. We flew operations over many other places as well such as Mandalay, Rangoon and Bangkok. Later when they told me I was being posted to the BBC I thought it was strange they were sending me to work with the British Broadcasting Company, but actually it was a Squadron which was part of RAF Transport Command called the Bengal and Burma Communications Squadron. This led to me undertaking many more wide-ranging operations, mainly in DC3 supply aircraft such as dropping vital supplies to the Chindits in the Burmese jungles, but also doing reconnaissance in a U.S Beachcraft light transport-spotter plane and flying suspected enemy collaborators and POW's in a Warwick, the civilian conversion of the Wellington Bomber, from Burma to India for our intelligence people to question them. On one of our supply drops to a place called Ramree Island we arrived and none of our lads appeared to greet us and unload as usual, then we heard a shout from behind some bushes saying 'get out the Japs have taken the other end of the runway' we didn't have to be told twice, we just turned round without unloading and flew straight back out with shots sounding behind us, lucky escape!"

An American built Consolidated B24 Liberator similar to the one in which Roland completed 32 Operations, here shown in British service and markings during World War Two. One of the aircraft he flew in was G for 'Goofy' as they lovingly named it, which had an 8–10-man crew depending on the operations being undertaken.

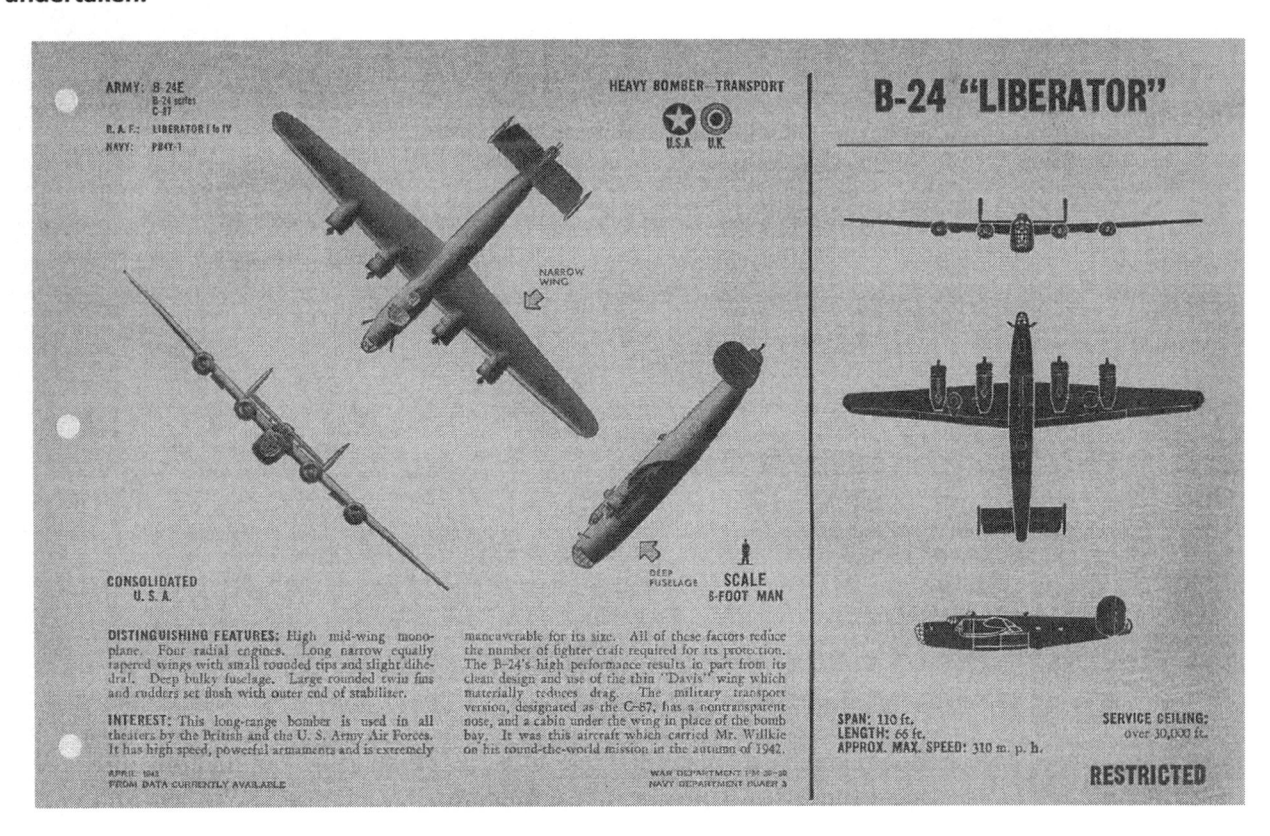

Wartime 'Restricted' Government/Military Recognition Drawings of the Consolidated B-24E Liberator. Note: Top centre, roundels indicating use by US & UK Bomber and Transport Commands.

"Then on what was to become my last operational flying, where we were given something really interesting and quite enjoyable when we were assigned to fly the popular entertainer George Formby and his wife Beryl who were part of the organisation ENSA to shows around Burma for a week in March 1945. These shows were all for front line troops in what really were front line areas, similar to what Vera Lynn used to do when she entertained the troops over there, sometimes whilst the show was going on you could hear the fighting which was less than a mile away, crazy when I look back at it now! We took them to all their shows, saw all their shows, and being a bit of a musician myself I appreciated the shows in many ways, all the crew spent time with them socially as well, a very nice experience to end my flying days." Even though his flying was over I knew his RAF service didn't finish there and I asked him to tell me more about what came after and he told me: "I remember being in Calcutta, India when V.E Day was declared and the news came through that the war in Europe was over, and we of course hoped the same would soon follow where we were! I was lucky because by then I was an instructor at the ASTR – Aircrew Signals Training Refresher School in Calcutta, doing radio conversion training for newly arriving aircrews, but that day I saw many men from the 14th Army who had come from the savage fighting in the jungle, they became known as 'The Forgotten Army', although the news was greeted with optimism in the bars they knew the war was still going on where they were and they didn't feel like doing too much celebrating as the war remained very real for them, especially when their leave was over! After kicking our heels during the last posting in Rawalpindi it was 1946, the war in the Far-East was over and it was time to return home, all of that journey from India to the Great Britain was made on another big and famous Cruise Liner the Franconia. Soon after returning I was de-mobbed at RAF Kirkham in my home county of Lancashire, bringing to an end five good years which were very well spent doing my bit."

A signed photo from George Formby to Roland saying: 'To Maxi thanks for a good trip George Formby and Beryl Burma 1945'. They got on so well by that time that George called him by his nickname 'Maxi' an abbreviation of his middle name Maxwell. George and Beryl, pictured, took Roland and the two other crew members of the DC3 for a special 'thank you' dinner at the prestigious Great Eastern Hotel in Calcutta before returning home to the United Kingdom.

# THE REMARKABLE TEAM

Behind Every Great Man is a Great Woman, so the saying goes and Rowland and Winifred Hill, nee Jervis certainly have been a real testament to that. Married 74 years at the time of finishing writing this part in Spring 2022, and as they were neighbours before that at Great Southern Street in Moss Side from 1938 they have been in each other's lives for a staggering 84 years! During the war Win played her part on the Home Front working in a reserved occupation as a Clerk in the cost office at Crossley Diesels on Pottery Lane, Gorton, Manchester, where the company made Diesel Engines for RAF Rescue Aircraft.

Thank you both for your contributions during wartime and after as part of a generation that really did in the words of a poem in this book put the 'Great' in 'Great Britain.' It was lovely to meet you both in May 2022 after 2 long years of the Pandemic and spend precious time with you again.

## Additional Information and Life After Service

**Rank upon finish of service** – Warrant Officer.

**Medals and Honours** – 1939-45 War Medal, 1939-45 Defence Medal, 1939-45 Star, Africa Star, Burma Star with Pacific Bar.

**Post War Years** – From 1946 until his retirement aged 70 in 1992 Rowland worked as a Salesman for many well-known companies such as Remington, Danish Bacon and Bookers Foods. Married Winifred at Christ Church, Moss Side, Manchester on the 3rd July 1948. Children; 2 Sons.

**Associations and Organisations** – Both members of St. Mary's Church, Davy Hulme, Manchester.

# LEADING AIRCRAFTMAN ROBERT WALSH

Served with – Royal Air Force 224 Squadron Coastal Command
Service Number – 1078027
Interviewed – Unsworth, Lancashire, 20th March 2019

### Service History and Personal Stories

- Born – 14th October 1922, Prestwich, Manchester, England, UK.
- Robert Walsh volunteered for the Royal Air Force aged 18 at the Dover Street recruitment office, Manchester in December 1940 around the time of the Manchester Blitz when the centre of the city was being devastated by enemy bombing. As he was already an apprentice electrician he was advised to go for a similar trade in the Royal Air Force as ground crew on essential aircraft maintenance as he had good transferrable skills.
- Next was RAF Padgate in Warrington for medicals and selection where he was chosen to become an AC – Aircraftman. But first basic training had to be undertaken, for this he was sent to Blackpool, billeted at St. Chad's Road at South Pier and sent to Blackpool Football ground to receive lectures and put through tough physical training by their Physical Training Instructor who happened to be one Stanley Mathews, the famous football League, European and later World Cup player, this lasted for 6 weeks taking Robert into early 1941.
- This was followed by his trade training, firstly at RAF Henlow in Bedfordshire under No.13 M.U - Maintenance Unit where he did 6 weeks of Aircraft Electrical training in Spring 1941, then

- onto No.60 O.T.U – Occupational Training Unit at RAF East Fortune near Edinburgh, Scotland where he was stationed for 10 months of hands-on training on various aircraft including the Westland Lysander, Bristol Blenheim and Boulton Paul Defiant's.
- Now trained as an Aircraftman Robert was posted to RAF St. Eval near Newquay in Cornwall as part of Royal Air Force Coastal Command on No.224 Squadron, and from early 1942 till spring 1943 he worked servicing electrical equipment on Consolidated B24 'Liberator' long-range heavy bombers, as these American made aircraft were starting to be used more widely within the service in the various roles that Coastal Command undertook.
- It was because of their long-range capability that the B24 flew on convoy escort duties and anti-U-Boat operations from RAF St. Eval over the North Atlantic and Mediterranean finishing down at RAF Gibraltar, then after servicing and re-fuelling doing similar operations as directed on the return journey back to their Cornish base in the U.K.
- RAF Gibraltar was short of all sorts of maintenance technicians, and Robert was one of those chosen along with various other ground crew from 224 Squadron to be posted out there from Spring until Autumn of 1943, those tradesmen sent consisted of Instrument Repairers, Armourers, Airframe Fitters, Mechanics and Electricians.
- Then in late of 1943 an opportunity arose on a B24 crew for an Air Gunner, and Robert finally seeing his chance to be part of a flying aircrew volunteered and was accepted for the temporary position. His gunnery training took place at RAF Gibraltar and included practice on in-air towed moving targets called Drogues, after all weapons training was successfully completed by the end of 1943 his active service duty as a Rear-Gunner took place for 8 months from Spring to Autumn 1944.
- His active flying operations consisted of giving very important air cover for shipping convoys and in relation to that tracking, engaging and attempting to destroy any U-Boats that were intercepted during those escort missions which ran from the Mediterranean back to the United Kingdom. During that time he was made a temporary Flight Sergeant.
- After completing his time as temporary Air Crew Robert was again transferred back to his job as an Electrical Engineer/Aircraftman and in late 1944 his next posting again took him somewhere completely different, this time out to what was then British Mandate Palestine to RAF Lydda near Tel-Aviv, where he served for 6 months until spring 1945. Over that period he also managed to pass the tests to become an LAC-Leading Aircraftman and worked giving ground vehicles and aircraft the maintenance they required.
- Just before the war in Europe ended Robert was transferred to the port city of Piraeus near Athens in Greece, where the allied forces were in control of the country after the German withdrawal. His skills were now required for something totally different when he was part of a team helping to get the ONON power generating plants up and running again, he was there when V.E Day arrived and remained working there until spring 1946.
- Upon return to the U.K his final posting was to RAF Leighton Buzzard in Bedfordshire, where along with many others he was given the task of destroying large amounts of material now surplus to requirements at this huge RAF Communications base, such as electrical equipment, batteries, cabling, and tools.
- Once this was completed he was released from service, and as his RAF Pay book shows his date of departure from Dispersal Centre was 26th July 1946 (at Wembley in London as Robert remembers), and his final release date was 19th October 1946, his last unit showing as No.26 OTU, 91 Group. *Note – Full service records were not available as Robert didn't have them at time of interview, hence most dates given by season not by months as all timings given by Robert are from memory.

I first met Robert Walsh in early 2019 when I did a talk about my work with veterans along with a book signing at B.O.B.V.A – Borough of Bury Veterans Association in Greater Manchester. The welcome I received from the association members and Robert who bought one of my books was very hospitable, as a result I am now a civilian member of B.O.B.V.A and Robert is a friend. When he came to talk with me I couldn't believe it when he said he was a World War Two veteran, he looked like he was in his 80's, not his 90's! He was of course telling the truth and he showed me some photos and we talked about his really interesting service in RAF Coastal Command where he served both on ground crew and air crew which is quite rare, I knew I just had to capture this in an interview if he kindly gave me permission to do so, which I am very pleased was the case. Since then I have got to know him well and even introduced him to WW2 AVRO worker Lilian Grundy who is in my first book and they became a couple, a beautiful thing indeed. On the 14th October 2022 Robert became a centenarian, and soon after everyone at the veterans association helped him celebrate this important milestone, a special day for a special veteran. So here is Robert's captivating story, starting from before his service right through to the end of it:

### FROM BEING A CIVILIAN IN THE BLITZ TO REPAIRING AIRCRAFT AND HUNTING U-BOATS IN THE RAF

"My experiences of war started on the Home front in Manchester and Salford before I went into the Armed Forces because I was still living at home on Walnut Street in Lower Broughton, Salford during what was known as the 'Manchester Blitz', and when we returned home after an air raid one time the roof of our house had been blown off and other houses around damaged, and further down the street very sadly people had been killed, those kind of things really effected everyone because in those days there was a real sense of community and all the street knew each other, grew up together, so it is not meant as a joke when I say those things really hit home! During that time I was working as an Auto Electrical Apprentice at a firm called Universal Auto Electric in the centre of Manchester and soon after when I arrived for work one morning there wasn't much of the place left, as it had been bombed as well, I still feel I was fortunate though, that when the Germans came calling both times I was out! When you saw things like that and your city under attack and burning, even as a civilian it really brought the war right to you but it also motivated me and many others I knew to want to take the fight back to the enemy, and so I volunteered for the RAF. I wanted to be aircrew at first but was persuaded to use the skills I had already learned as an electrician to become part of ground crew, but my first wish did come true for a while later on! Once I had been accepted and training was underway I found myself up in Scotland at RAF East Fortune, that's where we started to really get to grips with working on and learning about lots of different aircraft, including the Bristol Blenheim which I went up in once to check equipment on a test flight. After this I was posted down to RAF St. Eval in Cornwall and onto what would be my active wartime Squadron, No. 224, where we were responsible for servicing and maintaining all things electrical on the huge four-engine B24 Liberators on this Coastal Command Station. This comprised of doing daily inspection and maintenance checks of all electrical equipment on board aircraft before they went out on operations, on things like Navigational and Cockpit Lights, Bomb release mechanisms which were the electronic clamps that held the depth charges and the clamps that held the arming pins on munitions in the bomb bays, pre-flight we would work with the Flight Engineer on most of these things, he would also run up the engines so we could check the alternator that charged the battery in each engine was working properly by observing the instruments. Post-flight after operations the pilot would report any faults to the officer in charge, which would be relayed to us as the ground crew who would each work on our specialisation and repair what was needed such as instruments, fuel, radio, electrical etc. Once we even serviced Winston Churchill's aircraft and saw him when he was passing through RAF Gibraltar, a small claim to fame there."

I went on to ask Robert about some of the things he experienced and action he saw during his time as a Rear-Gunner on B24's undertaking convoy escort duties and anti-U-Boat missions, and he told me:

"I enjoyed my time as ground crew, but always wanted to experience being air crew, so when the chance came at RAF Gibraltar I jumped on it and trained to become an air-gunner, this led to me becoming a rear-gunner in a B24 heavy bomber, a real adventure that led to me being involved in operations to give air cover to essential shipping convoys and at the same time doing U-Boat hunting in areas around the convoys we were helping protect. We flew on a lot of outward and return missions over the 8 months I was involved on that temporary transfer in 1944, from RAF Gibraltar to RAF St. Eval in Cornwall, over the Mediterranean and North Atlantic Seas, we used sonar equipment to detect U-Boats that were still present and making kills even at that late time in the war, we would come in low and drop depth charges on those coordinates and if oil and wreckage came to the surface then it would be photographed to help confirm as a success once back at base. I once saw a U-Boat on the surface, we came back round to attack it, by which time it had dived, we still hit the target area with depth charges and had some oil come up but not wreckage so it wasn't a definite kill, but some were quite successful in our squadron." **Left – A U-Boat, similar to those that Robert and 224 Squadron hunted, this one escorted by allied tugs after surrendering at the end of WW2.**

Robert continued to tell me about another interesting episode that happened during his time on flying operations, which involved close combat with a German Fighter-Bomber: "Once when we were on escort duties back to the U.K we came under attack from what I think by the look of it was a Messerschmitt ME 110, a fast twin-engine aircraft with two crew, it took us by surprise, strafed us and shot out our forward undercarriage on the first run in, but when it came round again to attack for the second time I was ready and engaged it with the heavy twin machine guns I had at the back, giving it some good hard bursts of fire which made it brake off its attack. We were able to continue with our flight duties and at the break off point we left the convoy and headed onto our U.K home base at RAF St. Eval where we were forced to do an emergency landing, which the pilot did very skilfully by first touching down with the main or wing wheels that were okay, then dipping the huge aircraft onto its front belly scraping along until we came to a stop, we were all able to walk away unscathed so you can call that landing a successful one for sure!"

**A very interesting picture of Robert's B24 'Liberator' after its emergency landing with members of the 224 Squadron ground crew posing in front of it, as Robert recalls 'I think we were having breakfast when this was taken.' Note the distinct white aircraft colouring of RAF Coastal Command.**

Robert Walsh, World War Two RAF Coastal Command veteran, truly one of 'The Last Heroes' being presented by Peter Lees with an engraved ceremonial stick and framed picture with his No. 224 Squadron Badge on them, gifts from the Borough of Bury Veterans Association to mark his 100th birthday which was on the 14th October 2022. Robert was, at time of writing, the oldest attending veteran of B.O.B.V.A.

To finish, Robert it's a real pleasure to have met and got to know such decent and pleasant gentleman as you, the 224 Squadron motto; Fedele all' Amico - 'Faithful to a Friend' describes you very well.

## Additional Information and Life After Service

**Rank upon finish of service** – LAC – Leading Aircraftman.

**Medals and Honours** – 1939-45 Defence Medal, 1939-45 War Medal, 1939-45 Star, Palestine Medal.

**Post War Years** – After leaving the Air Force in 1946 Robert worked for Universal Auto Electric, then Kingsway Auto Electrical, then in the 1960's became a self-employed Auto Electrician for many garages until his retirement in 1992 aged 70. Married Vera in 1947 at Wrexham, together until her passing in 2010. Has 1 Son, 1 Daughter, 3 Grandchildren, 5 Great-Grandchildren.

**Associations and Organisations** – RAF Association – Bury Branch, B.O.B.V.A – Borough of Bury Veterans Association, George Formby Appreciation Society – Robert is a very keen Ukulele player.

# WARRANT OFFICER FREDERICK HOCKENHULL

Served with – Royal Air Force, 283 Squadron, Coastal Command
Service Number – 1086042
Interviewed – Didsbury, Manchester, 2nd September 2014

## Service History and Personal Stories

- Born – 19th October 1921, Cholton-on-Medlock, Manchester, England, UK.
- Frederick Seymour Hockenhull AKA Fred began his World War Two service when he joined the Royal Air Force on 17th April 1941 at the RAF Recruitment Centre at Padgate, Warrington, (RAF Padgate). After this extensive aircrew training took place over the next 2 years, listed here by year and courses until eventually he became a fully trained WOP/A.G – Wireless Operator/Air Gunner in RAF Coastal Command.
- In 1941 this consisted of 2 months at RAF Blackpool in Lancashire undertaking aptitude, selection and basic training, and once it was decided what he was going to specialise in Fred was sent to RAF Compton Basset in Wiltshire which was a major Radio and Radar Training School that was part of No.27 Group Technical Training Command.
- Following on from this in 1942 were higher level RAF Trade skills in Radio Communications which included Morse Code and equipment maintenance taught at RAF Bodorgan in Anglesey home of No.48 MU – Maintenance Unit, work was also carried out there on Percival Proctor, Airspeed Oxford and AVRO Anson aircraft for practical experience.
- Fred then went on in mid-1942 to train for six months in his other required operational skill as an Air Gunner and was sent to RAF Walney Island off the coast of Barrow-in-Furness, Cumbria, home to

No.10 Air Gunnery School. It was there whilst on an Air Gunnery course that he and others were trained using Ground-to-Air techniques firing from fixed turrets on the ground and Air-to-Air techniques when flying in Boulton Paul Defiant aircraft and shooting at moving target drones towed for both types of practices by Westland Lysander aircraft.

- ❖ These intense courses also taught the Gunners many other important and useful skills and practices such as; Aircraft recognition, gun sighting, pyrotechnics, clay pigeon and 25 yard range shoots, care and maintenance of many different calibre weapons such as .303 and .5 Browning machine guns and 20mm cannons, turret hydraulics, the use manipulation and operation of cine-camera guns, and by the end of 1942 having now successfully completed training as a Wireless Operator and Air Gunner Fred was awarded the rank of Sergeant.
- ❖ He now had the expertise to serve in either Bomber or Coastal Command, by early 1943 the branch of RAF service Fred would go into had been decided and he was sent to an RAF Coastal Command Operational base at RAF Long Kesh in Northern Ireland, and there was put on Bristol Beaufort Torpedo bombers to gain more of the required and specific skills for Coastal Command duties when he completed low-level torpedo attack and mine-laying training and was also able to practice as a WOP/A.G – Wireless Operator/Air Gunner.
- ❖ By the Autumn of 1943 Fred was chosen to join RAF 283 Squadron which was an ASR – Air-Sea Rescue Squadron, in preparation for this in October 1943 additional specialist training was undertaken for these tasks at the RAF Air Sea Rescue Training Unit which was part of No.16 Group at RAF Thornaby near Thornaby-on-Tees in the North Riding of Yorkshire.
- ❖ In March 1944 283 Squadron had received new Vickers Warwick aircraft and by April were operating them in an Air-Sea Rescue role around the Mediterranean theatre of operations on a mix of anti-submarine and air-sea rescue missions, as part of the latter they would locate downed airmen and drop rescue equipment to them and helped save many lives.
- ❖ One of those interesting ASR missions occurred when Fred and his crew were called out to help a vessel belonging to Neutral Spain that had sent out an SOS distress call in the middle of the night. This led to 2 Warwicks being despatched in a nigh time mission dropping flares to mark the position and then dropping life jackets and life boats to the crew stranded in the water, later other Warwicks took over and in the early daylight all the crew were saved and the vessel towed to a port for repairs, later a thank you message came from the Spanish Government to 283 Squadron for their help in the operation.
- ❖ April until October 1944 Fred and the crew of his ASR MK 1 Warwick, numbering 6 in total, were based at RAF Hal Far on the island of Malta, after which they were transferred for a short time to RAF Kalamaki (later renamed Hassani) near Athens on mainland Greece from November 1944 to January 1945, then they were assigned to a very special mission which would see them play their part in a very important historical event of World War Two.
- ❖ Late January to early February 1945 Fred flew as a WOP/A.G – Wireless Operator/Air Gunner in a special detachment consisting of 6 Coastal Command Warwick's that had been specially modified for long-distance travel with additional Air-Sea safety equipment in order to escort Winston Churchill from Malta on the huge 2750-mile round trip to Saki in the Russian Crimea and back for the Yalta Conference that took place between 4th-11th February 1945 between Churchill, Roosevelt and Stalin.
- ❖ It was at this vitally important conference that the future shape of post-war Europe would be decided, and the huge responsibility for the Prime Minister's travel and safety lay partly with Fred and his crew who escorted the plane that Churchill travelled in to and from this historic meeting of the allied leaders. More rare WW2 moments captured in this book.
- ❖ Once the detachment had completed their 'Special Mission' they returned to operate from their former base at RAF Hal Far under the command of AHQ – Air Headquarters Malta where they

- continued their life saving Air-Sea Rescue and other support work until RAF 283 Squadron (bearing the eight-pointed Maltese Cross as part of its squadron badge) finished its operational life there on 31st March 1946. During that time Fred who had now become a Warrant Officer also flew over to and completed some operational duties in North Africa at Algiers in Algeria.
- 2 weeks well-deserved leave followed for Fred and fellow crewmen which he described as MEDLOC – Mediterranean Leave Over the Continent, and after returning back to the U.K he was demobbed in his home town of Manchester on the 19th April 1946 bringing to an end exactly 5 years and 2 days service in the Royal Air Force and for his country.

When I conduct interviews with my World War Two veterans I always ask as an additional question of interest; "Have you ever met or seen any well-known or even famous person or people involved in that conflict from Military, Political, Royal or other backgrounds?" The reasons I ask this is because apart from it being generally quite interesting if it did occur it would of course normally come with its own personal little story attached to it that makes it even more appealing to any potential reader, and in Fred's case this was no exception because his story was not a little one but something quite big indeed, as he was with one of the six specially chosen aircrews from No.283 Squadron that flew, escorted and gave Air-Sea Rescue back-up for Winston Churchill on his trips to and from the very important Yalta Conference in the Crimea, Russia where between the 4th-11th February 1945 the fate and shape of post-war Europe was to be decided. Amongst the many people playing their parts at this hugely significant historical meeting between the 'Big Three' Allied wartime leaders Soviet Premier Joseph Stalin, British Prime Minister Winston Churchill and the President of the United States of America Franklin D. Roosevelt was Coastal Command Wireless Operator & Air Gunner Fred Hockenhull, who along with this very special experience now also shares with us other parts of his wartime service in his first ever interview since these events happened over seven decades ago that I was privileged to get, and which included his recollections in RAF Coastal Command of rescuing downed allied airmen, hunting dreaded Nazi U-Boats through to leaflet drops and much more as a:

<u>COASTAL COMMAND AIR-SEA RESCUE SERVICEMAN DURING WORLD WAR TWO</u>

"Our job in Air-Sea Rescue involved many different things and as a result led to many wide-ranging experiences in the course of our duties. We flew on specially adapted Vickers Warwick ASR Mark 1 aircraft that carried a lot of vital life-saving equipment called 'Lindholme' which included essentials such as food, water and dinghy's that we dropped to downed airmen in the sea after we located them at or near their last known co-ordinates, they ended up in the drink for a variety of reasons such as mechanical engine failure or damage caused due to enemy action, we had to locate them quickly because if we didn't then other potential factors such as water currents taking them away from their original known or approximate downed position or if at sunset a possible rapid loss of light could lead to a rapid loss of life! We flew a lot of the time out from our base at RAF Hal Far in Malta over the vast Mediterranean, it certainly could feel that way sometimes when trying locate people, although if we were lucky they might have been able to give coordinates before ditching or use visual aids such as flares or coloured dyes in the water when they saw us searching for them and other times tracking was made easier by other aircraft that may be looking for or that may have spotted them in the water radioing in recent coordinates to help us. It was always a good feeling to find and essentially help save these brave guys. Our aircraft or 'Kites' as we liked to call them could the same as all others used in Coastal Command be modified to take different sizes and kinds of loads, whether that be Air-Sea Rescue equipment or conversion by ground crew mechanics to carry depth charges to use in Anti-Submarine warfare, something we also did when called upon and ordered to do by Air Headquarters Malta which was one of the main commands that also implemented the war against the ever-present threat of Nazi U-Boats that existed in the Med, even in the latter part of the war. So the Warwick's of our 283 Squadron would sometimes conduct medium to long range search and destroy operations against them, something they were well-equipped to do and did well, guided through the use of radar equipment, positive and possible sightings or engagements with our forces or even pure luck and rare chance sightings when scouring 'hot areas' these deadly enemy subs could and sometimes would be detected, damaged or destroyed! This was something we all engaged in, coming in low, dropping our depth-charges on the U-boats whether they were on the surface, diving or already under, then circling back round looking for oil or wreckage to help confirm a potential kill! When we were on another posting in Greece in late 1944 at RAF Kalamaki near Athens and things were hotting up in what was essentially becoming a messy 'Greek Civil War' we were sent to drop a different kind of load that time which were leaflets I think were propaganda to hopefully let the civilian population know that we were there to help them now that the Germans had withdrawn and things like that, we also helped the Navy on mine clearance operations in harbours and photo reconnaissance at the Corinth Canal which the Germans had left in a right mess, anyway our cargos certainly changed depending on the different kinds of missions we flew!"

The Twin-Engine Vickers Warwick ASR (Air-Sea Rescue) Mk. 1, a special conversion of their famous Wellington Bomber. Fred Hockenhull served on these aircraft during his active operational time in Coastal Command when he was with No. 283 Squadron between 1943 to 1946. In its fully-developed Stage C version this aircraft was equipped with ASV Radar, additional fuel tanks, Lindholme life-saving supplies, and either the Airborne Lifeboat MK.1 produced by Uffa Fox, which weighed 771kg, was 6.1 metres long and could carry around 6 men and be dropped to them on three attached parachutes, or the bigger 9.1 metre long, 1633kg Heavy MK.2 Lifeboat which could carry ten men. The ASR Warwicks had three-gun turrets, one of which if required was manned by a duel-trained Wireless Operator/Gunner like Fred. The Warwick ASR MK.1 contributed very much to the ASR - Air Sea Rescue service run by RAF Coastal Command where it operated with 14 squadrons in many roles such as those described within this story.

In previous veterans RAF related stories I have written there have been airmen featured who flew in many types of World War Two heavy aircraft such as the Vickers Wellington, Handley Page Halifax, Short Sterling, AVRO Lancaster, Consolidated Liberator, but interestingly Fred was the first aircrewman I interviewed and have featured in a profile who served in the Vickers Warwick which as described before was specially modified for use in the RAF Air Sea Rescue service and was one of the big reasons that with further modifications it was chosen and used for the next big operation that Fred was engaged in, and along with other things he now tells us about:

### BEING PART OF CHURCHILL'S PERSONAL ESCORT TO THE YALTA CONFERENCE IN RUSSIA

"Our aircraft had been completely modified and the bomb bay totally re-assembled to have an airborne lifeboat fitted so if Churchill had come down in the Black Sea we could have dropped a purpose-built lifeboat to pick him up within minutes, our plane was also fitted with tarpaulins and all sorts of medical devices in case it was necessary, but fortunately they weren't necessary as it worked out very successfully, the whole mission. We took them out there safely as the escort and then had to wait for them in a place called Saki in the Crimea for a period of time and later we returned with Churchill safely back to Malta, where we were all thanked by him for our efforts, after which he travelled on I think with another escort. On the earlier outward journey we landed with Churchill, and Roosevelt had already arrived so we saw him as well, but on the return journey we took off with Churchill first so we didn't see the American President on the way back at all. Whilst waiting in Saki we enjoyed the delights of real Russian Vodka, it helped keep us warm I can tell you, much needed out there in February, and was that strong I'm sure you could fuel and run an aircraft on it! We flew in a Vickers Warwick's which was an improvement on the Vickers Wellington that had a crew of six and we'd also brought along a fitter and a couple of ground crew in case there was any maintenance needed which seemed to work out very well, we had an interesting crew, our pilot was a New Zealander, our Observer was an Australian and the rest of us from all over the U.K, our other aircraft had Canadians, South Africans and various different nationalities on board, a very diverse but good mix of people, that's how it was in the Royal Air Force during the war, multi-national, very nice that, folk from our country, the Commonwealth and countries that the Nazis had occupied who then came to join us, something which we benefitted greatly from because they became skilled airmen and made a great contribution to the allied cause, and the RAF was the place we were all united against the common enemy of Nazism. I was as you know a Wireless Operator and also trained as a Gunner to use the aircraft's guns if deemed necessary, but I never actually used them in anger at all, I worked mainly on the Wireless itself that was my main job on the aircraft, each crew member having more than one job he could do meant that if anything happened to others there was a good chance someone could cover it. Once our detachment had safely returned from our special operational journey on the Yalta conference, which I believe was 1375 miles each way, a long trip but we really did feel like we had taken part in a small but quite historical part of World War Two history, after that we returned to the Squadron at Hal Far in Malta for another year of operational duty during which time we also made aircraft maintenance trips to our base in Algiers in Algeria, North Africa. It was from there in March 1946 as our squadron was winding up everything that we were given granted leave on a government scheme called MEDLOC - Mediterranean Leave Over the Continent, designed to give servicemen who had been overseas for a long time a kind of free holiday on their return trip back to the UK. So off we went on our adventures visiting many places starting from Algiers in Algeria and crossing to Naples in Italy on the ship SS Argentina, then from Naples we went first to Rome by train, then up Italy to Milan, and continued all the way to Switzerland, through the Alps and onto France and eventually to Calais, following the sea crossing we got trains to our own home towns, after a few weeks moving around you were ready for a good rest and not long after that I was demobbed, my service days were over and that was that!"

**Fred, bottom row right-hand side kneeling, with other members of his crew whilst waiting for Churchill at the Yalta Conference with the sign behind stating their location; 'SAKI-CRIMEA-USSR'.**

## THE YALTA CONFERENCE – AN OVERVIEW

The very interesting history that Fred Hockenhull and his fellow aircrew were a part of when they were responsible for the safe transit and delivery of our wartime leader Winston Churchill to one of the most important wartime conferences ever held should not be understated, as his safe outward and return journeys were key to the hugely important negotiations and ratified post-war agreements that took place during that 8-day period from the 4th to the 11th February 1945. It is with these things in mind that we now look at some of the key points that the allies agreed upon during the conference which reflect the importance of the discussions that took place there which were effectively to carve out and shape the Europe that would follow after the fall of Adolf Hitler's Third Reich and the long overdue destruction of Nazism that was imminent at that time. It was also to be the 2nd and final meeting, the first having been at Tehran, Iran in late 1943 of what was known as the 'Big Three' of Churchill, Stalin and Roosevelt as very sadly the latter died soon after on the 12th April 1945, the final big Allied conference which would follow at Potsdam, Germany in July 1945 would be attended by Churchill, Stalin and the new U.S President Harry Truman. The Yalta conference AKA The Crimean Conference, Codenamed 'Argonaut' decided the following major points which laid the foundations for their initial post-war road map:

- Only final 'Unconditional Surrender' of Nazi Germany would be acceptable.
- After the war Germany and Berlin would be split into four occupied zones, these would be governed by Great Britain, United States of America, Union of Soviet Socialist Republics and *France.
- Stalin agreed that France could have a fourth occupation zone in Germany if it was formed from the British and American zones.
- A 'Committee on Dismemberment of Germany' was to be set up.
- Germany would undergo demilitarization and denazification, and also pay war reparations partly in the form of forced labour that would be used to repair damage that Germany had inflicted on its victims. *(However this eventually extended to tasks such as harvesting crops, mining uranium and much more in addition to that which was agreed).
- Creation of a reparation council which would be located in the Soviet Union.
- Discussions on the status of Poland were undertaken and recognition of the 'Communist Provisional Government of the Republic of Poland', which had been installed by the Soviet Union "on a broader democratic basis" was agreed to, (despite Churchill's reservations).
- The Polish eastern border would follow the Curzon (demarcation) Line and Poland would receive territorial compensation in the west from Germany.
- Stalin pledged to permit free elections in Poland.
- Roosevelt obtained a commitment by Stalin to participate in the United Nations.
- Regarding the United Nations Stalin requested that all of the 16 Soviet Socialist Republics would be granted UN membership, after consideration 14 of those republics were denied, Truman agreed to membership for only 2, they were Ukraine and Byelorussia while reserving the right, which was never exercised, to seek two more votes for the Unites States.
- Stalin agreed that the Soviet Union would enter the fight against the Empire of Japan "in two or three months after Germany has surrendered and the war in Europe is Terminated."
- Agreement was reached for the bombing of Japan which potentially could include American B-29's being based near the mouth of the Amur River which formed the border between the Russian Far East and North-eastern China (Inner Manchuria), but that did not eventuate, however Russian involvement against the Japanese to help bring about a swifter end to war in the Asia-Pacific region meant further territorial concessions were given to the Soviets.

- Nazi war criminals were to be found and put on trial in the territories in which their crimes had been committed. This later led to the War Crimes Tribunals being centrally and symbolically held at Nuremburg in Bavaria, ideological and conceptual home of the Nazi movement.
- Nazi leaders were to be executed. *In the end this pre-condition was carried out on most.

The Allied 'Grand Alliance' of World War Two that was the key to victory, shown here in a famous picture from the Yalta conference in February 1945. L-R Churchill, Roosevelt, Stalin AKA 'The Big Three', although unified in their desire to defeat the axis powers of Nazi Germany and Imperial Japan the alliance partners did not share common political aims, and they did not always agree on how war should be fought, based on a number of factors such as very different political ideologies of their own and territorial ambitions, things that would become very apparent and soon transpire in the cold war which would eventually follow in the post-war world.

Judging by the many varied tasks and operations undertaken and service given by Fred Hockenhull whilst he was in the special Air-Sea Rescue part of RAF Coastal Command, I think it is fair to say that he certainly achieved what the motto of his 283 Squadron stated, which was; Attende et Vigila – 'Be alert and on Guard'. As I do with all veterans I would like to thank you for your service.

## Additional Information and Life After Service

**Rank upon finish of service** – Warrant Officer.

**Medals and Honours** – 1939-45 War Medal, 1939-45 Defence Medal, 1939-45 Star, Italy Star.

**Post War Years** – From 1946 until his retirement in 1981 Fred worked as an Insurance Agent for the Prudential throughout Greater Manchester. He married Jean during the war on the 23rd October 1943 before his overseas posting to No.283 squadron RAF. They have 2 Sons and 4 Grandchildren.

**Associations and Organisations** – None.

# WARRANT OFFICER LES JOY

Served with – RAF Bomber Command – 460 'Australian' Squadron
Service Number – 1684799
Interviewed – Sutton, North Yorkshire, 29th October 2021

## Service History and Personal Stories

- Born – 16th March 1923, Bradford, Yorkshire, England, UK.
- Leslie Joy, Les to friends really yearned to play his part and serve his country during World War Two and he knew exactly which of the Armed Forces he wanted to join and what he wanted to do. It was the Royal Air Force and he aspired to become a Pilot, so much so that before joining up in addition to working full-time and doing extra night classes to improve academically in subjects such as maths he also joined the ATC – Air Training Corps to improve his chances of reaching these goals, a clever preparation which helped a lot.
- Once he was called up aged 19 in 1942 Les had to go in front of an ACSB – Air Crew Selection Board in Leeds and after a successful interview was accepted for air crew recruitment. In October 1942 his basic training began when he reported to RAF Padgate in Lancashire after which he went on to the ACRC – Air Crew Reception Centre at St. John's Wood in London, where aptitude and selection testing took place into November 1942.

- His next stop would be at an RAF 'Holding Area' in Ludlow in Shropshire where he would stay until December 1942 while the next stage of his training was being arranged then in that same month he was sent to an ITW – Initial Training Wing at Paignton in South Devon and after passing that course became an LAC - Leading Aircraftsman.
- By June 1943 Les was posted to 'Grading School' at RAF Clyffe Pypard in Wiltshire at No.29 EFT – Elementary Flying Training School where he was introduced to and learned to fly what he described as "the love of my life" – the DH82A Tiger Moth, and completed his first solo flight after just 4 hours instruction, a natural so it seemed! This was the place where the new recruits flying aptitude was assessed in order to sort them into different categories of aircrew such as Pilots, Navigators, Gunners, Flight Engineers and so on.
- In July 1943 all the recruits from that course were sent up North to an ACAC – Air Crew Allocation Centre at Heaton Park, Manchester, where they found out what they had been selected as, to his great delight Les was going to fulfil his dream and become a Pilot.
- This led in August 1943 to a big voyage across the Atlantic Ocean from the Clyde in Scotland to Halifax, Nova Scotia on the famous British super liner 'Queen Elizabeth', after which a big part of his training program would take place over in Canada as part of EATS – Empire Air Training Scheme, where thousands of aircrews were trained safely for the RAF.
- After this they were held at an ACHU - Air Crew Holding Unit at Moncton, New Brunswick then went on to No.5 EFTS – Elementary Flight Training School at High River in Alberta, near Calgary close to the foothills of the Rocky Mountains, where they flew on the single engine Fairchild Cornell and did flight training there for three months until October 1943.
- No.10 SFTS – Service Flying Training School in Dauphin, Manitoba near Winnipeg was where the next stage of flight training took place, now moving up to twin engine aircraft with the Cessna Crane AKA the Bobcat. Successfully completing this demanding course led to Les being awarded his well-earned Pilots Wings in February 1944, a very proud moment indeed for any flight trainee and a great achievement for a 20-year-old lad from Bradford.
- A great celebratory road trip followed when Les and his pal Reg travelled down to the USA and whilst there in March 1944 they visited New York and then celebrated Les' 21st birthday in Chicago. They later returned home on another super liner of the time the French 'Isle de France' and by April 1944 were back in the U.K and at an RAF Holding Unit in Harrogate, North Yorkshire. In May 1944 whilst on leave from there Les married Elsie (photo on the intro page), before being posted again and eventually being on active duty.
- By June 1944 Les was up in Scotland posted to No.15 AFU – Advanced Flying Unit at Perth, by August 1944 he was posted down to No.28 EFTS – Elementary Flight Training School in Wolverhampton until October 1944, in both places getting more valuable flying time under the belt in Tiger Moths, by then due to the continuing surplus of qualified pilots a number of them including Les were sent on a Flight Engineers Course at No.4 STT - School of Technical Training in St. Athan in South Wales, and upon completion were multi-skilled Pilots and Flight Engineers, great aptitudes that would be put to use in the coming months.
- In November 1944 he was posted to No.1667 HCU - Heavy Conversion Unit at RAF Sandtoft near Doncaster flying Halifax and Lancaster heavy bombers as 2nd Pilot/Flight Engineer with an all-Australian crew, this led to him being posted to No. 460 'Australian' Squadron at the end of January 1945 where he soon began active-duty operations.
- From 20th February 1945 to 10th May 1945 Les and his crew flew 21 missions in the legendry Lancaster Bomber from RAF Binbrook in Lincolnshire over war torn Europe and to many German cities, and undertook some special operations such as the bombing of Adolf Hitler's mountain HQ in Berchtesgaden, Bavaria on 25th April 1945, 'Operation Manna' dropping supplies of food to the

starving Dutch people on the 28th April 1945, 'Operation 'Exodus' bringing ex-Allied POWs back to England from Brussels, Belgium on 10th May 1945.
- ❖ The crew then took part in 'Cooks Tours' shortly after the war, flying RAF Ground Support personnel to see where RAF Bomber Command had operated during the conflict to view the enemy targets they had hit, giving them an idea of things from a different perspective!
- ❖ Sadly whilst Les was on leave in July 1945 a training accident killed 3 of his crew and injured others, these great losses having a profound effect on him. 460 Squadron was now named 'Tiger Force' and the Lancasters were being prepared for service out in the Far East for the ongoing war with Japan, the force was stood down after the A-Bomb drops.
- ❖ In September 1945 Les was posted from 460 Squadron to No.6 (P)AFU – Pilots Advanced Flying Unit at RAF Moreton Valence in Gloucestershire carrying out flight instruction in the Airspeed Oxford MK 1 Trainer, next by October 1945 he was at No.1540 BAT – Beam Approach Training course at RAF Weston Zoyland in Somerset flying on dual radio beam landing approach exercises for zero visibility and night flying purposes.
- ❖ By January 1946 he was back again on Oxfords, this time at RAF Wheaton Aston in Staffordshire on night flying landings, after which he was posted for his final few months to ground based admin duties whilst awaiting his demob, finally leaving the Royal Air Force as a Warrant Officer in October 1946 after 4 years of service with a very respectable 618 hours of flying time accumulated and having survived the perils of serving in Bomber Command and all the dangerous day and night flying that went with it, great service indeed.

Les Joy is another great example of a veteran with a story that differs somewhat from others as he was trained to be both a Pilot and a Flight Engineer, and whilst serving in RAF Bomber Command flew 21 operations as one of the few British servicemen in what was essentially the 'Australian' 460 Squadron. Although already a fully qualified Pilot on everything from single and twin-engine aircraft right through to the big 4 engine heavy bombers with a lot of flying hours under his belt, due to a surplus of Pilots in the RAF by late 1944 Les qualified for 2 roles within a bomber crew by also becoming a 2nd Pilot/Flight Engineer. This was a reverse of what happened when a qualified Flight Engineer would get some training that would allow them to be a 2nd Pilot and take control of an aircraft in an emergency and possibly be able to land it if needs be. During his many dangerous missions over Germany he undertook both roles, on the longer 'ops' although by then primarily a Flight Engineer he also took over from the 1st Pilot when the opportunity arose, giving him a break and at the same time allowing Les to keep his hand in on the flying side, something which was always good in case the 1st Pilot suffered injury or death whilst undertaking his duties. 19 of those 21 missions were day and night bombing raids over targets in Nazi Germany and the last 2 were humanitarian based, one to drop food to starving civilians in Holland and the other to bring back returning Allied servicemen who had been Prisoners of War in what had been occupied Europe. Amongst the bombing missions, the last one over Germany was particularly interesting when they tried to destroy Berchtesgaden, the mountain retreat and a major Headquarters of Adolf Hitler! Something covered in more detail later in this story. After the war Les continued to fly in the RAF until 1946 and eventually finished his service as a Warrant Officer in the Autumn of that year. He undertook his active-duty operations in the famous Lancaster Bomber and was reunited with one at RAF Coningsby in May 2011 which belonged to the BBMF – Battle of Britain Memorial Flight, this once again brought back numerous wartime memories for Les, as his interview with me did over 10 years later in July 2021, many of which he now willingly imparts to us about:

### BEING BOTH A PILOT AND A FLIGHT ENGINEER IN AN AUSTRALIAN SQUADRON

"For any young man who wanted to join the Royal Air Force and be involved in flying in any way, especially during a war as big as the Second World War I think the greatest ambition and aspiration was to be a pilot, it certainly was mine, so for a local lad from Yorkshire to finally achieve that after so much hard work was a real dream come true! Like everyone who was young we saw it all as a big exciting adventure, and to a certain degree it was, we were to share lots of good times and comradery with our crew on the squadron and make a lot of very good friends as well, but we also had a lot ahead of us including many of the realities of war, some of which as you would expect were not so good and would along with the better times always stay with you! Each stage of my training as a Pilot both in Canada and around the United Kingdom was challenging but thrilling, myself and the rest of the class received our 'Wings' in February 1944 when we finished at No.10 SFTS – Service Flying Training School near Winnipeg, we were all of course extremely proud to have got this far and now had wings and stripes to show for it, and most were like me 20 years of age, others around that, not bad going, but there was much more in store for us all! Then in March I had my 21st Birthday in America, and not long after returning to the U.K I married Elsie, the other great love of my life (Elsie and the Tiger Moth) in May, 1944 was shaping up to be quite a year! In October of 1944, owing to the continuing surplus of RAF Pilots we were sent on a Flight Engineers Course to No.4 School of Technical Training at St Athan in South Wales. This proved to be very interesting and useful as we were then not only qualified Pilots but also Qualified Flight Engineers too. This was another string to our bow and we were keen to learn new skills whilst we were waiting to get into operational service. My call came in November of 1944 and I was immediately posted to No.1667 H.C.U - Heavy Conversion Unit at Sandtoft near Doncaster back in my home county of Yorkshire. Here I flew in Halifax and Lancaster Bombers as 2nd pilot stroke Flight Engineer. We were quickly crewed up and I found myself with an all-Australian crew. It was Wartime, I was fully trained as a Pilot and the whole crew were also now fully trained in their particular area. The entire crew immediately got on really well together and there was a great feeling of camaraderie. It was very important to establish trust which we did quickly and that later proved vital when we were serving together on perilous missions. At the end of a cold January in 1945 we were all posted together as a crew to the 'Australian' 460 Squadron at RAF Binbrook, Lincolnshire for operations on Lancasters. I was one of only a handful of British born crew, in what was essentially an Australian Squadron under British Royal Air Force command. **The Crew, in one of Les' most cherished pictures from March 1945. Top from left; Harold Brown: Mid Upper Gunner, Kevin Quinn: Wireless/Operator, Les Joy: 2nd Pilot/Flight Engineer, Carl Johnson: Navigator. Bottom from left; Roy Rogers: Rear Gunner, Murray Nottle: 1st Pilot, Norman Small: Bomb Aimer.**

Between February to May 1945 we flew a total of 21 day and night missions, 19 of them specifically bombing operations, crews detailed to fly that immediate night were listed on the "Battle Order" which was posted up earlier during the day. Due to Allied advances on the ground by that time in the war those nineteen were all concentrated over Nazi Germany itself, hitting varied targets such as factories, ports and cities, a couple of them Chemnitz and Dessau in March were particularly long operations, over 9 hours each, as we were assisting the Russian Army during their invasion of the Eastern part of Germany. Then came two quite different types of missions, 'Operation Manna' dropping supplies of food to the starving Dutch people and 'Operation Exodus' to get ex-Allied POWs back to England from Brussels, we flew this our last op in relative safety and with great pride just after V.E Day, helping get our boys home was a great honour. There were of course a lot of dangerous moments for us and every crew in 460 squadron, despite being depleted in numbers by then the German night fighter force was well equipped with the latest radar-directed equipment. On one occasion when we were approaching the target area the enemy ground control had directed their night fighters above us and instructed them to release their flares simultaneously above the bomber stream. These brilliant white flares illuminated the whole night sky for miles around, it was like Regent Street at Xmas!

~ 231 ~

They lit up the whole bomber stream down each side, like daylight. We were lucky on this occasion as the fighters were busy picking off the Lancasters on the edges of the stream and we were fortunately in the middle, however on most operations there were many who were not so lucky and casualties in our squadron were very high! A lot of good men were lost! As I recount such experiences I wonder if we were slightly mentally anesthetised, a fair bit 'Flak-Happy' or both! But we were good together as a crew and were convinced we were going to survive in spite of some of our colleagues not coming back. When Crews didn't come back it was the most awful news and a constant reminder of the terrible war we were fighting. Whilst flying over Germany, the heart of the Hitler's Third Reich we came up against quite a lot of resistance, even at that late stage of the war, heavy anti-aircraft fire, day and night-fighter attacks, we saw Lancs go down, you could only hope and pray that the lads were going to be okay but couldn't dwell on it too much as we had to keep focused on the job at hand! The Lancaster we did most of our missions in was 'H for HOW'. When not on active-duty operations we were detailed for "Bombing Practice" over a bombing range called Donna Nook on the East coast, or "Cross Country" trips and other exercises which often entailed heading towards the German borders and then turning back, this was to act as a decoy so the enemy couldn't be certain which was the main bomber stream. During these forays towards the German border we used to drop large amounts of small aluminium strips called "Window". This showed up on the enemy's radar and appeared as many aircraft although there were often just a few of us doing it. Upon completion of our active duty I had flown 138hrs 45mins of combat operation hours and accumulated a further 47hrs 10mins of non-operational flying. Our Crew had stacked up over 185 hours of creditable daytime and night flights in our Lancaster, and survived the War and our operations across Germany!" **Pictured – Lancaster Bombers on an operation.**

There were of course lighter moments and some happy times as well, it wasn't all difficult operations and hard times for the Bomber Command crews, it was with this in mind and wanting to know how it was as a British airman serving with an Australian crew in what was pretty much an all Australian Squadron, something quite different, that I asked Les about his fond memories of things he shared with them in their 'down time', which led to this humorous tale: "The Australian's have a great sense of humour, our lot on the squadron were really fun-loving and liked to play whatever pranks they could get away with, whenever they could, here is one for you that you'll have to try and imagine in your mind's eye! We were playing a big, high stakes card game with drinks on the go in the mess room in Binbrook, our RAF Station, and some of the Aussie's managed to get hold of a whole bunch of sheep that they had 'Borrowed' from somewhere locally, as we were based in a rural area, and as most of them had been around or grown up with livestock in Australia that was not a problem for them I think! So we were all there and could hear something was afoot and right in the middle of our game they burst in and herded the flock with all the noise, bleating and mayhem, things getting knocked over, dirt flying around, the men jeering and whistling them on and running them right through the mess room and our game as if it was a normal thing, as if we were in the outback, meanwhile there we were smartly dressed Bomber Crew trying to sit there as straight faced as possible, hardly flinching, continuing with the cards and the drinking pretending they weren't there as they were trying their best to totally distract us with their mad surprise, funny, very funny scenario playing out there if you can picture it!? That was the Aussie's for you, that's what they were like, great jokers, so much fun to be around, we all needed lighter moments such as those to help relieve the stress that we were all experiencing whilst on active-duty operations."

In the many interviews I have done over the years with veterans of Bomber Command from British, Polish and now Australian squadrons, I have heard them list a lot of operations to both well-known and lesser-known targets all over Europe, indeed even when speaking to Les over the phone prior to my interview with him he had mentioned some of the targets he had been involved in hitting and said he had a special sheet that he had compiled about all of them in the correct order with information taken directly from his Flying Log Book and could do a copy for me. It wasn't until I was actually conducting the interview with camera rolling that he passed me the sheet which I read as he was continuing to give his story, as I worked my way down the list, which contained; Dortmund (x2), Duisburg, Pforzheim, Mannheim, Cologne, Chemnitz, Dessau, Kassel, Essen, Herne, Misberg, Hanau, Nordhausen, Lutzkendorf, Keil, Heligoland, Bremen, that much to my complete amazement near the end I saw that his last bombing mission was to Berchtesgaden in the Obersalzberg region of Bavaria in Germany! I nearly fell off my chair, Les hadn't told me that he was involved in this very special mission that occurred as a 'one off' attempt, carried out as a surprise attack on one morning near the end of the war to try and flatten Adolf Hitler's Berghof residence and major HQ and whilst hitting this key target to also attempt to eliminate top-ranking Nazis including the Führer himself should he be there! A mission deemed so important that Les flew in to undertake it with amongst others the Elite 617 'Dambusters' Squadron who started the raid by dropping the Barnes Wallace 12,000 pound 'Tallboy' bombs on the target area! So quite by chance here I was with the only veteran I had ever met who was involved in that particular World War Two operation, simply incredible! On the back of that and focusing on this special operation, here once again is Les Joy to tell us more about it in his own words, followed by some further information regarding this very interesting raid: "Berchtesgaden was our last active bombing operation of World War two and came almost right at the very end of the conflict, 25th April 1945 to be exact. In our briefing when we were told where we were going to bomb and that there were reportedly top Nazis in the target area and possibly Adolf Hitler himself we were elated! Can you imagine, not every day that you get told your being sent on a special mission that might take out Hitler and his cronies! Made it that extra bit better thinking we might get him! I guess a measure of how particularly important the operation was deemed to be was that the 'Dambusters' squadron were involved! Anyway later it became known that unfortunately Hitler wasn't there but we bombed a very important place that he could have run to and which could possibly have prolonged the war and Nazi resistance if he had, or if he'd got all the way down there who knows, Hitler like other top Nazis could have escaped Europe, anyway as history now tells us he died in his bunker in Berlin, but the intelligence we got ended up being partially true because we nearly got his second in command Hermann Goring on that raid! It was also quite a poignant mission for the Australian 460 squadron because coincidently the squadron's last op was also being carried out on Anzac Day, 25th April, the National Day of Remembrance for both Australia and New Zealand. Now here we are remembering it all these years later, very moving!"

The high-level target that Les, his crew and all the other squadrons involved were sent to 'Neutralise' was viewed as a very important one for many reasons and shouldn't be understated, the Berghof in the Obersalzberg of the Bavarian Alps near Berchtesgaden in Bavaria, Germany was not only Adolf Hitler's vacation home, but other than the Wolfsschanze (Wolf's Lair), his headquarters in East Prussia from where he directed most of his invasion of the Soviet Union, was the place he spent more time than anywhere else whilst Fuhrer of the Third Reich. Hitler's retreat and HQ encompassed a huge 256 acres and within it were contained houses for several of the Nazi party's hierarchy, such as Martin Bormann and Hermann Goering and Hitler's mansion the Berghof, it also had a hotel for other party officials, and a smaller but well-known house high up on its slopes called the 'Eagles Nest' and within the Obersalzberg mountain a three-kilometre long bunker system which apart from being used to shelter from air raids could also potentially be used as a command centre and as a strong hold if needs be! The Berghof was a location for major international diplomacy where, Adolf Hitler and British Prime Minister Neville Chamberlain met on the 15th September 1938 as part of the negotiations that led to the Munich Agreement to settle the 'Czechoslovakian Crisis', (pictured below), it was a place very well publicised by Joseph Goebbels' Nazi propaganda ministry and as a result became an important symbol of Hitler's leadership in the eyes of the majority of Germans. Other reasons for Bomber Command hitting the target included supporting Allied ground forces, helping to convince die-hard Germans that the war was defiantly lost, and obscuring the memory of pre-war appeasement policies that took place there like the visit of the British PM mentioned earlier, and also to attempt to destroy as much of the area above and below ground as possible that the Allies feared could potentially be used to command an 'Alpine Fortress' something which later proved to be a myth, it was however for all these reasons a cause of great personal satisfaction for the aircrews involved to be bombing such a prestigious target! The results of the operation were mixed but like the Germans before them mainly because of its symbolism and propaganda value it was well publicised by the Allies after being bombed!

An aerial photo taken during that raid by a Lancaster of No.460 'Australian' Squadron, note the bomb burst exploding on the upper left-hand side of the picture near Hitler's residence at the Berghof. This photo now released into the public domain by the Australian Government many years later for historical interest and use. On the day the area was attacked by a formidable force of 359 Avro Lancaster heavy bombers drawn from 22 squadrons of Nos. 1 and 5 Group RAF, 16 De Havilland Mosquito pathfinders from No.8 Group RAF, they were also escorted by fighters from 13 British RAF Fighter Squadrons and 98 North American P-51 Mustang fighters from the U.S 8th Air Force. 2 Lancasters were shot down by German A.A Guns, 1 from 460 Squadron and 1 from 619 Squadron. The 'Eagles Nest' is still there and along with the Dokumentation Obersalzberg Museum on the site can still be visited today.

N0.460 SQUADRON – As the Berchtesgaden mission was effectively the end of their active-duty operations, and with having included that story here, I have added some further information and statistics here about the squadron, which acts as a tribute to those who served within it, as follows: 460 is regarded as having been the most effective of the Australian Bomber Squadrons during World War Two and set numerous operational records. It maintained consistently higher serviceability records among its aircraft, flew the most sorties of any Australian squadron, 6,262, dropped more bomb tonnage than any squadron in the whole of Bomber Command – 24,856 tons! Sadly the flip-side to that was they lost 181 aircraft, suffered 1,018 combat deaths, 589 of whom were Australian, the highest number of any of the Australian squadrons, this meant it was effectively wiped out many times over during its existence! Regarding casualties, RAF Bomber Command represented only 2 per cent of total Australian enlistments during the Second World War but accounted for almost 20 per cent of its personnel who were killed in action! Bomber Commands' staggering losses reaching 55,573 for all nationalities who were represented within it. No.460 Squadron RAF was disbanded on the 10th October 1945 soon after the Second World War had come to an end. It was reformed again on 2nd July 2010 as a non-flying squadron of the RAAF – Royal Australian Air Force within the Defence Imagery and Geospatial Organisation – DIGO at an official ceremony held in front of the wartime Lancaster 'G for George' which is now on display at the Australian War Memorial, Canberra.

**Formal portrait of members of No.460 squadron commanded by Wing Commander C. E. Martin, in front of and lined up on the wing of Lancaster Bomber 'G for George' in August 1943. This aircraft carried out a staggering 90 operational missions over Germany and occupied Europe whilst with 460, a great symbol for the Squadron and also something which represents part of Australia's valuable wartime Commonwealth contribution.**

**Every time an aircraft went down there were seven aircrew with approximately 2 years of training each, 14 years between them, and for each one lost many extended family and friends who would mourn their loss, not just a burning aircraft and some statistics but young men with their whole lives ahead of them, many of whom were cut off in their prime as the information regarding the losses on No.460 squadron reflects in a big way. These losses took place for crews and servicemen even when not in front line operations such as the terrible accident that ended the crew Les served with, as he now recalls:** "In July 1945 after returning from leave I was greeted with tragic news. In my absence, my crew had been on a practice bombing exercise at Donna Nook on the Lincolnshire coast. During one of the runs tragedy struck; a bomb had "hung up" and exploded in the bomb bay. The Lancaster immediately caught fire and the wireless operator was killed instantly, the bomb aimer and the flight engineer bailed out successfully. The navigator's parachute harness got caught somehow and he was sadly killed too, the rear gunner bailed out alright but landed in a water-filled quarry and drowned, and finally the pilot got out but was burned as he had left it as long as possible in order to see the crew safe - a very brave man. The mid-upper gunner was not involved as he was not on the flight, he had been taken out to allow certain radar equipment to be installed. It was the most awful end to our Crew. I think the fact that when I returned from leave to find none of my colleagues around was very traumatic. I felt extreme loneliness and this made me reflect on the irony that fate had dealt such a cruel blow to my comrades with whom I had flown so many hours on dangerous operations over enemy territory. Somehow one can't help wondering; "If I had been there? Why did I escape?"

Near the end of the interview I asked Les having been on a squadron with high losses how he felt about the way Bomber Command and its servicemen were perceived, viewed and have been treated since World War Two, which from the various things I had read and been told personally from Bomber Command veterans that I'd spoken to was certainly not always good or fair, in answer to which I was told: "During one of the times I was in London the air raid sirens sounded and I was caught up in this wave of panicking people, virtually lifted and swept along with the masses as they headed down to the safety of one of the underground stations which were being used as make shift air raid shelters by a great many. So there we were, children crying, folks carrying all sorts, bags, food, blankets, and crammed in like sardines, in the distance up above you could hear the disturbing sounds of explosions and the like, and the poor Londoners they had been through so much of that before, days, weeks, months of it previously, and were still bravely maintaining the 'Blitz Spirit' from what I could see. Later on at different times when we were in various parts of London you witnessed huge amounts of chaos and damage that the enemy had brought to our capital and as we knew to many, many other ports, airfields, towns and cities, this was the reality of life on the Home Front in wartime Britain that Hitler and the Nazis had brought to us and many other countries, a reality that no one wanted, as a result the vast majority of people felt they had to do what they could to help the war effort, to strike back in the best way they could, and for me and a lot of other young men that ended up in Bomber Command we were giving back what had been meted out, and in the process a great many of those courageous boys had been horrifically maimed, injured or killed whilst carrying out their duties in order to counter the Nazi threat and then help the Allies win that war, one we had to win because the alternative or other outcome was an unthinkable one! So people who criticise the actions of Bomber Command would do well to remember all this before saying negative things about all those brave young men who gave the best they could in many ways and those who lost their lives undertaking the service their country asked of them! Other branches of the armed forces were lauded after the war, but not us, even Churchill had distanced himself from Bomber Command and from military tactics thought later by some to be a bit controversial, but acknowledged by many others to have been of great strategic importance, either way things he sent us to do! In time at least we have finally got somethings like an Aircrew Europe Medal and the Bomber Command statue in London, about bloody time, long overdue! Just don't forget all those heroic lads who didn't return from their missions and ever live to see even these things! I was one of the lucky ones, over fifty-five thousand others were not!"

As this very comprehensive story shows Les has led a very interesting and fruitful life, part of a generation that worked hard, served their country throughout a 6-year World War and despite living through difficult times kept on striving to improve their lot. In order to do this Les has certainly lived and succeeded according to the determined motto of his beloved 460 Squadron: 'Strike and Return'.

## Additional Information and Life After Service

**Rank upon finish of service** – Warrant Officer.

**Medals and Honours** – 1939-45 War Medal, 39-45 Defence Medal, 39-45 Star, France-Germany Star.

**Post War Years** – After leaving the RAF in 1946 Les had a few very different jobs in Civilian life, he worked in an Iron Foundry, then as a semi-skilled fitter for Crofts Engineering in Bradford, he joined Bradford City Police Force in the 1950's becoming PC 254 and after a few years left and went into Sales work starting as a door to door salesman ending up as Sales Manager at Better Ware Products, and eventually worked for Quango and Local Government as a Civil Servant in the Department of National Savings and Security and for the Nature Conservatory Council, 'officially' retiring aged 65 in 1988, but forever active he went on to do part-time bar work until aged 80 when he eventually retired in 2003. Les married Elsie in May 1944, they were together 62 years until her passing in December 2006. Children; 2 Sons, 2 Grandchildren, 3 Great-Grandchildren.

**Associations and Organisations** – None.

# FLIGHT LEUTENANT JOHN TROTMAN DFC & BAR

Served with – RAF Bomber Command, 150 & 692 Squadrons
Service Number – 1168608
Interviewed – By Phone, 25th March 2022

## Service History and Personal Stories

- Born – 9th September 1921, Winchester, England, UK.
- John Trotman volunteered for the Royal Air Force in April 1940 in Reading, Berkshire, and began his training in August of that year, and so started a very successful career which saw him undertake an almost incomprehensible 70 active-duty wartime operations in RAF Bomber Command during World War Two and time as an instructor as well.
- Everything started when John was told to report to Babbacombe in Devon, where vaccinations, further medicals, issue of uniform and some fitness and drill instruction was given for 2 weeks after which he and other trainees were sent on by September to an ITW – Initial Training Wing in Aberystwyth, Wales where he learned a lot of the RAF 'basics' such of theory of flight, navigation, Morse code, meteorology, enemy aircraft recognition, weapons maintenance and phonetical alphabet, all completed in 8 weeks.
- Now as an LAC – Leading Aircraftsman came the initial flying part of this basic training and on the 14th November 1940 they reported to a small grass airfield just outside Coventry that was called

RAF Ansty, which coincidently was the night the Luftwaffe decimated that city in a 13-hour bombing raid, the aftermath of which John and others saw first-hand.

❖ Flight training followed on the Tiger Moth and a variety of skills were taught and practiced such as instrument flying, cross-country flying, formation flying, map reading and navigation exercises, with the instrument flying part being undertaken in the air and additionally on the ground in an early form of flight simulator called the Link Trainer. In the latter part of the course John and the others were also taught aerobatics such as stall turns, spins, loops and rolls, with this course successfully completed by February 1941.

❖ The No.3 SFTS – Service Flying Training School at South Cerney near Cirencester in Gloucestershire followed where John took the next step up and began flight training in twin-engine aircraft which would take him in the direction of RAF Bomber Command rather than a lot more single engine training for aircraft of Fighter Command.

❖ There John began flying Airspeed Oxfords with an instructor and solo, practicing different flight patterns and various other skills, he passed everything and achieved the great accolade of being awarded his RAF 'Wings' and was now a qualified pilot and Sergeant.

❖ His 'Above Average Pilot' rating led to him next being posted to No.2 CFS – Central Flying School at RAF Cranwell, Lincolnshire in May 1941, home of the RAFC – Royal Air Force College, to train as an instructor instead of being sent to an OTU – Operational Training Unit like the other newly qualified pilots from the course.

❖ Whilst there John began learning to instruct on AVRO Tutor biplanes and Airspeed Oxfords, having to cover and learn the entire 28-part syllabus from the Instructors' Handbook of Elementary Flying Training, this included; Low flying, Action in the event of fire, Restarting engine in flight, Night flying, Precautionary & Forced Landings, Aerobatics.

❖ By July 1941 with the Instructors course finished John was posted to No.11 SFTS – Service Flying Training School at RAF Shawbury in Shropshire, where he trained pupils who had done their initial training on Tiger Moths on conversions to fly twin-engine aircraft, instructing on the Oxford. By early 1942 he had finally been posted to No.23 OTU – Operational Training Unit at Pershore in Worcestershire, a unit where Bomber crew who had already been trained in their particular skills came together to be 'crewed up'.

❖ At Pershore they were equipped with Wellington MK 1c Bombers which John went solo on after only 2 hours' instruction and after further day and night flying whilst there they were called up to be part of the first ever 1000 Bomber Raids which were over Cologne on 30/31 May 1942 and Essen on 1/2 June 1942. After this John was posted to No.150 Squadron at RAF Snaith in the East Riding of Yorkshire as part of a new 5-man crew on Wellington Mk III Bombers completing a further 28 operations from the 25th June to 23rd September 1942.

❖ Having now survived his first full operational tour over Germany and France, and additionally during this extremely dangerous time of early RAF Bombing over Europe, as was regular procedure surviving crews were usually withdrawn from front line service and sent to instruct on OTU's – Operational Training Units and HCU's Heavy Conversion Units within Bomber Command, for John this meant a posting to No.81 OTU at RAF Tilstock near Whitchurch in Shropshire undertaking flying instruction on Armstrong Whitworth Whitley Mk V Bombers teaching many skills including the use of the Beam Approach System.

❖ By January 1944 he had been posted to another airfield close by in Shropshire at RAF Peplow, AKA Childs Ercall home to No.83 OTU where he instructed using his familiar old aircraft the Vickers Wellington Mk III. Months later ready for a change and a new challenge John volunteered for a posting to the Pathfinder Force of Bomber Command and in September 1944 was sent to train to fly

- the De Havilland Mosquito at 1655 Mosquito Training Unit at RAF Warboys in Cambridgeshire, an original Pathfinder Force station.
- With this new flying skills and a 2nd Operational Tour would follow which between the 29th October 1944 until 2nd May 1945 led to a further 40 active-duty missions over Europe with No. 692 Squadron from RAF Graveley in Cambridgeshire, including 18 ops over Hitler's capital of Berlin in the new Mk XVI Mosquito High-Level Fighter-Bomber aircraft that would drop marker flares onto the targets for the bombers to follow up and hit with much better accuracy. On other operations they would also be bombing many targets in addition to pathfinding. The successful completion of 2 full operational tours led in 1945 to John being awarded a DFC – Distinguished Flying Cross for each, aka DFC & Bar.
- John was involved in the last 2 operations undertaken by Bomber Command in World War Two and after V.E Day, 8th May 1945 flew special 'Cooks Tours' taking ground crew to see devastated German cities and areas such as the Ruhr, Hannover, Bremen and Osnabruck.
- After V.J Day he went on to serve at RAF Upper Heyford in Oxfordshire again in an instructing role, training new intakes to fly the Airspeed Oxford and De Havilland Mosquito aircraft until March 1946 when he was transferred to RAF Cottesmore in Rutland in the East Midlands by which time he had become a Flight-Lieutenant. It was whilst there that John decided to leave the RAF and was demobbed a few weeks later in Spring 1946 bringing to an end approximately 6 years of very distinguished service in the Royal Air Force.

Over the years I have been extremely lucky and privileged to have interviewed World War Two Pilots who flew and other Aircrew who flew in most if not all the well-known aircraft of RAF Bomber, Fighter and Coastal Commands in active-duty operations during World War Two, in aircraft such as the Lancaster, Halifax, Sterling, Blenheim, Warwick, Spitfire, Hurricane, and even American Aircraft used in RAF service such as the Liberator, Dakota, Corsair and Mustang! However the two main aircraft that were missing from this list and the veterans who flew them were the Wellington and the Mosquito. You can imagine my absolute delight when I found John Trotman who was a 1st Pilot in both of those aircraft and who also completed a full tour of operations in both as well. An extremely rare RAF veteran because he had survived a staggering 70 missions whilst undertaking those duties in Bomber Command, more than any other Bomber Command veteran I have interviewed so far, and along the way John racked up over 2000 hours flying time, continuously survived the vicious ground and air defences of Nazi Germany on low-level and high altitude missions, had also been a flight instructor in different postings and was awarded 2 Distinguished Flying Crosses and very proudly received a telegram from the head of Bomber Command Air Chief Marshal A T Harris personally congratulating John on his actions, operations and outstanding service. Later on in life he was also decorated with France's highest accolade the Legion D' Honneur. So here is the story of an extraordinary aviator written after extensive phone conversations we had and with additional information gleaned with permission from his own brilliant autobiography aptly called 'J for Jonnie', telling the story of how it was:

<u>COMPLETING FULL OPERATIONAL TOURS ON THE WELLINGTON AND MOSQUITO</u>

I was interested to know what motivated John to want to become an RAF Pilot, and it was an infamous air raid during the Luftwaffe's 1940 Blitz that gave the answer: "In the early part of our training we were sent to RAF Ansty, a small airfield about 5 miles from the centre of Coventry, we got there in the afternoon but spent the night in an air-raid shelter as this was by chance the night that the German Air Force decimated Coventry in one of the most destructive air raids of that period which took place on the 14th November 1940, it lasted for a staggering 13 consecutive hours! The next morning we were sent to see what assistance we could give to the Civil Authorities, working with picks and shovels to clear roads and search for trapped people in cellars and assist in the grim task of extracting the dead from the rubble! The scene was absolutely anarchic and horrific with destroyed and smouldering buildings, broken sewage pipes and the disgusting smell that came from escaping effluence, leaking gas pipes also added to the dangers and the odours, the stomach-turning smell of burnt flesh and people walking around in a daze with nothing left apart from the clothes on their back! In the latter part of the day a lot of assistance had come from many of the neighbouring cities and areas such as Nottingham in the east to Wolverhampton in the west and our help was no longer required. That raid killed around 600 people and injured many more, and for us it was also a complete attack of the senses to experience such things first-hand, including seeing our own people dead like that! As a result I had no compunction about bombing Germany later in the war, as far as I was concerned I was giving back the same treatment they had ruthlessly dished out to the innocent people of Coventry and the other towns and cities of Britain that they bombed in the Blitz and throughout the war! It only fuelled our motivation to even the score, something we would get plenty of chance to do later!" Training and his first tour of operations followed, as John now describes in more detail: "Initially as you would expect pilots were trained to be competent to fly and be familiar with the aircraft they were going to be undertaking operations in, which in my case was the Vickers Wellington Mark III twin-engine long-range medium bomber, then the crews joined, in this case making a total compliment of five, which were myself as the Pilot, a Navigator, Wireless Operator, Bomb Aimer/Front Gunner and a Rear Gunner. Then as a complete team cross-country and bombing practices, both day and night were carried out, first under supervision and then on our own. Whilst we were still officially being trained at RAF Pershore we were drafted in to be part of the force that was used on the first 1000 bomber raids to Cologne and Essen in May and June 1942. In order to make up the numbers for these operations to happen 'Bomber Harris' had to pull in aircraft from everywhere, from Bomber, Coastal and Training Commands, so before we were even officially on a squadron we had already carried out 2 active-duty operations! Once training was completed we were posted to Number 150 Squadron, Bomber Command at RAF Snaith and our active-duty operations began in earnest with 28 more missions being successfully undertaken between the beginning of June to the end of September 1942. These were mainly hitting cities and strategic targets, they were (after the first two mentioned above, and reading from his logbook, some of which they bombed on more than one occasion); Bremen, St. Nazaire, Wilhelmshaven, Duisburg, Hamburg, Saarbrucken, Dusseldorf, Osnabruck, Mainz, Frankfurt, Kassel, Karlsruhe, Lorient.

The operations that we undertook to St. Nazaire and Lorient were quite different as we were on low-flying approaches to lay magnetic mines into river estuaries from only 100 feet to deter U-Boats, based in huge pens, from entering and leaving port, this required some precision flying under heavy fire." John explained more about one of the extremely dangerous St. Nazaire night raids: "As I guided our aircraft in, everything around was bathed in the glorious deadly white light of the searchlights, followed almost simultaneously by the thumping of the defenders anti-aircraft shells, this lethal fire came straight at us horizontally down the guiding beams of light! I could hear the ack-ack shells exploding everywhere, to the sides, behind us, above us, below us, my heart was beating fast as we heard and felt the red-hot shrapnel ripping holes in the bomber's thin canvas sides, rattling its frame, luckily for us the Wellington was very resilient and could withstand a lot of damage and still be able to continue its work, similar in those respects to the other wooden framed aircraft that I would fly on later missions, the Mosquito! The searchlights were blinding at such close quarters and I had to keep my head down in the cockpit and fly on instruments for a while, doing my utmost to maintain correct height and speed so that our bomb aimer Ed could lay the mines in the right position, in the meantime you had the sound of the ever increasing hails of cannon and shell fire as we got closer to the target area, the rattle of our engines continuing and the added noise of the rear-gunner Viv firing his four Browning heavy machine guns at the searchlights to try and take out the deadly beams we were trapped in that were trying to bring about our demise! I was sweating now, and then I felt our aircraft lift as the mines were released, something confirmed by Ed's voice in my headset, but it wasn't over yet and there was only one way out to safety and that was for us to keep going through that terrible barrage of A.A fire, it was simply hellish, we had to ride it out as we were still too low for me to turn and I dared not climb at that point or we would have been more vulnerable. Then as abruptly as the cockpit had been flooded with light the darkness folded around us again and we left everything behind, giving us an immense sense of relief, we could hardly believe that we were still in one piece! I called up each of my crew in turn to check that they were all right and to give words of encouragement as we headed back home, but also urging them to stay sharp and keep a lookout for enemy night fighters, another real danger that we came across many times during operations that also claimed many victims from amongst RAF Bomber Command Squadrons."

**Pictured – Wellington Bombers in formation, similar to the one flown by John, his having the apt call sign of 'J for Johnnie' and which sported 'Jane' a glamorous wartime comic strip heroine painted on the fuselage. These were key aircraft in the arsenal of Bomber Command in the early days of its missions over Europe.**

**This was just one incredible account from one operation at St. Nazaire, there were many others filled with a lot of different dangers such as these and more, but John and his crew had bravery, good luck and resilience on their side and as a result survived their first full tour, after which they were dispersed to go and instruct on Operational Training Units and Heavy Conversion Units as was standard practice in Bomber Command during the war. This led to John undertaking duties as a flight instructor at No.81 OTU at RAF Tilstock in Shropshire, but later he was yearning once again for the challenge of flying in active-duty operations which he volunteered for and after conversion training became a 1st Pilot once again, this time in a two-man Mosquito fighter-bomber that was part of the 692 Pathfinder Squadron, flying out of RAF Graveley in Cambridgeshire, where between late October 1944 until early May 1945 John undertook a further staggering 40 operations! With the unique nature of the Pathfinder Force of which No.692 Squadron and John was a part I have included a little bit of overview and background information regarding the two:**

The PFF - Pathfinder Force were special squadrons within RAF Bomber Command in the Second World War and acted in a target-marking and bombing capacity, during operations they were the first in ahead of the main bomber streams, locating and marking targets with flares that the main bomber force could then home in on and aim at, which then helped increase the accuracy of their bombing, this very important task and responsibility upon which the success of an operation could to greater degree depend meant that the PFF essentially became and consisted of 'Elite' squadrons and the nature of the Pathfinders work meant that they were normally the first to receive new advanced blind bombing aids such as Oboe, Gee and the H2S Radar. The early PFF Squadrons were expanded in January 1943 to become a group which was officially the No.8 (Pathfinder Force) Group. The initial PFF was comprised of 5 squadrons which later rose in size and strength to 19 squadrons. Although the majority of Pathfinder squadrons and personnel were from the Royal Air Force, the group also included many from the air forces of Commonwealth countries as well and very fittingly the Motto of the No. 8 (Pathfinder Force) Group was - 'We Guide to Strike'.

No.692 Squadron was formed on the 1st January 1944 at RAF Graveley originally as a light bomber unit equipped with the Mosquito Mark IV bombers, as part of the LNSF – Light Night Striking Force in the previously mentioned No.8 Group RAF. From March 1944 the squadron re-equipped with the newer Mosquito MK XVI bombers, until by June 1944 they had completely switched over to this more advanced variant that was fitted out to also undertake high altitude target-marking. It was the first squadron to carry 4000-pound bombs AKA 'Cookies' in Mosquitos, which they used in an attack on Dusseldorf. 692 also undertook low level operations which included minelaying, the first Mosquito unit to do so, and dropped 4000 lb bombs into the mouth of tunnels in the Ardennes during the German surprise offensive Dec 1944-Jan 1945. The squadron was disbanded on the 20th September 1945 shortly after the end of World War Two, at RAF Gransden Lodge in Cambridgeshire. **A picture of the De Havilland Mosquito B.XVI variant, top speed 415 miles per hour, the same aircraft in which John Trotman successfully completed his Second Operational Tour, plus an extra 10 missions, 18 of which were to Berlin. This very light, fast and agile aircraft was built in many variants which served in many roles with different kinds of armaments and munitions. It was originally conceived as an unarmed fast bomber, but during WW2 the Mosquito evolved greatly and was also used as a medium-altitude daytime tactical bomber, a high-altitude night bomber,** pathfinder, fighter-bomber, night fighter, intruder, and additionally operated in maritime strike and photo-reconnaissance roles as well as interestingly being utilised by the B.O.A.C – British Overseas Airways Corporation as a fast transport to carry small, high value cargo to and from neutral countries through enemy-controlled airspace for high speed conveyance. The DH.98 Mosquito with its wooden airframe was also known as 'The Wooden Wonder' and the 'Mossie'. It was manned by a pilot and a navigator, had room for every kind of 'cargo' in its sizable bomb bay including room for one person if needs be.

Having previously heard about one of John's operations whilst Piloting the Wellington Bomber on his first operational tour, I was now very interested to know and hear along with other things about some experiences from his second tour as a Mosquito pilot in one of the elite Pathfinder Squadrons and learned: "Whilst I was with 692 squadron I flew the Mark 16 Mosquito, which whilst being capable of undertaking any kind of mission had been updated and adapted specially for our use as a high-altitude night bomber and pathfinder and it was in these roles that I undertook a further 40 operations over Nazi Germany, dropping marker flares onto our targets with good accuracy with the help of advanced bomb-aiming equipment such as Oboe which significantly helped us achieve that task. We did most of that from high altitude, and occasionally dropped down lower if we needed to get below the clouds for any reason, once we had marked the target with flares, and also bombing when undertaken, this opened up the way for the main bomber force to do its job or sometimes were sent solely as Mosquito Squadrons to do the whole job ourselves using our 4000-pound 'cookies'. Ironically my first trip with 692 Squadron was with 49 Mosquitos on 29th October 1944 to Cologne which we had given a good battering when I was part of the first 1000 bomber raid back in 1942. The city may not have fully recovered but the defending night fighter force had come a long way since my last visit two years earlier, and technological advances on their side meant that they were now able to deploy jet fighters like the Messerschmitt ME 262, which were more than a match for the substantial speed of the Mosquito. Luckily we didn't lose any of our aircraft that night, and although I saw several of these fast jets at a distance, I wasn't sure exactly what they were! Once I had completed that first mission to Cologne the operations came thick and fast, mostly night but some daytime as well, there were 39 more of them to be precise, eventually making my final 2nd operation tour tally of 40, going 18 times to heavily defended Berlin and others to Hannover, Karman, Nuremburg, Duisburg, Karlsruhe, Mannheim, Erfurt, Kassel, Bremen, Dessau, Hamburg, Munich, Ludwigshafen, Husum and Kiel, and I flew on the last two operational missions of the war carried out by Bomber Command, they were an attack on an airfield at Husum on the 26th April 1945 from 7000 feet and the very last bombing attack which was on the dock area at Kiel on the 2nd May 1945 to prevent German troops who were massing in that port city, it was feared to cross over to Norway to possibly continue the war from there. Soon after on the 8th May 1945, V.E Day, I celebrated like most other people, and a couple of weeks later I flew ground staff over various wrecked cities in Germany at around 3000 feet in what were given the tongue in cheek nickname of 'Cook's Tours' where we viewed with astonishment the utter devastation of war, most places reduced to little more than rubble and ruined buildings, they certainly had 'reaped the whirlwind' which they had sown in places like Coventry years earlier! Incredibly I survived that conflict which for me meant 2 full operational tours, 70 missions, dropping bombs from 25,000 feet, laying mines at less than 100 feet, attacking targets over land and sea, facing night fighters, heavy flak and searchlights, surviving 3 crashes in 1941, 1942 & 1944, plus other near misses and contributing to the fall of Berlin late in the war! For this I was awarded with the Distinguished Flying Cross on two occasions, the first on 2nd January 1945 and the second came on 26th October 1945, both announced in the London Gazette."

**Undeterred by age and still having his deep-down love for flight John incredibly in early to mid-2022 at 100 years old was still flying, most likely making him the oldest pilot in the United Kingdom, a tribute to this amazing aviator who in the words of the No.150 Squadron motto has certainly proven to be: 'Always Ahead'. These great attributes still shone through when I finally had the honour of meeting and talking to this incredible 102-year-old veteran face-to-face at his home in Shropshire on the 29th September 2023 (pictured), and presenting him with a copy of The Last Stand. John, I and many others who really understand and appreciate your exceptional sacrifices and service sincerely thank you for them.**

## Additional Information and Life After Service

**Rank upon finish of service** – Flight-Lieutenant.

**Medals and Honours** – Distinguished Flying Cross & Bar, 1939-45 War Medal, 1939-45 Defence Medal, 1939-45 Star, Aircrew Europe Star with Bomber Command Bar, Legion D' Honneur (2018).

**Post War Years** – After leaving the RAF in 1946 John went on to work for the Hoover Corporation in their International Division, first as a Salesman later working his way up to an Upper-Management position, this job led to him working around the United Kingdom, Canada and the U.S.A up until his retirement in 1982. Incredibly John resumed flying again in his later years and after passing exams he earned a private pilot's licence at the age of 85! He was still flying on his 100th Birthday on the 9th September 2021 when he took a special flight at Sleap Airfield near his home in Whitchurch, Shropshire to mark becoming a Centenarian accompanied by his good friend and flight instructor Keith Walker, and as a result is still able to add this very impressive aviation milestone to an already superb and very distinguished flight logbook. John has been married 3 times, first to Audrey, then Joyce and now Olwen. He has 2 Sons, 1 Daughter and 2 Grand-Children.

**Associations and Organisations** – Sleap Aerodrome Flying Club, Member of Project Propeller and RAFA – Royal Air Forces Association, the Aircrew Association, Member of the Probus Club.

# ZN-S/PB304 – 'THE SALFORD LANCASTER'

# A LOCAL WORLD WAR TWO STORY

At 10.15 am on Sunday the 30th July 1944 there was a loud explosion that came from the direction of the playing fields near Littleton Road, Salford, Lancashire next to where the River Irwell flowed. This signified the last tragic moments of Lancaster Bomber ZN-S/PB304 and its crew of seven. Just prior to that locals had looked on in horror as the Pilot Flight Lieutenant Peter Lines had struggled to control his aircraft which was evidentially in trouble, as he tried to guide it with a hefty 9000-pound General Purpose bomb load to a safer place on open fields away from the densely populated local area in order to try and save the lives of the civilians below.

During World War Two Bomber Command lost 55,573 servicemen, more than all those who serve in the entire Royal Air Force today and around 12,000 Bomber aircraft of all types of which 246 Bombers were recorded as being lost in operational crashes, and of the 7377 Lancasters that were produced just under 50% were shot down during the conflict, staggering numbers, staggering losses! Here we focus on just one of those aircraft and its aircrew, and through information already available plus two eye witnesses accounts to the event that I have interviewed, the fate of this stricken bomber is featured here in The Last Stand, as something which varies from most other parts of the book as it is a story which is still shrouded in some mystery, much conjecture and with many theories as to what caused it to happen. I don't claim to have any conclusive answers myself but just adding a little more input and information whilst re-telling a very interesting and worthwhile story of an aircraft and its crew that subsequently many who live locally, of whom I am one, have taken to their hearts and which has become known as 'The Salford Lancaster'.

The Lancaster Bomber in question went by two identifying codes, either or both of which I will use to identify it by during the story, PB304 which was its allotted Registration and ZN-S, ZN being the Squadron Identifying Letters and S being the Aircraft Identifying letter. In the case of the latter these visible markings could be seen on RAF aircraft at the rear of the fuselage either side of the RAF Roundel. The code also formed the call sign for the particular aircraft in question. This one being S for Sugar, that was part of No.106 Squadron which at the time of this operation was based at RAF Metheringham in Lincolnshire. This Squadron **(badge shown with the Latin motto 'Pro Libertate' meaning 'For Freedom')** achieved a great deal during the Second World War, undertaking operations such as the 1000 bomber raids on Cologne, Essen and Bremen in 1942, the secret V-Weapons development centre at Peenemünde in 1943, a 1,900 mile round trip to bomb the German Baltic Fleet at Gdynia in 1944, it was also represented in the bomber force that pulverised the defences of Wesel in support of the Rhine Crossing into Germany in March 1945. During that time 106 Squadron won a total of 267 decorations, including the Victoria Cross awarded to Sergeant NC Jackson for conspicuous bravery during an attack on Schweinfurt on 26-27th April 1944, and from April 1942 until March 1943 it had Wing Commander Guy Gibson of later Dam Busters fame as its Commanding Officer who himself went on to win a VC for heading up that famous raid, and whilst he was C/O of No.106 Squadron was awarded the DSO – Distinguished Service Order in November 1942, and Bar to his DSO in March 1943. In total during World War Two the squadron flew operations on 496 nights, and 46 days, flying 5834 sorties, in doing so it lost 187 aircraft.

It was during one of those sorties that the loss of the relatively new Lancaster ZN-S occurred on the 30th July 1944 whilst involved in a bombing raid on strong German positions at Cahagnes in the Amaye-sur-Seulles battle area in Normandy, France, the attacking force was made up of 462 Lancaster and 200 Halifax bombers and 30 Mosquitos, but due to cloud covering the target area many were not ordered down through the cloud to bomb at low level as this would of course make them easy targets for enemy anti-aircraft fire, instead at around 8am the mission was called off and they returned to base still carrying their full bomb loads. To complicate things further they could not ditch their bombs in the English Channel as they might normally do due to huge concentrations of Allied shipping being present which were supplying the forces invading Western Europe.  So they had to make their way home with the added danger of carrying a full bomb load (comprising of eighteen 500lb devices) back to the U.K, something no Bomber crews liked doing because of the many potential hazards it could bring, which sadly in this case it did, eventually sealing the fate of this particular Bomber and its entire crew.

**An interesting and related picture showing aircrews of No.106 Squadron RAF photographed in front of Lancaster ZN-B, squadron markings clearly evident on the fuselage, signifying that it belongs to the same squadron as and is a sister aircraft of our ZN-S 'The Salford Lancaster.'**

Right from when ZN-S was undertaking its operation until now it is still not known exactly what had caused the problems that ended in its eventual demise, because of this the conjecture and theories start from as early as when they were over the target area in France, with the possibility it was hit by enemy flak which may have caused one of the engines and other important internal components serious damage, a regular occurrence for many aircraft involved in bombing missions everywhere during the air war.  Also if their position over Normandy was not precise due to circling in heavy cloud cover and with possible added wind drift this in turn could have had ever increasing knock-on effects and complications as they tried to return home with damaged navigational equipment, which also may help explain why they were seemingly so far off course on their return journey over the country. The Navigator would probably been using dead reckoning or estimated navigation which under those conditions could have easily led to overshooting either above or below Lincolnshire on the East coast where they were aiming to return, and looping in over the North-West coast of Blackpool where they were actually spotted on their way back.  Once they realised where they were as they broke cloud cover coming in over Blackpool, probably seeing the famous Blackpool Tower and then knowing they were over the wrong coastline it seems quite reasonable (when studying a map of the U.K) that they adjusted their course to then follow a gradually dipping Easterly line down from Blackpool via Manchester on to Lincolnshire in order to get back to their base at RAF Metheringham.

Whether returning via Salford was by choice or because further serious complications were arising such as a loss of fuel or a slow leak of the coolant called Goycol in the Merlin liquid cooled engines due to the damage of internal lines, also possibly sustained from enemy fire over France, is not known. What we must also bare in mind is when most air crashes are pieced together they don't normally occur as a result of any single failure or error, but as a chain of events which were normally beyond the control of those in the aircraft, especially when you factor in the massive amount of additional variables wartime conditions create that made everything far more difficult and dangerous for all airmen on every operation undertaken during the six years of that conflict. This can either help solve or add to the ambiguous nature of things when seeking answers as to why ZN-S or any aircraft came down in undetermined circumstances.

On board PB304 if things started to get worse and happen near or above Manchester it could have been their reason to try and land when and where the opportunity presented itself which may have been when they were coming over Salford? Very close by in flying terms was Heaton Park with much bigger parkland, 660 acres of it, but at the time landing there was quite impossible as it was RAF Station Heaton Park, a place where many Royal Air Force were being trained and with a large number of RAF personnel present there throughout the war, also as an ACDC – Aircrew Dispersal Centre many aircrew were being billeted between courses and postings, additionally it contained a Barrage Balloon anchorage and an AK AK emplacement and undulating land, making it far too dangerous for an emergency landing. There was also RAF Ringway, now Manchester Airport, not too far away from there but it may not have been possible to reach as things seemed to be getting much worse and were unfolding quite dramatically and rapidly at this point, with their hand being forced the crew seemingly had to make some very quick decisions to try and bring the Lancaster down safely ASAP!

The Flight Engineer Sergeant Raymond Barnes was local to the area and quite possibly suggested the open playing fields that he knew so well just off Littleton Road in the Pendlebury part of Salford as a good emergency place to land, and it is quite probable that he then helped guide the Pilot Peter Lines to that location. Witnesses have said that the Lancaster circled round twice in total, the first may have been a mini-reconnaissance run to see if and where they could put down or an actual attempt to land, either way they pulled up and went round again, a crew member believed to be Rear Gunner Sergeant Mohand Singh and a little later two others with him were seen peering out and looking around from the back door on the Starboard (right hand) side of the aircraft. It was on the second run that disaster struck, witnesses said along with the loud roar of the aircraft's engines they heard other smaller exploding sounds, like there was something obviously mechanically wrong and some said that one of the engines, which happened to be on the Port (left hand) side, looked like it was on fire! The key eye witness that I interviewed, Cliff Carr who saw almost everything that day, and later interestingly became a qualified career Engineer, thinks that the engine was misfiring as it became starved of fuel from near empty tanks and that the 'Fire' some people claimed to have seen were the flames that are sometimes ejected from what is essentially an engine trying to 'Cold Start' as it chokes out and that this was the key thing that brought it down! Very interesting and a very feasible prognosis from a man extremely qualified to deliver them as he was a Chief Engineer, Plant Inspector and eventual Manager of the Inspection and Technical Services Department at Shell Chemical Co Ltd, where he put in 25 years of service. Cliff does state though that despite his experience that these are still theories that he is putting forward. There are more thought-provoking ideas and suggestions regarding different aspects of the crash from him later.

Back to the last moments of Lancaster PB304 or ZN-S, as it came round on that second run very low over local houses it was really struggling to maintain height and whilst Flight Lieutenant Lines was trying to make it to the fields beyond S for Sugar clipped the roof tops of houses on Regatta Street and crashed very close by onto the embankment of the River Irwell, after a pause of about 30 seconds the 9000 lbs of bombs on board exploded, causing extensive damage to many houses and wounding many people caught in the blast zone!

A local newspaper, the Salford City Reporter on Friday 5th August 1944 stated, leading with these headlines:

## PLANE CRASHES ON RIVER BANK
### Many People Injured and Much Property Damaged
## EXPLOSION HEARD ALL OVER THE CITY

'About eighty people were injured, one of whom subsequently died, and considerable damage was caused to property when a British aeroplane crashed and blew up on the bank of the Irwell, near Langley-road, Pendlebury, about a hundred yards from the Salford boundary, and fronting on the Littleton-road Playing Fields on Sunday. The crew of the plane were killed.'

**A photograph taken soon after the crash showing some of the extensive damage at Regatta Street caused by the crash of ZN-S/PB304 and the explosion that followed it. As a result of this these houses were not inhabited again until the 1950's.**

Due to wartime restrictions only basic information was given regarding the crash and this was over a month later, the number of civilians killed was actually two in the end, a Mr George Morris and Mrs Lucy Bamford Grandmother of Joe Bamford who wrote an excellent and very detailed book on the crash released in 1996 called 'The Salford Lancaster'. 45-year-old George was an Air Raid Precautions Warden who was tending an allotment when PB304 came down close to where he was, causing him some serious injuries which he sadly succumbed to a few hours later in hospital. 72-year-old Lucy was at her home nearby in Langley Road when the blast and shrapnel from it ripped through her home, along with lots of glass which caused her many injuries, initially she was recovering well and was discharged from hospital but regrettably later died at her son's house on August 11th 1944. They were the fatalities as a result of the crash that day, 2 civilians, 7 crew, we now look in a little more detail about the crew who unfortunately perished and put faces to those names in order to try and hopefully bring alive those human losses a little, to show the real people behind the numbers we are so used to seeing when we read about any war or tragedy.

The standard crew of the Lancaster bomber numbered seven and each had a very important job to do within this huge machine of war, interestingly the varied British and Commonwealth nationalities represented within this one aircrew are a microcosm and very good example of the common place cross-section of those who served in Bomber Command crews during World War Two. To follow is some information about the crew of ZN-S/PB304 and also their positions in the Aircraft.

**The crew of the 'Salford Lancaster' pictured here in April 1944 during training at RAF Winthorpe, Lincolnshire, now Newark Air Museum, whilst with the 1661 Heavy Conversion Unit, the aircraft in the background being used is a Short Sterling.** After that they completed flying training at No.5 Lancaster Finishing School at Syerston, Nottinghamshire before joining No.106 Squadron at RAF Metheringham, 12 miles South-East of Lincoln in early July 1944 in what was known as 'Bomber County' due to its high concentration of RAF Bomber Stations/Airfields in that part of the country. From left to right the airmen were:

Bomb Aimer – 153263 Flying Officer John Steele from Bradford, Yorkshire. He had reportedly told his family of a chilling premonition he'd had that he would not survive the month! Part of his early training was actually at RAF Heaton Park close by to where he would sadly later die.

Mid-Upper Gunner – 515421 Sergeant John Bruce Thornley Davenport from Market Drayton in Shropshire. He had the longest service in the whole crew having joined the RAF on the 2$^{nd}$ December 1931 and up until the crash had already served an impressive 12 years, 7 months.

Flight Engineer – 542608 Sergeant Raymond Barnes from Pendlebury, Salford. Local to the area in which 'The Salford Lancaster' as it would become known crashed. Ray joined the RAF on the 28$^{th}$ July 1937 and already had a very respectable 7 years of service under his belt.

Pilot – 112751 Flight Lieutenant Peter Lines from Purley in Surrey. Peter's earlier training in April 1941 was at RAF No.5 Initial Training Wing in Torquay Devon, passing through the same course as George 'Johnny' Johnson who would eventually become 'The Last British Dambuster'.

Wireless Operator – 1337510 Sergeant Arthur Wilmot Young from Cardiff. He was of Afro-Caribbean descent, an accomplished musician who played Saxophone and Trumpet with a number of bands, and was married on the 18$^{th}$ March 1944 not long before the accident.

Navigator – J28851 Flying Officer Harry Reid from Toronto, Canada. Harry was studying Maths and Physics at the University of Toronto until he joined the air force on the 19$^{th}$ June 1942 for the duration of the emergency, sadly never returning to complete his degree course.

Rear Gunner – 1868785 Sergeant Robert Saul from Preston, Lancashire seen here in this crew picture was not on the raid because of illness, he had been replaced by Sergeant Mohand Singh, flying in what would be the last three operations of PB304 on the 26/27th, 28th and 30th July 1944.

Rear Gunner – 1324569 Sergeant Mohand Singh from the Punjab, India. Singh who was a medical student in London had been on operations since December 1943, this was his 27th, not far from completing the 30 needed for a full tour of duty which would have seen him posted to safer duties in line with RAF procedures. A sketch of him is shown here.

## The crew and their positions in Lancaster ZN-S/PB304

We now move on to the next part of what is essentially our 'Unsolved Detective Story' to hear from the two local witnesses that I interviewed, Mr Cliff Carr and Mrs Marion Garrod. Starting with Cliff who came forward after I went online to the website Aircrashsites.co.uk and put out an appeal for any witnesses of the crash to come forward for possible inclusion in a book I was writing. Having seen that the PB304 crash was already widely discussed on their forum it seemed like a very good place to try and I was not wrong and certainly not disappointed, when much to my delight Cliff Carr came forward who as a young witness had seen almost everything that day from a great viewing and vantage point where he overlooked and saw the last fateful moments of PB304. Later when I was lucky to interview Cliff at his home in Timperley, Cheshire on the 13th July 2018 he shared with me more about what he had seen that day and his later feelings about it all when he told me how it was:

### SEEING THE LAST MOMENTS OF THE SALFORD LANCASTER

"Yes I saw this plane crash. I was 12 years old at the time, me and two pals were playing in the field alongside the A666, Bolton Rd, Pendlebury. I lived at Number 124. The Lancaster came in very low with an engine making a strange banging noise but the propellers were turning on all the engines, as we looked down from our high point which was parallel to Langley Road close to where it came down, we saw it going in what was pretty much an Easterly direction towards the River Irwell.

It was losing height and was so low at that point that it was brushing over the tops of the trees, it continued to go straight, making what was to be its final approach, and then seemed to hit something, we didn't see what, but it spun the plane about 40 degrees, it continued a little as it twisted and then disappeared. After this a wing came up vertically and then flapped down gently out of view, this was followed by a few seconds of quiet then an enormous explosion accompanied by a huge tulip shaped cloud which was orange-red in colour reaching a great height. Incredible events to see as a child, things you don't ever forget.

These things were a source of great excitement as a kid and when you are young you don't think into or analyse events too much, it was one amongst many occurrences we saw during the war, also during that time most things were initially only passed on by word of mouth because the government was very careful about what it released in the press, and even though the wartime poster said 'Careless Talk Costs Lives' naturally local people who saw it and were affected by what was after all quite a traumatising event did talk low key about their experiences, points of view, theories and so on, and in cases like that of the Salford Lancaster I think it only added to the mystery of it all. It was only many years later when I had heard and read much more about the crash, also having seen pictures of the crew and by then thinking with an adult mind about it all, that I was very saddened when it dawned on me that what I was also witnessing at the very moment of that enormous explosion was the death of seven brave young men, it still upsets me today."

As mentioned earlier Cliff Carr **(pictured here holding a sheet I had made him showing the PB304 crew)** also had some additional thoughts and input regarding the crash which came thought in conversations we had and in e-mails that we sent one another where he said: "Some interesting points looking at it all now, knowing what we do, when we saw the plane apparently strike something that made it spin, well that by other witness accounts was as it struck the tops of houses at Regatta Street, whilst the pilot who we now know had a full bomb load was obviously by his line of approach aiming to put the Lancaster down in the open playing fields just over the river but didn't make it. Instead it crashed down that embankment by the houses where the bomber was seen momentarily stood up on its nose as it struck the ground by the river, that's when we saw the tip of the wing come up from the angle we were at before it disappeared followed by the explosion. That day I saw an aircraft with an engine mis-firing not on fire of that I am sure! From an engineering point of view this leads me to think it was starved of fuel. What also backs this up in my mind is that the huge Tulip shaped fire ball was bright orange-red in colour which would indicate bombs exploding, I don't remember seeing much if any black smoke in that eruption that would normally signify the presence of burning fuel! There may well have been more fuel used than normal on the return anyway, especially if they were lost whilst carrying the additional weight of a full bomb load, lots of factors to consider. We will probably never really know for sure what happened but these things seem to fit in well and in line with what we saw unfold that eventful Sunday morning."

After a very good and comprehensive interview with Cliff I thought it would be interesting to try and get another person as a second witness to what happened in order to have an additional perspective on those events. I tried different leads for months but admittedly wasn't successful. Then one Wednesday morning after a service at my church St. Paul's on Moor Lane, Salford which as it happens is also not too far from where PB304 went down, I was talking about the crash with a veteran from Broughton House for ex-servicemen and women where I have volunteered over the years and mentioned that I would really like to find and do a short supplementary interview with one more witness but just couldn't find one. When from behind me came the very familiar voice of Marion Garrod who said: "I saw that, I was close by there that morning!" I couldn't believe it, here was someone I knew as a fellow parishioner for over 15 years and all that time had never heard her ever talk about it, and as a result didn't know that whilst I was looking for someone who saw that piece of local history that there was a witness to it right there under my nose and around me all that time! Now that is what you call a small world I thought. Still gobsmacked at my luck I immediately started to talk to Marion about it and asked her if she would let me do a short interview sometime, which thankfully she agreed to do, so here is Marion's account of when she experienced:

## THE FRIGHTENING EVENTS OF THE 30th JULY 1944

"I lived at 109 South Radford Street and was 11 years old at the time of that crash. I was taking two younger children Beryl and Terry to Sunday School at St. Aiden's Church on Littleton Road, we were walking down Cheadle Avenue and had just got round the bend then we heard these terrible, terrible loud groaning and banging noises and as we gazed up we saw this aeroplane approaching from behind us that had flames coming from part of it, one of the engines I think, and the sound was unbearable. It flew over us nearly touching the roof tops and seemed like it could almost hit the chimney pots and was heading in the Littleton Road and Langley Road direction, I was stood there terrified with the kids watching it go over, not knowing what to do, I was only young, and a lady who lived nearby about three houses from where we were standing shouted frantically to us 'come in here, come in here.' I had the two children, one in each hand and we ran into the house, she closed the door and soon after we heard the horrific bang, the whole house shook violently, very frightening, the plane must have crashed. It was all over in a very short time, what felt like just a few minutes. I heard later it had crashed into the houses and the riverbank on the other side of the Irwell, right across the playing fields! We thought at first it could have landed on the playing fields but after that it would have been unable to because of all the piles of bricks that had been put in parts of it before to stop the enemy landing. It was a very, very sad incident, I didn't hear till sometime later because of course in those days we didn't have television, that there were people killed, and to think I saw those young men go over in what were the last moments of their life! **Marion Garrod, pictured, holding a map of the local area showing where she saw the stricken PB304 on its final descent.**

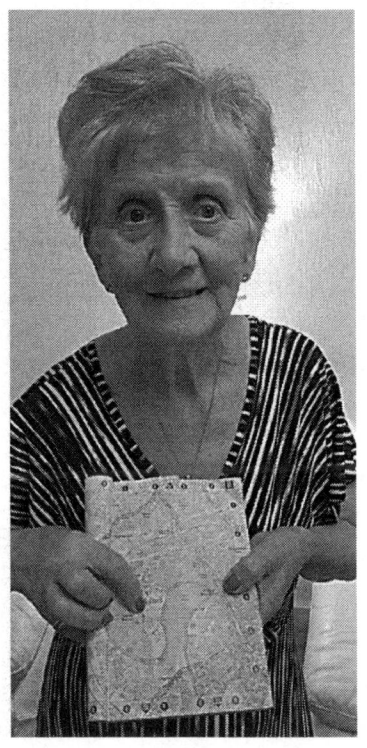

My sister May who was at home that day heard the noise and looked out the window and saw it come down, and when it exploded the noise was that bad she put her hands over her ears to protect them but still never heard properly again after that, later she had to have hearing aids, it semi deafened her for life! Whenever I close my eyes and think about it I can still see it very clearly, that plane coming at us, the noise, the fire coming from it, the explosion, we were lucky it missed us, some of the poor people on the other side of the river weren't so lucky!"

In a letter which has only come to light around the time of some later updating in 2021, this last approach was also recounted by George Eric Gordon who was the Rector of St. Paul's Church, Moor Lane, Kersal from April 1942 to December 1945, and was in the approximate flight path of the stricken Lancaster that was piloted by Peter Lines, incredibly an 'Old Boy' of the same Grammar school as the Rector, St. Olave's at Tower Bridge, London! In this correspondence from Mr Gordon in October 1945 which ended up with the Lines Family, part of it read: The photograph and the account of one pilot who lost his life soon after D-Day were of peculiar moment to us. He flew more or less over this rectory, then over many houses in one part of the parish. When he crashed the explosion shook this house and filled it with smuts, and it blew open the doors of the church the wrong way. So we have special reason to be thankful for his self-sacrifice, (eluding to him trying to land his fully laden bomber safely by the river because he knew they were over a densely populated area, and as a result the minimal casualties that arose from his brave actions)!

Very interestingly when I spoke to Marion about Reverend Gordon's letter in November 2022 she remembered him and had met him, because St. Paul's Church along with the old St. Andrew's and St. Aiden's church were all part of the same parish during the war years, and Marion recalls that each year on Mothering Sunday they used hire a Salford school bus and bring the children from St. Aiden's up the hill to St. Paul's, to the 'Mother Church' as Marion described it for that special service taken by Reverend George Gordon, amazing full circle connections that keep on occurring with this story!

Various eye witness accounts from local people who saw the last moments of ZN-S/PB304 that day put the aircraft at slightly different places as it circled round to make its last approach. It is very important to remember that these events were unfolding very quickly and that the people that saw the Lancaster coming down did so from different angles and places, in most cases for less than a minute before it disappeared out of their view in a direction where only seconds later it could well have altered its course somewhat before coming down. Add to this that these were sudden and shocking events and happened over 75 years ago and that people in retrospect can and do change their minds a little about things they have seen and events they witness in life, and certain details are or can become quite blurred in the years that follow and that people can even be influenced by what others say which leads them to change their minds about their account, then in that big mix you have the potential for all sorts to happen and be reported. Even with the greatest honesty and best intentions things are often reported both rightly and wrongly after an event which complicates things somewhat, and respectfully we should consider this case to be no different. As we all know you can have a number of people together in the same place all witnessing the same thing at the same time and still have varied accounts of what they saw and differences of opinion from within that same group of people.

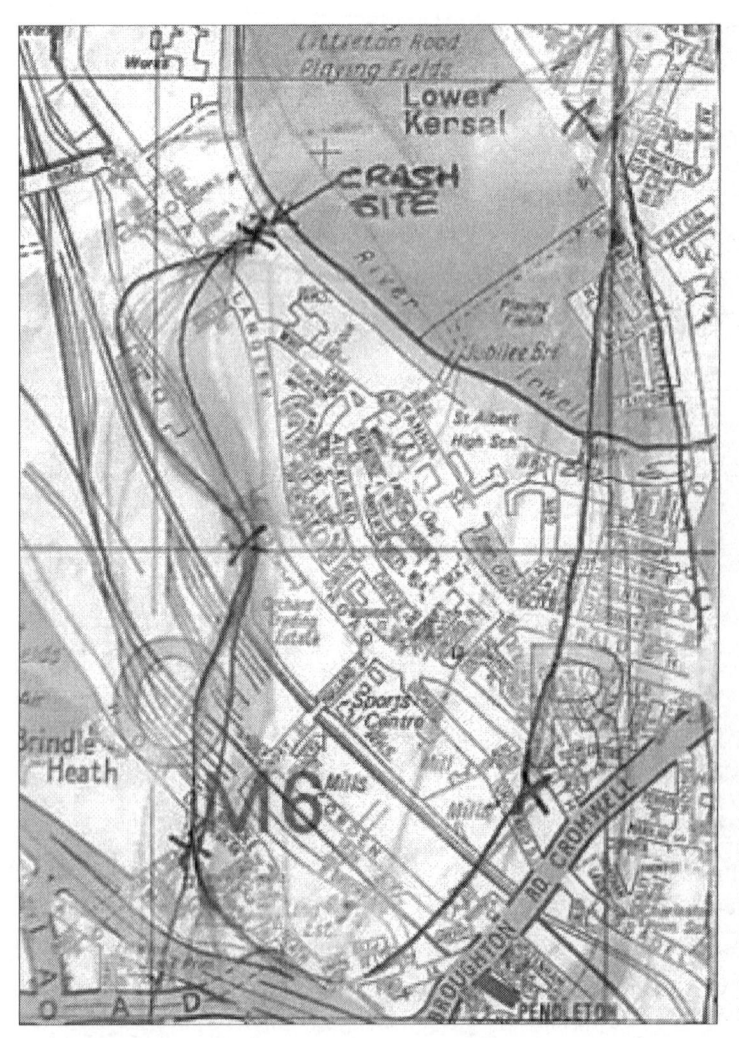

When viewing the map I have included here, with the top being due North, we need to take into account the points that have just been raised. I wanted to include a map just to show more than anything the local area where the crash took place, to give the story more meaning in a visual sense and to hopefully help provide a bit more clarity. Otherwise to anyone reading this who does not know this area, the local geography and its streets it will mean very little, with it we have a better idea for all those who read it a rough lay of the land where PB304 went down which helps bind this interesting local story and help it to make more sense. This close up map of the area around Pendleton and Lower Kersal in Salford, Lancashire was kindly sent to me by Joe Bamford and has lines marking out the last projected possibilities on the final fatal run up to and over Regatta Street, next to the crash site. These were based on various and slightly differing eye witness accounts, marked with crosses, of the aircraft's position as it came over just before it hit the houses and crashed. This map is an early projection and again it is very important to apply what I listed earlier about all the other variables that can and do come into play here, immediately demonstrated by the description that Cliff Carr gave, that would mean geographically the turning circle of the Lancaster would have to be wider and greater than shown marked out on this map, Cliff saw the PB304 after Marion once it had come down and round for its final run to try and land. The area which Marion Garrod gave her account of is near the cross in the top right-hand corner, Cliff Carr's account is further to the left-hand side and a little off this map opposite the cross directly in the centre.  Despite this, very importantly the final horizontal Easterly approach towards the Littleton Road Playing Fields and eventual crash site both marked here would still have been the same.  In the aftermath of the crash lorries and personal from RAF Heaton Park, mentioned earlier in the story, were dispatched to help with the clean-up operation as the direct local destruction was extensive and subsequently the explosion was heard up to eight miles away and damage reported in all the adjacent areas around Salford such as Swinton, Pendlebury, Lower and Higher Broughton, also the RAF quickly got involved because it was one of their own that they had just lost. Consequently it was one of the Medical Commanding Officers at RAF Heaton Park who signed the death certificates for all 7 crew members who had perished on that fatal day.

On Sunday the 28TH July 2019 the nearest Sunday to the 75th anniversary, many gathered at Agecroft Cemetery close where the crash happened and the site where the official memorial to the crew of ZN-S/PB304 can be found, this formed the centre piece of a moving tribute service to commemorate the crash and to remember the 7 crew and 2 civilians who died as a result of it.  During the service I recited live for the first time my new piece of poetry that I had written especially for the event called 'The Bomber Command Tribute' which is a generic tribute to all who lost their lives in RAF Bomber Command during World War Two, also incorporating into it is the story of this one crew so that we had both the bigger and the local picture being represented and remembered at the same time.

**The Lancaster Bomber memorial at Agecroft Cemetery, Salford, close to the Wartime crash site, listing the names of all the crew, pictured here on the 75TH anniversary in 2019 with poppy reefs, a permanent local tribute to the crew of AVRO Lancaster PB304 AKA ZN-S of 106 Squadron RAF.  To bring my coverage of this story to a conclusion, I feel that although what occurred here was something seemingly quite small in the much bigger picture of what was happening in the world at that time, relatively small losses compared to the thousands being suffered in the huge battles that were simultaneously raging around the world from Normandy to the Pacific, keeping alive the memory of each and every one lost that day is equally as important, no matter where or how they died, and that in the midst of all that went on in that devastating world conflict it is also good to remember a very profound local story, that of 'The Salford Lancaster.'**

I wrote this poem to honour all those who were lost in Bomber Command during World War Two, and integrating as a further mark of respect on a local level the loss of the crew of Lancaster ZN-S/PB304, AKA 'The Salford Lancaster' who were killed on 30th July 1944 whilst returning from an operation over Europe when their plane crash landed on the banks of the River Irwell in Salford, Lancashire. This poem being made all the more poignant having been written around the 75th anniversary of that event in July 2019 and is also a further link to the story of Lancaster PB304 featured here in 'The Last Stand - Memories of War'.

## THE BOMBER COMMAND TRIBUTE

Bomber Command World War Two
55,573 people who
Gave their lives in a war of attrition
With no thought of submission

Night after night, Operation after operation
Taking the fight to the enemy without hesitation
With just under 50 percent losses
They fought and perished for our nation

Hitting many targets, reaching Berlin too
In the Ruhr bringing down Dams and seeing their missions through
Giving back to Nazism what it had meted out to so many others
The saddest part, the loss of so many fine flying brothers

Flack, AK AK and Night Fighters they had to endure it all
The loss of aircraft and limbs, terrible burns and much more
Immeasurable sacrifices and bravery beyond belief
Giving more than their country asked, the courage never ceased

Wellington's, Sterling's, Halifax's and Lancaster's went
Diligently on 'Ops' to wherever they were sent
With their American allies Day and Night, up to 1000 strong
In the end good would prevail and triumph over what was wrong

So many crews lost, we should remember them all
The list is endless, so only one I will now recall
PB304 with its crew of seven
Lost on the 30th of July '44
Now with different wings they fly in heaven

**The 'Salford Lancaster' as it became known**
**Came down on the banks of the Irwell, its legend has grown**
**The boys that lost their lives that day shall not grow old**
**As long as we make sure their story is continually told**

**They completed their missions so let's make this one Ours**
**To remember them and all lost in Bomber Command, through their motto**
**Per Ardua Ad Astra, "Through Adversity to the Stars"**

Gary Bridson-Daley

17/07/19

The Salford Lancaster story is a great connecting point between the Royal Air Force and subsequent Civilian part of this book because it contains elements of both within it, an RAF tragedy witnessed by local people who I interviewed, which along with and after the accompanying Bomber Command Tribute poetry is a fitting run into the next part of the book regarding the remarkable and varied stories of Civilians who also experienced many different things during that conflict and whose lives and wartime narratives, as you will soon see, make stimulating reading.

# CIVILIAN VETERANS

**KEEP CALM AND CARRY ON**

# SINGER & ENTERTAINER DAME VERA LYNN DBE OSTJ

Served with – ENSA – Entertainments National Service Association
Visited – 31st May 2018, Ditchling, East Sussex

**ENSA**

## Service History and Personal Stories

- ❖ Born – 20<sup>th</sup> March 1917, East Ham, London.
- ❖ Incredible life detailed below.

Dame Vera Lynn CH, DBE, OSTJ, Forces Sweetheart, National Treasure, World Famous Singer, Icon of the Wartime Generation, Tireless Charity Worker and Centenarian with massive life achievements, a wonderful World War Two veteran to have in 'The Last Stand – Memories of War' and with which to start this chapter. During the Second World War whilst serving with ENSA (Entertainments National Service Association) the organisation responsible for entertaining and helping keep up the moral of the troops, Vera Lynn was very well known for performing out in various theatres of war, often near the front lines in places such as Egypt, India and Burma where there was very real danger from enemy action. This she would do to let the troops who were far from home, often for years at a time, know that they were not forgotten and that their service and sacrifices were truly appreciated by those back at home, by family, friends and the nation as a whole. It was this very special mission that would in time be one of her biggest legacies and something which struck a very real and poignant chord with the troops that she went to entertain, see and speak to, and did so in order to help in her own very special way during what were very difficult and demanding times in World War Two. It also endeared her to them so much that it earned her the title of 'Forces Sweetheart', and to this day Vera Lynn is still respected by many very grateful World War Two veterans and others from the generations that have followed throughout the United Kingdom and elsewhere who have echoed such sentiments, some of whom I have spoken to and interviewed over the years who knew her music, saw her perform or were also fortunate like me to have met her. Music equals memories and as soon as you hear timeless songs such as 'We'll Meet Again' or the 'The White Cliffs of Dover', 'A Nightingale Sang in Berkeley Square', and 'There'll Always Be an England' you are instantly transported back to another era, to that of wartime England, and in any conversation to do with the music of that period it will surely not be long before you hear her name lovingly mentioned in relation to those past times.

As the Entertainments National Service Association was a civilian run, recruited and based organisation, sometimes uniformed, sometimes not, that operated under the auspices of the Navy, Army and Air Force institutes and branches of those services, I have included this story here in the Civilian section of the book, to add to the interesting and varied mix of stories found within this chapter of it.

I didn't do a formal interview with Dame Vera about her life, instead I was very fortunate that the foreword to my first book 'The Last Heroes' was written by her, and after that we corresponded and I had contact with her through Vera's close personal friend and PA Susan Fleet who has been very kind and helpful with my requests, which has included having specific questions put forward by me and answered for special inclusion as part of her profile and this book, meaning some exclusive material resides within it. In addition to this I was very privileged to have been able to visit Dame Vera who was then an incredible 101 years of age and spend some time with her at her home in Ditchling, East Sussex, where we had a lovely chat about various things and where I was very warmly welcomed by both Dame Vera and daughter Virginia. It is something very special and means a lot to me to be able to have maintained this continuity and for her to be involved in and be a part of 'The Last Heroes' and 'The Last Stand' and to have very kindly validated my 'Debt of Gratitude Project' as a whole. So this is her story; a big story of a life very well lived:

**Dame Vera Margaret Lynn** née **Welch,** Singer and Actress was born in East Ham, London on 20th March 1917 to parents Bertram Samuel Welch (1883–1955) and Annie Martin (1889–1961), who had married in 1913. She began performing publicly at the age of seven in local working men's clubs, a tough circuit to start on at any age, and adopted her maternal grandmother's maiden name, Margaret Lynn, as her stage name when she was eleven. Her first radio broadcast, with the Joe Loss Orchestra, was in 1935. At this point she appeared on records released by dance bands including those of Joe Loss and of Charlie Kunz. In 1936 her first solo record was released on the Crown label, "Up the Wooden Hill to Bedfordshire". This label was absorbed by Decca Records in 1938. After a short stint with Loss she stayed with Kunz for a few years during which time she recorded several standard musical pieces. In 1937 she moved to the aristocrat of British dance bands, Bert Ambrose. Best known for her 1939 recording of the popular song "We'll Meet Again", written by Ross Parker and Hughie Charles, the nostalgic lyrics ("We'll meet again, don't know where, don't know when, but I know we'll meet again some sunny day") were very popular during the war and made the song one of its most emblematic hits, it resonated particularly with those who were separated when a loved one or someone special had to go away to serve their country. During the Phoney War in 1939-1940, the Daily Express asked British servicemen to name their favourite musical performers: Vera Lynn came out on top and as a result became known as "The Forces' Sweetheart".

In 1941, during some of the darkest days of the Second World War, Vera Lynn began her own radio programme, *Sincerely Yours*, sending messages to British troops serving abroad. She and her quartet performed songs most requested by the soldiers. Lynn also visited hospitals to interview new mothers and send personal messages to their husbands overseas. Her other great wartime hit was "The White Cliffs of Dover", words by Nat Burton, music by Walter Kent.

Vera Lynn joined ENSA at the beginning of the war and whilst a part of the organisation toured Egypt, India and Burma, giving outdoor concerts for the troops, in March 1944 she went to Shamshernagar airfield deep in Bengal to entertain the troops before the Battle of Kohima. Her host and lifelong friend Captain Bernard Holden recalled that she added a lot by; "her courage and her contribution to morale". In 1985, she received the Burma Star for entertaining British troops in Japanese-occupied Burma.

During the war years Vera also made appearances in three wartime films: 'We'll Meet Again' (1943), 'Rhythm Serenade' (1943) and 'One Exciting Night' (1944), where her versatile skills shone through when she proved to be a good actress as well as a singer. **Left – Vera Lynn performing at a munitions factory in 1941.** After the war her professional singing career continued and in 1952 "Auf Wiederseh'n Sweetheart" became the first record by a British performer to top the charts in the United States, remaining there for an amazing nine weeks! She also appeared regularly for a time on Tallulah Bankhead's US radio programme *The Big Show*. 'Auf Wiederseh'n Sweetheart', along with 'The Homing Waltz' and 'Forget-Me-Not', gave Lynn a remarkable three entries on the first UK Singles Chart, a top 12 (which actually contained 15 songs owing to tied positions). Her popularity continued in the 1950s, peaking with 'My Son, My Son', a number-one hit in 1954 which she co-wrote with Gordon Melville Rees. In 1960 she left Decca Records (after nearly 25 years) and joined EMI. She recorded for EMI's Columbia, MGM and HMV labels. She also recorded Lionel Bart's song 'The Day After Tomorrow' for the 1962 musical *Blitz!* She did not appear onstage in the play, but the characters in the play hear the song on the radio while they shelter from the bombs. In 1967 she recorded 'It Hurts To Say Goodbye', a song which hit the top 10 on the Billboard Easy Listening chart.

Vera Lynn was the subject of *This Is Your Life* on two occasions, in October 1957 when she was surprised by Eamonn Andrews at the BBC Television Theatre, and in December 1978, for an episode which was broadcast on 1 January 1979, when Andrews surprised her at the Cafe Royal, London. She hosted her own variety series 'The Vera Lynn Show' on BBC1 in the late 1960s and early 1970s and was a frequent guest on other variety shows, notably the 1972 *Morecambe & Wise* Christmas Show. In 1972 she was a key performer in the BBC anniversary programme *Fifty Years of Music*. In 1976 she hosted the BBC's *A Jubilee of Music*, celebrating the pop music hits of the period 1952–1976 to commemorate the start of Queen Elizabeth II's Silver Jubilee year. For ITV she presented a 1977 TV special to launch her album *Vera Lynn in Nashville*, which included pop songs of the 1960s and country songs. The Royal Variety Performance included appearances by Vera Lynn on four occasions: 1960, 1975, 1986 and 1990. Her last single, 'I Love This Land', was released to mark the end of the Falklands War in 1982. Dame Vera Lynn 'officially' retired in 1995.

Her final public performance took place outside Buckingham Palace that year as part of a ceremony to mark the fiftieth anniversary of VE (Victory in Europe) Day. Ten years later during the United Kingdom's VE Day Diamond Jubilee ceremonies in 2005 there was a concert in Trafalgar Square, London, in which Dame Vera made a surprise appearance. There she made a speech praising the veterans and calling upon the younger generation always to remember their sacrifice, and also joined in with a few bars of 'We'll Meet Again'. Later after that year's Royal British Legion Festival of Remembrance Lynn encouraged the Welsh singer Katherine Jenkins to assume the mantle of 'Forces Sweetheart', but of course when anyone remembers that title it is primarily Vera Lynn they still associate it with and to a greater degree always will do! In 2009, at age

92, she became the oldest living artist to top the UK Albums Chart, when *We'll Meet Again: The Very Best of Vera Lynn* reached No.1 and with this achievement she also surpassed Bob Dylan as the oldest artist to have a number one album in the UK.  When she released the album *Vera Lynn 100* in 2017, to commemorate her centennial year, it was a number 3 hit, which at that time marked the wartime singer's staggering 93 years in the industry, having made her stage debut as mentioned earlier at the age of seven!  It featured new re-orchestrated versions of her most beloved music alongside her original vocals and also intertwined in it as duets were a chart-topping line-up of British singers including Alfie Boe on 'We'll Meet Again', Alexander Armstrong on 'White Cliffs of Dover' and Aled Jones on 'As Time Goes By'.  In addition to this it included a previously unreleased version of 'Sailing', a surprise find as it was not widely known that she had recorded the track.  This album also made her the oldest continuous recording artist in the world and first centenarian performer to have an album in the charts, also the only artist to have a chart span on the British single and album charts reaching from the chart's inception to the 21st century.

Around the same time in March 2017 Parlophone which owns Dame Vera's later recordings from the 1960's and 1970's, released a collection of her songs recorded at the legendary Abbey Road Studios entitled 'Her Greatest from Abbey Road' which included five previously unreleased original recordings.  It doesn't stop there; Dame Vera is also a published author with her books 'Some Sunny Day' in 2009 and 'Keep Smiling Through' in 2017.  Her popularity never seemed to wane, this was again proven in October 2019 when a compilation album containing 14 of her best loved and legendary songs Remastered between 2017 to 2019 called 'Remastered Hits' was released.

**Dame Vera described becoming a Centenarian and her life in general in a lovely way when she said:** "It has been an incredible adventure of song, dance and friendship".

**Charity work** - Another very important part of Vera Lynn's life has been her charity work, something she has devoted much time and energy to over the years, with a lot of work connected to many causes very close to her heart. In 1953 Lynn formed the cerebral palsy charity SOS (The Stars Organisation for Spastics) and became its chairperson.  The Royal Air Forces Association and other charities also benefited greatly from her involvement and help over the years, and in recognition of all her valuable charity work she was awarded the OBE in 1969. The Vera Lynn Charity Breast Cancer Research Trust was founded in 1976, with Lynn its chairperson and later its president.  In 2002 she became president of the cerebral palsy charity The Dame Vera Lynn Trust for Children with Cerebral Palsy, AKA Dame Vera Lynn Children's Charity and hosted a celebrity concert on its behalf at Queen Elizabeth Hall in London.

**DAME VERA LYNN Children's Charity** — Discover together

**Logo of the amazing charity which Dame Vera Lynn was heavily involved in, devoted a lot of time to and which was close to her heart, one that in recognition for all she did still bears her name.**

In 2008 Dame Vera became patron of the charitable Forces Literary Organisation Worldwide and in 2010 the patron of the Dover War Memorial Project and additionally in 2010 patron of the British charity Projects to Support Refugees from Burma/Help 4 Forgotten Allies.  Burma and her time there having always been a very special part of her life. In 2013 Lynn joined a PETA (People for the Ethical Treatment of Animals) campaign against pigeon racing, stating that the sport was "utterly cruel". Dame Vera's amazingly kind and caring nature continued to shine through from her time helping servicemen and their families during the Second World War, right through into her 103$^{rd}$ year where she was still working from home and was actively involved in helping many of the charities listed here until her passing in June 2020.

As I was coming to the end of penning Dame Vera's part of the book I contacted her very helpful P.A Susan Fleet to put forward some questions especially from me to her for inclusion here, her interesting replies were another valuable up to date addition to this story, I received them shortly before her passing making them unique to this publication, as follows:

**Can Dame Vera tell us some of her favourite moments from when she used to go and entertain the troops during the war, from amongst the great many I am sure she has, any that particularly stick out and are good to include in my book?**

"I remember performing in Burma to our brave boys, and not having enough electricity to power the microphone. They hooked it up to a floodlight just so that I could perform! There was no running water either, and I remember hearing the sounds of the fighting in the distance but they always made me feel safe and I felt so happy to be there doing my part to bring them a piece of home."

**How does it feel to (rightly) be called and thought of as a 'National Treasure'?**

"I am not sure I can really comment, but it is very kind of you to say that Gary. I am delighted that people still enjoy my music, and it is encouraging to know that a part of history seems to have been kept alive by playing those nostalgic songs."

**At an incredible 103 years of age the honours and accolades keep coming, including being a part of 'The Last Stand' which is also jointly dedicated to you, how does that make you feel?**

"I am incredibly humbled that people still enjoy my music all these years later, and it is always overwhelming to receive an accolade. It is truly wonderful to hear from people around the world and hear their stories about those songs. I am grateful to have had such a long and diverse career, and I am incredibly fortunate to have achieved everything I could possibly have wanted."

**Sadly lives and memories fade, but the songs with their moving lyrics remain, and Dame Vera is captured in time now, as the voice of 'The Greatest Generation', preserving in her music remembrances from a Britain of a past age. I conclude this part with these words of wisdom given by the lady in question who draws upon and shares her extensive life experience when she says:**

"Stay true to yourself and keep on going. It is easy to give up or give in but if you are successful, you will want to be able to look back on your life and career without regrets, and be proud of the decisions you have made."

"We can't change the past but we can learn from history and remember the important things – the sacrifices our loved ones made, and the price of our freedom today."

# Additional Information and Life After Service

**Rank upon finish of service** – Private.

**Medals, Honours, Associations and Organisations** – **Some of the huge amount of her accolades and achievements are listed here, as follows;** Voted most popular singer in Britain in a Daily Express competition (1939), soon after also becomes known as the 'Forces Sweetheart', British War Medal 1939–1945 for service in WW2 (1945), appointed/became an OBE - Officer of the Order of the British Empire (1969), made honorary citizen of Winnipeg, Canada (1974), received Music Publishers' Award Show Business Personality of the Year, Grand Order of Water Rats, Ivor Novello Award, and was advanced to DBE - Dame Commander of the Order of the British Empire (all 1975), made honorary citizen of Nashville, Tennessee (1977), Freedom of the City of London (1978), granted honorary Doctor of Letters from the University of Newfoundland, Canada, M.Mus. - Master of Music, where she established the Lynn Musical Scholarship (1978), was President of the Printers' Charitable Corporation (1980). Awarded Commander of the Order of Orange-Nassau, named International Ambassador of Variety Club International, awarded Burma Star (all in 1985), became a fellow of the University of East London (1990), made an Officer of the Order of Saint John (OStJ)(1998), and in the Millennium year (2000) Dame Vera Lynn received a special 'Spirit of the 20th Century' Award and was named 'The Briton who best exemplified the spirit of the 20th century'. Later appointed a Member of the Order of the Companions of Honour (CH) in the (2016) Birthday Honours for services to entertainment and charity, awarded the prestigious 'Outstanding Contribution Award' at the Soldiering On Awards (2016). Since World War Two Dame Vera also remained a member of the Women's Royal Voluntary Service (WRVS) and a member of her local Women's Institute in East Sussex.

The honours and achievements keep on coming, at the Classic Brits (2018) held at London's Royal Albert Hall, the Classical world honoured her with the prestigious Lifetime Achievement Award, and a special Commemorative Coin has been struck to honour her in (2019). Also one of the new Transport for London ferries operating across the Thames from Woolwich entering service in (2019) has been named the 'Dame Vera Lynn' after the London born star, the vessel bearing her name is part of the fourth generation of ferries which has been running this free service since 1889, her name will now be linked to part of that great ongoing London tradition.

In addition to all of this she has a street named in her honour, Vera Lynn Close, which is situated in Forest Gate, London, and a preserved example of the WD Austerity 2-10-0 class of steam locomotives at the North Yorkshire Moors Railway is named 'Dame Vera Lynn'. All of these honours adding to the great affection and respect in which Dame Vera Lynn is held in the United Kingdom and throughout the world to this very day.

Her story continues, during the terrible Coronavirus Pandemic the world as everybody knows was gripped by Covid 19 and very sadly many thousands died here in the U.K (and a great many more around the World). In the spirit of a true 'Forces Sweetheart' Dame Vera being very aware of what was going on came forward and released a short video to mark her 103rd Birthday on 20th March 2020, where she took the opportunity to send some words of encouragement to everyone throughout the country affected by it, with the situation having a lot of parallels to and being very reminiscent of the Second World War in many ways including the nation having to truly pull together for the first time since that conflict, with these very poignant things in mind Dame Vera said:

"We are facing a very challenging time at the moment, and I know many people are worried about the future. I'm greatly encouraged that despite these struggles we have seen people joining together. They are supporting one another, reaching into the homes of their neighbours by offering assistance to the elderly and sending messages of support and singing into the streets. Music is so good for the soul, and during these hard times we must all help each other to find moments of joy. Keep smiling and keep singing."

In a very special and rare address to the nation by Her Majesty Queen Elizabeth II aired on Sunday 5th April 2020 the wartime spirit was again invoked as a rallying call to the country in order to help it get through the crisis. At the end of her speech the Queen very lovingly quoted and echoed the words of a Vera Lynn song when she said: 'We'll Meet Again.' At 103 years of age Dame Vera Lynn also responded in the best way she knew how, through the gift of music, when as one of the wartime generation, like Her Majesty the Queen, she again stepped up to do her bit at a time of national crisis by re-releasing that very same song on the 11th April 2020 less than a week after the Royal speech. This wartime classic being re-mixed as a duet with the new 'Forces Sweetheart' Katherine Jenkins and all monies raised by them going to the NHS Charities Together. Proving that her music was still reaching out, touching so many people's souls and doing so much good for so many others.

**The last parts of the incredible story of this wonderful lady were her passing on the 18th June 2020, a very sad day indeed, and at her funeral on 10th July 2020 the touching and fitting tribute of a Spitfire flypast to honour her. I feel so privileged to have met and had ongoing collaboration from and with our WW2 Forces Sweetheart and National Treasure, something I will always remember and be grateful for, and to have spent a little time with her means so much to me. Thank you for everything Dame Vera, your memory will be honoured in many places, amongst them here in my book. God Bless You. RIP.**

<u>Home Life</u> – In 1941 Vera married Harry Lewis, a clarinettist and saxophonist, and fellow member of the Bert Ambrose's orchestra whom she had met two years earlier. Harry went on to be Vera's manager for most of her musical career. They had one child, Virginia Penelope Anne Lewis. Harry died in 1998. After the Second World War Lynn and Lewis moved to Finchley, North London, after which they later moved to Ditchling in East Sussex in the early 1960s, where Dame Vera remained until her passing in 2020.

<u>Epilogue</u> – Having Dame Vera Lynn as one of the WW2 Veterans in 'The Last Stand' and with her wartime service in ENSA makes for a very interesting kind of story indeed, as their job was to help lift the spirits of the fighting men and assist in motivating them, an essential part of helping any Army physiologically to win a war, it is for this reason I am also including a short overview of this very unique and quite different kind of organisation that served within our forces in World War Two.

<u>ENSA (Entertainments National Service Association)</u> was established in 1939, it was set up by Basil Dean and Leslie Henson to provide entertainment for the British military during World War Two. The list of those who either were or would become stars that passed through and performed various kinds of acts for ENSA in front of all branches of the British Armed forces and many civilian services during the conflict is quite illustrious and includes; Arthur Askey, Tony Hancock, Eric Sykes, Spike Milligan, Lennard Pearce, Gracie Fields, George & Beryl Formby, Tommy Cooper, Joyce Grenfell, Kenneth Connor, Terry-Thomas, Peter Sellers, John Gielgud, Mantovani, the Sadler's Wells Ballet. In 1945 Laurence Olivier and Ralph Richardson were made 'Honorary Lieutenants' in the British Army, joined ENSA and embarked on a six-week tour of Europe performing plays by William Shakespeare.

The geographical extent of what ENSA tried to achieve in many theatres of war all over the world led to its skills frequently being spread very thinly indeed, but for every second or third-rate end-of-the pier act there were also class-acts to compensate! They were after all a civilian organisation operating under military rules and regulations frequently in very difficult and unsafe conditions. As a result ENSA was sometimes referred to tongue-in-cheek by the troops as 'Every Night Something Awful', which in many cases was not true, especially if you were lucky enough to get one of the great and talented performers listed above which also included of course our lovely Vera Lynn. ENSA paid those who performed for it £10 a week while those who worked in the chorus were paid £4 a week. This was very good money by the standards of the day. The first ENSA concert was in England on September 10th 1939 while the last performance was in India on 18th August 1946.

It was superseded by Combined Services Entertainment (CSE) which now operates as part of the Services Sound and Vision Corporation (SSVC).

Many women served and contributed greatly to the War effort in ENSA and many other branches of the military services and civilian occupations during the second world war, and in the Last Stand you will find the stories of women who were in a number of these branches represented and reflected within its pages, all of whom did very important work and all helping their country achieve victory in many different ways, therefore they deserve to be and are honoured rightly and equally alongside the men who served during that conflict.

**As you can see from her life story the legacy of Dame Vera Lynn is a huge one in so many, many ways, but the closing tribute that I am going to leave you with is from the lady to whom she handed the mantle of 'Forces Sweetheart', the amazing and highly talented performer Katherine Jenkins, who upon Vera's passing shared these very moving thoughts and feelings about her:**

**'I simply cannot find the words to explain just how much I adored this wonderful lady. Her voice brought comfort to millions in their darkest hours, her songs filled the nations hearts with hope, and her emotive performances, whether home or abroad, then or now, helped to get us through. It was she who chose the sentiments of her songs – she knew instinctively what people needed to hear, how to rally the morale and her spirit & strength created the soundtrack of a generation. There will never be another Dame Vera Lynn. Forces Sweetheart and our Sweetheart. An icon. A legend. An inspiration. My mentor & my friend. I will miss you greatly and I know we'll meet again some sunny day.' Katherine Jenkins**

**The Author Gary Bridson-Daley having a dream come true by sharing precious moments with National Treasure Dame Vera Lynn during his visit to her home in Ditchling, East Sussex on Thursday 31st May 2018, making a truly unforgettable 'Connection with History'.**

# BEVIN BOY HARRY PARKES BEM

Served with – Bevin Boys – Coal Miners

Service Number – 148 (Bestwood Colliery)

Interviewed – Nottingham, Nottinghamshire, 21st July 2018

## Service History and Personal Stories

- Born – 15th January 1927, Nottingham, Nottinghamshire, England, UK.
- Harry (in the above picture front row, right hand side kneeling) thought when his time came to serve he might be in the Army, Navy or Air Force but fate had something very different in store for him, as he found out in January 1944 after his 18th birthday when he was told to register for service at the local Labour Exchange in Nottingham City Centre where all forces interviews, selection and medicals took place.
- The Government later sent him a letter and a travel warrant and he was instructed to report to Creswell Colliery in Nottinghamshire for what he still believed was part of the selection and training process for the Army, only to find to his great surprise upon arrival that he'd been chosen by ballot to work as a National Service Conscript in a coal mine.

- This began with 4 weeks intense training from February to March 1944 which involved P.T instruction in the morning to toughen up the new recruits and work at the pit in the afternoon both on the surface and underground to gain practical experience, where they undertook various backbreaking tasks such as carrying props, filling and emptying wagons with stone, doing haulage and additional classroom theory in various aspects coal mining.
- Once Harry had successfully passed this 'Basic Training' he was then sent to Bestwood Colliery in Nottinghamshire where he served over 4 years from March 1944 until June 1948 becoming one of the 'Bevin Boys' named after Ernest Bevin, then Minister of Labour.
- Years of arduous and demanding work was undertaken as they strived to meet quotas and maintain production and output for a war economy that desperately needed this 'Black Gold' and Harry was one of the 48,000 conscripts that delivered what was required to win.
- During the time Harry worked in National Service within this industry it played a significant role in the British war effort, and he was a part of and experienced it right through to its Nationalisation in 1947 and after, as a result he was involved in and experienced many radical changes and restructuring at this pivotal time in its history.
- He continued on into a lifetime of work dedicated to coal mining, later becoming an Underground Mechanical and Electrical Shift Manager at Bestwood (part of Bestwood Coal & Iron Company) and eventually was Head Technician and Lecturer in the Department of mining at Nottingham & District Technical College, later University, his work also extended to major involvement in the Trade Union Movement with NALGO, NUM and UNISON.
- Harry's service to the Coal mining industry stretched from 1944 until his retirement in 1991, an incredible 47 years! On the 7th May 2013 a memorial to the Bevin Boys designed by Harry Parkes was unveiled by the Countess of Wessex at the National Memorial Arboretum at Alrewas in Staffordshire, based on the Bevin Boys Badge. All his efforts were rightly awarded that year with the BEM – British Empire Medal.

The story of Bevin Boy Harry Parkes is one of a very different type of World War Two service which was unique in many ways, in 1944 he was conscripted into the coal mining industry in Nottinghamshire, meaning his very interesting experiences regarding service on the Home Front during the Second World War vary greatly from other Home Front veterans I have interviewed who worked on the land or in factories, because for Harry and all the Bevin Boys like him their 'Frontline' was underground in the hard reality of a coal mine! These conscripts were pulled together from all walks of life regardless of status and included those who came from regular working-class families through to those from more privileged backgrounds like Public School boys. From 1943 to 1945 one in ten of all young men called up were sent to work in the mines, they were chosen by lot from all healthy male conscripts between the ages of 18-25, this eventually totalled 48,000 men sent with the purpose of increasing much needed coal production which had declined in the early part of World War Two. Some volunteered as an alternative to military conscription, most reluctantly joined but it was known to have caused a great deal of upset amongst them as many young men wanted to be a part of the armed forces believing that as miners their service would not be valued as much as their counterparts in the regular branches of the military services, something which in time proved to be quite true. Indeed during their time in the mines Bevin Boys were even targets of abuse from some members of the general public who mistakenly believed them to be draft dodgers or cowards, and they were frequently stopped by police as possible deserters! Unlike those who had served in the military Bevin Boys were not awarded medals for their contribution to the war effort and it took them decades to gain any kind of 'Official Recognition' for their hard and dangerous work, which was only first conferred by the British Government in 1995! After release from their service most left for further education or for employment in other sectors, one of the few who did the opposite and stayed within the Coal mining industry was Harry, who dedicated all his working life to it, he now tells us from his extensive experience about:

## THE IMPORTANT CONTRIBUTION OF BEVIN BOYS AND THE COAL INDUSTRY DURING THE WAR

"The contribution of hard-working coal miners, Bevin Boys and the coal mining industry as a whole during World War Two was huge and should never be underestimated, even though by many it was, in simple and stark terms no coal would have meant no fuel, no fuel meaning no power to run most aspects of the wartime industries in the United Kingdom, and to heat the houses of the nation on the home front! It also significantly helped keep the armed services going, from the bases in the U.K through to the vital shipping of every kind, that of the Merchant Navy of which most ships were still coal fed and consequently without whose precious convoys that brought and moved supplies to and around Great Britain plus men and material to fighting fronts abroad would not have arrived, and the vital means to continue fighting the enemy would have been greatly impeded, additionally many ships of the Royal Navy were supplied with coal at their British Port bases and went out from there to fight for our Maritime interests in every theatre of war on the high seas, importantly none of this could have functioned and no war could have been won without coal! My small part in this much bigger picture was at Bestwood Colliery in my home county of Nottinghamshire where the jobs I did entailed a lot of things, after training when I first began there as a regular full-time employee, for the first two weeks I was put on 'Surface Work' as a Coal Sorter with the pit women on fast moving conveyer belts, where we had to take out and separate the coal into small, medium and large sizes and filter out any stones and unwanted debris. Then I was moved to work underground and was the only Bevin Boy at that Colliery to be put in a team with coal miners sons, I would remain working underground for the rest of my time there all the way through till finishing in June 1948!

As we all soon found out no matter what job you worked on anywhere at a mine it was all very hard graft and as you would expect teams of miners did lots of different jobs at different points and places in the mining operation, all playing various but very important parts in the production process. So to explain in layman's terms for those who haven't worked or even been down a mine before, my part of the job, 8 hours a day, 5-6 days a week was roughly this; there were deep 'Air In and Air Out Shafts' down in the pit, one of each, I was on the Air Out Shaft also known as the 'Up-Cast Shaft' as one of the Haulage Operators sending up waggons full of coal to the surface. The coal travelled underground from the coal face, in our case as it was a well worked mine this was 4 miles away, and transported in trains of seven wagons pulled along by steel wire ropes on a pulley system to the shaft at the pit bottom which was half a mile down, from there the waggons were un-coupled before being sent up in cage lifts, 4 at a time, 70 waggons an hour, the cage lifts were operated by an additional mechanical pulley system that ran from outside the mine, this is the familiar structure with the big wheel that can be seen above a colliery in pictures, (such as the one shown in this and another picture later in the story). **An Interesting front cover of the Boy's Own Paper from November 1944 depicting rarely featured Bevin Boys.**

The mine worked 24 hours a day, as did these two huge shafts which each had express functions, the 'Air In or Down Shaft' brought in new fresh air and empty waggons down from the surface, and the coal that had been mined or 'Won' as we called it eventually made its way up to the surface along with the unclean old air that was being extracted via a huge fan at the top of the 'Air Out or Up Shaft', once the coal reached the top it was separated in the way I mentioned earlier called 'Screening'. Then it was put in storage areas and eventually taken out by steam trains on a railway network that also ran on coal, to its onward destination wherever it was needed around the country to help supply different parts of the war effort, sometimes having to make additional journeys by road and sea as well!"

# BEVIN BOYS – APPEALS FOR VOLOUNTEERS

Ernest Bevin, pictured, was appointed Minister of Labour and National Service on the 13th May 1940 by Winston Churchill and became part of his wartime coalition government. This was considered to be one of Churchill's most imaginative and effective appointments as premier, as Bevin indeed proved when he succeeded in transforming Britain into a 'total war' economy in the years that followed, maximising the British labour supply, for both the armed services and domestic industrial production, this he managed whilst minimising strikes and disruption as best possible, which as a result was a big contributory factor in the eventual final victory for the United Kingdom in World War Two.

The following year after his appointment Bevin made a broadcast appeal on 23rd June 1941 to former miners, asking them to return to the pits, essentially bringing years of experience with them, and with the aim of hopefully increasing numbers of mineworkers by around 50,000. He also cleverly issued a 'Standstill Order', to prevent more miners being called up to serve in the armed forces and as a result taking their much needed skills with them, something which especially in the first half of the war was certainly happening, so much so that a shortage of skilled and general labour in the essential coal mining industry led to a bigger recruitment drive later in the war as the need for coal increased, and on 12th November 1943 Bevin made a radio broadcast aimed at sixth-form boys, in order to encourage them to volunteer to work in mines when they registered for National Service. He promised the students that like those serving in the armed forces, they would be eligible for the government's further education scheme. The term 'Bevin Boys' is thought to originate from this broadcast, as follows:

'We need 720,000 continuously employed in this industry... This is where you boys come in. Each one of you, I am sure, is full of enthusiasm to win this war. You are looking forward to the day when you can play your part with your friends and brothers who are in the Navy, the Army, the Air Force... But believe me, our fighting men will not be able to achieve their purpose unless we get an adequate supply of coal... So when you go to register and the question is put to you 'Will you go to the mines? Let your answer be, Yes I will go anywhere to help win this war'.

Eventually he would get the numbers required anyway by introducing a lottery system which would be used to choose 1 in 10 of all new male recruits between the age of 18-25 from this time until the war's end in late 1945. This was done every month for 20 months by Bevin's secretary who drew numbers from his distinctive Homburg hat. If the number drawn matched the last digit of a man's National Service number, he was sent to the mines. This simple act would drastically change the lives of those chosen like Harry Parkes, who now tells us more about his time as a Bevin Boy: "It was a real shock to be chosen for the mines, you were conscripted like it or not and had to go on pain of imprisonment, and those who didn't go were jailed for up to 3 months initially, also you ended up with a criminal record because you were still considered a civilian and were tried in a civilian court! Those who still continued to refuse received fines and further imprisonment, and much to their disbelief after serving more time were sent directly back to the mines! Bevin also introduced Anti-Strike legislation Order 1305 which banned strikes and lockouts. Tough times! It was well-known that by the very nature of the work danger was ever present, and some terrible things did happen such as serious crush injuries, loss of limbs or deaths during the use of machinery or on waggon haulage or cages, also shot firing on the coal face triggering roof falls, and other dangers such as lung damage from the long term inhalation of coal and rock dust which scars the lungs, this was CWP – Coal Workers' Pneumoconiosis also known as 'Black Lung Disease', also if gasses were present and released they could lead to asphyxiation or poisoning! Despite all of this I never refused to go, I did my duty but I hated that time because I ended up mostly pushing heavy wagons around day in, day out for over four long years, what was there to like about that! But in the end it did pay off for me because after I finished my conscripted time in June 1948, not having a job to go back to but having been acknowledged as a very good worker, I got an opportunity from Bestwood Colliery to stay on and train as something much better. They paid for me to go to college and study Mechanical and Electrical Engineering one day a week whilst the rest of the week getting practical experience by servicing the machinery underground at the mine in a paid job, that's when it all became far more interesting, that laid the foundation for my future career, which I loved, it also gave me many more wonderful years helping educate others in the industry that I knew well, and it all started when I was a Bevin Boy!"

Bevin Boys talking to a Safety Officer outside the colliery during coal mining training in Ollerton, Nottinghamshire in February 1945. It was these 'Unsung Heroes' and many others like them that were hidden away underground throughout the country working hard to produce the coal that fuelled the British war economy!

On Tuesday 7th May 2013, a memorial to the Bevin Boys, based on the Bevin Boys Badge, was unveiled by the Countess of Wessex at the inspiring National Memorial Arboretum at Alrewas, Staffordshire. This poignant memorial was designed by former Bevin Boy Harry Parkes, front and side view shown here in this picture. It's made of four stone plinths carved from grey Kilkenny stone from Ireland. The stone should turn black over time, to resemble the coal that the miners extracted. The Inscription reads:

'The Bevin Boys were National Service conscripts, directed to work underground in British coal mines, providing unskilled labour to safeguard vital coal production to power the British war effort and produce coal for the nation.'

It was Harry's input on this very important memorial that amongst other things led to him being awarded the British Empire Medal.

During our many conversations Harry expressed the feelings that the Bevin Boys were 'Called Up and Sent Down, only to become the Forgotten Conscripts!' He also very kindly said; 'Gary you're vital, you're the link between history and the present day. People will read this in years to come and learn from it, your bringing history back to life from an age that's gone, by listening to people who are willing to tell their life stories and secrets before they too are gone.' Well Harry I hope my work does exactly that and in the process honours you and all the Bevin Boys who so rightly deserve recognition.

## Additional Information and Life After Service

**Rank upon finish of service** – Bevin Boy – Coal Miner.

**Medals and Honours** – Official Bevin Boys Veteran Badge (2008), British Empire Medal (2016).

**Post War Years** – 1948-49 at Bestwood Colliery working on servicing of pit machinery underground as a Mechanical and Electrical Engineering Apprentice whilst studying 1 day a week. From 1949-1952 went on to a full-time degree course in Mining at Sheffield University with in-depth theory and practical learning covering all aspects of the trade including Gas Testing. 1952-1961 Returned to Bestwood Colliery eventually becoming Underground Mechanical and Electrical Shift Manager for the South-East Area of the mine, and also on the pit Rescue Team. After having gained a huge amount of first-hand experience Harry now wanted to change and expand his career into education which he did for the next 30 years from 1961-1991. This started when he became a Technician in the Department of Mining at Nottingham and District Technical College, servicing and testing the machines used for teaching coal mining, Harry progressed over the years as the college became a Polytechnic and eventually the Nottingham-Trent University, where he became Head Technician and also a Lecturer in Mining Practice and Legislation, over those years he applied his vast amount of practical and theoretical knowledge to help train and educate others and was there so long in those capacities that he lovingly became known as 'The Coal Mining Mr Chips.' Whilst doing both those jobs he was also a Governor on the board of Governors at the University. He retired in May 1991. Married Enid in Nottingham, September 1950, together until her passing in 2003. No Children.

**Associations and Organisations** – Bevin Boys Association, NUM – National Union of Mineworkers, UNISON Trade Union; formally NALGO – National and Local Government Officers' Association.

# CORPORAL JEAN ARGLES

**Served with – FANY – First Aid Nursing Yeomanry**
**Service Number – 17897**
**Interviewed – Lancaster, Lancashire, 7th September 2018**

## Service History and Personal Stories

- Born – 7th November 1925, Lancaster, Lancashire, England, UK.
- Joined F.A.N.Y - First Aid Nursing Yeomanry in December 1943 aged 18 and trained to be a Code and Cypher Operator at the FANY HQ in Baker Street, London, learning different ways to de-cypher ever changing coded messages by using various code and log books and other methods to translate the incoming mixed letters and numbers into understandable text that were being received from the SOE – Special Operations Executive agents in Europe.
- During this intensive training Jean was dealing with Agents in Western and Northern Europe and did so well that by the end of January 1944 she had been posted overseas to the main Army/FANY HQ at Heliopolis in Cairo, Egypt, serving there till April 1944.
- After this from April 1944 until June 1945 Jean was posted to the Army/FANY HQ at Torre a Mare in Bari, Italy. At both locations her job was to work in the Cypher Section covertly decoding the messages and requests coming in from agents in the field, from areas around Southern Europe which incorporated the Balkans and Italy. After being looked at by senior officers for their intelligence these would then be quickly passed on to the central Baker Street HQ in order to be actioned ASAP to help the SOE Agents in their operations.
- Her important work supporting SOE agents in this way helped them carry out dangerous missions against the Nazis, where they operated with resistance networks, partisan units or sometimes alone to achieve success. Jean was demobbed at Baker Street in July 1945.

- Jean's family truly served in WW2, her sister WREN Patricia Davies worked as a Linguist on a Naval 'Y-Station' her intercepts going directly to Bletchley Park, and her father Colonel Cary Owtram was a POW on the River Kwai and British Camp Commandant of Chungkai.

Over the years as I have ventured around the United Kingdom interviewing World War Two veterans I have been constantly amazed at the variety of incredible stories that reflect the sheer scale of what was on every level truly a global conflict, and through the experiences imparted to me the many ways and means by which it was fought. I am again reminded of this when I begin writing about a veteran, which can be quite some time after the original interview, and as I review all the information, notes and videos made with and about them their incredible stories come to life once again. When the service history of someone is related to any of the intelligence services and their work is of a more secretive and undercover nature this adds another layer of interest and intrigue to a story. This certainly was the case with Jean Argles, who whilst working for the civilian /military organisation F.A.N.Y – First Aid Nursing Yeomanry was at the same time covertly working as a Code and Cypher Operator in conjunction with the SOE – Special Operations Executive, who were undertaking very dangerous clandestine and resistance related missions throughout Nazi Occupied Europe. Specially trained at their Baker Street HQ Jean was in one of the intelligence sections given the direct messages that had arrived in Code from the SOE agents 'Out in the Field', it was her job to then de-cypher and pass them on as quickly as possible so that they could be actioned without delay. These messages usually contained requests for more manpower or vital supplies to be parachuted in to help the SOE and the Partisan Fighters they were assisting in order to undertake many different types of operations against the Germans. This very interesting undercover work continued when Jean was posted overseas to the Cairo HQ, Egypt and later the Bari HQ, Italy, and again shows the diversity of roles carried out by women during that conflict and the extent and importance of their contributions, Jean now opens up and shares with us about:

### UNERTAKING COVERT WORK WITH F.A.N.Y TO ASSIST THE S.O.E

"I was only 18 when I joined the F.A.N.Y, and had already got a number of what I think were considered useful skills from being at The Triangle Secretarial College, where I had learned touch typing and knew shorthand, which was in itself like a code, after aptitude tests I was selected for special training that took place at their London HQ in Baker Street, all hush, hush of course, very exciting for a teenager to be involved in something covert like that! Even though I had to get the bus to work we were instructed to get off a stop earlier, supposedly so people didn't know where we were going, not sure if it worked but it added to the thrill of it all. We were taught all sorts of skills such as Morse Code, basic Radio Operation and various methods of Code de-cyphering and then from that found out what we were best suited to and would prefer, I ended up training to be a Code and Cypher Operator. Whilst I worked in Baker Street, which was the main HQ for FANY we covertly dealt with de-coding of messages from SOE Agents in places like France, Belgium, Holland and Norway who we knew were always risking and sometimes losing their lives undertaking many brave things to resist the Germans such as sabotage and working with Partisan fighters in all sorts of operations, you could work that out by some of requests they made and from what other people told us. So you were very aware about doing the best job you could because to a greater or lesser degree the lives of the Agents and Partisans out in the field depended on it! Later when I worked overseas in Cairo and Bari our coded messages came from places like Yugoslavia, Albania, Greece and Italy, the resistance and sabotage network was big and operated in so many countries, and it was my job to de-code the regular received messages and also when I had gained experience I got rather good at being able to sort out the broken, corrupted or unclear coded messages that were a lot harder to de-cypher and required clarification, eventually I got given a lot of those to do, which I guess was a bit of a pat on the back and satisfying work too, as each communication was seen as being potentially a valuable one which could help achieve objectives or in some cases even save lives elsewhere.

An example of one those from 'Out in the Field' French Partisan fighter Simone Segouin AKA 'Nicole' (seen here holding an MP40 'Schmeisser') who captured 25 Nazis in the Chartres area in August 1944, and was known to have liquidated many others during the fierce campaign to liberate France. As France was being freed by the Allies after the D-Day landings of June 1944 French resistance greatly increased, and after 4 years of harsh and oppressive German Subjugation for a lot of people the desire for freedom and also revenge was surfacing and coming to the fore! Jean's work helped many like Simone to rid their country of Hitler's forces of occupation, and to rightly return the country back to its people!

When I have been asked by people such as yourself Gary about why the SOE didn't just send all messages directly to Baker Street I think it was for a number of reasons, because different HQs would deal with different incoming transmissions and radio traffic from Agents in particular theatres of war, and an 'on the ground' presence relatively close to those areas was deemed necessary and important by those higher up. As far as I am aware Baker Street already having that with Western and Northern Europe dealt with them directly, but Cairo dealt with the Middle-East like Bari did with Southern Europe, each responsible for their own designated areas and countries. The overseas HQs would receive coded messages, then decipher, prioritise and send on those requests in another code mostly back to the main HQ at Baker Street in London to be acted upon, in the same way Y-Stations fed back intelligence to Bletchley Park except our organisation was dealing directly with SOE agents in the Field. This also meant it would be harder for the Germans and Italians to intercept because there was more than one code being used to transmit this vital information, moreover as it was sent in a slightly roundabout way basically in two parts, this also additionally helped protect where the messages were eventually intended to go, a broken link or two-part system if you like." Others in the book doing vital Intelligence related work only knew a piece or parts of the overall picture that they were involved in, Jean was aware of much more, knowing both ends, roughly where the information was coming from and based on the contents of the message where it would end up and who needed what, which could well have been of special interest to the enemy and as a result meant they had to be extra careful about everything, as Jean went on to explain: "We were officially and correctly part of the First Aid Nursing Yeomanry wherever we worked, and were uniformed accordingly and were granted official Army ranks because we were loosely affiliated to that service and when abroad went to work at legitimate Army HQ's which also housed FANY HQ's. There work was undertaken by some for the Admin and logistics of the organisation but many more of us did Signals or Code and Cypher work in the same building at the same time alongside and under the cover of those other activities, where we would have a Signals section for those on the radio sets who dealt with the initial incoming coded messages who then passed them on to us in the Cypher Section to de-code them, we worked on one of three 8 hour shifts that covered the complete 24 hour rotation. Our work was just another very secretive part of the many different things the FANY organisation did, and in order to try and keep things that way we would tell everyone else outside of our direct HQ and departments that we were Administration and logistics Staff and were all there in that capacity, this helped keep a lid on things and keep all concerned from us to the SOE Agents as safe as possible, after all we were dealing with things of a highly secretive nature and did our best to keep it that way! On top of that we were of course also duty bound by the Official Secrets Act as anyone dealing with sensitive intelligence information was, and rightly to! When the war was over even though we weren't allowed to talk about what we really did for a long time, I always felt that our contribution in the realm of intelligence was a significant one, which I think positively helped the SOE." **A key figure in the command structure of the SOE – Major-General Colin McVean Gubbins. Director of this veiled organisation from 1943 to 1946. Jean's 'Big Boss'. He had wide experience of commando and clandestine operations, and had played a major part in the SOE's early operations.**

S.O.E – Special Operations Executive was officially formed on 22nd July 1940 under the Minister of Economic Warfare Hugh Dalton, this surreptitious and very interesting organisation undertook guerrilla warfare, espionage and reconnaissance in many forms, and was originally charged by Winston Churchill to 'Set Europe Ablaze.' The Organisation was also known as 'Churchill's Secret Army' or the 'Ministry of Ungentlemanly Warfare' and was even involved in assassinations such as that of high-ranking Nazi Reinhard Heydrich in Prague in 1942 codenamed Operation Anthropoid. (Although they didn't officially have an insignia, the design shown here was created as a good representation). Few people were aware of the SOE's existence, those who were part of it or liaised with it, such as Jean Argles were sometimes referred to as the 'Baker Street Irregulars', after the location of its London headquarters (64 Baker Street). Its various branches and sometimes the organisation as a whole were concealed for security and secrecy behind names such as the 'Joint Technical Board' or the 'Inter-Service Research Bureau' or fictitious branches of the Air Ministry, Admiralty or War Office. So widespread was the SOE that it also had a branch office in New York City, which 'officially' came under the name of the 'British Security Coordination' which was headed by Canadian businessman Sir William Stephenson. This office, located at room 3603, 630 Fifth Avenue, Rockefeller Centre, was responsible for coordinating the work of the British SOE, MI5 and MI6 with their allies at the American FBI and OSS. The SOE operated in all territories occupied or attacked by the Axis forces from Europe to the Far East, except where demarcation lines were agreed with Britain's principal Allies, (namely the USA and USSR) and consisted of approximately 13,000 people of whom around 3000 were women who came from all backgrounds and nationalities and included amongst others the Free French, Polish and the Jewish Parachutists of Mandate Palestine. They also launched joint efforts with their U.S counterparts the OSS - Office of Strategic Services (later CIA) and liaised with Soviet Secret Service the NKVD – (Translated as) People's Commissariat of Internal Affairs. SOE and OSS cooperation led to the widespread 'Jedburgh' Operations across Western Europe 1944-1945 to disrupt the enemy as much as possible behind their lines before and after D-Day and also in support of Operation Market Garden in Holland where Jedburgh teams worked closely with the SAS. The 'Jeds' also operated out in South-East Asia under Lord Mountbatten's SEAC – South East Asia Command undertaking operations against the Japanese as Force 136. Many of their Agents, mainly in Europe, were parachuted into enemy territory to work with various resistance movements or sometimes as individuals transmitting vital intelligence back to London, and were all highly trained in many forms of sabotage, concealment, field craft, radio transmission, weapons and explosives, parachuting, hand-to-hand combat, silent killing and much more. These brave male and female agents undertook their duties at great personal risk, those who were caught by the Gestapo being brutally tortured, others being sent to Concentration Camps, lots executed. Many notables were recruited into the SOE including agents Noor Inayat Khan, Violette Szabo, Odette Sansom, Christopher Woodhouse and Fitzroy Maclean, it has been widely speculated that Ian Fleming used Maclean (who Jean worked for after the war) as one of his inspirations for James Bond. The SOE was dissolved on 15th January 1946, but nearly 300 were taken into the 'Special Operations Branch' of M16 where their very transferrable skills could be put to great use.

Whilst in existence the work of the SOE was closely and covertly supported on the signals, intelligence and logistical side by F.A.N.Y – First Aid Nursing Yeomanry of which Jean Argles as a Code and Cypher Operator was a part, and in many places where there was a FANY HQ there was in close proximity also an SOE HQ, this was true everywhere that Jean served such as Baker Street, London and overseas the SOE had subsidiary HQ's in Cairo, Egypt known as Special Operations Mediterranean or SO(M) and in Bari, Italy known as 'Force 133'. There were also a number of SOE Agents who were directly recruited from FANY who served with distinction in the field, 39 of the 50 women sent to France as part of the SOE's F Section were FANY's, after capture 13 paid the ultimate price! The Corps' strength during WW2 was 6000, of which a third of its servicewomen 2000 were in or attached to the SOE. At Beaulieu, AKA 'The finishing School for Spies', a mansion house with adjoining facilities similar to Bletchley Park and others throughout the country that had covert uses, this one being in the heart of the New Forest at Brockenhurst in Hampshire where they would learn the 'Dark Arts of Warfare' the Conducting Officers for the agents were also FANY's, further showing how these two very different organisations became intrinsically linked in a time of war Between 1939-45 as well as its work with the SOE the women of FANY undertook many other vital roles within the other organisations they served such as radio officers, personal assistants, drivers, radar operators, encryption specialists and of course nurses, they were also attached to various Red Cross associations. The Corps itself, now known as the FANY (PRVC) First Aid Nursing Yeomanry (Princess Royal's Volunteer Corps) is an independent all-female registered charity, formed in 1907 and active in both nursing and intelligence work during both World Wars, and over 100 years later still provides assistance to civil and military authorities in times of emergency. It is the world's longest established uniformed 'civilian/military' voluntary organisation for women, and today the only all-women unit left in the UK. Their Commandant-in-Chief since 1999 has been HRH The Princess Royal, hence the PRVC now incorporated in to its name. **Due to the First Aid Nursing Yeomanry Corps being a Civilian (Civil-Military Response) uniformed Organisation and British Independent Registered Charity Jean's story is included here in the civilian part of the book.**

**Noor-un-Nissa Inayat Khan** AKA Nora Inayat-Khan and Nora Baker. Born 1st January 1914, her father Inayat Khan, came from a noble Indian Muslim family, a musician and teacher of Sufism (Islamic Mysticism) and her mother Ora Ray Baker was an American from Albuquerque, New Mexico. Noor became one of the most well-known SOE Agents, who was originally in the WAAF – Women's Auxiliary Airforce, seconded to FANY then trained as an agent and went on to become a spy for the SOE F (France) Section. Noor was the first female Wireless Operator to be sent from the U.K into Nazi occupied France in that capacity to aid the French Resistance during World War Two. Codename: 'Madeleine' Call sign: 'Nurse' she arrived in France in June 1943 and became part of the 'Prosper' network in Paris and despite all the other wireless operator agents later being captured by the Gestapo Noor remained and at great danger to herself continued transmitting, until betrayed in October 1943. After capture she was tortured by the Gestapo but bravely never gave away anything, and after twice attempting escape was constantly shackled in chains and put in solitary confinement until sent to Dachau Concentration Camp where after all she had been through was executed by the SS along with 3 other female agents on the 13th September 1944, her last word was reported as "Liberte." She was posthumously awarded the George Cross, the highest civilian decoration in the United Kingdom for her service in the SOE.

**Kofferset 3 MK II portable radio transceiver, an essential piece of equipment for an operative for communication between SOE/Continental Resistance movements and their U.K-based HQ's, like those used by agents in the 'Prosper' network including Noor Khan. This radio set weighed a cumbersome 15 kg (33 lb) and required a long exterior aerial to transmit. It offered 4 or 5 crystal-controlled working frequencies in the 80-meter band and the 40-meter band. The frequency could be changed while transmitting. A radio operator had the most dangerous of SOE jobs in France, hence so many being captured during active service.**

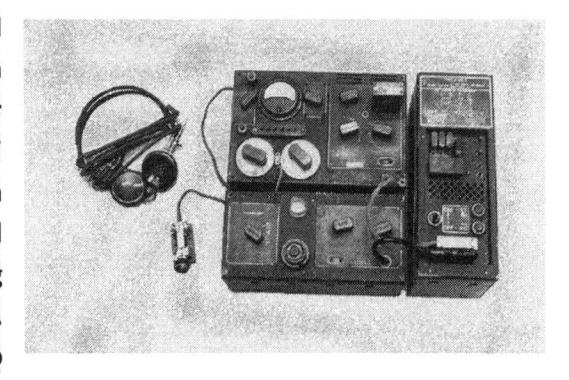

It was very brave agents like Noor that Jean and many others in FANY would be helping through their many different kinds of secret support and liaison work, and for this we express thanks to you all. Each and every one should and shall be remembered for your covert contributions to the war effort.

## Additional Information and Life After Service

**Rank upon finish of service** – Corporal.

**Medals and Honours** – 1939-45 War Medal, 1939-45 Star, Italian Star.

**Post War Years** – After World War Two Jean had some interesting jobs, including working as Secretary for Fitzroy Maclean MP for Lancaster (and Ex-SOE), as part of the United Nations Special Refugee Commission in Austria, Germany and Italy re-settling refugees from war-torn Europe, including ex-Concentration Camp inmates, forced labourers, displaced families, her language skills in French, Italian and German were very useful during that time. Later Jean worked at Lancaster University as a Careers Advisor and set up the Careers Service for the University. Married Michael in 1969. No children, but 4 Step-Children from Michael's previous marriage. Retired aged 58 in 1983.

**Associations and Organisations** – FANY (PRVC) Princess Royal Voluntary Corps Association.

# ELECTRICAL ENGINEER SAUL RUBINSTEIN

**Served with – Metropolitan Vickers Electrical Engineering Company**
**Interviewed – Salford, Greater Manchester, 23rd & 24th June 2021**
**Follow up Conversations 2021 & 2022**

## METROPOLITAN Vickers

### Service History and Personal Stories

- Born – 28th October 1919, Cheetham Hill, Manchester, England, UK.
- Saul studied from 18-21 years of age at the Municipal College of Technology which was the faculty of technology at Manchester University, he was there from 1937-1940 after which he was awarded a 1st Class Honours Degree in Engineering on the 2nd July 1940 at a time where war with Nazi Germany was in full flow and the Battle of Britain was taking place.
- After hearing about some of the injustices being perpetrated by the Nazis in Europe, especially against Jewish people Saul wanted as a Jewish man himself to enlist in the Armed services in order to hopefully take the fight directly to Hitler in some way. Being an Electrical Engineer it made sense to try and join the Army as part of the REME – Royal Electrical and Mechanical Engineers but the powers that be had different plans for Saul!
- Instead they had ear-marked him for a job in industry where they felt his know-how and skills could be put to very good use for general and later very specialist work that would help the war effort in some different and very interesting ways. So he was re-directed and sent to work in a 'Reserved Occupation' for the biggest Electrical Engineering company in wartime Britain called Metropolitan Vickers who had a huge site with a number of factories in the Trafford Park area of Manchester near the Salford/Manchester Docks. Metrovicks founded 1899 in Manchester, ceased operations in 1960.

- It was there that Saul first worked in some of the main factory buildings as a newly qualified Electrical and Mechanical Engineer from mid-1940 until Autumn 1942, gaining valuable experience whilst assembling various parts such as Dynamos to produce electricity, circuit boards for different instruments and much more that went into all manner of war materials such as military vehicles, aircraft, submarines and trains, some of which he recalls were being sent to Russia to help in the fight against the Nazis on the Eastern Front.
- By late 1942 Saul's high quality of work, ingenuity and attention to detail had been spotted and led to him being selected for an extremely important and very secret project that was being undertaken by Metrovicks which was the development of their version of a new cutting-edge technology, the Turbo Thrust Jet Engine.
- It was at the Metrovicks subsidiary factory known as the 'Barton Works Site' on Barton Dock Road in Stretford, Manchester that he was instrumental in developing the main Gas Turbine part of the F.2 and other versions of this revolutionary new form of propulsion Jet Engine, that under government licence were later combined with parts from other jet engine prototypes being developed by other companies at the time to become the Rolls-Royce Welland Turbojet Engine that powered the first British Jet Fighter the Meteor.
- The prototypes were flown in 1943 and the Meteor Mark 1 went into service as part of the new RAF 616 Squadron in July 1944 when this latest advancement in aviation technology was used against the new threat of incoming V1 guided missiles. Later from February 1945 it was deployed in Belgium and Holland and used in front line strategical bombing missions in support of Allied ground troops, and to potentially counter the opposing German threat of the Messerschmitt ME 262 Jet Fighter which had also appeared in the skies at that time.
- Essentially Saul's work on the Axial Jet Engine development project helped in the massive leap and milestone of taking us from the propeller to the jet age, and after finishing his time on that huge endeavour after the war's end in September 1945 he was transferred back to the main factory complex doing generic electrical engineering work, where he stayed until he got married to Pauline in 1950 having completed a reputable 10 years' service at Metropolitan Vickers and contributing significantly in his own way to the war effort.

I started writing this profile in earnest on the 28th October 2021 on Saul's 102nd birthday, this seemed to be a very fitting day to begin putting 'pen to paper' so to speak and to write his story in order to honour this remarkable Centenarian. Remarkable in his achievements both during World War Two and throughout the rest of his long life that he has been blessed to have. During the course of World history there are certain points where hugely significant leaps in invention and innovation have taken place and in modern times during the 20th century one of those was with the creation of the Jet Engine, the legacy of which is with us to this very day! So to meet, get to know and interview one of the very few people left in the world at time of writing who was historically at the epi-centre of such a great technological leap and who was partly responsible for it is nothing less than truly amazing! During the Second World War he would have been seen to passers-by as just another ordinary looking man on a bicycle on the way to work, which come rain or shine all year round he was, but once he arrived at his workplace this is when he became someone who was contributing to something quite extraordinary as part the Metropolitan Vickers development and research team working on a revolutionary jet engine project to try and keep us abreast or ahead of the Nazis hopefully before they could launch such technology against the Allies. These advancements once successfully delivered would become world-changing in their magnitude for both military and civilian application, and so here to explain how it all came to pass from his humble beginnings in the Jewish Community in Manchester through to the part he played in the war effort to help defeat Nazi Germany is Saul Rubinstein who now tells us how it was:

# WORKING ON THE METROPOLITAN VICKERS JET ENGINE PROJECT DURING WORLD WAR TWO

"I was born at number 3 Elizabeth Street, Cheetham Hill in North Manchester, not long after the First World War, sounds incredible saying that now, and grew up in what was already a well-established and vibrant Jewish community in that area, with Synagogues, Kosher food shops, Tailors and all manner of Jewish businesses present. But in general, unlike today, there wasn't much to go round as people were poorer in the 1920's and 1930's and we of course lived through what was called the 'Great Depression' and like most people had to make do and were happy for what we had and were fortunate to get, but back then as now there was a great sense of community in Jewish neighbourhoods. My education started with primary at the Jewish School in Derby Street, followed by secondary at Manchester Central High School in Whitworth Street, and at 18 I went on to study a degree in Engineering for three years at the Municipal College of Technology which was the faculty of technology at Manchester University. I began there before the war in 1937 and finished during the war gaining a first-class honours degree in 1940 becoming 'Bachelor of Technical Sciences' aged 21."

I went on to ask Saul about how things progressed as the clouds of war were looming and how being a Jewish man influenced his motivations, direction and choices, and was told: "In the years after Hitler came to power we began to hear about his anti-Semitic policies, hatred and bad treatment of the Jews, it was no secret with his vile speeches, passing of, what were they called... ah yes the Nuremburg Racial Laws, and what refugees who had been forced out of Germany had told many in the other countries they had fled too, including ours, it all filtered back and as I and others got older we heard and were told more about these terrible things, which of course only got worse for many more Jews and others who became trapped in the countries the Nazis invaded and occupied. Later on during the war stories of much worse persecutions and killings and the 'Death Camps' would also reach us! So for we Jewish who were lucky enough to live in Great Britain and not experience these things I think many felt a moral obligation to do whatever we could to play our part in stopping the evil of Nazism! That's why after I graduated I went to try and join the armed services, starting with the Army where I thought my knowledge as an Electrical Engineer could be put to good use in something like the REME where I could in my own way take the fight directly to Hitler! But that was not meant to be as I was soon directed to another place where those who made the decisions though I should serve and spend my war years, and so I ended up playing my part not in any 'Battle Front' but on the 'Home Front' which was in a reserved occupation at Metropolitan Vickers Electrical Engineering Company at Trafford Park in Greater Manchester. I would spend the rest of the war there, over 5 years helping the war effort on military related work, and after that a further 5 years there in civilian related work, all in electrical engineering.

There wasn't much Metrovick didn't make parts for, land, sea or air if it moved it probably had some if not all its electrical parts made by us, dynamos, transformers, circuit boards, lighting, we covered it all, parts for tanks, armoured cars, locomotives, submarines and various planes including the famous Lancaster Bomber! We heard that some of the military equipment we worked on and fitted out was bound for Russia and would be heading straight into battle zones on the Eastern Front, so we felt we were making some direct contribution to the war effort and the fight against Nazi Germany, that was a good feeling. I worked on these things and much more at different buildings in the huge MV complex in that industrial area from when I got there in the summer of 1940 until half way through the war in the Autumn of 1942, then after that they obviously thought I was good enough to be chosen for something else which was quite different and a bit special." I was intrigued and wanted to hear more because when I first met this humble man and asked him what he did during the war he said: "I just worked as an electrical engineer for the Metropolitan-Vickers heavy engineering company, that's all." 'Just' and 'That's all' were huge understatements as I found out when I conducted my 1st veteran interview of 2021 with him and went back on a number of consequent visits to see him at his home, becoming a friend, during which he elaborated more on the 'Special' parts of his time there, explaining: "By the back end of 1942 I had been transferred to Metrovicks 'Barton Works Site' at Barton Dock Road in

Stretford, where I became part of a research and development team working on a very secret project, extremely important cutting edge technology of the time, the new Axial Turbojet Engine, the part I specialized in, help develop and improve was the Gas Turbine which was a key component that helped provide the thrust that it required to operate, this was in the 'F-Series' of those Jet engines that we were creating. Other elements of that work included trying to find the best way to introduce the fine spray of fuel to the combustion engine, re-shaping the combustion chambers for maximum efficiency and how to best control the escaping force from the engine to harness it for the greatest power and lift possible! All of this was of course new and pretty ground-breaking work so we had trials and errors, successes and failures, but in the end we developed something that worked, and out of interest as I recall I was the only Jewish man working there throughout that time. Anyway, as we knew then we were not the only British Engineering or Aeronautical company working on this technology, also the Government was involved and it seemed they were very keen to get this know-how and equipment developed as soon as possible, I think scared in case the Nazis, who were working on this as well, could possibly get there first and use it significantly enough to influence the direction of the war, something new technologies are always capable of doing in wars! This innovative work had of course to remain as secret as possible in case of German spies and it was for that reason and because the Trafford Park Industrial area had been bombed before and could be targeted again by the Luftwaffe that all testing of the Gas Turbines and Turbojet prototype engines were done at other facilities safely hidden away in the countryside down in Cheshire, where I went on occasions to help set up and monitor progress of our work, it was all extremely interesting to see things evolving, and eventually testing took to the skies, something I didn't witness, but in the case of the new Meteor Jet fighter that our engines were attached to, I believe from feedback early testing went well."

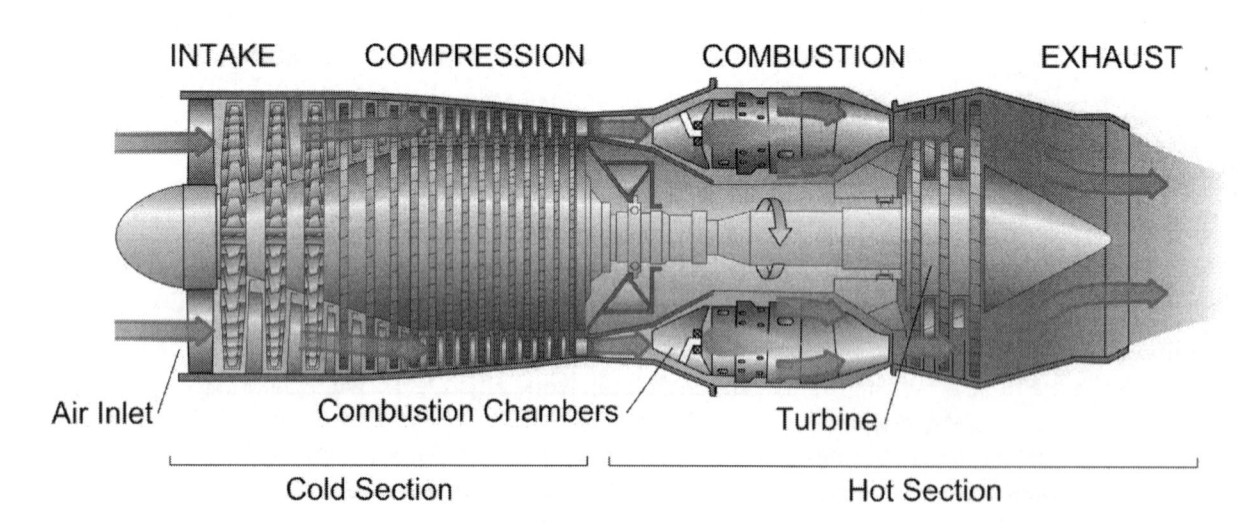

**Above – A diagram showing a Turbojet Engine with the various main parts labelled. This includes the Gas Turbine part that Saul helped develop on the Metrovicks version of this new technology. A Gas Turbine, also called a Combustion Turbine is a type of Internal Combustion Engine, which essentially helps to convert power into mechanical or electrical form to achieve in the case of Turbo Jets greater thrust-to-weight-ratio on afterburning engines and get the aircraft they are attached to airborne and flying at far greater speeds than earlier propellor aircraft were able to achieve, eventually years later taking aircraft into the supersonic realm of flight. Interestingly various types of Gas Turbines have been developed and are used to power not only aircraft but trains, ships, tanks, electrical generators, pumps and gas compressors. A few of the main companies tested their newer versions of Turbojet engines on a Meteor quite near together all in 1943, showing how close their work and advances in this new technology were, beginning with Power Jets in March, De-Havilland in June, and Metrovicks in November. Although not the first tests it showed good flying prototypes were available and that cooperation was the key to success.**

The main link that helped the British succeed in developing, flying and making their first Jet aircraft become a reality was the cooperation between the companies making Gas Turbine based Jet Propulsion Technology. Because it was shared, elements and knowledge of all the companies work involved in it were merged, integrated and carried forward into what was eventually the first successful hybrid Turbojet Engine of them all to be used and fly operationally on an RAF squadron Jet Fighter, the Rolls Royce 'Welland' which powered the Gloster Mark 1 'Meteor', the unique collaboration that was instrumental in bringing this about is explained in more detail below:

The major aircraft and engine companies had each been conducting their own research into combining gas turbines and jet propulsion, and with the threat of war government support arrived as gas turbines could give the Allies superiority in the air. The rapid development of the engine was the paramount consideration. The first aircraft to fly powered by a Whittle gas turbine was the Gloster E28/39, which had its maiden flight at RAF Cranwell on 15th May 1941. However, engine development was too slow and, to accelerate the process, (Harold) Roxbee Cox created and chaired the GTCC - Gas Turbine Collaboration Committee. This consisted of all the companies working on jet engine projects at the time, including Frank Whittle's company Power Jets, and was a forum in which they shared their design work and test data because at this pivotal time in history collaboration was far more important than trade secrets, with the British government encouraging any efforts that could give the Allies any edge in this worldwide conflict that was raging on many fronts. Initially Whittle was against the idea, but as he recollected in his book, *Jet - The story of a pioneer*:

*"...we later became enthusiastic supporters, and I am firmly convinced that Britain owes much of its technical superiority in this field to the Gas Turbine Collaboration Committee. There were many intrinsic difficulties in the proposal, but somehow or other, under the skilful chairmanship of Roxbee Cox, a good deal of thin ice was skated over very successfully."*

**Sir Frank Whittle, Aeronautical Engineer and Inventor, Royal Air Force Air Commodore.**

Roxbee later said that this was one of the most thrilling periods of his life and the formation of the GTCC proved to be a major milestone in the development of the jet engine, which it certainly did, and was quoted in more detail about this in his Autobiography 'A Wrack Behind' when he exclaimed:

*"I suppose that the most effective instrument in my jet propulsion development work was the Gas Turbine Collaboration Committee which I created in 1941. It held its first meeting in October of that year in the Midland Hotel in Birmingham. The situation was, that after the successful maiden flight of the E28/39, the interest of the aircraft engine industry was increased and several aircraft engine firms wanted to embrace the technology which Whittle had created. They all had ideas but hesitated to share them with Whittle or each other. I pointed out that if a firm patented any obvious extension of the technology it could safely share it with the others and that by sharing and discussing advances the whole technology would develop faster. This was understood and the Gas Turbine Collaboration Committee was a notable success. Meetings were held at the premises of the collaborators who were Power Jets, Metropolitan-Vickers, de Havillands (Halford), Ricardo, Bristol, Armstrong-Siddeley, and Rolls Royce, the last of which took the greatest advantage of the arrangement and in the end benefited most. Surprisingly, the Committee remained in existence for three years after the end of the war."*

**Roxbee Cox, Director of Special Projects, Ministry of Aircraft Production.**

Below is a timeline of events regarding the Metrovicks F-Series engines the development of which Saul was involved in, including the initial airborne tests of it briefly mentioned by him, through to the operational use of the first Hybrid Turbojet Engine with No.616 Squadron RAF on the first British Jet Fighter which its technology contributed towards, important aviation history & many great legacies:

1942 – A flyable version of the Metropolitan Vickers F.2/1 receives its test rating.

29th June 1943 – F.2/1 'Beryl' Axial-Flow Turbojet engine was tested on an Avro Lancaster (first test-bed prototype Lancaster, s/n BT308), mounted in the rear fuselage in place of the rear turret.

13th November 1943 – The prototype F.9/40M Gloster Meteor fighter (s/n DG204/G) equipped with F2 engines makes a successful flight from the RAE – Royal Aircraft Establishment, Farnborough. These were installed in underslung nacelles (external parts, in this case engines). This was the first time that a jet-propelled fighter aircraft with specific axial-flow engines had been flown in the UK.

1944 – The new more powerful version of the engine, the F.2/4 'Beryl' was test flown on the Avro Lancaster Mk II (s/n LL735) before being installed in the Saunders-Roe SR.A/1 Flying Boat Fighter.

1944 – Development of the F.2 ended with important parts of its design having been shared with the GTCC - Gas Turbine Collaboration Committee and as a result been integrated into the Rolls Royce 'Welland' project. Additionally parts of the F.2 basic concept that Saul worked on were also carried over into other later variants in the F-Series projects, eventually leading to the considerably larger and successful F.9 'Sapphire'.

12th July 1944 – After prior familiarization flying at RAF Culmhead at Churchstanton in Somerset, the first British Jet Fighter, the Gloster Meteor Mk 1 equipped with the Rolls-Royce 'Welland' Turbojet Engine officially enters service with RAF No.616 Squadron at RAF Manston at Ramsgate in Kent, making it the first operational squadron in the world to fly jets. *The Squadron Code was YQ at time of acquiring Jets and is in a photo shown later in this story, and the 616 Squadron Badge depicted here has the words (South Yorkshire) displayed on it as a reminder of its foundation at RAF Doncaster on the 1st November 1938.

27th July 1944 – No.616 Squadron engages in its first combat sortie against V-1 Flying Bombs that were en-route to London when it intercepts some of these incoming guided missiles which are part of Hitler's new 'Vengeance' weapons program.

4th August 1944 – The first victories came for the squadron in active combat operations when one V-1 was tipped over after a pilot's cannon jammed, a very skillful and tricky manoeuvre at extremely high speeds, and another V-1 was shot down.

January 1945 – Re-equipping of the Squadron with newly improved Meteor Mk. III begins.

February 1945 – A detachment of Meteor's is deployed to Melsbroek near Brussels in Belgium in an intended defence against German ME 262's which in the event they did not face.

April 1945 – The complete RAF 616 squadron moved to Gilze-Rijen in Holland, and on the 16th April they commenced ground attack sorties, which as the Allies advanced went on into Germany.

29th August 1945 – The squadron was disbanded in Lubeck, Germany. Despite having been reformed and disbanded again throughout its history it survives until today (2022), as the 616 (South Yorkshire) Squadron Royal Auxiliary Air Force (RAuxAF) based at RAF Waddington in Lincolnshire, to augment the RAF's Intelligence, Surveillance, Target Acquisition and Reconnaissance (ISTAR) Force and delivering a Combat Air capability.

1946 – Metropolitan Vickers cancel development when they sell their Gas Turbine business to Armstrong Siddeley, by which time Saul is transferred back to civilian Electrical Engineering at the main MV factories at Trafford Park.

1947 – Metrovicks also leave Jet Engine production, and their design team move to Armstrong Siddeley where parts of earlier Turbojet Engine development continues on into new projects.

1940–1950 – After 10 years of service during both Wartime and Peacetime in Civilian and Military Electrical Engineering Saul Rubinstein leaves MV for a new life and line of work.

New Technology in the Skies – Pictures shown for Comparison of the two adversaries in the era of the new Turbojet fighter, both of which interestingly had started to be seen in the skies over Europe from July 1944 onwards. Top: The British Meteor Mark 1 of No.616 Squadron RAF, seen here at RAF Manston, Kent on 4th January 1945, note the YQ Squadron markings on the aircraft behind indicating that squadron.

Bottom: The German Messerschmitt Me 262, this one, Werk-Nr. 111711, with its Junkers Jumo 004 axial-flow turbojet engines was the first intact Me 262 to fall into Allied hands on the 31st March 1945, seen here post-war during a test flight in the USA. Both aircraft saw frontline service at the back end of World War Two in 1944-1945 but they never came into contact or engaged each other in aerial combat. They were however the template for the revolutionary jet powered age that would follow.

To conclude, as a tribute to Saul, I am finishing with some quotes from him regarding his job at Mertovicks and how he and others generally viewed the war years and their contributions at that time, with a few words from me at the end: "It is very interesting looking back now as I talk to you Gary and tell my wartime story properly for the first time, no one has really gone into it in such detail as you and I've certainly never been interviewed before about my war years, and at this time in my life when I am over 100! Well at least it has been told now! Funny, although it seems I guess a pretty big thing now we look at it all in an historical context, at the time for me it was just a case of going to work every day, albeit quite a different job, and doing what I was directed to do based on the skills I had as an Electrical Engineer. We were all aware when doing the Turbojet Engine development that we were creating something special, that could potentially have great uses but at the end of the day it was our job, there was a war on and it was war work we were undertaking, our project was contributing to the war effort, as many other people did in their own ways, whether you were a soldier, a sailor, a pilot or an air raid warden, we all played our parts! After the war finished I continued to work for

MV's for around another five years until 1950, where I was seconded to different departments, then sometime after I got married I ended up in my wife's family furniture business, quite different! As with most people I knew of that generation once the war was over we concentrated on the life that came after, our families and other things, and didn't really think or speak much at all about the war years, Britain was re-building, and everyone was also continuing and building their lives, and because nearly everyone around you had served in one way or another in the war, most people, me included didn't think of ourselves as anything special, we had done what we had to do, did our bit and that's all. The only other things that impacted on my life directly during the war were things like rationing, air raids, and sometimes if we were at home having to hide in our Anderson Shelter in the garden when the bombing was happening until we heard the 'all clear', and once some kind of shell casing came through our roof! Central Manchester was not too far away from us and it got hit heavily in the Christmas Blitz, I remember because it was in the same year that I graduated in 1940! But again, things like that were common place and experienced by most people, not just me, and so you just got on with your life as best possible under the circumstances, you simply had to, going back to what I said before it is because we were all going through things like this that you didn't consider yourself special, you went to work, did your job every day until we finally, years later, won the war and I am happy to say beat Hitler and Nazism!"

**It is hard to follow such humble words, but what I will say is that there have been a lot of great legacies from the work Saul did during World War Two, many of which have been covered here within his profile. Quite simply to have met and know someone who was partly responsible for such an historical leap in aviation history and helped bring us into the 'Jet Age' for applications in military and later civilian use is simply quite remarkable, he certainly did play his part, more than I think he realized, and we all to this day still reap the benefits that came from the work that this incredible man carried out all those years ago. His work on the 'Home Front' also contributed alongside the efforts of those on 'War Fronts' to defeat an evil regime whose ideological hatred tried to destroy his race of people, so for this and much more myself and I know many others thank you for everything you have done in your extraordinary life. G-d Bless you Saul.**

## Additional Information and Life After Service

**Rank upon finish of service** – Electrical Engineer.

**Medals and Honours** – 1st Class Honours Degree, University of Manchester.

**Post War Years** – In 1950 Saul joined the furniture business belonging to his wife's family called Sterling & Company, Ltd. Based in Leigh, East Lancashire where he later became Director of the company, staying there until his first 'official' retirement aged 87 in 2007, after selling the company to Palestinian businessmen. But Saul ever the active man soon grew tired of retirement and came back to work on a voluntary basis for a number of charities and was involved in helping a Jewish charity shop back in his old area of Cheetham Hill and at Heathlands Village Jewish care facility in Prestwich, Manchester, he was also a driver for a charity 'meals on wheels' service that delivered to people's houses and to care homes "taking food to old people" as he put it with a grin on his face. Incredibly he continued in these giving roles for another 10 years, still driving up until his 'real official retirement' aged 97 in 2017! Further testament to the spirit and achievements of this incredible man. He married Pauline Sterling on the 22nd January 1950 in Cheetham Hill, Manchester and were together until her passing in 1972. Children; 2 Daughters, 2 Grandchildren, 3 Great-Grandchildren.

**Associations and Organisations** – Fellow of the Institution of Electrical Engineers (IEE), Freemason of the Ark Lodge, Manchester.

# SERGEANT WALTER LIEF

**Kinder Transport German Child Refugee and National Service Veteran**
Served with – British Army – Royal Army Ordinance Corps
Service Number – 227110
Interviewed – Whitefield, Manchester, 14th April 2022

## Service History and Personal Stories

- Born – 24th February 1932, Cologne, Germany. Pictured above, Left Walter, Right Kurt.
- As a young child Walter Lief grew up in a Germany that was undergoing radical changes after Adolf Hitler came to power on the 30th January 1933. Serious anti-Semitism and persecution of the Jews was sadly becoming common place and with the passing of the racial Nuremburg Laws in 1935 and the Crystal Nacht (Night of Broken Glass) in 1938 his mother Elly knew in order to survive they would have to try and escape Nazi Germany.
- It was these pressing circumstances that led to her having to make the heart-breaking decision to put her 2 twin boys on a Kinder Transport (Children's Transport) train out of Cologne, Germany

to what was then still a safe Belgium, a place which agreed to take them, in the hope that if circumstances permitted she would join them later.

- Initially from September 1939 to June 1940 they were sent to an Orphanage on the coast in Middelkerke, Belgium only 45.5 kilometres/28 miles from Dunkirk, France, where they witnessed the retreating BEF – British Expeditionary Force and their Belgian allies heading towards the French border on the way to Dunkirk to be evacuated in Operation Dynamo, and saw the British RAF battling it out in the skies above against the German Luftwaffe.

- After this with safety being the primary concern Walter, Kurt and other Jewish children were then moved to a bigger Orphanage in the Molenbeek-Saint-Jean area of Brussels in Belgium so that they could be hidden amongst other non-Jewish children, thus giving them a better chance of survival in what was now Nazi occupied Western Europe.

- This is where they would remain from 1940 through to the liberation of Brussels by Allied forces in September 1944 and after into the summer of 1945 until they could be re-united once again with their mother, who had fled to Great Britain but could not get her children out of Europe in time to join her before the German forces had overrun and occupied Belgium and France during the Blitzkrieg (lightening war).

- During the war years Walter and Kurt witnessed and experienced many things including being hidden for fear of being taken by the Nazis, and later the incoming V1 rocket attacks on the city, through to the liberation and eventual Allied Victory Parade in Brussels. Throughout that time with the help of the International Red Cross and the Orphanage a clever line of occasional yet ongoing communication was maintained between the children, via their uncle, to their mum at great risk to many involved, to help give some peace of mind for all.

- Eventually due to the dogged determination of their mother who contacted the British government at the highest levels to campaign for her children to be returned to her, this wish was facilitated by the Home Office and the Foreign Secretary and incredibly came true in late summer of 1945 when the twins were put on an RAF military transport aircraft with British Servicemen returning to the U.K, and a WAAF – Women's Auxiliary Air Force lady was specially assigned to the children to help aid their safe passage until they were back into the arms of their mother once again after nearly 6 long years!

- Then they were taken up to Glasgow in Scotland to join the Jewish community there where their mum Elly had already established herself, joining Hyndland Senior Secondary school to continue their education until the age of 18, becoming Naturalized Citizens in 1947. They then volunteered and served their adopted country by completing National Service from 1950-1952, and as Reservists from 1952-1956 both becoming Sergeants, and putting to use their linguistic skills in English, French and German whilst in the British Army.

- Walter and Kurt both served in the Royal Army Ordinance Corps, very sadly later on at the age of 29 Kurt died in an accident, but for Walter a long and successful life lay ahead full of big achievements in both his professional working and family life, and in time he also went on to become an officially recognised armed forces veteran of the United Kingdom being awarded the official 'Veteran's Badge' from the U.K Government.

- I was very fortunate to meet this amazing gentleman at the age of 89 at Broughton Leisure Centre in Salford where we both swim and keep fit, a place he drives to each week, and after a few conversations was amazed to learn about the fascinating life experiences of someone who arrived here with almost nothing but who has given a lot to his adopted home country of Great Britain, so it is a pleasure to honour him by having his story recorded here in my book, and I hope it is a story you enjoy hearing as much as I have done.

**The 24th February 2022 was a historically significant day, an aggressive Russia invaded the peaceful democratic country of Ukraine triggering war in Europe once again for the first time since the end of World War Two, and causing an unprecedented refugee crisis. It was also the 90th birthday of Walter Lief and on that day and others that followed he was again reminded of his own plight over 80 years before when he was made a refugee in a similar way having to flee his native Germany as a Jewish child with his twin brother Kurt as part of what were known as the 'Kinder Transports'. They were sent to Belgium, which was still considered a 'Safe Country' in 1939 but to their horror they again fell under the control of the Nazi tyranny that they fled from when in the following year Hitler's Blitzkrieg rolled over and occupied Western Europe in 1940, leading to more than 4 years of living in uncertainty and sometimes fear in a non-denominational orphanage in Brussels, whereas Jewish children they were hidden amongst the other children for their own safety. This only ended when the allies after landing on D-Day to take back and liberate those living under Nazi oppression had reached Brussels by September 1944. Finally after the war in Europe was over in May 1945 due to the frantic efforts of their mother who wrote directly to Winston Churchill about the plight of her children were they with the special help and intervention of the British Government re-united after nearly 6 years in the summer of that year, and with only a suitcase each containing all their worldly possessions Walter and Kurt came to their adopted country of Great Britain to begin a new life, because returning to a country they had to leave in the first place due to oppression and with their home eventually being destroyed later by the Allied bombings of Cologne meant going back was no longer possible. It was these very tough experiences which when he saw the plight of the refugees from Ukraine encouraged him to finally tell his story for the first time in over 8 decades, luckily to me, one which continued later when wanting to repay the country that took him in he served in the British Army during his national service for 2 years and after in the Army reserve for 4 years in the 1950's. So here are the remarkable experiences of a remarkable man Walter Jacob Lief who takes us on a journey:**

### FROM KINDER TRANSPORT REFUGEE TO NATIONAL SERVICE & RESERVIST VOLUNTEER

"Seeing the plight of those who flee Ukraine, who had a normal life before and then had it ripped away from them and forced to endure the turmoil of losing everything they had ever known, having their lives torn apart and needing to leave their family, friends and all they care about in order to survive is something I know about all too well! I have real deep empathy for them! It's the main reason I am talking to you now after all this time. The images and reports I see of those poor people on television, many of whom are innocent children, take me back to when we were forced to leave our home city of Cologne and the country we grew up in, Germany, both of which we loved but after Hitler and the Nazis came to power a country that became more and more difficult for all of us from Jewish origins to live in, and as the persecution of the Jews became worse and worse I think it was very obvious to our mum, on her own since the passing of our dad, that if we were to try and outlive this oppression we all had to leave to anywhere safe that would have us! It must have been so hard for her to put us on that train on that long platform at Cologne station in the late summer of 1939, not knowing when she would see us next, as a parent I couldn't imagine having to send my children somewhere far away in order to save their lives, but thank goodness there were these life-saving Kinder Transports or Children's Trains to do exactly that, without them I am sure myself and many other Jewish children would never have survived! Most people think that the Kinder Transports, which were set up by compassionate people who saw what was happening in Nazi Germany and knew the potential fate that could lie ahead for the Jews trapped there, and for many later did, went mainly from Germany to Great Britain, that was not the case as they also went to other European countries which were safe in 1938, 1939 and early 1940 and were not at that time occupied by the Nazis! For myself and twin brother Kurt our journey took us to Belgium where at first we were sheltered in an orphanage at a very nice place on the coast called Middelkerke, not too far from the French border and further down the coast from a place which would later become famous, Dunkirk!

My mother, Elly Lief was one of the last Jewish able to officially leave Nazi Germany because very luckily she had secured a work sponsorship in Edinburgh, Scotland, and on the way across Europe had come to see us at the coast before her onward journey to the United Kingdom, where once our official papers had been secured and everything was in place we would have followed, unfortunately for whatever reasons this did not happen in time and eventually much bigger circumstances overtook everything, namely the German invasion of Western Europe, mum herself was extremely fortunate as she made it to Britain on the day war was declared, 3rd September 1939! A few days later and she could well have been trapped in Germany with no means to get out, as all regular air and sea transport routes to the United Kingdom were closed once war was officially underway, then who knows what might have happened to her, thank God it didn't!"

**The Kindertransport rescued around 10,000 Jewish children from Nazi persecution which eventually led to the much bigger and systematic horror of the Holocaust, the picture showing Jewish children on a train is a scene similar to that, but with this one taken after the war showing the slogan 'Hitler Kapout' (Hitler is Finished)! Walter and Kurt were a part of that special evacuation programme which in their case initially reached Belgium, but later as described in their story they eventually got to the United Kingdom and as a result enjoyed the refuge that came thereafter. Those in the Kindertransport travelled by train, boat and some by aircraft, the first arriving in the Port of Harwich in Essex on the 2nd December 1938 on board the passenger and freight vessel TSS Prague, the last escaped from Ijmuiden, Holland on the 14th May 1940 on board SS Bodegraven which was noted to be the very last ship to leave the harbour as the invading German armies advanced and the Dutch harbours were being closed, the following day Holland capitulated to the Nazis. Despite the ship carrying 74 Kindertransport children and about 200 other refugees it still came under attack and was strafed by the Luftwaffe as it departed for Great Britain. These transports took predominantly Jewish children from Nazi Germany, Austria, Czechoslovakia, Poland and the Free City of Danzig and eventually for those that came to the United Kingdom placed them with British foster homes, hostels, schools and farms around the country, and as a result by the end of the war they were in many cases sadly the only members of their family who survived the Holocaust. Smaller numbers of children were taken in via the programme by other countries such as Holland, Belgium, France, neutral Sweden and Switzerland, among them as mentioned before were the Lief twins.**

I was fascinated to hear stories from a very different perspective that occurred during the conflict, those things seen and experienced whilst in Belgium between 1939 to 1945 and from inside what was most of the time a part of Nazi occupied Europe during that conflict, and interestingly something which to a certain degree mirrored many experiences recounted to me by veterans on the home front in the United Kingdom during those war years, which included rationing, opposing air forces in the skies above and also those I interviewed who witnessed the V1 'Doodlebugs' attacking Great Britain, Antwerp and with Walter's accounts also Brussels! We now continue with further interesting stories from Walter regarding some of the wartime history he witnessed as a child refugee: "Next we were moved to 'The Happy Village' orphanage in the Molenbeek-Saint-Jean suburb of Brussels, where for approximately the first two years from 1940 until half way through the war in 1942 we didn't leave the premises because we as Jewish Children were purposely being mingled and hidden amongst the other Non-Jewish children in the place, there were about 12 of us in the midst of about 100 kids in total. We were taught French with good pronunciation and a local accent so we could be further thought of as being from Belgium to help with our cover and didn't begin going out as part of short organised walks until the teachers were more than happy that we were very proficient with that! We had to be extremely careful for all the obvious reasons, if we were ever to come under the slightest suspicion then as with Jewish everywhere else we might get a visit from the Gestapo or the SS and could be taken away and that would be the end for us, and most probably have meant deportation to a Concentration Camp and eventually almost certain death! And we knew it! Not a normal childhood for sure, but then again these were not normal times that we were living through, this was a 'World War' in every true sense and it effected every aspect of everyone's life in one way or another, no matter what their age or background! To add to things there was even a German Army base just up the road from us, they sometimes came round knocking on the windows of the orphanage and asking the teachers if they could use the playground to park vehicles, hairy moments, but very luckily that was as close as it got to any kind of 'visit', I don't fully know why we were so lucky, maybe we were hidden in plain sight and did nothing out of the ordinary to attract unwanted attention, but also the brave lady who ran the orphanage called Denise Vandenbrook was doing a lot behind the scenes to ensure our safety, she really was our main 'Guardian Angel' during those dangerous years, a 'Female Schindler' if you like, she was a key factor in our survival, we were so fortunate to have her, because as we found out later millions of others from Jewish communities in Europe were not so lucky and were completely wiped out by the Nazis."

Having spoken to Walter on a number of occasions both in person and on the phone I knew a number of other interesting and varied wartime related experiences took place whilst he was in Belgium, some of which he now shares with us: "My mother knew how we were doing because of the two-way communications that took place between us via our uncle that went through the International Red Cross in Switzerland a couple of times a year, we were only allowed a very brief 25 words per telegram and not to give away anything of real importance that could potentially endanger us, also 2 or 3 times a year we saw our Uncle who lived in Brussels, he also checked up on us, so these things combined I believe helped her live with our separation a bit better, at least she knew we were alive and well. I also think that this was of additional importance when other things happened as well such as the Allies advancing on Brussels which brought with it the possibility heavy fighting breaking out in the streets, and the very real danger when V1 rocket attacks were taking place as anyone could randomly be killed by those, add to it the Jewish angle we talked about earlier and our poor mum must have been going out of her mind sometimes, helpless all those miles away. We saw the 1000 Bomber raids going over on occasions and the sky filled with British and American aircraft as far as the eye could see, a vast armada in the air, not knowing until much later that one of the first big targets they really decimated was our lovely home city of Cologne **(depicted in this dramatic painting by W. Krogman, in the background the silhouette of the twin steeples of the famous cathedral are visible).** We also saw the Germans shoot some of them down with their big Anti-Aircraft guns and the white parachutes floating to the earth in the distance, we hoped the airman would survive and be okay. If Bombers were going over in the night then the sky would be lit up with searchlights and you could sometimes briefly see the silhouettes of Allied planes caught in their beams, and the sounds of the big Nazi guns roaring in the distance and shells exploding up in the air, thundering sounds that made things, and sometimes us, shake!

We had a home-made deep dug shelter in the grounds of the orphanage that was covered over with all sorts and if needed we would sometimes go in there to keep safe when air raid sirens were sounded, later in the war when the V1 Flying Bombs came and fell on Brussels it really was dangerous and the shelter was used again but we still managed to see some of them as they came over, looking like a flying tube with small wings and an engine on top which had fire spitting out, one blew up a house not too far from us and during one of our guided walks into town we saw that the house it hit and area around it were totally destroyed."

**A very interesting picture taken at the back end of World War Two showing a downed or captured V1 on public display, similar to those Walter witnessed over Brussels during his time there. This menacing V-1 Flying Bomb, in German the 'Vergeltungswaffe 1 or Vengeance Weapon 1' was nicknamed 'The Doodlebug' and the 'The Buzz Bomb' by the Allies and their civilian populations due to the noise it made in flight just before it cut out and fell upon its target area. This early Cruise Missile was at the time the only production aircraft to use revolutionary Pulsejet technology for its power, and it did so with devastating results!**

So many fascinating experiences from the Belgian Home Front as seen through the eyes of a child, but the stories didn't end there: "As the war eventually got into its later stages we of course heard about the Allied forces landing on D-Day and slowly but surely they advanced over Western Europe and liberated much of France including the capital Paris (25th August 1944) and came on into Belgium where they finally did the same when they reached our capital Brussels (3rd September 1944), in the evening we had gone out to greet the liberators and when they thought it was safe enough they put many of us children on their tanks and let us have the great fun of siting and climbing on them for a little while as the Germans had left without hardly any resistance. The next day when Belgian and British tanks and armoured vehicles passed through the Centre of Brussels in their big Victory Parade (4th September 1944), we were all walked down from our 'Happy Village' Orphanage in straight lines to go and be part of this historical event where we were in the cheering crowds, I have seen Pathe' news footage reporting on it, and we certainly were happy because for us all it was freedom at last! Interestingly we had seen them going both ways, when they were retreating and losing in 1940 and when they were returning, advancing and winning in 1944."

**Brussels – Changing Armies; Walter saw them come and go. Right – German Army Victoriously Parading in the centre of the city on the 24th July 1940. Left – Tanks of the liberating Allied forces on the 4th September 1944 parading through Brussels with men, women and children riding on them amidst scenes of complete jubilation, and somewhere in the celebrating masses were Walter, Kurt and all the other Jewish children that had survived 4 years of Nazi occupation. These liberating units consisted of the British Guards Armoured Division and symbolically the Belgian Brigade Piron.**

The war in Europe dragged on for another 8 months until May 1945, within that time the Germans launched the huge offensive in the Ardennes region of Belgium to try and reach the strategically vital port city of Antwerp which became known as The Battle of the Bulge, this brought war back into Belgium again from the 16th December 1944 until the country was finally and completely cleared of Nazi troops by the 4th February 1945. The V1 and V2 terror weapons rained down on Belgium from October 1944 until March 1945, hitting Antwerp, Brussels and Liege and proving that even with the capital liberated the danger was far from over. During and after these massive events were happening Walter and Kurt's mother was undertaking her own personal battle to try and get her children back, as Walter explained: "My mother was very persistent and went right to the very top of the British government by writing to No. 10 Downing Street a few times, and directly to Winston Churchill himself about the plight of her boys, we don't know if he ever saw the letters asking for help but it certainly touched the heart of someone high up because our case was passed to the Foreign Secretary at the time Anthony Eden who instructed people in his Foreign Office to organise safe passage for us, and later arrange our full immigration status! So we were collected from our orphanage, taken to Brussels airport, put on a military transport aircraft with returning troops, and escorted all the way by a special liaison officer who was assigned to us from the Women's Royal Air Force (WAAF), she stayed with us until we got all the way to the United Kingdom, landed at Croydon Airdrome in London, were we ran into the arms of our mother who had not seen us since the age of 7 in the Autumn of 1939, it was now the late summer of 1945 we were both 13 years old, can you imagine we had not held each other for nearly 6 years, and that is how it happened, with all the things that occurred in between we were now all together once again, safe in our newly adopted country, which would be the final stop for we who had been refugees in transit for a very long time. In our own country we had been persecuted, in our absence our city had been devastated, our home almost completely destroyed, extended family killed and the old life swept away, gone, so with nowhere to really return to, and add to this the chaos of post war Europe, we were determined to make the most of our new life and new opportunities here in Great Britain, something we never took for granted and that I am extremely grateful for even now nearly eight decades later!

When we were taken to Glasgow in Scotland by our mum to start our new life and joined our new school called Hyndland in September 1945, we became known as 'The Belgian Boys', better we were thought of that way I think, because Germans as you can imagine were not too popular just after the war! We learned English very quickly, within a year and excelled in our subjects, and eventually had 3 languages, French, German and English, with a Scottish accent, (which Walter has always kept), we were there from 13 to 18 years of age. Later as part of our gratitude to the country that gave us so much we both completed our National Service between 1950 to 1952, serving together in the Royal Army Ordinance Corps, posted most of the time at a huge Army depot at Bistor near Oxford, involved in the supply and issue of almost any and everything needed and requested by the Army, also having to undertake clerical duties as well. After this we both volunteered continuing as British Army Reservists for 4 more years from 1952 to 1956. Many years later acknowledgment for that service came from the British Government when they sent me the official Veterans Badge."

The R.A.O.C – Royal Army Ordinance Corps was the branch of the British Army which was responsible for the procurement, storage and issue of material classified as 'Ordinance Stores'. In 1993 it amalgamated with other Corps to form the R.L.C - Royal Logistics Corps. Ordinance Stores was defined to include; Personal & Unit Equipment, Armaments, Small Arms Ammunition, Explosives, Signals Stores, Armoured Fighting Vehicles, Motor Transport (except vehicles used by the R.A.S.C – Royal Army Service Corps), Tractors, Motor Transport Stores including Spare & Replacement Parts, Clothing, Personal Accessories, Workshop Tools, Medical and Veterinary Stores, All else as directed. *Expendable Supplies, such as Food, Animal Fodder, Petrol, Oil & Lubricants was the responsibility of the R.A.S.C.

**The R.A.O.C Motto is 'Sua Tela Tonanti' commonly translated as 'To the Warrior his Arms' and a fitting tribute to a man who has battled, strived and worked hard to survive and achieve a lot in his life despite many trials, from refugee to Armed Forces Veteran and much more, a shining example of perseverance and success, well done Walter.**

## Additional Information and Life After Service

**Rank upon finish of service** – Sergeant.

**Medals and Honours** – Official British Veterans Badge.

**Post War Years** – After finishing secondary Education 1945 to 1950, and National Service 1950 to 1952 Walter worked for Ideal Furniture Enterprises in Glasgow as an Export Sales Correspondent and because of his languages travelled extensively with his job, later rising to Sales Manager. After this he worked for British Carpets Limited in Glasgow as a Sales Manager. Retiring and moving down to Manchester to be closer to his family in 1997. Married Arline on 31st July 1961 at Langside Hebrew Congregation Synagogue in Glasgow, they had their 60-year Diamond Anniversary in July 2021. Interestingly Arline herself a twin like Walter was evacuated to the countryside in the U.K during the war and saw WW2 from the other side over here! They have 1 Son & 1 Daughter, 5 Grandchildren.

**Associations and Organisations** – Fellow of The Chartered Institute of Linguists (Fcil), Graduate of the Institute of Export.

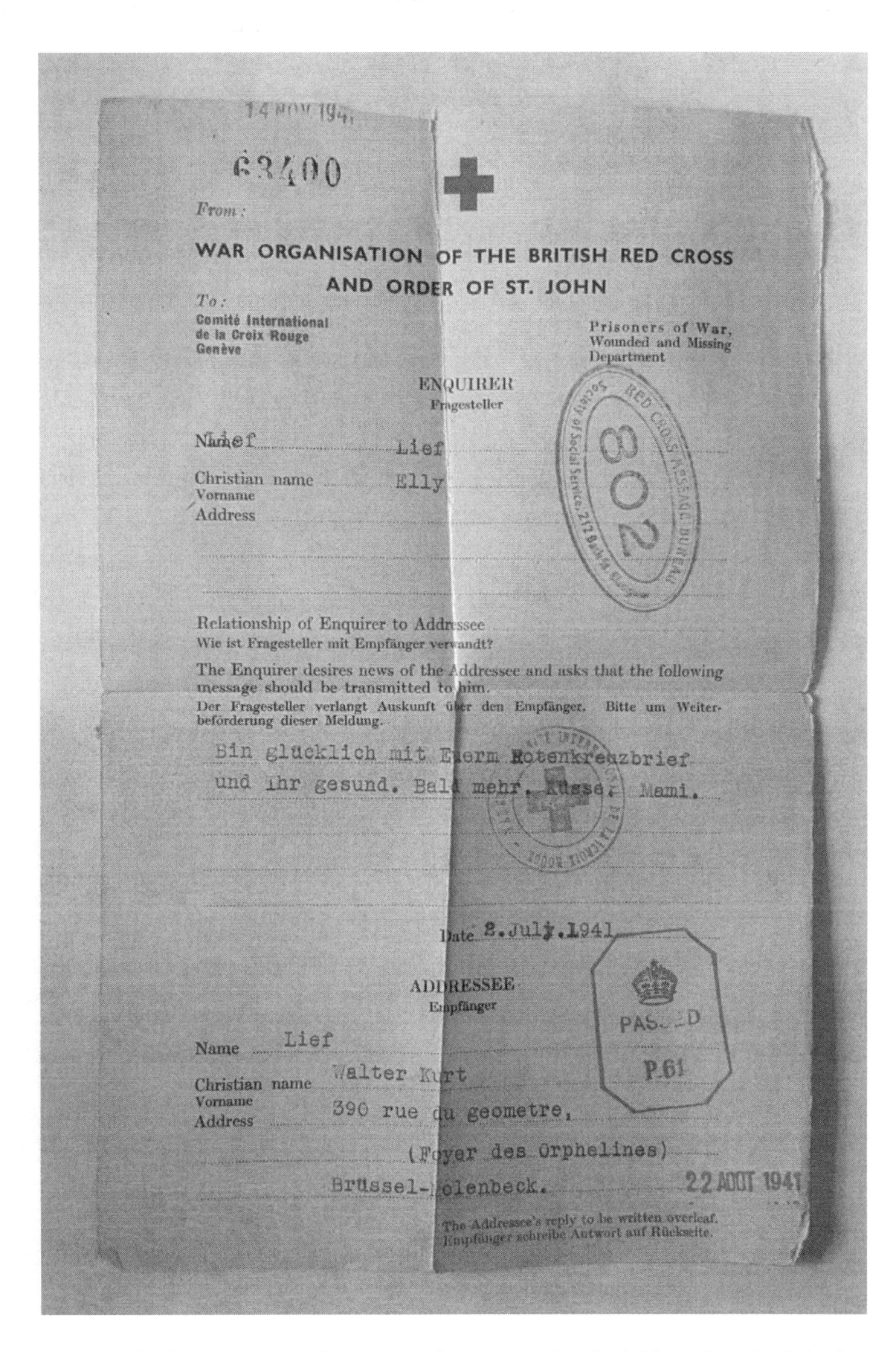

Above – One of the short International Red Cross telegrams sent by Elly Lief from the United Kingdom to her sons Walter and Kurt in Belgium in July-August 1941. A little piece of World War Two history from the 'Prisoners of War, Wounded and Missing Department' of the I.R.C and a special piece of family history kept as a reminder of Walter's days as a refugee.

# A VERY DIFFERENT WORLD WAR TWO STORY FROM A SURVIVOR OF THE HOLOCAUST WITH RELATED CHAPTER & WW2 TIMELINE

# HOLOCAUST SURVIVOR MAYER HERSH MBE

**Visited/Interviewed – Heathlands Care Village, Prestwich, Manchester - 2015 & 2016**

In contrast to the other kind of veterans related stories in this book, the World War Two experiences captured here detail a very different reality that existed for many at the same time in parallel to other events whilst the conflict unfolded between 1939 to 1945, and because of its equally important and relative historical significance this chapter has been included as part of the book in order to also preserve the content for posterity alongside the other narratives found within its pages. This is the incredible and harrowing story of a Polish born Jewish man, Mayer Hersh, who by some miracle survived the horrors of a staggering 9 Concentration and Labour Camps during the Holocaust including 18 months in Auschwitz, despite the unimaginable terror of the events he witnessed and the brutal things he had been subjected to himself, he was unbelievably one of the luckier ones in his family. His Father Isaac, Mother Riwka, four of his siblings and his entire extended family in Poland, numbering nearly one hundred, were all murdered by the Nazis, only Mayer and his elder brother Jakob survived the Holocaust.

For many years Mayer kept silent about his losses and his experiences during World War Two, but as the years went by and the living witnesses were declining in numbers he dedicated himself to Holocaust education, speaking out loudly about that devastating part of Jewish and World history and his part in it, and as an ageing survivor of that tragedy he made sure he spoke out as much and as often as he could and in as many places as possible, in order to reach and educate as many people as possible, so much so that during the last 30 years of his life he became one of the foremost UK-based witnesses of that unparalleled catastrophe.

He explained his mission and motivation when he said: "To me, this is a fulfilment. But why is it a fulfilment? Because I'm talking about my family, whose lives were extinguished and whose voices were obliterated. The perpetrators also wanted the memory of these people to be obliterated, and that's something I don't want to happen. I want their memory to be preserved for eternity."

I was very fortunate to get to know Mayer, he was someone who I spent quite a bit of time with on a few occasions in his last years whilst at the Heathlands Village care facility in Manchester. A survivor of one of the biggest genocides in modern world history, he was a man I sat with, talked to, shared emotional and sometimes quite upsetting moments with as he imparted his heart-rendering stories of the horrors he witnessed and things he suffered, family and friends he lost, someone who rolled up his sleeve and showed me his tattooed number from Auschwitz on his left arm, very real and chilling moments, yet moments I was honoured to share, and very importantly he allowed me once again to 'Connect with History' first-hand, this time with the very disturbing history of the Holocaust.

As touched on earlier, this by its very nature as you would expect is a completely different kind of story and part of the Second World War which is being looked at and covered in this chapter of the book, and I must say in advance to those about to read it that some of the things contained within it could be a bit difficult or disturbing, however they are facts and accounts which truly reflect what was going on and are documented here to capture some of the terrible wrongdoings undertaken by the Nazis, which again reinforces the importance of why Nazism had to be defeated and what all the veterans in this book, each in their own ways, stood up to and fought against. This section is one which I have extended in a number of ways from what began as a profile about one person like the others but ended up as a whole related and detailed chapter about the Holocaust, and as a result became a much bigger piece of 'The Last Stand'. It is divided into eight parts, as follows; **1)** Mayer's personal story. **2)** A General Overview of information and statistics about the Holocaust including a detailed 'Persecution Timeline'. **3)** 'Number of Deaths in the Bigger Holocaust', updated statistics from the United States Holocaust Memorial Museum in Washington D.C giving a bigger picture regarding the Jewish and non-Jewish victims of this huge travesty. **4)** 'Insights into Twisted Minds of the Nazi Perpetrators'. **5)** The 'Pulse of Death', some relatively new research and data published by Mathematician Prof. Lewi Stone from Tel-Aviv University. **6)** 'Schindler's List - Making a Conscious Connection', touching on the acclaimed 1993 Steven Spielberg film which was released whilst I was travelling in the Middle East and was at that time living in Jerusalem, this section includes a bit of my own story regarding this subject and the film. **7)** 'Past to Present Day - Dealing with the Aftermath of the Holocaust', bringing this history up to recent times by including insightful thoughts and feelings expressed by people in the Jewish Community in North Manchester with whom I conducted mini-interviews, done in order to find out about how Jewish people have in a broad sense absorbed and processed such a cataclysmic event in their people's history. **8)** 'Holocaust Conclusion Linking to History on a Knife Edge in 1942', this section connects it to the next relative and important part in the book, a factual essay I wrote called 'History on a Knife Edge in 1942' about how close Nazi Germany actually came to winning World War Two, (whilst at the same time in duality undertaking the Holocaust), and which essentially details one of history's great 'What If's'.

So let's start with the story of one person, before expanding it outwards, that of Mayer Hersh, during one of my interviews with him he told me he saw Adolf Hitler when his motorcade passed through the Lodz region of Poland in September 1939, a region where Meyer lived and had extended family, and he is the only person I have interviewed face to face who so far actually claims to have seen Hitler first hand. Mayer was 13 years old at the time, little did he or the rest of the world know at that moment what murderous crimes the Nazis would perpetrate in the lands they would occupy, starting in Poland, the first country to be invaded by the armed forces of Nazi Germany in World War Two. Also Meyer was not to know that he would have five years of pure hell ahead of him during the worse and biggest attempt at total annihilation of the Jewish, and for that matter any race in history, chilling to think all this to come because of the Anti-Semitic policies of the man this young Jewish teenager was looking at as he passed by in his car, this man Adolf Hitler who would be directly responsible for so much pain to his people, his family and eventually in many ways to Mayer himself!

Mayer was from the town of Sieradz in central Poland, it was from here in the spring of 1940 that he and his brother Yakob were taken by the SS along with others from their town to become slave labourers, there was no time for goodbyes, they were taken during the night and that was it, they would never see their family again! Meanwhile the brothers were put to work building a railway that a year later would be used to supply what would become the Eastern Front, whilst doing so they were incarcerated at Otoczna Concentration camp, then later Guttenburg, Lusenheim and Poznan, they were taken from camp to camp as the railway was extended, eventually he and his brother got split up, in May 1943 Mayer found himself in Auschwitz, where he survived unimaginable and horrendous experiences for 18 months (during which time he again found Jakob in August 1943), he was then moved from there in November 1944 and taken with many others to work on other gruelling forced labour tasks that the Nazis subjected them to whilst keeping them ahead of the impending Russian advances that were steam-rolling Westward towards Germany.

As he was moved on Mayer became an inmate of other Concentration Camps such as Stutthof near the Baltic Sea, then to a camp called Ohrdruf-Nord AKA Gotha, where he worked in an underground bunker loading ammunition on to trucks. It was from there in April 1945 he was put on a forced 'Death March' to Buchenwald Concentration Camp, the last part of it through mountainous terrain where anyone who stopped would be instantly executed! A month later he and others were on the final part of their continuous 'Road to Hell' to what would be Mayer's final Concentration Camp, Theresienstadt, this is what Meyer had to say about that infernal journey and the things he witnessed: "With the allies approaching, they took us Jews and the Russian prisoners of war on open coal wagons to Theresienstadt in Czechoslovakia, a hundred men to a wagon, standing up packed like sardines, whilst Germans with machine guns guarded over us ready to kill in an instant anyone who tried to escape. Because the lines were clogged with troop movements, we spent days in sidings and a journey that should have taken a few days took three weeks. We had no food or water and were always freezing and constantly shaking with a combination of the bitter cold and pure fear, because of these things plus starvation people were dying like flies. Whenever the train stopped, we would get off and have to dispose of the dead who for long parts of the journey could be pushed up tightly against you, obviously beginning to decompose! Then if we had a chance to pick up a few leaves and grass to eat and some snow for water we did. Some men tried to roast the leather from their shoes over an open fire I even saw Russian prisoners of war turn to cannibalism. There was no flesh on the bodies, so they had to eat the organs. I couldn't do it myself, but nor could I blame them."

Mayer was there for a few weeks and was down to a pitiful four stone in body weight, he was amongst thousands of other internees who historically were present when Theresienstadt became the last of the Nazi Concentration camps to be liberated in World War Two on the 8th May 1945 (V.E Day) by the Red Army, although it was a very different V.E Day than most in Europe were having with huge celebrations, it was still certainly cause for him to feel victory, a great personal victory of surviving all the pure anguish, misery and torment he had been through and seen, and all the camps he had endured including this, his last!

During his 5 years of hell Mayer and others saw and were subjected to the most barbaric cruelty and conditions, they were regularly and mercilessly beaten, worked almost to death, malnourished, lice ridden, regularly contracting numerous ailments, illnesses or diseases, working in all weather conditions, frequently in sub-zero freezing conditions with little clothing and with their shoes worn until they fell apart and with their bare feet being ripped to pieces until they could take shoes from the dead who no longer had use for them. If not working hard enough they could be shot on the spot, constantly seeing many around them die in many vicious and sadistic ways, in some camps seeing countless innocent people, some of whom he knew being hung or randomly executed, others selected for gas vans or taken to the gas chambers and crematoria, all the while feeling helpless to do anything and with the fear of death constantly hanging over them, this was the terrifying reality for many of those that lived for any period of time during the Holocaust!

Mayer stayed alive through hard work, intelligence and sheer luck and in Auschwitz on a few occasions came face to face with one of the most evil and sadistic perpetrators of the Holocaust Doctor Josef Mengele AKA 'The Angel of Death' but was never chosen by him for extermination. People to the left and the right of him, many his friends, were chosen to die or selected for horrific experimentation by Mengele but incredibly not Mayer! Inmates, some twins, had returned to his block in riving agony after having been sadistically operated on without anaesthetic with sown up parts of their body from where things had been removed in Mengele's notorious Block 24. During the holocaust he had seen and experienced things no human being should ever have seen or been subjected to and yet miraculously survived all of these horrific occurrences, and when finally liberated he was almost incomprehensively still only a eighteen-year-old teenager! **Above – Magen David (Star of David) Representation of the faith for which so many including Mayer were persecuted. In the middle of it are the words 'Juud' or Jew, something the Nazis forced the Jewish populations in the countries it conquered to wear as a means of identification, and all part of the process of discrimination, intimidation and subjugation leading to eventual extermination!**

Mayer very sadly found out the fate of the rest of his family after the war, in August 1942 his father was gassed upon arrival at Auschwitz, his mother and three youngest siblings were murdered in gas vans in Chelmno Extermination Camp after being taken out on the last transports from Lodz ghetto in August 1944, and his other sister Kayla had died on board one of three prison ships that were sunk in the Baltic Sea in early 1945. Many years later when he went to visit Chelmno knowing that his Mother and other members of his family met such a terrible end there, he described his visit as: "That day the rain fell and the tears fell."

For any of us it is extremely hard to deal with the loss of a single loved one from our family, the pain of losing nearly 100 family members is almost beyond comprehension, yet this was Mayer's reality, this on top of all the personal torment and suffering he had been through. To get a further insight into what Mayer was subjected to and saw during the war years, a war which was very different for him than others in this book, we now hear more of his harrowing experiences, these things don't make for easy reading but come as a 'Warning from History' about very sadly what human beings are capable of inflicting upon and doing to other human beings, this is what Mayer had to say about:

### SUFFERING AT THE HANDS OF THE NAZIS DURING THE HOLOCAUST

"At Auschwitz I was tattooed with the number **158528**, from that moment on that was what I became, a number not a person, this what the Nazis did, it was all part of their bigger Master Plan, (touched on earlier) which was Humiliation, Enslavement, Dehumanisation, Death!

When we were building the railways German foreman and supervisors who were civilians oversaw the job. Some were real swines as well, some beat you ruthlessly. They were highly educated people but it made no difference to their ruthlessness, to their hardness and the hate they had for us. People were driven to suicide. Every day we had to carry home collapsed people. When the railway line next to us was completed, people committed suicide on the lines. If anyone was caught in time they would be beaten, then forced to continue work again later in the next place. We completed one section and were moved to another. In Otoschno the gassing waggons would come and anyone who wasn't well was taken away in them. We knew what they were! In the camp people had escaped, for this the penalty was death, before execution they were given more beatings, one day they put up 52 hooks for hanging in the shower room. I remember they read out the details and we had to watch the executions taking place, more physiological terror tactics!

In the bigger camps like Auschwitz the Germans always delighted in picking Jewish holidays as days of special treatment for us and special punishment. They always speeded up liquidations on those days, like Rosh Hashanah. It was part of their enjoyment, they delighted in it. They did it with such vindictiveness, I really don't know why, we had never harmed them, they never met us before! We were normal people; I don't understand how they could be like that? What crime had these children committed against them? And they killed so many innocent, beautiful children every day. They carried out their 'orders' but they went beyond their orders because they committed so many cruelties before the people were executed that were so unnecessary! These people were barbaric! Shortly after my arrival in Auschwitz the block leader said: 'Listen, you men, do you think Auschwitz is a holiday camp? Nobody survives here. Can you see those crematoria chimneys over there? That's where you are all going to end up!' Sadly for many men, women and children that we saw coming in every day that was their terrible reality. At night you could see the chimneys with fire spewing out, they worked 24 hours a day to try and destroy all traces of our people, with it came the smell of death which was constantly around! We would see, hear and smell it, and it was sickening, and most people, myself included, wondered how long until it was me in those flames?"

**THE BRAVE POLISH:** Amongst those who tried to stop these horrors was an incredibly heroic Polish Cavalry Officer turned Spy and Resistance Fighter called Witold Pilecki, pictured, who became a 'Volunteer for Auschwitz' to be midst the horrors of it all in order to gather evidence of the existence of the industrialised scale of the murder being undertaken as part of the Nazi Extermination program. For 2.5 years he managed to get his information out of the camp via released and escaped prisoners and civilian workers to the Polish Underground Resistance movement that was called the ZOW – Związek Organizacji Wojskowej who then passed it on to the Polish Government-in-Exile in London, who in turn saw to it that these direct reports landed on the desk of Winston Churchill in the hope that he would act to save many innocent people, such as Mayer Hersh, from the potential or actual fates that awaited them! Such was his great courage and exploits I felt he should be remembered here as his story is connected directly to that of Auschwitz! He is also included in the 'Persecution Timeline' at September 1940-April 1943.

Back to Mayer who went on to impart further painful memories:

"In the summer of 1944 Hungarian Jews were arriving by the thousands, almost every day they came, and were being murdered at an accelerated and almost frenzied rate, they destroyed the inhabitants of every cattle truck that turned up in endless shipment after shipment, each processed then quickly disposed of in 'The Showers'! But not only Jews suffered this fate, whole areas of the camp where the Roma Gypsies stayed were cleared out and the people exterminated almost overnight. You could hear the lorries arriving and the Gypsies screaming, many thousands of them all rounded up and taken, the screaming was unbelievable, by the morning not one Gypsy was left in the camp. They were all gassed! No one was safe, no matter who they were, during 1944 even German civilians arrived, they were classed as Jews by Hitler although they classified themselves as Messianic Christians, this made no difference, they were murdered just like all the rest and along with all the rest! When you entered Auschwitz, like many other camps the words above the entrance read 'Arbeit Macht Frei – Work Makes You Free', the only way you were free is if you were worked to death as so many were, this was the only release that set them free! The only other way was if you were one of the extremely lucky ones who by some incredible set of circumstances or miracle managed to get through to the very end and be freed by the advancing Allied armies, like me." Once liberated from his final camp Theresienstadt by Soviet forces in May 1945 where in his words he was: "a filthy, emancipated skeleton suffering from typhus" Mayer was transferred to a hospital where he spent some time recovering and building up strength, the patients were released once they could walk and eat properly again.

May 1945, Allied Liberation! Shown here at Mauthausen Concentration Camp, Austria by the 11th Armoured Division of the U.S 3rd Army. This was one of the camps where later Nazi hunter Simon Wiesenthal was held. Note the surviving inmates wearing the notorious 'Stripped Pyjamas' uniform. The banner states: 'The Spanish Anti-Fascists Salute the Liberating Forces.' Scenes like these were playing out all over the newly liberated countries inside mainland Europe in late 1944 into Spring 1945.

Then he and others were passed into the hands of the Jewish Refugee Committee that selected 300 children who after all their traumas were sent to the United Kingdom for rehabilitation, of which Mayer was one. He arrived in Windermere, England in August 1945 where he recalls being looked after very well, he continued to recover and resumed religious teachings, (something quite remarkable after what he had been through, and which shows the importance of strength through faith which is touched on later in this chapter). It was also a place as Mayer recalls where they were welcomed and where the local people showed them kindness and hospitality, something that had been virtually non-existent for the last five years of his life, they were also interested in the stories of the survivors which when shared left them almost 'numb in disbelief'. In time they became known as the 'Windermere Children' as depicted in the excellent and very informative 2020 film and documentary of the same name. After about two months in Windermere they were sent to a hostel in North Manchester on Middleton Road and then to Singleton Road where they learnt English and further religious studies, a year later Meyer and others were boarded out to live with families in areas of the city where many Jewish communities could be found, such as Cheetham Hill, Higher Broughton, Sedgley Park, Prestwich and Whitfield, all this as part of their long rehabilitation process. After the war, as you would expect, Mayer had frequent nightmares and suffered from 'survivors guilt', 'why them not me' being something he wrestled with for a long, long time, living as many did under 'The Shadows of the Shoah'.

His first job was in the 'Rag Trade' in a clothing factory in Charlotte Street, Manchester then he found a job with a tailor in Fountain Street, these places being familiar to those who know our city. Mayer was ambitious so he moved on to other tailors to learn more about this professional end of the trade and began working for himself and eventually owning a bespoke tailoring business and later even employing others to work for him. In 1965 he married Judith Cooklin from Manchester, but regretted not having any children after all the family he lost during the war. From the 1970's onwards Mayer became an increasingly important voice in Holocaust education, eventually dedicating over 30 years of his life to the 'Importance of Remembrance', constantly touring, mainly schools, where he regularly did up to three a week, it is estimated by those who helped organise his trips over three decades that he had spoken to around 100,000 children during his time, no mean feat for an ageing yet very determined survivor who only retired from public speaking just a few months before his passing. Having survived nine camps, Mayer was much in demand to verify archival material, and recorded his testimony many times, most notably in 1997 for the University of Southern California Shoah Foundation, established by the film director Steven Spielberg in 1994 after making Schindler's List, apart from the film itself another great legacy of his work.

Mayer passed away on the 10th October 2016 at Heathlands Care home in Prestwich, Manchester aged 90, but left a great legacy in Holocaust Education behind him. He was also part of the 45 Aid Society, set up to help 'The Boys' who were the eventual 732 orphaned Holocaust survivors who came to the UK in 1945, founded with the aim of giving something back to the country that gave them a new home after the war, this they did by raising and giving money for various UK charitable causes. Amongst his many accolades Mayer was made an 'Honorary Fellow' of Edge Hill University, Liverpool when awarded his Honorary Doctorate of Education (DEd) in July 2012, he was later made an MBE in the Queen's 2013 New Year Honours for services to Holocaust Education, and a special ceremony was held at Manchester Town Hall on 1st May 2013 in acknowledgment of him becoming an MBE - Member of the Most Excellent Order of the British Empire.

Very fittingly I conclude the last part of Meyer's story with tributes, first from Rabbi Jonathan Guttentag who said of Meyer at his funeral; "Bearing witness – not with anger but with compassion – had become his vocation. In spite of what he had been through, he was not bitter or negative – he was positive and faith-filled; he was wise, he was inspirational… By constantly being prepared to tell the story of his experiences, he was upholding the memory and the dignity of his family, his friends, his community and his people."

My accolade and closing mark of respect to him here in this part of the book is that this was a great man who did great things in relation to his passion for Holocaust Education. I feel privileged to have known him and spent time with him and humbled by what I learnt from him. It seems most fitting that Mayer should finish his own incredible story with his own words, so I leave you with this poignant quote from him – *"SURVIVORS HAVE A DUTY TO EXPLAIN THEIR HISTORY, HISTORIANS HAVE A RESPONSIBILITY TO TELL THE TRUTH!"*

**Above – Mayer Hersh working away quietly and peacefully as skilled Bespoke Tailor in 1960 with his name on the windows of his business. In this serene picture, from the outside looking in, who could ever imagine what hell he had been through and the horrors he had seen and experienced!**

# THE AUTHOR'S TRIP TO AUSCHWITZ – 14TH FEBRUARY 2023

In order to be closer to the story of Mayer and to understand better from a real historical perspective all those I have written about in the Holocaust part of this book and to connect with their journeys, I thought it was very important to try and get the best possible first-hand idea, true understanding and emotional sense I could by making a visit to Auschwitz in Poland. It was there that I was given further in-depth information from an experienced and very knowledgeable tour guide about the Holocaust and the very sad and horrific things that took place and happened in that place, and also something that was beyond words, the feelings and overriding emotions which sweep over you in moments of epiphany as you realise the magnitude of the history that you are taking in and walking amongst in the most well-known Concentration/Extermination Camp of the Shoah, a place where over 1 million people's lives were taken just because of who they were! One which was liberated by Soviet Armed Forces on the 27th January 1945, a date which is now set as the National Holocaust Memorial Day in the U.K and many other countries. For these things I give thanks for understanding and having experienced. Again I remember and venerate all those who were taken as a result of this unimaginable travesty. May You All Rest In Peace. GBD.

# THE HOLOCAUST – 'ORIGINS TO OUTCOME' – AN OVERVIEW

The persecution of Jewish people and anti-Semitism has been going on in one form or another for thousands of years and knows no borders. In the biggest and most modern of these it was undertaken on such a massive level it can only be described as Genocide on a truly and wholly industrial scale! This as we all know was carried out essentially by the Fascist Regime of Nazi Germany but also with help from some of its wartime allies and others, its origins or a frightening pre-curser of which were contained in the pages the Adolf Hitler's book 'Mien Kampf' (My Struggle), where he mainly blamed the Jews for Germany losing World War One and for perpetrating other bigger ongoing world conspiracies. As always especially in a dictatorship a main 'Scape Goat' is required to hate and blame for any or all of the country's ills or the state of the world in general at any given time in history. This of course provides a 'Common Enemy' or enemies which that dictatorship can then oppose, detest and focus itself on and with the manipulation of propaganda turn and brainwash the majority of its nation to do as well, and whilst that distraction is in place and that policy being perused then seize and consolidate power for itself which it can then manipulate for its own ends and means whilst carrying out its other policies and greed driven goals such as increasing totalitarian rule and expansionism normally first by political and then by military means.

In the case of Adolf Hitler and the Nazis that strategy worked very well indeed, but went on much further than that when it tried to achieve the wholesale annihilation of a race of people, the Jews, it is also very important to remember that although the Jewish race were the main target of Hitler's 'Final Solution' that they were not solely chosen for liquidation, as any who were not deemed as racially or otherwise pure for any reason, this included Slavs, Gypsies, Homosexuals, Communists, Other political & religious opponents, Disabled and many more for various reasons were also exterminated by them. This build up started off in Germany as attacks on people and the damage of property, and continued to be escalated by the Nazis with other things such as the passing of official race laws. Then later with wartime expansion and the territory gained by invasion which brought tens of millions under their control, leading to the outright slaughter of millions which by then had become 'Policy!' Any mind that is inquisitive about these events for any reason must wonder how did this happen on such a massive scale, as these cataclysmic things didn't just occur overnight they were the product of over two decades of directed hatred, from Hitler's early anti-Semitic/race theory writings through to the height of their destructive implementation during the Second World War.

To help us understand this better and shine some light on these earth-shattering events I have outlined in greater detail in this Holocaust - 'Origins to Outcome' section generic overview information laid out in the form of a 'Persecution Timeline', put together from my research into the Holocaust with material drawn from many sources which shows the historical progression of the accelerated programs that the Nazis undertook, the content of which is not exhaustive. Starting from the creation of 'Mein Kampf' in 1924 to Hitler attaining power in 1933, through to the 'Final Solution' taking place during WW2 through to the eventual liberation of the camps, defeat of the Nazi regime and end of the Second World War in 1945 and some important related occurrences and events that came after, taking us right up to when this book was completed in 2023 (and beyond if more is added). The term Holocaust is derived from the Greek word 'Holokauston', which means sacrifice by fire. This in modern terms refers to the Nazi's premeditated persecution and slaughter of the Jewish people and others considered by so called 'True Germans' to be inferior, those they saw, classified and disgustingly deemed as 'Untermenschen' or 'Subhuman'! The Hebrew word also used to describe this genocide is Shoah, which translated means ruin, waste or devastation.

# THE HOLOCAUST – ORIGINS TO OUTCOME – PERSECUTION TIMELINE

Along with the history of the Holocaust this Timeline also contains some key events of the Second World War in the 1939-1945 parts of it in order for the reader to see and know the duality of what was happening as the back story to the Shoah, and as that conflict progressed and the fortunes of war changed how it influenced the actions of the Nazis in response to everything, such as the speeding up of programs, dismantling of camps and movement of people, all things that happened as the bigger picture of world events changed.

**Pre-War**_____

**1924** – After the failed Munich 'Beer Hall Putsch' of 9th November 1923, whilst in Landsberg Prison, Bavaria Adolf Hitler dictates to his Deputy Rudolf Hess what would become his book/s 'Mein Kampf' or 'My Struggle', which became the bible of National Socialism (Nazism), in it were outlined his political and race beliefs, it would also serve as his Anti-Semitic manifesto and blueprint for his later actions.

**30th January 1933** – Adolf Hitler Becomes Chancellor of Germany. A nation with a Jewish population of 556,000.

**22nd March 1933** – Less than 2 months after coming to power Dachau the first Concentration Camp, in German: Konzentrationslager (KZ) is set up to imprison enemies of the state.

**10th May 1933** – Burning of Books throughout Germany deemed to have 'Un-German' ideas.

**2nd August 1934** – German President Paul von Hindenburg dies and Adolf Hitler becomes absolute dictator of Germany under the title of 'Fuhrer' or 'Leader' paving the way for the creation of his new 'Third Reich' controlled by his NSDAP – National Socialist German Workers Party or Nazi Party.

**1935-1939** – German Pre-War Territorial Expansion begins, Saarland (January 1935), Rhineland (March 1936), Austria – 'Anschluss or Annexation' (March 1938), Czechoslovakia (October 1938 and March 1939) bringing hundreds of thousands of Jews under Nazi control.

**15th September 1935** – German Reichstag passes the Nuremberg Race Laws, and the Swastika Flag (Hakenkreuz), the black Swastika on a white circle with a red background became the national flag of Germany, although the Swastika symbol itself was originally a religious emblem of the Buddhist, Jains and Hindus it had been used by the Nazis since the early 1920's, but to this day it symbolises for many the most evil regime in history.

**March 1936** – SS Death's Head Units 'Totenkopfverbände' are formed to guard concentration Camps.

**17th June 1936** – Heinrich Himmler is appointed Chief of the German Police – Reichsführer-SS.

**1st-16th August 1936** – Nazi Germany hosts the Olympic Games, officially known as the XI Olympiad, held in Berlin that summer, during which Hitler orders the visible relaxation of the implementation of racial laws in order to showcase his regime in a positive light whilst the eyes of the world were on his country. When the showpiece games were finished and the attention of the world was averted elsewhere oppression within Germany would begin again.

**6th-15th July 1938** – At Evian in France the U.S convenes a League of Nations conference with delegates from 32 countries to consider helping Jews fleeing from Hitler, but results in total inaction as no country will accept them. In addition to these 24 voluntary organizations attended and some 200 international journalists were also present. This inaction will in time prove to be a key contributory factor to the needless death of so many who were denied the means to flee the Holocaust as 'Victims of Nazi Oppression'.

**30th September 1938** – Munich Conference between Germany, Italy, Great Britain and France allows Hitler and the Nazis to annex the Sudetenland area of Czechoslovakia in order to avert war. Bringing a further 3 million mainly German Speakers under their control, and leading the British Prime Minister Neville Chamberlin to declare "Peace in our Time", a peace that would not last for long! In violation of the agreement Germany takes the rest of the country six months later, only then was it confirmed that Hitler had deceived them.

**9th November 1938** – 'Kristallnacht - Night of Broken Glass' Nazi Anti-Semitism intensifies as Jewish homes, businesses and synagogues are attacked, looted and burned throughout Germany and Austria.

## 1939

**30th January 1939** – Hitler threatens the Jews during a Reichstag speech, openly talking about and with foreboding declaring intentions for: "The annihilation of the Jewish race in Europe."

**23rd May 1939** – The British Government under Neville Chamberlain puts forward the 'White Paper of 1939' which is passed by the House of Commons. This puts a strong quota on the amount of Jewish refugees allowed to enter British Mandate Palestine and prevents them from buying land there, a further blow to refugees after the Evian Conference.

**1st September 1939** – Germany invades Poland and World War Two begins, the Jewish Population of over 3 million, the largest in Europe falls into Nazi hands. In the 6 years that followed wherever the conflict spread to it would prove to be a war waged against both the Allied forces on one hand and the Jewish race on the other, something reflected within the timeline which as mentioned earlier also shows some key military events alongside the unfolding tragedy of the Holocaust to reflect this overall duel course of the war.

**September 1939** – SS (Schutzstaffel or Protection Squads) activity begins. Reinhard Heydrich, Himmler's second in command issues instructions to SS Einsatzgruppen (Special Action Squads) to gather Jews into Ghettos near railroads for the future "Final Goal" later 'Solution'. Heydrich is given control of the RSHA – (Reich Main Security Office) which combined the SS Security Service (SD), Secret State Police (Gestapo), Criminal Police (Kripo), and Foreign Intelligence Service, this enormous centralized organisation would soon terrorize the entire continent of Europe and beyond, where they would conduct mass murder on a scale unprecedented in human history.

**September 1939-May 1945** – The 'Aktion T4 Program' of mass murder by involuntary euthanasia is undertaken by the Nazis in psychiatric hospitals in Germany and elsewhere in occupied Europe. By the end of the war it is estimated between 250,000-300,000 patients deemed 'Unfit and Unworthy to Live' were murdered. Adolf Hitler personally sanctions the program as he signs a document called the 'Euthanasia Note.'

**23rd November 1939** – Yellow stars required to be worn by Polish Jews over the age of 10.

## 1940

**1940-1945** – A network of Concentration Camps and Extermination Camps is set up and operated in many areas that Nazi Germany occupies, leading to the death of millions of Jews, Soviet POW's and other 'Undesirables'. *Further figures on this later in this chapter.

**April-June 1940** – More conquests of countries in Europe and Scandinavia such as Denmark, Norway, Belgium, Holland, Luxemburg, France leaves hundreds of thousands more Jews at the mercy of the Nazis. The same year Hungary joins the Axis powers, later on in 1944 this has devastating consequences for the Jews in that country. In July Romania also allies itself with Hitler. All these conquests and alliances, and those yet to come would lead to unimaginable destruction and upheaval for the Jews who would fall under Nazi control, their world or the worlds that they once knew, their towns and communities would be destroyed so quickly and so completely by extreme violence instead of gradually and normally changing by the natural passing of time!

**1940** – A big example of the above, the Ghetto system begins to be used as mass 'Containment Areas' for Jews in places like Lodz, Krakow and Warsaw in Poland before later transports will carry them on to Concentration and Extermination Camps in other occupied areas of Poland and Europe. The largest ghetto was Warsaw. At its peak in March 1941, some 445,000 were crammed into an area just 1.3 square miles in size.

**September 1940-April 1943** – Brave Polish Resistance Spy Witold Pilecki 'Volunteers' for Auschwitz' to uncover and document the horrors he sees there, he becomes inmate 4859 and sends messages and reports out by various means such as the resistance network which successfully as intended reach allied leaders, amongst them in late 1942 Winston Churchill, but sadly they are not acted upon. *More about the reasons for this in the – 'Conclusion linking to History on a Knife Edge in 1942' part of this chapter. After 2.5 years Witold escapes from Auschwitz and incredibly goes on to take part in the Warsaw Ghetto uprising and other courageous actions.

**27th September 1940** – The Tripartite Pact Signed in Berlin between Germany, Italy and Japan essentially forming the main part of 'The Axis Alliance' and strengthening each of these regimes.

**3rd October 1940** – The Vichy collaboration government of Southern France passes its own version of the Nuremburg Laws and would later deport Jews to death camps elsewhere in occupied Europe.

## 1941

**March 1941** – Hitler's 'Commissar Order' authorizes the execution of anyone suspected of being a Communist official in territories that will be seized from Soviet Russia.

**March-June 1941** – Bulgaria joins the Axis powers, German conquests continue now in the Balkans, with invasions of Yugoslavia, Greece, Crete and Greek Islands, as a result the Nazis procure many more Jews. April; The newly created Independent State of Croatia joins the Axis alliance, between 1941-1945 in the territory it controlled there existed 22 Concentration Camps, two Jastrebarsko and Sisak held only children!

**16th May 1941** – Marshal Phillipe Pétain of Vichy France approves collaboration with Hitler in a radio broadcast, as a result of this in the years that follow many thousands of Jews would perish.

**22nd June 1941** – Nazi Germany invades Soviet Russia and the Baltic States in Operation Barbarossa the biggest land invasion of the Second World War, which net millions more Jews and others in the process. As the German Army makes huge advances SS Einsatzgruppen follow as Special Extermination Squads and begin to conduct the mass murder of Jews behind the front lines in seized lands. Meanwhile in other parts of the 'Occupied Territories' more Ghettos come into existence in places such as Minsk, Belarus; Riga, Latvia; and Vilna, Lithuania. The 'Lebensraum'(Living Room) being created by the invasion of Russia was a key part of Adolf Hitler's overall plan of world domination, he envisioned a '1000 Year Reich', luckily for the world this invasion which he implemented would lead to that same Reich (meaning Realm, Kingdom or Empire or in this case realistically signifying a Regime) lasting less than 1500 days after this undertaking and had led to its total destruction by 8th May 1945.

**Mid 1941** – Kommandant Höss is summoned to Berlin by Himmler who tells him "The Führer has ordered the Final Solution of the Jewish Question. We, the SS, have to carry out this order… I have therefore chosen Auschwitz for this purpose." This demonstrated that if you want to see what Hitler was thinking, see what Himmler was doing and ordering, as it was all done with Hitler's permission!

**29-30th June 1941** – Romanian troops carry out a pogrom against Jews in Jassy, Romania, murdering 10,000, pogroms like it would follow in this and other countries allied to or conquered by the Nazis.

**31st July 1941** – Göring instructs Heydrich to prepare for the 'Final Solution.'

**3rd September 1941** – The first test use of Zyklon-B gas at Auschwitz.

**29th-30th September 1941** – 33,771 Jews executed at Babi Yar near Kiev in the Ukraine by SS, SD and Ukrainian Auxiliary Police, as in many occupied territories other nationalities aided the Nazis in carrying out mass liquidations such as these in the years that followed.

**December 1941** – Japanese attack the United States at Pearl Harbour (7th), followed by the U.S and Great Britain declaring war on Japan (8th). Hitler and Germany declare war on the U.S (11th), and America retaliates by declaring war on Germany (11th).

## 1942

**20th January 1942** – High ranking SS and SD meet at the Wannsee Conference near Berlin, chaired by RSHA leader Reinhard Heydrich to coordinate the "Final Solution" to what they deemed 'The Jewish Problem.'

**February-March 1942** – Regular Killings of Jews using Zyklon-B gas begin at Auschwitz-Birkenau.

**1942** – Himmler orders Einsatz Reinhard - Operation Reinhard, forced mass deportations of approximately 2 million Jews from Poland to Extermination Camps. It ran from Autumn 1941 until Autumn 1943, seriously gaining momentum throughout 1942 as the 'Final Solution' rapidly speeds up and expands. Jews from many other occupied countries in Europe such as Belgium, Holland, France, Croatia, Slovakia, Germany and Scandinavian Jews from Norway are also arriving and being disposed of en masse at various camps. Meanwhile aiding this is the fact that in 1942 the Third Reich is militarily at the height of its territorial and global conquests, with more Jews and others who it considers sub-human now under its control. Also the Nazis construct six 'Extermination Camps' made for the almost immediate mass murder of victims upon arrival, all of these were in Poland: Chelmno, Belzec, Sobibor, Treblinka, Auschwitz and Majdanek. (Auschwitz and Majdanek were both concentration and extermination camps.) In other infamous 'Concentration Camps' such as Bergen-Belsen, Buchenwald, Dachau, Sachsenhausen, inmates were shot, starved and worked to death and/or died of disease during the time they operated.

**27th May 1942** – Operation Anthropoid, an assassination attempt on Chief of the Secret Services (RSHA) Reinhard Heydrich, AKA 'The Hangman' takes place in Prague, a combined operation between the British SOE – Special Operations Executive and the Czech Resistance movement. Heydrich one of the highest ranking and most feared of Hitler's henchmen dies of his wounds on 4th June 1942, in retaliation the Nazis executed around 5000 civilians in the Czech villages of Lidice and Lezaky.

**5th June 1942** – SS report 97,000 persons have been "processed" in mobile gas vans. Many more would die this way before the permanent Death Camps with fully operational gas chambers were in wholesale use.

**30th June and 2nd July 1942** – The New York Times via the London Daily Telegraph reports that over 1,000,000 Jews have already been killed by the Nazis.

**Mid 1942** – After receiving information from a German industrialist regarding the Nazi plan to exterminate the Jews, Swiss representatives of the Jewish Congress pass the information on to both London and Washington, no significant action of any kind is taken in response. On the battle fronts, at sea the Nazi U-Boats are sinking more ships than ever, on land the German Armed forces are sweeping forward in both North Africa with the Afrika Korps taking Tobruk and moving towards Cairo, and in Southern Russia German Army Group South has taken Sevastopol and the Crimean Peninsula and is heading for the oil fields of the Caucasus, should these two arms of a potential giant pincer be able to meet, taking the oil fields of the Middle East along the way then the outcome of the war could be quite different, this is covered in much more detail in the '1942 History On A Knife Edge' essay later in this book. It also could have meant a prolonged war which would have been even more catastrophic for those caught up in 'The Final Solution', leading in the long term to many more victims!

**9th September 1942** – The decision is made to exhume and cremate 107,000 bodies at Auschwitz to prevent fouling of ground water. These were the twofold realities at that time, whilst horrific occurrences such as these were unfolding within the camps ongoing in-action from the allied powers continued outside. Coincidently it was around this point when the Nazi empire was at its height and reaching its greatest extent in terms of land conquered, territories occupied and peoples' it rules with an iron fist and extreme cruelty.

**29th October 1942** – A public meeting at the Royal Albert Hall in London presided over by the Archbishop of Canterbury and with international political figures in attendance registers outrage over the Holocaust.

**17th December 1942** – British Foreign Secretary Anthony Eden tells the British House of Commons that the Nazis are "now carrying into effect Hitler's oft repeated intention to exterminate the Jewish people of Europe." The U.S declares those crimes will be avenged. It is now no secret what is happening, but the true extent of it will not be known until the end of the war when the complete network of camps and their horror has been fully uncovered over 2 years later.

**December 1942** – Exterminations cease at Belzec after an estimated 600,000 Jews had been murdered up until that point, then the camp is then dismantled, ploughed over and planted.

# 1943

**29th January 1943** – Nazis order all Gypsies arrested and sent to Extermination camps.

**2nd February 1943** – The encircled German 6th Army Surrenders to the Russians at Stalingrad, with 91,000 Axis prisoners being taken, signalling a major military reversal which is a sign of things to come for the Axis powers.

**27th February 1943** – Jews working in the Berlin armaments industry are sent to Auschwitz, proving once again no one no matter where they are or what they do are safe from the Nazis.

**March 1943** – The start of deportation of Jews from Greece to Auschwitz, lasting until August.

**14th March 1943** – The Krakow Ghetto is liquidated; more and more ghettos will follow as the war grinds on and the tide turns with Germany being pushed back on the Eastern Front.

**19th-30th April 1943** – The Bermuda Conference takes place as U.S and British representatives discuss the problem of refugees from Nazi-occupied territories, and despite now knowing of the mass murder taking place, once again as with the Evian conference of July 1938 it results in inaction regarding the plight of those being slaughtered by the Nazis.

**19th April-16th May 1943** – Warsaw Ghetto Uprising. Jewish resistance fighters hold out against the Nazis for 28 days, longer than many European countries had been able to withstand Nazi onslaughts.

**13th May 1943** – All Axis forces in North Africa surrender, and Rommel's Afrika Korps is no more, eventually approximately 250,000 German and Italian troops are taken prisoner, many more than at Stalingrad! Another truly disastrous military defeat for Hitler and Nazi Germany in a relatively short space of time, the tide had certainly turned for the Axis! Yet elsewhere the mass killing in the Holocaust continues apace!

**19th May 1943** – Nazis declare Berlin 'Judenfrei' (cleansed of Jews).

**11th June 1943** – Himmler orders the liquidation of all Jewish ghettos in occupied Poland. Other ghettos are also liquidated such as Vilna, Minsk, Riga, those not killed in or near the ghettos are shipped out to extermination Camps such as Chelmno where eventually approximately 300,000 are murdered, the ever-constant numbers of victims continues to beggar belief!

**5th July -23rd August 1943** – Operation Citadel – The Battle of Kursk, German Summer offensive in the East leads to the biggest tank battle in history, eventually Nazi forces in Army Group Centre would lose this attempted giant pincer movement incurring massive losses and from there on would never regain the military and strategic initiative on the Eastern Front. Elsewhere, also in July 1943 British and American forces would successfully invade and take Sicily in Operation Husky, meaning the allies had their first foothold in Europe! This would lead to the further allied invasions on mainland Italy in September, Operation Avalanche at Salerno and Operation Baytown at Calabria.

**2nd August 1943** – Two hundred Jews escape from Treblinka Extermination Camp during a revolt. Nazis hunt them down one by one. Later that month liquidations cease at Treblinka where there were an estimated 870,000 people murdered.

**4th October 1943** – Himmler talks openly about the Final Solution to SS Group Leaders in Posen, occupied Poland. An excerpt of which is included in this Holocaust chapter.

**14th October 1943** – Massive escape of 300 prisoners from Sobibor extermination camp, only 50 survive, after 250,000 deaths all killing at Sobibor ceases, in the following weeks all traces of the Death camp are removed and trees planted over it to hide the Nazi crimes.

**3rd November 1943** – Operation 'Harvest Festival' or Aktion 'Erntefest' launched by SS and Police units in response to uprisings and escapes in places like Warsaw, Treblinka and Sobibor. In 2 days approximately 42,000 Jews were shot and put into mass graves in the Lublin District of Poland. The killings at Majdanek on Nov 3rd was the largest single-day, single location massacre during the Holocaust with 18,000 people being murdered by execution squads with continuous music being played loudly to cover the sounds of their crimes.

**4th November 1943** – Quote from the virulently Anti-Semitic Nazi newspaper Der Stürmer that said in part: "It is actually true that the Jews have, so to speak, disappeared from Europe...."

**11th November 1943** – Auschwitz Kommandant Rudolf Höss (also spelt Hoess) is promoted to Chief Inspector of concentration camps. His camp at Oswiecim (Auschwitz) near Krakow, Poland was the largest concentration and extermination camp built. It is estimated that a staggering 1.1 million people were murdered there. Auschwitz consisted of Auschwitz I (the original Concentration Camp), Auschwitz II– Birkenau (a combined Concentration /Extermination Camp), Auschwitz III–Monowitz (a labour camp to staff of the IG Farben factory), and 45 satellite camps, 15.44 square miles of Nazi torment, killing and hell. Amongst its many products IG Farben chemical and pharmaceutical company first discovered the nerve agent Sarin and one of its subsidiaries supplied the poison gas Zyklon B that killed over one million people in gas chambers during the Holocaust. Certain names would remain strongly associated with Auschwitz such as Adolf Eichmann Chief Logistics Coordinator of the final solution and Doctor Joseph Mengele known as the 'Angel of Death' and the 'White Angel' due to the white Doctors coat he wore when undertaking his ghastly work, he selected prisoners for execution in gas chambers and led horrific medical experiments on inmates.

## 1944

**3rd January 1944** – Russian troops reach the former Polish-Soviet border.

**March-July 1944** – Nazis occupy Hungry on 19th March (Jewish population 725,000). Eichmann arrives with Gestapo 'Special Section Commandos' to organise the deportation and killing of as many Jews as possible in the shortest time possible. By May Rudolf Höss and Adolf Eichmann return to Auschwitz to personally oversee the killings. Something also witnessed by Mayer Hersh the Holocaust survivor featured in this chapter of the book. The first Hungarian Jews arrive in Auschwitz in May and from then until July over 425,000 are murdered in highly accelerated killing, Auschwitz-Birkenau with more Gas Chambers and Crematoria now in use records its highest ever daily number of liquidations at just over an incomprehensible 9000 Jews being gassed and cremated every 24 hours! Upon arrival at Auschwitz the selection process took place on the rail platforms, and within minutes families were separated and loved ones were torn apart there and then, never to see one another ever again. If deemed fit enough by SS 'Doktors' such as Joseph Mengele to be worked to death as slave labour they were sent to the right, if deemed for whatever reason not to be fit enough to be used as slave labour then they were sent to the left, the fate of most, that line led directly to the gas chambers where they were gassed, cremated and in most cases all traces of their very existence erased WITHIN ONE HOUR!!

**7th April 1944** – Two Jewish inmates escape from Auschwitz-Birkenau and make it safely to Czechoslovakia. One of them Rudolf Vrba submits a full report to the Papal Nuncio in Slovakia detailing the horrors of the extermination program being undertaken there, this is forwarded to the Vatican in mid-June. As with other similar reports previously submitted to the Allied powers virtually nothing was done in relation to it.

**6th June 1944** – D-Day – Deliverance Day; Operation Overlord, the allies land in Normandy, France opening up a new front, the Nazis are now fighting on 3 battle fronts against the allies in the West, East and the South, plus losing the war in the air above, the sea below and all zones in which it is engaged! Further signs of things to come for the Nazis as the net continues to close in on all sides.

**12th June 1944** – Alfred Rosenberg, Reich Minister for the Eastern Occupied Territories orders Operation Hay Action 'Heuaktion', the kidnapping of 40,000 Polish children aged 10-14 for slave labour in the Reich. The traumatic experience involved them being imprisoned at Auschwitz before transfer to Germany where they are ruthlessly put to work.

**22nd June 1944** – Operation Bagration - The Massive Red Army Summer Offensive destroys German Army Group Center eventually causing the loss of over 400,000 Nazi troops, and with big territorial gains the Russians move ever closer to the Concentration and Death Camps.

**23th June 1944** – A delegation of the ICRC – International Committee of the Red Cross visits Theresienstadt after the Nazis have carefully prepared and 'Beautified' the Camp for inspection in order to fool the delegation about the treatment of the Jews and others. This results in a favourable report which of course does not in any way reflect the true picture.

**20th July 1944** – Operation Valkyrie AKA 20 July Plot, an attempt to end the war and stop more killing on the front lines and in the concentration camps by assassinating Adolf Hitler and seizing power, undertaken by brave German Conspirators, many military, led by Colonel Claus von Stauffenberg unfortunately fails, leading to nearly 5000 Germans being executed and no mercy shown, proving yet again that no one was safe from the evil of Nazism, not even their own!

**24th July 1944** – Russian troops of the 8th Guards Army liberate the first Concentration Camp at Majdanek where over 360,000 had been murdered.

**4th August 1944** – Anne Frank and family are arrested by the Gestapo in Amsterdam and sent to Auschwitz. Later Anne and her sister Margot are sent to Bergen-Belsen where Anne dies of Typhus on the 15th March 1945. The story of and focus on the plight of this one little girl later comes to represent for many the tragedy of the millions killed in the Holocaust.

**17th-25th September 1944** – Operation Market-Garden, The Allied plan to shorten the war by a bold attempted push over bridges in Holland into Germany fails, leaving the British 1st Airborne Division decimated at Arnhem, this stalls but in the long run does not stop the Allies winning the war.

**7th October 1944** – A revolt by Sonderkommando (Jewish Slave Labourers) at Auschwitz-Birkenau results in complete destruction of Crematory IV.

**28th October 1944** – The last transport of Jews to be gassed arrives at Auschwitz from Theresienstadt, around 2000 in number.

**30th October 1944** – Last use of gas chambers at Auschwitz.

**October 1944** – Oskar Schindler saves 1200 Jews by moving them from Plaszow Labour Camp in Poland to the Brünnlitz Labour Camp in his hometown of Brünnlitz in Czechoslovakia. His story would later become famous and the subject of Steven Spielberg's film 'Schindler's List' in 1993.

**25th November 1944** – Himmler orders the destruction of the crematories at Auschwitz.

**16th December 1944** – Germans launch a massive surprise counter-attack through the Ardennes area of Belgium to try and cut the advancing Allied armies in two, it becomes known as 'The Battle of the Bulge' and is Hitler's last 'roll of the dice' major offensive, but by January 1945 it has failed.

## 1945

**Early 1945** – As Allied troops advance the Nazis conduct ruthless 'Death Marches' of Concentration Camp inmates over vast distances in sub-zero temperatures away from outlying areas, many die or are executed if unable to keep up along the way.

**27th January 1945** – Russian troops liberate Auschwitz the Extermination/Concentration Camp in Poland, site of over 1 million murders, there they uncover the full horrors of the biggest of the Nazi Camps, which are then revealed to the world.

**January-May 1945** – In late March British & U.S troops cross the Rhine: Operation Varsity/Plunder. In the East and the West the liberation of the camps continues, revealing the scale of the Camp system and extent of the Nazi machine of mass murder. Some more of the key dates and camps to follow.

**4th April 1945** – Ohrdruf (sub-camp to Buchenwald) near Gotha in central Germany is the first occupied Concentration Camp to be liberated by Allied forces in the West. General Eisenhower later visits the camp on the 12th April with Generals George S. Patton and Omar Bradly and later wrote – 'The things I saw beggar description. I made the visit deliberately, in order to be in a position to give first-hand evidence of these things if ever, in the future, there develops the tendency to charge these allegations merely to propaganda.'

**11th April 1945** – Buchenwald Concentration Camp judged second only to Auschwitz in the horrors it imposed upon its prisoners is liberated by the Americans, one of the inmates saved is Elie Wiesel, who would later go on to win the Nobel Peace Prize in 1986.

**15th April 1945** – Around 40,000 prisoners freed by the British Army at Bergen-Belsen Concentration Camp, one official account reported "Both inside and outside the huts was a carpet of dead bodies, human excreta, rags and filth." Amongst the liberators was Neville Foote who as one of the veterans featured in this book gave me a graphic first-hand testimony of his experiences at that horrific place which I have included in his story.

**16th April 1945** – Russians launch the 'Berlin Strategic Offensive Operation' incorporating 3 Soviet Armies.

**24th April 1945** – Berlin is encircled and flanked by the Russian Armies and the Battle of Berlin, the final part of the last Red Army offensive in Europe begins.

**29th April 1945** – U.S Army liberates Dachau, the first ever Concentration Camp which has been in continual operation since 1933.

**30th April 1945** – Ravensbrück Concentration Camp liberated, this camp housed nearly all female prisoners between 1939 and 1945 of which around 20,000-30,000 perished.

**30th April 1945** – Adolf Hitler commits suicide in his underground bunker in Berlin.

**2nd May 1945** – The Battle of Berlin concludes with Marshal Georgy Zukhov 's success, by the 2nd May 1945 the Russian flag flies over the German Reichstag building and the Nazi forces in Berlin have surrendered but at a very high cost with the Russians having lost around 80,000 and the Germans 50,000, again reflecting the staggering numbers of losses in every aspect of this war! In just over two years since the Battle of Stalingrad Stalin's Soviet armies have advanced over 1300 miles to reach Hitler's capital in order to destroy their arch enemy Nazi Germany. Along with the Allied forces advancing from the West and all uncovering the horrors of the Holocaust, a time of reckoning now rightly awaits the perpetrators of those heinous crimes!

**7th May 1945** – Initial Unconditional German surrender signed by General Alfred Jodl at Reims, France.

**8th May 1945** – Theresienstadt in Czechoslovakia is liberated by the Russians on V.E Day and is the last of the Nazi camps to be revealed to the world, one of the inmates is Mayer Hersh. In Berlin the final and definitive document of Unconditional surrender of all German forces is signed by Field Marshal Keitel.

**9th May 1945** – Hermann Göring captured by members of the U.S 7th Army in Bavaria. Known mainly for being Head of the German Air Force (Luftwaffe) and not generally associated with the Holocaust, but he was also named as Adolf Hitler's successor in 1939 and Reichsmarschall in 1940. It was with these powers he ordered Security Police Chief Reinhard Heydrich to organize and coordinate a 'Total Solution to the Jewish Question.' Tried and found guilty at the Nuremburg war trials for 'Crimes against Humanity' he commits suicide by taking cyanide two hours before his scheduled execution on the 16th October 1946.

**9th - 16th May 1945** – The Channel Islands are freed by Allied Liberation Force 135. Alderney having the only Concentration Camp on British soil called Sylt, a sub-camp of Neuengamme Concentration Camp in Hamburg. Here the 'Agents of the Holocaust' undertook murder showing the true ongoing intention of the Nazis had they successfully taken Great Britain!

**23rd May 1945** – SS-Reichsführer Himmler takes his own life by biting on a cyanide capsule whilst in British custody at the headquarters of the Second British Army in Lüneburg, Germany. Soon after the head of the organisation responsible for the death of millions is very fittingly buried in an unmarked grave near Lüneburg Heath so it doesn't become the place of a future martyr for Fascist Sympathisers.

**Post War**

**20th November 1945** – The Nuremberg International Military Tribunal begins. It will run from 1945 until 1949 with the main Nazi leadership being tried between 20th November 1945 until 1st October 1946 by a court consisting of judges from the allied powers of Great Britain, France, the Soviet Union and the United States of America. After these main trials the U.S held 12 additional trials of high-level officials that included a cross-section of the Nazi apparatus from Government, Military, Leading Industrialists, Medical Professionals to the SS and their Einsatzgruppen leaders. The trials were undertaken symbolically in the Bavarian city of Nuremberg as it was the spiritual capital of Nazism where the famous Nuremberg Rallies had been held and its race laws passed, having the trials there apart from the practicality of facilities was to bring accountability to the regime that had brought about so much death and destruction to the world and to metaphorically indicate the end of Hitler's Third Reich.

**16th October 1946** – The first execution of top Nazi leaders takes place, 10 in total, of which one, Hans Frank (former head of the Nazi General Government in Poland) repentantly states: "A thousand years will pass and the guilt of Germany will not be erased." Frank and the other high-ranking Nazis; Jodl, Ribbentrop, Keitel, Kaltenbrunner, Rosenberg, Frick, Streicher, Sauckel, Seyss-Inquart are all hanged.

**16th April 1947** – After a trial in Warsaw the former Auschwitz Kommandant Höess is hanged by Soviet authorities. Over 100 people including high officials from the ministry of justice and former prisoners are witnesses. The sentence was emblematically carried out next to the crematorium of the former Auschwitz I Concentration-Extermination Camp. This was the last public execution in Poland.

**18th July 1947** – Given a life sentence at Nuremburg Rudolf Hess, Deputy Führer 1933-1941, who signed into legislation the Anti-Semitic Nuremburg Laws of 1935 is taken to Spandau Prison, Berlin, as prisoner Number 7 he will symbolically remain there until his death by suicide on 17th August 1987 aged 93. The prison was then demolished to prevent it from becoming a Neo-Nazi shrine.

**Post Nuremburg Trails – 1949 Onwards** – At the end of the war many of the top perpetrators of the Holocaust escaped from Europe to havens mainly in South America through what were known as 'Ratlines' aided by alleged organisations such as ODESSA (Organisation of former SS members), and Die Spinne (The Spider) the latter run in part by Hitler's SS Commando Chief Otto Skorzeny. The hunting of escaped Nazis directly responsible for their part in The Final Solution and other war crimes continues in the decades that follow, organisations such as MOSAD (Israeli Secret Service) and many determined individuals such as Simon Wiesenthal sustained their hunt for the perpetrators of the Holocaust with a number of successes such as the capture of Adolf Eichmann in Argentina on the 11th May 1960. Eichmann a key figure in the implementation of The Final Solution was then symbolically put on trial from 11th April – 14th August 1961 in Jerusalem the Jewish capital of Israel where he was found guilty of crimes against the Jewish People, Crimes against Humanity and War Crimes, and on the 1st June 1962 was hanged at Ramla near Tel Aviv. In 1994 relatively big war criminals such as SS and Gestapo Commander Erich Priebke, then in his 90's were still being caught and successfully tried for their crimes, he died in 2013 aged 100 whilst serving life imprisonment under house arrest in Italy, rightly proving that no matter how much time has passed and regardless of their age those responsible for their horrific crimes against humanity must be punished, it is the least that can be done to honour the memory of their victims!

**23rd July 2020 – Frankfurt, Germany** – Much to their credit the German judicial system is still finding and bringing some of those who participated in and helped facilitate the Holocaust forward to face justice. A former SS guard at Stutthof Concentration Camp called Bruno Dey, aged 93 at his time of sentencing was convicted of 5232 counts of accessory to murder that occurred near the end of the war. He was handed a two-year suspended sentence, and was told by the judge when delivering the verdict, whose name is interestingly Anne Meier-Göring, "The concentration camp and the mass murder that took place inside was only able to take place with your help!" Germany's Central Office of State Justice for the Investigation of National Socialist Crimes, which examines historical records in search of further cases to bring to trial and searches for those still alive who participated in that genocide, says it is looking into a further 14 individuals over crimes they were a part of in the Concentration and Extermination Camps during the war years with the intention of bringing them to trial in the coming years.

**February 2021 – June 2022 – Neuruppin, Germany** – In February '21, prosecutors at a court held in that city charged Josef Schuetz with assisting directly in the murders of a staggering 3518 people! The accused was a former SS guard at Sachsenhausen Concentration Camp between January 1942 and February 1945. Whilst there he took part in the shooting of Soviet prisoners of war, and was also an accessory to murder of prisoners through the use of the lethal Zyklon B gas and the deaths of prisoners through maintaining life-threatening conditions in the camp! Cyrill Klement, a prosecutor in Neuruppin rightly said about the case 'It took a long time, which has not made things any easier because we are now dealing with such elderly defendants, but murder and accessory to murder have no statute of limitation.' Those very important sentiments were echoed by Alex Drecoll, director of the Brandenburg Memorials Foundation who said 'The charges are a late, but important sign that such crimes will be brought to justice.' **101-year-old Josef Schuetz has so far been the oldest person tried on Nazi-era charges, he was convicted to 5 years in prison on the 28th June 2022, for accessory to murder, again proving that heinous crimes such as these have no set time limitations when it comes to justice, and never should! *So beware those who have done such things since World War Two, are committing crimes against humanity now, or may choose to do so in the future!!**

This ongoing atonement for the huge collective sins of their wartime generation is a brave thing for modern Germans to still be doing, and something that many in the world don't seem to know is still happening! It is another ongoing legacy of the Second World War, which in this case is a very important one as these are parts of the last justice of the silent dead, they who do not have a voice of their own yet await these final historical reckonings on their behalf! It must also serve as a signal to modern Neo-Nazi and extreme Right-Wing organisations that their existence like those of their Nazi predecessors cannot and will not be tolerated in a modern world. One of the greatest lessons to be taken from World War 2 and history as a whole should be the need for greater tolerance between all in the world today if in the long term the human race is to have any real chance of peaceful co-existence and long-term survival! GBD.

Pictured here are two key figures mentioned in the timeline from opposite sides of the Holocaust Spectrum. On the right Adolf Eichmann, a chief instigator in the Final Solution, who was tasked with facilitating and managing the logistics involved in the mass deportation of Jews to Ghettos and Extermination Camps in Nazi occupied Eastern Europe. On the left a determined looking Simon Wiesenthal, survivor of Gross-Rosen, Mauthausen and other concentration Camps turned Nazi Hunter who dedicated his life after the war to capturing people such as and including Eichmann.

**Below - From War Hero and Reichsmarschall to War Criminal stripped of all rank and eventually Sentenced to death for amongst other things 'Crimes Against Humanity'** – This was the rise and fall, life and fate of Hermann Göring! The two pictures showing those contrasts, left in an official portrait from 6th January 1943, and right his Detention Report Card with Mugshots from 22nd June 1945 registering him at the Nuremburg War Trials and clearly showing his fall from grace as his Civil Occupation is listed merely as a 'Regular Army Officer' and his Prisoner Number 316 350013 also clearly evident on the board in front of him! He was heavily involved in the Holocaust where as one example he gave clear instructions to **Reinhard Heydrich** to implement the Final Solution, that order quoted in **'Insights Into Twisted Minds Of The Nazi Perpetrators'**.

*"The world will not be destroyed by those who do evil, but by those who watch them without doing anything."* – Albert Einstein.

> BERLIN, DEN 1. Sept. 1939.
>
> ADOLF HITLER
>
> Reichsleiter B o u h l e r und
> Dr. med. B r a n d t
>
> sind unter Verantwortung beauftragt, die Befug-
> nisse namentlich zu bestimmender Ärzte so zu er-
> weitern, dass nach menschlichem Ermessen unheilbar
> Kranken bei kritischster Beurteilung ihres Krank-
> heitszustandes der Gnadentod gewährt werden kann.
>
> [signature: A. Hitler]
>
> [handwritten note: Von Bouhler mir übergeben am 27.8.40 — Dr. Gürtner]

It was very rare indeed to see Adolf Hitler's personal signature on any document in relation to the Holocaust. This example which gives another insight into 'The minds of Monsters' is regarding him giving permission to grant euthanasia to what were termed incurably sick patients, a term that was very loosely applied to many with mental and physical conditions who became victims of the 'Aktion T4' Program, which is briefly outlined within the 'Persecution Timeline' in this chapter.

Written on Adolf Hitler's personal stationery, this carefully worded edict issued on 1st September 1939, the day Nazi Germany invaded Poland triggering the Second World War, in English reads:

"Reich Leader Bouhler and Dr. Brandt are entrusted with the responsibility of extending the authority of physicians, to be designated by name, so that patients who, after a most critical diagnosis, on the basis of human judgment [*menschlichem Ermessen*], are considered incurable, can be granted mercy death [*Gnadentod*]. -- A. Hitler"

The translated comment: "given to me by Bouhler on 27.8. [August] [19]40; Dr. Gürtner"

Franz Gürtner was Minister for Justice (Reichsjustizminister) from 1932 to his death in 1941. Philipp Bouhler was an SS-Obergruppenführer and leader of Hitler's Chancellery (Kanzlei des Führers; KdF).

# NUMBER OF DEATHS IN THE 'BIGGER HOLOCAUST'

The following statistics have come from and are credited to the United States Holocaust Memorial Museum in Washington D.C and released by them via their USHMM website into the public domain. Their extensive ongoing research into the Holocaust provides what are widely acknowledged to be the most comprehensive and up to date figures available on this particular part of World War Two history at time of writing. All numbers are approximate based on the documentary evidence available and as new information is discovered and more records come to light these statistics may well change, more than likely continuing to increase as has been the case over the years thus far. The figures shown here include all those killed by various terrible means such as mass shootings and those that died directly in Labour, Concentration and Extermination Camps who were from every kind of background and met their sad fate due to wide-ranging circumstances and reasons, this includes Jewish, Non-Jewish, Prisoners of War, those of all nationalities in lands invaded and occupied by the Germans and their allies and that were essentially caught up in the overall Nazi program of extermination, all of whom were victims and therefore are counted here as deaths in the 'Bigger Holocaust' and as such have been incorporated into these statistics in order that they are all rightly and equally acknowledged and remembered amongst those who suffered as a result of the misguided ideology of Nazism.

Staggeringly this combined number reaches more than 17 million victims of Nazi Atrocities and Genocide!! 6 million of these were Jews, approximately two-thirds of all Jews living in Europe at that time, of which over 1 million were children. When people think of the word Holocaust they associate it mainly if not completely with the Jewish victims, but as these figures demonstrate it was not only limited to them hence the term used here of the 'Bigger Holocaust', because these were truly 'Crimes Against Humanity' undertaken on a vast scale. This was a true indication that a very different kind of war was being waged in the Second World War, one that included but was not limited to or solely fought along military lines but also being undertaken by some along ideological and racial lines, where total obliteration of huge parts of civilian populations was seen as a component of the overall strategies that were being implemented in different ways, such as the Holocaust, the War of Annihilation against the Soviet Union and Nazi Security Warfare (Anti-partisan/Guerrilla operations that led to many atrocities). These mind-numbing revised and estimated figures in relation to this part of the conflict are as follows:

- 6 Million Jews.
- 5.7 Million Soviet Civilians (an additional 1.3 Soviet Jewish civilians are included in the 6 million figure for Jews).
- 3 Million Soviet Prisoners of War (including about 50,000 Jewish soldiers).
- 1.9 Million Polish Civilians (non-Jewish).
- 312,000 Serb Civilians.
- 250,000 or more people with disabilities.
- 196,000 to 220,000 Roma Gypsies.
- 1,900 Jehovah's Witnesses.
- At least 70,000 Repeat Criminal Offenders and 'Associals' including Homosexuals.
- An undetermined number of German political opponents and activists.

**Total = Over 17 Million!**

A rare picture of the 'selection' process in action from the 'Auschwitz Album' found at Mittelbau-Dora Concentration Camp in 1945. It shows Hungarian Jews during the last period of Hyper-Intense killing in May-July 1944 where over 400,000 deportees arrived and most were gassed almost immediately. In the spring of 1944 just prior to their arrival a new extended railway line and ramp were completed directly inside Auschwitz II-Birkenau to bring the condemned almost directly off the train and into the Gas Chambers after the 'Selection' shown here. In the background is the infamous entrance the so-called 'Gate of Death' at Auschwitz-Birkenau II, most people who passed through there were never seen again. Note; all ages are present in this transport, sadly few would be spared!

Auschwitz, the biggest camp of them all, a present-day view from above at the main 'Gate of Death' entrance, this gives some idea of how vast this Extermination/Concentration camp really is, and here we only see part of it! An unnerving insight into the mind-boggling industrial scale of killing that took place here! And this being one of many camps that ran throughout Nazi Occupied Europe during the war.

# INSIGHTS INTO TWISTED MINDS OF THE NAZI PERPETRATORS

What kind of people can organise and undertake genocide on such a huge scale we might ask? How do they rationalize and validate such actions? What mind-set was it that allowed those who were signing the orders from behind desks far away from the crimes they were initiating to do so with a convenient detachment from their wrongdoings, and others who saw first-hand what they were facilitating to continue with it whilst remaining indifferent to the suffering they caused and witnessed? In an attempt to try and understand these things, even in a limited way, I searched for quotes from some of the top perpetrators of the Holocaust in order to gain an insight into their twisted ways of thinking, racial theories and anti-Semitic ideologies which led to the death of millions of innocent victims. Here is a cross-section of those pre to post war quotes from some of the key Nazis responsible for the 'Final Solution'. Starting with the leader of the Third Reich Adolf Hitler whose hate driven ideologies shaped and directed what eventually became the Holocaust, the quote shown here was made in the early years of his political career and summarises in one short yet unequivocal sentence his entire future plan for the whole Jewish race. That way of thinking and lack of regard for human life is also reflected in the words of Reichsmarschall Hermann Göring, Reinhard Heydrich head of the SD, Heinrich Himmler head of the SS, Chief SS Logistics Co-ordinator Adolf Eichmann, between them they reveal the 'Minds of Monsters' as they proclaimed prophetically these frightening things which to a large degree came to pass:

"Once I am in power, my first and foremost task will be the annihilation of the Jews"

Adolf Hitler 1922, Munich, Bavaria, Germany.

**I hereby charge you to carry out preparations as regards organizational, financial, and material matters for a total solution (*Gesamtlösung*) of the Jewish question in all the territories of Europe under German occupation. Where the competency of other central organizations touches on this matter, these organizations are to collaborate. I charge you further to submit to me as soon as possible a general plan of the administrative material and financial measures necessary for carrying out the desired final solution (Endlösung) of the Jewish question.**

Hermann Göring in a Letter sending a direct order to Reinhard Heydrich, 31 July 1941. This communication making him undoubtedly complicate in the Holocaust at the highest level.

**"To take the place of emigration, and with the prior approval of the Führer, the evacuation of the Jews to the East has become another possible solution. Although both courses of action (emigration and evacuation) must, of course, be considered as nothing more than temporary expedients, they do help to provide practical experience which should be of great importance in the view of the coming Endlösung (Final Solution) of the Jewish question."**

Statement by Reinhard Heydrich on the 20th January 1942 at the Wannsee Conference, Berlin, where the course of action for the deadliest part of the 'Final Solution' was decided upon. Interestingly, if there has ever been any doubt, this statement directly confirms the order to implement this has come with 'approval' from the Führer himself, (who intriguingly signed hardly any documents or written orders relating directly to the final solution but openly verbalised his intent to destroy the Jews and others who didn't fit Nazi racial profiling), this lays the biggest responsibility for the eventual mass murder of millions squarely at the feet of Adolf Hitler as it was obviously all part of his final plan for a New World Order!

**"We expect of the SS super human acts of inhumanity, it is the will of the Führer!"**

A quote from Himmler in relation to the murderous and barbaric acts undertaken by his SS during the holocaust and war in the East that shows the utterly ruthless mindset adopted to undertake these tasks.

"Whether the other races live in comfort or perish of hunger interests me only in so far as we need them as slaves for our culture; apart from that it does not interest me. Whether or not 10,000 Russian women collapse from exhaustion while digging a tank ditch interests me only in so far as the tank ditch is completed for Germany."

Heinrich Himmler's thoughts regarding all slave labour in a speech to SS Leaders, October 1943 in Posen, occupied Poland, where he also reminded them of their duty according to their ideological SS oath; 'Meine Ehre heisst Treue' meaning 'My Honour is Loyalty.'

"The only good enemy of the Reich is a dead one! In particular I have to add, when I received an order, I always carried out this order with the executioner, and I am proud to say of that to this day...."

A remorseless post-war quote from Adolf Eichmann, regarding the Holocaust and the zeal with which he carried out his terrible duties, these words came from the 'Argentina Audiotapes' of 1957, showing there was still no repentance from one of the biggest instigators of mass murder in history. These original tapes are now stored in the State Archives of Germany.

"To sum it all up, I must say I regret nothing!"

Words Eichmann defiantly and chillingly uttered whilst awaiting trial in Israel, quoted by LIFE Magazine, 5th December 1960. It was unrepentant comments such as these that led to his well-deserved death sentence!

The top perpetrators of the holocaust each quoted earlier, L-R: The Führer Adolf Hitler, Reichsführer SS Heinrich Himmler and Reinhard Heydrich Chief of the SD (far right), on their hands the blood of millions! Adolf Eichmann and Hermann Göring pictures can be found at the end of the 'Persecution Timeline.'

---

**For God will bring every deed into judgement, including every secret thing, whether good or evil. Ecclesiastes 12:14**

---

## AN ARTISTIC DEPICTION OF NAZI PERSECUTION FROM JEWISH PAINTER ARTHUR SZYK - 1942

This very strong and hard-hitting painting from Polish-Jewish artist Arthur Szyk shows the image of Adolf Hitler, which he aptly entitled 'Anti-Christ', with skulls reflected in his eyes and the words "Vae Victis" - Latin for "woe to the vanquished (ones)" in his black hair. The detailed watercolor is filled with figures and war imagery: uniformed Nazi soldiers, men in manacles, a field of skulls, and a skeleton with a banner with a line from a National Socialist song: "heute gehört uns Deutschland / morgen die ganze Welt" (today Germany is ours, tomorrow the whole world). Its generic message depicting that with Nazism comes only violence and death, on the battlefield, in occupied lands and in the death camps! The painter being both Polish and Jewish was fully aware of the many different ways in which Hitler and the Nazis had brought all of this to bare, and this work is also a very good example in the form of a graphic representation that again serves to show 'Insights into Twisted Minds of the Nazi Perpetrators'. It was an image I found to be quite chilling but for all the reasons stated in the description above I decided to include it here as a relative part of the book and because quite fittingly it is the work of a Jewish artist undertaken during World War Two.

# HOLOCAUST 'PULSE OF DEATH' AUGUST TO OCTOBER 1942

In a comprehensive study undertaken by Mathematician Professor Lewi Stone of Tel-Aviv University in Israel and featured in the January 2019 AAAS (American Association for the Advancement of Science) publication 'Science Advances' of which the main information in this part is credited, he claims that approximately one third of all Jews murdered in the Holocaust, 1.47 million of around 6 million Jews overall, were exterminated in roughly 100 days of 'Hyper-Intense' killing which took place between August to October 1942 at a time (which is covered in much more detail later in the book) when Nazi Germany was at the zenith of its powers and territorial conquests in World War Two. This (first) 'Pulse of Death' period as Mr Stone called it in his report brought a spike in the killing which was far worse than previously believed. It came after Adolf Hitler ordered the Death Camps to step up operations, which they did significantly, with the chilling results being outlined here, and which I have included in an effort to shed some new light and incorporate newly researched content and information in to my book on a subject which generically is already historically well documented.

It is now estimated according to Mr Stone's research that around a mind-boggling 15,000 people a day were eliminated by the Nazis around this period, this almost incomprehensible figure is based on the available data that he was able to find and study from surviving German Reichsbahn train records mainly in relation to what was codenamed Operation Reinhard, which showed that the very highly coordinated executions using train transports and gas chambers killed ten times more people than is commonly believed during that period! He stated that: 'The Reichsbahn railway network was a critical component of the Nazi's blueprint for genocide and destruction, records of train schedules and movements, fragmentary as they are, have since become an important source of data used to estimate the spatial and temporal patterns of victims who were shuttled to the death camps. The Nazis' extremely efficient extermination machine presumably could have continued to run smoothly for many more months at the kill rates identified here had there been a continuous supply of victims in Nazi Occupied Poland.'

Indeed without the Reichsbahn Hitler could not have undertaken the mass movement of people for any of his aims whether they were for military use, territorial expansion or genocide, but additionally the frightening and sickening fact that made these figures possible is that in Death Camps such as Auschwitz-Birkenau, Sobibor, Belzec, Chelmno, Majdanek and Treblinka the SS had managed to perfect a horrifically efficient system of extermination to such an extent that from arrival, to the stripping of all possessions and clothing, gassing and cremation, hundreds, sometimes thousands of Jews from one transport entered these camps as human beings and in approximately 60 minutes their very existence was erased as thousands of communities and hundreds of thousands of individuals were completely obliterated! Incomprehensively at the height of its sickening efficiency during this time Auschwitz for example was liquidating up to 4500 victims a day! This number would almost double in that particular camp in later years around the time of the second hyper-intense killing that followed in May-July 1944 with the extermination of the majority of Hungarian Jews.

As outlined here these mass murders were being perpetrated on an almost unbelievable and industrial scale, hard for any sane, decent and normal human being to comprehend, sadly the killing was so vast that it is mainly represented by numbers and that is when people can easily become detached from the horror of what happened, it is ironic that this is epitomised in the words of Joseph Stalin who himself was responsible for the death millions, when he said *"A single death is a tragedy; a million deaths is a statistic."*

**But on a human level if the stories of individuals are when and where possible captured, written and documented, as in this book, then as a result continually read or re-told, hopefully all those people and their suffering might never be forgotten, and also those who denied it ever took place will be unequivocally reminded that it most definitely did!**

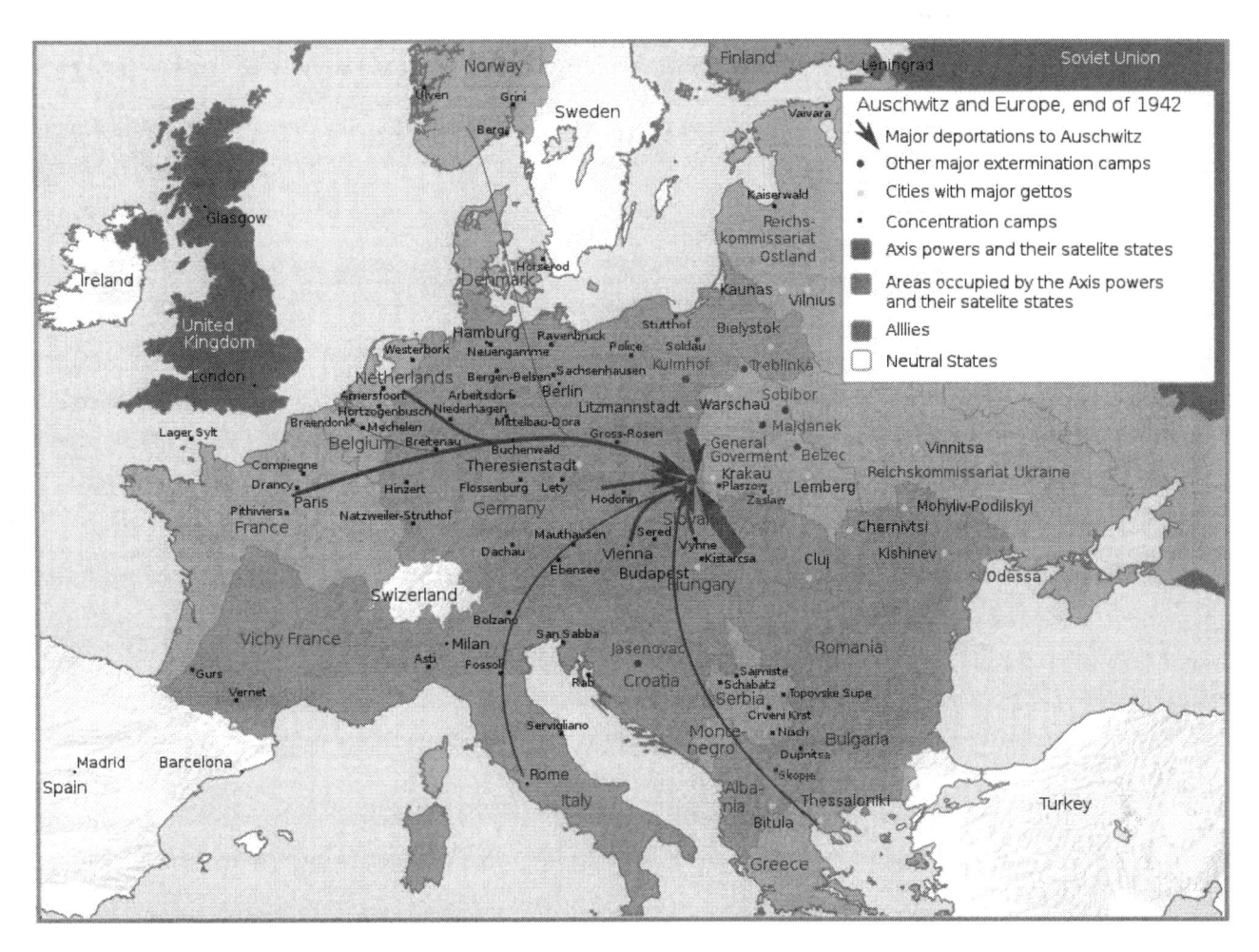

A map showing major deportations to the largest Concentration/Death Camp Auschwitz during the first 'Pulse of Death' period, the greatest movement of people being from Poland are indicated by the thickest arrows. Other main Death Camps, Concentration Camps and Ghettos already in operation are also shown here, at a time when the extent of the Nazi Empire was at its greatest.

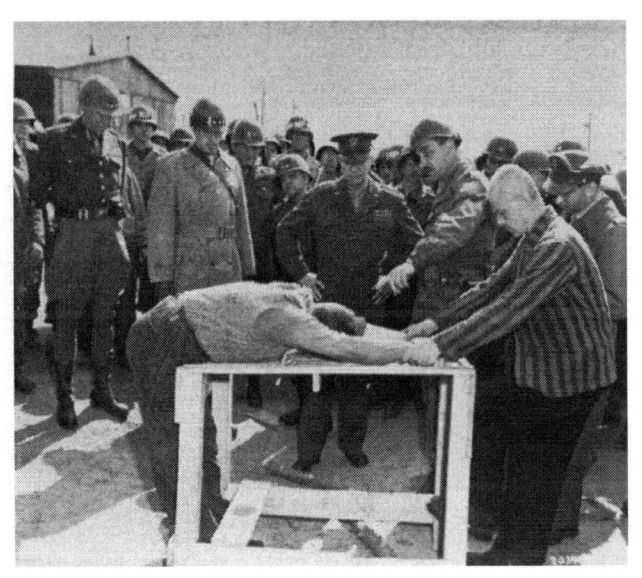

Survivors of Ohrdruf Concentration Camp at Gotha, Germany, a subcamp of Buchenwald, demonstrating torture methods used in the camp by the Nazis, to General Dwight Eisenhower (Centre), General Omar Bradley (Second from the left), and General George S. Patton (Left). Jules Grad (Far Right), 'Stars and Stripes' pool correspondent is taking notes. The Moustached soldier who is pointing at the demonstrated torture victim is Alois J. Liethen of Appleton, WI, (Wisconsin) who served as the interpreter for the tour of Ohrdruf. The things the Generals saw would stay with them for the rest of their lives! It also led to 'Ike' becoming determined that the world should know and see these terrible things in order to remember what the Nazis did to countless victims, the message being; if the world didn't see it would potentially not learn, and if it didn't learn then it could possibly repeat these horrors in future years and future wars!

*"The world must know what happened, and never forget."* – **General Eisenhower, whilst visiting liberated Nazi Death Camps, 1945.**

# SCHINDLERS LIST – MAKING THE CONSCIOUS CONNECTION

As part of the ongoing continuity in this holocaust chapter of the book, and following on from the last piece 'Pulse of Death' is this relative element, which I wrote for inclusion over the U.K National Holocaust Remembrance Weekend in January. It is written with the duality of understanding and making the conscious Human connection with what happened in the holocaust, and to acknowledge that these as mentioned earlier were not just numbers, they were real people who had families and were themselves parts of families; Mothers, Fathers, Sons, Daughters, Brothers, Sisters, Aunties, Uncles, Nephews, Nieces, Cousins and dear friends who were lost forever, they were loved and mourned by many and still are! Also in this chapter there is a bit about my own personal story and reflections in relation to this film and subject, which due to the nature of where I was at the time made for very powerful experiences in their own right. I write this piece not with any political or religious affiliation but to convey the very important feelings and message that the systematic murder of any human beings in cold blood regardless of who they are is simply categorically wrong and abhorrent, and leaves a huge nasty stain on our human history!

Steven Spielberg in his 1993 film 'Schindler's List' very cleverly brought it home to anyone watching it that these really were people not numbers, when in his mainly black and white film he gave the character of a beautiful and very young girl a bright red coloured coat so that she distinctly stood out. This made the conscious connection and some form of attachment between the viewer to an individual in the film, very discernible whilst making her way through all the chaos, people and killing that is going on around her in a Ghetto, and you naturally hope she will survive it all somehow! Later the body of the young girl is seen in her red coloured coat on a wagon stacked with many other bodies in black and white, that striking moment brought home to most, hopefully all, that this was a real human being that had been murdered, and like so many others, a child!

By making it one person, not one million, enabled the human brain to be able to emotionally comprehend what was going on in a more personalised way and help to process it more realistically!

I saw that film for the first time during my travels in the Middle East soon after it was released, in a public cinema in Jerusalem, capital of the modern Jewish state, as you would expect the impact was massive, there was only silence throughout the entire film and for some time after, and when the music from the film score had finished no one moved and this complete quietness and stillness was only broken by the sound of an ever-increasing amount of people openly crying!! I will never forget it, in an audience, predominantly Jewish as you would expect, but with a lot of people from other countries present, such as myself from Britain and my then girlfriend Rikke Rasmussen from Denmark there was not a dry eye in the house, ours included, the impact and magnitude of the that terrible history was of course made far greater by where we were when we watched it and by the very high probability that many in the audience had relatives who perished in that travesty.

In the days that followed we made it an absolute mission to find the grave of Oscar Schindler, who as we eventually discovered was buried in the Roman Catholic Franciscan Cemetery on Mount Zion in Jerusalem. We went there as the survivors their children and grand-children did at the end of the film and put stones on his grave in the traditional way as a mark of respect to this very brave man, something that was again a very moving and real moment of connection with the story and the history in quite a poignant way. When I went to Krakow in Poland in February 2023 it was a very heart-rending trip, where I visited Auschwitz and also the Oskar Schindler Factory Museum, both those places brought things full-circle for me regarding the Shoah, interviewing the survivor Mayer Hersh and all the Schindler related things mentioned above, and so it seems fitting to add this quote from the man himself, which shows the compassion which drove him to help others:

**'Life makes sense as long as you save people'. (From the Factory Museum in Krakow). Oskar Schindler.**

**The dedication on his grave in Jerusalem, shown here, reads; Oskar Schindler 28.04.1908 – 9.10.1974 Followed in Hebrew by 'Righteous Among the Nations' and then in German with 'The Unforgettable Lifesaver of 1200 Persecuted Jews'.**

Schindler was a successful businessman, opportunist, war profiteer, member of the Nazi Party turned great humanitarian and personal rescuer of those workers under his care after realising the potential fate that awaited them. At the end of the war he was given a ring made by some of those who he helped save, (depicted in the film) on it were inscribed some very touching words from the Torah which said: **'He who saves one life saves the world entire.'** One lengthier interpretation of those words that I had passed on to me whilst in the Holyland was that this means: 'From the one life saved many more can or will come through the generations of their family that will follow, and as a result of that the continuity of those or any people helped and the world itself will be assured and thus saved!' Powerful words and real food for thought!

On the 8th May 1962 Schindler, **pictured left**, was present when a carob tree was planted in his honour on the 'Avenue of the Righteous' at Yad Vashem in Jerusalem and on the 24th June 1993 he and his wife Emilie were named 'Righteous Among the Nations', an award bestowed by the State of Israel on non-Jews who were actively involved in the rescue of Jews during the Holocaust.

Returning to our part of the story we decided to finish that huge Holocaust related week with something that seemed very much in keeping with everything when we visited The World Holocaust Remembrance Centre called 'Yad Vashem' (literally meaning 'A Monument and a Name'). This massive 44.5-acre complex is Israel's official memorial to the victims of the holocaust that is located in Jerusalem, which included the haunting 'Children's Memorial' where the faces of many of the 1.5 million children murdered by the Nazis appear, with their names and where they were killed being whispered in the background! Despite being very heavy going to do all these things in the same week we managed it and after taking days to properly absorb everything we were of course glad we did it all, and as non-Jews it was still a form of pilgrimage and it increased our understanding of this very traumatic yet very significant part of our world history.

As mentioned earlier the story of the little girl in the red coat brings to life in more vivid terms the plight of one person amongst the millions who suffered at the hands of the Nazis, because of this it is for me in many ways similar to the story of Mayer Hersh, again one amongst millions who suffered in the Holocaust but in this case one who somehow against all the odds managed to survive it.

Of all the numbers quoted in the many books written about the tragedy of the Holocaust (and those approximate numbers quoted in this book), here is one person who brought this history to life by sharing it with me, and for this I will always be very grateful, thank you Mayer, now may you rest in eternal peace, a peace after all you have been through that you truly deserve and I sincerely hope that by putting your story here in my book, as promised, that I can help in some way keep alive your historical account and your mission to preserve the memory of those who were lost. Amen. GBD.

# PAST TO PRESENT DAY – DEALING WITH THE AFTERMATH OF THE HOLOCAUST

I believe it was very important to capture the story of a survivor of the Holocaust, as this is an individual's first-hand testament to that tragic history. But I also thought it would be a very interesting and significant thing to try and capture in some way a different modern historical perspective about the on-going psychological effect which the Holocaust has had on the Jewish people, and how they have been processing such an enormous catastrophe ever since.

At the time of writing this part of the book I was very lucky to be living close to a big local Jewish community in North Manchester, the second largest in the UK, and as a result had a unique opportunity to have access to many people I could potentially have conversations with and gain varied and valuable opinions and views from regarding this subject matter. This ranged from Orthodox Rabbis to other more Liberal and less Religious Jewish people in their community. As a result of this I was able to ascertain some extremely interesting perspectives and very thought-provoking insights into the mindset of those who were as a race of people most directly affected by the Holocaust, I feel the contributions from these mini-interviews which I have collated here in relation to this huge part of WW2 history help bring the story of the Holocaust up to date in a more comprehensive way and has provided some fascinating and insightful feedback in relation to what for obvious reasons is still a painful or/and challenging thing for many to talk about. **This is what they shared with me:**

"The Holocaust or Shoah as we call it, is as you can imagine a huge and very difficult subject to deal with, it is still very real for many because there are still the last of the survivors amongst us in our communities, although that will not be for very much longer, also there are many, many Jewish families who have lost loved ones in the Holocaust and that is something which of course will never go away, as it is a very sad part of their family history!

To have so many of your family, friends and wider community murdered by one of the most evil regimes in history just because you are viewed as different is not an easy thing to deal with, it wouldn't be for any community of any faith if it happened to them, no matter who they might be.

In the end it is vitally important that we don't forget the many millions of innocent men, women and children who were victims during that time, and it's true to say that there is still much debate about the Shoah in Jewish communities throughout the world, that is because Jewish people are still processing and coming to terms with it right to this very day!"

**Rabbi M Cohen - OYY Lubavitch School, Higher Broughton, Salford, Greater Manchester.**

"There have been many Jews who have forgiven the Germans for what they did during World War Two and many who have not! Especially for those who were in it, coming to terms with the Holocaust is a real case of faith, and a real test of an individual's depth of belief and their ability to forgive.

Historically as most people know the Jews have been continuously persecuted, but what Nazi Germany did during the Holocaust and the industrial scale on which they did it was so horrific it is almost too hard to comprehend!

In the bigger picture the Nazis perpetrated an enormous 'Crime Against Humanity' not just to the Jews, as this included many other people of many other religions, political affiliations, nationalities and ethnic backgrounds who were murdered by them as well, unfortunately for us it was mainly targeted against our people!

I've spoken to many in our community over the years and a big consensus was that like them or not the Germans would again become a major power in Europe one day, which they now have, and because of the things that have happened in recent history this has I think been greeted by many with the mixed feelings of fear and admiration! Fear that if the climate and circumstances were right that they could once more pursue such a policy and maybe try and do something like it again, and admiration for their general ability as a nation to be very disciplined, efficient and get things done, which is only good if those attributes are not channelled into destructive directions or horrific goals as they have been in the past, the last thing we want is a repeat of history, but very worryingly right wing Nationalism is once again on the rise in many countries in Europe, including Germany!"

**Maurice Wallman - Whitefield, Manchester.**

As I had further insightful conversations with different people who I met and knew in the community I asked, with their consent, some quite probing questions, such as why do they think God would allow something of this magnitude to happen to the Jewish and other peoples? Some extremely interesting thoughts were revealed in relation to this question. One gentleman who said he had never talked to anyone about this subject outside of his faith before was he felt ready to share his feelings and also an anecdote based on the importance of having and keeping faith of any kind, especially when it helps get us through the most difficult and testing of times and assists us in staying alive, he said:

"Even if they try I don't think anyone can really give a fully comprehensive answer as to why the Holocaust happened and why God would allow such things to transpire. They could only offer theories and there are a great many of those out there, expressing almost countless points of view. Anyway who are we to question the reasoning and judgement of the great all creative power that made all life in this universe including us, we can only get an insight into the nature of God through the laws, words and teachings passed down to us over thousands of years, and in relation to all of this how could we as mere humans even begin to understand the thought processes of something so much more superior and advanced in every way than ourselves. In short the answer is we can't, and so I don't think we will ever really know how such a devastating occurrence was permissible." He then imparted this little gem:

"I am however happy to pass on to you this short story which is left purposely open-ended for you to draw whatever conclusions you wish from it.

During the Shoah there were three Rabbis in Auschwitz who decided to put God on trial, a very big and audacious thing to do, each one acting out an important courtroom role, one as the prosecuting attorney, one the defending attorney and one as the judge, and all three did so very seriously because of the horrors and killing they saw around them every day, they thought it was something of great significance that they felt very moved to do.

After hearing all the very heavy and fiery arguments and counter-arguments, the presiding judge found God guilty of 'Abandoning his People', an extremely serious verdict indeed!!

This was followed directly by all three discussing where they should hold afternoon prayers...

Take from it what you will..."

**Avram Klyne - Adath Israel Synagogue, Salford, Greater Manchester.**

Continuing on from this are these very insightful words of a well-read Jewish lady I spoke to who articulated:

"Across history devastating events of one kind or another have and still are happening to every kind of person all over the world right to this very day, from people contracting cancer or other dreadful diseases, to dealing with the death of loved ones, to being victims of tsunamis, hurricanes, earthquakes, war or famine, whether they are seemingly natural or man-made disasters they are things that all people affected by them have to come to terms with and try and deal with as best possible, in the same way as we Jewish people have had to constantly do.

Many others have also been victims of evil powers, regimes and rulers throughout time, for example the Armenians, Christians, those in Cambodia, Rwanda and Syria but interestingly though in our case the Jews have been continually tormented and struck by hard and re-occurring calamities in our history, in ancient times by the Babylonians, Egyptians, Romans, later during the Crusades and the Inquisition, through to the Russian Pogroms, Nazis and the Shoah, as it says in the book of Ecclesiastes 'There is nothing new under the sun', but we have in every case out-lived and out-lasted all the empires and perpetrators of wrong doing that have tried to destroy us, that in itself is a great enduring victory, so looking at this in a more philosophical way it seems that God has a bigger plan for us if after everything he continues to allow us to survive like this!

It also serves to remind us that both good and evil, darkness and light, exist in different forms and levels in this world, and that both are sent to teach us many kinds of lessons and guide us in many apparent and not so apparent ways, it is up to us singularly and collectively to try and make sense in the best way possible what we can from these experiences and to learn from them! The ability, capacity and choice to do good or evil is within all of us, every human being, but remember what comes with that choice is always one way or another the responsibility for our actions, and if bad the punishment that follows, in this life or the next!"

**Ayelet – Israel/Manchester.**

During the proof reading of this part of the book, which came quite some time after it was written, I was once again deeply moved a number of times by many things in it, and also had to pinch myself when thinking that I personally recorded the testimonies of one of the few Holocaust survivors still alive at that time, it also reminded me of the importance of preserving this history. All of these things were beautifully encapsulated with these words from literature regarding the Holocaust that was lent to me by a certain Rabbi Paley after I asked him for some input, which read:

There is an old saying which is: 'Others may fear what the morrow may bring, but I must tell the world what happened yesterday. We owe it to the dead to keep their memory alive by reminding the world of its responsibility never to forget. For to face the future one has to understand the past!'

To conclude these amazing insights are the slightly humorous words of wisdom and advice very kindly given to me regarding my 'Debt of Gratitude' Project, when a gentleman from the community who knew of my work said:

"Gary, God is Omnipotent! He has created everything and can do anything, apart from change the past! It is for that reason he created historians! This is vitally important work you are doing! So keep on interviewing all kinds of survivors from that conflict whilst you can, and carry on capturing the past for those who will come in the future!"

**This chapter of the book is written for and dedicated to those from all backgrounds, nationalities and religions who perished in the Holocaust and were victims of Nazi tyranny. GBD.**

## WORDS OF HOPE AND LIGHT IN A TIME OF ADVERSITY AND DARKNESS

Even during times of utter despair and utter disbelief when things are happening to people and they can't believe and don't know or truly understand why, even in those darkest moments the true strength and spirit of humans can find a way through to express itself! Real proof of this has been included here in a noted inscription that was carved on a wall by an unknown victim of the Holocaust! It reads;

*"I Believe in the Sun,
even when it is not shining.
And I believe in love,
even when there's no one there.
And I believe in God,
even when he is silent.*

*May there someday be sunshine.
May there someday be happiness.
May there someday be love.
May there someday be peace."*

## HOLOCAUST CONCLUSION LINKING TO 'HISTORY ON A KNIFE EDGE IN 1942'

As we saw earlier in the part called 'Pulse of Death' relatively new figures based on a study at Tel-Aviv University estimate that the first horrific and one of the biggest spates of killing in the Death Camps reached its climax in around August to October 1942. The frightening ultra-efficiency of the Germans made this possible, and even though Churchill and the allies knew about what was happening at this time they chose not to do anything about it. This may be hard to comprehend, will always be controversial and of course seems very harsh to say the least, but in the bigger picture at this point in the war everything was still truly hanging in the balance, and coincidently running in parallel with the unfolding horrors of the holocaust was the fact that the Germans were at the height of their powers and were still winning the war at that time and were mainly on the offensive whilst the allies were mainly on the defensive. The Allies would not even win their first land battle of the war against the Germans until November 1942, and consequently would not be winning the land war significantly enough to directly be able to reach and liberate any of the camps for nearly another two years (by which time the vast majority of the killing had already been undertaken), as a result of this the only other option realistically left open for them to take the fight to the enemy and/or try to disable the Final Solution in any significant way was by attack from the air.

However the massive amount of bombing required by the Allied air forces to take out the immense rail networks of the Concentration Camps, Death Camps, Sub-Camps and the vast supporting infrastructure that was scattered all over Europe and also possibly attempt very dangerous low-level operations to hit key parts of the worse camps themselves, which were mostly in Poland and meant at great risk passing over most of heavily defended Germany to get there and back would have taken huge resources away from the allied air forces that were critically needed elsewhere at this pivotal time in the war and thereafter, and would have cost a great many more lives of their bomber crews who during that conflict had the highest attrition rate of any of the services, and potentially cause the death of many camp inmates that they were trying to save if direct bombing of those targets was undertaken! Other sobering factors that the allies had to consider that influenced their very difficult decision making in relation to this was that their over-stretched air forces were already engaged and continuously needed in all other theatres of the war and many other operations that they deemed directly both 'Tactically and Strategically' more Important to the war effort, such as the bombing campaign over Europe and the many battles that were raging simultaneously everywhere else around the world during that pivotal time.

Tactical being the aerial bombing of targets of immediate military value such as combatants, military equipment or installations to reduce its most direct and immediate means to wage war, Strategic bombing being that of attacking enemy factories to cripple future military production and cities to destroy infrastructure and try and break the morale and will of enemy civilians to support their country's war effort, and overall the economic ability of the adversary to produce and transport material to the various battle fronts throughout that conflict in order to try and debilitate the enemy's long-term capacity to wage war. Sadly for those caught up in the Extermination and Concentration camp system they didn't really fall into either of those categories, ostensibly further big reasons for the in-action of the Allies in relation to the Final Solution. The Allied decision makers simply could not justify the re-allocation of significant amounts of valuable forces in either the short or long term for operations that were seemingly not going to tip the scales in their favour or positively influence the outcome of the war for them in any way, and which would certainly result in further high losses of men and material.

In fact it could have had quite the opposite effect, if the Germans due to the direct pressure of the intentional bombing of these targets decided to put the Final Solution on hold and to divert the vast amount of manpower, rail freight and logistical resources involved that were specifically 'dedicated and directed' to the efforts of that mass killing then this especially during the pivotal crises period of 1942 (and also at later critically important points of the war for that matter, for example on the run up to D-Day), could have been disastrous for the allies. Had these very substantial pinned-down assets and energies been effectively re-directed into the Nazi war effort on other fighting fronts it could have made a significant difference to the longevity or even outcome of the war! This is something the allied decision makers were fully aware of and that figured in their thinking and the choices they made, as they did not want to give Hitler any possible advantage whatsoever in this conflict where realistically the fate of the world was hanging in the balance and so much was at stake! These are not meant as justifications for the deaths of so many innocents but an overview of the hard unfortunate realities of that conflict which led to the way things unfolded.

All of these strongly linked factors lead directly to the next part of the book, a big essay called 'History on a Knife Edge in 1942' where we look in much more detail about the events and far bigger picture of what was happening in the world during the pivotal year of 1942 that influenced the decisions being made on every front, even in relation to the horrific and expanding Holocaust that was taking place at that time. This continues to focus further on the Axis side of things, which I know a lot of people who have a keen interest in this conflict also find very thought-provoking, and in doing so gives some balance in a book whose main focus through the stories of its veterans is on the Allied side of the conflict. It also shows that once again it was truly an 'Inter-Connected World War', where the brutal reality of having to focus on winning it meant that very hard decisions had to be made by world political and military leaders that would affect the outcome for many in a favourable way and unfortunately for many others meant the complete opposite. Hard Times required Hard (if not always correct) Decisions! With the benefit of hind sight we can draw many conclusions and put forward many arguments about the validity of any decision made by any leader in World War Two, (or any part of world history for that matter)!

But one thing is for sure, if the allies had not focussed militarily with all the resources at their deposal on their priority of beating the very powerful and tenacious Axis War machine on all fronts in order to win the Second World War, then there is no doubt that Nazi Germany would have had more time to continue pursuing its mass extermination programs and millions more people would have been victims of their terrible and disgusting racial and political policies, with almost unimaginable consequences and effects on world history and the generations that followed! It is with these considerations in mind we move on to my detailed factual essay 'History on a Knife Edge in 1942' which takes us back to look at this critical time in our not-so-distant past, which is hard for us in our relatively peaceful lives today to really comprehend! One still within 'living memory' of the oldest generation in our country when this piece was written. A time where it is no exaggeration to say the future of the world was being decided in the middle of that six-year conflict, a year where the Nazi and Axis powers came so close yet in the end were denied their goal of an ultimate victory.

# HISTORY ON A KNIFE EDGE IN 1942

# HISTORY ON A KNIFE EDGE IN 1942 – THE FATE OF THE WORLD IN THE BALANCE

Think about this, sometimes history is on an absolute knife edge, fate and fortune could go either way, destiny favouring either side in a conflict, one example of this is in 1940 during the Battle of Britain when Great Britain stood alone holding on and staving off Nazi Germany for its very survival and everything a free world stood for, at a time when it was still very much a 'European War'. However by 1942 it was truly a 'World War' with brutally-fought, closely contested titanic struggles taking place on a global scale, and by the mid to latter end of that year Nazi Germany was at the zenith of its power and conquests and as a result was realistically a massive threat to the world in every way!

A true 'Life and Death Battle' was being fought simultaneously on every front, land, sea, air and also by clandestine means, on different continents and terrains, in jungles, deserts, mountains, fields, in villages, towns and cities, over and under seas, in the air, in top secret establishments and extended to all places of production from farms to factories and shipyards, with involvement in one way or another by most of the countries on the planet, by men and women in both military and civilian capacities, and there was a real danger that Germany might win, in fact many people don't release how close the Third Reich nearly did come to winning the Second World War!

1942 was a real pivotal and deciding year in the balance of power, and the last one in which Nazi Germany and those fighting alongside and for Hitler could have possibly swung that balance in their favour if they had consolidated key objectives before the might of America combined with that of the other Allies started to make a significant difference, and before being overstretched on all the fronts on which the Axis had committed itself, things that could (and later on eventually would) combine and conspire to reverse and overwhelm them in every way. But incredibly it would still take the direct combined military and economic might of the biggest countries in the world, once these sleeping giants had been awoken, namely the U.S.A, the Soviet Union, Great Britain and her entire Commonwealth/Empire to beat Nazi Germany and her allies, (some of whom became a liability), and in addition that of China, mainly against Imperial Japan but still one of the Allies. Such was the sheer magnitude of this all-consuming, all-encompassing conflict and battle of total annihilation, that in the end it raged for six years and took on average over 12 million lives a year before it was concluded and the Axis forces were beaten! **Left – 'United Nations Fight For Freedom' poster. This depicts as mentioned the vast combined forces needed to totally defeat Nazi Germany and her Allies.** What fascinates me and led to me writing and including this extended essay is that Nazi Germany potentially winning the war up to this point, despite some setbacks, was not so much an historical 'What If' scenario, it is a realistically 'Could Have Been' fact! Also because I know that there is a great deal of interest in the opposing forces in World War Two, amongst whom were also many brave men and women, many having been conscripted and essentially forced to fight and take part in the war, resulting in this further representation of that Axis side.

So to help understand how close it truly was at this point we will now look in greater detail at things that were going on and went well mainly in favour of the Nazis and their Allies during the vitally important year of 1942 and that helped bring it to a near attainable victory for them in pursuit of their ultimate goal of a 'Thousand Year Reich!' This is a more detailed snapshot of this vitally important year both in World and War history. Nazi Germany's New Order had been on the march since entering the Saarland in 1935 and the Rhineland in 1936 and by this point in the war in 1942 had conquered vast swathes of territory, carving out an empire on all points of the compass that stretched from the Baltic to North Africa and from the Channel Coast of France to Black Sea in the Soviet Union. It was in Russia on the Southern front the Axis powers were again victoriously on the move when in May 1942 in the Second Battle of Kharkov the Germans encircled and destroyed 3 Soviet Field Armies, culminating in over 250,000 Russians killed, wounded or captured, amongst the dead were 3 Russian Generals, leading to the Commander of the 38th Army, Kirill Moskalenko quoting an anonymous soldier when he said "these fascists woke up after they hibernated" (from subsequent Soviet Winter and Spring offensives). These operations greatly helped give the Germans the upper hand in preparation for their main Summer Offensive called 'Case Blue', launched on the 28th June, which went on to make large territorial gains including taking the vitally strategic and historical port city of Sevastopol on the 4th July 1942, where they netted a further 90,000 Soviet prisoners in the process, and as a result of this gaining complete control of the Crimean Peninsula, and in another part of Case Blue in Southern Russia they were getting closer to capturing their main objectives the valuable oil fields of Maykop, Gronzy and Baku in the Caucasus, which would have been an absolute life line if all had been reached and had been taken in reasonable working order and possibly utilised to help fuel the Axis war machine, these valuable assets would have potentially allowed them much greater means to carry on the fight and realise their greater objectives. **This Nazi 'Eastern Front Specific' propaganda poster depicts a German Soldier symbolically slaying a Red Dragon using two lightning bolts and states: 'Deutschlands Sieg, Europas Freiheit' which translated means 'Germany's Victory, Europe's Freedom', interestingly indicating that Germany was acting in the role of a Liberator when in fact the Third Reich was pursuing a total 'War of Annihilation' against Russia on the Eastern Front.**

Such was the absolute danger posed by the Germans at that time that on the 29th May 1942 the Soviet Foreign Minister Vyacheslav Molotov had arrived in Washington to meet and try to convince President Roosevelt to open a 2nd front in Western Europe to help relieve the immense pressure on Russia at that particular time, knowing full well that the Soviet Union could still loose the war on the Eastern Front! After having that meeting on the 30th May Roosevelt, to try and pacify the Russians, made the remarkable statement: *'Inform Mr Stalin that we expect the formation of a Second Front this year.'* Essentially promising what he knew was the impossible at that time in the war, something that Churchill had already told Molotov when he visited him for meetings in the U.K directly before his onward journey to the U.S.A.

Hitler understanding the importance of capturing valuable natural resources, especially oil, dramatically stated on the 1st June 1942 to Major General (later Field Marshal), Friedrich Paulus commander of the 6th Army: *"If I don't get the oil of Maykop and Gronzy, then I must finish this war."* The Russians would have undoubtedly continued to sabotage their oilfields and oil extracting and producing facilities rather than letting these vital assets be captured and utilised by the Germans, but as proven elsewhere the Nazis were very quick to brutally use and exploit slave labour of any kind in their occupied territories to serve their purposes and meet their goals, and had no problem with working them to death if needs be and to liquidate those that did not comply to their demands, which essentially meant that oil production would have once again begun as soon as they could humanly make it possible in order to help feed their war in and against Russia, as long as the Wehrmacht (combined armed forces) could also keep their flanks safe-guarded and transport links running and continued to run effective anti-Partisan operations to counter that additional and very dangerous menace that already existed in most conquered areas. A tall order, but the seemingly impossible had already been achieved by Germany up until that point in the war! During the campaign in the Caucasus region the Germans also reached a symbolic goal and propaganda victory when on the 21st August 1942 Alpine troops of the 1st and 4th Mountain Divisions (Gebirgsjäger) had reached the top of Mount Elbrus, the highest and most prominent peak in Russia and Europe (5,642 metres/18,510 feet above sea level) and conquered it for the Third Reich by placing the Reich War Flag with its Nazi Swastika on the summit! **(Pictured).** Seemingly 'On Top of the World' with the dizzy heights of success now being achieved in many ways! All in the pursuit of Lebensraum 'Living Space' and the continuing expansion of Adolf Hitler's Gross Deutsches Reich 'Greater German Realm or Empire'.

In that part of Southern Russia had Hitler stuck to his original plan, which was going very well, and continued concentrating all the forces he had initially committed to the capture of the oilfields they would have fallen into his hands and the Middle East and its oil would have potentially been opened up to him from that direction as per the bigger plan of 1942. Instead as history now recalls the lure of the city bearing the name of his arch enemy Stalin was far too great for him, and just like the year before when he diverted his armies that were within reach of Moscow he again interfered with and changed the initial strategic plan, leading to a similar result, when diverting most of his forces and key armoured elements up towards what would later become their nemesis, Stalingrad!

Meanwhile in the Western Desert Campaign Rommel was busy conquering most of North Africa and had overrun the strategically important port city of Tobruk in Libya on the 21st June 1942, this resulted in the capture of 35,000 British and Commonwealth troops that included the entire South African 2nd Division, after which a jubilant and confident Rommel stated in his 'Order of the Day' – "Now for the complete destruction of the enemy." Such was the impact of this loss that Churchill later said: *"This is one of the heaviest blows I can recall during the war. Not only were its military affects grievous, but it had affected the reputation of the British Armies."* Later on when Rommel was at El Alamein in Egypt his forces were only 162 miles from the capital city of Cairo, and 248 miles (or to bring things into sharp focus, if unimpeded, 1 day's drive on well established roads) from the vital Suez Canal waterway, an essential supply and lifeline of the British Empire.

Had this vital artery been reached and cut it would have been catastrophic for the Allies and almost certainly finished their ability to wage war in this theatre of operations by removing a huge additional reinforcement route to North Africa and the Middle East. It would also have severed Great Britain's closest and best means of material and troop movement to and from the rest of her empire in the Far East. Around that pivotal time if Rommel had been allotted just another 1 or 2 additional Divisions by Hitler history may well have played out differently and might have led to these goals being achieved by the Desert Fox, which in turn could have opened up the way as hoped to Palestine and beyond! During the summer of 1942 the Axis forces were advancing significantly and fearing the worse many allied Diplomats in Cairo were in panic and evacuating the capital, and it was rumoured that Rommel was so confident of victory at this point that the Germans had phoned the exclusive Shepheard's Hotel in Cairo to book him a room ahead of his imminent arrival. The Axis offensives were also helped by successful secret intelligence gathering and covert eves-dropping in the desert from his stealthy mobile monitoring unit the 621st Signals Battalion and also for 6 months up until late June 1942 from the interception of vital information sent by an unwitting provider who Rommel called: *'die gute Quelle'* (the good source), who was Brevet Colonel Bonner Frank Fellers, the U.S. military attaché in the Egyptian capital who sent detailed military updates to Washington every day, he had become completely compromised due to the special 'Black Code' (the material used by U.S. military attachés and ambassadors worldwide), and its accompanying super-encipherment tables that he operated with already being known to the Axis. His messages held all the information on allied strength on the ground, its displacement, reserves, supplies and intentions all being picked up, de-cyphered and fed back to Rommel by the Chiffrierabteilung (military cipher branch of the Abwehr, the German military Intelligence Service), via its intercept stations, the 'Desert Fox' then used this massive advantage as part of his operational planning, until the allies found out where this huge security breach was coming from and dealt with it. Rommel knowing full well the situation on the ground and being a brilliant strategist, despite becoming over-extended still wanted to maintain the advantage and continue pressing home for more victories and said of Hitler's accolades around that time: *"I rather he would have given me one more division"* (instead of being made a Field Marshal), as with so many things for Nazi Germany that year it was thank goodness a case of: 'So Near, Yet So Far'! **Field Marshal Erwin Rommel AKA 'The Desert Fox', respected by both Axis and Allied troops alike, one of the very few of Hitler's men who was, due to his great ability in conducting battle and his fairness in dealing with those who he encountered. He would later be forced by a paranoid Hitler to commit suicide in October 1944, suspected of being involved in the July 1944 bomb plot to kill him.** Also, in the extended Mediterranean theatre of operations, Malta the British forces based there and her civilian population were under almost constant attack during what became known as 'The Siege of Malta' where in 1942 they endured 154 consecutive days and nights of bombing with 6700 tons of explosives dropped on them over that period! At certain times during that year this extremely strategically crucial little Island was the most bombed place on earth and only just held by the Allies! To give some idea of the intensity of what the island and its inhabitants went through, in March and April of 1942 alone, the joint air forces of the German Luftwaffe and Italian Regia Aeronautica dropped more bombs on the island than had been dropped on London during the entire Blitz of 1940 & 1941 combined! These attacks along with approximately 54,000 sea mines laid by the Axis forces around the island greatly helped ease pressure on the Afrika Korps who were doing so well by the summer of 1942 that the Germans had planned in conjunction with everything else to undertake Operation Hercules, the proposed invasion through air and sea landings on the islands of Malta and Gozo, which they hoped would eliminate Malta as a key British air and naval base and as a result secure an uninterrupted flow of supplies across the Mediterranean Sea to their forces in Libya and Egypt and greatly help Axis domination in the Mediterranean theatre of war and aid their push on into Middle East. Such was the importance of continually being able to subdue or possibly even capture this geographically very significant island that Rommel was quoted as saying: *"Without Malta we will lose the war in the desert!"* In recognition of the many trials, tribulations, suffering and bravery of the people of Malta during that time and throughout all periods of the siege King George VI bestowed the very highest civilian honour possible, the George Cross, upon the entire island, something still proudly displayed to this very day, by being incorporated into their flag. **The civilian services in both Malta and the United Kingdom worked under extremely dangerous conditions and were under massive pressure trying hard to save people and property throughout the relentless bombardments of the Axis Air Forces, and whilst doing so, as this picture shows, trying continuously to maintain that other important factor; morale!**

In the bigger picture, despite these being enormous objectives, had these two arms of this giant pincer had the full resources required at the right times and places to have been able to successfully connect by an enormous push down from Southern Russia and up from North Africa, and/or an additional proposed push from invading Nazi forces coming through the country of Axis ally Bulgaria then through neutral Turkey, meeting and taking the Middle East and their many oil fields in the process, then this big potential German war aim of 1942 could have set World War Two on a distinctly different course altogether and could possibly have created an entirely different outcome! The sheer scale of conquest that Hitler envisioned is reflected and the above plan confirmed in parts of the secret 'Führer Directive 32' which came directly from Adolf Hitler to those in the highest ranking positions who had to implement it and was issued as early as 11$^{th}$ June 1941 just prior to his invasion of Russia which stated: 'The struggle against the British positions in the Mediterranean and in Western Asia will be continued by converging attacks launched from Libya through Egypt, from Bulgaria through Turkey, and in certain circumstances also from Transcaucasia through Iran.'

Interestingly later in that same directive in relation to these aims it says; 'To this end plans must be made to assemble in Bulgaria as soon as possible sufficient forces to render Turkey politically amenable or to overpower her resistance.' Incredibly it shows that the neutrality of any country, even a potential ally as Germany viewed Turkey, would not be allowed to stand in the way of Nazi territorial ambitions, essentially the attitude and approach was simple 'collaborate or be conquered.' Turkey however was biding her time as the war ebbed, flowed and progressed, playing very careful and clever 'wait and see' tactics, courting and liaising with both the Allied and Axis sides as most 'Neutral Countries' such as Portugal, Sweden and Switzerland also did during the war, and having backed Germany in World War One and ending up on the losing side which contributed to the loss of her Ottoman Empire she was fearful to commit again! But had they have backed Hitler during this crucial period then frighteningly this could have released massive additional manpower and natural resources and the use of extremely strategic territory that could have been utilised for the Axis cause which would have made Hitler's plan even more achievable! The realistic implementation of all this depended on how things played out with German advances in Operation Barbarossa, the invasion of the Soviet Union, and became more of a possibility later on in 1942 due to the German offensives in the Caucasus region, and also the simultaneous victories taking place in North Africa. It could easily have gone either way, especially whilst Nazi Germany had the upper hand in the war, as it did at that time (and as it was reaching its greatest extent between Sep to Nov 1942), but what it also shows is that Hitler and the Nazis really were thinking on the biggest scale possible, that of true World Domination! This 'Greater Plan' as demonstrated by Hitler's military expansionism chillingly and essentially being - *'TODAY WE RULE GERMANY, TOMORROW THE WORLD!'*

**The 'High Tide' map showing the Nazi Empire in black at its fullest extent, and the intended Nazi 'giant pincer strategy' for 1942 incorporating the seizure of key oil producing regions, indicated by the Easterly heading arrows, that could help make winning the war a reality. As to this very day oil playing a vital part in the power plans of Nations.**

Also within that bigger picture other very interesting and unlikely alliances had come into play as the Germans advanced throughout both Southern Russia and across North Africa with the anticipated continuation of what could essentially become a Blitzkrieg into the Middle East, leading to certain other power players from that Middle Eastern Region who had their own agenda and some shared goals with the Nazis such as strengthening and expanding a realm for their own people plus other motives to position and aligned themselves with Hitler. One of those who had such intentions and who was seen by Hitler as being useful with implementing potential Arab uprisings and insurrections in order to help him destabilise the Allied presence in that region when the time was right which could help aid the Nazi goals of conquest in 1942 (leading as mentioned before to eventually taking and using its vast oil reserves for the Reich) was the Grand Mufti of Jerusalem Haj Amin al-Husseini, who as the top Muslim Cleric in the Holy Land had influence and held sway with many in that region, and who due to his affiliations with the Axis powers had already fled to Nazi Germany in 1941. Whilst there he had met with Hitler in Berlin on the 28th November that year to discuss a number of these 'shared issues' and their mutually beneficial 'duel cooperation' during which Hitler foreseeing a Nazi victory interestingly reflected on both the bigger military and ideological ambitions that he had, asking al-Husseini "to lock …deep in his heart" these points; "When Germany has defeated Russia and broken through the Caucasus into the Middle East, it would have no further imperial goals of its own and would support Arab liberation", but Hitler did have one big common goal with al-Husseini as he went on to say; "Germany's objective would then be solely the destruction of the Jewish element residing in the Arab sphere under the protection of the British power" (as it was at that time, prior to an anticipated German victory that both men were hoping to bring about, as it would greatly benefit their general and personal ambitions). Had the Germans advanced into the Middle East this mutual cooperation could have helped pave the way for an Axis victory in that region, but whilst looking promising for a while in the end as the tide turned it didn't quite work out that way! **Here the Grand Mufti in Berlin meeting with volunteer soldiers from the Muslim Azerbaijani Legion on the 19th December 1942. As the war progressed there were many foreign units being formed in the German Wehrmacht from a lot of nations, especially within the Waffen SS (combat branch of the Schutzstaffel or Protection Squads which eventually numbered divisions in size and strength). This photo an example reflecting some from the large array of nations, backgrounds and religions that fought on both the Axis and Allied sides during World War Two.**

The points touched on here being exactly what is outlined in both this 1942 chapter and Holocaust chapter of the book. However, it is very important to note that the big plans of the Mufti do not necessarily reflect the thoughts and ideologies of all those in the Middle East, many of whom were opposed to Nazism and some who bravely fought against it, but what this essay continues purely from an historical interest and perspective to highlight and again show is that all areas, cultures and peoples in the world during that conflict were to a greater or lesser degree involved, influenced or pulled into what was happening during those cataclysmic times, how could they not be as the war and Nazi Germany's territorial ambitions were spreading outwardly, engulfing country after country! Another insight into the Nazi hierarchy mind-set and their bigger overall plans, where the conquest of Europe as a springboard to eventual world conquest was further reflected and later confirmed in part of a speech made by Joseph Goebbels, the Reich Minister of Propaganda where he said: *"The Fuhrer gave expression to his unshakable conviction that the Reich will be master of all Europe. We shall yet have to engage in many fights, but these will undoubtedly lead to most wonderful victories. From there the way to world domination is practically certain. Whoever dominates Europe will thereby assume leadership of the world."* Indeed this global fight was like a giant chess game, with each move that either side played equalling one of the key battles, and with the eventual winner potentially attaining the final and greatest prize, that of total victory and world governance!

*Out on a Long, Long Limb*

**Above - The big Axis attempt at world domination led by Adolf Hitler with Hideki Tojo of Japan and Benito Mussolini of Italy in tow, as depicted in this interesting World War Two caricature drawing, indicating how real this threat was perceived by the Allies, who portrayed as Uncle Sam try to 'fell them' as they reach 'Out on a Long, Long Limb' and greedily strive to take it all! Although this was Allied propaganda it was also a true expression and reflection of what to a very large degree was actually happening at that time, a fascist and Imperialist land grab on a truly monumental scale!**

By 1942 the Nazis were already the 'Masters of Europe' and ruling it with an iron fist with the help or support of collaborationists like the Vichy Regime of Southern France and the other Fascist Allies of Italy and 'neutral' Spain, and further countries aligned with her such as Bulgaria, Romania, Hungry and Finland, and additionally the rule of terror, control and ruthlessness enforced by the sophisticated apparatus of the SS, SD and the Gestapo within the huge spheres of influence in the countries it occupied. This backed up by a terrible network of concentration and extermination camps set up to liquidate those seen as enemies of the Third Reich was the realisation of its frightening 'New Order', it was also a sign of the reality of what awaited any country and indeed the world itself should the evil of Nazism prevail. Had the United Kingdom been taken at any time during the conflict there is little doubt that this system of harsh rule and camps would have been implemented on the British mainland, this was proven by the existence of a Concentration Camp called Sylt which was officially the only one to ever exist on 'British Soil' and its 3 supporting Labour Camps of Helgoland, Norderney and Borkum, all located on the Channel Island of Alderney and where as with all others in the Nazi empire people were murdered and had perished in various ways, here this happened to slave labourers brought in from many places from a far afield as Russia, France, Poland and Algeria to work on huge fortification projects. The Sonderfahndungsliste G.B 'Special Search List Great Britain' later known as 'The Black Book' had also been complied by the SD and SS, containing the names of nearly 3000 mainly prominent British Nationals and European Exiles who were to be rounded up, utilised and/or executed upon the Nazi conquest of mainland Britain.

Whilst Nazi Germany was in firm control of Europe and Hitler's power at its height and he was unchallenged by any around him, in the U.K there were signs of disquiet regarding their leadership, which through the democratic due processes of parliament led to some MPs from his coalition government putting forward during 1942 two motions of 'No Confidence' in Winston Churchill and his handling and direction of the War. One was in January the other in July, both of which thank goodness Churchill survived resoundingly with his characteristic resilience and determination, but the signals it sent out of what seemed like a wavering government must have been a further confidence boost to Germans and all the Axis powers at a time when they were effectively 'Riding High' on their wave of successes, especially when they heard about things that some in the British parliament were saying such as: *"Churchill wins debate after debate, yet losses battle after battle, the country is beginning to say that he fights debates like a war and the war like a debate!"* Damaging words from Labour MP Aneurin Bevan, which during very difficult times certainly didn't help moral, the British war effort or the allied cause in any way whatsoever! Also the kind of rhetoric that was a gift to the Nazi propaganda ministry!

Other things were going on at this time that were very much in their favour and adding to the knife edge events of that year, in the covert intelligence war the 'B-Dienst' a department of the German Naval Intelligence Service, which specialised in cryptanalysis and the deciphering of enemy and neutral states message traffic, had managed to already break the British Naval Combined Cypher No.3, which effectively allowed them to encrypt all communications for allied North Atlantic convoys from October 1941 until June 1943, some of their biggest breakthroughs coming in early 1942. In addition to this they could regularly read the British and Allied Merchant Ships (BAMS) Code. These combined advances and successes allowed them to know and be able to plot the course of nearly all allied convoys in The Battle of the Atlantic during those periods, 1942 being the main year in which they could still tip the balance before later allied advances in technology and tactics went on to make significant differences against them in that theatre of war.

In tandem with this the British code breakers of Bletchley Park, undoubtedly the best intelligence gatherers of the Second World War were unable to continue breaking the German Naval Codes of the Enigma Machine because the Germans had added another wheel to the Naval version of this highly sophisticated piece of equipment on the 1st February 1942, essentially meaning it had become immeasurably harder to crack the secret messages, orders and coordinates sent from the German Navy High Command to its surface vessels and U-Boats. They were essentially 'Locked Out' of all direct communications traffic for that branch of the German Armed Forces and their ability to directly eves drop on that extremely dangerous part of the Axis strike force was gone! So for the best part of 1942 there was no way from that source to know what the German Navy (Kriegsmarine) and its U-Boats were doing, also when and where their dreaded 'Wolf Packs' would strike. It greatly contributed to what U-Boat commanders called 'The Second Happy Time' where the rate of sinking's and losses of allied vessels mainly from the Merchant Navy were some of the highest of the war. Only indications from Luftwaffe interceptions when they were in support of sea operations might give a slight and limited clue to some German naval activity. Essentially this was the destructive product of the intelligence war where the German Naval intelligence were doing particularly well, and which could have led to the Nazis achieving their ultimate goal of effectively 'Choking the Lifeline' of Great Britain and potentially forcing her to sue for peace by 'Starving Her Out'! This was something that the German U-Boats were making real headway in doing with over a frightening 4,000,000 Tonnes of war materials lost and 1000 ships sunk between January and June 1942, and a further 3,600,000 Tonnes of war materials lost and 675 ships sunk between July and December 1942, even on the last day of that year 31st December sadly the Royal Navy lost a ship, HMS Bramble, she went down with 'All Hands', 113 sailors and her Commander H.J Rust during the Battle of the Barents Sea. In general had overall losses such as those detailed here continued at this or and increased rate they could have become quite unsustainable for the United Kingdom and put an even greater strain on the country, which in turn could have led to a very different outcome to the war. Such was the threat, reality and danger of this possibly happening that Winston Churchill said nothing frightened him more during World War Two than the U-Boat Menace! It showed that although the British Royal Navy were certainly ruling the ocean waves on the surface, it was a very different story down below!

**Above Left - The fear, as expressed through an Allied wartime message: 'A careless word… …A needless sinking'. Above Right – The reality, a ship in its last seconds as seen through the periscope of a submarine as it disappears with its crew below the ocean waves. Right – The reality that still remains, one which again shows the diversity of those who helped our country during World War Two, and one of the many who paid the ultimate price, the Merchant Navy grave of Salem Mohamed, Fireman and Trimmer on the vessel SS Gracefield is a very good example of service and sacrifice. He is buried at Western Cemetery in Cardiff, Wales. The MN insignia can be clearly seen on his gravestone. This picture was taken on the 20th May 2020.**

~ 339 ~

Many Allied shipping convoys suffered terribly as a result of these devastating U-Boat attacks, the absolute mauling of two convoys in particular were very good examples of the way things were going in general at that time, Arctic Convoy PQ17 and Malta Convoy WS 12S. In July 1942 PQ17 lost 24 of its 35 merchant ships during seven days of coordinated daylight attacks by U-Boats and aircraft, the effect of these losses was so bad that the allies stopped the Arctic convoys for over two months after PQ17, this had the knock on effect of a vital flow of much needed supplies to the Soviet Union for use on the Eastern Front at a time of the German summer offensives there was temporarily lost, this helped the Nazis and again added to the overall precarious balance of things at that time. Meanwhile in the Mediterranean in August 1942 supplies of everything including desperately needed fuel for aircraft were running so low on the vitally strategic island of Malta that there was a real possibility of the island surrendering, and so a desperate attempt by Great Britain to reach and supply her with the heavily defended WS 12S Convoy was undertaken, this was given the code name 'Operation Pedestal'. In six days 13 vessels were lost in total, and only 5 of the original 14 Merchant Navy vessels made it to the Grand Harbour in Malta to try and help maintain her lifeline, in addition to this the Royal Navy lost the aircraft carrier HMS Eagle, the Destroyer Foresight and the cruisers Manchester and Cairo along with more than 500 Merchant and Royal Navy sailors.

The Mediterranean, Atlantic and Baltic were not the only places where the U-Boat threat was being felt in a significant way, incredibly they also reached and operated as far away as the East Coast of the United States of America and into the Caribbean! Where for over half a year until around August 1942 they were sinking huge amounts of American shipping almost at will, U.S shipping now being a legitimate target since they entered the war after the December 7th 1941 attack on Pearl Harbour by the Japanese, followed by Adolf Hitler declaring war on them on the 11th of that month in support of their Tri-Partite Pact ally Imperial Japan, and on the same day America declaring war on Nazi Germany. On the U.S East Coast they attacked mainly at night, helped greatly by the illuminated coastline of a country which at that time did not understand the importance of a 'Black Out'. The U-boats attacked using all the deadly weapons at their disposal, torpedoes, surface guns and they even laid mines in known shipping lanes, these combined weapons & tactics cost the allies hundreds of ships, thousands of lives and over a million tonnes of valuable cargo. Most of the vessels they were sinking formed part of the vital Atlantic shipping routes and their supplies were bound for battlefields thousands of miles away in North Africa, the Mediterranean, Europe, the UK, the Far East and elsewhere, as a result of the loss of these ships the knock on effect was influencing the direction and sometimes outcome of vitally important strategic battles and events far away across the world, reminding us once again about the vast scale of this conflict, one which as we continue to see here was truly international and inter-connected through events that were playing out simultaneously around the globe. For many months the Nazis seriously threatened this Atlantic lifeline whilst a lot of the U.S Navy and their vast resources were directed to and focused on the new war in the Pacific against the Japanese, it was only when a convoy system was organised and introduced, based on the one the British were using with land, sea and air cooperation that things started to change, but until this really kicked-in and began to work, which took until August, the situation was very precarious indeed with U-Boats achieving massive killing rates, contributing and further adding to the immense 'Knife-Edge' drama playing out in '42.

The confidence of Nazi Germany was further boosted by events taking place that year on the other side of the world in that region with their other Ally Imperial Japan, who were also reaching the extent of their powers in the Asia-Pacific areas where they were rampaging through that part of the world and also having victory after victory up until mid-1942. They had taken many Allied land possessions and parts of the British Empire and were threatening many others, such as Australia and India whilst continually increasing their Geo-Strategic influence, further options and overall confidence in their ability to wage war and conquer new territories successfully. During the course of these victories they had also inflicted the biggest ever defeat experienced by the British Army in its entire history when they captured Singapore on 15th February 1942, with its surrender the Japanese took over 80,000 British and Commonwealth Prisoners of War. Adding to Allied problems during that period of the Japanese Blitzkrieg in Asia and the Pacific was the invasion of Burma, January to Mid-May 1942 which led to the longest retreat in British military history when the last of the British and Burmese forces there completed a 1000-mile fighting withdrawal eventually crossing up into the safety of India, at least this time its badly weakened forces escaped to fight another day! At sea in that part of the world the allies were not fairing much better either, during Naval battles near Java in late February and early March a number of ships from various allied Navies were lost, these included Destroyers and cruisers such as HNLMS Kortenaer (Netherlands), HMS Electra (U.K), HMS Jupiter (U.K), HNLMS De Ruyter (Netherlands), HNLMS Java (Netherlands), HMAS Perth (Australia), USS Houston (USA), HNLMS Evertsen (Netherlands), HMS Exeter (U.K), HMS Encounter (U.K), USS Pope (USA), HNMLS Witte de With (Netherlands), USS Pillsbury (USA), USS Edsall (USA), the Aircraft Carrier USS Langley (USA).  These ships were all part of ABDACOM – The American-British-Dutch-Australian Command, which was a short-lived supreme command for all Allied forces in South-East Asia that was activated in January 1942 in response to the ever-increasing Japanese threat in that region.  Devastatingly as the ships listed above indicate the main ABDA Naval force was almost totally destroyed, with over 2000 sailors lost!  This in part led to the Japanese occupation of the entire Dutch East Indies and the Allied campaign to defend them by land, sea and air was totally lost by March and ABDA had been disbanded and ceased to exist! It was later superseded by SEAC – South East Asia Command. The Japanese victories in the Java area battles meant they had secured vast resources of the Southwest Pacific, and it also allowed them to establish a big defensive perimeter along an arc of islands in that part of the Pacific region, putting them in a very strong strategic position indeed, they were now the new masters of the Asia-Pacific rim, and up until losing the Battle of Midway in June 1942 for their new Empire it truly was the time of 'The Rising Sun.'

In the meantime back in Europe on the 19th August 1942 came the tragic and ill-fated Operation Jubilee, an attack on the heavily fortified coastal town of Dieppe in France.  This operation undertaken mainly by the Canadians with some combined British forces and a small contingent of the newly formed U.S Rangers was meant to test a well-defended enemy held beach area, adjoining town and occupied part of coastline, with the objectives of taking and holding this small but tactically important German controlled area for a short time, and to be a trial run for any potential and much bigger sea borne invasion that might follow later such as a hopeful 'Second Front', instead it proved that the Allies were woefully ill prepared in many aspects of such an operation.   It was also intended to provide a great moral boost to the Allies and their civilian populations at home, who sought any good news and desperately needed victories during what was still quite a desperate time for them in the war.  Instead what they got was a landing force that suffered horrendous casualties and was horrifically mauled!  In total during 9 hours on that one day in August 1942 from just over 6000 men landed the Allies lost over 3,500 men, either killed, injured or captured, 106 RAF aircraft downed and the Royal Navy Destroyer HMS Berkeley lost, in an operation with almost none of the tactical objectives achieved! It was the first large-scale daylight assault undertaken on a strongly held objective in Occupied Europe and up until that point the largest Allied amphibious landing since 1915 in Gallipoli during World War 1, resulting in a similar outcome, a bloody disaster!  Many important lessons were learnt that day which would help the Allied armies later, but the immediate one was that they were nowhere near ready or capable of launching a much bigger second front sized seaborne invasion on mainland Nazi occupied Europe any time in the very near future, despite huge coercing from Stalin and the Russians to do so in order to relieve the enormous strain they were under on the Eastern Front, but without a doubt for those young servicemen on the beaches of Dieppe during Operation Jubilee these 'lessons' came at a very sad and high cost indeed!

Elsewhere around the globe in many other theatres of the conflict lots more Allied ships were sadly being lost during that year, each one an interesting story in itself, a good example of this is the Town-class cruiser HMS Edinburgh.  She was involved in many Naval actions during WW2 including the hunting of the famous

German battleship the Bismarck in May 1941, later HMS Edinburgh which was the flagship of Rear-Admiral Stuart Bonham Carter was torpedoed and damaged in the Barents Sea by German Submarine U-456 on the 30th April 1942 whilst escorting Artic Convoy QP 11 from Murmansk back to the UK. On board was a top-secret consignment of gold which was being transported to the UK as payment from Stalin to the Allies for war materials used to help supply Russia in her war against Germany. On the 2nd May the badly damaged ship was abandoned having lost 57 men and was finished off by the destroyer HMS Foresight with her last torpedo, sending nearly 5 tons of Gold bullion to the bottom with HMS Edinburgh, worth about 1.5 million in 1942, at time of writing in 2021-2023 that equates to over £70 million! The gold was eventually salvaged in two operations, the first in 1981 and the second in 1986.

Back to 1942, and at the same time running behind and alongside all of this was a world equally as shadowy as that of intelligence which was that of secret weapons development, where in October 1942 from the top secret facility of Peenemunde on the Baltic Sea in Northern Germany Wernher Von Braun and his scientists who were working on the Vengeance weapons program, successfully launched a V2 Rocket into the earth's atmosphere and returned it under monitored conditions making it the world's first ever inter-continental ballistic missile, and the first man-made object in space, technology way ahead of anything the Allies had, and of anything in the world at that time. If Hitler had not interfered by ordering that the V2 **(Pictured taking off)** be enlarged to carry bigger deadly payloads, significantly setting this development program back and losing the Nazis a huge opportunity of bringing this lethal key weapon into general service in great numbers far earlier in the war, they could if utilised and used strategically and with reasonable accuracy have potentially made a real difference to the direction or outcome of World War Two, because as proven later in 1944 when they did strike, unlike the V1 they were unstoppable! The V2 rocket that took off from Launchpad No.7 on the 3rd October 1942 created what was essentially the birthplace of spaceflight, a dream which was ultimately attained decades later in July 1969 when after many years working for the Americans at NASA the very same Wernher Von Braun and his team had developed the Saturn V rocket that successfully took man to the moon! **Right – Von Braun wearing a civilian suit in a picture taken with some high-ranking German officers at Peenemünde, he was a member of the Nazi party from 1937-1945, was also part of the Allgemeine-SS and personally awarded the Iron Cross for his work by Adolf Hitler. The use of slave labour to build the V2 rockets was known to him. Later in the U.S.A he worked under and knew both Presidents Eisenhower and Kennedy!**

During 1942 another quite realistic train of thought for Hitler relating to everything was that most of the resources of the their other biggest enemy the United States of America were as mentioned earlier in this essay starting to be channelled to their war in the Pacific to engage the Japanese, which he thought would mean less pressure on Germany whilst the Soviet Union was being 'dealt with', and Britain held off and starved into submission by his U-Boats, all of these and other things in the bigger picture of 1942 further influenced the key military decisions being made by Adolf Hitler on all fronts where his forces were engaged, thus making this an even more climatic and momentous year in world history, one with eventual huge consequences for the Third Reich. In that year the forces of Nazi Germany did not have it all their own way, of course over that same 12 month period they also suffered very high losses in both men and material on all fronts, also the first allied 1000 bomber raids had pounded some German cities, Bletchley Park was still able to listen into and decipher the top secret communications of the German Army and Air Force and use that vital information against their Nazi foe, the output of the combined war factories of the Allies was already outstripping those of their enemies, organised resistance within occupied areas of both Europe and Russia was significantly on the increase, as was Special Forces activities, more forced labour was having to be put into war related production due to manpower shortages on the Axis side, something which became more acute as the war went on, whilst Allied forces would only become stronger over time. But for most of 1942 the consolation for the German and other Axis servicemen was at least one of outwardly being on the winning side for most of that time, and also being driven by a sense, rightly or wrongly, that victory was tantalisingly close and potentially attainable for them. The first main cracks only began showing late in the year with the 'Hinge of Fate' starting to swing in favour of the Allies after the second battle of El Alamein in November, when they suffered their first defeat of World War Two in a land battle against British and Commonwealth troops (and units made up of soldiers from other occupied countries) during Operation Lightfoot and Operation Supercharge, the very hard fighting that ensued cost the Allies a heavy 13,560 Casualties, of which 2,350 men had been killed, 8,950 wounded and 2,260 missing in just 20 days! A victory that took the Allies 3 years, half way through WW2 before they could achieve it! A very important British & Commonwealth triumph obtained at a high price, but the Germans and Italians although beaten at El Alamein and with over 20,000 casualties were not finished in North Africa. Each clash of armies in this decisive year producing staggering casualty numbers such as these. Soon after the U.S led Operation Torch landings in Morocco and Algeria in November 1942 further exasperated things for the Germans who responded by invading and taking the rest of (Vichy) France in order to secure its Southern Mediterranean flank which expanded its empire even further to what would essentially be its greatest extent.

More cracks showed with events unfolding that month at Stalingrad in Russia with the German 6$^{th}$ Army surrounded and cut off by the Soviet Operation Uranus further compounding the Axis situation on the Eastern Front (eventually leading this Army and its Führer to the same fate as Napoleon before them). Then with the initiative truly lost by Hitler and with the last chance of World domination having slipped from his grasp with both ends of the giant German pincer in both North Africa and Russia now blunted, the most worrying period had passed for the Allies, and as Churchill said that November – *"NOW THIS IS NOT THE END. IT IS NOT EVEN THE BEGINNING OF THE END. BUT IT IS, PERHAPS, THE END OF THE BEGINNING."*

**Interesting extremes; Left - German Soldiers on their 'Victory March' in Paris 1940 with the Arc de Triomphe behind them, part of the units marching are from the 6$^{th}$ Army. Right – Parts of that same 6$^{th}$ Army on a 'March of Defeat' as they are led past a factory into captivity by Soviets at Stalingrad just over 2.5 years later! From the victorious highs of Axis victory at Tobruk in Libya and at the summit of Mount Elbrus in the Caucasus in the Summer of 1942 to decimated armies in the heat of the Western Desert and cold of the Russian ice and snow in the Winter of 1942/early 1943! The fortunes changed as Hitler's over-reaching dream of world domination ground to a halt, but for a while it did seem so obtainable for the Germans!**

In the long run though one of the biggest reasons for the Nazi war machine going from the potential closeness of achieving victory to its eventual demise in World War Two was not any lack of ability or determination on the part of its regular fighting forces, but from the ruinous meddling, bad decisions and unrealistic orders given by its extremely self-defeating Commander-in-Chief Adolf Hitler.

**Shown here in the famous Nazi propaganda poster 'Ein Volk, Ein Reich, Ein Führer!' It was this belief, held by many, in what this slogan was proclaiming 'One People, One Empire, One Leader!' that helped reinforce the cult of Hitler and the sense of destiny that the Nazi Party claimed made him the saviour of Germany and Father of the German people, and it was as a result of these ingrained beliefs, their oath of allegiance to the Führer and other contributory factors that meant that most would follow him from the great victories and high points of 1939-1942 through to the lost victories and bitter end in 1945!**

These are detailed examples of some of the colossal fights which the Axis and Allied forces were engaged in during that year, there could of course be varying alternative views to the overall picture I am painting here from the Allied side and state of affairs if studied in much greater detail, but the bigger generic overview is very much as you have read it in this essay. Also for most of those serving in the very dangerous front lines and on the home fronts who were very busy and focused on their day to day survival and who mostly could only see their individual part at any given time, their personal struggle would have probably felt pretty much the same in 1942 as it was most other war years, continuous hard work or ongoing dangerous operations and battles with possibly the men at front later increasingly sensing a change as more Allied victories occurred, but for many only when the end was really in sight in 1945 would they have maybe felt that things were about to become very different. Most would mainly get their war news from the mainstream medias and see their bigger picture from there, which for the sake of Allied morale had to be very carefully managed and presented or in the case of certain bad news scaled back or kept from the public altogether. For those in possession of overall and more precise facts and who had a much better idea of how things were really going throughout the war, such as those who were high ranking in military and political circles, the bigger picture up until the end of 1942 was a much more troubling thing, and for the reasons highlighted in this overview and more, it was as some of those in the know later said a time of; *'Deep war and bitter perseverance'* and *'a very close call indeed!'* However, it is important to also remember and separate to a certain degree the regular fighting man at the front who was fighting for his country, some believing in the Nazi ideology that they represented, some not, like all other soldiers from all sides and nationalities in the conflict doing what they volunteered or were conscripted to do, unlike the others involved in different aspects of it such as the Holocaust, something which interestingly Oskar Schindler reflected upon when he said; "We must differentiate between guilt and duty. The soldier on the front, like the common man, who does his duty everywhere, should not be held responsible for the actions of a few who also called themselves Germans." Of course no one is completely blameless in war and atrocities were carried out even by some regular troops as well, the sad repetitive nature of conflict!

Interestingly as we now know looking back, at the same time the Nazi war machine was reaching the height of its conquests and coming close to what seemed like an attainable victory, it was also simultaneously reaching the furthest extent of what it was potentially capable of achieving, huge conquests on one hand, dangerously over-extending on the other! All this whilst dedicating immense resources to their simultaneous dual pursuit as mentioned previously of also trying to reach the goals it had set itself in carrying out the Holocaust, again proving that this conflict also had another dimension as it was one which due to the immoral ideology of Nazism was by its very nature a completely different kind of struggle, an absolute fight to the actual death, and where it was essential for righteousness to prevail.

A German propaganda wall newspaper, this one issued 29th April 1942 which reflects the Nazi mindset, proclaiming; "Wir haben alle nur einen Willen, Sieg um jeden Preis!" – "We have only one goal… Victory at all Costs!"

Even though in the war years that lay ahead many more very tough battles were yet to be fought, 1942 was the year when the fate of the world truly 'Hung on a Knife Edge' and where eventually it began to be the 'Turning of the Tide', something that has been written about and reflected upon here around the time of the 80th anniversary of these events (2022), but will of course through historical facts and human interest remains timeless. It was one of those extraordinary periods where the outcome of the monumental battles fought within it would itself dictate the direction and course of that war, and as a result the outcome of world history and the future shape of our world depending on who would ultimately be victorious! The legacy of which would be either a world with freedom, democracy, hope and light or that of a global totalitarian dictatorship, oppression, the continued mass extermination of those the Nazis and their Allies deemed 'Unfit to Live' and a time of continuing darkness. Sadly human nature seems to dictate that history to a greater or lesser degree continually repeats itself, as it has done since time immortal, with everyday people caught up and drawn into numerous conflicts time and again. And now here we are in the 21st century with other emerging Super Powers who share similar ideologies rooted in Socialism/Communism making modern bids for World domination by any and all means possible, some interesting parallels to the earlier history outlined here I think, with the other 'ism' that was attempting to be a dominant global superpower! But that is another story, for another day, in possibly another book!

**A visual representation of different aspects of World War Two shown here in this collage which depicts a war fought on Land, Sea and Air and illustrates many of the destructive aspects of it.**

All the World War Two veterans in 'The Last Stand' played their part in tipping the balance in favour of the Allied cause. The invaluable contributions of each of these men and women helped bring about that final victory, one which three long hard-fought years later, as we will see next, Winston Churchill in his V.E Day speech gave credit to the British people for achieving by saying - *"This is your Victory."*

Thank God it was one for the powers of good over those of evil.

# THIS IS YOUR VICTORY
## INSPIRING WORDS BY WINSTON CHURCHILL

The great wartime leader Winston Churchill made speeches on the 8th May 1945 to declare the end of the 'War in Europe' and to mark a great victory, brought about by a nation that unified when it mattered most and did so for the greater good, so it seemed very fitting to include some of his inspiring and uplifting words near the end this book in relation to this after the words of the military and civilian veterans whose stories have been featured within The Last Stand – Memories of War.

This gives a snap shot of a hugely important moment in World War Two and World History through the words of one of the most eminent orators that ever lived and a measure of the spirit of that moment and a great victory won. A people's victory!

Backdrop – German armed forces surrendered unconditionally on May 7th 1945. Hostilities in Europe ended officially at midnight, May 8th 1945.

First are parts of the broadcast made to the nation by Churchill and which was also later given to the House of Commons in a slightly expanded form, as follows:

"Yesterday morning at 2.41 am at Headquarters, General Jodl, the representative of the German High Command, and Grand Admiral Dornitz, the designated head of the German State, signed the act of unconditional surrender of all German Land, sea, and air forces in Europe to the Allied Expeditionary Force, and simultaneously to the Soviet High Command. The German War is therefore at an end! Almost the whole world was combined against the evil-doers, who are now prostrate before us. Our gratitude to our splendid Allies goes forth from all our hearts in this island and throughout the British Empire. Advance, Britannia! Long live the cause of Freedom! God save the King!"

This feeling of such a great victory attained, albeit at a very high cost was again reflected when Winston Churchill later appeared on the balcony of the Ministry of Health in Whitehall where he proclaimed to a jubilant crowd:

"My dear friends, this is your hour. This is not victory of a party or of any class. It's a victory of the great British nation as a whole!"

He later went on to say in his famous galvanising speech making voice:

"God Bless you all. This is your victory! It is the victory of the cause of freedom in every land. In all our long history, we have never seen a greater day than this. Everyone, man or woman, has done their best. Everyone has tried. Neither the long years, nor the dangers, nor the fierce attacks of the enemy, have in any way weakened the unbending resolve of the British nation. God Bless You All."

After Churchill said the words: *"THIS IS YOUR VICTORY"* the crowd roared back: *"NO - IT IS YOURS."* A great mark of respect for the man who had taken them by the hand and led them through some of the darkest, hardest and most desperate years that our country had known in its modern history, and brought them through to that victory!

This was followed by the crowd gathered below singing 'Land of Hope and Glory' conducted by Churchill, this historical day became known as V.E Day – 'Victory in Europe Day'.

That left only Japan to be dealt with, which after the dropping of the atomic bombs on Hiroshima on the 6th August 1945, followed by Nagasaki on the 9th August 1945, led to Japanese Emperor Hirohito announcing the surrender of Japan in the 'Jewel Voice Broadcast' on the 14th August 1945, 15th August in Europe with the time difference, making that V.J Day – 'Victory over Japan Day', which meant another huge party in London in just over three months, and also in many other cities of the victorious nations around the world.

When our American Allies across the ocean in the USA began celebrating, Life Magazine reported it was: 'as if joy had been rationed and saved up for three years, eight months and seven days since Sunday, Dec 7, 1941' (the day of the Japanese attack on Pearl Harbour). Finally the formal Unconditional Surrender of Imperial Japan came on the 2nd September 1945 on USS Missouri in Tokyo Bay, Japan, with General MacArthur overseeing the historical event, bringing to an end, almost to the day, six long, hard years of global conflict and the almost incomprehensible loss of over 70 million dead, but ended in the defeat of two of the most malevolent and destructive powers the world had ever seen. **Pictured here; Winston Churchill on the balcony of the Ministry of Health at Whitehall, V.E Day, 8th May 1945 giving his trademark 'V for Victory' sign on this most victorious of days!**

### Preliminary Unconditional Surrender Document – 7th May 1945

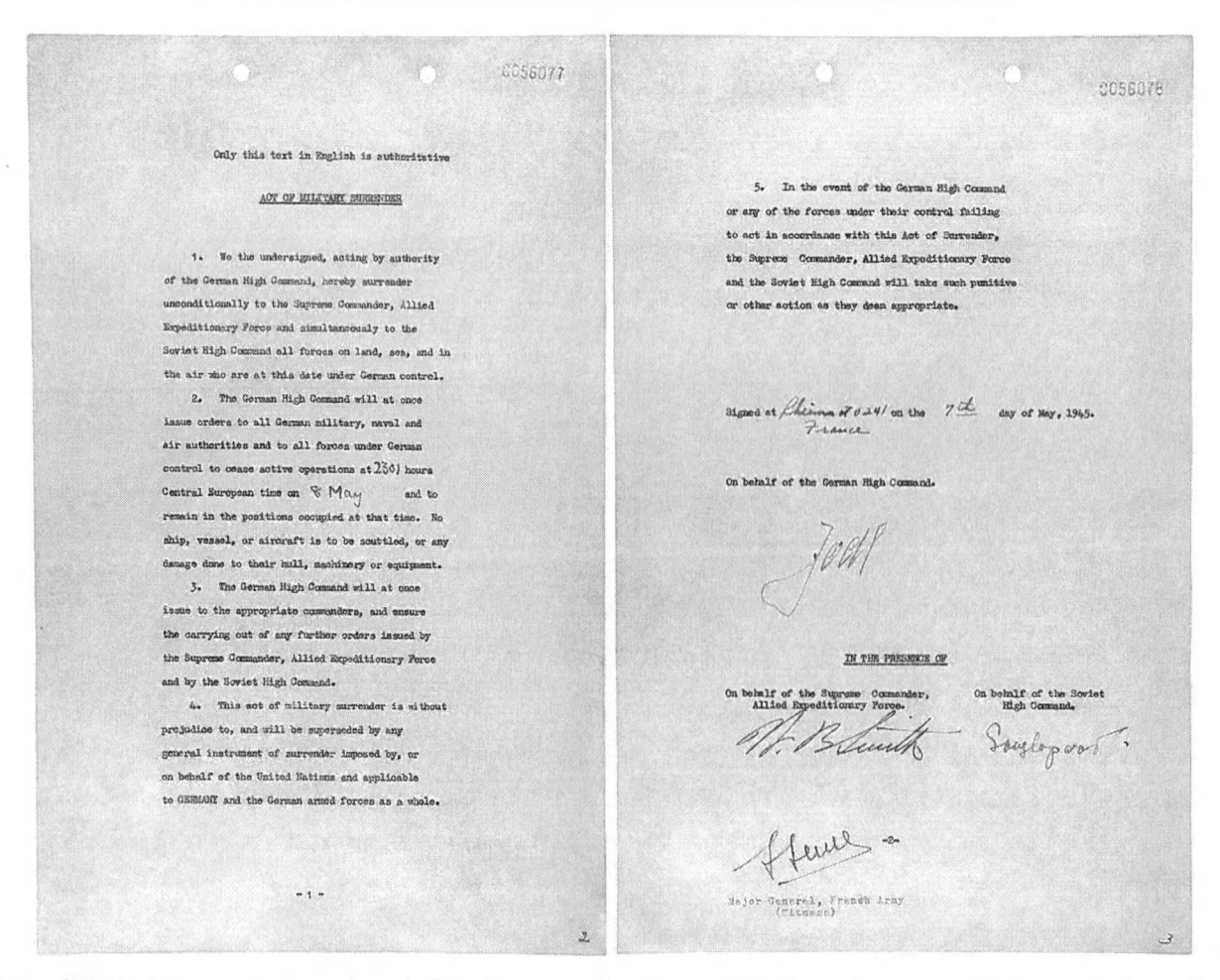

**This official document was signed for Germany by General Jodl and representatives of the Allied Expeditionary Force, Soviet High Command and a French Major-General as an official Witness.**

# Definitive Unconditional Surrender Document – 8th May 1945

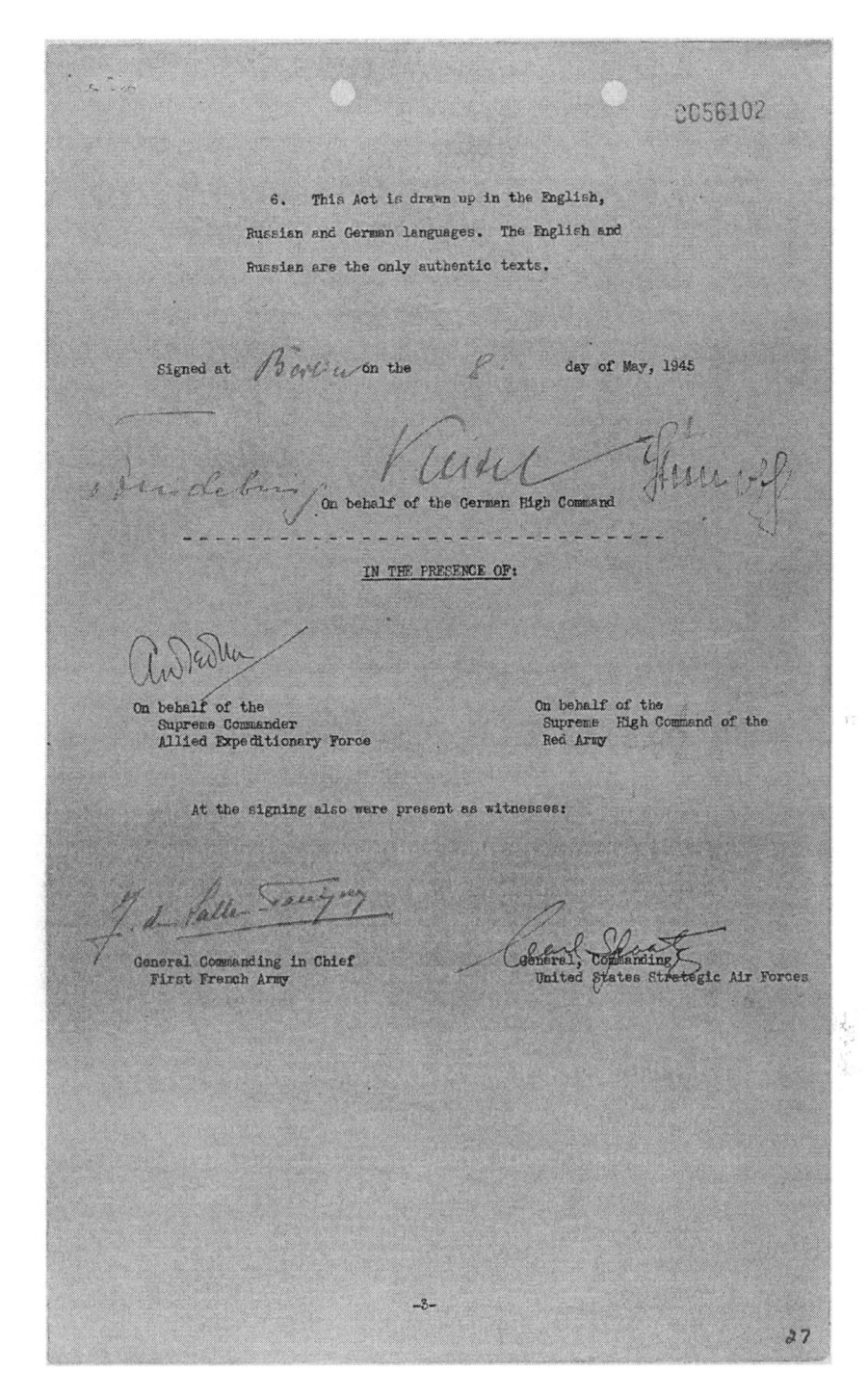

> 6. This Act is drawn up in the English, Russian and German languages. The English and Russian are the only authentic texts.
>
> Signed at Berlin on the 8. day of May, 1945
>
> *[signatures]*
> On behalf of the German High Command
>
> IN THE PRESENCE OF:
>
> *[signature]*
> On behalf of the Supreme Commander Allied Expeditionary Force
>
> On behalf of the Supreme High Command of the Red Army
>
> At the signing also were present as witnesses:
>
> *[signature]*
> General Commanding in Chief First French Army
>
> *[signature]*
> General, Commanding United States Strategic Air Forces

**The Third and Last Page of the Instrument of Unconditional Surrender of the German Armed Forces signed in Karlshorst, Berlin, dated 8th May 1945, effective at 23.01 hours, this legal document effected the extinction of Nazi Germany and ended World War II in Europe. Its signatories were Generalfeldmarschall Wilhelm Keitel, Generaladmiral Hans-Georg von Friedeburg, Generaloberst Hans-Jurgen Stumpff on behalf of the German High Command, Marshal Georgy Zhukov (very feint and barely legible signature) on behalf of the Supreme High Command of the Red Army, and Air Chief Marshal Arthur William Tedder on behalf of the Allied Expeditionary Force. Present as witnesses & signatories General F. de Lattre-Tassigny, Commander in Chief of the First French Army and General Carl Spaatz, Commander of the United States Strategic Air Forces. There were 3 language versions of the surrender document (first 2 definitive) – English, Russian, German, actually signed on the 9th of May local time, backdated to the original date it was intended to be signed and in line with it most European countries celebrated as V.E Day 8th May, Russia still marks V.E Day on 9th May.**

# The Journey – A Short Story from Gary Bridson-Daley

# 'THE JOURNEY'
## (A personal short story from the Author)

It wouldn't be too difficult to write a book about the making of my books based on the many remarkable experiences I had and incredible people I have met on that long and fascinating journey. There would easily be enough personal back-stories to do this, but as I realistically think it is more important to keep writing about the veterans and rightly keep the main focus on them with only some interwoven input from or regarding me that I have included just one stand-alone 'personal interest-insight' story in this follow up book to continue giving different and varied content within it.

When I was visiting East Anglia in 2015 to interview Battle of Britain Fighter Pilot Ace Tom Neil I was staying in a small town called Beccles in Suffolk. Whilst there I was taking a stroll and getting some fresh air, I walked through the small town, had a look at the ancient local church of St. Michael's with its very interesting three-sided clock tower, with the side facing Norfolk being the one with no clock face, the funny story as I was told by some of the towns' inhabitants was that this was about old rivalries between the counties, and symbolised one not wanting to give any time to or having any time for the other! I also went around the churchyard to check out the lovely views from Suffolk overlooking Norfolk at this highly recommended viewpoint. As I was taking in the beautiful landscape a lady who was walking her dog came towards me, we said good morning to each other and hearing I was definitely not a local she inquisitively asked me where I was from and I told her 'Manchester.' She exclaimed in a broad Anglian country accent: *'you are a long way from home, what brings you here to the back of beyond?'*

This led to a conversation about the book and me being there to interview a World War Two Air Force veteran. As I was telling her about the different veterans I had been interviewing I could see that she was listening intently and was becoming quite moved. Then she told me that her favourite Uncle who she admired and loved very much as a child was in the Royal Air Force during the Second World War and was a Navigator in a Lancaster bomber which got shot down, and that tragically he was killed during that operation over Europe. Whilst telling me this she began crying and just waved to say goodbye as she was not able to continue talking. She departed quickly leaving me standing there in the graveyard, finding myself very moved by our brief encounter and absorbing what she had just shared with me.

What impacted me the most was the fact that over 70 years after the event her pain for the loss of a family member was still so raw, and that under the surface the scars of World War Two, a conflict that had been over for decades brought about an almost instant outpouring of grief! I thought to myself this was one person still mourning a loss of one serviceman from Bomber Command, and that this feeling would have been multiplied and shared by many more family and friends of that one and every other lost serviceman, and knowing there was a staggering 55,573 Bomber Command casualties during the Second World War the amount of people it must have affected and pain it caused is almost incomprehensible. These losses were in just one branch of the RAF, increase this by including all those also killed in the Army and Navy, over 380,000 in combat and around 70,000 civilians killed, mainly from enemy bombing! All of that immeasurable hurt being absorbed by our small island nation, with more than one loss in many families! Almost too much to grasp!

That momentary chance meeting triggered all these thoughts and feelings within me, it showed and confirmed to me that this conflict from so long ago was still affecting people even now and as a result was not truly over, I found this very touching indeed and wondered how many other people must still be walking around harbouring similar stories, thoughts, feelings and pain? That same day I went on to interview Tom, a veteran who was in combat and in the thick of it in front line action in the Battle of Britain, and who helped save our country during one of the darkest times in our modern history and who saw first-hand many of his friends and fellow servicemen shot down and lost in battle and had to himself absorb and deal with that whilst going back into combat day after day!

This is just one story of a great many experiences that occurred whilst I have been undertaking the 'Debt of Gratitude' project from 2014 onwards, this poignant example which is part of the 'back drop of events' as I have moved around the United Kingdom, serves as a reminder of my own personal journey and the journeys of those whose lives and paths have crossed with mine along the way, such as the lady in the churchyard.

# Interesting Observations – A Short Story from a WW2 Service Veteran

# **INTERESTING OBSERVATIONS**

This story is conveying and encapsulating the feelings that quite a few veterans shared with me in one way or another regarding conflict during my interviews with them and those who I met at veteran related events over the years, one such random meeting with a very articulate WW2 veteran at an event led to an extremely interesting conversation where he expressed this exceptionally insightful narrative that I wrote down for future use, and which I feel is very good to include at the latter end of this book to give a different perspective on the experience of warfare.

"These poignant observations of mine were made when I was a Junior Officer during the Italian Campaign, I was in an ancient city after a fierce battle and when the smoke had cleared and as the dust was settling, from amongst all the carnage, death and destruction we saw very old depictions of warriors in action carved on stone facades from antiquity, and after some deliberation I said quite pensively to a good pal of mine, who had just been through the same dreadful ordeal as me, look mankind never learns!  Over 2000 years have passed and we are still doing the same horrible things to each other!

The only things that have changed are the uniforms and means of transport to get into battle and the some of the weapons used to kill.  Even the reasons to wage war have remained pretty much the same at the end of the day, greed, domination, the lust for power, wanting what another person, ruler or kingdom has got and as result of that causing the seemingly never-ending wars and all the pain that goes with them!  And us, we are just pawns in a much bigger strategic board game!

Just imagine I said how much better the world would be if all the time, money and energies that were spent perusing war were instead channelled towards peaceful, positive and creative activities!  After my open sermonising or should I say big rant my pal just looked at me gob smacked and still a fair bit shell shocked from our own fierce fighting said: 'bloody hell your right, we never learn do we.'

I was always known as a bit of a deep thinker, and that day I really was one, helped and encouraged I reckoned by a good university education, being well read and having a great need and curiosity to know much more about life, to try and make sense of the madness I was seeing around me which we were all experiencing almost every day whilst on active duty and in front line combat!

But I don't believe that my observations were wrong and looking at the world around me today I still consider the same to be true!  From my experience of battles and war I can say that there are truly no real winners or losers, only survivors!

Although it is true to say that our war, the Second World War was as understandable as a war could be, purely because it was truly a war against dark powers and unjust enemies hell bent on world domination and eradicating anyone or anything that stood in the way of that goal, who also undertook the wholesale murder of innocent civilians based on racial, religious, political and other differences.

We all knew to varying degrees that because of these and other reasons the evil ideology of Nazism had to be crushed.  However I think the morality and Justification of some other wars since has been to a greater or lesser extent more questionable.

The root cause of all these wars from the beginning of time until this very day, as I was once told and still hold to be true is;

>'That in this life there is enough of everything for everyone, but not enough for everyone's greed!'

I'm proud to have served my country, to have stepped up and contributed when needed and maybe I shouldn't be saying some of these things, because they don't sound very patriotic and maybe even a bit controversial, which is why I don't want to be quoted by name here. But all war is terrible for those involved or caught up in it and affected by it, mentally, physically, emotionally, whether that war is thought of as justifiable or not, but thank God our precious Island Nation has had generations of brave servicemen and women who have been and still are willing to defend us all.

To finish I will quote these words that I picked up some time ago and feel, especially as I have grown older, greatly express my emotions regarding war and conflict of any kind;

There is no way to Peace

Peace is the Way

Beautiful and so true I think, I hope you think so to?"

# Tribute Poetry from Service Veterans

# ARNOLD 'ARNIE' HUTCHINSON MBE 7th BATTALION
## 6th AIRBORNE DIVISION

In this part of the poetry section are featured pieces of poetry written by World War Two Veterans who are featured in this book. When I wrote 'Ode to Comrades and Old Friends' it was inspired by and dedicated to the many veterans I had interviewed over the years, and to one in particular who was a great inspiration as he like myself wrote poetry on a regular basis.

That man was was Arnie Hutchinson, WW2 Paratrooper of the 7th Parachute Battalion, 5th Brigade, 6th Airborne Division who was involved in the Battle of the Bulge in the Ardennes, Belgium in December 1944, Operation Varsity the airborne drops into Germany to help secure the bridgeheads over the Rhine in March 1945, India-Malaya-Singapore 1945-46 and later as part of the forces sent to undertake policing in Palestine in 1946. Arnie is a prolific and very good poetry writer with nearly 300 pieces to his name, some giving glimpses into the mind of a young man and his experiences of serving as a Para and other related things from his life.

Featured here are 5 pieces of his poetry which Arnie allowed me to select and gave permission for me to include here, they are diverse, moving and are an important contribution to this book having been written by a veteran of the Second World War and again show the depth of thought, emotion and humour conveyed through this medium.

# BATTLE MORN

This short but poignant piece was written by Arnie on the morning of the 24th March 1945, just prior to going into battle in Operation Varsity, the Airborne drops over the Rhine, with the aim of helping secure bridgeheads in Germany and supporting the other ground actions of Operation Plunder that were intended to help speed up Allied victory.

Scribbled on the back of a leaflet, these were the thoughts and fears of a young 20-year-old man going into battle for the first time, not knowing if he would survive it!

A truly unique and significant piece of poetry as it comes directly from the veteran who wrote it during WW2 itself, now passed on to me to be featured here in 'The Last Stand', another real example of 'Connecting with History' and the continuity that comes from it.

## BATTLE MORN

Ah Death! Though safe a haven
How best can we evade thee?
Ah Life! In war so freely given
We pray to God who made thee

That we may cling with every limb
To thee, through battles cruel and grim
O God, who'll hear our pleading hymn
Thou light, no hell can shade thee

24/3/45

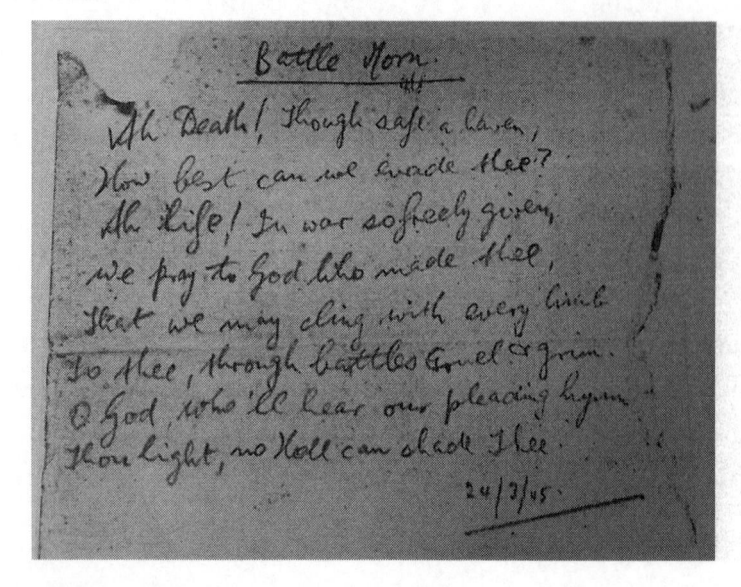

**The original 'Battle Morn' as written by Arnie on the eve of battle**

**Written to honour the memory of his good friend Private Thomas Cairns, who was one of 38 men from the 7th (L.I) Battalion, Parachute Regiment who was killed in action at the Bridge in Neustadt Am Rubenburge on 7th April 1945, and laid to rest with 24 of his Brothers-in-Arms in the Becklingen War Cemetery, Soltau, Germany.**

## YOUNG FRIEND TOMMY

Tommy my pal was just a lad like me
Young soldiers thrown together, had a beer
Wondering what the next day's jobs might be;
Good, another parachute jump? That's naught to fear!

Fit, adventurous, ready for a lark
Enjoying life as hardly ever before
We earned the wings, but now soon to embark
To drop amongst the Germans in the war

These days of hell, thank God you'll never know
Such hideous fears and dangers, would we survive?
Perhaps every minute there would be no more!
God only knows the answer, dead or alive?

It's been now seventy years since Hitler's crimes
I look at a war grave, a friend's face I see
Who never had the long happy family times
Tommy, nineteen, got killed – but why not me?

**18/10/14**

A poem written about 7 Para as a unit of occupation whilst in South-East Asia under S.E.A.C – South East Asia Command, just after the war, enjoying the 'wonders' of the Far East, yet longing to return home. This piece was written by Arnie exactly a month to the day after the Unconditional surrender of Japan.

## THE SEVENTH IN S.E.A.C

Occupation is our lot
We'll show Malaya what we've got
And peace on earth gives plenty time
To learn French prose or English rhyme

Football will make our sportsmen sweat
But we'll be playing it, and get
Some games and jazz recordings hired
The "Seventh Echo" is admired

At six o'clock the CSM
His wrathful anger fails to stem
"Where've you been, lad? Quick, double in,
Stand easy, take your mepacrine!"

In Singapore we see again
The wristlet watch, the fountain pen
And treasures of the Mystic East
But in the shops a private's fleeced

Majestic pillars, domes and towers
Pagodas, palms and flashy flowers
All these things were Hirohitos's
Ants, fleas, lizards, bugs, mosquitos!

'Neath a net of jungle green
In seclusion like a queen
On the hard stone floors we kip
Wake with aching ribs and hip

But no hardship can deter
The tough Seventh Para lads, No sir
However sick the blokes may be
Of Blanco white of dysentery

The Jap has gone where went the Hun
The Allies set the Rising Sun
And now the Pegasus unfurls
Where Tojo taught the Chinese girls

From Singapore one day we'll go
To Pontypridd, Perth, Plymouth Hoe
Ipswich or Ilkley Moor 'baht 'at
At home there there'll be the welcome mat

02/10/45

A poem about the comradery and sense of belonging shared with Airborne veterans and their families at the monthly Parachute Association meetings, and how that fellowship and care is extended to all who need it, long after every conflict was over.

## OUR AIRBORNE BROTHERHOOD

On every first Tuesday I know where to go
Three walks, waits and bus rides to meet Jack and Joe
At Short Heath, then back, takes me almost eight hours
Well worth it, so I bring a lady some flowers

Occasional socials with eats, drinks and song
And sometimes a dance but that can't last too long
Those excellent sarnies and cakes the girls bring
Then read the minutes, our silence, an efficient meeting

We're friends of charities we support with good will
We celebrate birthdays and visit the ill
Our standard is lowered as we say "goodbye"
To wonderful comrades whose time came to die

Now what day every month could be better spent?
In sincerity, good faith and contentment
Our brotherhood means that we all play our parts
In preserving the ideals close to our hearts

Care for the ageing, remembering those gone
Achieving our purposes as we carry on
In difficult times, which we hope some fine day
Will make the world better, because we passed this way

(No Date)

A poignant piece about the four seasons of life, the four seasons of man. Starting with the springtime at war and the losses it brought, through to better times and a much happier thought!

## THE FOUR SEASONS

In Germany that Spring of Forty Five
Still fighting fit, good just to be alive
Thousands were killed, right in their prime of life
Forever lost, no future, kids or wife

Somehow though later, when the war was won
Played Summer games of cricket in the sun
Enjoyed the closeness of our family lives
From which each other joy in life derives

In Autumn, when the green trees turn brown
Through cool and misty pathways stroll to town
Are you too busy with your seasons' 'shop'?
Be careful! Now's when even strong folk drop

But good old Christmas snow falls, Winter's here
So after church have plenty wine and beer
To keep your spirits up and see you through
To the panto, not only kids, it's for us too!

21/08/16

# DON HITCHCOCK ROYAL NAVY HMS NARBROUGH

I met WW2 Royal Navy Veteran Don Hitchcock on the 6th June 2019 at a Royal British Legion event at Bayeux Cemetery in Normandy, France during the 75th Anniversary of the D-Day landings. We struck up a conversation, got on very well and in a very short time I learned a lot about his very varied and interesting service history, and also much to my delight found out he also enjoyed writing poetry, some of which he very kindly and radiantly recited there and then. On the 20th July 2019 I interviewed Don (pictured here with original U-Boat Captains' Binoculars) at his home in the West Midlands where we had a delightful day, along with capturing his great story I was also given 3 pieces of his poetry by Don for use in this book.

During the Second World War Don served on the Captain Class Frigate HMS Narborough as a Code & Cypher Operator during which time he was involved in de-cyphering incoming classified communications to his ship, then sending out coded replies to other ships in the surface fleet during operations and to the Admiralty in London. He was also involved in weather mapping on the run up to D-Day, during and after the Normandy landings he was involved in 34 D-Day related escorts to all 5 landing beaches, and on the 7th June 1944 was involved in the rescue of 2689 mainly U.S soldiers from the stricken troop ship USS Susan B. Anthony. Later Don and his ship served in the latter part of the Arctic convoys and he finished his time in Germany at Naval Establishments in various places such as Hamburg where he worked on the 'Type X' Cypher Machine undertaking more secret de-coding.

This first piece of poetry was written by Don in 2011, sixty-seven years after D-Day, it incorporates some of what he saw and his feelings regarding those experiences, poignant reflections from a D-Day veteran.

## A POEM TO REMEMBER THE EVENTS OF D-DAY

We whom remain remember
Those friends who shared a life
Of white capped waves
And wind-whipped spray
That shredded our duffles
With a cruel knife.

How we joked and bantered
On sun-drenched decks,
With innuendo course and lewd,
While we remember the silken motion,
And soon forgot how we retched and spewed.
When yards were held in bitter fingers
And metal tore the ungloved hand,
We struggle through time
To a once-bright morning,
And fetched up close to the burning sand.

An old man now stands on that sodden shore,
Looking out where he once looked in.
He remains to remember sights of sinkings
Of unknown men caressed by the tide.
They came from afar and so soon they left us,
Omaha is the place they died.
Their Styx was our Channel, nowhere to hide.
Now it is empty, endeavour has gone.
He remains to remember alone, not yet gone.

'Crossing the Bar' is a term generally used by military or ex-military and more specifically the Royal Navy to politely inform and advise of a person who has died or crossed over to the other side. This poem was written by Don as a tribute to those fellow servicemen who had 'Crossed the Bar' in the Captain Class Frigate Association of which he was a member.

## CROSSING THE BAR

A tear, a smile and a fond farewell
Mark our passage over the bar
The storms are passed and a gentle swell
Breaks the still quite with the creak of a spar

Proudly, in youth like the Captains of old,
Remember their battles well fought long ago,
We too faced the heat and the Arctic's chill cold

And kept open the seas from the menace below,
The fate of our fleet, long shrouded in mystery
No longer forgotten, lives on in proud history.

Written by Shipmate Don Hitchcock
Ex HMS Narborough K578

HMS Gould (K476) was a British Frigate of the Captain Class. She was sunk North of the Azores on 1st March 1944 by German U-Boat U-358 Captained by Rolf Manke with the loss of 124 men including her Commanding Officer Lt. Daniel William Ungoed, RN. During this fierce engagement U-358 was forced to the surface and sunk only 20 minutes later by gunfire and depth charges from HMS Affleck (K362), and as a result only one crew member survived, 50 others including the Captain died. Don found all of this very moving and as a result wrote this piece to commemorate the demise of this fellow Captain Class Frigate and entitled it 'Loss of the Gould.' *In the text Zephyr means a breeze or wind.

## LOSS OF THE GOULD

They who had the power to hurt
Can hurt us no more
For our eternity it lies
Upon the Ocean floor

On that brave day Zephyr teased up
When between the waves
We slipped away for ever
To join the chartered graves
Our epitaph is terse at best
Forty-five North by Fifteen West

But now a miracle has taken place
Neptune's jewels our face
While in the sunlight far above
Great Whales perform their rites of love

We cannot move and far from land
Save for faint stirrings of the sounds at hand
For ever locked in endless time
We rest content, in death sublime

**Revised by Chris Hitchcock (Son)**

# KEITH QUILTER DSC 1842 SQUADRON ROYAL NAVY FLEET AIR ARM

Navy Fleet Air Arm Fighter Pilot Keith Quilter was awarded the Distinguished Service Cross for his brave actions whilst serving in South-East Asia in WW2, it was there and in other theatres of war where he mainly flew the Vought F4U 'Corsair' carrier-based fighter-bomber aircraft.

He flew from the aircraft carriers HMS Formidable and HMS Victorious, he helped give 'Top Cover' on raids against the German Battleship 'Tirpitz' which he dive bombed in August 1944 in Norway in 'Operation Goodwood', later he was with the British Fleet in the Pacific and was involved in 'Operation Iceberg', the invasion of Okinawa. Whilst in a dive bomber mission against a Japanese base in the Pacific he was shot down, crash landed his plane in the sea and was miraculously picked up and saved by an American submarine!

The piece of poetry he gave for inclusion in the book is called 'Veteran Pilot's Memories' and is about former pilots and other service veterans during get-togethers in bars and members clubs and their nostalgic reminiscing of former days and past glories, where many shared stories and their sentimental preference for the older type propeller engine aircraft that they once flew in many well-known missions and Operations during World War Two.

It is an adaptation from a similar short poem penned by his friend Mr C Rutter Fletcher with permission to be added here, and both are credited for this piece.

# **VETERAN PILOT'S MEMORIES**

In outmoded smart-casuals they chat at the bar
Or dine in the local pub's mess
Each man has won, in peace or war
The world's esteem – success

They talk of twin Cessenas or twenty ton yawls
And of other successful men
Or of capital gains, till someone recalls
"Do you remember when....."

Then memory plays with far off days
When planes dragged their tails and were bold
With adventures half lost in a distant haze
Which is more than tinged with gold

And of all the increasingly splendid jets
That they've flown in the years between
It is true perhaps, for those veteran chaps
Some old prop fighter's still queen

Keith Quilter & C Rutter Fletcher

# Tribute Poetry from Gary Bridson-Daley

# THE IMPORTANT CONTRIBUTION OF POETRY

As we are all aware creative writing comes in different forms, of which I feel poetry is a very special one, as it can be and often is a very profound form of self-expression, where the writer is really allowing his or her deepest thoughts and feelings to be truly articulated and opened up to the outside world. The messages a poet conveys through verse are often very poignant, many good pieces stand the test of time and continue to touch and influence those who read them many years after they were written. I hope the poetry of the veterans who I am privileged to feature in my book along with the veteran, conflict and remembrance related poetry I have written which is contained here in this part of it will do the same for some of those who read it. GBD.

Above – Author and Poet, Gary Bridson-Daley on the 6th June 2019 with Prince, later after his mother Queen Elizabeth II passed on the 8th September 2022, King Charles III and Camilla The Duchess of Cornwall, later Queen Camilla, at Bayeux Cemetery in Normandy, France. Right – Also on the same day with the then Prime Minister Theresa May presenting her with a copy of my 1st book 'A Debt of Gratitude To The Last Heroes'. Everyone in attendance at this and at other ceremonies on the 75th Anniversary of D-Day came to pay tribute to all who served in Operation Overlord on that famous 'Deliverance-Day', and also to remember all those who fell both on that day and during the Normandy Campaign as a whole. As a result of these very important meetings with Royalty and the head of our political establishment I had managed to get my very important message of Remembrance and honouring veterans through my book into the hands of people at the highest level and get copies of it into both Buckingham Palace and Downing Street. In addition to this I have written a number of veterans related articles which have been featured in the Independent (i-paper) and Sunday Express in both the physical Newspaper & Online, done Radio and had ITV & BBC appearances on special WW2 reports. Not bad for a local lad from Manchester/Salford!

This opening poem has been written as a tribute to our former Monarch HRH Queen Elizabeth II to coincide with her Platinum anniversary year, but due to the nature of it covering her service in World War Two when she was Princess Elizabeth through all the years that have followed as Queen Elizabeth makes it an abiding and ageless tribute, linked to her dedication and wartime story also found in this book. In some parts of the poems in my section, due to type setting, there may in some cases be slight overlaps where a word or words have continued on to the line below it, I hope this doesn't lead the reader to lose the flow, or the hopeful enjoyment of the content.

## HER MAJESTY THE QUEEN

Her Majesty the Queen
No Greater Monarch hath the country ever seen
Only fully devoted service to her nation
No half measures or anything in between

Been reigning over us since 1953
Through the many storms this country has weathered
Continuing a noble historical link of 1000 or more years
Ever constant, never severed

Even playing her part during World War Two
Then as a young Princess in the ATS, learning to be a driver and a mechanic,
as you do,
The only ruling sovereign in the world who served in that conflict so long ago
Like all others she saw around her at that time, stepping up with pride and a
willingness that she did show

From one service to another, from Princess to Queen
With a continuity across the decades, never failing under pressure, through trials
and tribulations, remaining supreme,
And as many around you have sadly come and gone
From Churchill to the Duke of Edinburgh, still you continued to work on

Second World War Veteran, Commander of our Armed Forces, Head of State
In these and other capacities providing a stability to which many can relate
Been with us throughout many conflicts since that of which she was a part,
A symbol of some of the greatest things this country stands for and a special place
at the centre of this nation's beating heart

Her Majesty's landmark years marked by Jubilees in the past
In 1977 Silver, 2002 Gold, 2012 Diamond, and in 2022 Platinum,
70 years on the throne, a feat no reigning Queen in history has ever surpassed,
So I honour you in my book, which is primarily dedicated to you
As one of many countless people sending heartfelt thanks for all that you have done,
for remaining steadfast and staying true

You promised in your youthful years that your life would be dedicated to the service
of your people in this island nation
As history now testifies a commitment you have fulfilled in many ways
and without hesitation,
For the betterment of our realm doing things both seen and unseen
So from those in this country and the Commonwealth all that remains to be said,
even though you are now gone is respectfully 'God Save the Queen'.

Gary Bridson-Daley

2022

A poem I wrote to honour The Last British Dambuster George 'Johnny' Johnson, only a few days after his passing and near the completion of this book which I am very honoured to say has his Foreword as a great validation and his name forever linked to it. I was very privileged to have spent precious time with him as a guest at his home in Bristol when I interviewed him for my 1st book 'A Debt of Gratitude To The Last Heroes' in which his story is featured, to have dined and shared wine and laughter with him, to also have met him at a veterans event where my favourite picture used with the foreword in this book was taken, and to have kept in touch and had lovely phone conversations with him, all these things mean a lot to me. Thanks Johnny for your kindness, your decency, your service, RIP.

## FOR 'JOHNNY'

George 'Johnny' Johnson the 'Last British Dambuster' from 617
All his earthly operations completed he has now flown to heaven,
Greeted by the boys from the squadron who were all part of Chastise
Reunited and once again with his full crew he soars and flies

A great 101 years that he lived to the full, achieving so much
Many lives he inspired, helped and beautifully touched,
Humble man always thinking of and praising others
Continually looking to elevate and remember his serving brothers

On that faithful night in May '43 he struck the Sorpe Dam
Bomb Aimer in 'T for Tommy' hit his target, what a man,
Using the Barnes Wallace 'Bouncing Miracle' they got the job done
A poke in the eye for Hitler and a step closer to getting the war won

But he wasn't a crewman of just one mission, no 50 he completed
Awarded a DFM for his valour and kept going until the Nazis were defeated,
Bomber Harris' boys sent on mission after mission, away they would go
Courage and determination is what they would all show

Over 20 years in the RAF, Squadron Leader he became
Having served in wartime a King, in peacetime a Queen, never seeking fame,
It found him anyway as the Dambusters legend grew
He took it in his stride like everything else in his life that he put his mind to

Success in many ways and great legacies he has left behind
A beautiful big family, WW2 history and all those to whom he has been kind,
I feel blessed to have been one of those with whom you shared your time
For that and your service I thank you for being simply sublime

Missed by many, and remembered by many more
In hearts and minds you will stay that is for sure,
So this is my tribute to you in the best way I know how
Using words to express and to honour you forever, not just for now

A poem for Johnny to say thank you and goodbye
When I see a Lancaster I'll be thinking of you as I look up at the sky,
And as you look down over us with a smile on your face
May you find eternal peace in that most special place

For 'Johnny'

(25th November 1921 – 7th December 2022)

Gary Bridson-Daley

12/12/22

The wreck of this Second World War Merchant supply vessel is like an incredible time capsule that for those lucky enough to have dived her transports you back over 80 years! Built by J.L Thompson and Sons in Sunderland, County Durham in 1940 for the Albyn Line, and sadly was destroyed by a German Heinkel HE 111 Bomber in the Autumn of 1941 whilst trying to deliver her valuable cargo of war materials to help Montgomery's fight against Rommel in the Western Desert Campaign. This amazing wreck is now classed as one of the top 'must do' Scuba Diving destinations in the World. I count myself as very fortunate and privileged to have dived her on 3rd January 2007 whilst working out in Egypt. The experience is another great and this time underwater connection to WW2 history and one undertaken with reverence as she is an official war grave, and now many years later as a PADI Master Scuba Diver I hope to re-visit her again one day. In December 2022 after seeing some documentary footage about the ship I was moved to write this poem which I have decided to include here in this poetry chapter along with a couple of pictures from the dive, so here is my tribute to the Thistlegorm and those who lost their lives on her.

## THISTLEGORM

SS Thistlegorm, casualty of a war on the sea
Sitting in her watery grave now, tranquil as can be
British Merchant Navy vessel sunk in Egypt 6th October 1941
With the loss of 9 brave souls forever gone

From Glasgow via Cape Town and onto Alexandria she was to steam
But fate had something else in mind or so it would seem
For this was to be her last journey and whilst at a 'Safe Anchorage' she lay
Struck by two bombs from the enemy, unfortunately easy prey

This only her fourth sea voyage when spotted by an adversary from above
Luftwaffe Heinkel dropped its deadly payload showing no love
Her cargo destined for the Eighth Army to fight the Nazi foe
To try and stop the Afrika Korps but instead to the bottom it would all go

A Defensively Equipped Merchant Ship with Captain Ellis at the helm
Didn't stand a chance that night and so now occupies a different realm
Struck at hold 4 near the stern of the ship
Into obscurity and the history books she would slip

Yet the story of this vessel was not destined to be over that's for sure
As Jacques Cousteau rediscovered her in the 1950's once more
Fast forward decades and in Ras Muhammad she does still reside
A gem of the Red Sea she is proclaimed to be, her name elevated with pride

Now amongst the best wreck sites in the world and therefore living on
History comes alive for those fortunate to dive what's left, of which I was one
A visitor seeing the World War Two treasure that lies around and about
Trucks, Motorcycles, Armoured Cars, Locomotives a marvel without a doubt

Crewed now only by the creatures of the deep
In an aquatic world at around 30 metres she does sleep
Remembered by many now her fame has grown
As it should be in perpetuity the name Thistlegorm will always be known

Gary Bridson-Daley

December 2022

### TO THE MEMORY OF THE CREW LOST ON THE SS THISTLEGORM
(27° 49' 03" N, 33° 55' 14"E)

Arthur Cain – Aged 26.
Archibald 'Archie' Giffin – Aged 18.   Alfred Oswald Kean – Aged 68.
Donald Masterson – Aged 32.   Joseph Munro Rolfe – Aged 17.
Kahil Sakando – Aged 49.   Christopher Todds – Aged 25.
Alexander Neil Brian Watt – Aged 21.   Thomas Woolaghan – Aged 24.

R.I.P

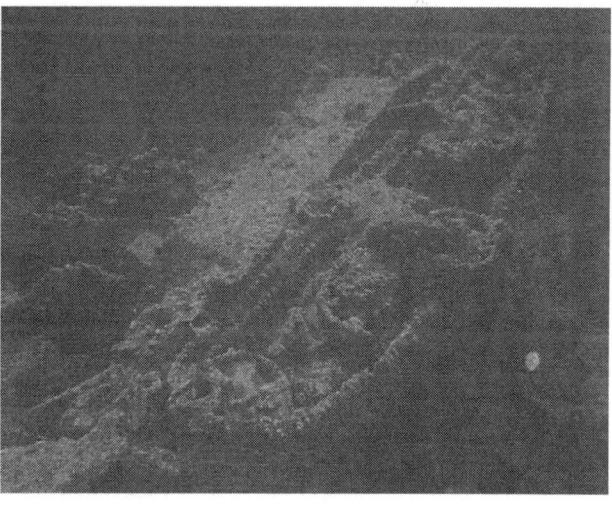

Left – The Author at the main gun on the stern of the ship.  Right – A Bren Carrier still very discernible in the wreckage.  Poignant memorials to a war fought over eight decades ago!

A moving piece that was written especially for the centenary of WW1 to mark that very important anniversary in 2018. Relevant and applicable not only in the centenary year but any time we remember the fallen of WW1 in the years to come. Likewise it is also significant as this book intentionally carries stories of some WW1 relatives of WW2 veterans featured within it, this being done in order to maintain the continuity of remembrance for all who served from past to present day that my 'Debt of Gratitude Project' seeks to honour.

## 100 YEARS HAVE PAST

Behind every name on every stone
Is a story waiting to be told
100 Years have passed since the last blast
That decimated a generation so bold

Their bodies rest in peace
Whilst their souls march on over fields filled with poppies bright red
Silent witnesses they have become in a war so painfully won
As long as they are remembered they will never be truly dead

Brothers in arms who whispered Psalms
Whilst waiting for the whistle to blow
Over the top they went to wenst they were sent
Into an inferno of lead and shrapnel they would go

Bayonets fixed, hearts pounding fast
Ordered forward once again
Having seen the fate of the friends that went before them
And praying they wouldn't meet the same

Sadly fortune rarely smiled
And so millions of good souls were lost
Their pain through the years still resonates
As we still count the cost

But my God the bravery of our boys
As onward they went
Fear overcome by the will to survive
To serve and be victorious
Upon this they were hell bent

They did their duty to the bitter end
So it is our duty now to be like a friend
To show we care and won't forget
With continued remembrance and no regret

We owe it to them all these years later
To make sure their memory does not diminish
But only becomes greater
To carry the torch and keep alive their flame
And pass it on to the next generation
So they can do the same

And as we continue to honour them over a century on
Think of each as a precious flower like the poppy we don
Something which is a symbol of pride and brings an occasional tear
Yet reminds us of the freedom that they bought, which we hold so dear

Continue to do this and their ultimate sacrifices will not have been in vain
Don't forget the peace we have today is partly due to them
So maintain and show respect time and again

And make sure it does last
This year and every year
Keep remembering
Until another 100 years have passed!

Gary Bridson-Daley

09/11/18

Verses saying thank you to those who defend us through wars of the present and those who will be defending us in the inevitable wars of the future. They who defend our todays and our children's tomorrows. A different poem than the others, as it is looking from the present moving forward in all it is wishing to express!

## **THANK YOU FOR OUR TODAYS**
## **AND OUR CHILDREN'S TOMORROWS**

So here we are once more
Another battle, another war
Each blaming the other for the hell that has broken lose
The continuation of diplomacy by different means
Further suffering and for many unspeakable abuse

More regimes and ideologies arise
Evils that need to be destroyed that many rightly despise
For in their wake only death they bring
Once again decent men and women must mobilise
To destroy this terrible thing

The enemies outside and those within
Unfortunately the sin of killing must take place in order for good to win
Because sadly, for evil to triumph it only takes good people to hold back
History has shown to destroy bad, good must make a stronger attack

So be grateful that there are those that will undertake
What many of us would not do
And remember if it wasn't for them
There would be no freedom for me and you

Pursuing peace without going to war we should always firstly try to do
Then if all else fails take on and get rid of terror that opposes all that is true
We are so fortunate that throughout time
We the many have been defended by 'The Few'

It is those few that we remember here today
And in future for more like them we should pray
Because without them all that is wrong would overcome all that is right
And future generations would not sleep safely at night

I salute you all now through words such as these
Those with us, those not, all those who believe
Believe that freedom is worth fighting for until the bitter end
Knowing the peaceful days that it brings are a true God send

Thank you all, those who have played and still play your parts
From myself and many others in our nation
With gratitude from the bottom of our hearts

For our todays and our children's tomorrows
Because of your service and sacrifices
We will continue to have far less sorrows

God Bless and keep you all
For your service you deserve to stand proud and tall

Gary Bridson-Daley

24/05/18

An interesting poem which encompasses the life of a veteran soldier from WW1, following his journey and that of his sons throughout the years, on to WW2 and later as they all become much older, until his 'Final Roll Call' where his brothers-in-arms who were lost in battle wait for him at Heavens gates to be re-united forever.

## THE FINAL ROLL CALL

The guns of war fall silent
Now we hear only the pipes of peace
From tortuous years of fighting
We are finally released

It's the 11th of November
And it's all over now
Soon free to go home
Hard to believe somehow

Now we are going back to Blighty
But not many of the original Pals are left
A sense of uncertainty awaits us all
For those who we lost I am bereft

To return home and rebuild new lives
This is what we must do
I no longer know what is right or wrong
I've been to hell and back
Now nothing seems true

That is until I arrive back to the green grass of home
See your face, feel your warm embrace
My Goodness how the children have grown
Once again my heart is warmed by this familiar place

Despite all of this there is not a day that passes by
Where I don't think of friends lost and wonder why
We went to war as innocent boys, came back as shattered men
Every night I relive it, moments of darkness from way back then!

The years numb the feelings and soften the memories somewhat
Having to accept that was my past and this is now my lot
The boys have become men
Now I am horrified that it's all going to happen again
Hitler and the Nazis, same nation back for another go
Part two of that horrific show

Part one was the Kaiser and I played my part
In this second instalment I see my sons go to war and it breaks my heart
Knowing what they will go through and the terror they will face
Wondering if they will ever return home to see this place

I had four years of hell, this time we all got six
But both sons returned and for this I give praise
They have seen the trauma of war, it's in their gaze
Something that will remain with them for the rest of their days

So now we all sit together as older men, around a warm fire
Also as family and veteran soldiers, sharing stories
About our conflicts and friends in a place much higher

Each one of us an ageing warrior
With bonds of friendship forged in battle
One day to be reunited with our pals of both world wars
Their faces forever young and still wearing the same tackle

When I close my eyes for the last time I know it will be clear to me
That guarding the gates of Heaven is where they will be
Waiting with smiles and salutes for us all
Last battle over, waiting to share The Final Roll Call

Then we will take our place once again next to our mates
And march together through those golden gates
Eternal peace with all who we know
A beautiful end to the final show

Gary Bridson-Daley

15/01/18

This is written about the everlasting bonds of friendship formed between those who served and experienced so much together. This piece was influenced and inspired by the many veterans I have interviewed, and around the time of writing by one in particular whom I had just spent two days with whilst interviewing him down in Stafford. 7 Para, Operation Varsity veteran and Poet Arnie Hutchinson. So this poem is a dedication to all veterans and in this case especially to Arnie. Thank you all for your service.

## ODE TO COMRADES AND OLD FRIENDS

Comrades and old friends, they are true God sends
By us in battle they stood firm and resolute
Actions more than words when it mattered most
I've heard servicemen and veterans say
At times they have felt protected by the eternal host

The fellowship that was so binding and can never be denied
As they fell in battle, some injured and some who died
Words used as poetry by those who were there and those who simply respect
All that has been done for them and who wish to honour and reflect

Days spent with old Soldiers, Sailors and Airmen with many stories shared
They were proud to serve and wonder why they were spared
From conflicts, hard moments whilst in the thick of the fight
Somehow they summoned inner courage to be counted and not take flight

Thank God they did or the world we inherited would have been much worse
As the Nazi tyranny and many others since they did disperse
Good against evil the eternal struggle goes on
If they hadn't stood together good would never have won

In service as in life it is true friendship that continues to bond
And any threats to those who we love and care about we do respond
Whether as a Band of Brothers on the battlefield or with your closest at home
It means the world to all that they don't stand alone

So remember comrades both old and new
Don't ever forget what they have done for us all and continue to do
Make new friends, but keep the old
For the new ones are Silver, the old ones are Gold

With these words I thank Servicemen, Servicewomen and Veterans alike
Those who I have never met and those who I know stood for what was right
Those who out of self-sacrifice passed out of the sight of men
Proving that good prevails time and again

I ask you all to join me for one minute, two minutes and many more
To remember, not only in November
But for as long as the sea meets the shore

For as long as they protect us, each and every one
We should always remember them
At the going down of the sun...


Gary Bridson-Daley

28/11/17

# **FOR ALL THOSE WHO HAVE AND CONTINUE TO SERVE**

A 'Poem of Remembrance' that spans and incorporates a Century of conflict. It honours and pays tribute to all our servicemen and women, past to present day. The first line is in Latin, followed directly by its translation into English, which the poem stays in thereafter.

## **THE ETERNAL LEGACY**

### (The Centenary Poem)

Aut si quid est in vita in Aeternum Resonat
What we do in life echoes in eternity
From those who lost their lives in the mud of Passchendaele
To those cut down on the beaches of Normandy

More than endless lines of crosses or names carved in stone
Each life lost meaning another was safe far away at home
Their pain, not in vain
Those lost on the Somme, at Dunkirk and at El-Alamein

Men and Women of all services
Lost in many conflicts over time
Allowing the generations that follow to live full lives
Like yours and mine

Korea, Suez, Falklands and Iraq
Throughout history they have had our back
In continuous struggles they persevered to the bitter end
As a protector, a brother, a sister and a serving friend

Army, Navy, Air Force, Intelligence and Home Front too
Doing what they felt was right
To protect our families, our nation
And the likes of me and you

On the distant shores of Gallipoli, in the streets of Northern Ireland
And in the burning deserts of Afghanistan
Baptisms of Fire
Where many a boy became a man

Don't let their sacrifices be lost
Like tears in the rain
Keep their Eternal Legacy alive
By remembering them again and again

They gave their tomorrow for our today
And by honouring them we don't throw that precious gift away
For peace is what most pray for in our troubled times
But until it comes 'Lest we Forget'
That it is those who serve that hold the lines...


Gary Bridson-Daley

13/11/17

Always wear your poppy with pride.
When you observe the 2 minutes silence try and think of the 1st minute as being for those who have served their country, and were sent off to wars.
Try and think of the 2nd minute as being for those who served their country, were sent off to wars and never returned!

Armistice Day – 11th November 2023

Equally as important on this and every other time of Remembrance to come. GBD.

# Tribute Poetry from the Homeless Poet Jamie Smith

Jamie is originally from Rhyl in North Wales, a plasterer by trade. When a set of very unfortunate circumstances led to him becoming homeless in 2016 he ended up living in a tent at the back of Piccadilly Station in Manchester.

I met Jamie on Market Street, Manchester back in 2018 who I spoke to after seeing his touching sign saying - I'm trying to sell my poems instead ov begging. Something I really respected. After speaking to Jamie who within a short space of time I really liked, he gave me one of his poems which was well crafted. I then gave him a donation and brought food and drinks for us both and we sat, ate together and talked about our shared love of creating poetry and shared views on many other things such as life, Brexit, the state our country, homelessness and homeless veterans, and despite his situation I liked his positivity and strong morals, his dislike of bad behaviour and rude people, which he sees a lot of on the streets, and his appreciation for those who serve and help others in all capacities, these were some of the many qualities I admired in him.

He never asks for money, and if anyone chooses to donate he will immediately offer them a piece of his poetry. As his sign rightly says; #Homeless… But Still Human…

I have made sure since then that each time I am in Manchester City Centre I look out for Jamie and if I find him I will buy food for him, give what money I can spare and spend time with him, which he really appreciates. After one such visit I thought if he was happy to do it, how different and interesting it would be to have a piece of poetry written by him about veterans from his street perspective to include in this book, which would also be something special that would mark his positive contribution to things, he agreed, and so here it is, a short piece called 'A Veteran's Tale' from Jamie Smith AKA 'The Homeless Poet', thank you Jamie you're a good man, God Bless you and stay safe.

## A Veteran's Tale

People don't think how this country was built
But the veterans that made it home
Put the 'Great' back in to 'Great Britain'
Kept us safe and gave their lives to protect this country
That's why this poetry has been written

They gave us morals and made us proud
Our Grandparents still live with this moral code
That we should all live by day after day
But life went on and all these things seem to be lost, gone astray

Veterans homeless on the street
No help, No thanks for your service, very bleak
Where did it all go wrong?
Have we lost the 'Great' in 'Great Britain'
By failing those who once served us
Are we no longer strong?

We need to think and help our veterans back on their feet
Because we all need a helping hand every now and then
Especially those on the street!

Jamie Smith

2019

# FOR THE FALLEN

## BY ROBERT LAURENCE BINYON

# Robert Laurence Binyon and his Famous Poem

'For The Fallen' a poem by Robert Laurence Binyon English Poet, Dramatist and Art Scholar (10th August 1869–10th March 1943) was published in The Times newspaper on the 21st September 1914.

The poem was written by Binyon whilst sitting on a cliff-top, taking inspiration as he looked out to sea over the dramatic scenery of the north Cornish coastline in mid-September 1914, a few weeks after the outbreak of the first World War and soon after the British Expeditionary Force had suffered heavy casualties following its first encounter with the German Army at the Battle of Mons on the 23rd August, and at the subsequent battles that followed such as the First Battle of the Marne 5th and 9th September 1914.

This was a portent for Binyon, which sadly became all too true in the terrible battles which followed throughout the First World War, Laurence said in 1939 that the four lines of the fourth stanza (verse) came to him first. It is the words of this fourth verse which have become especially familiar and famous, having been adopted by the Royal British Legion as an exhortation for ceremonies of Remembrance to commemorate fallen Servicemen and Women of all conflicts.

Despite being considered too old to enlist in the military forces, being 45 soon after the outbreak of World War One, Binyon volunteered to work for the Red Cross as a medical orderly and in 1915 he was sent to a British Military hospital for French soldiers, the Hôpital Temporaired' Arc-en-Barrois in the Haute-Marne area in France, where he saw, worked with and directly experienced some of the aftermath of the horrors of trench warfare, he returned there again in 1916 helping take care of soldiers taken in from the Verdun battlefield and later wrote about his harrowing experiences in 'For Dauntless France' (1918).

Binyon lost several close friends and his Brother-in-law during WW1 so the tragedy of that conflict was also very personal to him and impacted him deeply, something that was expressed through his writing.

He did however leave behind what is now one of the best known and most quoted pieces of remembrance poetry when he wrote 'For The Fallen'.

I have included it in this book in its entirety as it is rarely seen and read as such and still remains one of the greatest tributes to all those who gave the ultimate sacrifice. Additionally this poem is a great legacy and tribute in itself to the talented man who wrote it!

Above- A Sketch drawing of Robert Laurence Binyon by William Strang in 1901.

# FOR THE FALLEN

## By Robert Laurence Binyon

With proud thanksgiving, a mother for her children,
England mourns for her dead across the sea.
Flesh of her flesh they were, spirit of her spirit,
Fallen in cause of the free.

Solemn the drums thrill; Death august and royal
Sings sorrow up into immortal spheres,
There is music in the midst of desolation
And a glory that shines upon our tears.

They went with songs to the battle, they were young,
Straight of limb, true of eye, steady and aglow.
They were staunch to the end against odds uncounted;
They fell with their faces to the foe.

**They shall grow not old, as we that are left grow old:**
**Age shall not weary them, nor the years condemn.**
**At the going down of the sun and in the morning**
**We will remember them.**

They mingle not with their laughing comrades again;
They sit no more at familiar tables of home;
They have no lot in our labour of the day-time;
They sleep beyond England's foam.

But where our desires are and our hopes profound,
Felt as a well-spring that is hidden from sight,
To the innermost heart of their own land they are known
As the stars are known to the night;

As the stars that shall be bright when we are dust,
Moving in marches upon the heavenly plain;
As the stars that are starry in the time of our darkness,
To the end, to the end, they remain.

# EVERLASTING SACRIFICE

## Words of tribute for those who died in all conflicts

They lie dead in many Lands
So we may live here in Peace

Tranquil they now Lie
Their Knightly Virtue Proved

But there is a link death cannot sever
As Love and Remembrance last for ever

****

*Lest We Forget*

****

## Act of Remembrance

Let us remember before God, and commend to his sure keeping:
Those who have died for their country in conflict;
Those who we knew, and those whose memory we treasure;
And all who have lived and died in the service of humanity.

We Will Remember Them.

****

# LEARNING FROM THE LESSONS OF THE PAST

## Concluding thoughts and words from two of the greatest peace makers of the 20th Century

*"When I despair, I remember that all through history,
the way of truth and love has always won.
There have been murderers and tyrants,
and for a time they can seem invincible.
But in the end they always fall.
Think of it – ALWAYS."*

*MKGandhi*

# **LOOKING TOWARDS THE FUTURE**

*"We must learn to live together as brothers or we will perish together as fools"*

# AKNOWLEDGEMENTS

In this short life where we bring nothing in to this world and cannot in a physical sense take anything out with us, there are only a few accomplishments that can possibly remain as a legacy and a form of posterity for a person. Namely these:

Great memorable or historical acts of any kind, Serving your country, Positive Discovery or Invention, Children, Works of creativity; literary, musically, art or otherwise. It is surely a great thing to have achieved any or some of these, because if done well they are truly something to be proud of, and in time all that will be left to mark our very existence.

The veterans I have been privileged to interview, both military and civilian, have already created a very honourable legacy through their service to the nation and the many forms of self-sacrifice they have given whilst undertaking their duties.

I feel the writing of a book is the act of passing down information, stories and in this case also history from one generation to the next, and in doing so ensuring the preservation of that history, it is like leaving a personal footprint on the earth, something you have created from deep inside you which is a reminder of your time here, a special achievement.

In time I hope that the books I have written will be a lasting tribute to our veterans to thank them for all they have done for us, a meaningful contribution to World War Two and military history, and also a significant part of my legacy as well.

Gary Bridson-Daley

Those who sow with tears will reap with songs of joy – Psalm 126:5

The author would like to thank and acknowledge the following people, organisations, associations and charities whose help and co-operation contributed in making this book possible and is greatly appreciated.

Dame Vera Lynn and Susan Fleet, Tom Robin and Blind Veterans UK, Lorna Dorrell and BLESMA, Lt. Commander Nigel Huckstable and the Royal Naval Association, Kenneth Kirk and the Royal Engineers Association, Captain (Retired) Andy Harris and the Royal Regiment of Fusiliers Association (incorporating the Lancashire Fusiliers Association), Dick Goodwin and the Taxi Charity for Military Veterans, Kieran Whitworth and the IWM, Tamsin Stares and the Royal Marines Association, Terry White and the Borough of Bury Veterans Association, Nicky Barr and the International Bomber Command Centre, Daniel Scott-Davies and The Spitfire Society, Elizabeth Todd and The Bevin Boys Association, Johnny Wallis and the Parachute Regiment Association, Catherine McGrath and Bovington Tank Museum, Guillaume Dormy and the D-Day Museum at Arromanches in Normandy France, Alexandra Cropper and the Jewish Museum Manchester, All staff & Management at Broughton House, Claire Wright and the Trafford Veterans Breakfast Club, Owen Hammond and all at the Salford Veterans Breakfast Club, Helen Kay, Veterans Sweetheart Sarah Dennis, Samir Hardy, The Wilson Family, Delia Mangligot, Jamie Smith 'The Homeless Poet'.

Rabbi M Cohen, Rabbi Paley and all at OYY Lubavitch School Manchester, you have been caring, thoughtful and supportive throughout my journey with my 2nd book, for this and so much more I thank you. G-d Bless you, each and every one of you.

Joe Bamford for his very kind input and permission to use 5 photos he provided for the 'Salford Lancaster' part of the book, including the map of its last approach marked out by him.

George 'Johnny' Johnson and his daughter Jenny for their help with the foreword, and Terry Buck for permission to use his picture of myself and Johnny.

Dame Vera Lynn 100 Photo – Courtesy of Liz Mills.

A big thank you to Alice Kouzmenko and Carver PR for their help regarding Sir Captain Tom Moore and the modern photograph provided by them for use in this book.

The U.S National Holocaust Museum, for some statistical data quoted in the Holocaust chapter of this book. Adolf Eichmann Photo – DIZ Muenchen GMBH, Sueddeutscher Verlag Bilderdienst. Image ID: 00126367. Holocaust Mathematical data from Professor Lewi Stone of The George S. Wise Faculty of Life Sciences at Tel-Aviv University. Sketch Drawing Auschwitz-Birkenau – Lubomir Rosenstein.

Wikimedia Commons for the use of selected copyright free photos, the author acknowledges and thanks all contributors from that source. Rommel portrait – Bundesarchiv, Bild 146-1973-012-43/Unknown/CC-BY-SA 3.0. R.M Commandos on exercise – Open Government Licence version 1.0. Attribution: Photo: POA (Phot) Sean Clee/MOD. Soldier Poppy Pic – SAC Andrew Morris. M3 Lee Tank in Burma – No.9 Army Film & Photographic Unit. Robert Blair Mayne Photo – Seb.cestari.16. Commonwealth Soldiers in Tobruk: 22nd Oct 1941 – www.awm.gov.au/collection/C273600. RN crew sat on 15" Guns of HMS Nelson – IWM Collections, Photograph A4606 by Coote, R G G (Lt), Royal Navy Official Photographer. Royal Air Force, 54 Squadron, Spitfire Group Photo - IWM Collections, Photograph CH2710 by Woodbine G (Mr), Royal Air Force Official Photographer. HRH Princess Elizabeth, ATS, April 1945 – IWM Collections, Photograph TR2832 (Cropped), Ministry of Information Official Photographer. Surrender Documents – Office of War Information (U.S) & Joint Chiefs of Staff (U.S). Anti-Christ (1942) Painting – The Arthur Szyk Society, Burlingame, CA, 94070. Candle – WO2 Daniel Harmer GBR Army/MOD. Gravestone of Merchant Navy Sailor Salem Mohamed – No Swan So Fine. Dornier DO17 & Spitfire – Bundesarchiv, Bild 146-1969-094-18/Speer/CC-BY-SA 3.0. Any Shutterstock pictures used have been purchased by the Author.

High Tide 1942 Map - "Cornell University – PJ Mode Collection of Persuasive Cartography."

First Aid Nursing Yeomanry Insignia courtesy of FANY via Jean Argles.

All military insignias, logos and crests from all services on the MoD portal and through historical branches 'Reproduced with permission of the MoD'. With special thanks to all at the DIPR. Historical decommissioned insignia, logos and crests: Crown copyright, MoD. Air Historical Branch (RAF) & Crown copyright, and MoD Courtesy of Royal Naval Historical Branch.

All families of the veterans for their kind assistance and the veterans themselves for permission to use all materials included in this book, such as their stories and related information, photos, documents provided and poetry. Also everyone who kindly donated through my GoFundMe page.

Mike and Jean Dyson for welcoming me into their 'Extended Family' and giving me a peaceful haven and the right environment to make this book a reality, thank you and God Bless you both for that invaluable help and your kind understanding.

To contact the author about 'The Last Stand' and 'Debt of Gratitude Project' please email him at; bookoftheveterans@gmail.com or arealdebtofgratitude@gmail.com. You can also find 'A Debt of Gratitude to The Last Heroes' page on Facebook, and follow the author on Twitter, @bridson_daley.

# THE AUTHOR

Gary Bridson-Daley, is a Manchester born author who previously worked as a Tour Manager in travel and tourism for over a decade and the half all over the world. He has been inspired to interview and write about World War Two veterans after meeting some of them in the WW2 related places that he was lucky enough to work or visit over the years, such as all 5 D-Day Landing Beaches and their museums at Normandy in France, El Alamein in Egypt, Pearl Harbour in Hawaii, Arnhem in Holland, Maleme & Souda Bay in Crete, Risiera di San Sabba Concentration Camp in Italy, Auschwitz-Birkenau in Poland, Jersey War Tunnels German Underground Hospital Complex in the Channel Islands, the site of Adolf Hitler's *Führerbunker* in Berlin, Germany. Additionally Gary has scuba dived on the WW2 shipwrecks of the SS Thistlegorm in the Red Sea, Egypt & HMS Maori in Malta, and in the U.K has also visited and spent time at; Bletchley Park, Biggin Hill Heritage Hanger, All the Imperial War Museum Sites, RAF London and RAF Cosford Museums, Churchill's grave at Bladon, Bentley Priory: Home of Fighter Command HQ during the Battle of Britain, Western Approaches Atlantic Convoy Museum, Stockport Underground Air Raid Shelters, The National Memorial Arboretum, Cannock Chase Commonwealth and German WW1 & WW2 War Cemetery, and many more WW2 related locations. During and since then he has continued to honour the sacrifices of servicemen & women for posterity and in perpetuity through the books he has written on this fascinating subject. Following on from 'The Last Heroes', 'The Last Stand' continues to pay tribute to those who Gary greatly respects for the precious gift of freedom they have given us all over the years as a result of their service and their actions on behalf of our country.

Throughout his Debt of Gratitude Project the motivation of the author resolutely remains, as expressed in his first book, to pay tribute to and write books that are:

*ABOUT VETERANS*
*FOR VETERANS*
*TO HONOUR VETERANS*
*BECAUSE TO REMEMBER IS TO HONOUR.*

# OTHER WORKS

> 'A wonderful tribute to our World War Two servicemen and women, very well written with real compassion and understanding.'
>
> DAME VERA LYNN

## A DEBT OF GRATITUDE TO THE LAST HEROES

VOICES OF BRITISH AND COMMONWEALTH VETERANS

GARY BRIDSON-DALEY
FOREWORD BY DAME VERA LYNN

***A DEBT OF GRATITUDE TO THE LAST HEROES
THE AUTHOR'S FIRST BOOK***

***STILL AVAILABLE FROM AMAZON, WATERSTONES AND ALL OTHER GOOD OUTLETS IN HARDBACK (1ST EDITION), PAPERBACK (2ND EDITION) & KINDLE VERSIONS***

Printed in Great Britain
by Amazon